MANAGEMENT:
A BEHAVIORAL APPROACH

SECOND EDITION

MANAGEMENT:
A Behavioral Approach

EDWIN B. FLIPPO
University of Arizona

ALLYN AND BACON
BOSTON

TO

J.G.F.
R.D.F.
S.J.F.
S.J.F.

Preface

The objective of this book has not changed in its second edition—an attempted integration of traditional and behavioral approaches to management. It is based on a belief that both approaches have much to contribute toward more effective management, and the task is one of diagnosing situations to determine the optimum mix. Since there are few if any effective measures of appropriate mix, the approach of this book is one of contrasting, side-by-side, the values, methods, and philosophies under the "umbrella" framework of the management functions of planning, organizing, directing, and controlling.

In a sense, equal time has been allocated to the two approaches; the number of chapters devoted to each are equally divided. Each of the four major management functions are divided into two portions. Section A under each function deals with the rational, scientific concepts, while Section B is concerned with behavioral modifications and substitutions. For example, Section A of the organizing function deals with the formal relationships of responsibility, authority, and accountability and their resulting structures. Section B is concerned with informal and unofficial relationships which serve to alter the formal, such relationships as power, feelings, and status. Section A of the control function presents the essentials of formal control theory, encompassing such elements as standards, collection of data, evaluation, and corrective action. Section B presents the reactions of people to these controls which serve to impinge upon the human ego. Accommodations which might be achieved between formal controls and human needs are discussed.

The organization of this book allows the professor to deal first with formal management theory by covering the four Section A's in sequence. He may then concentrate upon the behavioral and informal by developing the four Section B's as a unit. It is apparent that the writer feels that such an approach, though feasible, is likely to result in the creation of two courses within a course, and that a function-by-function integration is more likely to force student and professor to face the issues.

Among the major changes in this second edition are the following:

1. Emphasis is placed upon a systems viewpoint where appropriate. This takes the form of both a "total" systems approach for the organization, as well as supporting subsystems which may work against, as well as for, the total system and other subsystems.

2. Greater attention and space are devoted to quantitative aids in decision making. This is covered briefly and simply in Chapter 4, the only new chapter added to the book. The help of Professor Gary Munsinger of the University of Arizona is acknowledged in this area, though the mistakes of commission and omission are, of course, the property of the author.

3. More illustrative material has been included, thereby adding to the length of the book. Professors using the text have found the basic framework to be valuable in teaching, but many have indicated that students require more supplementary information.

4. Major research efforts of recent years have been incorporated into this edition, e.g., Herzberg's theory and its validation, research on the effectiveness of sensitivity training, and the contributions of the socio-technical systems field.

5. There has been a complete revision of supplementary readings to reflect the literature of the past four years. Many of the discussion problems have been revised as well.

In addition to the above, there has been, of course, considerable review, updating, and revision of many smaller portions of the text. As examples, project structure has been given a more elaborate treatment; recent events in the social problem of integrating minority groups have been noted; and additional models of integrating the behavioral and traditional approaches have been added.

The author is still indebted to many people for help provided in preparing this book. The many comments of users and reviewers are very much appreciated and have affected this revision to a considerable degree. The initiation of this integrated approach by the management faculty of California State College at Los Angeles at the suggestion of Dean William Voris, now of the University of Arizona, is again acknowledged. The greatest continuing stimulation to the author is the reactions of various college students, both within and outside the classroom. The contrasting of apparently conflicting approaches to management seems to stimulate a markedly high degree of thought, interest, discussion, and at times, heated debate. In the detailed, time consuming, and demanding area of manuscript preparation, I am again indebted to my wife, Jean Gwin Flippo, for the initial editing, and to Donna Brammer for her rapid and accurate typing.

It is my sincere hope that this book will stimulate a greater attempt on the part of managers, professors, and students to integrate the many values of both traditional and behavioral approaches to management theory.

Edwin B. Flippo

Contents

PART FOUR   DIRECTING

PART SIX   CONCLUSION

Part One

INTRODUCTION

Management is fundamentally a process of planning, organizing, directing, and controlling activities which will lead to an effective fulfillment of corporate objectives. The approach used in executing these functions can be scientific, humanistic, or both. In this introductory chapter, the development of both approaches will be examined as a basis for the organization of the book.

1

The Nature of Management

In the modern business economy, there is probably no single factor as significant as that of management. Whether viewed as a concept or as a particular
group of people, management is concerned with establishing and operating
organizations for the execution of work. Organizations are social and technological devices which enable the accomplishment of objectives that are too
large and complex to be executed by a single person. Business organizations
are established largely for the purpose of accomplishing economic goals—the
creation of values of form, place, ownership, and time.[1] As we shall see in the
following chapter, certain other types of goals have been suggested as being
pertinent to an effective business organization.

It should also be apparent that organizations are created to accomplish goals
in other areas such as the military, religious, educational, and governmental.
To some, modern society has become an "organizational society."[2] In all such
cases, the necessity for management of the organization and its activities is
inevitable and essential.

As suggested in Fig. 1–1, an organization can be viewed as a unit that
processes certain inputs from the environment for the purpose of creating
certain specified outputs valued by society. The organization is a unit that
transforms resources into other forms, e.g., the hospital changes sick patients

[1] To take the simplest kind of example, let us look at the housewife who wishes to preserve
food for future use. A refrigerator constitutes for her a value of "form." When it is
transported from factory to home, it has acquired the additional value of "place." When it is
provided at the time desired and becomes the property of the housewife, it has taken on the
further values of "time" and "ownership."

[2] Cf. Robert Presthus, *The Organizational Society* (New York: Alfred A. Knopf, 1962).

FIGURE 1–1   ORGANIZATION AS A SYSTEM

into healthy ones, the school transforms uninformed students into knowledge-able ones, and the manufacturing firm converts steel, aluminum, glass, and rubber into automobiles. This transforming unit, the organization, must be controlled and directed by a management. Not only does a management establish and direct the organization toward specified goals, it also monitors the resulting outputs and corrects the unit should it deviate from the prescribed path.

MANAGEMENT FUNCTIONS

As a concept, management is defined as the planning, organizing, directing, and controlling of the enterprise's operations so that objectives can be achieved economically and effectively.[3] As Fig. 1–2 indicates, these functions can also be viewed as a subsystem of the total organizational system.

The manager begins by taking various human and economic resources from the environment in the form of labor, materials, equipment, and money. To the extent that he is unable to completely control the quality and amounts of these inputs, he is part of an "open," rather than "closed," system. The environment also establishes various types of constraints which can be affected but not completely controlled by the manager, e.g., the political system, the state of technology, and the mores and ideals of society.

The first function of the manager is that of *planning*, that is, the specification of goals and means. The resulting plan is composed of goals, policies, procedures, standards, and any specification in advance of what is to be done. To implement this plan, an organization must be created. Human and economic resources are divided and allocated to various work areas within the enterprise, and relationships are established among the resulting sub-units. The management function of *organizing* is concerned with developing a structure or

[3] There are various breakdowns of the major management functions presented by theorists, such as plan, organize, and control; plan, organize, command, coordinate, and control; plan and control; and plan, organize, actuate, and control. The differences are in emphasis rather than in content.

FIGURE 1-2   MANAGEMENT AS A SYSTEM

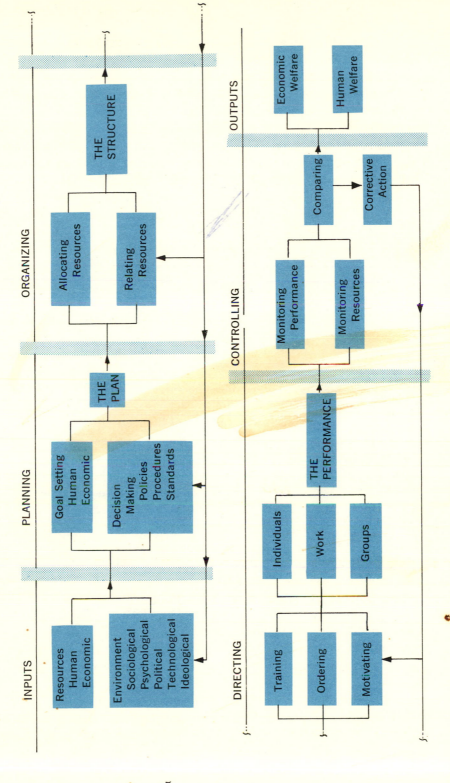

5

framework which relates all personnel, work assignments, and physical resources to each other and to the enterprise objective. This framework is usually termed *organization structure.*

The third basic management function is that of *directing*, which is concerned with stimulating the organization to undertake action along the lines of the plan. As such, it deals with the dissemination of orders and the acceptance and execution of these orders. This acceptance and execution usually necessitates managerial attention to training and motivating of individuals and groups that make up the organization. At this particular time in the system, the execution of operative work takes place. In Fig. 1–2, this is labeled "performance."

The final function of management is that of *control,* or regulating whatever business action results from direction. The objective of control is to assure proper performance in accordance with plans. It requires the monitoring of operative performance and the effectiveness of resources utilization. This monitoring provides the management with performance information that can be compared with predetermined plans. In the event of unsatisfactory execution of work, corrective action can take such forms as retraining and remotivating of organization members, altering the allocation of resources through reorganization, and altering the basic plan itself. In some instances, the manager may decide to go outside the organization to alter the supply of inputs, e.g., a shortage of engineering talent in the 1950's led the General Electric Company to attempt to influence high school students to elect courses in the physical sciences. Thus, the control function closes the system loop by providing information feedback to the manager so that he may replan, reorganize, and redirect the enterprise.

The outputs of the organization are both human and economic in the case of the business organization. It is by these outputs that society judges the success of the enterprise. In a sense, organizations exist by permission of society, and will fail or be abolished if the values produced are deemed inappropriate or excessively costly.

These broad and rather basic management functions are in direct contrast with more particularized operative functions. Thus, operative functions may include anything from production, sales, and purchasing to transporting goods on barge lines or processing an insurance application. The manager of any of these operative functions must plan the work, establish job assignments and relationships, issue orders and instructions, and insure that the operative work is accomplished in accordance with the plan. Successful managers in one operative area should be able to transfer to other areas and become similarly successful as they make use of their basic management skills.

The people concerned with the basic functions are known as the management or administrative group. They include anyone who is organizationally superior to another, and who is in a position to issue orders and presumably exact results. Consequently, the first-level supervisor in any operative area is a part of management, as much as is the topmost official in an organization, the president. Of course, the manner and specific content of planning, organizing, directing, and controlling will vary according to the organization level on which it is done. For lower levels, planning is short term, organizing is limited in scope, and the major emphasis is upon direction and control. For the higher levels, planning is of extreme importance and of a long term nature, the function of organizing is crucial, and direction and control are more impersonal.

MANAGEMENT APPROACHES

In the opinion of the author, there is no such thing as a science of management. It is still largely an art resting upon various philosophical bases. This does not mean that the scientific method of investigation cannot be used in making managerial decisions, but the resulting truths are not so many or so exact as to merit the label of science. In addition, the openness of the total organizational system precludes effective managerial control of the environment and the various input resources.

As a result of this inexactitude of concept, various philosophical approaches to management have been developed over the years, so many that one author has termed the resulting array as "the management theory jungle."[4] The oldest and perhaps most widely accepted among practitioners in business has been called the *classical* or traditional school. It is from this group that the sequence of management functions described above was derived. The focus is upon the manager as he determines what should be done and sets about the process of making it come true. It tends to lead to managerial decision making, control, regimentation, and autocracy, however benevolent in its intent.

A second major school of management thought has developed through an emphasis upon the organization members *other* than the manager. The manager may prescribe and command, but there is no guarantee that the resulting action will be in accordance with the prescription. This approach emphasizes the power that lies in the hands of organization members through the extending or withholding of initiative and cooperation. This school is largely populated by psychologists, sociologists, anthropologists, and political scientists, and is generally labeled *behavioral* in its approach. It would add a consensus formation system to the rational decision-making system of the classicist.

In addition to these two basic approaches, various other more specialized emphases have been projected. There is the *decision* school that views all management through the keyhole of managerial decision making. There is a

[4] Harold Koontz, "The Management Theory Jungle," *The Journal of the Academy of Management,* Vol. 4, No. 3 (December, 1961), pp. 174–188.

related *quantitative* school that utilizes mathematics and statistics in attempting to improve the entire management process. It is this school that has developed advanced college degrees in "management science." Some even split the behaviorists into the sub-schools of *psychological*, emphasizing the individual, and *social*, emphasizing the group.

It could well be that we are again experiencing the fable of the three blind men and the elephant. Each approach is dealing with a portion of the truth, thereby requiring an integration and relating of the values of each. Of all the approaches, the first two, classical and behavioral, seem to be most in conflict. The emphasis upon the manager and the resulting autocracy of the classicists will clash with the emphasis upon human relations and the resulting democracy of the behaviorists. This apparent clash is the basic reason for this particular text in management theory. It is believed that some degree of integration can be effected.

BACKGROUND OF THE CLASSICAL MANAGEMENT MOVEMENT

Many business historians mark the beginning of industrial management problems with the Industrial Revolution of the eighteenth century. This period saw the onset of the factory system, where many people were brought together under one roof to operate capital equipment provided by the owner. This was in marked contrast to the handicraft system, where the craftsman worked with his own tools in his own home. When groups of people are brought together for the purpose of working for someone else, utilizing someone else's equipment, and depending primarily or totally upon someone else's favor for their livelihood, many management problems are thereby created. Formal lines of authority, systems, and procedures must be established to provide a basis for coordinated effort. In the past a major complaint was that too often these structures were established poorly and without apparent thought. There was little or no attention devoted to such problems as insecurity, loss of pride in work, adjustment to change, and informal relationships. It was merely a matter of riding roughshod over any objections, with a heavy reliance upon the fear motive.

From the latter part of the nineteenth century through the beginning of the twentieth, there was an intensified and dedicated interest in management as a process and as a possible science. It was apparent to many, particularly Frederick Taylor, H. L. Gantt, Frank Gilbreth, and Henri Fayol, that the management of the past had not been enlightened. The marked increase in the amount of management research that took place in this period was such as to merit the title of "a second industrial revolution" or "the rise of scientific management."

The essential thesis of Taylor, who is generally recognized as the "father" of scientific management, is that management is a process in which the scientific method can be used. Instead of abdicating responsibility for establishing standards, for example, management would scientifically study all facets of an operation and carefully set a logical and rational standard. Instead of guessing or relying solely upon trial and error, management would go through the arduous process of logical study and scientific research to develop answers to business problems. Taylor stated many times that scientific management would require a "revolution" in thinking on the part of both the manager and the subordinate. His motives were not confined solely to advancing the interests of the manager and the enterprise. He believed sincerely that scientific management practices were for the mutual benefit of the employee and the employer through the creation of a larger productive surplus. There was therefore a mutuality of interests in terms of output and monetary income.

The greater bulk of Taylor's work was oriented toward improving the management of production operations. The classic case of the pig-iron experiment illustrates his approach as well as the resulting widely accepted management techniques.[5] The task was simple, so much so that most managers would tend to ignore it. Laborers would pick up 92 pound pigs from a storage yard, walk up a plank onto a railroad car, and drop them at the end of the car. In a group of 75 laborers, the average output was about 12½ tons per man per day. In applying the scientific method of study to this problem of getting work done through others, Taylor developed an improved method of work (motion study), a prescribed amount of rest on the job (fatigue study and rest periods), a specific standard of output (time study), and payment by the unit of output (incentive wages). Using this approach, the average per man per day output rose from 12½ tons to 48 tons. Under the incentive system, the daily pay rose from $1.15 to $1.85, an amount substantially higher than the going rate in the community.

The dedication of Taylor to the systematic planning and study of processes pervaded his entire life. With a specially designed tennis racket, he became part of the National Doubles Tennis Championship team. When he played golf, he used uniquely designed clubs for any predictable type of lie. When he used a particular putter, his friends refused to play because of its accuracy. A famed novelist reports that Taylor died of pneumonia in a hospital with his watch in his hand.[6]

Other pioneers of scientific management were Frank and Lillian Gilbreth who concentrated upon motion analysis to develop "the one best way," and H. L. Gantt who developed a control chart which is used to this day in production operations.[7] In contrast with Taylor, Gantt, and Gilbreth, Henri Fayol

[5] Frederick W. Taylor, *The Principles of Scientific Management* (New York: Harper and Bros., 1911), pp. 41–47.
[6] John Dos Passos, *The Big Money* (Boston: Houghton Mifflin Co., 1960), pp. 19–22.
[7] See Chapter 20.

attempted to develop a broader theory, concerned with general management.[8] His book is the forerunner of this and other modern textbooks that deal with the principles of management. Fayol's thesis was that the fundamental functions of any manager consisted of planning, organizing, commanding, coordinating, and controlling. He attempted to evolve empirically a number of general principles which, if followed, would improve the practice of general management.

The primary concept behind the work of these men, then, was an attempt to rationalize business. A logical, objective approach to all management problems would greatly enhance the possibilities of success, particularly in contrast to the more conventional approaches. Scientific management is still the basis of modern management in America. The systems, structures, and frameworks that resulted from this concept have played a large part in increasing general productivity and our standard of living. The power of this approach should not be sold short.

BACKGROUND OF THE HUMAN RELATIONS MOVEMENT

In the 1920's and 1930's, there were some observers of business management who became concerned with what they felt was a short-sightedness and incompleteness in the scientific management approach. Elton Mayo and F. J. Roethlisberger in particular began to point out that the systems advanced by the scientific manager were not necessarily the most efficient, nor did these systems always work as intended.[9] The essentially *human* character of business organizations had been largely ignored. Organized research was begun and from such work there issued the field of human relations, with Mayo as the recognized "father."

The project that had the most to do with the beginning of human relations as a separate area in business was the Hawthorne experiment, 1927–1932, of the Western Electric Company. In this experiment, the researchers attempted to prove the validity of generally accepted principles of management. A behavioral scientist would introduce a variable into what he thought was a perfectly controlled situation, and then would attribute the observed result to that variable. For example, a rest period would be introduced where there was none before. Increased productivity resulted, thus "proving" Taylor's thesis that a properly introduced rest period will benefit operation results. Several

---

[8] Henri Fayol, *General and Industrial Management* (New York: Pitman Pub. Corp., 1949, trans. from the French originally published in 1916).

[9] See Elton Mayo, *The Human Problems of an Industrial Civilization* (Cambridge: Harvard University Press, 1933) and F. J. Roethlisberger and William J. Dickson, *Management and the Worker* (Cambridge: Harvard University Press, 1939).

principles were thereby tested under these controlled conditions. To clinch the case, various factors, such as rest periods, that had been introduced were removed; the scientists expected a decrease in productivity. Contrary to these expectations, production still continued to improve in most instances. Obviously, everything had *not* been controlled in the experiment; the human mind was still free and uncontrolled. Mayo and Roethlisberger followed up these experiments with an intensive counseling program and an investigation of the myriad of informal cliques, groupings, and relationships initiated by the members of the organization. Thus, the new field was born.

There are various reasons for the expanded interest in human relations problems in the past three decades. In the first place, certain other phases, such as production, marketing, finance, and engineering, had been developed intensively prior to 1930. A theory of business is *not* usually developed equally well on *all* fronts simultaneously, and since the human element had been largely ignored prior to the 1930's it was logical that some group would attempt to fill the gap.

Secondly, in the 1930's and 1940's, two of the previously noted factors behind the acceptance of more constructive human relations came to the forefront. These were government and labor. The union movement grew five-fold in a decade and the amount of governmental regulation of business seemed to grow in an equally significant manner. This, coupled with the development of mass production factories, the association of large groups of people in work situations, and the demonstrated connection between society and a fluctuating economy during the depression of the '30's, resulted in an increasing recognition of the significance of effective human relationships in our business system. The work in this field of management research has been largely among psychologists, sociologists, anthropologists, and physiologists. Management, like engineering, takes from many disciplines but has the inescapable obligation of applying that specialized knowledge to a particular situation.

If one analyzes the writings of some of the pioneers of scientific management, he will find a number of concepts and principles which might come under the heading of human relations. For example, there are Fayol's principles of "equity," "welfare work," "non-financial incentives," and "stability of tenure of personnel."[10] Still, contemporary behaviorists, while not denying that there is concern for the human factor among scientific managers, feel that it is of a type that will not lead to the greatest creativity and productivity. They feel that impulses, humanistic or otherwise, too often issue from the manager *down* to the subordinate in the scientifically managed enterprises. The "new" theory that has been advanced by some in the human relations field is that

[10] Fayol, *General and Industrial Management,* pp. 32 and 38.

there must be a reversal of this directional flow. They feel that the organization should be more people-oriented with less emphasis upon formal structure, policy, and control, no matter how humane these formal frameworks may be.

The behavioral approach to management is neither very old, nor very well developed. Yet the potential value that lies in our human resources is well worth the struggle, effort, and confusion that must accompany the development of any new field. There has, of course, been the usual tendency to overdo a good thing, and this has led to criticism of the humanistic approach. Such criticism in many cases is well deserved. Overenthusiasm, misinterpretation, and misapplication of concepts going under the guise of "good human relations" have done much to prevent acceptance by management of those phases that are sound and constructive. Eventually, however, the most valued aspects of the human relations approach will receive the imprimatur of management, to the point where this approach will truly be looked upon as an essential portion of the process.

Nature of Human Relations

The term "human relation" is widely used in our society. "Human relation groups" have been established to mediate disputes concerning charges of discrimination in housing, schools, and public accommodations. "Human relation commissions" have been set up to administer state and local fair employment practices acts. The term has also been applied to cultural interchanges among nations. As used in this text, it is viewed as a significant portion of the management process. As long as people are a part of business organizations, there will be the task of integrating interests, a task we have labeled "human relations."

Thus, human relations, as it applies to management, is primarily concerned with the *integration of people into a work environment* in a manner which facilitates *cooperation, creativity*, and *productivity*. Researchers in the behavioral sciences have suggested substantial modifications of these traditional approaches to management. Any such changes would, of course, have to be encompassed within the framework of the fundamental management functions mentioned earlier.

The objective of the human relations or behavioral phase of management is the same as that of the classical or traditional approach, that is, the economical and effective achievement of basic organization objectives. Behaviorists, however, have appropriately pointed out that more emphasis upon the behavioral approach in an organization will advance the organization's efficiency; that reasonable satisfaction of the needs and desires of those people who work *within* and contribute to the enterprise will lead to greater results. The best functional arrangement possible and the latest in capital equipment can go for nought if personnel are not reasonably cooperative. A management approach which ignores or de-emphasizes the human element will usually result in half-accomplished objectives, reduced creativity, and general dissatisfaction.

The traditional approach of the past was not wrong, it was merely incomplete. We must build on the philosophies and approaches of the past to develop a more farseeing and enlightened approach which adjusts to modern conditions. This writer cannot accept the thesis advanced by some behaviorists that we must disregard the traditional approaches to organization theory; that we must have an entirely new approach since the old was so authoritarian and restrictive; that this new approach must emphasize the informal groupings, shared authority through participation, and adjustment of the superior to the subordinate. That these should be considered *substitutes* for the old rather than *supplements* and modifications is inconceivable. One wonders how much work would be accomplished in a firm of hundreds or thousands of people if formal organization structures, systems, and procedures were discarded completely for the newer informal approach. Indeed, one wonders if it could be called an organization. To repeat once more, we shall attempt an integration of management theory, as developed for the basic management functions, with a proper concern for the attitudes, sentiments, and relationships among the personalities within the organization. The marriage of the two approaches is more than merely possible; it is necessary.

Importance of Human Relations

The reasons for the unavoidably greater emphasis upon human relations in management are several in number. Foremost is the thesis that serious recognition, study, and proper control of these relationships will simply contribute to greater creativity, productivity, and effectiveness, much as does the investigation of formal organization, procedures, systems, equipment, and the like. Various research studies have attempted to isolate one or more of the "humanistic" elements in management to determine their effect upon productivity. Though no invariable correlation has been discovered, the cumulative results of these experiments, in addition to the conclusions derived from practical experience, lead to an acceptance of the thesis that improved human relations will benefit organizational productivity.[11]

The second reason for devoting greater attention to human relations in

[11] Cf. Rensis Likert, *Motivational Dimensions of Administration* (Chicago: Public Administration Service, 1954), and Robert L. Kahn and Daniel Katz, "Leadership Practices in Relation to Productivity and Morale," in *Group Dynamics Research and Theory*, ed. Cartwright and Zander (Evanston: Row, Peterson, 1953), and Rensis Likert, *New Patterns of Management* (New York: McGraw-Hill Book Company, 1961).

management is somewhat negative. If management does little or nothing in the area of human relations, or on the contrary gives evidence of a negative attitude toward human relations, there is the possibility of an organization being created to oppose and countermanage the management group. With the assistance of our federal government, the labor union has become a major influence in our economy. Much of the force behind the labor union movement can be traced to mismanagement of the human factor. Thus, if management does not accept the idea that constructive human relationships will make a net contribution to organization productivity, the fear of possible containment by a labor organization may elicit more favorable consideration for this idea. A union, of course, works to protect the interests of the worker, and such an organization has obviously greatly altered the approach of many managements.

The third basis for activity in the human relations area is the possibility of government intervention in the affairs of the firm. History has shown that mismanagement of the business in general, and of the personnel factor in particular, has led to increasing governmental participation in business operations. A prime example is the many state and federal Fair Employment Practice laws which attempt to prohibit discrimination against employees because of race, religion, sex, age, or color. Society feels that its members, who are under the control of management, have certain rights and privileges that cannot be transgressed. If there is serious general mismanagement of human relationships by private management, it is not at all unlikely that society will feel that its trust in private management has been misplaced. Thus, proper concern for effective human relations is of great assistance in keeping the management of business firms relatively free of government intervention.

One final argument justifying the significant role of human relations in management rests on moral grounds. Though an economic unit such as a business organization has necessarily economic objectives, it is undeniable that certain concomitant objectives of a moral nature must be met. The attainment of economic objectives cannot under any circumstances trample moral values. We cannot literally be our brother's keeper, but concern for others as fellow human beings, a concern which must be reflected in many of our actions, has to be present if we are to preserve the system, enjoy its fruits, and keep the respect of ourselves and others.

MANAGEMENT: A BEHAVIORAL APPROACH

We have now come to the point where we can begin to analyze the four basic functions of management in terms of both the behavioral and more traditional studies of organizational and management theory. The classical management functions have been chosen as the vehicle for presentation. It is believed that they have proved sufficiently viable and flexible to incorporate both the behavioral and traditional contributions. Perhaps a better title would be a "neo-classical" or "neo-traditional" approach as a result of their alteration in the light of behavioral research.

Planning. Planning is logically the first duty of a manager. Someone must undertake the task of thinking through the phases of the business problem under consideration. The tangible results of this intellectual process take various forms. Plans can be classified as *single-use plans* or *standing plans.* Single-use plans are determinations of desired actions for projects which either will never recur, or will recur under greatly altered circumstances. Standing plans are those covering repeating situations. Examples of the latter are programs, objectives, policies, and procedures. Chapters 2 to 5 will cover the management principles and concepts of planning as developed by practitioners and theorists in scientific management.

Immediately following the presentation of the theory of planning, we will examine the nature of the human element in these situations. It has become apparent that planning must take into consideration the needs, desires, sentiments, attitudes, and possible reactions of personnel to the scientifically designed programs and policies that are established. These reactions can be influenced not only by the particular details of the presented plan, but also by the general tenor of attitudes and morale in the organization. Chapters 6 and 7 will present the outline of major psychological and sociological factors that will affect business planning, reactions of personnel to plans imposed from above, and a discussion of the means whereby management can assist in effecting more productive reactions and attitudes.

Organizing. Concern here is with establishing the basic conditions for effective performance. All organizations are made up of three fundamental components: people, functions, and physical factors. In organizing, the manager must procure these personnel and capital goods, divide the work up, and relate all three components to each other and to the common organization objective, while utilizing certain procedures. The formal ties that bind these components together are those of responsibility, authority, and accountability. Basic principles and concepts governing the process of formal organizing are discussed in Chapters 8 through 10.

Sociologists and psychologists have been pointing out that the formal structures established by management are always altered in some respect by the particular people who man that structure. Various informal groupings and ties are established, not by management alone, but by all personnel in the enterprise. The creation of such relationships is inevitable, and their complete destruction is neither desirable nor possible as long as there are people in the organization. Chapters 11 through 13 will examine the various facets of informal organization, emphasizing such subjects as cliques, reward and favor systems, status, effects of specialization, and the impact of particular work systems and procedures upon people. Certainly, we look through only one eye if we view the organization simply in its formal character. We need both the informal and the formal points of view if we are to understand organization structure with any degree of depth and perception.

Directing. In the older approaches to defining fundamental management functions, many writers followed a three-part breakdown as follows: planning, organizing, and controlling. In the last three decades, because of the impact of the behaviorists, there has been an emphasis upon identification of a fourth function, that of direction. It is not assumed today that if we have sound plans and excellent structures, personnel will automatically begin to work. Directing, or the activating of an organization through motivation and stimulation, is a major management function which is equal in importance to planning, organizing, and controlling. There must be some directive leadership undertaken because of the very pyramidal organization structures designed by management. In Chapters 14 through 16, various aspects of formal direction will be discussed with attention devoted to leadership, the role of the immediate supervisor, and two major formal methods of stimulation: compensation and training.

As indicated above, the leader is expected to move and direct his subordinates. In recent years, such initiation has often been met with various forms of subordinate resistance. Consequently, formal direction may have to be altered and supplemented with various approaches which find their basis in employee reactions. It has been advocated that the leader permit a sharing of his directive function through various forms of subordinate participation. The suggestion is that when the leader talks, he is not always, or even usually, getting through to the subordinate; in short, he fails to communicate. Thus, in looking at the reverse side of the direction function, in Chapters 17 through 19, we shall examine such specific subjects as employee participation, communication, and group dynamics.

Controlling. The function of control is concerned with the regulation of business activities in accordance with the original plan. In Chapters 20 and 21, we shall discuss the basic theory of formal control, including the establishment of control standards, the collection of information about employee activities, and the alteration or correction of those activities which do not conform to the wishes of the manager. The manager often views control as one of his most important functions. Other functions can be split and submerged to a degree, but the process of control is to many the essence of management. In Chapter 21, one particular type of control correction will receive emphasis: disciplinary action.

The reaction of subordinates to managerial controls is as varied as the differences between people or between environments. Certain basic patterns and problems have been identified, revolving particularly around the issue of effectively integrating the viewpoints and interests of members of the organization. Again, the power of the subordinate group has demonstrated that pure force and authority have to be altered in response to individual and group reactions. The manager who attempts to control actions without regard to possible and probable results is rapidly creating more problems than he is solving. He must be concerned with the viewpoints of his personnel. If he and the organization are to measure up to formal responsibilities, these viewpoints have to be integrated to some degree to make the necessary cooperation possible; otherwise, the organization as a whole will inevitably disintegrate. Thus, in this final section, we shall examine specific aspects of the general problem of integrating viewpoints and effecting group cooperation toward the goals established by management. In Chapters 22 through 25, such specific problems will be discussed as the introduction of change, the integration of minority groups and viewpoints, counseling, and the formalization of those once-informal groups into labor unions.

In the final chapter, various other philosophies and techniques of integrating traditional and behavioral approaches to management will be examined. This writer believes that an alteration of the traditional definitions of planning, organizing, directing, and controlling is inevitable if the organization is to be most effective. These four compartments, and their subsections, are not water-tight; neither management functions nor human personalities are that simple. But such a framework will at least lead us towards a management philosophy which combines both the "rationalistic" and the "humanistic" approaches.

SUMMARY

All organizations constitute processing units for input resources from an open environment. All organizations require management to insure that such processing results in satisfactory outputs. Information feedback and correction are essential in the total organization system as well as within the managerial subsystem. Management can thus be defined as the planning, organizing, directing, and controlling of the activities of an organization to the end that objectives are achieved with economy and effectiveness. The pragmatic, or rationalistic, study and development of managerial functions was begun by such pioneers as Taylor and Fayol, and much progress has been made in further objectifying the process of decision making in a business environment.

A half-century after the initiation of the scientific approach in American business, a major element of the management process was extracted for study. Elton Mayo and other behavioral scientists pointed out the significance and variability of the human element in the rational, economic, and rather rigid situations visualized by the scientific manager. Increasing concern for this element was and is necessary in order to improve the economy and operating effectiveness of the enterprise, avoid undue trouble and interference on the part of labor unions and governmental units, and fulfill certain human obligations which transcend the economic environment.

A prime contention of this text is that the execution of the four major management functions must be altered significantly to conform with the anticipated interaction between formal regulation and regimentation and the human personality. Our purpose is to examine each of these functions in turn and cover both the necessary formal execution as well as possible alterations to accommodate that significant element, the human personality.

DISCUSSION PROBLEMS

1. In what way is the external environment of an organization an open one?
2. In what way is the internal environment of an organization a closed one? an open one?
3. Distinguish between the behavioral and the classical approaches to management.
4. What are the similarities among the following organizations? (1) a hospital, (2) a university, (3) a prison, (4) a business firm, and (5) a city government. What are the differences?
5. In what way or ways would Elton Mayo disagree with Frederick Taylor on how to manage an organization? Would Taylor agree with Fayol?
6. What is a management approach? Why are there so many? Which ones are in most apparent conflict?
7. Can human relations be studied in controlled, experimental situations? What are the possible gains? the difficulties?
8. In what way does the field of management resemble the field of engineering?
9. Would the management functions be performed any differently in a free enterprise business system than they would under a socialistic state? Would there be any similarities in managing a Russian tractor firm and an American one?
10. What would you say to convince a "died-in-the-wool" classical manager that he should consider a more behavioral approach to his management functions?

SUPPLEMENTARY READING

Churchman, C. West, *Challenge to Reason,* Chap. 2. New York: McGraw-Hill Book Company, 1968.

Cleland, David I. and William R. King, *Systems Analysis and Project Management,* Chap. 1. New York: McGraw-Hill Book Company, 1968.

Goodman, Richard A., "A System Diagram of the Functions of a Manager," *California Management Review,* Vol. 10, No. 4 (Summer, 1968), 27–38.

McGregor, Douglas, *The Professional Manager,* Chap. 1. New York: McGraw-Hill Book Company, 1967.

Mockler, Robert J., "The Systems Approach to Business Organization and Decision Making," *California Management Review,* Vol. 11, No. 2 (Winter, 1968), 53–58.

Ways, Max, "Tomorrow's Management: A More Adventurous Life in a Free-Form Corporation," *Fortune* (July, 1966), 84–87, 148–150.

Young, Stanley, "Organization as a Total System," *California Management Review,* Vol. 10, No. 3 (Spring, 1968), 21–32.

Part Two

PLANNING

The first function of management is to determine what is to be done, where it is to be done, how, when, and by whom.

Section A

Formal Planning

The first approach to planning should be essentially logical, with emphasis on the objectives of contemplated actions (Chapter 2), the rational process of decision making (Chapters 3 and 4), and the resulting policies, procedures, and standards (Chapter 5).

2

Organization Objectives

The management process must start with a specification of objectives, must end with an evaluation of how well the objectives were accomplished, and must be ever aware of the guidance value of these objectives. To break the process down even further, we may say that planning involves the determination of objectives; organization is constructed to accomplish the work necessary to fulfill objectives; direction is concerned with the stimulation of organization members toward the objectives; and control compares results with objectives to measure the degree of effective achievement.

IMPORTANT OF OBJECTIVES

Before we can plan programs and determine what is to be done and where and when that action should take place, we must, of course, know what it is we hope to accomplish. Knowledge of and familiarity with the objective facilitates comprehensive and integrated plans covering all facets of activity.

Organization implies the existence of at least one objective held in *common* by all members of the enterprise. Consequently, business objectives must be examined to determine specifically the nature of *the* common objective that will provide the basis for guiding *all* efforts, as well as the specific goals of particular individuals and groups within the large framework. All subsidiary goals must be integrated with this common, general objective.

The objective has great influence on the execution of the direction function.

Not only does it indicate the proper course of action; it also indicates the reasons for that action. When one knows *why* he must do something, he is usually more willing to undertake the necessary activity. In addition, such knowledge gives him some criteria to judge the propriety of acts not specifically covered by the directions of his superior, and he is able, therefore, to contribute a little self-direction.

Similarly, the objective is also important in that it provides the basis for eliminating action that makes no contribution toward its accomplishment. Instead of the work becoming all-engrossing and an end in itself, it is viewed from a larger perspective as a means to an end.

Organization objectives also provide the basis for cooperation and the development of good morale. Each member of an organization has slightly differing, and often conflicting, personal goals or values for joining the organization. The gathering of these diverse individuals and groups into one framework presupposes at least *one* common objective seen as important by all. Various interests are thereby subsumed by the common objective and a rationale is developed for cooperation.

Finally, the objective is important in that it sets up a standard for effective control. The goal establishes the results desired from organized, coordinated, and cooperative action. When the basic goals are broken down into specific objectives such as deadlines, targets, and standards, we have the practical, tangible, and operating basis for control. If the objectives are hazy and fuzzy, control will be loose and erratic. If goals are well defined and thought out, control of action will be greatly facilitated.

TYPES OF OBJECTIVES

One of the first things recognized by most managers is that an organization has more than one objective. This, of course, presents to the manager one of his major tasks, that of integrating all these goals so that coordinated and cooperative action results. At least four main goals of a business organization can be identified as follows:

1. Creation of economic value in the form of products and services.
2. Survival and growth of the organization as an entity.
3. Creation and distribution of values desired by participating individuals and groups within the organization.
4. Creation of values, other than economic, desired by general society.

Each of these will be set forth and discussed in the following sections.

Economic Service Objective

Society needs and must have various economic values, and the creation of these values constitutes the prime purpose or *economic service objective* of particular organizations within the whole economy.

The broad service objectives of one firm can be broken down into a hierarchy of service objectives for its component divisions, departments, and individuals. Thus, the general service objective of the "XYZ" corporation could be the manufacture and distribution of a refrigerator, to use a prosaic example. Similarly, the manufacturing division's service objective could be the creation of values of form; the service objective of the sales division is the creation of values of place, possession, and time. Within the manufacturing division, the objective of a major department could well be the building of a motor to run the refrigerator. Another department's service objective may be the construction of the insulated cabinet. Within the motor division, the service objective of a section could be the construction of the motor housing. And within this section, a single worker's service objective might be the creation, by use of a milling machine, of a particular surface.

Thus, there is the *general* service objective of creating and placing a refrigerator into the hands of a member of society at the time and place he wants it. There is a *major* objective of creating the form of the refrigerator, *intermediate* ones of constructing a motor and a motor housing, a *minor* one of accomplishing milling work on the housing, and an *individual* one of forming a particular surface on this housing. All add up to total value to be enjoyed and consumed by society. Throughout this sequence, it is a duty of management to insure that the hierarchy of service objectives is logical, consistent, and integrated.

Davis points out that service objectives within the organization be classified in two ways: (1) according to groupings within the enterprise, such as division or department, and (2) according to steps in operation procedures.[1] Regarding the second classification, a procedure or method is established to accomplish a particular project service objective. For example, the manufacture of a motor housing may involve a number of operations executed in order. Each operation within the project sequence has a service objective which must fit in and add to the final objective. These intermediate operation service objectives may be portrayed by a series of process drawings showing the product in various stages of completion; the final drawing of the housing would then represent the final objective of this particular procedure. Each intermediate service objective represents varying values placed into the product by different

[1] Ralph C. Davis, *Industrial Organization and Management,* 3rd ed. (New York: Harper & Bros., 1957), pp. 26–29.

operations. Again, no work should be undertaken that does not result in some contribution to the final objective.

Thus, Joe Doakes, a milling machine operator, has an *individual organization service objective* on a long-term basis, doing various types of milling work on a number of different projects and procedures. He reports to and is rated by his section head for this work. At the same time he has *multiple intermediate operation service objectives* depending upon the particular procedures in which he is involved. For one type of housing, he may perform step number 20, for another, step number 15. A sequence of operation service objectives usually cuts across organization lines, and the accumulation of these in any one job, section, or department constitutes that job's, section's, or department's *organization* service objectives. Chart 2–1 represents the vertical and horizontal relationships of organization and operation service objectives.

In summary, the economic service objective of a business organization is the creation and distribution of certain economic values. In the large firm, the general service objective must be broken down into subservice objectives. Each man and each unit of the firm has a service objective, the accomplishment of which justifies the receipt of individual reward in the form of money or such nonfinancial returns as status, recognition, and power. This hierarchy of service objectives must be well defined and integrated if maximum coordination and cooperation is to be forthcoming. After organization service objectives have been defined, work methods or systems must be specified. These methods and systems usually cut across organization lines as particular projects are undertaken and accomplished. Thus, there are operational service objectives which include intermediate objectives for each step and the final operational service objective for the entire project.

Survival and Growth

If we begin by saying that an organization has at least one objective held in common by all, we may also note the existence of an all-important second objective, one which in some cases might even dominate the thinking of the organization. This objective is survival and growth of the enterprise. Whether an organization is producing desired economic value or not seems to take second position to just staying alive. The organization is here and now, and the higher objective of service to society often assumes a secondary importance.

All organizations require a certain minimum level of income in order to exist. In times of prosperity, other goals assume greater importance, but in times of depression, survival, in the hope of better conditions in the future, becomes the prime consideration. In many cases, meeting next week's payroll takes precedence over conforming to ethical practices or contributing to society.

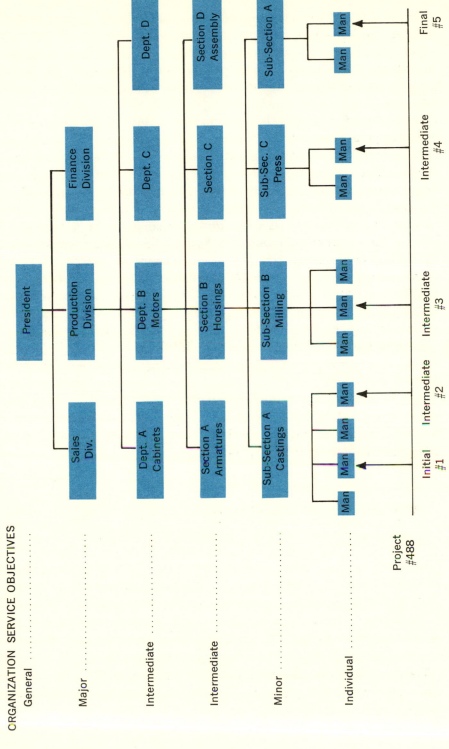

CHART 2–1   ORGANIZATION AND OPERATION SERVICE OBJECTIVES

ORGANIZATION SERVICE OBJECTIVES

General ....

Major ....

Intermediate ....

Intermediate ....

Minor ....

Individual ....

President

Sales Div.   Production Division   Finance Division

Dept. A Cabinets   Dept. B Motors   Dept. C   Dept. D

Section A Armatures   Section B Housings   Section C   Section D Assembly

Sub-Section A Castings   Sub-Section B Milling   Sub-Sec. C Press   Sub-Section A

Man   Man   Man   Man   Man   Man   Man   Man   Man   Man   Man

Project #488   Initial #1   Intermediate #2   Intermediate #3   Intermediate #4   Final #5

OPERATION SERVICE OBJECTIVES

Organizations also become infused with values with the passage of time and with the development of attitudes and relationships among their members. An organization personality, character, or "image" begins to assert itself. Thus, an individual or group may wish to preserve an enterprise for personal, nontangible reasons, even though the economic situation may demand its discontinuance.

Survival must, of course, be accompanied by growth—in sales, investment, employees, etc. Mere survival restricts and constricts the organization, leading to its eventual demise. Thus, growth, sometimes at the expense of real economic service and profits, becomes an important objective of the organization. Better service and higher profits and salaries are indeed a function of growth, but growth, nevertheless, often seems to become an end in itself. Growth can become a major objective of a firm for such reasons as the following: (1) to become the *biggest* organization of its kind in the city, state, nation, or industry; (2) to insure against stagnation and eventual decay; (3) to provide a tangible and specific goal which will stimulate organization members to greater activity; and (4) to acquire the economic advantages which come from size, such as more efficient methods of production and distribution and increased power and influence in the various markets in which the firm participates.

From society's viewpoint, survival and growth are justified only in the sense that they contribute real and desired economic values to society. The firm that survives and grows without returning economic values constitutes economic waste. In a sense, society applauds when firm "A," which cannot produce values or products of equal worth with other firms, goes bankrupt and dies. The resources that are thereby freed flow to the firms that can more effectively utilize them to create greater economic values.

Objectives of Organization Members

The organization as an entity is one thing. Its members, separately considered, are another. These members have various personal goals or objectives which they hope to achieve through organization activity. If these personal goals are not achieved to a reasonable degree, these members will withdraw from the organization. If the organization is to survive and grow, it must also return value to its members in order to retain their services. Personal goals of organization members thereby become organization goals.

There are several groups of organization members which have various and often apparently conflicting personal objectives. Among these groups and their personal goals are the following:

Organization Members	Member Goals
Stockholders	Profits
Management	Salaries, bonuses, etc.
Employees	Wages and bonuses
Bondholders	Interest on investment

It is not unusual for particular groups or members to feel that their personal goals are in conflict with the personal goals of other members. Some stockholders believe that if there are to be higher wages, there must be lower profits. Many employees feel that if there are to be higher management salaries, there must be lower employee wages. Though there is no economic justification for such feelings, it is a management task to integrate interests and reconcile conflicts, whether or not these conflicts are real. If any one group believes that its personal goals are not being satisfactorily accomplished, it will seek to withdraw from the organization. Stockholders can sell their stock, bondholders can transfer their investment elsewhere, and management and employees can resign or strike.

In addition to the above-listed goals of organization members, there are also certain non-monetary, or psychological, objectives which most people have. Not only would the stockholder like to have reasonable dividends, he also would want to feel proud of the organization of which he is part owner. The employee or manager would like to feel that he is a significant part of the enterprise and that the job he is doing is worthwhile. Such psychological goals are examined at length in another part of this book.

Objectives of Society

As indicated earlier, society has an economic stake in every business enterprise. But there are other objectives of society which a business organization can and does affect, a fact which thereby makes them business objectives. The business system is but a segment of general society, a society with certain goals which transcend all lesser objectives. For example, a goal of society is to insure care for its older members once they are retired and no longer earning income. Since the business segment of society can contribute to that general objective, social security thus becomes an objective imposed upon the business firm by society. If a business organization does not recognize and voluntarily provide for these social goals, statutory legislation and regulatory agencies are usually established to insure that they do so anyway.

There are many firms whose policies reflect a stronger obligation to society than that required by statute. These organizations encourage, for example, employee participation in community activities. The organization itself also tries to be a "good citizen" by supporting various civic groups, private and public educational institutions, and charitable organizations. These noneconomic objectives also become collateral social objectives of the business firm.

PROCESS OF ESTABLISHING OBJECTIVES

Objectives are established *by people* for the organization. Consequently, goal establishment involves all members of the organization as well as certain groups outside the enterprise. Classical theory contends that top management and the board of directors for a corporation determine the major objectives. Lower managers then develop more specific goals that are in consonance with general objectives. The result is a unified, effective, and efficient combination of efforts directed toward clear and consistent objectives.

Behaviorists are more concerned with identifying *real* goals as compared with *stated* goals. Objectives are often the result of power plays and pressures that issue from various places—the board of directors, outside creditors, lower managers, employees, major stockholders, and labor unions. The neat, logical hierarchy of classical goals is often significantly altered by particular individuals and groups who seek to adapt the organization to particular purposes.

To determine the real goals of an organization, one must look at the actual decisions and actions that occur day-by-day. What functions or groups actually receive the lion's share of the resources? What type of behavior is accorded the greatest rewards by management? If the administration of a prison, for example, specifies its major goal as rehabilitation of prisoners, the presence of only two counselors and five hundred guards would indicate otherwise. "It is the decision to commit resources for certain activities and to withhold them from certain others that operationally defines the organizational goals . . . the speaker must put his resources where his mouth is if something is to be considered a goal."[2] The reading of lofty goal and policy statements of an organization will not usually provide an accurate picture of real, actual, operating objectives.

To add to the difficulty, it must be emphasized again that all organizations have multiple and somewhat conflicting real goals which must be balanced and integrated by management. There must be developed some type of goal hierarchy to assist in conflict resolution. In a survey of 1,072 business managers on varying organizational levels, England attempted to determine the goals

[2] Vernon E. Buck, "A Model for Viewing an Organization as a System of Constraints," in James D. Thompson, *Approaches to Organizational Design* (Pittsburgh: University of Pittsburgh Press, 1966), p. 109.

FIGURE 2–1   BEHAVIOR ANALYSIS OF ORGANIZATIONAL
GOAL CONCEPTS

Total Group (N = 1,072) Goals of Business Organizations	% High Importance	% Successful 1st Ranked
Organizational Efficiency	81	71
High Productivity	80	70
Profit Maximization	72	70
Organizational Growth	60	72
Industrial Leadership	58	64
Organizational Stability	58	54
Employee Welfare	65	20
Social Welfare	16	8

Source: George W. England, "Organizational Goals and Expected Behavior of American Managers," *Journal of the Academy of Management* (June, 1967), p. 108.

that were deemed to be important as well as those deemed to be essential to success of the enterprise.[3] The results are presented in Fig. 2–1. Though eight specific goals were listed, manager reactions resulted in four major classes: (1) general efficiency in pursuit of economic goals, (2) associate status goals of growth and stability, (3) employee welfare, and (4) social welfare. It is interesting to note that the organization comes first in the eyes of management, with employee welfare a distant second, and social welfare in third place. It should be noted that though 65 percent believed employee welfare was of high importance, only 20 percent deemed it essential to success of the organization. Behavioral management theories receive much lip service in the form of stated goals, but little in the way of significant influence on decisions where organizational and human values appear to clash.

In recent years, a specialized sub-field in management theory has arisen under the label "social responsibility of business." In England's survey, social welfare ranks a distant last in the estimation of business managers. In another survey where the managements of three hundred large companies were asked to rank the groups to whom they felt the greatest responsibility, the order resulting was (1) stockholders, (2) employees, (3) customers, (4) creditors, and (5) society.[4] On the other hand, observation of managerial behavior reveals an increasingly large and varied array of organizational expenditures in such social welfare areas as jobs for the hard-core unemployed, establishing

[3] George W. England, "Organizational Goals and Expected Behavior of American Managers," *Journal of the Academy of Management,* Vol. 10, No. 2 (June, 1967), pp. 107–117.
[4] Arthur W. Lorig, "Where Do Corporate Responsibilities Really Lie?" *Business Horizons,* Vol. 10, No. 1 (Spring, 1967), pp. 51–54.

and financing enterprises in ghetto areas, support for colleges and universities, and urban redevelopment. Yet, many feel that these social welfare goals are only stated goals, and cannot become real ones except insofar as they are translated into the language of business—dollar profits. The England survey also revealed that company presidents as a class reported higher relevance scores for both social and employee welfare than did all other types of managers.[5] This could reflect both the social class of presidents and the influence of their position which requires them to represent their firms to society.

At present, there is no well developed, usable theory of decision making in the social responsibility area. There is, however, a growing sense or feeling of responsibility for various societal problems among American managers. Among various causes for this change of attitude are increasing levels of education of both managers and the work force, and outside pressures from groups and governments. As business firms become more affluent in an affluent society and more independent of threats from customers, investors, and creditors, there is a tendency to move from a profit *maximization* decision base to one of profit *satisfaction*. The result is the accumulation of resources that may be allocated to secondary goals in the social and employee welfare areas. This is a major point made by Galbraith in *The New Industrial State*.[6] However, in any head-on clash between social or employee welfare and the economic well-being of the enterprise, it is probable that the latter will prevail, at least in the short run.

GOAL COMPLEXITIES

In addition to the problem of distinguishing between real and stated goals, there are a number of other difficulties that often arise. First, the economic service objective is not as simple to define as it first appears. Should it be defined in terms of short-run or long-range service values, or both? Should, for example, General Motors define its service objective as the manufacture and distribution of automobiles, or, rather, as the manufacture and distribution of transportation? Defining the objective in terms of an automobile is good only for immediate purposes. There is no guarantee that the customer will always want to be transported by automobiles. If better means of transportation are developed, the customer will no longer purchase the products of the automobile industry. This industry, then, should define its basic service objective in such a manner that it is not unalterably committed to the combustion engine automobile. It should, in short, be customer-value oriented, rather than

---

[5] England, "Organizational Goals and Expected Behavior of American Managers," p. 114.
[6] John K. Galbraith, *The New Industrial State* (Boston: Houghton Mifflin Co., 1967).

product-oriented. Using this approach, General Motors could develop entirely new concepts of transport such as fuel-cell units or solar-energy conversion systems. Or the ground vehicle may largely disappear in favor of air transport even for single individuals. If the automobile industry refuses to view its objectives in this light, it is certain that other more farsighted industries and organizations will. Thus, as stated by Levitt, each firm and industry should engage in "creative destruction," that is, destroying one's own current and immediate assets by finding newer and better products to provide the ultimate values desired by the customer.[7]

A second difficulty occurs when it is determined that there are often *multiple* service objectives. What, for example, is the major service goal of a university? Is it the instruction of students, or research to advance the state of knowledge? In some universities, research is given the first priority in money, manpower, and privilege. In others, the teaching goal is dominant. In still others, an attempt is made to be all things to all people. In any event, effective accomplishment of service goals requires some specification of priority that cannot be altered too frequently. "Management by drive" is an attempt to maximize all goals, one at a time; e.g., this year is the "teaching year," next year is for research, to be followed by counseling students and community education programs at designated intervals. In industry, such an approach is also quite common in the form of sales contests, safety drives, scrap campaigns, cost reduction programs, etc. Man's attention and efforts are limited, and a poorly defined set of goals usually leads to management by drive. One can debate the priority of goals for such institutions as (1) a mental hospital (therapy or confinement), (2) a church (religion or social relationships), (3) a prison (rehabilitation or confinement), (4) a vocational high school (skill development, general education, or keeping young people off the streets), (5) a hospital (treatment, research, or teaching), and (6) an aerospace firm (research information or usable hardware). The specification of priorities will have far reaching and drastic effects upon the type of personnel required, the style of management appropriate, and the development of a distinctive organization character or image.

A final complexity with respect to goal determination is the myriad of opportunities for *goal distortion*. The more quantitative the goal, the greater the attention and pressure for its accomplishment. Production managers *must* meet specific quotas and schedules; personnel managers have more subjective goals and consequently less pressure. In universities, research and publication are far easier to measure precisely than is teaching ability. If the most important goal is also the most measurable, then little distortion will take place. If

[7] Theodore Levitt, "Marketing Myopia," *Harvard Business Review,* Vol. 38, No. 4 (July–August, 1960), pp. 45–57.

the reverse is true, the organization is likely to be pushed in the direction of the more quantitative, but less important, goal.

In addition, organization members lower in the hierarchy often experience confusion between goals and means. To effectively accomplish goals through the efforts of large numbers of personnel, there must be developed a pattern of means consisting of supporting procedures, policies, and standards. The definition of a pathological bureaucrat is one who inverts ends and means. He is not so much concerned with accomplishing the goals of an enterprise as he is in making sure that he is correct according to the book, the means specification. Books become out-of-date as goals and environments change, but the bureaucrat sticks to the letter of the law. This phenomenon suggests important managerial questions. Do we want all organization members to be well informed concerning organization goals? Do we want them to willfully violate established supporting procedures and policies if, in their opinion, they do not contribute to organization goals? Or do we want them to do precisely as they are told and leave the thinking and decision making to top management? The answers to these questions will contribute much in determining whether one is basically a classicist or behaviorist in managerial philosophy.

PRIMACY OF THE ECONOMIC SERVICE OBJECTIVE

Extended analysis of the various major objectives of a business firm leads to the conclusion that the economic service objective is *primary* in nature. In the final reckoning, it must be regarded as more fundamental than survival or various personal objectives, including profit. There are at least three reasons for this, reasons which we shall call "societal," "organizational," and "economic."

Societal Basis

The political rationale finds its basis in the idea that an economic system is a means to an end. The end is the creation of economic values to be consumed by society. In America, our society has chosen the profit system to create these values, and the right of private property has been delegated to individuals within society. These individuals are to use this right to produce economic goods. If these goods are not forthcoming, or are produced at excessive costs or in a manner deemed undesirable, the right of private property and the profit system will be abridged and possibly even abolished. Thus, we receive the right to start a business organization from society. They granted that right, not so we *could* make a profit, but rather so we *would* make a product. If profit motivation does not work satisfactorily, society will search for a new motivating force in order to achieve the desired economic values.

All countries have some type of economic system to produce economic values. A Russian tractor firm's primary service objective is the creation of a tractor. The motivation to produce has, at least until recently, tended to be based upon fear. The International Harvester Company's primary service objective is also the creation of a tractor. The motivation or system to get this done for society is profit. It is believed in the United States that more economic value can be created at a lesser cost by means of profit than by orders and punishment. Thus, the objective of the business firm, as society views it, is to create economic goods, and *not* to make a profit. From the view of the businessman, the order of importance may be different. But in the final analysis, society makes the rules of the game.

Organizational Basis

The second reason for supporting the primacy of the service objective has been called "organizational." We have noted the principle of organization which states that there must be at least one objective held in common by all members of an organization. The only objective that fills this requirement is the economic service objective. As indicated in Fig. 2–2, the objectives of various groups are personal in nature: dividends for stockholders, wages for laborers, salaries for executives, and interest for bondholders. The objective of the *organization* is the creation and distribution of economic values, and each group must contribute to this common objective in order to profit, in whatever way, from the organization. All members should be interested in the enterprise attracting the customer's dollar. After this has been accomplished, many of the

FIGURE 2–2   ORGANIZATION AND OPERATION SERVICE OBJECTIVES

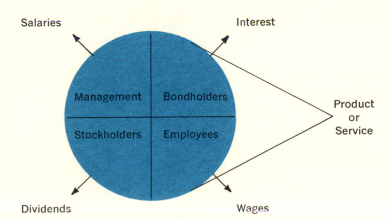

personal conflicts cited earlier come to the fore and must be reasonably well reconciled in order to effect the necessary cooperation.

In an analysis of individual and group goal satisfactions for ninety-seven business firms, it was discovered that though there is conflict among these goals, it is not of sufficient magnitude to disrupt organized activity. Correlations of goal satisfaction were computed among seven groups—owners, employees, creditors, suppliers, customers, government, and community. "The lack of any significant *negative* correlations is gratifying and indicates that the satisfaction of any one party does not immediately imply gross dissatisfaction for any other party-at-interest."[8] However, the absence of high *positive* correlations demonstrates the difficulty of fulfilling the management responsibility of reasonable reconciliation and integration of multiple goals.

Economic Basis

The third argument, economic in nature, rests upon the rationale of the free enterprise system. In the competitive system, the customer is relatively free to choose among the products and services offered by various business organizations in the market place. The theory of the system is that the resources will flow through this market to the business organizations that are producing the best goods and services. The competitive system is designed to reward the firms creating the values desired by society and drive out those that do not.

Rebuttal to Thesis

It would be well to look at the reverse side of these questions and point out the weaknesses in the arguments. There is a substantial number of businessmen who establish and defend profit as the primary goal of business. In rebuttal to the first argument (recognition of the source of authority for establishing a business), one could state that the system could be taken as a *given fact* from the view of the businessman. From the perspective of society, the objective has to be service. From the perspective of the businessman, the objective of his business unit *within the framework* established by society is profit. He believes that society knew what it was doing when it set up the profit motive. As a motive, it is powerful and effective. Society feels that if he pursues profit, he will *automatically* pursue the service objective. Viewing the individual firm as it is managed and operated on a day-to-day basis, rather than from a broad sociological perspective, we could conclude that the

[8] Hal Pickle and Frank Friedlander, "Seven Societal Criteria of Organizational Success," *Personnel Psychology*, Vol. 20, No. 2 (Summer, 1967), p. 171.

immediate and society-approved major objective is profit. The system is given; the businessman merely operates within the confines of this framework.

The organization argument cited earlier also has certain defects. It is true that all organizations are composed of various individuals and groups with different and often conflicting personal goals. It is true that there is only one real common objective—the product or service. However, one particular group, the owners, has been a dynamic and important segment of the enterprise. This group started it and may ultimately end it. Thus, it is difficult for members of this group to subordinate their personal interests to the interests of someone else or of the entire organization as an entity.

The third argument, the economic, has a number of deficiencies. The theory of the competitive system is that the efficient operation is rewarded and the inefficient is penalized, and that free market choice enables this process to occur. Consequently, to the extent that free market choice is inhibited, to the extent that monopoly and oligopoly are established, the system does not work as intended. Instead of markets making business decisions, many observers would conclude that prices and resource allocations are administered from outside. Thus, a firm in a monopolistic or oligopolistic position could well pursue the profit goal to the detriment of the service objective if left unregulated by the state.

One Viewpoint

Recognizing the power of the immediate profit objective in our economic system, we must still strive for understanding of the service objective. An excessive pursuit of the profit dollar can and does lead us into paths not approved by society. Each time this happens, there results another law, another administrative ruling, or another regulatory agency. Too avid an interest in the immediate profit objective may lead ultimately to a completely government-regulated economy without the businessman's ever really understanding how this came about. In addition, because of the slowness of governmental processes, some individuals are tempted to pursue profit to the detriment of service. Their success "proves" that profit was the basic objective. Of course, such actions often leave gaping holes in the free enterprise system which are then filled in with another law, ruling, or agency. We require a greater understanding of this concept of service and the role of profit. We should like to keep the dynamic and powerful characteristics of the profit goal while retaining as well some regard for and appreciation of the nature of the economic system and its role in society. In other words, we would like to see an *intelligent* pursuit of profits.

Events have occurred which give rise to the prospect that this intelligent pursuit of profits can be effected. In the past, many firms have been operated primarily for the exclusive interest of the owner group. In recent decades, however, there has been an increasing separation of ownership from management with the latter attempting to establish itself as a profession and to increase its power. The modern professional manager recognizes that *all* groups are necessary to accomplish the service objective, and he must insure equitable remuneration of *all* participating members. Management views itself today more in the light of a trustee and balance wheel of all groups rather than the representative of only one, the stockholder.

Finally, despite the difficulties of operating a perfectly competitive economy and the regulations that have been effected through government action, the essence of the profit system still exists. More economic values at lower costs will be produced by a system that utilizes the profit motive as much as possible. True, the public interest is paramount, and any time that there is a clash of interest between profit and the public interest, freedom and profit will be restricted. But the intelligent pursuit of long-run profit, which means a proper consideration for the service objective, will return a maximum in economic values to society.

Principles Behind the Service Objective

The principle of the primacy of the service objective is important for proper understanding of relationships within the business organization, the business system, and between these two and the society which encompasses them. In addition, there are several other principles which are of assistance in managing effectively an enterprise. Some of these have been referred to earlier and others will be repeated later, but it is helpful to note those which bear directly at this point upon the objective. Among these principles are the following:

1. *All activity undertaken in the organization should contribute in some way, directly or indirectly, to the accomplishment of the objective.* The determination of necessary functions must rest upon an analysis of the objective to be achieved. Much confusion and working at cross purposes could be minimized or eliminated by frequent reference to and definition of basic organization objectives.

2. *The more exact and definite the statement of objectives, the greater the effectiveness of organization and operation.* Fuzzy thinking and implied objectives contribute to a well-meaning but wandering organization and operation. The clearer the goal, the more effective the management process.

3. *The more respect and confidence accorded the objectives of an enterprise, the more they are accepted and, thus, the greater the likelihood of accomplishment.* This principle is violated when objectives are set up which conflict with

the desires of society, or when the objectives have not been successfully communicated to the people concerned. People do not work well toward goals in whose worth they do not believe.

4. *The establishment of reasonable goals provides incentive to accomplish those goals.* If an objective is within reach without unreasonable effort and sacrifice, its very establishment will tend to stimulate attempts to succeed. Management should make clear the goals of the enterprise, its various divisions, and the many specific jobs. Each member should know what is expected of him so that a basis is established to judge his performance. Modern merit rating, rather than an evaluation of personal characteristics, has become the accepted means of analyzing performance in relation to specific job goals.

5. *Participation in goal establishment by the members of an enterprise makes for greater understanding and acceptance of these goals, as well as a greater correctness in their determination.* Management and ownership do not have a "corner" on the brains in the enterprise, and a tapping of the human resources that exist within the organization can often lead to a better conception and statement of objectives. In addition, such participation often contributes to the above-cited principles of confidence in and respect for the organization objectives, reasonableness and attainability, and employee acceptance of the legitimacy of the goals.

SUMMARY

One of the most important elements of the process of management is the establishment of the organization objectives. These objectives constitute the organization's raison d'être. When the objectives are abolished or completely accomplished, all need for the organization disappears. Consequently, serious study of the nature of organization goals is necessary to effective management.

There are four major goals of the business organization: the economic service objective, personal objectives, survival, and society's objectives which are imposed upon the business organization. From the broad perspective of society, we conclude that the basic objective of the business organization is to produce and distribute an economic good or service. From the narrower viewpoint of the individual owner or manager of a business firm, the profit objective looms as the most important in the immediate sense. The profit economic system is taken as given, and the manager operates within this existing framework. It is important, nevertheless, that the modern business manager understand his role in an economic system which is a part of a larger society, and that he understand the possibility of change in economic systems.

In establishing a set of compatible objectives for the enterprise, the task of management is exceedingly complex. Both goal statement and execution are usually altered through informal and formal pressures of people within and without the enterprise proper. Real goals often differ from stated goals. Organizations can get off track by pursuing too avidly the more quantitative goals, confining efforts to short-run values, and inverting ends and means. The task is made more difficult by apparent conflicts in interest among the several parties. It is a central responsibility of management to maintain a viable balance among all groups—stockholders, fellow managers, employees, bondholders, customers, suppliers, and the general public.

DISCUSSION PROBLEMS

1. Discuss the difference between real and stated objectives of an organization.
2. If an organization's management is seemingly torn between two or more service objectives, what types of problems are likely to occur?
3. How can clearly defined objectives become twisted and distorted in the process of their accomplishment?
4. What is the nature of the managerial task of balancing, reconciling, and integrating multiple objectives of an organization?
5. Defend the thesis that the primary organizational objective of a business enterprise is the economic service goal. What are the objections to this thesis?
6. Distinguish between short- and long-run economic service objectives. Of what importance is this distinction?
7. Why is the concept of objectives of such great importance to a theory of management?
8. In what way has the separation of ownership and management in the modern large corporation contributed to a change in organization objectives?
9. Is the survival and growth objective an example of goal displacement or distortion? Does a firm's management distort basic objectives when it attempts to pursue profit satisfaction rather than profit maximization?
10. What is the social responsibility of the private businessman? Is it any different for the small firm than it is for the large?

SUPPLEMENTARY READING

England, George W., "Organizational Goals and Expected Behavior of American Managers," *The Journal of the Academy of Management,* Vol. 10, No. 2 (June, 1967), 107–117.

Etzioni, Amitai, *Modern Organizations,* Chap. 2. Englewood Cliffs: Prentice-Hall, Inc., 1964.

Galbraith, John K., *The New Industrial State,* Chap. 15. Boston: Houghton Mifflin Co., 1967.

Henderson, Hazel, "Should Business Tackle Society's Problems?" *Harvard Business Review,* Vol. 46, No. 4 (July–August, 1968), 77–85.

McGuire, Joseph W., "The Finalité of Business," *California Management Review,* Vol. 8, No. 4 (Summer, 1966), 89–94.

Miles, Raymond E., "The Affluent Organization," *Harvard Business Review,* Vol. 44, No. 3 (May–June, 1966), 106–114.

Pickle, Hal and Frank Friedlander, "Seven Societal Criteria of Organizational Success," *Personnel Psychology,* Vol. 20, No. 2 (Summer, 1967), 165–178.

3

Decision Making

The study of management philosophy and procedure has been subjected to various approaches. Schools of thought emphasizing mathematics, human relations, the purely pragmatic, or the functional, have applied their talents to the analysis of management systems. One of the most recent approaches has been that of the so-called "decision-making" school.[1] In *all* philosophies of management, decision making occupies a crucial position; the growth of scientific methodology has, in fact, placed the decision-making step at the center of the management process. The essence of scientific management, as advocated by Frederick Taylor, for example, was the development of more accurate tools of decision making.

In this chapter, we wish to examine the nature of the decision-making process as performed by the modern manager. This will entail a discussion of the logical process of thought, as well as some consideration of "creative" thinking and operations research. In Chapter 5, various kinds of long-range, or standing, plans, such as policies, procedures, and standards, will be discussed in terms of their derivation from this decision-making process.

ELEMENTS OF DECISION MAKING

The process of decision making that has been proposed in classical management literature typically involves a sequence of activities such as the following:

[1] Herbert A. Simon, in particular, has been an advocate of this approach as reported in such writing as James G. March and Herbert A. Simon, *Organizations* (New York: John Wiley & Sons, Inc., 1959) and Herbert A. Simon, *Administrative Behavior,* 2nd ed. (New York: The Macmillan Company, 1957).

recognizing a problem, determination of tentative solutions, collection and analysis of data, and making and implementing the decision.[2] It is essentially a logical and rational process that assumes that the world is an orderly place where cause and effect are operative. If man is to be rational in making decisions, he must usually be concerned with the following basic elements:

1. Awareness of difficulties and disharmonies.
2. Criteria for successful resolution of difficulties and disharmonies.
3. Relevant alternatives.
4. Developing expectations of alternative outcomes.
5. Choice.

Awareness. An effective manager requires a sensitivity to organizational actions and attitudes which do not meet his standards and expectations in either the short or long run. This sensitivity comes not only from a well developed set of interrelated experiences, but also from a personality drive that moves him toward excellence, improvement, and growth. The experienced manager will see more problems than an inexperienced one, provided he can throw off, from time to time, the inhibiting effects of the status quo and an undue worship of past successes. He is more aware of problems that are now buried, but which will rise up in all their horror for him and the organization if left unattended. His perceptual skills enable the collection and interpretation of cues from the environment which would be totally ignored by those without background in management or in the operative field concerned, e.g., production, sales, engineering, etc. Those with poorly developed conceptual frameworks and limited perceptual skills can live in organizational messes for years, completely oblivious of major discomfort.

It is apparent that no decisions will be made when no trigger cues are picked up from the environment. In some instances, no decision is the correct decision—time heals all ills. But in most cases, a blind, unperceptive manager who can see only the obvious is leading his organization toward trouble.

The manager must also be able to distinguish between cause and symptom of trouble to get beyond the mere surface manifestations of the problem. As in medicine, failure to make such a distinction will lead inevitably to a recurrence

---

[2] Other sequences suggested are (1) William Newman and Charles E. Summer, *The Process of Management* (Englewood Cliffs: Prentice-Hall, Inc., 1961), p. 261: (a) making a diagnosis, (b) finding alternative solutions, (c) analyzing and comparing alternatives, (d) selecting the plan to follow; (2) R. W. Morell, *Managerial Decision Making* (Milwaukee: Bruce Publishing Co., 1961): (a) uncertainty, (b) analysis and definition of the problem, (c) development of alternatives, and (d) verification; and (3) Ralph C. Davis, *The Fundamentals of Top Management* (New York: Harper & Bros., 1951), p. 60: (a) recognition of the problem, (b) preliminary observation and analysis, (c) developing tentative solutions, (d) testing and analyzing proposed solutions, (e) developing the correct solution, (f) testing the selected solution, (g) intelligent compromise, and (h) installation of the plan.

of the original difficulties. A treatment that is confined to manifest difficulties with no regard for latent sources is tantamount to inventing rubber gloves in order to write with leaky fountain pens. Thus it is that the executive must constantly strive for a thorough identification of the real problem.

Criteria of Acceptable Decisions. The manager must also specify what constitutes satisfactory handling of the perceived difficulty. He must visualize, and preferably quantify, the state of affairs that he would like to see effected. His desire to move the organization to this new outcome state is the cause for decision making, e.g., a higher return on investment, meeting a particular output schedule, reducing the level of absenteeism and turnover, becoming the industry's leader, increasing the share of market, and so on.

As indicated in the preceding chapter, most decision problems require the attainment of multiple objectives, thereby necessitating multiple criteria. The conflicts that exist in goals and criteria constitute one of the crucial elements of the decision-making process. The manager's concern is for overall effectiveness which necessarily leads him to a desire to optimize, rather than maximize, any one goal. Thus we should speak of a criteria mix encompassing multiple, ordered, and related specifications that define the optimum outcome situation.

Relevant Alternatives. The generation of relevant alternatives that may lead the organization to the desired outcome state is largely the product of men's minds, individually and collectively. In a survey of a dozen major users of digital computers, no company reported that computers were utilized for the definition of possible courses of action.[3] They were more frequently used in the identification of problems or opportunities, and the evaluation of relevant alternatives supplied by other means.

In the classical approach to the development of alternatives, it is often envisioned that *all* possible alternatives are to be considered. This will then insure that the final choice will naturally be the best choice. However, the study of actual decision processes in business firms reveals no such complete, scientific approach. Managerial behavior is more often one of searching for a *satisfactory* solution rather than the best solution.[4] Man's rationality is limited by inherent psychological and environmental factors which lead to a stopping of search activities as soon as a satisfactory alternative has been discovered.

In a depth study of a transportation method decision by fourteen middle-management executives, an average of 2.8 alternatives per decision maker were developed.[5] The largest number of alternatives discovered by any one executive was less than one-third of those possible. In addition, though all were

[3] Rodney H. Brady, "Computers in Top-Level Decision-Making," *Harvard Business Review,* Vol. 45, No. 4 (July–August, 1967), p. 71.

[4] Cf. Richard M. Cyert and James G. March, *A Behavioral Theory of the Firm* (Englewood Cliffs: Prentice-Hall, Inc., 1963), pp. 44–47.

[5] John E. Fleming, "Study of a Business Decision," *California Management Review,* Vol. 9, No. 2 (Winter, 1965), p. 52.

experienced and devoted ample time to the problem, *six* different satisfactory solutions were found and actually adopted by these executives. Any theory of scientific management that proposes to lead to the "one best answer" for each problem may just be a theory as far as actual practice is concerned.

Nevertheless, logic would suggest that the greater the number of alternatives, the greater the chance of selecting a satisfactory one. As one author states, we are attempting to apply the "principle of multiple hypotheses."[6] Logic and experience have their place in idea generation, but *imagination* can also make a significant contribution. Specific methods of organizing and applying imagination to business decision problems will be discussed later in this chapter. It is sufficient here to point out that new looks at old problems through the eyes of other people, often neophytes, frequently suggest answers which make sense to the experienced manager. Often, the neophyte does not really know or understand what he is suggesting; he may supply a new approach or insight, but its use is dependent upon the decision maker who is actually involved in the problem situation.

Development of Expectations. If the decision maker knows the nature of the desired future state and knows a number of possible alternate routes to that state, he is in a position to develop a set of expectations for each alternative. In a few instances, expectations can be developed with some degree of exactitude—a mathematical analysis, with or without the assistance of a computer, will quickly reveal the one alternative that best meets the specified criteria. In most cases, however, the projected expectations involve some degree of risk and uncertainty, thereby leading the manager into the realm of probability.

In actual practice, the typical manager relies heavily upon an intuitive approach based on years of education, experience, and study of actual cases. If asked how he goes about selecting an alternative, replies such as the following are not unusual: "I don't think businessmen know how they make a decision. I know I don't. You don't know how you do it. You just do it."[7] Certainly, the business decision maker is judged by his number of actual successes. Those who survive have usually come up with a majority of satisfactory answers, or at least a few crucially important successes.

In recent years, there have been developed approaches and techniques that purport to systematize and quantify the analysis leading toward the development of expectations. Some of these quantitative techniques will be presented in summary fashion in the following chapter. This latter approach is entirely consistent with the classical management philosophy, and sometimes leads to a seeming transformation of uncertainty into certainty. At the least, quantification should provide the manager with a greater measure of confidence in the correctness of his choice.

[6] Ralph C. Davis, *The Fundamentals of Top Management*, p. 65.
[7] John McDonald, "How Businessmen Make Decisions," *Fortune* (August, 1955), p. 84.

Choice. Though the manager can seek the assistance of specialized personnel and various decision-making aids in all other elements of the decision-making process, choice is his alone. He may abdicate his responsibility to a computer program, a mathematical formula, or a toss of the coin, but even this abdication is a management choice. As a former president said, "the buck stops here!" Choice is the inescapable responsibility of the manager.

Often, none of the proposed solutions is completely adaptable to the problem after fact collection. The best solution may constitute a synthesis of two or more hypotheses, or portions of hypotheses. The solution may not be among the proposed hypotheses, or if it is, the best hypothesis does not meet certain requirements in terms of practicability, finances, or talent available. Thus, *intelligent compromise* is often an essential element in business decision making. The theoretically perfect solution may have to give way to an *answer,* less than perfect but more acceptable. Behaviorists have long accused classical managers of being too heavily committed to the *quality* of a decision, and too little concerned with its *acceptability* by those responsible for execution. The values of cooperative and understanding behavior should not be overlooked in the executive's drive toward technically correct solutions.

LIMITATIONS OF THE RATIONAL PROCESS

The above-described series of decision-making steps represents an ideal, "all-knowing" approach to business problems. As such, it is representative of the traditional viewpoint. But there are many limitations to this process which issue basically from man's lack of complete knowledge of all aspects of an event, both before and after.

One of the first limitations involves the issue of social *values.* If all could agree upon a certain set of values, then the decision-making process could be more fully sustained as rational. But there are multiple and often contradictory sets of values in operation which lead to prolonged and emotional arguments over decisions. For example, should a firm embark upon the project of administering lie detector tests to persons applying for positions with the organization? One manager may feel that the most important value is organizational efficiency, and that if the test enables a more accurate prediction of future employee success, then it should be given. A second manager may be equally strong in his belief that the lie detector test constitutes an excessive invasion of individual privacy not warranted by proved increases in efficiency. It is apparent that these two managers operate with different scales of social values even though both recognize a need for efficiency. If values can be agreed upon, the decision-making process from *that* point can be scientific. Before that point, however, we are in the field of morals and ethics, a field which is not subject to fixed and incontestable statements.

A second limitation is the inability of any model to encompass the never-ending chain of repercussions and events that would ensue from any selected choice or decision. Let us assume that the company has decided to institute the lie detector test. An improvement in the accuracy of the selection process has been effected as anticipated. But what else will happen as a result of a higher percentage of successful employees being hired? Will the number of voluntary resignations increase because of a greater supply of outstanding employees in relation to the opportunities available? What about the grievance rate, the demands for increased salaries, the difficulties of supervising higher caliber personnel, and the possible misuse of skilled personnel? What about the effect of the lie detector test upon the morale of present employees and the attitude of the general community? If the community reacts negatively, what effect will this have on sales, and on further recruitment? And finally, what would have happened to all these items had the company management decided *against* the policy of using this type of test? Perhaps with the continued improvements in the modern digital computer, all the possible chains of events can be programmed and analyzed before the choice is actually made. Until that day arrives, we would have difficulty in labeling the decision-making process as completely rational or scientific.

APPLICATION OF THE DECISION-MAKING PROCESS

This suggested sequence of rational decision-making steps requires some illustration in terms of a specific problem in order to be fully meaningful. Let us assume, as was the actual case in one company, that a problem has been identified as being one of generally inadequate performance by first-level supervisors. In arriving at this conclusion the observers, through experience, are able to rule out the influence of the environment as the controlling cause of trouble. In addition, comparison with other supervisors in similar circumstances indicates that the performance of those under observation is below par. Thus, the problem, as developed from the decision maker's conceptual framework, supplemented by observation and study of the actual situation, is established as one of substandard supervisory performance in managing the work of the various departments. Requirements for successful supervision could be established in a specific manner such as reducing the number of grievances, increasing the quality and quantity of products, and/or conforming to established budgets. Furthermore, time and expense requirements could be set up which would govern any particular solution. For example, a possible solution might be one that resulted in a 10 percent reduction in manfacturing costs within the next twelve months.

The second stage of establishing possible answers can be tackled when the problem is clearly in mind. On a logical basis, it is hypothesized that the substandard performance issues from two fundamental sources: (1) inadequate ability, or (2) inadequate motivation. Under the ability hypothesis, other possible solutions could be set up such as replacement of supervisors, retraining, and education. Under the subsolution of training, several possible training programs could be considered which would provide the skills necessary to achieve the requirements of step one. Under the motivation hypothesis, a number of tentative solutions could be established. Incentives of both the monetary and the nonmonetary types could be considered. Under the monetary type, various possibilities could be charted, such as bonus plans based on departmental productivity, profit sharing, and stock options. These are the traditional and well-known possible solutions. Imagination may suggest unusual ideas which, with further investigation and the application of logic, may be of value. These hypotheses can be arranged in a pyramidal form, from the very broad, such as ability and motivation, to the very specific, such as a course in budgets or a supervisory bonus plan.

After the possibilities have been examined, evaluation must be made. Some of the hypotheses can be rejected very quickly on the basis of the requirements for successful solution. Wholesale replacement of supervisors, for example, may be rejected as a solution, with little or no fact-finding being necessary. Other possibilities will require extensive investigations. For example, the profit-sharing arrangement may look good to the decision maker. Research will have to be undertaken on both profit-sharing plans, and the adaptability of these plans to this particular firm. In addition, it will have to be determined whether or not the profit motive can elicit the effort necessary. Perhaps sharing in profits motivates only an interest in the profit-and-loss statement, and does not stimulate greater supervisory effort. The fact-finding should also include interviews with the supervisors to ascertain their views on possible solutions. This is particularly necessary if the solution lies in the area of motivation.

As a result of the long, difficult, and often tedious fact-finding process, the decision maker may well conclude that no one solution will solve the problem. Fact-finding may reveal that there are both specific skill deficiencies, which can be in part remedied by certain training, and a lack of involvement, which can be aided by more supervisory participation in higher management decisions. Thus, the program or solution that is developed may be the synthesis of a number of solutions designed to meet the requirements necessary for successful solving of the problem.

DECISION-MAKING AIDS

As indicated in the preceding discussion, there are techniques and approaches that have been developed through research and experience that help improve execution of various elements of the decision-making process. One of these approaches, quantitative analysis, requires more space and will be discussed in the following chapter. The values of creative thinking, concepts, and strategies as aids in decision making will be presented in the following sections.

Creative Thinking

Creative thinking is of great assistance in all functions of management, but it is of particular value in the development of relevant alternatives from which the decision maker can exercise choice. Creativity is a highly valued asset in most progressive organizations. As political, technological, sociological, and economic environments change, the organization must innovate, adapt, or die.

Typical definitions of creative behavior involve such characteristics as the following: (1) development of innovative or new ideas or products, (2) sensitivity to gaps in knowledge and disharmonies, (3) high self-motivation and persistence, and (4) nonhabitual behavior encompassing a seeming rejection of conventional norms. Maslow sees two types of creativity.[8] The first, primary creativity, refers to the unconscious processes of insight, incubation, seeing things from within, inspiration, and the like. Secondary creativity deals more with logic, science, planning, and a calculated research for new combinations of existing ideas. Secondary creativity is that sought in an organized fashion by research and development departments in business firms. It is also the type which usually issues from artificial creativity techniques such as brainstorming, checklists, and the Gordon technique.

If the executive desires more creative behavior within the organization, he can first seek out and hire personnel who seem to possess primary creativity, and secondly, he can attempt to develop an organizational climate which facilitates both primary and secondary creativity. With respect to the first, there has been much research directed toward identifying and measuring characteristics of the creative person. A summary of several studies has revealed such characteristics as:

1. Creative people do not differ significantly from less creative in terms of intelligence. Intelligence is necessary for creative thinking, but its presence does not assure that it will occur.
2. The more creative are more likely to view authority as conventional rather than absolute. They therefore are able to reduce the external inhibitions upon their thinking processes.
3. Creative people tend to make fewer black-and-white distinctions. They have a more relativistic and less dogmatic view of life.

[8] Abraham H. Maslow, *Toward a Psychology of Being* (New York: D. Van Nostrand Co., 1962), p. 175.

4. The creative are more willing to consider and express their "irrational" impulses.
5. They are usually less anxious.
6. They tend to have a better sense of humor than the less creative.[9]

In summary, the more creative persons exhibit a general pattern of behavior that is freer and less rigidly controlled.

Creative people can be stifled by an organization that insists upon complete rationality and close control of actions. If the executive desires to enhance creative thinking in his organization, he must develop an atmosphere of freedom among organization members. In a sense, freedom is the antithesis of organization. An atmosphere of insecurity and fear of failure, induced through overt or implied threats, will effectively eliminate both creative people and creative thinking. In a research and development department where creativity is highly prized, the executive must move closer to the behavioral approach in his style of managing. The need or desire for creativity on a production assembly line is far less and we are more likely to encounter classical management. Similarly, universities and colleges are more likely to be behaviorally managed than are business organizations as a class. The need for creativity in thinking is deemed to be higher in the former. If creativity is a greatly needed and prized asset of an organization, it must be both sought out and nurtured in an atmosphere of freedom, security, trust, and nonconformity.

In addition to general atmosphere, the manager can structure certain decision-making situations to focus upon the imaginative powers of organization members. In all these contrived techniques, the emphasis is upon imagination rather than judgment, and security rather than criticism. In a sense, they constitute "organized random searches" of new ideas and combinations of old ideas. Some also incorporate the concept of interpersonal stimulation within a group of people working on a common problem. It has been suggested that we experience a so-called "imagination regression" from childhood to adulthood, as we construct a set of inhibitions on the basis of what others consider to be good or bad thinking and behavior. The use of such devices as brainstorming, the Gordon technique, and forced relationships can once again bring the individual to the point where he can conceive of the daring innovation, the new idea, the radical approach.

Brainstorming. The brainstorming approach is one developed by Alex Osborn in his work in the advertising field.[10] It can be adapted to many types of problems. The approach is based upon free association, unrestricted interaction with others, and complete restraint of criticism. A problem is presented

[9] Bernard Berelson and Gary A. Steiner, *Human Behavior* (New York: Harcourt, Brace and World, Inc., 1967), p. 195.
[10] Alex F. Osborn, *Applied Imagination* (New York: Charles Scribner's Sons, 1953).

to a group, the members of which have varying degrees of knowledge and ability about the subject. The issue might be, for example, ways in which a firm can reduce the amount of worker time away from the job. Quantity, rather than quality, of ideas is emphasized. For a certain time period, any idea that comes to mind is voiced. One idea suggests another. Ridiculous and unrealistic ideas are stimulated and not repressed. No criticism of any idea is permitted and all are recorded faithfully. Concerning lost work time, there may be such suggestions as (1) raise the pay, (2) improve the working conditions, (3) pipe coffee to the desks, (4) provide two spigots on each desk, one for cream and one for black, (5) provide formfitting chairs, (6) arrange it so that soft music plays when you sit at your desk, etc. Most of the ideas in any brainstorming session will be rejected by logic and judgment after the session is over. It may be that none can be considered as is, but the creative process may be continued by further modifications of one or more ideas. For example, the piping in of coffee is somewhat impractical, but many firms have found that a mobile coffee cart has reduced the amount of lost work time.

Brainstorming is an attempt to "storm" a problem quickly with the various brains of a group. Ideas come off the top of one's head, and some have characterized the process as "cerebral popcorn." This approach has a place in solving business problems, particularly when fact-finding and analysis have been exhausted with no solution forthcoming. A fresh new look by the uninhibited, utilizing free association, is often worth the effort expended.

Gordon Technique. This technique was developed by William J. J. Gordon of Arthur D. Little, Inc. It is much more indirect and lengthy than a brainstorming session, and perhaps also less inhibiting in effect. Whereas a brainstorming leader will announce that the problem is one of developing an employee recreational program and the ideas would immediately start to flow, the Gordon leader would announce that the group should discuss "play" in general. The real and specific subject is withheld and a general one is picked that is related to it. The brainstorming technique consumes short periods of time and places its emphasis upon a large quantity of ideas. The Gordon technique discussions take a much longer amount of time and are directed toward producing *one* radically new idea. Discussing "play" may move the group far beyond the bounds of traditional recreational programs. Only the leader knows the true problem to be solved and thus the group is *less* inhibited by tradition, custom, and practice in the employee recreational field. The leader is of relatively little importance in a brainstorming session. In a Gordon discussion, however, he is a key individual for only he can determine the usefulness of suggestions produced by the group.

Forced Relationships. A new idea often consists of a new arrangement of old ideas. Innovation is sometimes the new application of an old technique to a problem to which it had never been applied before, e.g., applying time study to sales positions instead of the traditional factory job. To aid in this type of creativity, forced association can be utilized. A list of attributes of a product or a list of factors in a problem situation is first established. Then, each item can be paired with every other item and an association be forced. This process continues until all items have been related to all other items and the nature of the relationship examined.

A similar approach has been used by cartoonists in obtaining new ideas.[11] A catalog of items is selected and two of the items in it chosen at random. A relationship is then forced between these two items to form the basis of a new idea for a cartoon. The forcing of relationships requires one to seek the new and the unusual, especially when custom and experience tell us that there is no relationship between the two items.

Whether or not we use any of the creativity devices described above, we all experience the flash of illumination that comes unexpectedly. Yet even the unexpected contains what some authors have identified as the "incubation" and "illumination" stages.[12] The manager starts with the scientific decision-making method and struggles with the problem, its hypotheses, and related facts. It has been demonstrated that creativity is frequently not forthcoming under pressure, that we should disengage ourselves occasionally from our problems. Even during this period of disengagement, often labeled "incubation," the subconscious retains hold of the issue. Illumination may occur at any time and any place—while tramping from one golf tee to another, while shaving, or upon waking up in the middle of the night. It would appear that the subconscious developed the new idea (incubation) and was finally successful in thrusting it through to the conscious (illumination). For this reason, many executives always carry paper and pencil to record these thoughts which may appear at any time of the day or night.

Concepts and Strategies

Every man has a conceptual framework which helps him make decisions in his work and everyday life. Developing this framework solely through experience is a tedious, time-consuming, and yet effective process. To speed up this development, the decision maker should become acquainted with certain concepts and strategies that have been evolved from other peoples' experiences and, in some cases, through controlled research. Again, we can only roughly

[11] Charles Whiting, "Operational Techniques of Creative Thinking," *Advanced Management,* Vol. 20, No. 10 (October, 1955), p. 28.

[12] Frederic D. Randall, "Stimulate Your Executives to Think Creatively," *Harvard Business Review,* Vol. 33, No. 4 (July–August, 1955), p. 122.

indicate the nature and extent of these concepts. Examples of these are as follows:

1. Before attempting to plan any course of action, the objective should be clearly stated.
2. The cost of taking any one alternative can be measured by that which was given up to make that alternative possible.
3. The facts of the situation, if one can obtain them and have the courage to face them, often indicate the proper alternative course to take.

In the area of strategy, the *time* factor is quite important. It is apparent that the correct alternative initiated at the wrong time can be as disastrous as adopting the wrong alternative.

It is sufficient here to note that logical and creative answers based on the scientific method, operations research, creative thinking, and various concepts are not enough. The successful decision maker must supplement this with a skill in strategy which includes such maneuvers as making a small beginning when a total program is unacceptable, implanting an idea in a junior executive in order to get to the senior executive, and sponsoring gradual evolutionary changes in programs rather than revolutionary ones. Each of the strategies of timing and maneuver make sense in themselves. Often, however, they conflict with each other, e.g., the mass concentrated offensive versus gradual evolution (fabianism). It requires a shrewd and knowledgeable executive to determine when the situation is appropriate to a particular strategy.

TYPES OF PLANS

In a broad sense, the decision that is finally determined can be labeled a "plan." Plans may be detailed or vague, permanent or temporary. There are various types of semi-permanent or standing plans that are used in business. Among these are (1) objectives, (2) policies, (3) procedures, and (4) standards. We have already discussed one type, organization objectives, in the preceding chapter. It should be apparent that these plans are not restricted to any one level of organization. Thus, there are objectives of the firm, of divisions, departments, and jobs. There are company-wide as well as departmental policies. We have standards established governing the operation of the entire firm as well as those for judging the performance of any one individual. A set of *related* objectives, policies, procedures, and standards may be termed a "program." This program may in itself be composed of a hierarchy of plans according to both organizational level and chronological time. These standing plans, because of their importance and prevalence in business organizations, demand more consideration.

SUMMARY

Management is many things to various practitioners and theorists. To all, however, the making of decisions is of crucial importance to success. Decision making should first rest upon a base of rational analysis. This analysis must be preceded by an awareness and sensitivity to problems requiring solution. Final decision choice should be based on a foundation of concrete criteria for successful solution, development of relevant alternatives, and determination and projection of reasonable expectations for all relevant alternatives. Aiding in this rational process of decision making are such techniques as quantitative analysis, creative thinking, and various strategies and concepts. Creative thinking involves the use of imagination to develop new ideas and new combinations of old ideas. An atmosphere of freedom, trust, and security is necessary for the obtainment and nurture of creative talent. Various concepts and strategies of timing and maneuver, largely developed through distilled experience, also play an important role in the decision-making process. The third major aid, sometimes referred to as operations research, will be discussed at greater length in the following chapter.

The executive attempts to develop the perfect plan for his particular situation, personnel, and time. These plans may be temporary for nonrecurring situations. They may be standing in the sense that they cover events that will occur again. The standing plan types of policies, procedures, and standards will be discussed in Chapter 5 after the completion of the decision-making discussion in the following pages.

DISCUSSION PROBLEMS

1. In what ways does an executive develop a sensitivity or awareness to difficulties requiring decision making?
2. Of the various elements of decision making, which is the inescapable obligation of the manager? Why?
3. Discuss the scientific manager's quest for the "one best solution" to decision-making problems.
4. What objections do behaviorists have concerning the manager's search for the highest quality decision?
5. What is the role of creative thinking in the rational decision-making process?
6. Distinguish between primary and secondary creativity. In what ways can creativity be introduced into the firm?
7. Is creativity a generally prized asset of all organizations? Cite illustrations.
8. If the executive wishes to enhance creativity in his organization, what type of atmosphere should he wish to establish? Does this atmosphere clash with the concepts of classical management?
9. Compare and contrast brainstorming, the Gordon technique, and forced association on such elements as leadership, procedure, and inhibiting factors.
10. How do differing scales of values complicate the decision-making process?

SUPPLEMENTARY READING

Brady, Rodney H., "Computers in Top-Level Decision Making," *Harvard Business Review*, Vol. 45, No. 4 (July–August, 1967), 67–76.

Churchman, C. West, *Challenge to Reason*, Part 1. New York: McGraw-Hill Book Company, 1968.

Dauw, Dean C., "Creativity in Organization," *Personnel Journal*, Vol. 45, No. 8 (September, 1966), 465–474.

Drucker, Peter F., "The Effective Decision," *Harvard Business Review*, Vol. 45, No. 1 (January–February, 1967), 92–98.

Henderson, Bruce D., "Brinkmanship in Business," *Harvard Business Review*, Vol. 45, No. 2 (March–April, 1967), 49–55.

Wallace, William H., "Some Dimensions of Creativity," *Personnel Journal*, Vol. 46, No. 6 (June, 1967), 363–370.

4

Quantitative Aids in Decision Making

The past few decades have seen a considerable increase in the level of quantification of business decision making. As a general label, this approach to management has been termed "operations research." To some, it is old wine in a new bottle with a fancy label—merely Taylor's old scientific management approach to business problems. To others, however, it represents an additional and highly specialized tool that can be placed into the manager's decision-making kit. Some briefly define operations research as the application of advanced statistical and mathematical techniques to business problems. But in many instances, it also involves a change of viewpoint. This viewpoint is characterized by (1) research, for facts underlying the relationships used to manage a business, and (2) a comprehensive rather than segmented view of the problem. Operations research is done more by the scientist than the businessman. The businessman is the decision maker, but the scientist provides the unbiased facts and analysis. He does not recommend what to do; rather he says, "if you do that, this will probably happen."

Operations research requires a view of the problem in its entirety. Instead of labeling it an engineering or sales problem, the analyst tries to achieve *overall* optimization of results for the total interests of the organization. An attempt is made to avoid the pitfalls of suboptimization, that is, maximizing return in one area, with little regard for its impact upon other areas of the business. This approach often requires a team of research scientists, rather than a single researcher, in order to deal with the various facets of the problem.

Thus, operations research is an approach that aids in making more scientific the decision making process. It is characterized as being heavily mathematical in its analytical techniques, research minded rather than management minded, and as being more concerned with overall optimization rather than sub-optimization.

TYPES OF DECISION-MAKING PROBLEMS

The degree of quantification that can be effectively utilized varies with the conditions surrounding the decision maker. Three basic states of nature have been identified as follows.[1]

1. *Certainty:* It is assumed in this case that there is complete and accurate knowledge of the consequences of each choice.
2. *Uncertainty:* In this case, the consequences of each choice cannot be defined by a correspondence relationship even within a probabilistic framework.
3. *Risk:* In this case, it is assumed that some knowledge exists about the probability distribution of the consequences of each alternative.

When there is certainty, the decision maker is completely aware of the exact nature of the post decision situation that will develop. This very attractive state of nature is rare in social situations and is a holdover from the physical sciences. In many cases, managers *act* as if they were operating in a state of certainty even though the facts belie the assumption. Though the manager must cope with an open system, particularly with reference to the external environment, he attempts to increase the level of certainty *within* the enterprise, hoping to be able to use deterministic, closed models of decision making. He hopes to create security and accuracy for both himself and organization members. A particularly interesting closed decision-making framework used in allocation problems is that of linear programming. A simple illustration of this type of decision making will be given later in this chapter.

Despite the yearning of the manager for a certain and calculable environment, the facts usually indicate that he is operating in situations involving some degree of risk and uncertainty. The manager cannot be absolutely certain that he will know the post decision conditions in advance. If he is unable to determine even a small degree of probability with respect to which of several conditions are likely, he is said to be operating under conditions of uncertainty. In this event, his quantification attempt may well consist of *assuming* that all identified future states are *equally possible*—the Laplace criterion.[2] Other

[1] James G. March and Herbert A. Simon, *Organizations* (New York: John Wiley & Sons, Inc., 1959), p. 137.

[2] P. S. de Laplace, *A Philosophical Essay on Probabilities,* translators F. W. Truscott and F. L. Emory (New York: Dover Publications, 1951).

strategies to be considered would be selecting the alternative with the highest minimum payoff (maximin), "going for broke" by selecting the one with the highest possible payoff (maximax), or choosing the one that minimizes the maximum dissatisfaction that could take place *after* he knows the actual outcome (minimize regret).[3] A comprehensive illustration involving all these strategies will be presented in a later section of this chapter.

The greater bulk of the situations in which the decision maker operates involves a degree of risk. Some, though not complete, knowledge exists concerning the likelihood of the outcomes of various decision alternatives. This knowledge may be based on a large number of similar experiences in the past from which *objective probabilities* can be developed. Or it can come from the informed, best judgment of knowledgeable decision makers who have successfully digested past experiences and can propose *subjective probabilities*.

Risk implies that usable and reasonably accurate information exists that the manager can employ to improve his choice. Objective probabilities are based upon the relative frequency of events that tend to stabilize in distribution after a large number of occurrences. In the case of a coin flip, for example, observation of its construction would suggest the likelihood that heads will appear 50 percent of the time. After a large number of flips, assuming no unusual weighting and design of the coin, the number of heads and tails will be almost equally divided. Thus, we say that the probability of heads is 50 percent, ½, or .50. The probability of throwing a five on one toss of a die would be about ⅙ or .17. Such objective probabilities are used in predicting rainfall by the Weather Bureau, deaths and accidents by insurance companies, generator station breakdowns by electric power companies, and "no-show" reservations by airlines.

Most decisions facing the business manager have no history of occurrences like those mentioned above. They are somewhat unique in character and present the greatest difficulty in arriving at an objective, nonintuitive solution. In this case, subjective probabilities can be developed by the knowledgeable manager. These are "betting odds," or the degree of confidence that he places in his prediction of outcome states. Subjective probabilities can be improved through consultation of multiple personnel who have the requisite background and experience to merit some confidence in their judgments. They can also be revised with the obtaining of more partial information as the situation unfolds.

Though the concept of subjective probability is quite old, dating back to the seventeenth century, it has been only in recent years that a new interest has been taken in this approach. Though the resulting estimates of probability are undoubtedly affected by such factors as the importance of the decision, degrees of revocability, and the decision maker's tendency toward optimism or

[3] L. S. Savage, *The Foundations of Statistics* (New York: John Wiley & Sons, Inc., 1954).

pessimism, their use is based on the lack of usable alternate ways of obtaining probabilities. A systemization of one's estimates of probabilities and their resulting implications is far more likely to lead to a consistent, more successful approach to decision making. In the absence of relative frequency histories and objective probabilities, we are left with the choice between unrecorded and variable intuitive feelings, and a consistent and systematic subjective estimate. This forces the manager to remain true to his original estimate when developing subsequent estimates, or to reappraise and revise his original judgment if he moves toward inconsistent directions.

MODELS

The concept of a model for decision makings is a favored one of the quantitative school of thought. However, models have been used by all managers for many years. A model is an *abstraction* of the real world—it is *not* the real world itself. Consequently, it is an imperfect representation of reality since it incorporates only a portion thereof. This imperfection constitutes its major value since simplification enables the manager to deal with that portion of the real world more effectively. It is important, however, that the model incorporate *significant* aspects of reality in order that any predictions resulting may have practical application.

A model is ordinarily developed with some specific use in mind. For example, a model airplane that sits on a child's desk incorporates from the original only significant features of outer design and dimensions.[4] These are the only elements of reality that the child wants for his purposes. On the other hand, the ground airplane trainer is also a model. It does not have the dimensions and proportions of the child's model; rather, it includes components that are contained in the aircraft's cockpit. The model responds in a similar way to which a real airplane would act in actual flight, thus enabling the accomplishment of training.

Most of the models used by the manager are *symbolic* models. The organization chart is a model that shows formal positions and levels of authority for an enterprise, but it is only a small fraction of the total relationships that are developed. This chart model has come under heavy attack by behavioral theorists as being untrue and misleading. Such attacks are merited only if the manager has equated the model with the real world. If he uses it as a model of a small portion of reality, and uses it for the specific and narrow purpose for which it was designed, the behavioral criticisms are not merited.

The models proposed by those who would quantify decision making are

---

[4] William R. King, *Probability for Management Decisions* (New York: John Wiley & Sons, Inc., 1968), p. 16.

usually of the symbolic numerical type. They consist of sets of equations and matrices, and enable the decision maker to concentrate more effectively upon a portion of his total problem. To the degree that the model is not in accordance with reality, either in terms of accuracy or comprehensiveness, to that same degree the decision maker must discount its use. Management decision making is not a blind acceptance of the mathematical and statistical analyses of operations researchers. Symbolic quantitative models are undergoing constant improvement as we learn to identify and measure more accurately. It is doubtful, however, that they will become so effectively related to reality that a true management science can be developed.

LINEAR PROGRAMMING

Decision situations where linear programming can be utilized are usually problems of allocation. The manager is faced with scarce funds, materials, or capacities, and must allocate resources among various users. Though all can use these resources, the total desired exceeds that available. The manager then attempts to allocate in such a way that a desired objective is maximized, e.g., highest profit, least cost, greatest output, etc. In addition, linear programming assumes that the relationships between two or more uses of a scarce resource is linear, that is, in a straight-line relationship. Perhaps a simple illustration is the best way to make these ideas clear.

Let us assume a firm that manufactures two products that can make use of the same capacity resources, e.g., stereo record players and monaural players, or color and black and white television sets. To enter the realm of certainty that linear programming requires, we must also assume that, due to temporary market conditions, we can sell all that we can produce of either product. The contribution to fixed overhead and profit (Z) per unit of the stereos (S) is $30 and that of the monaurals (M) is $10. This is the goal to be maximized in the allocation problem and is expressed in the following formula:

$$Z = 30S + 10M$$

This company is basically an assembler and the major restraints are the capacities of the chassis assembly and set assembly departments. Time study, from the certain world of the classical manager, indicates that it requires 10 man-hours of work to assemble the chassis of a stereo, and 3 man-hours to put together a monaural. The total daily capacity of this department is 900 man-hours. This linear relationship can be expressed in the following manner:

$$10S + 3M \leqq 900$$

This means that the total hours expended on both products each day can equal or be less than 900. It cannot be greater.

The set assembly requires .5 man-hours for both types of products. With a total daily capacity for this department of 100 man-hours, the linear relationship is as follows:

$$.5S + .5M \leqq 100$$

We now have all of the essential elements to maximize profits through allocating capacities to the two products. These linear relationships are portrayed graphically in Fig. 4–1. Product S is plotted on the vertical axis, with product M on the horizontal.

If all the capacity of the chassis assembly department is allocated solely to product S, as it can be by definition, then we can produce 90 stereos daily. If it is completely allocated to monaurals, we can produce 300. We can also produce any amount on the line connecting these two points since the capacities are completely interchangeable as to product. We cannot produce any amounts to the right of this line on the chart; the feasible decisions are now enclosed in the right triangle.

FIGURE 4–1   A LINEAR PROGRAMMING DIAGRAM

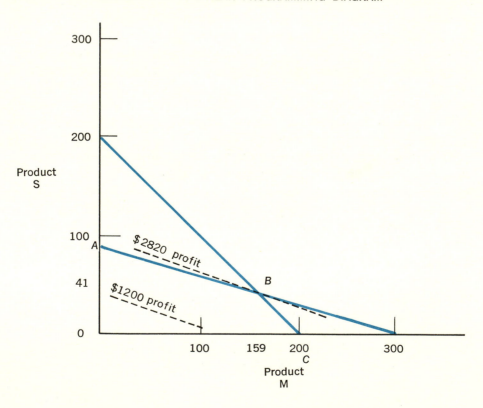

If all the set assembly capacity is allocated to produce S, 200 can be produced. This is also the case to produce M. Because of interchangeability, any combination of outputs along the straight line connecting the two extreme points is also possible. Obviously, we cannot have set assembly of stereos of any amount in excess of 90 even though we have a capacity for 200. Nor can we have set assembly of monaurals in excess of 200 even though 300 could be turned out by the chassis department. Our feasible solutions area has been further reduced to the portion identified by points O, A, B, and C.

It will be recalled that the profit function is also linear and can be visualized in the form of dotted lines on the chart in Fig. 4–1. To effect a return of $1200 for example, it would require 40 stereos *or* 120 monaurals, *or* some combination on the line connecting these extremes. Obviously, we wish to maximize profits, so a point will be selected within the feasible area that is on a profit line farthest away from zero. In Fig. 4–1, this is at point B where an output of 41 stereos and 159 monaurals will return a contribution to overhead and profit of $2820. The return at points A and C are $2700 and $2000 respectively. All the capacity of the set assembly department (100 man-hours) has been utilized at point B. There are, however, 13 hours of excess capacity in the chassis assembly department.

There are numerous examples of successful applications of the linear programming model in decision making. For example, various grades and types of coffee beans can be ground and mixed to create a coffee with specified qualities of strength, acidity, caffeine, aroma, and body. As the supplies of incoming beans vary in quantity and price from time to time, linear programming can determine the optimum mix to maintain the desired quality at minimum cost. Oil refineries have long used linear programming in the selection of crudes and blending of gasolines and fuel oil stocks in order to maximize profits. In the raising of cattle, the mixing of various feeds can be determined to meet specified nutritional values.

When the problem is large and complex, the use of computer programs is advisable. Perhaps a third product could be diagrammed in Fig. 4–1, but additional ones would require the use of mathematical equations. Algebraic methods for solving linear programming problems are beyond the scope of this text, but the general process as executed by a computer using the "simplex" program is quite easy to understand. It consists of a series of steps that, when repeated again and again, will finally produce the optimum answer. It begins with the assumption of zero production for all products, and then computationally moves up the vertical axis of Fig. 4–1. On reaching point A, it begins to compute any possible net advantage derived from moving along the line to point B. This series of high-speed calculation steps is usually referred to as an "algorithm." It will quickly identify the one combination that will optimize the objective.

DECISIONS UNDER RISK AND UNCERTAINTY

A second and final simple example will illustrate the use of quantitative approaches in making decisions under conditions of risk or uncertainty. These two states of nature are far more likely to be the conditions under which a business manager makes most of his decisions.

Let us assume that the decision maker is a retail merchant with the task of determining how much of a given product he should stock for a given time period.[5] His primary goal in making this decision is to maximize profits on this one item. To further simplify the problem situation, he will incur no customer ill will if he is unable to meet demand, and is not able to reorder the item if the actual demand is in excess of supply. The retail manager must order *now* in anticipation of consumer demand. However, he is confident that the total amount demanded will not exceed four units during this designated time period. Thus, the post decision demand states that could occur are five in number:

$$S_1 = 0; S_2 = 1; S_3 = 2; S_4 = 3; \text{ and } S_5 = 4.$$

In the light of the above conditions, the various alternative courses of action are obvious. He can order any number up to a total of four. These possible decisions can be labeled D_1 for ordering no units, D_2 for ordering one unit, D_3 for two, D_4 for three, and D_5 for four units.

In developing the expectations for each possible decision alternative, the costs and rewards must be determined. Let us assume that the cost per unit is $100, the selling price is $200, and salvage value of unsold units is $50. With this information, ruling out all other cost considerations, the relationships between the decision alternatives and the payoffs for the possible post decision states are as indicated in the matrix Fig. 4–2. The figures in each cell show the profit or loss that results from the interaction of the decision alternative and the demand states. The formula for their determination is as follows:

$$\text{Profit (loss)} = (\$200 \times \text{units sold} + \$50 \times \text{unsold units}) - (\$100 \times \text{units purchased})$$

For example, if he decides to order one unit (D_2), the retailer will lose $50 if the demand is zero (S_1), and will have a $100 profit at all other levels of demand. If he decides to buy three units (D_4) with a resulting demand of two

---

[5] Credit for this example must go to Professor Gary Munsinger of the University of Arizona as presented in "A Systematic Approach to Decision Making," *Arizona Review*, Vol. 17, No. 11 (November, 1968), pp. 1–7.

FIGURE 4–2   CONDITIONAL PAYOFF MATRIX

Alternative Decisions	S_1: Demand is zero units	S_2: Demand is one unit	S_3: Demand is two units	S_4: Demand is three units	S_5: Demand is four units
	States of Nature				
D_1: Order zero units	0	0	0	0	0
D_2: Order one unit	(50)	100	100	100	100
D_3: Order two units	(100)	50	200	200	200
D_4: Order three units	(150)	0	150	300	300
D_5: Order four units	(200)	(50)	100	250	400

(   ) indicates loss.

(S_3), the two units sold will return $400 and the unsold unit to be salvaged will return $50 for a total of $450. The profit derived will be $150 after subtracting the $300 purchase price for 3 units.

If the retailer were operating under conditions of certainty concerning the post decision states, he could easily choose the decision alternative that would yield the maximum profit. In the typical case, however, he does not know with certainty what state will occur. If he is *completely* uncertain concerning the likelihood of the actual occurrence of the five possible states (S_1 through S_5), he may elect to follow one of a number of strategies. One possible approach, termed *maximin,* is the selection of the alternative for which the minimum payoff is maximum. He selects the *best* of the worst possible outcomes. The first alternative, D_1, yields the maximum of the minimum payoffs which is zero. Only the more pessimistic decision maker would elect to use the maximin strategy of stocking no units under conditions of uncertainty.

A more optimistic manager would choose to follow the *maximax* strategy which requires selection of the decision that will have the highest maximum payoff—the best of all possible returns. Under this approach, he would order 4 units, D_5, with the possibility of obtaining $400 profit.

A third possible strategy under conditions of uncertainty is that of minimizing the maximum regret (minimax regret). When we find out what actually happened in a situation, many of us tend to look back and see what we have lost by not following the best decision alternative. The term "regret" is used to denote the dissatisfaction that accrues as a result of not being certain concerning post decision states. Thus, a strategy can be selected in advance which will tend to minimize the maximum possible amount of this dissatisfaction. Fig. 4–3 shows the regret matrix for the retailer. The best decision for each state shows a regret of zero. All other decisions for this particular state involves some loss of satisfactions as determined by subtracting that payoff from the maximum payoff. For example, the maximum payoff for S_2 is $100, and if D_2

FIGURE 4–3   REGRET MATRIX

STATES OF NATURE

Alternative Decisions	S_1	S_2	S_3	S_4	S_5	Maximum Regret
D_1	0	100	200	300	400	400
D_2	50	0	100	200	300	300
D_3	100	50	0	100	200	200
D_4	150	100	50	0	100	150*
D_5	200	150	100	50	0	200

* Minimum

had been actually adopted there would be no regret. If, on the other hand, we had actually ordered no units (D_1), we would have lost and regretted $100. If we had actually ordered two units, we would have profited only $50, with a resulting regret of $50 as compared with the maximum possible of $100.

As shown in the matrix, the maximum regrets for the five decisions are:

$$D_1 = \$400; D_2 = \$300; D_3 = \$200; D_4 = \$150; \text{ and } D_5 = \$200.$$

Therefore, if the retailer following the strategy of minimizing his possible maximum regret, he would choose alternative D_4 and order three units.

A final strategy that can be used under conditions of uncertainty would be the adoption of the Laplace criterion—assignment of equal probabilities to each possible post decision state. Since there are five possible states, the probability for each would be .2 (1.0 divided by 5). *Expected values* of each can then be derived by multiplying the probability (.2) times the monetary value of each decision under each of the possible states. The expected values of the alternative decisions would be as follows:

$$(D_1) = (.2)\,(0) + (.2)\,(0) + (.2)\,(0) + (.2)\,(0) + (.2)\,(0) = 0$$
$$(D_2) = (.2)\,(-50) + (.2)\,(100) + (.2)\,(100) + (.2)\,(100) +$$
$$(.2)\,(100) = 70$$
$$(D_3) = (.2)\,(-100) + (.2)\,(50) + (.2)\,(200) + (.2)\,(200) +$$
$$(.2)\,(200) = 110$$
$$(D_4) = (.2)\,(-150) + (.2)\,(0) + (.2)\,(150) + (.2)\,(300) +$$
$$(.2)\,(300) = 120$$
$$(D_5) = (.2)\,(-200) + (.2)\,(-50) + (.2)\,(100) + (.2)\,(250) +$$
$$(.2)\,(400) = 100$$

Since D_4 would have the highest expected value of $120, it is the Laplace decision. The retailer would stock three units.

In all the above four decision strategies, we have been assuming complete ignorance concerning the post decision state that is likely to occur. More often, the retail manager will have some information that will enable him to make predictions concerning the likelihood of each of the five states. Thus, he is not completely uncertain and can develop a prior probability distribution that reflects his judgment of relative likelihood. This would be a subjective probability distribution as contrasted with the objective probability distributions of classical statistics. The use of subjective probabilities is sometimes termed the "Bayesian approach" as it is based on a theorem developed by an eighteenth century English clergyman, Reverend Thomas Bayes.

Let us suppose that on the basis of the retailer's knowledge of his customers' consumptive habits, he feels that the chances favoring a demand of three units are greater than any other level. He also judges that the chances of selling none are very small. If he can be led to systematize his feelings and judgments, they can be portrayed in the form of a probability distribution as follows:

$$P(S_1) = .10; P(S_2) = .15; P(S_3) = .20; P(S_4) = .40; \text{ and } P(S_5) = .15.$$

When combined with the monetary values of the decision alternatives, the *expected values* are as follows:

$$
\begin{aligned}
(D_1) &= (.10)(0) + (.15)(0) + (.20)(0) + (.40)(0) + (.15)(0) = 0 \\
(D_2) &= (.10)(-50) + (.15)(100) + (.20)(100) + (.40)(100) + \\
       &\quad (.15)(100) = 85.0 \\
(D_3) &= (.10)(-100) + (.15)(50) + (.20)(200) + (.40)(200) + \\
       &\quad (.15)(200) = 147.5 \\
(D_4) &= (.10)(-150) + (.15)(0) + (.20)(150) + (.40)(300) + \\
       &\quad (.15)(300) = 180.0 \\
(D_5) &= (.10)(-200) + (.15)(-50) + (.20)(100) + (.40)(250) + \\
       &\quad (.15)(400) = 152.5
\end{aligned}
$$

Following the subjective probabilities, the retail decision maker would choose to stock three units with an expected value of $180. This approach provides a convenient means of incorporating both managerial intuition and objective research evidence into a systematic approach for selecting alternatives.

THE ROLE OF QUANTITATIVE AIDS IN DECISION MAKING

As indicated previously in this text, the crucial and inescapable function of the manager in a decision-making situation is that of *choice*. He can use all types of specialized support personnel and all types of mathematical and statistical aids to assist him, but in the final analysis the choice is his and his alone.

Inasmuch as his supporting advisors often have "tunnel vision" because of their specialization, and the various quantitative models are *not* duplicative of the real world, the manager must fill in the gaps with his personal computer (his brain). He selects the alternative which he *thinks* optimizes all legitimate interests. Certainly, the use of quantitative aids will improve his decision, but they do not automatically specify the choice he should select.

It should also be apparent that we are not able as yet to quantify all significant aspects of most decision problems. The subjective probability approach described above is a useful approach that helps bridge the gap between objective evidence and executive intuition. It is particularly difficult to quantify with accuracy the area of human values, e.g., loyalty, attitudes, confidence, trust, and so on.

The manager's unique position in an organization affords a more general view and perspective than nonmanagement positions. For example, a specialized technician using quantitative techniques will approach a queuing problem in a post office, bank, or supply room in a particular manner. His goal is to minimize costs while providing adequate service to customers of the post office and bank, or employees using the supply room. How many attendants or processing stations are necessary to achieve the goals of service and costs? He requires knowledge of the average arrival rate of customers, the average servicing time per customer, and the costs of both waiting time and servicing time. For example, if the average arrival rate at a post office window is 20 per hour, and the average servicing rate is 30 per hour, then the average idle time of the attendant will be ⅓ (excess of 30 over 20). The average queue length will be two customers (20/30 divided by 1−20/30) with an average waiting time of 4 minutes per customer (1/30-20−1/30). We can then compute the costs of servicing by the attendant in terms of both idle time and work time. We can estimate the costs of dissatisfaction accruing from customer waiting. This would be higher for a bank that must compete with other banks than it would in the case of post office monopoly. If it were a supply room problem, we could determine specific costs of employee wages consumed while waiting in line for supplies. With quantitative techniques, the appropriate number of servicing stations could be set up to provide adequate service at minimum cost.

The above described quantitative information is highly valuable data to the manager. However, his position should provide a broader view that would lead to posing such questions as the following: Could the servicing attendant be given other tasks to perform when there are no customers waiting? Could the customer's dissatisfaction in waiting be minimized by providing free coffee thus stimulating conversation and interaction with other waiting customers? Can the customer's arrivals be controlled in some way by the manager? Could special express windows be set up to reduce overall waiting time of the total number of customers? Or can the queue be eliminated altogether by establishing some other method of giving the customer the service he requires?[6] It is *this* view of the environment which distinguishes the manager from his more specialized assistants.

SUMMARY

Quantification of data is a hallmark of progress in any field of study. The degree of this type of progress is not very great as yet in management theory, but intelligent use should be made of quantitative decision-making aids that have proved of value in practice. If the manager is able to create or assume an environment characterized by certainty, then powerful quantitative models such as linear programming can be applied to identify the optimum answer in allocation problems.

More often, the manager operates in an environment characterized by risk and uncertainty. In the case of risk, objective probabilities based on many like experiences of the past are most helpful to the manager. When the decision-making problem is more unique and identical past experiences are lacking, he can quantify by establishing a subjective probability distribution for post decision states. This combined with the monetary values of possible decision alternatives will provide an expected value distribution that will help identify the choice with the highest probable return.

In situations involving a high degree of uncertainty, the manager can only elect to follow one of several basic strategies such as maximin, maximax, minimax regret, or the Laplace criterion. In all cases, quantitative aids are just that—*aids* to the decision maker. The manager is stuck with the responsibility for *final choice* and cannot abdicate that responsibility in favor of a perfunctory acceptance of the results of a quantitative model.

DISCUSSION PROBLEMS

1. In what ways would an operation researcher's viewpoint differ from a manager's viewpoint? Are these differences significant in management theory?
2. Distinguish among the following states of nature: certainty, risk, and uncertainty.
3. What is the relation between the states of nature and the selection of quantitative decision-making aids?
4. What types of decision-making problems are most adaptable to linear programming? What characteristics of the decision-making problem are essential to the use of linear programming?
5. What is a model? a quantitative decision-making model? What are its strengths and weaknesses?

[6] Cf. C. West Churchman, *Challenge to Reason* (New York: McGraw-Hill Book Company, 1968), p. 24.

6. When the manager is operating under conditions of uncertainty, what types of strategies are available to him?

7. Is the manager more optimistic when he elects to minimax regret than when he elects to maximin? Why?

8. What is the difference between objective and subjective probabilities?

9. What is the argument for using subjective probabilities in management decision making?

10. In a queuing problem, what things should a manager see that his quantitative analyst is not likely to see?

SUPPLEMENTARY READING

Alexis, Marcus and Charles Z. Wilson, *Organizational Decision Making*, Chap. 3. Englewood Cliffs: Prentice-Hall, Inc., 1967.

Emory, C. William and Powell Niland, *Making Management Decisions*, Chaps. 6, 7, and 9. Boston: Houghton Mifflin Co., 1968.

Hammond, John S., "Better Decisions with Preference Theory," *Harvard Business Review*, Vol. 45, No. 6 (November–December, 1967), 123–141.

King, William R., *Probability for Management Decisions*, Chap. 1. New York: John Wiley & Sons, Inc., 1968.

Stockton, R. Stansbury, *Introduction to Linear Programming*, 2nd ed. Boston: Allyn and Bacon, 1963.

Thimm, Alfred L., "The 'New Management Sciences' and Managerial Behavior," *Personnel Journal*, Vol. 46, No. 7 (July–August, 1967), 427–433.

Wiest, Jerome D., "Heuristic Programs for Decision Making," *Harvard Business Review*, Vol. 44, No. 5 (September–October, 1966), 129–143.

5

Plans

A plan can be defined in a general sense as any specification of factors and interrelationships which provides the foundation for future action. Planning constitutes an attempt to foresee the future and to specify events and actions which are desired when the future becomes the present.

There are many kinds and varieties of plans. They can be classified on several bases, one of which is the degree of permanency. *Single-use plans* are those determinations which are highly temporary in the sense that the event is not expected to recur. If it is decided that the problem is recurring in nature, it is more efficient to establish a semi-permanent plan usually characterized as a *standing plan*. When the event does recur, the person concerned attempts to apply the previously tested decision to the situation.

Single-use plans are very commonly used in business situations. Too often, the manager does not recognize that he has a recurring situation, and therefore approaches every event as an entirely new one. Not only is much time wasted in repetitive decision making, but the time allocated to each decision is often inadequate. Thus, we may have several poor decisions made several times. If one is able to recall the previous decision and the resulting action, the values of trial and error may be applied to all ensuing decisions.

There are, of course, many events and problems which either never recur, or, if they do, take place in such a radically different form as to preclude the use of the standard approach. The amount of time and effort devoted to decision making in these instances will vary according to the degree of importance of the problem and the time available for study. For example, the determination of new plant location may occur seldom enough to term it a single-use plan.

Yet it is of sufficient importance to merit a complete and thorough job of fact-finding and analysis. On the other hand, a parking lot flooded by heavy rains in a normally arid climate would merit little in the way of time, effort, and importance for decision making.

If events and problems are recognized as being of a recurring nature, the manager must determine whether or not a standing plan should be developed. There are many recurring actions which can be left to the intelligence and initiative of the subordinate without specific decision on the part of management. It is this area of delegated freedom which constitutes a field of controversy between traditionalists and behaviorists in management theory. If freedom cannot be granted and uniformity and consistency of action is desired, a plan must be evolved.

In theory, the first plan to be established is the overall long-range, strategic program for the enterprise. In practice, this is seldom the case, particularly for the small enterprise. Nevertheless, for conceptual purposes, we will begin the discussion of plans with this overall approach. This will be followed by coverage of the more typical, narrower standing plans: (1) policies, (2) procedures, and (3) standards.

LONG-RANGE PROGRAMS

In recent decades, business executives have become increasingly concerned with long-range plans or programs for their enterprises. It has been estimated that there are at least 1000 companies that have established a specialized, formal planning department for the purpose of developing five-, ten-, and fifteen-year programs for their organizations.[1] Such programs encompass not only broad, long-range goals, but also a supporting framework of decisions and actions deemed feasible within the constraints of organizational resources available. A comprehensive program would include: (1) corporate plans of diversification through acquisition and merger, (2) possible divestments of existing functions and facilities, (3) basic product research and development related to selected, strategic markets, (4) marketing plans adapted toward determination and development of demand, (5) basic production plans geared toward supplying the anticipated demand, (6) financial plans concerned with the generation of sufficient capital to implement all portions of the general program, and (7) a general administration plan concerned with developing the kind and size of organization that can meet program requirements. In view of the increasing tempo of change in modern civilization, the executives of larger firms in particular feel that they can protect and promote the enterprise

---

[1] David W. Ewing, "Corporate Planning at a Crossroads," *Harvard Business Review,* Vol. 45, No. 4 (July–August, 1967), p. 77.

primarily through anticipating and adapting to significant trends in technology, markets, governments, and societal values.

The adoption of a systematic approach to long-range planning helps, but does not assure, the effectuation of desired results. In some enterprises, the planning department has produced reams of paper with little effect upon actual operations. It is as if the planners viewed their success in terms of the number, length, comprehensiveness, and complexity of plans developed, rather than with respect to their actual execution. This is not an unusual problem when planning is specialized and divorced from execution. To overcome this difficulty, some executives have moved to involve operating managers in the process of plan development. In too many cases, these managers are not convinced of the merits of "crystal ball gazing," and look upon demands for such plans as dreary chores that detract from the efficiency of current operations. A third difficulty often encountered is that the programs turned out by the planners are in excess of organization capacities and capabilities. It is always easier to plan than it is to execute. In this event, an atmosphere of continued failure and perpetual inadequacy will be created, thereby leading to behavior indicative of frustration.

Most long-range planning has centered around analysis and prediction of future economic conditions. The view has been that the enterprise must adapt to these anticipated conditions. Undeniably, this type of analysis is valuable and is necessary for controlled growth or even survival. But specialized economic planners would do well to consider the behavioral implications of long-range plans. Operating officials must be convinced of the merits of the process. Small successes, perhaps of a shorter range, should precede larger, longer-term attempts. This helps to develop a favorable attitude toward the entire planning process. Consideration should also be given to the *manner* in which information is collected in order to foster a greater involvement. Careful formulation of budgeting and reporting procedures should help prevent resistance or even outright sabotage of plans by those being judged against their content. As many as possible should have some confidence that planned goals and actions are within the realm of practicable accomplishment. The development of consensus on program desirability is as important as the accuracy of its content.

Finally, all members of an organization should develop a tolerance for error in planning. It must be remembered that our economy is becoming increasingly complex. Our general affluence makes the prediction of specific demand far more difficult; we are beyond the basic food and shelter stage. In addition, the base of competition is becoming wider, e.g., plastics compete with steel in various products which have traditionally been composed of the latter. Competition is becoming more intense as more and more managements are undertaking the above described process of long-range planning. Though it does not insure success, progressive managements must plan on a long-range basis whether or not it is done systematically, accurately, or in a formalized fashion. The alternative is to rely on luck, and the odds are steadily getting worse.

POLICY

Policy is a word that is in every manager's vocabulary. As a result, there is much confusion and miscommunication, for the term has a number of different interpretations. To some, policy can be made only by top management. To others, all managers, low or high, can formulate policy. Some confuse policy and principle, while others have difficulty in separating policy and procedure. As far as this text is concerned, the following definitions are presented in the interest of more accurate communication.

Policy can be defined as a predetermined, general course or guide established to provide direction for ensuing action. As such, it should be based upon a thorough analysis of enterprise objectives.

A *rule* is a very specific and detailed guide to action which is set up to direct and restrict action in a fairly narrow manner. In a sense, policies and rules are at the opposite ends of a continuum, as shown in Chart 5–1. There is no clear-cut distinction in the center of this scale. Most would accept the contention

CHART 5–1   POLICY-RULE CONTINUUM

Policy			Rule
General Basic Guides— Organization wide	Specific Guides— Organization wide	Specific Guides— Organization element	Specific Detailed Guides for the Individual

that a decision not to employ female employees anywhere in the enterprise has to do with policy. On the other hand the decision to dock an employee's wages for lateness in excess of ten minutes would be termed a policy by some and a rule by others.

Both policies and rules are designed to direct action toward accomplishment of objectives, since, by definition, only work or functions can accomplish objectives. If we could be assured that the persons doing the work were thoroughly conversant and in agreement with basic objectives, we could do without intervening policies. However, it is apparent from Chapter 2 that objectives are not only nebulous, they are often controversial. Thus, all organizations have need for policies and rules which can and should be more definitive and understandable than the objectives on which they are based.

A *procedure* is a series of steps or functions established for the accomplishment of some specific project or endeavor. For most policies, there would be an accompanying procedure to indicate how that policy should be carried out. Take, for example, the following: "It is the policy of this firm to practice no discrimination on the basis of race, creed, or color in hiring, promotion, and retention." Such a statement by itself does not ensure that the course of action prescribed will be followed. If, however, accompanying procedures for hiring, promotion, and layoff are created to help assure nondiscrimination, we have directed action more closely and definitely. In a sense, policy can be characterized as the creation of substantive law, while procedure can be categorized as a means of execution of the law. Such a distinction is, at best, only a general indication of the difference, for it is undeniable that the manner in which a procedure is designed and implemented can invade the substantive areas.

Principles of Policy Formulation

There are sales policies, product policies, personnel policies, financial policies, etc. To formulate policies, the manager must have knowledge of and skill in the operative function concerned. However, there are certain generalizations that are broadly applicable to the formulation of all types of policies.[2] One of these has already been stated above: that policies must be based upon an analysis of objectives of the enterprise. Other generalizations, or principles, which are applicable are as follows:

1. Policies should be based on known principles in the operative area concerned.
2. Subordinate policies should be supplementary to superior policies.
3. Policies should be complementary to coordinate policies.
4. Policies should be definite, understandable, and preferably in writing.
5. Policies should be flexible and stable.
6. Policies should be reasonably comprehensive in scope.

With respect to the first statement, it must be recognized that policies are man-made laws to govern the operation of the organization. Insofar as possible, these laws should be based upon facts and truths. Some state this principle by dividing policy into two elements: (1) the guide which tells *what*, and (2) the principle which tells *why*. For example, it may be the policy of a firm not to force one division of the firm to buy materials and components from

2 See Ralph C. Davis, *Industrial Organization and Management,* 3rd ed. (New York: Harper & Bros., 1957), p. 41.

another division. This policy rests upon the principle that competitive purchasing will insure minimum costs as well as stimulate divisions to perform as well as, or better than, outside firms. Certainly, from the human angle, the individual finds it less difficult to accede to policy or rule if he knows the principle behind it. It is the policy which appears to have no good reason that is difficult to accept.

A major difficulty in basing man-made policies on man-discovered principles and truths is that there are vast areas where the truth is not yet discovered. For example, is it true that employees with high morale will outproduce those with low morale? If we definitely knew, policy making in the field of human relations would be considerably simpler. Many of our personnel policies constitute legislation in areas where truth is either unknown or in such hazy form that rational men can differ. So the manager bases his policy decisions on principles insofar as they are determinable. In areas where principles are lacking, he relies on intuition and good business judgment, for policies, nevertheless, must be present to provide direction and uniformity.

The second stated generalization is one of those truisms usually taken for granted. If a division policy, for example, directly conflicts with a company policy, not only is the division contributing to a lack of organization and coordination, its manager may also be considered insubordinate.

The third statement, that policies should be complementary, is more difficult to apply. That management should supplement top management is obvious, and is enforceable through the chain of command. That one division manager should coordinate his decisions with a second division manager is less obvious and less enforceable since they are on equal organization levels in two chains of command. Yet, from the view of management theory, managers "A" and "B" are a part of a single organization, which has at least one common objective. For example, what should the policy be on comprehensiveness of the product line to be offered to the market? Sales managers tend toward a policy of diversification, emphasizing completeness of offering to attract customers. Production managers favor product simplification in the interests of longer production runs and reduced costs. How often should product quality specifications be altered? Both sales and engineering managers favor frequent changes in the interests of enhanced sales and higher engineered quality. Production managers, again, favor fewer changes for reasons of economy. Should the firm follow a policy of buying raw materials from customers whenever possible? Sales managers tend to favor a policy of reciprocity. Purchasing agents do not want their choices in materials markets unduly restricted by a sales argument. In all three instances, there is conceptually an answer that strives toward *overall* organization optimization, rather than the particular optimizing of sales, engineering, purchasing, or production. Thus, the vice president of sales should not make sales policies which levy an unduly heavy burden on production unless that burden is necessary for the overall advancement of the organization. To effect this complementary relationship, one must rely upon two basic approaches: (1) the coordination through the chains of command by the common superior, and (2) the education of the coordinate managers concerning the facts of organized life.

That policies should be definite, understandable, and in written form is a generalization so frequently stated that it, too, may fall into the category of a truism. However, it has been suggested by one writer that the art of imprecision in policy statements is of great assistance in achieving flexibility.[3] It is felt that public commitment to a specific set of policies makes it far more difficult to persuade organization members to change when conditions require it. The writer contends that the executive should possess a sense of direction and policy, but not necessarily announce it in detail. Thus he is able to (1) avoid organized attacks upon the appropriateness of policy, (2) avoid time spent in arbitrating disputes concerning policy application, and (3) avoid frightening organization members with respect to the magnitude of major policy shifts since they are passed out in small doses when the opportunity permits. He suggests "muddling with a purpose" by taking advantage of all unanticipated events that enable actions directed toward his conception of proper policy directions. For example, one manager, who wanted to move to a significantly higher level of product quality, was able to do so by taking advantage of three unforeseen opportunities: (1) the present, only adequate quality manager asked for a transfer, (2) the personnel department asked for a new training program and he made sure that quality work was emphasized, and (3) a large error on a valued customer's order provided the necessary excuse to install a completely new system for inspecting and testing. In all of these opportunities, the barriers to resistance were down, and the manager was able to make significant strides forward. Following these tactics is consistent with the classical idea of manipulative control. The manager has determined what is best and uses this approach to move the organization in that best direction. His decisions and actions will slowly reveal the general nature of the policy without a definite specification that will tie his hands. The necessity for policy and direction is not denied; only the tactics of implementation are being debated.

The usual classical literature, however, emphasizes the directive advantages of definite, complete, and written policy statements. If policy is to guide action, the persons responsible for providing that action must be aware of the guide as well as understand it. In the absence of this standing guide, the manager must interject his specific decisions.

[3] H. Edward Wrapp, "Good Managers Don't Make Policy Decisions," *Harvard Business Review*, Vol. 45, No. 5 (September–October, 1967), p. 94.

Committing the policy to writing has a number of values. It provides a common body of law equally available to all concerned. It protects the organization from the ravages of turnover that would occur if policies were only carried in the executives' minds. Written policies are also more likely to be thought through and worked out. One is usually more careful of what he places on paper than of what he says informally.

The requirements of policy stability and flexibility are not contradictory; rather one is a prerequisite to the other. Stable policy changes only in response to fundamental and basic changes in condition. Needless to say, policy should not be altered daily or weekly. If it is, the executive is kidding himself that he does have a policy, rather than a single-use decision. The higher the organization level, the more stable the policy must be. Changing the direction of the enterprise is an infinitely more complex and time-consuming task than changing the direction of a department or section. The higher the organization level, the more policy resembles principle. The lower the level, the more it resembles or becomes a rule. The Armco Steel Corporation, for example, has a set of policies currently applicable which were first formulated and approved December 12, 1919.[4]

The larger the organization, the greater the need for policy stability and flexibility. Policies are more adaptable than rules, and principles are more adaptable than policies. This is why the Armco policies resemble principles, a necessary characteristic if they are to last through depression and prosperity.

If the organization is so large that principles are not sufficiently flexible guides, one might move to the philosophy level. A philosophy is a particular approach, set of attitudes, and general theory of attacking business problems. One hears of the "Army way" or the "Navy way." We are sure that there are General Electric and General Motors management philosophies which are taught to the various division managers. Philosophies also serve in a similar capacity as policies, principles, and rules in guiding the actions of the members of an organization to desired ends.

The final generalization of policy formulation facilitates the use of the exception principle. This principle is cited often in management literature. The manager should organize his work in such a way that subordinate personnel can handle the routine and predictable, while he devotes most of his time to the exceptional events and problems. If the body of policies is reasonably comprehensive, the cases that arise which are not covered by policy constitute exceptions. These latter can be submitted to the executive for decision. If the exceptional case arises again, consideration can be given to the desirability of establishing a standing plan, or policy, governing such cases. If the policy body is not reasonably comprehensive, then *most* cases that arise must be

[4] See *Armo Policies,* Armco Steel Corporation, pp. 14–20.

submitted for executive decision with a consequent heavy burden upon him. Policy conserves the executive's time by making available a previously determined decision. Standing plans of all types are essential prerequisites to the use of the exception principle.

The Policy Process

All policies, regardless of the functional field concerned, should be formulated in accordance with the above-cited generalizations. After formulation is complete, however, the job is far from done. The purpose of policy, it will be recalled, is to guide behavior or work along certain lines. Consequently, the next step is to disseminate the policy to the persons responsible for its application. This requires a choice of media such as memoranda, group meetings, word of mouth, handbooks, policy manuals, and the like. This dissemination has a concomitant requirement of explanation and education. If one expects subordinate personnel to be guided by these standing plans, they must understand the reason or principle behind the policy. At times during its application, questions will arise as to interpretation. A policy may be applicable to a case but the fit is not perfect. When these questions do arise, the subordinate must refer it to his superior for interpretation. This interpretation is a continuance of the education process started earlier.

The final stage of the policy process would be some assurance that action is in reality being guided by the policy. The policy-making executive must be assured that his decision is being applied as he intended. Thus, some channel of communication must be established whereby he can obtain information concerning action. General observation, regular reports, and unsolicited complaints are some of the means of policy control. In a department store, for example, the management may use an employed shopper to determine the effectiveness of certain policies upon sales personnel.

Professor Ralph Davis summarizes the policy process in the following sequence of steps.[5]

1. Policy formulation.
2. Policy dissemination.
3. Policy education.
4. Policy acceptance.
5. Policy application.
6. Policy interpretation.
7. Policy control.

[5] Ralph C. Davis, *The Fundamentals of Top Management* (New York: Harper & Bros., 1951), p. 190.

Each of these events occurs roughly in the order indicated. It is apparent that much work follows the original decision that was reached during the first step of policy formulation.

PROCEDURES

Most organizations do not find policies capable of providing a sufficient amount of direction and control. They are usually supplemented with more detailed specifications of *how* the work should be executed. These specifications are referred to as procedures. Thus, a procedure is a series of steps or functions set up for the accomplishment of any specific project or undertaking, anything from processing a claim to establishing a budget. Standing plans governing the matter in which work is to be done can be and are designed for all types of work, managerial and operative. Thus, the enterprise must not only have organization charts in order to allocate the work load, it must also have procedures to show the manner of operation.

The Value of Procedure

Standing procedures for an organization are valuable from a number of points of view. In the first place, they provide the basis for coordinating the elements of the enterprise. Coordination involves a correlation of separate activities on the basis of time and order of events. Thus, on a particular work project, if there is to be an orderly accumulation of values and a proper utilization of each element, all elements must be tied together and correlated. There is little to be said for doing an excellent job on one phase of a project if the job is done at the wrong time or completely duplicates or counteracts the efforts of another element. To schedule effectively a project, one must establish an appropriate series of steps which lead up to the desired conclusion.

A second major value of standing procedures is in the labor saved because of improved methods, elimination of work, and facilitation of training. If a job is assigned and the manner of execution not specified, the first method that comes to mind is usually the one adopted. It is not unusual to have effort expended which is worthless. If procedural analysts would intensively study the job with the objective of ascertaining the most effective method, effort would most likely be eliminated, and remaining procedures will no doubt be more effective. In addition, the availability of a written standing plan is of material assistance in training new personnel, with self-training facilitated through study of the standard method. Teaching is also aided in that a logical outline is available.

Most managers believe that work cannot be left to chance. The study of work and its proper execution is conducive to material savings in all segments of the firm. Though most attention has been allocated to production and clerical procedures, value can be derived from a study and redesign of managerial and control methods as well.

Procedure Design

All managers have a responsibility for the effective execution of work in their organization areas. As such, they should have a skill in work design. Many organizations have, for this purpose, utilized procedural specialists. In production work, these people are often called motion analysts. In administrative and office work, they may be referred to as procedural analysts.

There are certain basic generalizations applicable to these two types of work. In the production field, such principles of procedural formation, or motion study principles, as the following are often stated.[6]

1. Continuous and curved movements are preferable to straight motions involving sharp changes in direction.
2. Movement of the hands and arms should be simultaneous, symmetrical, and opposed in direction.
3. The most effective method usually involves the least movement.

In the office and administrative type of work, such generalizations as the following are of some use (these are also of value in analyzing the work flow in production):[7]

1. Provision should be made for the effecting of accountability for each step in the procedure. Clear-cut delineation helps to reduce confusion, overlapping, and conflict.
2. The capacities of each step in the procedure should be balanced in terms of manpower and capital equipment in order to effect a smooth progression of work.
3. Provision must be made for combining an operative procedure with its management control procedure. This involves establishing reports and records appropriately designed with respect to critical information and the timing of its receipt.

[6] See such basic books as Benjamin W. Niebel, *Motion and Time Study*, 4th ed. (Homewood: Richard D. Irwin, Inc., 1967) and Ralph M. Barnes, *Motion and Time Study*, 6th ed. (New York: John Wiley & Sons, Inc., 1968).

[7] Cf. Adrian M. McDonough, *Management Systems* (Homewood: Richard D. Irwin, Inc., 1965).

4. The form that initiates a procedure should be designed to meet the needs of all elements of the organization that will be involved in the project. This precludes the necessity for additional paperwork to be initiated in later steps in the procedure, and thereby reduces confusion and overhead.

In the redesign and improvement of any procedure, the first step is usually an attempt to analyze the present work flow. In production work, there are available a multitude of study forms and standard symbols such as manufacturing diagrams, flow process charts, man and machine charts, left- and right-hand forms, and simocharts. In the office and administrative category, a procedural flow chart is often used. Any chart which clearly depicts the present flow of work in a manner capable of being absorbed by the analyst is of use. There is also ample room for original creation by the analyst.

STANDARDS

The fourth example of a type of standing plan is perhaps the most comprehensive. A standard can be defined as a model or criterion to which something can be compared. Thus, in a sense, all plans are standards. Perhaps the most common use of the term is when it is restricted to performance results, thus concentrating upon the end objectives of plan execution. However, as we shall see, the term has been broadened to include the process of plan execution.

The values of having standing models lie heavily in the area of control. The model or standard itself can be characterized as a *significant* element of the plan. The application of the model is accomplished through the management function of control, that is, the comparison of action and results to the standard, and the effecting of necessary adjustments. The more precise and quantitative the standard, the more accurate the comparisons, and the closer the control can be.

Types of Standards

Standards can be classified into two main types: (1) those specifying the end action results, and (2) those specifying the nature of the elements of the action. Sub-categories of these two main classes would appear as follows:

I. Performance Results Standards
   1. Quality of work.
   2. Quantity of work.
   3. Time to complete.
   4. Cost of work.

II. Process Standards
   1. Personnel standards.
   2. Functional standards.
   3. Physical factors standards.

In establishing a program of standardization, the place to start is with end actions. Quantity and quality standards of output should be established if possible. Time study is a specific means of establishing a standard of quantity. Establishing requirements for a staff function is a much more complex process. The personnel department for example, may be given such standards as not more than 1 percent labor turnover, or a specified number of grievances reaching a selected stage. It becomes readily apparent that not only are quantity and quality standards difficult to prescribe, but such standards that are established cover only a portion of the overall plan and action.

Though it is difficult to establish quantity and quality standards in areas like personnel and public relations, it is easier to set up standards governing time and cost. Thus, a staff department is given a *budget*, under which it must live, as well as certain schedules for accomplishing particular projects. But even here, indirect functions are sufficiently nebulous so as to require that these standards be established on a joint basis between the general manager and the departmental manager. The more objective and definitive the function, the easier it is to have performance standards imposed unilaterally from above.

Every organization and manager has standards of performance. They may not be altogether spelled out, but they nevertheless exist. When a manager observes the results of an act and is dissatisfied, he has reached this conclusion by comparing what he sees to what he would like to see in terms of quantity, quality, time, and cost. Realistic establishment of such standards usually calls for intensive study and, often, joint participation on the part of subordinates and superiors. In addition, the labor union is also very interested in the standards established for personnel who are also union members. It is estimated that in many companies, over half of all grievances concern the standards of performance established by time studies.

If it is difficult or impossible to establish accurate standards of performance, or if resulting action does not comply with such performance standards as do exist, it is logical to move to a consideration of the *action process*. There are three basic components of all organizations: people, jobs or functions, and physical factors. Therefore, even though one does not know enough to be able to establish accurate standards of performance results, he may attempt to specify and control these action-process factors. For example, we may try to hire for this job a person who possess the highest qualifications; this would be a standard of personnel. Or we may study and develop the best method or procedure for executing the job; this is a standard of function. And finally, we may attempt to provide the best in the way of physical equipment and working conditions; these would be standards of physical factors. Thus, the best people using the latest in methodology and equipment might result in maximum efficiency without necessarily establishing *standards* for these latter variables.

To effect a complete program of standardization, one would establish models of performance results, personnel, functions, and physical factors, thereby providing the basis for controlling the process as well as the result. Examples of personnel standards are the hiring specifications and particular levels of employee morale desired. The standards of function can be divided into two types: (1) those dealing with organization arrangements, such as job descriptions and organization charts, and (2) those concerned with methods of doing work, examples of which are the many standard procedures discussed in the preceding section. If an employee violates his job description by doing more or less than that prescribed, he has violated a standard. If he uses a method different from that laid down in the procedural manual or standard practice instruction sheet, he has violated a standard. Thus, one can control not only the skill-level and type of person assigned to do the job, but his methods and content of work as well.

The third component, physical factors, deals with an area that we know more about. Textbooks on industrial management covering such subjects as equipment selection, layout, and working conditions deal primarily with the problem of establishing the best standards of physical factors.

Values and Disadvantages of Standardization

It is difficult to visualize how one could manage an activity without standards. As we have mentioned, such standing plans provide the basis for effective control. In addition, the establishment and communication of performance standards serve as an incentive for those concerned. Most people want to achieve the ends which have been established as the goals of their activities. If these standards are reasonable and known, they in themselves constitute a stimulus toward accomplishment. Serveral firms, for example, have dropped their piece-rate incentive systems and yet have retained the standards of performance established by time study. These standards were still of considerable value in stimulating above-average performance even without the impetus of money.

A third value issuing from a program of standardization is that uniformity and dependability are introduced into the environment. There are values as well as drawbacks to uniformity. Uniform treatment of personnel in hiring, for example, promotes greater acceptance of decisions concerning whom to hire. This is particularly true with respect to the attributes of race, religion, color, and nationality. Uniformity in the size of component parts is an absolute essential for efficient management of production and assembly. Holding all elements and conditions uniform for a period of time permits a greater quantity of work to be accomplished. If we are to change daily the specification of results or the means of accomplishment, even though the change constitutes an improvement in quality, the volume of output will be materially reduced. In one narrow subject area, Frank Gilbreth found long ago that if working conditions, regardless of level, were merely held *constant* so that the employee could become familiar with them, a significant increase in output would result.

On the other hand, standardization does freeze conditions and thus in a sense retards progress. For a period of time no change may be permitted; but as indicated above, this is essential for the sake of quantity. The implication is not, however, that there should never be any alteration of standards; the introduction of such improvements should be on a planned basis and timed in such a manner as to obtain the optimum in quality *and* quantity.

Standardization also suggests certain disadvantages in terms of adjusting to individual differences. Perhaps there is no single best method of work for everyone. Certainly a standardized chair does not fit everyone equally well. In addition, the introduction of standardization may repress innovations and originality. The existence of specific and approved standards suggests an environment where the new and nontraditional will be somewhat suspect. It is always easier to retain the status quo, a retention which becomes more crippling when it is documented on the basis of past intensive and systematic studies.

In theory, one can have his cake and eat it, too. In practice, however, it may be difficult to work out a balanced program of standardization without completely sacrificing values in the areas of improvement, innovation, and flexibility. Certainly every enterprise must avail itself of standards, as long as these standards are not overused and misused.

PLANNING, CONTROL, AND HUMAN RELATIONS

The manager is responsible for the effective accomplishment of a group objective. He cannot merely announce the goal to his subordinates and rely upon their good will to make it come true. He attempts to insure accomplishment by providing a blueprint which will chart the direction to be followed by the group. The traditional manager is inclined toward "playing it safe" through a high degree of detailed planning. These plans, policies, procedures, and standards serve to regulate effectively subordinate activity. This regulation is achieved not only through informing personnel of what is expected of them in advance, but also through providing the basis for close control of the ensuing action. The manager collects information of operating results and compares these data with his various plans, programs, and standards. Thus the manager, who cannot do all of the necessary work by himself, attempts to insure that his subordinates will do the work in a prescribed manner with predictable results.

Though the manager is more comfortable in the security of his detailed planning and restrictive regulations and controls, the subordinates who must execute the plan are forced to give up a large measure of individual freedom. Thus, the stage is set for a clash between the organization's need for coordinated direction and the individual's need for recognition and self-direction. There is a natural tendency for the ego to rebel against regulations, and particularly the detailed regulations in which many traditional managers place their trust. In theory, a perfect balancing of the needs of personnel and the needs of the organization can be developed. In practice, it is a difficult art to effect this optimum arrangement. In later chapters, the reaction of subordinates to the detailed plans and controls of the organization will be examined in greater detail.

SUMMARY

To be against planning is akin to being against motherhood and for sin, according to most writers of management theory. In any event it would be difficult to contend that management should *not* think through problems in advance and make what provisions they can to handle them. This is the essence of the scientific management movement.

We can define a plan in its broadest sense as the determination of anything in advance of action. Long-term planning encompasses time periods as long as five, ten, or fifteen years. The classical manager likes to leave as little as he can to chance, and predictions concerning the state of the world to come are useful in reducing the importance of chance. The successful introduction of long-range programs requires consideration of behavioral as well as economic implications.

In this chapter, we have been involved primarily with three of the basic types of standing plans. *Policies* are general guides to action established for the enterprise and its major segments. Well-formulated policy is based upon an analysis of objectives, conforms to known principles in the area, is stable and flexible, complementary and supplementary, and reasonably comprehensive in scope. A *procedure* is a series of steps or functions which indicates how the policy should be applied or the project executed. Well-formulated procedures are flexible, balanced, efficient in the uses of resources, and subject to organized control in each of their steps. A *standard* is a model or criterion to which action can be compared for purposes of assuring compliance with plans. Standards are of two types: (1) performance results, and (2) performance process. Examples of the former are specifications of quantity, quality, time, and cost. Concerning the process, standards can be established for (1) personnel, such as job specifications; (2) functions, such as job descriptions and procedures; and (3) physical factors, such as lighting and equipment.

All of the above are standing plans designed to guide the organization through reasonably repetitive operations. They enable the use of the exception principle by prescribing for the predictable, leaving time for the manager to handle the exceptions to these standing plans. It is apparent that these exceptions call for single-use decisions for their resolution. If these exceptions seem to reappear from time to time, consideration should be given to the possible development of a standing plan to cover the problem.

DISCUSSION PROBLEMS

1. What difficulties are often encountered in the introduction of long-range planning approaches in business firms? How can the impact of these difficulties be reduced?

2. What are the advantages and disadvantages of having definite and written organization policies? What approach do you suggest?

3. Cite business policies that are likely to engender conflict and disagreement among various members of the firm. What is the basis for these disagreements?

4. In what way does the manager's penchant for planning conflict with the needs of individuals and groups within an organization?

5. Distinguish among the following: (1) objectives, (2) policies, (3) procedures, (4) standards, and (5) principles.

6. Of the two basic types of standards, performance results and process, with which type is a behaviorist most likely to take issue? Why?

7. Relate the exception principle to the concept of standing plans.

8. Why should a manager be highly concerned with the proper establishment of procedures?

9. What possible losses are derived from a program of standardization in any organization?

10. After formulation of policy by management, what happens next? Assume an example such as "no discrimination in hiring based on race, religion, nationality, age, and sex."

SUPPLEMENTARY READING

Ewing, David W., "Corporate Planning at a Crossroads," *Harvard Business Review,* Vol. 45, No. 4 (July–August, 1967), 77–86.

LeBreton, Preston P., *General Administration: Planning and Implementation,* Chaps. 2 and 4. New York: Holt, Rinehart, and Winston, 1965.

Litschert, Robert J., "Some Characteristics of Long-Range Planning: An Industry Study," *Academy of Management Journal,* Vol. 11, No. 3 (September, 1968), 315–328.

Schaffer, Robert H., "Putting Action Into Planning," *Harvard Business Review,* Vol. 45, No. 6 (November–December, 1967), 158–166.

Steiner, George A., "Approaches to Long-Range Planning for Small Business," *California Management Review,* Vol. 10, No. 1 (Fall, 1967), 3–16.

Wrapp, H. Edward, "Good Managers Don't Make Policy Decisions," *Harvard Business Review,* Vol. 45, No. 5 (September–October, 1967), 91–99.

Section B

The Human Element

Of all the components of organization, the most complex is the human being. Before plans can be established in a realistic manner, knowledge of people, their needs and "need patterns," and their surrounding cultures is essential (Chapter 6). As a person enters the business environment, his needs are translated into specific wants, while at the same time he adapts in various ways to the rational plans established by management (Chapter 7).

6

The Human Element

We have frequently stated that there are three basic components of all organizations or enterprises: *functions* or tasks, *personnel* to accomplish these tasks, and *physical factors* that implement accomplishment. In this and the following chapter, we will examine that most important of all components, the human being. We shall first be concerned with the basic nature of people as identified and described by psychologists and sociologists. Though individuals are different, basic patterns of need-motivated behavior have been identified. To a large extent, one's philosophy of management must rest upon basic assumptions regarding the nature of man, and we must judge the appropriateness of any management approach in light of these assumptions.

IMPORTANCE OF THE HUMAN ELEMENT IN BUSINESS

The human relations movement has developed, particularly over the last three decades, partially in response to the extraordinary increase in technical knowledge. For these very advances in science have underscored the need for socially-oriented solutions to technically-created problems (one need only consider the implications of automation, for example).

American private enterprise has been seriously concerned with this movement, and for several reasons. These reasons were briefly listed in Chapter 1, but deserve further elaboration and emphasis here. In the first place, two pressure sources have arisen in the form of labor unions and government agencies of all types and levels. Though the beginning of the labor movement in the United States can be traced to the 1700's, its basic strength has been developed only in the last three decades. It is safe to say that prior to this time large portions of private managements had not gauged accurately the importance and role of the individual worker in business enterprises. His needs were often ignored and frustrated either because of ignorance on the part of managers or because of a conflict of short-run business objectives with employee objectives. This mishandling of the human factor took place over a very long period, and most attempts to restrict management through union organization were unsuccessful. In the 1930's, passage of the Wagner Act provided the protection necessary to the development and continuation of a strong labor organization. As a result, the numerical strength of the movement in the United States increased from 2½ million in 1933 to over 15 million in 1945. Present strength is approximately 19 million, in a work force of over 78 million. Thus, human needs are presented to management with a force that cannot be ignored. Labor organization not only affects the significance of the human factor in those firms in which there are unions, but also in the remainder of the economy as well. Fears of potential labor organizations and a desire to remain competitive in the labor market have led much of private American industry to alter its policies in regard to personnel.

The various levels of government in the United States have also had a considerable impact upon American industry. In addition to the Wagner Act, there are many specific laws dealing with such specifics as minimum wages, hours of work, old age and survivor's insurance, workmen's compensation, and nondiscrimination on the basis of race, creed, or color. These laws are a result of changing attitudes of society; hopefully, management will recognize these changes and voluntarily undertake the study of human problems with a view toward development of private solutions rather than solutions imposed upon them by society. For, in the final analysis, the interests of society must prevail.

There is also a substantial amount of research concerning the relationship between certain management approaches to personnel and the productivity and morale of these personnel. The uncertain results have posed a question concerning the proper role of human values in a management philosophy. They may be regarded as means, ends, or combinations of both. As means, the manager would view "good human relations" as a causal factor leading to greater productivity, creativity, and profit, these being more closely identified with the basic end objectives of the business organization. Regardless of the impact of unions and government, *if* it were proved through research and widely accepted that humanistic approaches *always* resulted in higher productivity, it is certain that they would be adopted by most managements fairly quickly. Concerning the research, some studies have shown a positive relationship between morale and output, but others have not. Results of these studies have been summarized by Brayfield and Crockett in 1955, Herzberg in 1957, and Vroom in 1964.[1] Though most tend to show a meaningful relationship between member attitudes and such variables as absenteeism and turnover, the one conclusion expounded by all three reviews is that there is *no strong relationship between employee attitudes and productivity*. The studies reviewed by Vroom, for example, show a median correlation of plus .14 between employee satisfaction and output. Though the direction of correlation is that hypothesized by the behaviorists, the level is quite low. Rensis Likert suggests that this low correlation is a result of varying time spans. The effects of altered human relationships are slow to become apparent, and it may require as much as three years before a true measurement can be made.[2] He suggests that some studies were made early in this cycle, with consequent low correlations, while others were made much later, thereby producing significant positive correlations. In a dynamic business economy, it is difficult to wait for two to three years, particularly in the smaller enterprises. If a decision must be made in allocating investments between a technological improvement and a humanistic innovation, the one with the shorter, more assured payoff is likely to be chosen. It should be noted, however, that many managements are more convinced of a payoff of humanistic approaches when dealing with higher caliber employees on jobs that cannot be highly structured and controlled. Thus, a portion of the enterprise may be managed behaviorally, while the larger remainder may be approached in the usual classical manner.

If human values are to be viewed as *ends*, rather than means, then the above described search for payback is not so important. If this is the case, it is often the result of *outside* pressures from governments and unions to force the firm to seek *other values* besides the economic. Thus, it may well be that some human values are viewed and utilized as constructive means to economic ends of the enterprise, while others, lacking such a proved relationship, will be imposed from without as the price of continued approval and cooperation. If the approaches suggested by behaviorists are unsuccessful in terms of costs, quality, quantity, and creativity, it is likely that only the outside forces of union, government, and/or personal codes of ethics will result in changes favorable to the human element. If, however, research and experiment in the future demonstrates a greater mutuality of interests, then we will have the positive driving force of profits behind these programs.

[1] Arthur H. Brayfield and Walter H. Crockett, "Employee Attitudes and Employee Performance," *Psychological Bulletin*, Vol. 52 (September, 1955), pp. 396–424; Frederick Herzberg, et al., *Job Attitudes: Review of Research and Opinion* (Pittsburgh: Psychological Service, 1957); and Victor H. Vroom, *Work and Motivation* (New York: John Wiley & Sons, Inc.), p. 183.

[2] Rensis Likert, *The Human Organization* (New York: McGraw-Hill Book Company, 1967), Chap. 5.

HUMAN NATURE

Since the human element is becoming more important to the modern manager, it is necessary that it be studied more carefully and systematically than is the case in usual manager-subordinate relationships. Most psychologists are in agreement that human behavior is not completely disorganized and without motivation. The human personality is composed of various elements which are structured and related to achieve some degree of balance. Thus, in a sense, each person is an organization with his own internal organizational problems.

The usual explanation of human behavior rests upon the study of basic human needs. The specific list of needs varies from author to author, but disagreement appears to be more a matter of terminology than content. The list of needs can become rather long, and it has been suggested that they be classified into three main categories: physiological, social, and egoistic.

Physiological needs have to do with sustaining life. Man must have food, water, air, rest, shelter, and the like. These needs can be met in a modern society by wages or salary. It goes without saying that these needs should be met on a continuing basis, and that man feel secure that such will be the case.

Social needs are those that issue from man's inherent gregariousness, the opportunity to be with and derive satisfaction from association with others. Within this category, there are three prime needs: (1) physical association and contact; (2) acceptance; and (3) love and affection. Most people desire to live with and relate to others. The hermit feels little need of this, but modern cities demonstrate the strength of this drive.

Physical contact and association are usually not enough. Most people are desirous of being affiliated with and *accepted* by some group or groups. It has long been noted that modern society has tended toward the formation of multiple groups and that one man is simultaneously a member of several. We often must deal with conflicts among such affiliations, e.g., a business organization whose policy requirements conflict with the ideals of a particular profession to which the man belongs. Groups will be formed by people in all walks of life, whether officially permitted or not. Such activity issues from a very strong need of acceptance by one's fellow man.

The need for social acceptance is met by many—a group or groups; but the need for love and affection can be satisfied only by few—one's immediate family and circle of friends. There is no requirement, and usually no desire, that one be loved by all of his fellow associates. However, most people have a definite need for love and affection from a few people. Thus it is that we form and maintain ties of family and friendships.

Egoistic needs have to do with satisfying one's self or ego in a certain manner. The social needs are concerned primarily with one's relationships with others. At the same time, however, other people can also be adapted to the satisfying of ego needs. Among the identifiable egoistic needs are the following: (1) recognition; (2) dominance; (3) independence; and (4) achievement.

Though man desires acceptance from the group, he does not usually wish to merge with it to the extent that he loses his identity. He has a difficult problem of balancing his desire for acceptance with his need for recognition. If he accepts a promotion and thus derives recognition, he risks loss of old friends and their acceptance of him. These two sets of needs are not mutually exclusive, but they do pose, as we said, certain problems of balance for both the individual and the organization.

Younger people tend to be relatively submissive. As the human being matures, however, the need to dominate becomes more apparent. Dominance may well be an extension of the need for recognition, with the ultimate objective being autonomy and independence. The ego demands that we have some measure of control of our life and future. This is particularly true of mature and educated people. Both social and egoistic needs are usually labeled secondary needs in contrast with the primary nature of the physiological.

Many psychologists contend that most people also have within them a need to achieve some goal beyond a kind of vegetation survival. This is one of the higher needs and is not felt until most of the previously mentioned needs have been reasonably well-satisfied.

The above-described three categories tend to cover most of the identified needs of men and help to explain much of observable human behavior, because these needs set up within man certain tensions which can be relieved and satisfaction effected only through behavior. If the man is able to satisfy a need in a manner acceptable to society, he is termed "adjusted." If, on the other hand, he is unable to satisfy this need in any manner whatsoever, or only in a manner unacceptable to society, he is labeled "maladjusted." (These labels are, of course, relative.) One form of maladjustment, known as "frustration," results when the individual can find absolutely no means of satisfying his needs, whether these needs are approved by society or not. As a result, behavior which seems pointless does actually serve to release accumulated tension. Examples of behavior exhibiting frustration are *aggression* (useless assault upon the obstacle or any other convenient item), *regression* (resort to tears and childlike behavior), *fixation* (repetition of acts previously determined as useless), and *resignation* (wholesale surrender of self).

The modern manager must be sufficiently aware of basic human nature in order to understand much of the behavior he observes. He must not assume that all people are alike, or that they are like himself; there are individual differences. If he is aware of the theory of need-motivated behavior, he is less apt to leap to the conclusion that the observed behavior is without reason, irresponsible, or dangerous. He is also in a better position to review the possibilities for integrating human needs with the organization needs of economy and effectiveness of operation.

NEED PATTERNS

Even taking into account individual differences, many psychologists believe that there are certain patterns or configurations of needs. A common approach to establishing this need pattern is that of developing a hierarchy according to priority. Abraham Maslow has proposed one widely-accepted pattern as follows:[3]

1. Basic physiological needs.
2. Safety.
3. Love.
4. Esteem.
5. Self-actualization.

All psychologists are agreed that the basic physiological needs are first in priority. Man must have food, water, clothing, shelter, and air to maintain his existence. Once these needs are satisfied to a reasonable degree, he becomes *aware* of needs which were below the immediate threshold of consciousness, and which now become apparent after satisfactory fulfillment of more basic needs.

In Maslow's list, security is second in the sequence. Man wants to assure himself that satisfaction of basic needs will be continued; in short, he desires safety. Once the necessities for continued existence have been met, the three higher needs come into prominence. There is some disagreement concerning the classification and priority of these higher needs. Maslow suggests that the need for love is next, a need which includes the desire for affection and association with others. Once this is gratified to an acceptable degree, man then feels a need for some esteem, the satisfaction of which, according to Maslow, derives from social approval, self-assertion, and self-approval. Other psychologists would separate and rank these needs more finely and place the social needs for acceptance and association higher in priority than the needs of the ego for self-assertion and self-esteem. *All*, however, are agreed that the need of lowest priority is that of self-actualization or self-fulfillment. This is the need to realize one's capacities and potentialities by achieving some very definite goal. As indicated earlier, perhaps the low priority of this need provides us an excuse for not contributing to society (we have not sufficiently

[3] Abraham Maslow, *Motivation and Personality* (New York: Harper & Bros., 1954).

gratified needs for survival, security, acceptance, and recognition; ergo, why bother with something higher?). Man is never completely satisfied on any need level, but a sufficient amount of gratification of higher priority needs must be forthcoming if he is to perceive a lower priority need. Maslow suggests a hypothetical example for an average citizen who is 85 percent satisfied in his physiological needs, 70 percent in his safety needs, 50 percent in his love needs, 40 percent in the self-esteem category, and 10 percent in his self-actualization needs.[4] Needs that are reasonably well-satisfied, such as the physiological and safety needs, cannot be prime motivators of behavior.

Some field research has been done which tends to substantiate the hierarchical concept of needs. In contrasting the levels of need satisfaction of lower- and middle-level managers, Porter discovered that the former perceive significantly less need fulfillment in the security, esteem, and autonomy categories.[5] Both groups tended to perceive greater deficiencies in the lower priority needs (autonomy and self-actualization) than in the higher priority categories (security and social). The physiological needs were not examined on the assumption that both types of managers were receiving reasonable gratification. Contrary to expectations, both middle and lower managers were equally dissatisfied in the self-actualization category. The level of organization is not the only factor affecting need satisfaction, but the differences discovered lend some support for the Maslow hierarchy. A study of clerical employees by Beer with respect to need satisfaction deficiencies resulted in a rank-order correlation of .80 with the order for lower-level managers as found by Porter.[6] Evidently, needs of self-actualization and autonomy are also felt by operative employees in business firms. Self-actualization was the least satisfied category for both clerks and bottom-level managers.

Other patterns of needs have been presented which vary from the above. Louis Barnes accepts the priority of the basic physiological and security needs, but suggests that the other needs of lower priority are to be grouped into one category, all having direct relationship with the need for security. His pattern would appear as follows:[7]

1. Basic physiological needs.
2. Safety.

[4] *Ibid.*, Chap. 5.

[5] Lyman W. Porter, "Job Attitudes in Management: I. Perceived Deficiencies in Need Fulfillment as a Function of Job Level," *Journal of Applied Psychology*, Vol. 46 (1962), pp. 375–384.

[6] Michael Beer, "Needs and Need Satisfaction Among Clerical Workers in Complex and Routine Jobs," *Personnel Psychology*, Vol. 21 (1968), pp. 209–222.

[7] Louis B. Barnes, *Organizational Systems and Engineering Groups: A Study of Two Technical Groups in Industry* (Boston: Division of Research, Harvard Business School, 1960).

3. Balanced, subsequent opportunities for:
   a. substantial self-direction and self-esteem
   b. wide range of warm, accepted relationships with others
   c. some degree of reciprocal influence relationships with superiors and equals.

If one or more of the needs of the third category are blocked off, this serves to *reactivate* the safety need. This is in line with psychological theories that hold that when man is frustrated, he will revert to lower, more basic need levels such as security. Thus, Barnes suggests that if a man is blocked in his desire for reasonable independence, he may direct much of his energy to developing more social contacts with others. However, the development of improved social relationships with others may in itself not be evidence of a higher need, but rather may be motivated by a continuing search for security. In general, Barnes emphasizes action motivated by anxiety over security.

THE MATURATION PROCESS

In addition to recognizing certain need patterns, behaviorists have also pointed out that human nature is, at least partially, a function of maturation. Chris Argyris, for example, has established the following as the dimensions of maturity of the human personality.[8]

1. Development from a state of passivity as an infant to a state of increasing activity as an adult.
2. Development from a state of dependence on others as an infant to a state of relative independence as an adult.
3. Development from a state of being capable of behaving only in a few ways as an infant to being capable of behaving in many different ways as an adult.
4. Development from having erratic, casual, shallow, and quickly-dropped interests as an infant to having deeper interests as an adult.
5. Development from having a short time perspective as an infant to a much longer time perspective as an adult.
6. Development from being in a subordinate position as an infant to aspiring to occupy an equal and/or superordinate position as an adult.
7. Development from a lack of awareness of self as an infant to awareness and control over self as an adult.

Each of these dimensions is in the form of a continuum. Any individual can be in varying states of maturation on each of the dimension continuums. Note

[8] From p. 50, *Personality and Organization* by Chris Argyris. Copyright © 1957 by Harper and Row, Publishers, Incorporated. By permission of the publishers.

that this pattern of human characteristics and behavior is not to be taken as a substitute or contradiction of the need patterns presented above. These latter constitute merely one portion of the total human personality, but a portion which is highly significant to the business enterprise.

As will be discussed in the following chapter, this theory of maturation establishes the basis for certain clashes between business organizations as traditionally structured and the mature human personality as described above. We are not suggesting that all adult employees in industry are mature in the sense of having fully developed all of the dimensions cited. The only generality that applies is that as one increases in age, one *tends* to move from the infant end to the adult end of the scales.

ASSUMPTIONS CONCERNING THE NATURE OF MAN

Philosophers have long been fascinated and puzzled concerning the apparent contradictory and dual nature of man. Man appears to have a capacity for tenderness, sympathy, and love while at the same time possessing tendencies toward cruelty, callousness, hate, and destruction. If man is basically the former, he needs little external regulation. If the latter, he must be closely controlled and regimented for the good of society.

There are well-known writers and theorists on both sides of the controversy. Freud saw in man an instinct for aggression resulting in anxiety as his basic nature clashed with the requirements of society.[9] Interpreters of Darwin's theory attempted to apply the survival of the fittest concept to man, thereby favoring the strong and aggressive. Biologists, such as Robert Ardrey and Konrad Lorenz, also tend to emphasize built-in tendencies toward aggression, particularly with respect to the defense of territory and space.[10]

On the other hand, various theorists emphasize the fundamental goodness of man. At the least, he is born neutral with a "blank page" to be written upon by society. John Locke, for example, viewed man as being basically cooperative in nature, as does also the anthropologist Ashley Montagu. The latter suggests that "it is not human nature, but nurture that is the cause of human aggression."[11] He concludes that so-called differences in human nature are in fact differences in cultural experiences. This latter view of man would lead to efforts to develop, enhance, and tap his potential, as contrasted with creating devices and methods to control his negative drives.

[9] Sigmund Freud, *Civilization and Its Discontents* (New York: W. W. Norton & Co., Inc., 1961).

[10] Robert Ardrey, *The Territorial Imperative* (New York: Atheneum Press, 1966), pp. 289–305.

[11] M. F. Ashley Montagu, *Anthropology and Human Nature* (Boston: Porter Sargent, 1957), p. 36.

The theorist responsible for the introduction of this dual theme into management theory is Douglas McGregor. In observing practices and approaches of traditional managers, he inferred that they were based on the following assumptions about human nature.[12]

1. The average person has an inherent dislike for work and will avoid it if he can.
2. Because of this human characteristic of dislike of work, most people must be coerced, controlled, directed, and threatened with punishment to get them to put forth adequate effort toward the achievement of organization objectives.
3. The average person prefers to be directed, wishes to avoid responsibility, has relatively little ambition, and wants security above all.

Obviously, McGregor believes that the traditional approach of management, which he labels Theory "X," is based on a belief that the average man is *not mature* in the dimensions proposed by Argyris. He suggests that even though the personnel hired are over the age of twenty-one, they are regarded by most managements as approaching more nearly the infant end of the maturity dimensions.

As an opposing set of assumptions regarding the degree of maturity of people in business organizations, McGregor submits an alternative theory, called Theory "Y."[13] He believes the following to be a more realistic assessment of people:

1. The expenditure of physical and mental effort in work is as natural as play or rest.
2. Man will exercise self-direction and self-control in the service of objectives to which he is committed.
3. Commitment to objectives is a function of the rewards associated with achievement.
4. The average person learns, under proper conditions, not only to accept but to seek responsibility.
5. The capacity to exercise a relatively high degree of imagination, ingenuity, and creativity in the solution of organizational problems is widely, not narrowly, distributed in the population.

An examination of these two sets of assumptions, Theories "X" and "Y," helps to explain some of the controversy between the management theorists called traditionalists and those labeled behaviorists. It largely adds up to *what type*

---

[12] Douglas McGregor, *The Human Side of Enterprise* (New York: McGraw-Hill Book Company, 1960), pp. 33–34.
[13] *Ibid.,* pp. 47–48.

of subordinate each assumes to be present in the work situation. Our major point here is that the manager must have a *philosophy of human nature*. This philosophy or basic attitude toward people inevitably affects his view of management problems and the techniques he selects to solve them.

Theory "Y" assumptions represent the behaviorist's boundless faith in the capacity and potential of man. This would lead them to create conditions under which *all* people would have the opportunity to self-actualize, whether it is a changing of the ghetto environment for the black teenager, or the loosening of rigid procedures and rules for the apathetic assembly line worker.

On the other hand, there are those who feel that a small percentage of the world's population must do the world's work, that those who can will ride on the backs of the others. Whether this irresponsibility, selfishness, and apathy is a result of basic human nature or human nurture is not important to the manager who lives primarily in the present. If man does exhibit such characteristics, whether he was born with them or is a victim of the system, such managers maintain that the fact of the matter is that *they do exist* in his organization. And thus, he concludes, restrictive controls are necessary. He would protest that the nurturing of today's employees started many years ago in the home and the school system, and that a fundamental social change in one's views toward work and cooperation lies outside the control of the single business enterpriser.

And so the controversy rages. It is true that what a manager can do in the present is largely restricted by what has happened in the past. It is also true that no management practitioner or theorist holds himself bound inseparably to the past; if one concludes that undesirable human characteristics are a product more of nurture than nature, it then behooves all managers to undertake a change in the nurture. Such changes, it must be admitted, will be painfully slow and difficult to accomplish. And when the change involves changes in basic cultural values, patience is a prime requisite.

CULTURE

Action is undertaken to satisfy needs with the overall tendency being in the direction of self-actualization. These particular acts, for which the motivation lies within the human psyche, must take place within a particular culture. Culture is concerned with the human-created elements of life, and includes such diverse components as customs, beliefs, laws, habits, and knowledge. Whether or not one is aware of it, there is a constant interaction between an organization or individual and the surrounding cultures.

The modern manager requires a specific knowledge of the total culture and specific subcultures that surround him and his organization. We have, for example, a certain culture in the United States. We also have a specific subculture in XYZ firm. Certain subcultures cut across organizations (e.g., the engineering profession or the business management group). Knowledge of these cultures enables one not only to understand and predict behavior of members of these cultures, but also to determine what actions are *not* possible. Specific managements have encountered difficulties in directing engineering subordinates to undertake specific acts which were incongruous with professional requirements. The engineer may be a member of the XYZ firm "culture" but he is also affected by the standards and customs of his profession. When these two cultures are in conflict, the individual must make a decision favoring one or the other. To the surprise of some managements, professional people often hold a greater loyalty to the profession than they do to the particular firm with whom they are currently associated. These are sometimes labeled "cosmopolitans," as contrasted to "locals" or "provincials" who accept the value system of the particular firm. To the cosmopolitan, the firm is a temporary stop where he may practice his profession. The manager's orientation toward the firm's profit objectives often leads to misunderstandings and clashes with professionals whose orientation is often toward development of competence, self-control, and colleague, rather than manager, influence. Consequently, it is necessary for industrial managers to study the characteristics, standards, and customs of the subcultures whose members they wish to utilize within their business organization. Just as the individual has certain predicted patterns of behavior and reactions, a group also develops recognizable characteristics which assist in predicting the general behavior pattern of that group.

One of the easiest ways to appreciate the effect of culture upon the practice of management is to contrast the cultures of various countries in the world. In a cross-cultural study of Peru and the United States, it was found that employees of the former nation favor close supervision while United States workers do not.[14] Peruvian employees react favorably to strong pressures to produce, while U.S. employees do not. Peruvians operate individually and do not see themselves as part of a work group, while U.S. workers tend to rely more on teamwork. It is apparent that behavioral management approaches emphasizing group participation would be less usable in Peru than in the United States.

Other cultural comparisons have been made with various nations. In interpreting these, Argyris concludes that participation approaches are less workable in Norway, South America, and Europe.[15] German managers tend to view power and authority as more of a natural right, and consequently are more directive and less anxious and defensive about it. United States cultural beliefs

---

[14] Lawrence K. Williams, William F. Whyte, and Charles S. Green, "Do Cultural Differences Affect Workers' Attitudes?" *Industrial Relations*, Vol. 5, No. 3 (May, 1966), pp. 107–108.

[15] Chris Argyris, *Integrating the Individual and the Organization* (New York: John Wiley & Sons, Inc., 1964), Chap. 1.

of freedom and equality make the acceptance of authority more difficult for both manager and subordinates. Japanese employees look upon impersonal, contractual, and formal relationships as immoral and distrustful. Such an attitude would cause some difficulty for the classical manager who would attempt to plan and codify job descriptions and procedures.

If the United States manager is to operate in a foreign culture, he will certainly have to understand and adapt to its requirements to some extent. If he is to manage subcultures in this country, such as professionals and blue-collar workers, he will also have to understand and adapt. Yet, management is not simply adapting. It also must involve change if progress is to occur. To the degree that he attempts to change a culture, the manager is a revolutionary.[16] In trying to change a family and hereditary system of employee selection to a merit system, he is bucking centuries of tradition in some nations. Yet, the latter system will tend to enhance economic values. As noted previously in this text, similar clashes and contradictions are present within any organization. Whether to adapt to a culture or to alter it is a question involving considerations of both immediate and long-range values.

An understanding of the total culture and various subcultures of which all individuals are a part is an essential skill prerequisite to a sophisticated understanding of human behavior. People do not behave in a vacuum. To the knowledge of individual behavior provided by the psychologist must be added the knowledge of group behavior provided by the sociologist and anthropologist.

SUMMARY

We have been focusing on that most important and essential ingredient of all organization, the human being. The importance of the human factor has been forced upon business management through greater activity and power on the part of labor unions and government, as well as through a gradual realization that a more *effective* utilization of people could be conducive to increased profitability. A general knowledge of people is prerequisite to the specific task of managing them.

Human behavior is not completely random and unmotivated. Psychological researchers have developed theories of behavior revolving around the physiological, social, and egoistic needs of man. The specific needs within these categories have been projected as being patterned in a hierarchical manner based on priority. One such pattern could be as follows: (1) health; (2) security or safety; (3) love; (4) social acceptance; (5) esteem; and (6) self-actualization. In Maslow's hierarchy, social acceptance and esteem are grouped into one class. Before man can be unduly concerned about and motivated by a higher need,

---

[16] Richard N. Farmer, "The Revolutionary American Businessman," *California Management Review*, Vol. 9, No. 4 (Summer, 1967), pp. 79–84.

the lower needs must be reasonably well-satisfied. Man is motivated by unsatisfied needs, not by those that have been fulfilled.

It has been hypothesized that as man grows older, his behavior patterns exhibit a certain degree of maturity. As an infant, the human being is passive, dependent, shallow, short-sighted, subordinate, and unaware of self. As he matures, he tends to become active and independent, and he develops deeper interests and larger perspectives; he desires equal or superordinate status and is more aware of self. This process of maturation, as well as certain fundamental assumptions as to the basic nature of man, have a profound effect upon a manager's approach to his personnel. Sociologists, psychologists, and anthropologists differ as to the basic nature of man, whether he is essentially good and cooperative, or indolent and in conflict. Various practicing managers are also in conflict on these points; the point, however, is that their respective philosophies inevitably and drastically affect their managerial approach.

To complete this brief survey of the basic nature of man, one must recognize that human behavior cannot be fully understood and accurately predicted apart from a knowledge of the various cultures in which this behavior takes place. The ego, for example, can be satisfied in ways unacceptable to a culture. Individuals acting in such a manner are usually labeled "maladjusted." The manager should realize that his own organization constitutes a specific subculture, with its own traditions, customs, values, and habits, within a larger total culture. The manager should become aware that he must deal with various other specific subcultures that cut horizontally across his organization, such professional subcultures as engineering, law, and medicine.

Discussion Problems

1. Does the Maslow hierarchy of needs have anything to do with current emphases upon human relations in business organizations? Are human relations programs a creation of moralistic business managers?
2. Contrast human values as both a means and an end.
3. If the discovered correlation between employee morale and productivity is a plus .14, should managers attempt to do anything about morale?
4. How does one's philosophy of human nature affect his managerial practices? Cite illustrations.
5. What is the nature and significance of the Argyris dimensions of maturation to the manager?
6. What is meant by the concept that man is motivated only by unsatisfied needs?
7. What approach should be used by a manager who believes in the essential goodness of man (Theory "Y") but is convinced that he must deal with a group of Theory "X" subordinates?
8. What is culture? Of what significance is this concept to a manager?
9. Are behavorial approaches to management usable in nations throughout the world? If they are not, does this mean that we have encountered Theory "X" people?

10. Does the development of a subculture for the engineering profession help or hinder the management of a specific firm? Discuss.

SUPPLEMENTARY READING

Farmer, Richard N., "The Revolutionary American Businessman," *California Management Review,* Vol. 9, No. 4 (Summer, 1967), 79–84.

Gibson, James L., "Organization Theory and the Nature of Man," *Academy of Management Journal,* Vol. 9, No. 3 (September, 1966), 233–245.

Haire, Mason, Edwin E. Ghiselli, and Lyman W. Porter, *Managerial Thinking* (New York: John Wiley & Sons, Inc., 1966).

Knowles, Henry P. and Borje O. Saxberg, "Human Relations and the Nature of Man," *Harvard Business Review,* Vol. 45, No. 2 (March–April, 1967), 20–38, 172–178.

Landsberger, Henry A., "The Behavioral Sciences in Industry," *Industrial Relations,* Vol. 7, No. 1 (October, 1967), 1–19.

Rosenzweig, James E., "Managers and Management Scientists (Two Cultures)," *Business Horizons,* Vol. 10, No. 3 (Fall, 1967), 79–86.

Sarachek, Bernard, "Elton Mayo's Social Psychology and Human Relations," *Academy of Management Journal,* Vol. 11, No. 2 (June, 1968), 189–197.

Williams, Lawrence K., William F. Whyte, and Charles S. Green, "Do Cultural Differences Affect Workers' Attitudes?" *Industrial Relations,* Vol. 5, No. 3 (May, 1966), 105–117.

7

The Human Element in Business Organizations

As indicated in the preceding chapter, the behavior of human beings is need-motivated and is affected by the customs, mores, and practices of the surrounding culture or cultures. We are here primarily concerned with the culture of business organizations. We have seen how management attempts to specify and control the environment through planning, decision making, and policy formulation. We have also recognized the necessity for identifying and allocating special attention to one important aspect of these plans, the human element. In this chapter, attention will be devoted to the ways in which human needs are made evident in business organizations. Consideration will then be given to the reactions and adjustment of human beings to the essentially rational and somewhat mechanistic environment established by traditional managements. In some manner or another, people must be merged or fused with the formal organizations in our society; the one should not function independently of the other.

EMPLOYEE WANTS

The human being in a business firm is usually called an employee. Human needs as expressed in a particular environment are termed "wants." Thus, management should be concerned with employee wants, that is, with the manifest needs of individuals and groups in business organizations.

Though the number of employee wants are unlimited in practice, certain of these are identifiable as being fairly prevalent in business firms. Though again, the order of importance will vary from time to time and place to place. If a want is being met reasonably well, then other wants will begin to assume primary importance. For example, in various companies the want of pay, which works toward satisfaction of the hunger and shelter needs, is ranked lower in importance by the employees than other wants, such as opportunity to advance or recognition for work accomplished. This does not mean that pay is unimportant or that hunger and shelter needs are no longer primary as compared to social and egoistic needs. It does mean, however, that this particular business organization has satisfied reasonably well the want of pay, and that *other* wants rise in importance in the estimation of the employees.

Among the commonly cited human wants in business organization are the following:

1. *Security of job.* This particular want is high on the list of employees in many companies. It issues, of course, from the basic need for general security and becomes most desired when threatened. Meeting this want has taken such diverse forms as guaranteeing no job loss due to technological change; use of seniority as a controlling element in decision making; and pensions.

2. *Pay.* Inasmuch as pay enables one to satisfy physiological needs, it will always be an important employee want. It should also be pointed out that the pay cup has "social handles,"[1] i.e., pay is an indication of status and prestige, and relative pay may be more important to a particular individual than the absolute amount. Thus, pay is an employee want that assists in fulfilling ego and security needs as well as physiological needs.

3. *Comfortable and attractive working conditions.* The provision of comfortable, safe, and pleasant working conditions also helps to ease physiological and psychological needs. The individual might want security, but he also desires the prestige associated with a certain type and level of physical environment.

4. *Congenial associates.* The desire for congenial associates issues from the need to be accepted by the particular people with whom one must work. The need for love can be met by one's family, but the need for acceptance must be met by one's associates in work or play.

5. *Credit for work done.* Man has both a need for recognition and a need for acceptance. To some degree the two are conflicting. Receiving credit for one's accomplishments is a want issuing from egoistic needs, and such recognition can be accorded by means of oral praise, letters of commendation, and merit ratings. Frustration of this want often produces undesirable effects in terms of morale and cooperation. And yet, its gratification may lead to a lessening of satisfaction of social needs since it tends to separate the individual from his

[1] Whiting Williams, *Mainsprings of Men* (New York: Charles Scribner's Sons, 1925), p. 58.

associates who have not been so recognized. In these times, conflict within the individual is not an unusual occurrence.

6. *Opportunity to advance.* The desire for opportunity to advance to higher positions also issues from the egoistic needs. In the United States, two of the basic tenets of our culture have been those of freedom and opportunity. Supposedly, a man can go as far as his ability and energy will take him. He prefers to see that avenues upward are open to him even though he may never attempt to embark upon the journey.

7. *Competent and fair leadership.* The desire for skillful and just leadership in an organization issues from a number of needs. The wish for justice and equitable treatment comes, in part, from the security need. Competent leadership also inflicts less injury upon the subordinate's ego—it is less difficult to subordinate oneself to persons accorded higher status. And finally, competent leadership helps to assure the success of the enterprise, thus enabling the continuing gratification of other wants such as pay, job security, and the like.

8. *Appropriate job requirements.* Many people want jobs that are interesting and that permit the use and development of their particular talents. Working for the paycheck only and viewing work as the penalty for such pay are admittedly attitudes too often found in business firms. Such attitudes often result from such things as poor design of jobs, faulty matching of individual abilities to job demands, and the conditioning of attitudes by one's family and associates. Some complaints about job demands can issue from lack of satisfaction of social or ego needs; e.g., the work layout that prohibits conversation. But other complaints could well issue from a lack of opportunity to make a significant and worthwhile contribution in life. Work should have some meaning other than money.

THE APPRAISAL OF EMPLOYEE MORALE

Morale can be defined as the attitudes of individuals—and particularly of groups—that determine the degree of voluntary cooperation in concerted endeavors. When morale is high, there is an evident increase in loyalty, interest, initiative, pride, discipline, and voluntary cooperation. When morale is low, there is an equally evident and observable increase in discontent, discouragement, dislike of job, destructive conflict, surliness, and outright insubordination. Determining the level of morale between the two extremes of high and low often calls for finer instruments of measurement than mere observation.

Management cannot dictate that another person or persons shall have high morale. In all probability, the degree of morale hinges heavily upon the degree of employee want satisfaction present in the business environment. However, it is important to distinguish between constructive morale and mere content-ment. A very happy, congenial group could very well be a lazy and incompe-tent one. They may have low absenteeism and tardiness rates, but their positive contribution to the organization may be low. Constructive morale would encompass attitudes of voluntary cooperation toward organization objectives and the willingness to work even in the face of adversity. Construc-tive morale would not necessarily mean the absence of *all* conflict, for conflict often leads to reevaluation and constructive thinking. We do not seek rosy optimism, happiness, contentment, and satisfaction with no thought for the degree of accomplishment in organization tasks. We do seek a reasonable level of employee satisfaction which will lead to long-term productivity and creativ-ity in the organization.

If one is interested in organizational effectiveness, one must, therefore, be concerned with the level of employee satisfaction. There are several methods of appraising morale, but all rest upon the successful attainment of truthful information about employee attitudes. Among the many methods of appraising morale are supervisory observation of subordinate behavior, systematic non-directive interviewing by personnel counselors, "exit interviews," and the analysis of objective data such as the number and type of grievances, level of absenteeism, production quantity and quality effected, and degree of labor turnover. The discussion from this point on will be confined to a single method of appraisal in order to illustrate the nature of the process: the anonymous questionnaire survey.[2] We are not implying that this is either the only way or the best way of appraising the level of morale.

If we are to obtain truthful information concerning attitudes, the employee must feel comfortable, secure, and confident in giving answers to the questions posed. Usually this is most likely to occur if his anonymity is preserved. Many firms employ the services of an outside consultant to administer the survey, guaranteeing that no individual's answers will be revealed to the organization. Two basic types of questionnaires can be used: (1) the attitude survey, and (2) the opinion survey. The attitude survey is usually of the objective, mul-tiple-choice type. Various subjects, usually issuing from the list of employee wants that management feels are important, are selected and a question is prepared with a series of possible answers. Thus, *management* usually selects not only the subjects, but also the array of possible answers. The attitude survey requires a scaling of these answers according to some set of values established through research.[3] Higher scores are accorded answers reflecting

---

[2] Other means of appraising attitudes are counseling interviews; analysis of such data as absenteeism, grievances, and turnover indices; and anonymous complaint systems. Any channel which will reveal truthful information about employee sentiments can be used to appraise the morale level.

[3] See Joseph Tiffin and Ernest McCormick, *Industrial Psychology*, 5th ed. (Englewood Cliffs: Prentice-Hall, Inc., 1965), Chap. 10, for a description of scaling techniques.

attitudes which are more conducive to cooperation and productivity. Examples of such questions appear below.

1. How do you feel about the opportunity to advance in this organization?
   a. If one works hard and does a good job, he will get ahead in this company.
   b. The only way to get ahead in this company is to know someone with "pull."
   c. Hard work and loyalty to the company is not rewarded in this organization.
   d. If you stick around long enough in this company, you'll get ahead.
   e. There is no opportunity to advance in this company.
   f. Usually the best man wins out, but occasionally "pull" is more important.
2. How do you regard the way that pay is handled in this company?
   a. This company pays as little as possible while remaining within the law.
   b. This company is generally competitive in its level of pay.
   c. In general, the pay is good, but there are several cases of gross unfairness.
   d. This company pays better than the others in the area for the same work.
   e. My pay and the pay setup is a complete mystery—there is no rhyme or reason.
   f. The pay system is set up to advance the interests of employees and is competitive with the better companies in the area.

The opinion questionnaire differs only in the absence of scaling. Answers are reported in percentages of replies, that is, 45 percent indicates choice 1; 30 percent, choice 2; etc. The company obviously has preferences among these lists of choices also, but this preference is not scaled through a systematic weighing process.

The appraisal of the results of these anonymous surveys can be handled in various ways. However, it is significant to note that resulting scores are primarily of value only in *relative* terms, such as are listed below:

1. Scores for the entire organization now and in the past.
2. Scores for other entire organizations if the same measurement instrument is used.
3. Scores for each department now and in the past.
4. Scores by organization level.
5. Scores by seniority of employees.
6. Scores for men as compared to those for women.
7. Scores on each want covered by questions.
8. Scores for each question for each category of personnel cited above.

It should be noted that there is no provision for scores by individuals. An individual's morale can be measured, but usually not by management in this particular manner.

Thus, a survey may have resulted in a total score of 80 for the organization as compared with a 70 in the past. All we know is that it is improving as indicated by the criteria covered in the measurement instrument. If the identical survey had been administered to other companies by a consultant, and the industry average was also 80, one could conclude that we are reasonably competitive with respect to employee morale. If departmental scores are 95, 75, 85, 70, 80, 95, 95, and 40, we obviously know there is trouble in the department last cited. Other techniques may be used within that department to ascertain the source of the difficulty. If a score of 10 for all persons on the subject of "pay" and a 3 on the subject of "competent and fair supervision" are obtained, one should spend more time to improve the quality of supervision.

Conducting a morale survey has many values for the management truly interested in the degree of acceptance by the employee of his business environment. However, the process is not without its problems. Some contend that such a survey will only provide fodder for the union with which management may be attacked, that attitudes change daily and even hourly at times, that employees are needlessly stirred up and trouble is created rather than revealed, and that the process is too inexact to be relied upon. Each of these objections has some truth. However, if employee attitudes are deemed important, then the use of one of the effective, though admittedly imperfect, instruments of appraisal is justified. In fact, there is often an important side-benefit to the organization: the employee has been shown that management is interested in his feelings and beliefs after all!

EMPLOYEE REACTIONS TO BUSINESS PLANS

Thus far we have been speaking generally of the human element in the business organization. In order to follow the original design of this text, we will now consider the impact of traditional management planning on employee attitudes and behavior.

Few managers are naïve enough to believe that every plan will be put into actual practice without change. They have always been aware of the vagaries of unforeseen circumstances, changing market conditions, unexpected equipment breakdowns, unpredictable weather conditions, and the like. Too often, however, an additional element is overlooked, namely, that human personalities are variable and that, for better or worse, human behavior cannot be programmed as precisely as can a computer. As Selznick indicates, "we are inescapably committed to the mediation of human structures which are at once indispensable to our goals and at the same time *stand between* them and ourselves."[4] The devising of a plan is restricted only by the availability of technical information, but its execution must involve people and their minor, and sometimes major, adaptations and qualifications of the original plan. Thus, the manager must live with uncertainty issuing from human sources and has to accept the fact that deviations from the original plan are *not* necessarily mistakes to be corrected. Some deviations will occur because of unforeseen objective circumstances, and we require at this point that the participants be flexible and adaptable. Other deviations will result from misinterpretation of orders and information, thus emphasizing once again the need for skills in communication.[5] But still others will result from an attempt on the part of the employee to *personalize* his tasks. Few people desire merely to fill a slot, operate like a robot, and react only when and if the correct button is pushed. The needs of the ego, and perhaps those of self-actualization, dictate the desire to *alter* in some manner the orders, policies, and procedures dictated from above.

The manager should be aware of these human tendencies to alter original plans. He should also be aware of the advantages as well as disadvantages that may issue therefrom. Among the former are a transformation of an unrealistic plan into one that adapts to the reality of the place and time of execution; the increased satisfaction of the employee in being able to control some small portion of his business life; and the tapping of new sources of enthusiasm and interest in work. The opportunity to alter some portion of the job may result in better acceptance of that larger portion rigidly controlled by the organization.

The disadvantages of deviating from organization plans rest on the assumption that scientific management produces the best possible plan to achieve organization objectives. Quite possibly, alterations of the plan by employees would result in failure to achieve rational organization goals or in achieving these goals but at greater expense. If the costs of employee deviation from the plan are greater than the returns, whether immediate or long term, such deviation will have to be corrected. On the other hand, it is frequently found that permitting personalization of tasks, at some cost to the organization, facilitates a greater *net* contribution to the firm through its beneficial effect upon morale.

Among the major problems that scientific management planning can create for the employee in business organizations are the following:

1. A reduction of independence and opportunities for self-control.
2. Possible boredom and apathy.

---

[4] Philip Selznick, "Foundations of the Theory of Organization," *American Sociological Review*, Vol. 13 (1948), p. 33.

[5] See Chapter 19 for a more complete discussion of communication.

3. Lack of opportunities to participate in plan formulation.
4. Lack of perspective in relating oneself to the plans of the organization.
5. Conflicts between organizational demands and individual needs.

Reduced Independence

Scientific planning hopes to anticipate every eventuality in order to reduce or eliminate uncertainty. This very process, however, results in a reduction in the degree of independence of organization members. This is ego threatening and often stimulates an attitude of rebellion against the system. When the subordinate *knows* that an order issuing from the plan is unrealistic and will not work, yet takes great delight in following it to the letter to insure failure, such rebellion takes the form of malicious obedience. The establishment of rigid standards might reduce effectively the opportunities for deviation. Yet there remain tangible evidences of rebellion, attempts to thwart these standards. The rebellion may not necessarily be against a bad or unworkable plan. The needs of the ego lead to a degree of rebellion against *any* plan imposed from without.

Boredom

A related problem is the possible resultant employee states of boredom and apathy. If every detail of the work plan is covered in standard practice instruction sheets, policies, orders, etc., and if such specification results in a high degree of transfer of skill requirements from man to system, the worker is called upon to contribute less and less. The result may well be boredom with the job and consequent disinterest in both the job and the organization. The job has been "engineered out." Pay, under these circumstances, may very well be a reward for the penalty of work.

Limited Participation

The lack of opportunity to participate in plan formation results in losses for both the employee and the organization. One of Taylor's tenets deals with the responsibility of management to determine how the work should be executed; this should not be left to chance or to the worker. Thus, the plans are made in detail and the results are the problems cited above. But these problems are now compounded by having such plans made *only* by management personnel. The subordinate is to be involved only in execution. In a later chapter, we shall examine this problem and a suggested solution of encouraging greater subordinate participation in decision making. But it is sufficient to point out here that nonparticipation can play a part in contributing to unrealistic and incomplete plans and to general apathy and disinterest.

Reduced Perspective

This lack of participation in plan formulation also contributes to another problem, the lack of perspective and understanding by the employees of policies, plans, and objectives. As indicated in the discussion of objectives, coordinated effort requires an understanding of the relationship between the organization objective (economic contribution) and the personal objectives (wages, interest, and profits). To facilitate this understanding and perspective there must be a greater degree of subordinate involvement in planning programs and policies.

Limited Need Gratification

As a final, summarizing problem, the planning function as practiced in many scientifically managed organizations tends to work against the fulfillment of certain human needs. Basically, the organization is attempting to restrict and regulate human behavior on rational grounds. This restriction does not serve to thwart those needs of a physiological or security nature; in fact, it may enhance the fulfillment of these needs. But this restriction *does* tend to work against fulfillment of the egoistic needs of independence, recognition, dominance, and achievement. When the lower needs are reasonably well satisfied, detailed planning tends to invite deviations in execution since people are now aware of and affected by other needs in the hierarchy.

THE MEANING OF WORK

As far as the traditional manager is concerned, the employee comes to an organization to perform work that will contribute to basic organizational goals. The employee, on the other hand, views work as a means of multiple need gratification. In either case, the work is performed in a particular environment that is officially structured by management and considerably affected by human interactions and feelings.

One of the most stimulating and controversial theories of work and motivation proposed in recent years is that credited to Frederick Herzberg.[6] It grew

[6] Frederick Herzberg, *Work and the Nature of Man* (Cleveland: World Publishing Company, 1966).

out of research directed toward ascertaining the employee wants that lead to satisfaction on the job. The usual approach is one of examining a multiplicity of factors such as the work itself, pay, working conditions, supervision, status, security, and the like. The underlying assumption is that there is a *single* continuum ranging from job dissatisfaction on the one end to job satisfaction on the other. The factors listed above are the determinants of particular locations on this continuum.

The Herzberg theory proposes that there are in reality *two* significantly different classes of factors and thus two different continuums. One class, referred to as "hygienic factors," makes up a continuum ranging from *dissatisfaction* to *no dissatisfaction*. Examples of these are pay, interpersonal relations, supervision, company policy and administration, working conditions, status, and job security. Herzberg indicates that these factors do *not* serve to promote job satisfaction, rather their absence or deficiency can create dissatisfaction. Their presence can only serve to eliminate dissatisfaction.

The second class of factors, referred to as "motivators," makes up a continuum leading from *no job satisfaction* to *satisfaction*. Examples of this class are the work itself, recognition, achievement, possibility of growth, and advancement. All these are concerned with the work itself, rather than its surrounding physical, administrative, or social environment. If the worker is to be truly motivated, the job itself is the major source of that motivation. All the other hygienic factors can serve only to "clean up" the environment and prevent dissatisfaction.

The method of research used in developing this theory was not the usual anonymous objective questionnaire type. Rather, each subject was asked to recall a time when he felt exceptionally good or a time when he felt exceptionally bad about his work. These incidents or stories were analyzed to ascertain the particular factors mentioned as contributing to the exceptional satisfaction or dissatisfaction. A significant preponderance of the motivator factors dealing with the work itself was mentioned when the subject was describing a time when he felt exceptionally good. And the times when he felt very bad were marked with a significantly large number of hygienic factors.

This type of study has been duplicated by other researchers on many occasions. In a summary of 12 investigations encompassing 1,685 employees, incidents describing job satisfaction involved 81 percent motivator factors and only 19 percent hygienic factors.[7] In cases describing job dissatisfaction, 69 percent involved hygienic factors as compared to 31 percent motivator factors.

The Herzberg theory has been criticized by some as being method bound; that is, individuals will tend to blame environmental factors for job failure and consequent dissatisfaction, and take credit for any job successes that occur. A

[7] Frederick Herzberg, "One More Time: How Do You Motivate Employees?" *Harvard Business Review*, Vol. 46, No. 1 (January–February, 1968), p. 57.

few objective questionnaire studies are in agreement with the theory, but most are not. Others have criticized the Herzberg type of study as being primarily concerned with the higher, technical jobs whose usual occupant is better educated and more interested in his work. However, there have been studies of various types of jobs such as lower-level supervisors, hospital maintenance personnel, nurses, food handlers, agricultural administrators, accountants, Finnish foremen, Hungarian engineers, and military officers.

It is apparent that this approach to employee satisfaction rests on two assumptions concerning the nature of man: the need to avoid pain and the need to grow. Hygienic factors prevent dissatisfaction and pain by providing a good work environment. Motivator factors enable growth and movement toward some degree of self-actualization. Both sets of needs should be met in the business organization. If the manager desires employee interest and enthusiasm in the job, efforts devoted toward improved fringe benefits, congenial and understanding supervisors, security, and good working conditions will return little. If he wants cooperation, reasonable subordination, and constructive apathy, hygienic efforts will produce a great deal. There is a serious question as to whether an organization can actually restructure all jobs to enable the motivator factors to be felt. There is also a question concerning whether an organization desires *all* personnel to be creative, enthusiastic, and enterprising. Examination of these questions will be pursued in the following section.

THE MATURE EMPLOYEE IN THE BUSINESS ENVIRONMENT

The individual brings to the business organization various needs which he hopes to gratify through behavior within the rational organization framework. As indicated in the previous chapter, there have been various assumptions concerning the nature of the typical individual in the business organization. The assumptions of Argyris were that human personality changes with growth and that the more mature tend to move from states of passivity and dependence to states of increasing activity and independence. Then in examining the nature of scientific management, he concludes that there is a basic incongruity between the demands of the mature personality and the demands of the business organization. Argyris suggests that if plans, policies, procedures, and rules are prescribed in detail, there is a necessity for a submissive and passive plan executioner. The demand is for the subordinate to concentrate on the orders as given and not question or attempt to understand these orders in a broader perspective. In brief, such a detailed prescription may ask individuals to work in an environment where "(1) they are provided minimal control over their workaday world; (2) they are expected to be passive, dependent, and subordinate; (3) they are expected to have a short time perspective; (4) they are induced to perfect and value the frequent use of a few shallow abilities; and (5) they are expected to produce under conditions leading to psychological failure."[8] The last suggested effect is concerned with the lack of opportunity for the individual to achieve since the conditions are those where life has been prescribed in full by someone else.

When the mature employee encounters the above-described conditions, frustration will lead to a number of possible actions. He may try to escape through quitting the job, absenting himself from work, or attempting to climb to higher levels in the organization where the structure is less rigid. It is suggested that the most typical reaction is one of adaptation through an attitude of apathy or indifference. Pay becomes the compensation for the penalty of working. If frustration continues, employees may band together and exert pressure upon the structure through informal organization.[9] Still later, these informal organizations may be transformed into formal labor unions which can help to meet some of the ego needs of employees.

William H. Whyte, Jr., has broadened this analysis of conflict to include the effects upon attitudes and off-the-job activities as well. In *The Organization Man,* he establishes the thesis that the organization insists upon member conformity to organization modes of behavior and thought.[10] Not only is he highly regulated through rational policies and procedures, he is also expected to dress a certain way, act in a certain manner, live in a home in a designated environment, and possess a certain type of personality. This is to insure predictability and control of human behavior, supposedly for the benefit of cooperative organized activity. Whyte suggests that the individual must *fight* to preserve his identity within the organization and resist where he can the inroads of unnecessary and excessive conformity. This is made doubly difficult in that one of the basic needs of man is, as we have seen, to conform and be socially accepted by his associates.

OTHER EMPLOYEES IN THE BUSINESS ENVIRONMENT

Certainly the picture presented by Argyris and Whyte with respect to the mature employee is rather black. As has been repeatedly demonstrated in this text, analysis of human needs and behavior in organizations is not simple. Are *all* employees mature as defined by Argyris, Theory "Y" types as defined by McGregor, or responsive to motivator factors as described by Herzberg? Many

---

[8] From p. 66, *Personality and Organization* by Chris Argyris. Copyright © 1957 by Harper and Row, Publishers, Incorporated. By permission of the publishers.
[9] See Chapter 11.
[10] William H. Whyte, Jr., *The Organization Man* (Garden City: Doubleday and Co., 1957).

have granted the importance of these concepts when dealing with more highly educated professional, technical, and managerial white-collar employees. For example, in a study of 692 employed adults engaged in a wide variety of occupations, intrinsic job components or motivators were valued over environmental, hygienic factors by the white-collar group.[11] The opposite was true for those engaged in blue-collar occupations. A study of 1,468 civil service workers revealed that only medium- and high-status white-collar workers placed primary importance on the work content elements.[12] With advancing age and seniority, there was a tendency for all types to value the environmental factors more highly. Utilizing Dubin's Central Life Interest Schedule, it has been found that employees of various occupations exhibit different attitudes toward the job. The job was found to be of central interest to only 24 percent of a group of industrial workers, to 54 percent of a group of bottom- and middle-level supervisors, and to 79 percent of a group of professional nurses.[13]

Strauss has suggested that the theories advanced by behaviorists are more indicative of the need structures of highly educated, behavioral theorists than they are of rank and file blue-collar employees.[14] Security may mean more to the industrial worker than to the highly educated professional. The former often values the freedom of thought permitted by the highly structured, repetitive, simple task which may be boring to others. It has also been observed that many people are more comfortable when working in a highly defined situation. In addition, the need to self-actualize may not be so widely spread in the population as hypothesized by Maslow and McGregor. One study of 83 workers (bench hands, testers, wiremen, machinists, toolmakers, electricians, etc.) in a firm of 8,000 employees revealed a positive correlation between need satisfaction and job structure, that is, the higher the structure, the greater the need satisfaction in such areas as achievement, affiliation, autonomy, and recognition.[15] Strauss suggests that perhaps we should say "Thank God for the number of people who have made an apparent adjustment to routine jobs. Would that there were more!"[16]

Behaviorists reply that the preceding analysis is an attempt to rationalize a

[11] R. Centers and D. E. Bugental, "Intrinsic and Extrinsic Job Motivations among Different Segments of the Working Population," *Journal of Applied Psychology*, Vol. 50 (1966), pp. 193–197.

[12] F. Friedlander, "Motivation to Work and Organizational Performance," *Journal of Applied Psychology*, Vol. 50 (1966), pp. 143–152, and "Importance of Work Versus Non-work among Socially and Occupationally Stratified Groups," *Journal of Applied Psychology*, Vol. 50 (1966), pp. 437–441.

[13] John G. Maurer, "Work as a 'Central Life Interest' of Industrial Supervisors," *Academy of Management Journal*, Vol. 11, No. 3 (September, 1968), p. 333.

[14] George Strauss, "The Personality-versus-Organization Theory," in Leonard Sayles, *Individualism and Big Business* (New York: McGraw-Hill Book Company, 1963), p. 70.

[15] William P. Sexton, "Industrial Work: Who Calls It Psychologically Devastating?" *Management of Personnel Quarterly*, Vol. 6, No. 4 (Winter, 1968), pp. 3–8.

[16] Strauss, *op. cit.*, p. 79.

mechanical structure seemingly made necessary by the demands of large-scale organization. In the optimistic view of man, we do him harm when we not only cut off his potential for growth, but also make him like it. It has been suggested that possible frustration of future generations is reduced through teaching one's children not to expect too much in the way of freedom, self-control, and achievement in large organizations. Thus if any group of men view their lot in highly structured organizations as satisfactory, we have in effect created a group of lower class men—the gammas of Huxley's *Brave New World!*

Robert Dubin may well be taking a middle position when he suggests that we can distinguish between necessary and voluntary behavior. He declares that most people can and will adjust even to those tightly regimented work situations which Argyris contends would demand immature personalities. Dubin sees the individual as "caught up in necessary behaviors that are organizationally relevant and imperative, but normatively *neutral* in their consequences for the individual. Voluntary behavior implies some choice among alternatives on either rational or affective grounds. Necessary behavior, on the other hand, implies no such choice."[17]

Thus, necessary behavior is regarded by subordinates neither with repugnance nor enthusiasm, but rather with indifference. Dubin accepts indifference as a normal characteristic of many employees. It would be very difficult, if not impossible, for everyone to sustain high interest in every activity, every day. The individual has many opportunities to achieve self-actualization off the job, particularly with the shorter and shorter work days and weeks. He concludes that no serious damage will be done to human personalities by scientific managers for man is basically a flexible and adaptable creature. Perhaps we set an impossible goal if we attempt to stimulate *all* employees to a constant high pitch of excitement.

AN APPROACH TO THE DILEMMA

Thus we are caught between two sets of demands which on the surface appear to be completely contradictory. The conflict is there, yet some type of compromise is not out of the question. The individual must accept the necessity of subordination to group goals and coordination of efforts when *many* must contribute to central objectives. However, there is no necessity for complete subordination. For example, the subordinate will almost always have additional information of significant value which can aid in realistically modifying the plan or its implementation. The superior should also recognize the

[17] Robert Dubin, *Human Relations in Administration*, 2nd ed. (Englewood Cliffs: Prentice-Hall, Inc., 1961), pp. 60–61.

values which issue from permitting deviations from plans, both those that are due to original information deficiencies and those arising from morale factors. The degree to which this can be permitted by management depends both upon the type of individual and the situation. If we have the type of individual that McGregor assumes in his Theory "Y" (those eager to contribute and capable of self-control toward organization objectives), more freedom can be granted. Certainly we cannot afford to manage the highly educated and skilled employees in the same manner as those of lesser abilities. If we are to retain and utilize the creativity and knowledge of the professional, we must manage along the lines suggested by behaviorists. The immediate objective is development of an internal commitment to the work and aims of the organization. Such a commitment is likely to come only from an environment characterized by free communication, development of consensus, influence based more on competence than formal position, and intelligent acceptance of emotion and conflict. If we have the apathetic and disinterested person described by Argyris, management cannot afford the same degree of freedom, regardless of who was at fault in creating this apathy. Even in this latter event, however, there is a responsibility, and a possibility of future gain, for the management to begin a gradual modification of the environment, and thereby of the individuals within that environment, in the direction of greater participation and permissive deviations. Someone must take the first step and it will admittedly be the beginning of a long process. In other words, neither of the extremes—complete regimentation or complete freedom—can be rationally defended. Some balancing of values must be effected, and this balancing process is ever continuing.

The situation and environment are also major factors affecting the degree of control and freedom that can be effected. Where sequences of action must be precisely related and where time is of the essence and the possible losses high, the more the emphasis must be placed upon traditional, scientific controls. When the opposite is true, there is greater opportunity to treat personnel along the lines suggested by McGregor and Argyris. The general climate of the organization is also a modifying factor. Certain firms can be characterized as bustling and efficient, others as cold and impersonal, and still others as flexible and adaptable. These varied general atmospheres are doubtless the net overall result of hundreds of specific acts. However, the resultant climate in turn determines human behavior. To be more specific, if there is a general approach or feeling on the part of a firm's management that their personnel are of high caliber and can be trusted, it is under this type of climate that we are more likely to breed the Theory "Y" type of men. If we have good men and our general attitude is one of distrust and doubt, we will either lose them or transform them into Theory "X" types. Again, the problem may well be, how do we transform our present set of Theory "X" men into Theory "Y" men in a firm engaged in price competition with other enterprises in a free economy? The least we can do is to *begin*.

FUSION PROCESS

As long as the individual and the organization stay together, there will be effected a degree of merger or integration. The process whereby this happens has been called the *fusion process*. This term has been defined by Bakke as the "simultaneous operation of the socializing process by which the organization seeks to make an agent of the individual for the achievement of organizational objectives, and of the personalizing process by which the individual seeks to make an agency of the organization for the achievement of his personal objectives."[18] Thus the organization has goals or objectives as specified in Chapter 2. The individual has needs as described in Chapter 6. In this process, the individual and his behavior are altered to suit the needs of the organization. He must subordinate, coordinate, and cooperate to some degree toward common organization goals. At the same time, the organization's plans and structure are not so rigid and unchangeable. The individual can and does alter these original specifications as he attempts to adapt the organization to meet his physiological, social, and egoistic needs. If both the organization and the individual are satisfied, there is successful fusion. If either is dissatisfied, we have, of course, a lesser degree of fusion. Perfect fusion is both impossible and probably undesirable inasmuch as progress is enhanced by conflict as well as by cooperation and agreement.

Bakke and his fellow researcher, Argyris, have applied this fusion model to various enterprises.[19] Through a series of scales representing organization requirements and a separate series for individual requirements, scores have been obtained which indicate the degree of fusion in a particular organization or portion of an organization. In the teller department of a bank, for example, high fusion scores were obtained. Less conflict between the individual and the organization was felt by personnel in this type of work. In the bookkeeping department, on the other hand, the fusion was low. The demands of the job and organization were fairly precise and formal. The desires of the groups of young girls working in this department were for freedom to talk, visit, etc. The turnover in this department was very high as compared with the tellers, thus illustrating the tangible indication of the conflict that existed.

These fusion scores suggest another way out of the dilemma posed by Argyris in his maturation theory. There are in the American economy a wide variety of jobs and organizations. Obviously, not all people are identically alike, nor are they all at either extreme of the maturation scales. If freedom of movement does exist in our job markets, individuals will tend to seek jobs and

[18] E. W. Bakke, *The Fusion Process* (New Haven: Yale University Labor and Management Center, 1955), p. 5.
[19] Chris Argyris, *Organization of a Bank* (New Haven: Yale University Labor and Management Center, 1954), pp. 189–201.

organizations where fusion can be highest, and quit jobs and organizations where conflicts are most felt. To the degree that freedom of movement does not exist, through such factors as pension arrangements, seniority systems, and family ties, conflict and low degrees of fusion may be forced upon both the individual and the organization. In addition, if one believes that the *typical* job is the repetitive, boring one, and the *typical* organization is the completely autocratic and preplanned one, then freedom of choice is also thereby restricted. However, many pictures of jobs and organizations in the American business system have been painted excessively black by some psychologists and sociologists, and a variety of jobs, organizations, and industries still provide sufficient choice to permit a greater fusion of personalities and organizations.

Summary

Perhaps the extreme of the traditional viewpoint in planning can best be expressed in a statement by Frederick Taylor: "Each man must learn how to give up his own particular way of doing things, adjust his methods to the many new standards, and grow accustomed to receiving and obeying directions covering details, large and small, which in the past have been left to his individual judgment."[20] The substitution of careful and scientific planning for rules of thumb and impromptu action was certain to result in improved performance and goal accomplishment. The scientific management movement led by Taylor should not be sold short.

We should, however, avoid the pitfalls to which a too-enthusiastic acceptance and application of scientific planning will lead. Or rather, we should incorporate new data into this scientific study to make more realistic the prediction of future events. These new data are concerned with the nature of the human element through which scientifically planned action must take place. The individual seeks to gratify his needs through organized activity. Failure of reasonable gratification of these needs, identified as wants in the business situation, will usually result in the creation of blocks to goal accomplishment. Thus, the management of an organization should be concerned with the level of want satisfaction and make some attempt to ascertain and appraise the level that exists.

Once the necessary attention has been paid to employee needs and wants, there should be an integration of scientific plans and human execution. The manager will not automatically assume that people are mechanical instruments, operating within the confines of mechanical plans, with results foreseen perfectly in advance. He will accept the necessity for some individuality in operation, the personalizing of a job by the incumbent. The inherent dangers of such personalization are primarily two in number: (1) failure to satisfactorily accomplish organization objectives, and (2) accomplishment of objectives at an excessive cost. It therefore becomes a problem of balancing the gains from personalization with the possible costs to achieve the maximum net return to the organization.

---

[20] Frederick W. Taylor, *Shop Management* (New York: Harper & Bros., 1911), p. 133.

Greater freedom and trust will be accorded to the mature, Theory "Y" employees who respond to the challenge of self-actualization. Behaviorists recommend that more of our employees are of this type than traditional managements have generally assumed.

The manager will also seek to create an environment where the social and egoistic needs of man can be satisfied along with organization goal accomplishment. Objective systems may have to be bent slightly to provide the room in which these needs can be realized. Such specific acts as job redesign to adapt to human personalities and permitting and stimulating subordinate participation in plan formulation may be undertaken.

Yet, in this new concern for the human element in business organizations, we must not forget the rational demands of organized activity. In any successful fusion of the organization and particular individuals, it is likely that any head-on clash of interests will be resolved in favor of the organization. But even with this guiding philosophy as a basis, there is still ample room to accommodate the human element in the organization.

DISCUSSION PROBLEMS

1. When employees report that pay is not their number one want, what does this mean in terms of Maslow's hierarchy? in terms of the organization's pay program?
2. Describe the Herzberg theory of work motivation. Relate this to the Maslow hierarchy of needs.
3. Describe the traditional and behavioral positions on dealing with a group of admittedly Theory "X" men.
4. What is Argyris's maturation theory and what implications does it have for the manager? How does Dubin's identification of necessary and voluntary behavior alter these possible conclusions?
5. Does it matter whether an employee self-actualizes on the job or off the job? Discuss conditions in which it does and does not.
6. The scores of morale surveys are significant only in relative terms. Explain.
7. What are the values and drawbacks of allowing employees to personalize a job?
8. What advice does William H. Whyte have for the mature individual caught up in the large, structured organization?
9. Distinguish between human needs and wants. Relate examples of particular wants to these needs.
10. What do the theories of Maslow, McGregor, Herzberg, and Argyris have in common? In what way does Dubin both agree and disagree?

SUPPLEMENTARY READING

Behling, Orlando, George Labovitz, and Richard Kosmo, "The Herzberg Controversy: A Critical Reappraisal," *Academy of Management Journal,* Vol. 11, No. 1 (March, 1968), 99–108.

Chartier, Roger, "Managing the Knowledge Employee," *Personnel Journal,* Vol. 47, No. 8 (August, 1968), 558–562.

Fielden, John S., "The Right Young People for Business," *Harvard Business Review,* Vol. 44, No. 2 (March–April, 1966), 76–83.

Herzberg, Frederick, "One More Time: How Do You Motivate Employees?" *Harvard Business Review,* Vol. 46, No. 1 (January–February, 1968), 53–62.

McGregor, Douglas, *The Professional Manager,* Part I. New York: McGraw-Hill Book Company, 1967.

Stanton, Erwin S., "The Individual and The Corporation: Are They Really in Conflict?" *Personnel,* Vol. 45, No. 1 (January–February, 1968), 33–37.

Strauss, George, "The Personality-versus-Organization Theory," in *Individualism and Big Business,* ed. Leonard Sayles, pp. 67–80. New York: McGraw-Hill Book Company, 1963.

Urwick, L. F., "Organization and Theories About the Nature of Man," *Academy of Management Journal,* Vol. 10, No. 1 (March, 1967), 9–15.

Cases for Part II

EDWARD LANE

At the age of twenty-four, Edward Lane was awarded a bachelor's degree in hotel management and administration by a large state university. He was immediately hired by Hotelo Corporation, a firm possessing a contract to operate various hotels and motor inns located in a number of national parks. His first assignment was as manager of one of the motor inns in a large park. The company attempted to establish and operate the inn manager's job on a decentralized basis through delegation of the authority to hire and discharge all regular personnel, and authority to hire and discharge key personnel with approval of upper management. Key personnel were considered to be cooks, gift shop employees, campstore managers, and auditors. The great majority of regular employees were young college graduates working during the summer months.

Edward Lane arrived at his assigned motor inn early in June, about two weeks before the season began. He discovered that the inn had a total personnel allotment of fifty-five, and that, unlike most inns, the gift shop and campstore were under the control of a single supervisor, George Locke. Lane's first impression of Locke was somewhat negative. In his words, he said, "Locke struck me right off the bat as someone who might be difficult to get along with. Maybe it was because he is about fifteen years older than I, but I received the impression that he didn't want me or anyone else meddling in his affairs. He had been a justice of the peace. He also had some limited experience in running a small retail store with the help of his wife. As his supervisor, I felt that I should be available for advice and assistance. Before the season started, I would drop in on the campstore daily and ask him how things were going. Inevitably, his only answer would be a muttered 'no problems.' He would not engage in any form of casual conversation."

When the season opened, a personnel problem quickly arose in the campstore. As one of the young campstore employees said, "Apparently Mr. Locke and his wife do not trust us. There is never a minute when one of them isn't present. Even at lunch time, they always eat separately so that the store can be watched. It kind of bothers us, because we like to think that we can be trusted to handle the store alone once in a while. They rarely operate the cash registers themselves, so there really isn't any reason why they can't leave us alone." A more pressing personnel problem was the excessive grumbling about Locke's split-shift schedule. Employees were scheduled to work the morning and evening of one day, and the afternoon of the next, thereby averaging sixteen hours every two days. The effect of this schedule was to prevent them from going on long hikes or hitchhiking around the park, a valued fringe benefit of these summer vacation jobs. Lane learned of these adverse reactions during casual chats in the dining room. While he had the authority to order George Locke to make any adjustments, he merely suggested that the split-shift schedule be abandoned. Locke refused the suggestion, saying that he thought the employees worked better with some rest between shifts. Lane did not pursue the matter further.

During the second week of the season, Locke "locked horns" with the inn auditor, Pete Fuller. Locke had been following the practice of sending all receipts, including all change, to the auditor for preparation of the daily revenue statement for forwarding to the accounting department located in the main hotel in the park. Fuller, a young man of twenty-five, received a call from accounting to instruct Locke to send no more than one dollar in change in each daily envelope. When Fuller contacted Locke to pass on the instructions, the latter said that he could not keep all the change that he was getting in his registers. He also said that he would not follow the order unless Fuller could figure some other way for him to get rid of his change. The following day, Fuller offered to buy his excess change at the end of each working day with bills from the safe. Although Locke agreed to this arrangement, his daily contact with Fuller was distinctly unpleasant. As Fuller said, "The old buzzard really didn't like me. I think it was partly because Ed Lane and I got along so well with each other."

More difficulties were forthcoming during the third week. In his capacity as inn manager, Edward Lane approached Locke with some suggestions for altering procedures for ordering campstore supplies. The main supply department had called Lane to complain about Locke's current practice. Again, Locke was reluctant to cooperate, and Lane doubted if he could change his method. Later in the day, Lane took a new employee into the campstore and introduced him as a newly hired clerk. Locke just said, "He doesn't work for me!" He turned on his heel and went to another part of the store. Lane attempted to reduce the embarrassment by explaining that Locke was very weary from working fourteen hours a day, and that he should not be judged by this initial encounter.

The next morning, George Locke strode into Edward Lane's office, threw his keys on the desk, and said, "I'm done working at this place." When asked for his reason for leaving, he indicated that he had never seen so much lack of cooperation in all his working experience. When informed of his resignation, Lane's superior called Locke by telephone to see if he would reconsider and finish out the season. He refused to do so, and he and his wife left the park that afternoon.

THE AJAX CORPORATION

The Ajax Corporation is a manufacturer and distributor of various electronic devices. One of its departments is concerned with assembly of two volume items—the Trans-X and the Trans-Y. The equipment and personnel of the department are quite flexible and can manufacture each product equally well. At the present time, the market is such that any volume produced can be sold. The profit per item of Trans-X is $5 and for Trans-Y is $15.

The processes of the Assembly department are subdivided into three sections: (1) Pre-assembly, (2) Assembly, and (3) Inspection. There are three employees in Pre-assembly who work a 40-hour week. Each Trans-X requires .5 man-hour for Pre-assembly, while the Trans-Y requires .8 man-hour.

In the Assembly section, there are 22 full-time employees, who work a 40-hour week, and 1 half-time employee. Each Trans-X requires 3 man-hours of assembly time, while a Trans-Y requires 9 man-hours.

The final section of Inspection has two employees, one working a 40-hour week, the other 41. Each Trans-X requires only .25 man-hour to inspect while each Trans-Y demands one full man-hour.

The department head of Assembly feels that some simple graphing technique can be used to calculate the number of Trans-X's and Trans-Y's that he should produce to effect the greatest weekly profit. His goal is to develop the optimum mix since his facilities and manpower are completely interchangeable.

THE JONES-WILLIAMS COMPANY

The Jones-Williams Company has just been formed. It constitutes a merger of the Jones Company, a manufacturer of ceramic ash trays and figurines, and

Williams Enterprises, a producer of dishware and ceramic lamp bases. The newly formed company employs approximately 1000 persons, but is expected to expand rapidly in the next three years.

Both companies were financially sound and moderately successful upon merger. Williams Enterprises is older and has been directed by professional managers hired by its board of directors. The Jones Company was founded and directed to its present position by the Jones family. The son, a progressive and active leader, has been very much in favor of the merger.

While Williams approached Jones on the merger, the latter was thus favorably disposed for a number of reasons: The owner, Mr. Hiram Jones had been considering retirement and this offered a very good solution to his problem of what to do with the business. He was offered a position on the new board, instead of complete retirement. In addition, production could be stimulated if both lines were produced together. With minor additions and changes at the Williams site, such a set-up could be achieved. The Jones Company also faced a new outlay for additional equipment to meet competitive outputs and prices. The necessity for this outlay was avoided by the merger, as Williams equipment was in excellent condition and was purchased only two years before. The scrap value of the old equipment would help in meeting merger costs.

Williams Enterprises had been administered through a series of management committees. All future and past operations were discussed and changes in policy and production were analyzed before any action was taken. Reports on scheduling, production control, engineering, etc., were reviewed by the executive committee and suggestions for improvement were studied. Staff meetings among supervisors were held bimonthly.

The Jones Company had had the traditional board of directors structure. Executive control came from personal contact and presidential direction. Each supervisor had authority over his department and ran it accordingly. The only committees were those concerned with the annual budget and labor grievances. Executives consulted each other on related activities, but concentrated on doing their specific duties.

When the merger was completed and the new board of directors met, Mr. Sawyer of Williams Enterprises explained how they had used committee action for leadership. He stated that committees are extremely helpful and suggested that a similar plan be used in the new firm. Personnel, sales, production, and other major fields should be represented by committees meeting at regular intervals. The secretary would attend all committee meetings and send reports to the board of directors, who would meet for control and direction of the newly formed company.

Executives from the Jones Company had no experience in this management approach and stated as much at the meeting. They also expressed doubt as to whether or not this type of system could give as much time to detailed processes as was suggested by Mr. Sawyer. They contended that action, rather than extended discussion, was essential in a company of the size of Jones-Williams. When controversies do arise, the president could always resolve them, just as Mr. Jones had done for the Jones Company for so many years. Mr. Jones, as chairman of the new board, tended to support the individual executive approach, feeling that the board of directors would provide the breadth of control needed. Executives from Williams Enterprises were much disturbed by this sudden revelation of management philosophy.

A POLICY EXPANSION

John Nelson is one of six superintendents in the production division of a large manufacturing firm. Three years ago, one of the secretaries in the division had been able to negotiate a deal with a well-known candy manufacturer to purchase 1000 pounds or more at a special discount rate. Because of the complexity of administration, it was decided that this discount would be available only to office and managerial employees. The following expresses the feelings and actions of John Nelson in his own words.

"No fuss was made about the way the candy purchase was handled, but the whole deal was one of those things that somehow go against my grain. I resolved at that time to do something about it the following year, although I wasn't sure just what I would do.

"Last year I did it. Around the first of December a bulletin was circulated throughout the offices that once again candy would be available at the special reduced rate. Without permission, I typed out several subscription lists, then wrote in the department turnover book that candy was available to *anyone* at the price of $1.10 a pound if he wished to sign up for it. Our department, with 120 employees, 8 supervisors, and 25 quality inspectors, comprises better than 50 percent of the production division. Within 24 hours, production employees signed up for more than $600 worth of candy. Supervisors were told that I would handle and be responsible for collection of all monies. I did not consider this a risk in any way.

"The cat was let out of the bag in a beautiful manner. The following day a union steward and several other employees stopped the division production manager as he walked through the department and told him that they thought it was absolutely wonderful of the company to make the candy available to the production employees. I was called into the office a few minutes later and asked to explain my action. I did, using as an excuse my belief that gestures of this nature were the best employee relations activities that we could undertake.

The people who had stopped him and expressed their thanks reinforced my statements, although I didn't know it at the time. I was told that it was too late to undo what I had already done, but that the responsibility for collecting the money and for distributing the candy was all mine. Fears that turnover, absenteeism, and general human perverseness would cause me to turn up short on money when the candy was delivered were freely expressed. The use of any part of my working day, or that of my supervisors, for activities of this nature was also roundly condemned, despite protestations that it was well worth the small amount of time required in promoting better employee relations.

"The employees came through wonderfully. They paid their money promptly, although some of them had purchased as much as $25 worth of candy. On the day that the order was delivered, the supervisors sent the people to my office in an orderly and well-planned manner, spacing them at correct intervals. The entire order was distributed in less than 30 minutes, and there were many people from other departments eagerly awaiting the possible defection of any purchaser so they could purchase any candy that was left over. There was none.

"Through proper use of the informal organization, many members of the management were stopped in ensuing days by production employees and thanked profusely for giving everyone the opportunity to purchase candy.

"This year the announcement was made in the form of an inter-office bulletin that candy was once again available to anyone who wanted it, and no question was raised about the production employees; they have, as a policy, become part of the plan. In all departments of the production division the candy was made available to anyone. Every part of the subscription and collection proceeded without incident.

"I am proud of my part in this incident; my faith in people was once again confirmed."

THE CUSTOMER MIX-UP

The Jones Lumber Yard is a small concern that distributes not only lumber but concrete blocks and various items of hardware as well. Mr. Jones runs a one-man operation as far as the firm's management is concerned. One summer, his nephew worked for the lumber yard during the college vacation period. Mr. Jones was hopeful that his nephew would join the company upon graduation and ultimately replace him as manager. The following is the nephew's report of an episode that occurred that first summer.

"Last year while working at my uncle's lumber yard a problem came up which was very unusual and annoying to our customer and to a neighboring resident. The problem was that we had delivered four hundred 8 x 8 x 16 cement blocks to the wrong address. It all happened on a day during which our normal yard supervisor was ill, leaving an unfamiliar yard-hand in charge. This delivery of four hundred blocks was to be unloaded at 4000 West Fernfield in Rolling Hills, but by mistake they were taken to 4000 *East* Fernfield. About 30 minutes before the delivery truck was due back in the yard, a phone call was received from our customer saying he had not received the blocks and that he had workmen waiting who were being paid by the hour. The fellow in charge of deliveries at that time explained we had sent out the loaded truck and that possibly the driver had become lost. Ten minutes later we were given the same story by the same customer. This time we were forced to load another truck and deliver it. By the time the second truck had been loaded the original truck returned. After talking the matter over the error was discovered, but by this time we were so far behind in deliveries we were forced to forget momentarily about the original blocks. As was figured, the man owning the house where these had been delivered called the yard around 5:30 P.M. Since this was closing time, another fellow and I went out to load these blocks again. After we had loaded approximately three hundred, the owner came out and loudly began to complain about his lawn, flowers, and inconvenience. The fellow with me was of little help in calming him down so I took it upon myself to make the agreements. I explained to him we would replace all damaged flowers, replant the part of his lawn where many of the blocks were stacked, and we would leave him twenty-five blocks which he said he needed to enclose an area in the back of his lot.

"After taking the three hundred seventy-five blocks back to the yard I called my uncle and told him about the agreements. He literally blew his top. He said that I had no authority to make such agreements and that the cost of the 25 blocks would be deducted from my salary. Naturally I was upset with his reaction, but he impressed me that I must always consult with him before making such major decisions. He did not feel that the blocks had to be given if repairs to the lawn been made. He has invited me back to work again next summer, but I am not sure if I want to accept."

Part Three

ORGANIZING

Once objectives and plans have been established, the manager must develop an organization capable of accomplishing the prescribed goals. This development is structured officially by the manager (Section A) and unofficially by organization members (Section B).

Section A

Formal Organization

All organizations are composed of people, functions, and physical factors. In Chapter 8, the principles and processes of functionalization are developed. The manager must then prescribe formal relationships among the functions, personnel, and physical factors (Chapter 9) to the end that a structure is created which will enable accomplishment of organization goals (Chapter 10).

8

Functions and Functionalization

After the manager has formulated his plans, with or without substantial subordinate participation, the next logical step in the process is that of organizing. The immediate objective of the organizing process is the creation of a human mechanism that will be able to carry out established plans. If one man can effectively accomplish the designated goals, there is no need for organizing. If it requires more than one, someone, presumably a manager, must attempt to combine and relate these multiple personnel into an effective working unit. A major portion of the organizing process will thereby consist of the establishment of working relationships.

We have previously noted the three basic organizational components: personnel, physical factors, and functions. Organizing can be defined as *the process of establishing relationships among these components to the end that all are related and combined into an effective unit capable of being directed toward accomplishment of common goals.* Thus, to understand the nature of this process, one requires knowledge of (1) components, (2) relationships among components, and (3) objectives. In Chapter 2, a discussion and analysis of organization objectives was presented with emphasis upon the common objective of economic service. In Chapter 6, we examined in summary fashion the basic nature of the personnel component. There will be no specific coverage of the physical factor or capital component, though Chapter 13 will deal with the human problems that issue from technology in business organizations. In this chapter, the third component of functions will constitute the primary subject.

After we know something about objectives and the components which enable the accomplishment of those objectives, the process of combining and relating these elements will be presented in the following chapter. The immediate result of this process is the creation of a structure which can encompass these components. These various alternative formal structures are covered in the chapter following the organizing process. Thus, systematic coverage of the basic function of organizing will include analysis of objectives, personnel, physical factors, functions, relationships, and resultant formal structures.

FUNCTIONS

What is a function? This term is a very flexible one and usually must be preceded by an adjective to have meaning, e.g., the *sales* function or the *accounting* function. A *function* is *work* that can be identified and separated from other work. The determination of what work should be undertaken must issue from the goals of the enterprise. Thus in broad terms, one can talk about the function of the "XYZ" Corporation, which may be the creation and distribution of refrigerators that provide certain desired services for customers. As Fig. 8–1a indicates, within the firm we can identify and distinguish certain broad functions such as *manufacture* of the refrigerator, *sales* of this product, and *finance*, or the provision of capital for its manufacture and sale. Any one of these three major functions can be further subdivided into smaller ones. Manufacturing, for example, may be further divided into such functions as product design, process design, materials provision, personnel provision, production control, quality control, and the actual production process. This is illustrated in Fig. 8–1b. Proceeding further, the production process can be broken into such smaller functions as lathing, drilling, milling, and the like, as shown in Fig. 8–1c. The milling function, in turn, may be divided into still smaller functions which are usually termed "operation elements." As indicated in Fig. 8–1d, the functional sequence could be: (1) pick up piece out of tote box; (2) place piece in lathe fixture; (3) operate the lathe; and (4) extract piece from fixture and set aside. We can proceed one step further in functional analysis and break each of these operation elements into still smaller functions which Frank Gilbreth called "therbligs."[1] A *therblig* is the smallest function that can be identified and separated from other functions. It is a fundamental unit motion and is ordinarily used only in detailed motion studies. Gilbreth discovered and identified seventeen of these therbligs, some of which are:

[1] Frank B. and Lillian M. Gilbreth, "Classifying the Elements of Work," *Management and Administration*, Vol. 8, No. 2 (August, 1924), p. 151.

1. Search—the eye turning to look for the part.
2. Transport empty—the hand moving toward the part.
3. Grasp—the taking hold of the part.
4. Transport loaded—moving the part to the fixture.
5. Position—turning the part for proper orientation.
6. Assemble—placing the part into the fixture.

FIGURE 8–1 FUNCTIONAL DIFFERENTIATION

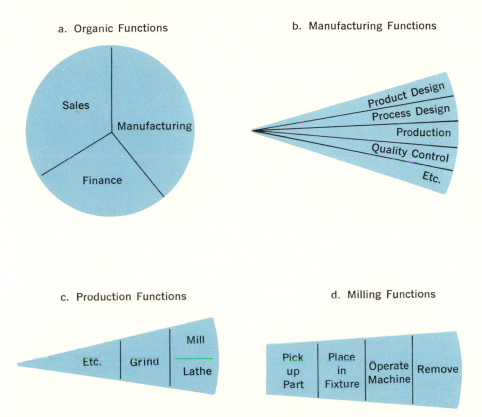

a. Organic Functions

b. Manufacturing Functions

c. Production Functions

d. Milling Functions

Pick-up and Placement Functions

The segmentation and measurement of such small functions often requires the utilization of motion picture photography.

Thus it is apparent that function is a flexible term. If a unit of work can be distinguished from other work, it can be identified and described. The largest function in an enterprise is the total work of the organization; we can distinguish the "XYZ" Corporation from the "ABC" Company. The smallest function is the unit motion or therblig.

ORGANIC FUNCTIONS AND THE LINE

In trying to establish a science of management, certain writers and researchers have attempted to attach varying values to functions performed. Though there are many specific acts that a manager executes, we have identified planning, organizing, directing, and controlling as organic, vital, and major management functions.

With respect to business functions, the determination of what is organic is basic to distinguishing between primary and secondary functions. Primary functions will obviously differ from industry to industry. In manufacturing, for example, at least two functions are ordinarily designated as basic: *production* and *sales*. Logic would defend this choice since production creates values of form for the customer, and sales creates values of place, time, and possession. Other authors identify the function of *finance* as primary. Justification of this rests upon empirical evidence. Since the top level of an organization is the presidential one, analysis of the second level should indicate the functions which those firms deem of major and vital importance. In one survey of over 400 Ohio firms, it was found that executives heading the functions of production, sales, and finance reported to the president or executive vice-president in over 90 percent of the firms.[2] Other functions were present on this second level significantly fewer times, e.g., purchasing in 39.6 percent of the firms, engineering in 38.6 percent, and personnel in 26.2 percent. Thus it would appear that the greater bulk of manufacturing firms deem production, sales, and finance to be the primary functions of the organization around which the remaining ones are to be grouped.

Naturally, the organic functions of an enterprise will vary according to its objectives. The objectives of a university, for example, are to contribute toward the development of people and to advance the fund of knowledge. The organic functions are education and research. Thus, the professor is performing a primary or line function in the university. If that same professor joined a refrigerator manufacturing firm as an instructor in the personnel department, he would be performing a secondary function since the primary objective of

---

[2] James H. Healey, *Executive Coordination and Control* (Columbus: Bureau of Business Research, Ohio State University, 1956), pp. 79–82.

this organization is producing and distributing refrigerators, and *not* the education of its personnel. Similarly, the organic functions of a retail department store could well be buying, selling, and finance, and those of a railroad, maintenance, traffic, and finance.

Thus, what is basic and vital depends upon the objectives of the organization as well as upon interpretation of those objectives by its leadership. Objectives do change and thereby affect the designation of functions. For example, in the aircraft industry of two to three decades ago, production of planes was certainly one of the primary functions, and product research and design could well have been labeled secondary. Today in this same industry, now called "aerospace," objectives have been enlarged from producing aircraft to include the accumulation of research information for the government. Thus, the research and development function in the modern aerospace firm may well have to be designated as an organic function.

This analysis of functions provides the basis for a definition of *line* and *staff*. If the performance of a function leads directly to an accomplishment of basic organization objectives, it is usually called line. Thus any person directly preforming primary functions and those in the direct chain of command above these functions are line personnel. In manufacturing, the production worker, the salesman, the treasurer, the vice-presidents of production and sales, and the president are all line personnel. Functions other than these three are labeled secondary or staff. This does not mean that they are unimportant or make no contribution to enterprise objectives. However, the incidence of this contribution is secondary, at least one step removed from the basic objective. The personnel department, for example, performs a staff function of providing personnel for the line and other staff activities. Providing personnel is *not* the basic reason for the organization's existence. The maintenance department performs a staff or secondary function as it services the equipment of the organization. But servicing the equipment is again *not* the basic objective of a manufacturing organization.[3]

Some theorists contend that this distinction between line-and-staff functions is no longer pertinent in the modern, complex, and dynamic world of large-scale organizations.[4] The bases of this contention are (1) organizations usually have multiple objectives whose value will vary from time to time, (2) line and staff designations imply first- and second-class citizenship, and (3) staff functions are usually manned by highly knowledgeable and professional personnel whose true influence usually outweighs any artificial specifications of authority. Nevertheless, it can be contended that a firm's management cannot and will not allocate equal attention and importance to all functions simultaneously. An

---

[3] It could well be the basic objective of a separate maintenance service company, in which case mechanics and janitors would constitute line personnel in the service company.

[4] Gerald C. Fisch, "Line-Staff is Obsolete," *Harvard Business Review,* Vol. 39, No. 5 (September–October, 1961), pp. 67–97.

organization is a rational instrument designed to direct all efforts toward some set of objectives. This necessitates some ordering of priorities which can, of course, vary from time to time. It matters little whether this ordering is labeled line and staff, primary and secondary, or basic and support; the significance still remains. The line or primary personnel represent the general objectives of the organization. Specialized staff support personnel represent valuable activities whose particular impact upon objectives must be filtered and monitored in the light of those objectives. As objectives change, so can this primary and secondary ordering of contributions. Some orderings change infrequently; e.g., plant maintenance rarely is elevated to primary status in a manufacturing firm, and secretarial service does not usually take precedence over teaching and research in a university. Each specialized person probably feels that his contributions are not fully appreciated in terms of attention and resources, and this feeling usually results from perceptual limitations inherent in that very specialization. *Someone* must take responsibility for the whole. Despite the ideals of various behaviorists, it is not likely that democratic group consensus will always identify the nature of that whole. Thus, there is always a need for line management whose responsibility is the final judging of all functional contributions.

FUNCTIONALIZATION

Functionalization is the process of splitting and differentiating functions as the organization grows. All functions, in embryonic fashion, are contained within the one-man enterprise. He designs the product, procures the material, makes it, sells it, and provides the necessary financing. As the volume of business grows, the work required will increase beyond the capacities of one man. Thus the process of functionalization begins.

Functional differentiation with growth can be made in two directions, downward and outward. In the following sections, each of these two types will be discussed.

Functional Differentiation Downward

Beginning with the one-man firm, as the volume of business necessitates the addition of another person, certain functions will be differentiated and allocated to the second man. For coordination purposes, two levels of organization will be created, an operative and a managerial. The latter will perform operative work in addition to directing his hired employee. It is not unusual at the start for the manager to retain the sales and finance functions, and allocate the

FIGURE 8–2   FUNCTIONAL DIFFERENTIATION DOWNWARD

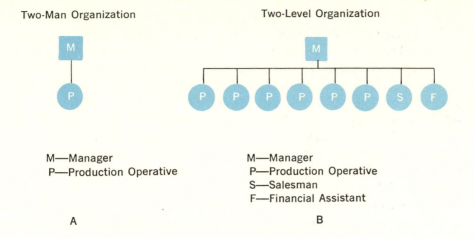

Two-Man Organization

M—Manager
P—Production Operative

A

Two-Level Organization

M—Manager
P—Production Operative
S—Salesman
F—Financial Assistant

B

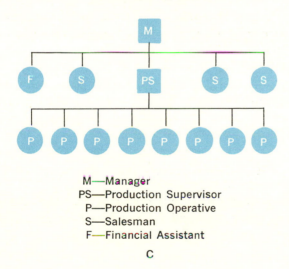

Three-Level Organization

M—Manager
PS—Production Supervisor
P—Production Operative
S—Salesman
F—Financial Assistant

C

production work to the new man. As indicated in Fig. 8–2a, we have differentiated a function and allocated it downward under the control of the original
man.

As the volume continues to expand, other personnel will be added and more
operative functions differentiated and allocated. Thus as shown in Fig. 8–2b,
the original man may now be fully a manager with operatives performing the
basic functions of sales, production, and finance—a two-level organization.

This process of adding personnel to the second level has its limits. This limit is usually referred to as the *span of control*. This principle is an organizational generalization based largely on a theory of human limitations. Obviously, one man cannot directly and effectively supervise a thousand people; yet he probably can supervise more than one. Somewhere between these two obvious extremes lies an ideal answer for a particular manager in a particular situation.

The span of control concept deserves further discussion, which will be presented in the following section. It is sufficient to note here that this concept *forces* further functional differentiation downward, and leads to the creation of a third level of organization. One of the operatives is designated a supervisor, and subordinates are placed under his control. We can now start to utilize his span of control, and, as indicated in Fig. 8–2c, there are now three levels. Were there no such limitation as the span of control, we would require only two—the chief and all the Indians reporting to him.

Span of Control. There is a considerable amount of controversy over the essential nature and implications of the span of control concept. Originally, it was designated as a principle of organization by writers of traditional or classical management theory. Lyndall Urwick credits General Sir Ian Hamilton with the first public statement and indicates that it entered management literature during the 1920's,[5] when General Hamilton suggested a specific span limit of three to six persons per manager.[6] V. A. Graicunas substantiated this limited span through a mathematical analysis of relationships.[7] He recognized three types of relationships among personnel in an organization: (1) direct single; (2) direct group; and (3) cross contacts. The number of such relationships is an indication of the difficulty of control. The formula for determining the number of relationships for varying numbers of direct subordinates is as follows:

$$R = s\left(\frac{2^s}{2} + s - 1\right)$$

Thus, with two subordinates, there are six relationships. This increases to 44 for four, 1,080 for eight, and over a half-million for sixteen. Graicunas supports Hamilton's contention that spans should be limited to approximately six subordinates.

In recent years, it has been customary to distinguish at least two different kinds of spans, depending upon whether one is supervising operatives or other managers. Thus, Ralph Davis suggests that if a manager is supervising subordinate managers, the work is difficult and the span should be limited to

[5] Lyndall F. Urwick, "The Manager's Span of Control," *Harvard Business Review*, Vol. 34, No. 3 (May–June, 1956), pp. 39–47.

[6] Sir Ian Hamilton, *The Soul and Body of an Army* (London: Edward Arnold and Co., 1921), p. 229.

[7] V. A. Graicunas, "Relationship in Organization," in *Papers on the Science of Administration*, ed. L. Gulick and L. Urwick (Institute of Public Administration, Columbia University, 1937), pp. 183–184.

approximately 3 to 9.[8] If one is supervising operative employees, acceptable spans are from 10 to 30.[9] Keith Davis suggests a third type of span, designated a "policy span," for situations when less supervision is required and subordinate managers require only *access to* the executive. He suggests that such spans of executive control include from 6 to 15 other managers.[10] Evidently, these varying spans are based not only upon the varying types of work being supervised, but also on what is meant by control in the label "span of control."

One study of American business organizations was confined to counting the number of personnel reporting directly to the president of each organization. The median number was 8, with a range from 1 to 24.[11] Another study in Ohio found a modal number of 6 and over 93 percent with less than 9 immediate subordinates for the president.[12] Thus, it would seem that actual practice tends in the main to be influenced by the traditional philosophy of more limited spans.

In recent decades, the relatively limited spans advocated by traditional writers have come under attack by various behaviorists.[13] If the span is limited, it obviously provides a greater opportunity for closer supervision and regimentation, and affects the number of levels of organization necessary for a given number of personnel. The longer the spans, the fewer the levels of organization and the greater the degree of freedom for the individual subordinate. The shorter the spans, the greater the number of levels that will be required and the closer the supervision can be of each individual. We come back again to the controversy between the traditional manager wishing to be assured of coordination, control, and predictability, and the behaviorist wishing to trust subordinates to act responsibly and with self-control. Regarding the latter, Worthy recommends a very wide span to literally *force* a manager to delegate authority since he could not possibly peer over the shoulders of everyone.

It should be emphasized that no one, traditionalist or behaviorist, denies the existence of the span of control concept. No one has advocated the two level organization for all enterprises regardless of size. There has to be some limit. The exact limit varies, and the figures cited in the various studies are either suggestions based on experience or reports of actual practice. Perhaps the

[8] Ralph C. Davis, *The Fundamentals of Top Management* (New York: Harper & Bros., 1951), p. 276.

[9] *Ibid.*, p. 271.

[10] Keith Davis, *Human Relations at Work,* 2nd ed. (New York: McGraw-Hill Book Company, 1962), p. 226.

[11] Ernest Dale, "Planning and Developing the Company Organization Structure," *AMA Research Report No. 20* (New York: American Management Association, 1952), p. 57.

[12] Healey, *Executive Coordination and Control,* p. 65.

[13] James C. Worthy, *Big Business and Free Men* (New York: Harper & Bros., 1959), pp. 100–112, and Waino Suojanen, "The Span of Control—Fact or Fable," *Advanced Management,* Vol. 20, No. 11 (November, 1955), pp. 5–13 are two examples.

sounder approach is to realize that the correct span of control is affected by a number of factors. Among these are the following:

1. The complexity of the work being controlled.
2. The degree of similarity to other work.
3. The degree of interdependency with other work.
4. The stability of the organization and situation.
5. The degree of standardization.
6. The caliber of the manager, including his spans of attention, energy, and personality.
7. The caliber of the subordinates.

Thus, a series of "sub-principles" can be proposed. The more complex the work, the shorter the span of control. This helps to explain why the span of executive supervision, 3 to 9, is shorter than the span of operative supervision, 10 to 30. The more similar the jobs being supervised, the longer the effective span. The more closely interlocked and interdependent the jobs are, the greater the problem of coordination, and thus the more limited the effective span of control. The more unstable the situation is, the more limited the span may be. The establishment of numerous standards increases the degree of predictability and provides the basis for effective control, thus resulting in an expansion of the effective span. There are also differences in people; and the greater the capabilities present, the longer the effective span can be. In other words, the capable manager can effectively control more people than can those lacking in ability, energy, and personality. As a corollary, the more able the subordinate, the less supervision he requires.

The "correct" span for one man in one situation at a particular time may be nine; for another man, situation, and/or time, the answer will be different. Though this analytical approach is probably the more correct one, its practicality is limited by the difficulty in effecting such studies. As Chart 8–1 indicates, the Lockheed Missiles and Space Company has developed a measurement tool that implements this approach. Utilizing six factors which have bearing upon the effective span, measuring sticks have been devised to indicate various degrees. Point totals are utilized as a guide in determining the appropriate number of personnel and functions. Though the application of this tool has been limited, its immediate effect was to lengthen most of the spans studied. However, the spans for middle managers still ranged from 4 to 11 and for first line supervisors, from 8 to 22.[14]

Most managers will probably continue to be influenced by the traditional views on the span of control. They may be persuaded by the behavioral

[14] Harold Stieglitz, "Optimizing Span of Control," *Management Record* (September, 1962), p. 22.

scientist to experiment by gradually adding more personnel to existing spans. When this is done, there will be an attempt to balance possible costs against incremental values. We must go back again to the basic needs of man and the basic demands of the organization for coordinated and controlled effort. We have to realize that the specific answer concerning the span of control affects not only the supervisory relationship between superior and subordinate, but also the shape of the organization structure.

Functional Differentiation Outward

The first direction of organizational growth from the one-man enterprise is usually downward. Because of limitations on the span of control, sheer numbers of personnel and functions will demand additional organization levels. The net result is a chain of command from the top executive through intervening levels of management to the various specialized operatives.

At some point in the process of growth and functionalization, there will occur a splitting-out of functions from the original chain of command. Personnel executing these functions are *not* a part of the original chain of command even though they may be performing functions formerly executed by a manager in that chain. Ordinarily, this splitting-out occurs because the original manager finds that the function can be performed more effectively and economically by a specialist.

There is shown in Fig. 8–3 a functional growth downward of the three organic functions of a manufacturing firm. In the production area, we have indicated a splitting-off of a training function. In our terminology, this becomes a secondary or staff function. When training was performed by the supervisor of a production department, it was a line function. Now it has been separated out because the supervisor is unable to find the time to do an effective job of training. If training is then allocated to a specialist not in the chain of command, that training then becomes a secondary or staff function. The training specialist cannot give orders to line operative personnel and will very likely work on a service and advisory basis. Inasmuch as he is the expert in training, however, it is highly probable that his advice will, in most cases, be accepted.

Professor Ralph Davis has identified one of the forces behind the process of outward functional differentiation as the "law of functional growth." This law is defined as follows: "The various functions of an organization increase in scope and complexity, as well as in the amount of work and the technical requirements for their proper performance, as the volume of business grows."[15]

[15] Ralph C. Davis, *The Fundamentals of Top Management,* p. 232.

CHART 8–1 SPAN OF CONTROL SCALE

Span Factor		Degree of
Similarity of Functions	Identical 1	Essentially Alike 2
Geographic Contiguity	All Together 1	All in One Bldg. 2
Complexity of Functions	Simple Repetitive 2	Routine 4
Direction & Control	Minimum Supervision & Training 3	Limited Supervision 6
Coordination	Minimum Relationships With Others 2	Relationships Limited to Defined Courses 4
Planning	Minimum Scope & Complexity	Limited Scope & Complexity 4

POINT VALUES ASSIGNED TO FACTORS

Similarity of Functions

One point—identical. Employees would be of the same occupation doing the same type of work. In a typical situation, a particular function (such as assembly) would be organized by teams or groups working on identical units or giving identical service.

Two points—essentially alike but having distinguishing characteristics in the nature of the functions. This rating would be applied to those components which perform similar work or work of the same nature at different geographic locations.

Three points—similar but with distinct differences in approach or skills required. Typically, each employee or component would be doing work in a general classification (e.g., general accounting, physics, manufacturing engineering) but in different segments of that field (nuclear physics vs. ionic physics, or payroll accounting vs. property accounting, etc.).

Four points—inherently different but with common purpose. This rating would apply, for example, to those components (such as development manufacturing) which are closely tied to a single end product or result but where each component performs different phases of the total process (such as development assembly, electronic assembly, final assembly and production control within a development manufacturing activity).

Five points—fundamentally distinct, with different areas of responsibility and requiring entirely different types of personnel skills. The scope of responsibility is fairly broad and the components are organized on a functional basis, each function requiring specialized skills and knowledge.

Geographic Contiguity

Location of personnel or subsidiary components are: one point—in one contiguous area in one building; two points—in separate locations within

Similar	Inherently Different	Fundamentally Distinct
3	4	5

Separate Bldg's One Plant Location	Separate Locations One Geographic Area	Dispersed Geographic Areas
3	4	5

Some Complexity	Complex Varied	Highly Complex Varied
6	8	10

Moderate Periodic Supervision	Frequent Continuing Supervision	Constant Close Supervision
9	12	15

Moderate Relationships Easily Controlled	Considerable Close Relationship	Extensive Mutual Non-Recurring Relationships
6	8	10

Moderate Scope & Complexity	Considerable Effort Required Guided Only By Broad Policies	Extensive Effort Required Areas & Policies Not Charted
6	8	10

one building; three points—in separate buildings within a plant location; four points—in separate buildings in a geographc area (in different cities of one country); five points—in widely dispersed geographic areas (in several separate parts of the state or country).

Complexity of Functions

Two points—simple, repetitive duties which require little training (less than six months) and which follow simple and well-defined rules and procedures. Examples would include typing, stock handling, mail handling, simple assembly.

Four points—routine duties of little complexity requiring individuals to exercise some but not a great amount of skill and/or judgment in following rules and procedures. Examples would include production machine operations, reproduction operations, receiving and shipping.

Six points—duties of some complexity requiring two or three years' experience and training and which require the application of reasonable judgment and/or skills. Examples would include production planning and scheduling, equipment maintenance, accounts payable, etc.

Eight points—complex duties involving a variety of differing tasks, requiring four–six years' experience and training and which require the application of considerable creativity, judgment and skills. Examples would include personnel administration, management planning, industrial engineering, buying, financial planning, test mechanics, special tool builders.

Ten points—extremely complex duties which might involve a wide variety of tasks and which require long training and experience (eight–ten years). Abstract or creative thinking and/or the necessity for consideration of many factors.

Source: Harold Stieglitz, "Optimizing Span of Control," *Management Record*, September, 1962.

FIGURE 8–3   DIFFERENTIATION OUTWARD OF TRAINING FUNCTION

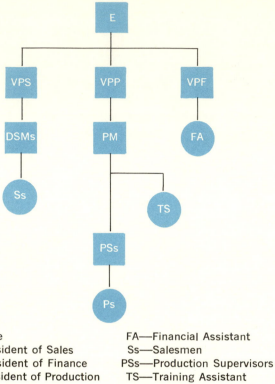

E—Executive
VPS—Vice President of Sales
VPF—Vice President of Finance
VPP—Vice President of Production
DSMs—District Sales Managers
PM—Production Manager

FA—Financial Assistant
Ss—Salesmen
PSs—Production Supervisors
TS—Training Assistant
Ps—Production Operatives

Training one new employee may well be within the capabilities of the line supervisor. Training a dozen new employees within a rapidly expanding department is probably beyond him because of the pressure of other duties. In addition, if new and technical jobs have been created, a training specialist is required to provide a more adequate knowledge and skill than the line supervisor could supply. Yet the training specialist is still a part of the organization and must relate to its basic objectives. The basic objective is not to have more and better training; rather it is to create and distribute better products for a profit. Improved training can contribute to the economy and effectiveness of that production and distribution.

If one can assume a gradual growth of the organization, the first step will be differentiation outward of one function from the line, and allocation to a *single* man. The particular functions that are most likely to be split off are those *most complex* and *least similar* to other functions performed in the line. For example, the production manager is most likely to hire quickly a specialized engineer for the product development and design function. He will be inclined to delay on the industrial engineering function since, though complex, this work of methods and layout of production is more closely related to his usual responsibilities. On a different level, the typing of letters is likely to be differentiated quickly both because of its complexity and its dissimilarity.

If the organization still continues to grow, the staff specialist will find that the volume of *his* work exceeds the time available. Thus, the second stage of functional differentiation outward is likely to be the creation of a staff unit or department. He is given a subordinate in the function, and thus the process of functional differentiation *downward* begins within the specialized training function. A *secondary* chain of command has thereby been created. Further growth in the amount and complexity of training will lead to further differentiation downward. The span of control applies here also, and thus two or three levels of organization could well be developed within the training area.

We have been concentrating upon the growth of the training function. While this has been going on, it is likely that other functions have undergone a similar process. Thus, an employment specialist may have been added along with a labor relations representative. There are frequent news reports about reorganizations of business firms because of the necessity for realignment at various stages of growth. It could well be that training, employment, and labor relations will be grouped together under a single head, a personnel manager. This will serve both to reduce the span of the line executive and to add to the coordination among the functions having to do with personnel. Thus, in the third stage of outward differentiation, we have developed a larger, integrated staff department, as indicated in Fig. 8–4. An example is also shown of an industrial engineering staff department.

Though these stages of differentiation do not occur in precise order, a fourth one has been observed if growth of the firm still continues. Functional differentiation outward *within* the staff department can occur, thus creating a staff to serve a staff, which in turn is serving the line. Thus, for example, at some point we may feel the need for specialized personnel research in training, employment, and labor. If that research is performed by persons doing the hiring, training, and labor relations, there is no functional differentiation outward within this staff unit. If, however, it is decided to establish a specialized research section to provide data and help for the people doing the training and hiring, there is then functional differentiation outward *within* the staff personnel department. The personnel research function is tertiary, since we have labeled line as primary and training and hiring as secondary.

Finally, it is not unusual to change the organization level of the differentiated staff function. Staff or secondary functions can be split off at *any* level in the organization. Ordinarily the personnel department splits off from a *production* chain of command. Because of sheer numbers of personnel and the nature

FIGURE 8–4   DEVELOPMENT OF STAFF DEPARTMENTS

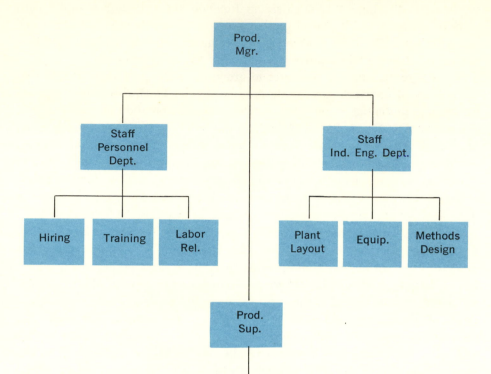

of problems to be solved, the need is usually felt here first. As the function develops and the enterprise grows, the department may be *elevated* from the production division to the second level of the organization in order to serve sales and finance along with production. Subsidiary service sections in personnel may still remain *within* the divisions, as indicated in Fig. 8–5, thus creating a parallel arrangement of the same function on multiple levels. The central staff personnel department serves as a clearing house, provides central services, and acts as directive force for the lower personnel sections. Thus a parallel, but specialized, channel of *communication* is created. Problems of dual allegiance sometimes arise between central personnel and the line executive to whom the lower personnel section reports.

It should be apparent that the concepts of objectives, organic functions, and functional differentiation downward and outward provide the basis for distinguishing between line and staff functions. The level of organization does *not* matter in determining the difference. There are *line* vice-presidents and *staff*

FIGURE 8–5   PARALLEL STAFF

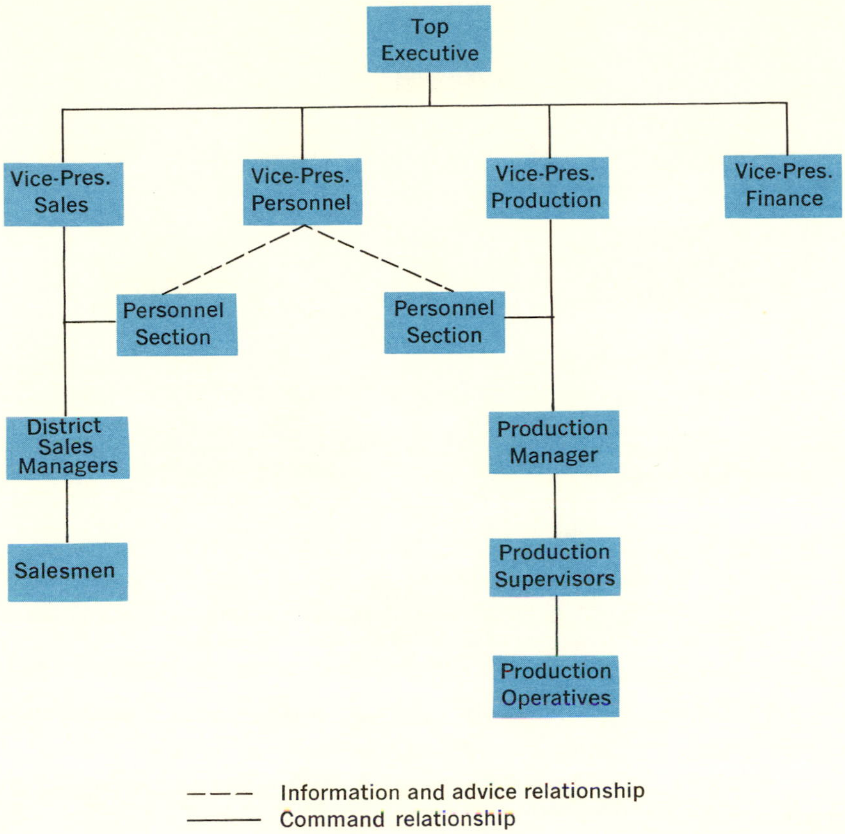

——— Information and advice relationship
———— Command relationship

vice-presidents. Just because the personnel manager is elevated to vice-presidential status does not change his designation from staff. The objective of the organization remains the controlling factor.

This distinction between types of functions is important to the manager since a balanced organizational perspective demands interrelating of functions on some basis. On a football team, one needs to know who is to carry the ball and who is to run interference. In industry, we need to know the basic functions around which to organize. These emphases will shape the image and character of the firm as well as provide a basis for coordination of the many functions necessary.

In summary, the distinction between line and staff relies primarily upon the relative incidence of service in relation to the organization objective. If the service is primary, the function is line. If the function serves and assists those engaged in the primary work, it is staff or secondary. If the function serves and assists those fulfilling a staff function, it is staff-to-staff or tertiary. If one is

FIGURE 8–6   BASIC GROWTH PATTERN

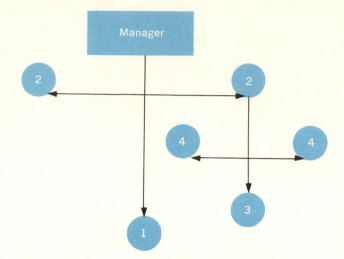

1—Primary functional differentiation downward
2—Secondary functional differentiation outward
3—Secondary functional differentiation downward
4—Tertiary function differentiation outward

aware of the basic pattern of growth, as shown in Fig. 8–6, he will be able to predict the future development of the organization. Its expansion or contraction will result in functional differentiation or integration along the lines indicated.

FUNCTIONAL BALANCE

The ideal result of the process of functionalization is the development of functional balance. This is primarily a theoretical concept but it does possess advantages for background purposes. Each function in an organization should be developed, through manpower and capital allocation, to the point where its return in value produced is at least equal to, and preferably greater than, its cost. For example, if a firm has approximately 2000 employees and there has been no functional differentiation outward of personnel management, it is probable that this function is out of balance. Too little is being allocated in this area. If certain phases of personnel management, such as hiring or labor relations, were to be separated out and given to staff specialists, the chances are great the values derived would exceed the costs expended.

On the other hand, if in this same firm it was decided to establish a new personnel department of some 200 members, it is highly likely that we would still be out of balance. All reports of experiences in industry indicate that 10 percent of total personnel being placed in the staff personnel function would be an excessive amount. Theoretically, there is some stage of development for each function in the organization that would be correct with reference to the size of the enterprise and its rate of growth.

There are many factors which contribute to a state of functional imbalance. First and foremost is the inability to measure precisely the values of further functionalization. What is the value, in dollars and cents, of creating a new industrial engineering department by splitting off such functions as methods design and plant layout from the line supervisor and allocating them to staff specialists? We know the amount of money it would cost the firm. Or do we? We know the cost of salaries paid and equipment purchased, but do we know the costs of attempting to sell the new service to the line, the cost of interrupting the work of supervisors and employees in making staff studies, and the costs of overcoming resentment of supervisors at the loss of functions formerly under their control? Against these costs, one must attempt to compare values derived from improved layouts, more efficient methods, and the like. Are they more economical and effective than those methods and layouts formerly developed by line supervisors? Should the new industrial engineering department be further enlarged because the firm is still out of balance on the low side? Or should it be cut back or possibly even eliminated with the function being reintegrated in the line? Matching costs with values is easier to state in theory than it is to effect in practice.

The *timing* of further functionalization is a problem related to the task of determining values and costs. It was stated earlier that as a business grows in size, the functions increase in scope and complexity, leading to the process of functional differentiation outward. *When* should a function be separated out— at 200, 300, or 400 employees? When are we large enough to justify the addition of a new department? There is again no precise answer. Surveys of actual practice provide information concerning the sizes of staff departments in firms of varying sizes. For example, one survey revealed that the ratio of personnel department employees to total employees varied with the number of separate plants in the company. For firms with single plants, the median ratio was 0.66; for those with multiple installations, it was 0.74.[16] Such figures can be used as guides in determining competitive functional balance.

It is interesting to note that European business firms tend to differentiate fewer staff personnel than do American firms of comparable size. A European

[16] Roberta J. Nelson, G. W. England, and Dale Yoder, "Personnel Ratios and Costs, 1962," *Personnel,* Vol. 40, No. 1 (January–February, 1963), p. 19.

manager transferring to an American firm would protest that he is immobilized by being forced to consult and work with innumerable staff experts. An American manager transferring to a European firm may be upset in not being able to consult so many staff experts for advice prior to making a decision. It is also interesting to note that during World War II every American fighting man was backed up by ten or more support personnel. The Russian Army, on the other hand, had a much higher percentage of personnel in the line.

Since the values of staff operation are so difficult to measure, their development is largely affected by one's philosophy of management. In the United States, with the emphasis upon scientific study and measurement, there is a strong belief in the probable high economic return from utilizing specialized experts. Certainly few profit-motivated firms will knowingly spend more money than necessary to effect a desired level of service. The steady increases in productivity in American industry, with its consequent impact upon a rising standard of living, also give some comfort to those advocating the scientific and specialized approach to business problems.

There are other sources of difficulties besides the inability to measure precisely costs and returns on increased functionalization. Managerial biases can lead to the overdevelopment of one function to the detriment of another. These biases often issue from the background of the leader concerned. A company president with a heavy background in engineering is likely to listen favorably to the engineering department on requests for expanded budgets and manpower. He is less able to understand and less inclined to accede to requests from other petitioners. Organizational politics also serve to confuse perspectives and contribute to imbalance. The executive who seeks to construct an empire is more interested in numbers and less concerned with balancing costs and values.

Perhaps the correct balancing of all functions is an unattainable objective. But a proper organization perspective requires that some attention be devoted to the problem and particularly to the typical sources of possible imbalance. No one function should be given a blank check without regard to proven values.

Summary

A function is work that can be distinguished from other work. The organization objectives determine the nature and content of the work to be performed. Functions that contribute directly to the accomplishment of primary goals are labeled primary or line functions. Those that contribute to these goals through assisting in the performance of primary functions are called secondary or staff. In manufacturing, the line functions are usually those of production, sales, and finance.

Functionalization is the process of functional differentiation and specialization that accompanies an increasing volume of work. Growth in volume beyond the capabilities of the one man will start this process downward. Gradually, there will be a separation of management functions from operative functions. The span of control will then force a further differentiation downward, resulting in the addition of multiple levels of organization.

At some point in the process of growth, economy and effectiveness of operation can be enhanced by functional differentiation *outward* from a primary chain of command into secondary or staff functions. The initial separation is usually to one man whose purpose is to provide specialized assistance to the original function, e.g., a methods engineer. These staff personnel are creating secondary values to be consumed by the organization (better hiring, more efficient methods). Further growth leads to downward differentiation of functions within the staff department, thereby creating a secondary chain of command. Thus the basic pattern of growth is first downward, then outward.

The objective of the process of functionalization is to achieve functional balance in the allocation of manpower and capital. This balance involves an attempt to match costs of further differentiation against possible values issuing from specialization.

Discussion Problems

1. How do you distinguish between primary and secondary functions in an organization? Why do it?

2. Does the distinguishing between primary and secondary functions result in the creation of first- and second-class citizens in the organization? Is it possible for a particular staff person to make a more valuable contribution to organization objectives than a particular line person?

3. What are the behavioral and classical views on the span of control concept? Why do they take these views?

4. Discuss the multiple factors that affect the effective length of the span of control. How does Lockheed go about the process of determining appropriate spans?

5. What effect does the span of control have on the number of organizational levels?

6. Explain the reasoning of Graicunas in determining the appropriate span of control.

7. Start with the one-man manufacturing concern and trace the theoretical development of functional differentiation to the point of establishing a staff personnel department headed by a vice-president.

8. What is functional balance? What factors tend to effect functional imbalance?

9. What is a function? How far can functional analysis be pursued?

10. Discuss the parallel development of staff functions on multiple levels.

Supplementary Reading

Davis, Ralph C., *The Fundamentals of Top Management*, Chap. 7. New York: Harper & Bros., 1951.

Delbecq, Andre L., "The World Within the 'Span of Control,'" *Business Horizons*, Vol. 11, No. 4 (August, 1968), 47–56.

Efferson, C. A., "In Defense of the Line-Staff Concept," *Personnel,* Vol. 43, No. 4 (July–August, 1966), 8–15.

Fisch, Gerald C., "Line-Staff Is Obsolete," *Harvard Business Review,* Vol. 39, No. 5 (September–October, 1961), 67–97.

Nelson, Edward A., "Economic Size of Organizations," *California Management Review,* Vol. 10, No. 3 (Spring, 1968), 61–72.

Nowotny, Otto H., "American vs. European Management Philosophy," *Harvard Business Review,* Vol. 42, No. 2 (March–April, 1964), 101–108.

Suojanen, Waino W., *The Dynamics of Management,* Chaps. 2 and 3. New York: Holt, Rinehart, and Winston, 1966.

9

The Process of Organizing

The process of organizing involves the establishment of conditions necessary for effective accomplishment of corporate goals. When these goals require the efforts of multiple personnel, we are concerned with the crucial job of establishing some type of relationship among them, and between the group and the common goal.

In this chapter we shall be concerned with the three basic *formal* relationships: (1) responsibility, (2) authority, and (3) accountability. These are designated as formal since they are predetermined and predefined by management as the appropriate ways of relating and combining the diverse elements of the enterprise.

RESPONSIBILITY

Responsibility is defined as the *obligation* to execute functions or work, and is a derivative of functions. The latter are in turn a derivative of objectives; one cannot decide what work should be performed unless one knows what is to be accomplished. All these three factors—obligation, functions, and objectives—have to be as closely integrated as possible if there is to be a viable business operation.

They are usually documented in some fashion, thereby establishing a model which has previously been designated as a standard of function. The myriad of informal and unofficial relationships will be discussed in a later section of this book.

151

Delegation of Responsibility

The source for delegating responsibility is one's superior in the organization. When a superior delegates responsibility to a subordinate, he creates a relationship based on obligation between himself and the subordinate. (A similar relationship with *his* superior remains unchanged.) By delegating, one cannot relieve oneself of any portion of the original responsibility; delegation only allows for someone else to do the work.

This concept of delegation creates a risk for the manager, for he is ultimately responsible for either the success or the failure of an operation. As a result, some managers have attempted to reduce the risk by avoiding delegation and doing tasks themselves. When this is done, it may sometimes be construed as an admission of managerial failure.

Thus, the president of a firm delegates responsibility for production, sales, and finance to his vice-presidents, even though the board of directors still holds the president accountable for total performance. A departmental supervisor delegates to the machine operator responsibility to work on a particular project. If the project fails, the supervisor is answerable to his own superior and so on up the ladder. Responsibility is thus a series of obligations established between any two *contiguous* levels of organization.

Division of Responsibility

As indicated in Fig. 9–1, the objective determines the work to be performed. The total work load must be divided among the available personnel. Individual jobs, or units of responsibility, are created by selecting and grouping functions into individual assignments. The basic guide that governs this process is that of "functional similarity." In Fig. 9–1, functions L, Q, and J are shown to be sufficiently similar in objectives and content to make a logical job assignment; therefore, one person with the skills and abilities necessary to execute this job can be found. (There are, as we shall discuss shortly, instances where dissimilar functions are combined.)

The same principle also guides us in the creation of sections, departments, and divisions. Jobs with similar objectives and requirements are grouped to form a section. A section manager with the background to supervise these functions properly can be found. We should, for example, seek to avoid creating a department concerned with personnel management, purchasing, and machine maintenance. It would be difficult to man properly, and, because of a lack of specialized attention, would contribute to wasteful expenditures.

Various factors modify the application of this basic organizational guide.

FIGURE 9–1   JOB DESIGN

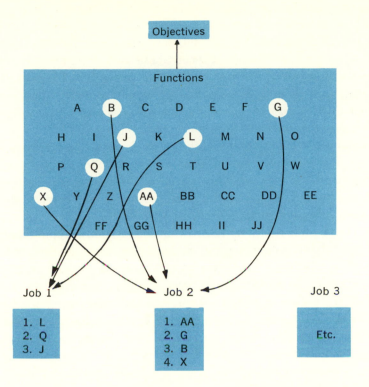

There must, of course, be a sufficient volume of work to enable some speciali-zation. In the small firm, personnel will have to cope with a wide assortment of jobs. But, with increases in volume, the concept can be applied more rigor-ously. In such situations, jobs are created which consist of one function performed over and over again, such as placing headlights on automobiles on a continuous assembly line. Behaviorists have been quite critical of industrial jobs designed along the lines of functional similarity.[1] Nevertheless, volume is a prerequisite to specialization, and specialization often leads to economies of operation.

A second factor that may work against the concept of functional similarity is that of present personnel qualifications. By following the demands of objec-tives, functions, and functional similarity, the manager will derive a unit of responsibility based upon the capabilities of the "typical" person. (The actual capabilities of present personnel may be something quite different.) One view is that the manager should organize around the people he has and divide up the work, not according to principles, but, rather, according to the peculiar

[1] See Chapter 13.

backgrounds and abilities of present personnel.[2] This will ensure a better matching of man to job. The opposing view emphasizes that people are temporary while functions are permanent. If an illogical assignment has been created, it will be difficult to find another person to fulfill it. Undoubtedly, there is some middle ground between these two extremes. One organizes around *both* functions *and* personnel available, but in the order stated. Thus, a logical assignment of units of responsibility should be created first as a desired framework. After this, certain modifications may have to be made to match available personnel to the job more effectively.

A third complicating factor is that the particular function in question is often similar to other functions. As one example, the function of inventory control would appear to fit logically with the purchasing function. The purchasing department *buys* the material and thus has need for records of inventory levels. However, production *uses* these materials and, in scheduling, must work with these same inventory records. Inventory control could then go either way. In cases of this type, either the "most use" or "most interest" criterion can be used. If production control has the most pressing need or the greatest interest in inventory records, these records can be assigned to that unit of responsibility. Another example of the similarity of functions is the function of safety. Obviously, all parts of the organization need rules of safety. However, the function of greatest need is again that of production, and the safety engineer is usually assigned to this division. In all these examples, individual interest is another legitimate factor when functional analysis has indicated that logical assignment can go either way.

A fourth complication is the occasional necessity for *separating* similar functions for purposes of control or motivation. For example, inspection is a function that is intimately involved in production; inspectors frequently work side by side with production personnel. Inspection is a judicial function, however, and should not be unduly influenced by the production executive's interest in quantity and cost. Thus, inspection, though similar to production, should be separate from it to protect its own independence. There are times, also, when a firm wishes to make use of internal competition to stimulate its workers. Units doing similar work are separated organizationally, and operating results are compared. In the General Motors Corporation, Buicks, Oldsmobiles, and Pontiacs compete at the same price level.

Finally, there are occasions when two dissimilar functions must be combined for purposes of effective action and control. Though purchasing is clearly differentiated from selling in a factory organization, buying and selling are so interdependent in department stores that one person is often made responsible for both. The theory is that a well-bought dress or hat is half-sold.

[2] See K. K. White, "Understanding the Company Organization Chart," *AMA Research Study 56* (New York: American Management Association, 1963), pp. 26–27.

Another example of combining dissimilar functions would be internal transportation among production units in a factory. Since transporting goods is different from manufacturing them, economy and effectiveness may be enhanced by specialization in separate units. However, production is so dependent upon internal movement from station to station that coordination by one executive is often deemed essential. As some writers have noted, there is no "clean break" between the functions.[3]

Other Guides in Dividing Responsibility

The concept of functional similarity is basic to the process of dividing and delegating responsibility. In addition, there are other guides; among these are (1) avoiding overlaps, (2) avoiding gaps, and (3) avoiding delegation of responsibility for work that does not contribute to the objective.

An overlap in responsibility occurs when two or more persons are made responsible for the same function. This often happens when there is an unclear specification of responsibility limits or when work is unknowingly duplicated in different parts of the organization. The larger the organization, the greater the chance for such duplication. In theory, we should be able to match units of responsibility with required functions so precisely that there will be no known or unknown overlapping. In practice, however, we find this exceedingly difficult. As a further complication, if the overlap is known, each person may attempt to obtain the function clearly for himself; or, if the task is undesirable, he may attempt to divorce himself from it. In either event, we have laid the foundation for controversy.

A gap in responsibility results from a failure to foresee all requirements for effective accomplishment of goals. A function *should* be performed but has been assigned to no one. As a result, it may not be accomplished, and the organization suffers. Or the organization politician, who searches for power, may leap in and volunteer to take on the job even though it bears no similarity to his main task.

The third guide cited above would appear so obvious as to be implicit. However, there are many examples of activities that in no way contribute to organization objectives, often as a result of a change in those objectives.

Once any organization, or element of it, is established, it is very difficult to abolish. Government is often accused of starting agencies and then continuing them long after the need has disappeared. This can also happen in private business organizations, where sheer size of organization can easily lead to gaps, overlaps, and performance of work that is unnecessary.

[3] See Harold Koontz and Cyril O'Donnell, *Principles of Management: An Analysis of Managerial Functions,* 4th ed. (New York: McGraw-Hill Book Company, 1968), pp. 285–286.

AUTHORITY

Just as responsibility is a concept based upon and derived from functions, authority is a derivative of responsibility. Authority is a right: the right to decide, to command, or to perform. In this writer's suggested framework, no authority should be delegated unless there is a prior obligation justifying the possession of rights. This is in direct contrast to a viewpoint that contends that rights are established first, and that certain obligations are then sought.[4] This writer contends that a philosophy of management which emphasizes business obligations, which in turn justify the acquisition and use of authority and power, is a more balanced and justifiable concept in the eyes of general society.[5]

Source of Authority

The ultimate source of formal authority in business is organized society. Society delegates to individuals the right to own property. Owners of property in turn delegate rights to boards of directors, who themselves delegate to the president, the vice-presidents, and so forth. Thus authority is a *legal, institutional right to decide, command, and/or perform.* Such rights are obtained from a superior source.

It is important to note that any authority delegated by a superior can be retracted. We have seen in Chapter 2 where society delegated a substantial amount of authority to private individuals and organizations. According to the derivative relationships established and noted above, this delegation of authority in business can be justified only on the basis of recognition and acceptance of a prior obligation, such as the creation and distribution of economic goods and services.

The right of a manager to direct people to do things can be defended on bases other than the legal and institutional. "The real source of managerial authority is the substitutional and essential *need* for authority in a specific situation."[6] If the subordinate lacks knowledge and skill, the manager must substitute his superior knowledge to provide answers and actions needed by the organization. With training and development, substitutional authority is self-destructive. Of course, some managers tend to abuse this type of authority

---

[4] In Mooney's model of formal organization theory, authority is given a more central role as the basis of the all-inclusive coordinating principle. See James D. Mooney, *The Principles of Organization* (New York: Harper & Bros., 1947), p. 6.

[5] See Chapter 11 for a discussion of power and its distinguishing differences from authority.

[6] Robert Albanese, "Substitutional and Essential Authority," *Academy of Management Journal,* Vol. 9, No. 2 (June, 1966), p. 140.

as they chronically underestimate the abilities of subordinates. Behaviorally oriented managers tend to possess a more optimistic view of man's potential and will move more rapidly toward elimination of substitutional authority.

Even in the unlikely event that all organization members are perfectly able and informed, there will still be a need for authority. Essential authority rests upon the necessity for choice among multiple acceptable alternatives. Theory "Y" personnel of great ability and good intentions will not always agree concerning what constitutes the best decision. If there is to be united, purposeful group action, some agency must finally decide the course to be followed. Where the group cannot or will not identify the selected organizational choice, the manager must exercise his essential authority to enable the group to act.

The behaviorists have submitted a view of authority based on a different source. This view is labeled "informal authority," and its source in the organization structure is from *below*. Acceptance of decisions and orders is a crucial part of this theory, which will be discussed later in this text.

Division of Authority

Since authority is a derivative of responsibility, its division should be along the same lines. This is made evident in a widely accepted basic guide, the concept of "parity of responsibility and authority." This guide indicates that a delegation of responsibility should carry with it a commensurate amount of authority to allow for its fulfillment. If one has an obligation and no legal justification for it, certain obvious difficulties would ensue.

The concept as stated is a truism. Yet one of the most common complaints of first-level supervisors is that they have more responsibility than authority. On the other hand, there are very few complaints about having an excess of authority. Authority seems to be more desired by organization members than responsibility. Yet if the derivative relationships suggested above are sound, they would indicate that the member who seeks additional authority should first concern himself with enlarging his obligations.

Authority deals with rights, and these must be made specific in terms of the responsibility delegated. For example, if a supervisor is made responsible for manning his department, he can be delegated any one of the following levels of authority: (1) rights of recruitment, screening, and hiring of all personnel; (2) rights of recruitment, screening, and hiring subject to prior approval from above; (3) no rights of recruitment and screening, which have been allocated to a staff personnel department, but rights of accepting or rejecting candidates; or (4) no rights of hiring since he must take whomever the personnel department sends to him. In the last instance, there would be grounds for contending that a state of inequality of responsibility and authority exists.

McGregor has pointed out that even though the parity relationship should be true in theory, it is rarely, if ever, true in practice.[7] The facts of business life, he contends, place most managers in a position where they cannot control everything that affects the results they are obliged to achieve. Among the uncontrollable factors are unexpected changes in consumer preferences, actions of labor unions, new legislation by government, unusually high absenteeism, and the vagaries of the business cycle. Admission of these difficulties, however, still would not destroy the value of the concept. If the superior is reasonable, he will make allowances for unforeseen and unusual events outside the control of the delegate.

Another author has suggested that a new, untrained employee's responsibility should be made purposefully greater than his authority.[8] Then, as he acquires skill and his superior's trust, the amount of authority can gradually be increased to equal the responsibility. However, if the new man makes a major mistake, do we hold him accountable in the same manner as we would an older, more skilled, and trusted subordinate? The answer is usually "no." Thus in fact we expect *less* of the untrained, resulting in a temporary reduction in responsibility until he acquires the necessary proficiency.

Delegation of Authority

Just as an employee receives his responsibility from his superior and is thereby obligated to perform, he also receives his institutional rights from the same source. However, many superiors are considerably more reluctant to release authority to subordinates than to delegate responsibility to them. As was pointed out previously, there is no way that the superior can reduce his own responsibility through delegation. The risk that must be assumed by a manager is usually the factor behind his reluctance to delegate authority.

Other reasons for refusing to delegate are as follows: (1) real or presumed unavailability of qualified subordinates; (2) enhancement of one's own indispensability to the enterprise; (3) lack of delegating skill; and (4) fear of possible threats from subordinates who learn too much from the exercise of delegated rights and responsibilities. Most, if not all, of these reasons, however, do not constitute sound grounds for refusal to delegate when the work load requires the efforts of others. In fact, the ability and willingness to delegate authority to others is the essence of being a manager.

[7] Douglas McGregor, *The Human Side of Enterprise* (New York: McGraw-Hill Book Company, 1960), p. 158.

[8] Michael J. Jucius, *Personnel Management,* 6th ed. (Homewood: Richard D. Irwin, Inc., 1967), p. 80.

ACCOUNTABILITY

Accountability is a logical derivative of authority. If one has been delegated a sufficient amount of authority to enable fulfillment of his responsibility, one is reasonably answerable to a superior for results. If the authority given has been insufficient, the delegate has been provided with an excuse for poor performance; he cannot be held accountable for those activities not within his realm of authority and control.

In exacting results from a subordinate, we should make sure, first, that he understands the responsibilities thoroughly; second, that he is personally capable of fulfilling the obligation; and third, that sufficient organization rights have been granted. If failure of accomplishment then ensues, answerability can logically be imposed upon the delegate. The manager must determine if the results effected constitute an acceptable accomplishment of organization goals.

Perhaps the most widely known guide governing the relationship of accountability is that of "single accountability." Each person should be answerable to only one immediate superior—one boss to each employee. If this relationship is effected, the result should be better coordination and understanding of what is required, and improved discipline. If, on the contrary, a man has two or more bosses, the likelihood of contradictory orders is increased. If the subordinate executes the orders of supervisor "A," he may not be able to carry out the requirements of supervisor "B." Thus we place the subordinate in the unlikely position of having to coordinate his superiors.

A second reason for the adoption of this guide of single accountability is to promote coordination. The chances for consistent and coordinated action throughout the firm are enhanced if orders are issued from a single source and if accountability is exacted to that same source. Obviously, this emphasizes the importance of the manager in integrating the various functions.

Though this concept of single accountability is sound, it does have certain limitations. The foremost one is that it requires extremely capable managers who can keep the enterprise under control. As the size of the organization increases, such control becomes more difficult. One man may not find it easy to personally evaluate, clear, and issue consistent orders as president of a firm of 100,000 employees. To help him, staff elements are often established in various technical and specialized areas. In theory, all staff suggestions and advice clear through the central manager, who evaluates, coordinates, and transforms them into his own orders, thus preserving single accountability. But in many organizations, this singleness of accountability is no doubt a fiction; actually, in many instances a man is accountable to more than one boss. The military organizations preserve the fiction by issuing orders over a by-line—"by order of the commanding officer." Yet these orders are often cleared, coordinated, and written by the commanding officer's adjutant.

When an organization becomes large, its sheer size requires more than one manager, and we begin to speak in terms of the manager's "office." In effect, it may adopt a plural manager—for instance, the commanding officer *and* his adjutant or chief of staff. As far as the subordinate is concerned, when he hears the adjutant speak, he is in effect hearing the commanding officer's voice. Aside from subtle differences (which only experience within the organization will reveal), the overall effect is indeed some alteration of single accountability.

Single accountability is often given the alternate title of "unity of command." This appears to be the same concept differently defined—one order-giver as contrasted with one boss to whom to account. However, there may be important differences. Unity of command emphasizes the rational, logical coordination of the diverse units of the enterprise. Is it not possible to violate single accountability while still preserving unity of command? In the "A" and "B" illustration above, if managers "A" and "B" work well together, could they not preserve *unity of command for the subordinate* even though he is accountable to both? The answer to both these questions is that single accountability, though highly desirable, may have to be violated as the enterprise grows in size and complexity. However, unity of command will *always* be necessary if there is to be organized action. Though unity is *easier* to effect with a single head, it can still be preserved even with multiple bosses, provided these bosses have a close and coordinated working relationship.

Almost 50 years ago, the E. I. duPont de Nemours and Company pioneered in the adoption of the concept of a plural executive office. Its executive committee of nine members divide and execute the work of the presidential office. Each member acts as an adviser to one of the nine operating departments and one or more of the dozen staff departments. Department heads are appointed by and report to the committee as a whole. By combining their advisory functions with planning and control activities, the committee acts as a daily working board.

In recent years, the increasing complexity of decision making on the top level in various large corporations has led to reorganization of the presidential office. Significant movements toward the concept of a plural president have been reported in such organizations as General Motors, General Electric, Union Carbide, Allis-Chalmers, Scott Paper, Gulf Oil, Continental Can, Armstrong Cork, and Caterpillar.[9] Pressures toward this change stem from human limitations of time and expertise. A single person, no matter how able, cannot spread himself effectively over the large number of activities that must be undertaken in the huge organization. Answers to this problem in the past have included

[9] "Management Outlook," *Business Week* (December 23, 1967), p. 40.

sharing decisions with subordinates (decentralization), development of the positions of "assistant" or "assistant-to," and development of specialized head-quarters staff units. The latest attempt involves a blossoming of the presidential position itself. Though the formal president is still ultimately accountable, he surrounds himself with several men who are in effect associate presidents. The latter are selected for special complimentary talents, and are encouraged to act as a president in particular areas. It is apparent that members of the group must develop effective and close interpersonal relationships in order to preserve the necessary unity of command.

There are, then, two guides in this area of organization. Both single accountability and unity of command are highly desirable and should be applied as long as possible. However, only the second, unity of command, is absolutely essential regardless of the size and complexity of the organization.

CENTRALIZATION AND DECENTRALIZATION

The concept of parity of responsibility and authority has already been presented and defined. A related problem in organization is that of determining the *amount* of responsibility *and* authority that should be delegated, assuming that these two relationships are always equal. If small amounts are delegated, the enterprise is usually characterized as being *centralized*. If large amounts of rights are delegated to subordinate levels, the enterprise is described as being *decentralized*.

Centralization and decentralization are the opposite ends of a continuum with many different degrees. The real question is not "whether" one should decentralize, but rather "how much." In determining the actual amount of decentralization existing in an organization, the nature and locus of decision making must be assessed. Other things being equal, the degree of decentralization will be greater when:

1. The decision is made at a lower organization level.
2. The decision is important as judged by (a) possible risk if wrong, and (b) impact on various portions of the enterprise.
3. The decision is not subject to restraints either before or after. For example, decisions subject to no check are evidence of greater decentralization than those subject to check after the fact. The latter in turn are evidence of more decentralization than are decisions requiring approval before being placed into effect.

Centralization and decentralization are not ideals. They are neither good nor bad, though the fashion of the day seems to favor the latter. Decentralization is consistent with recommendations made by behaviorists advocating a greater share in management decision making by subordinates in the organization. If *all* decisions and orders issue from one central source, organization members tend to act as robots and unthinking executors of someone else's commands.

In addition to the human-relations implications of decentralization and centralization, there are other factors that will affect a manager's decision in this regard. Centralization produces uniformity of policy and action, lessens risks of errors by subordinates who lack either information or skill, utilizes the skills of central and specialized experts, and enables closer control of operations. On the other hand, decentralization tends to make for speedier decisions and actions on the spot without consulting higher levels, and such decisions are more likely to be adapted to local conditions. Usually, there is also greater interest and enthusiasm on the part of the subordinate to whom the authority has been entrusted. These expanded jobs provide excellent training experiences for possible promotion to higher levels. And finally, the central executive's time can be better utilized for more study and consideration of the basic goals and policies of the enterprise.

Additional factors to be taken into account then, are the following:

1. Size and complexity of the organization.
2. Dispersion of the organization.
3. Competency of personnel available.
4. Degree of repetitiveness and standardization.
5. Adequacy of the communication system.

As indicated above, the larger the size of the enterprise, the more authority the central manager is forced to delegate. Size requirements exceed human limitations, even when supplemented by numerous staffs, plural executive offices, and various committees. If the firm is engaged in numerous separate businesses, the limitations of expertise will usually lead to decentralization of authority to the heads of these units. Each major product group is likely to have different production problems, varying kinds of customers, and varied marketing channels. If speed and adaptability to change are necessary to success, decentralization is a must.

When the difficulties of size are compounded by geographic dispersion, it is very evident that a greater degree of decentralization must occur; General Motors Corporation is a prime example of decentralization because of size and geographic dispersion. However, not every decision or every function must be decentralized. Control of *operations* may have to be pushed down to lower levels in the organization, while control of *financing* may still be centralized. Because of the increasing complexity of labor laws and unionization, centralization of *labor relations* is often established for purposes of uniformity throughout the enterprise. Increasing automation and more effective data processing are likely to cause centralization of the logistics system, that is, the flow of raw material, work-in-process inventories, and finished goods inventories at warehouses and dealers.

A major limiting factor in many organizations is the adequacy or inadequacy of present personnel. If the enterprise has grown up under centralized decision making and control, past experience has often ill-equipped subordinate personnel to start making major decisions. They were hired and trained to be followers, not leaders and decision makers. And those personnel inclined toward more independence of thought and action may well have been driven away from the centralized firm. Either new personnel will have to be obtained, or the painful process of instituting behavior changes may have to be undertaken through a carefully planned management development program.[10]

Let us recall the previously cited tendency of the manager to seek to retain control since he can never escape his responsibility. Size and geographic dispersion again may force his hand and lead to more delegation, with its accompanying increased risks. On the one hand, standardization and improved communication systems may enable him to overcome these forces to some degree and to retain a greater amount of centralized authority. On the other, size, complexity, and geography mean that the central manager cannot make realistic decisions for the point of operations, since he is not on the spot. However, if a large measure of repetition and standardization of operations can be introduced, events can be predicted much more accurately. Thus, authority can be reclaimed and recentralized. In addition, if the speed, accuracy, and capacity of the communications system can be improved to the point where the central manager can be immediately apprised of changed local conditions, he has basis for reclaiming authority. Some management theorists have predicted that, though size and complexity have led us to the era of decentralization, the computer and integrated electronic data processing systems will halt this trend. Presumably, this would not be looked upon with favor by the behaviorists.

Naturally, management wants the best possible mix of centralization and decentralization on all decisions and functions so as to enable a long-run maximization of return to the enterprise. But there must be *some* central control to provide for unity of command and coordination. If all personnel thought alike, through long training and indoctrination programs, decentralization could be facilitated. Then the central manager could be comfortable with the thought that subordinates would approach a problem in much the same manner as he. But the additional organization information and the broader

10 See Eli Ginzberg and Ewing W. Reilley, *Effecting Change in Large Organizations* (New York: Columbia University Press, 1957).

perspective that can come only from the central management position would be lacking. Thus some overall control must always be present for general coordination.

DOCUMENTATION OF RESPONSIBILITY AND AUTHORITY

If the scientific manager is to obtain the maximum from his logical division and delegation of responsibility and authority, these relationships should be diagrammed in some fashion. Documentation introduces a much greater degree of formality than oral instructions do. Recording also provides for a degree of permanency, which helps to overcome possible memory losses, misunderstanding of instructions, and turnover of personnel. The job is defined, rights indicated, and lines of accountability definitely stated.

There are those who prefer a minimum of formalization and wish to rely more heavily on the informal, often impromptu relationships that evolve among personalities. The considerable value of these informal relationships will be discussed at length in later chapters. However, it would be difficult to imagine how large numbers of personnel could effectively relate to each other and the common goal on a purely individualistic basis. Someone must seek to identify primary tasks, specify who works for and with whom, and allocate the institutional rights. This "someone" is usually the leader or manager. The larger the enterprise, the more detailed and elaborate documentation tends to become. Though this reduces flexibility somewhat, it does not preclude it. And in any case, flexibility presupposes some set design. Having no set course is not flexibility; it is, rather, confusion and chaos.

There are various instruments of documentation used in business to record the basic formal organization relationships. Perhaps the most common is an organization chart. There are the usual types of *pyramid* or *inverted tree* charts which have been used in the preceding chapter. Sometimes these charts are dressed up with the titles and/or pictures of the job holders. Usually they cover only job or departmental titles (which give an indication of responsibility), along with lines of accountability. In addition, there are *circular charts*, where the president's position is placed in the center and subordinate jobs fan out in concentric circles from there. Or the *line chart* can be adopted, as shown in Chart 9–1. Needless to say, all of these charts present only fragmentary information concerning the basic relationships. However, incomplete as they are, they do provide a quick, comprehensive conception of the entire organization with fairly accurate information as to lines of accountability.

Another suggested technique is the Management Responsibility Matrix. A series of charts are designed to show the relationship between various positions

CHART 9–1   LINE ORGANIZATION CHART

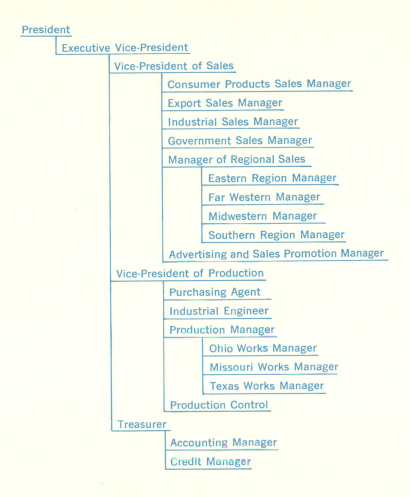

President
  Executive Vice-President
    Vice-President of Sales
      Consumer Products Sales Manager
      Export Sales Manager
      Industrial Sales Manager
      Government Sales Manager
      Manager of Regional Sales
        Eastern Region Manager
        Far Western Manager
        Midwestern Manager
        Southern Region Manager
      Advertising and Sales Promotion Manager
    Vice-President of Production
      Purchasing Agent
      Industrial Engineer
      Production Manager
        Ohio Works Manager
        Missouri Works Manager
        Texas Works Manager
      Production Control
    Treasurer
      Accounting Manager
      Credit Manager

or units, and the major tasks or key functions. For each of several major tasks listed down the left side of the chart, a responsibility relationship is designated for the various affected positions listed across the top of the chart. The chart will indicate, through a set of symbols, such varying responsibilities as who (1) performs the task, (2) directly supervises the task, (3) provides general supervision of the task, (4) must be notified when the task is done, (5) may be consulted about the task, (6) must be consulted, and (7) must give approval. Each executive fills out the matrix for each major duty. The greatest value of this approach is the confrontation of all interrelated executives as they discuss the confusions and contradictions that result when the various matrices are compared. The classical manager hopes to derive an agreed upon set of detailed relationships from this discussion. As indicated by one author, the

CHART 9–2   KAISER STEEL CORPORATION SALARIED POSITION DESCRIPTION

Position:	Labor Relations Representative
Department:	Labor Relations
Location:	Fontana
Code:	834-06-210

Primary Function:

Under the general supervision of the Assistant Director and/or the Director, Labor Relations is engaged in assisting in the development, administration, and maintenance of a satisfactory labor relations policy in the plant, and in the negotiation and administration of collective bargaining agreements and their interpretation.

Scope:

Duties encompass all labor relations activities and related problems at Fontana. Is responsible for maintaining uniform and consistent labor relations policy throughout various mills and locations, and interpretation of collective bargaining agreements for plant personnel as required.

Position Content:

1. 100%—Assist in matters pertaining to Labor Relations and related problems.
    a. Assists and advises all levels of Supervision and Management on matters pertaining to Company-Union relations.
    b. Analyzes trends, situations, and personalities in order to advise and make recommendations to Management and Supervision on action to be taken to insure a sound labor policy.
    c. Interprets Company Policy to Union Representatives and Supervision.
    d. Recommends disciplinary action to be taken for violations of plant rules and regulations.
    e. Assists in negotiating basic labor agreements with Unions representing Company employees at Fontana.
    f. Conducts investigations in the resolution of Step Three and Step Four grievances.
    g. Advises and assists supervision in resolving Step One and Step Two grievances.
    h. Meets with Labor Relations groups from other companies to discuss mutual problems.
    i. Uses considerable diplomacy in all contacts in order to create a favorable relationship with all employees and their collective bargaining agents.
    j. Participates in conferences in regard to wage negotiation, contracts, etc.
    k. Counsels and assists employees in individual and personal problems.
    l. Answers inquiries from public and governmental agencies.
    m. Reduces to written form all departmental agreements, etc.
    n. Prepares Monthly Labor Relations Activities Reports, as required.
    o. Makes daily contacts with departmental superintendents and other supervisors, as assigned, to maintain a detailed, current working knowledge of local labor relations, activities and conditions.
    p. Attends and records proceedings of meetings of Company and Union representatives.

Working Conditions:

1. Sitting 50%; standing 15%; walking 35%.
2. Normal work days.
3. Normal office and mill conditions.

responsibility matrix "requires detailed analysis of interrelated responsibilities and the specific determination of who is going to do what."[11] With everyone checking each other out, a check and balance system is thereby developed.

To supplement the basic organization chart, *job descriptions* are often used to document responsibility and authority. As indicated earlier, business organizations tend to do a more effective job of defining the responsibilities of a job than they do of designating the authority. Chart 9–2 shows a typical job description, specifying the major duties of the incumbent. A few firms have attempted to develop and use a type of job description that specifies, first, the duties and obligations of the job and, second, the *corresponding* organization rights for each obligation. Thus, if it is the obligation of the jobholder to review and approve requests for capital budget expenditures, the corresponding specification of authority may indicate that he has (1) the right of *approval* up to $5000, provided funds are available in the budget; and (2) the right to *recommend* approval for expenditures in excess of $5000. In this manner, the job incumbent knows his formal rights for each of his duties. Too often, however, he is told only of his obligations, and there follows a period of trial and error while he attempts to ascertain just how much authority his superior intends to let him have. Hopefully, he does not make too many mistakes, out of either excessive caution or extreme daring, before he discovers the scope of his authority.

Finally, it is important to note that these job descriptions are significant in many areas other than that of assisting in the establishment of organizational relationship. They can be used for orienting and educating new employees; as standards for control; and in many personnel activities, such as screening, training, merit rating, and job evaluation.[12]

Summary

Organizing is the process of establishing the required conditions for carrying out the plans of the enterprise. It involves the establishment of relationships among functions, personnel, and physical factors for the purpose of harnessing and directing efforts toward common goals.

Through observation and practice, various generalizations have been evolved to assist in the design of effective organization structure. In dividing and delegating responsibility, the concept of functional similarity is basic if work specialization is to be at all valuable. The manager also tries to avoid responsibility gaps and overlaps. Authority is a derivative of responsibility, and its division should follow closely that of responsibility. The concept of parity of responsibility and

[11] T. M. Hamilton, "Clarifying Responsibility Relationships," *California Management Review*, Vol. 10, No. 3 (Spring, 1968), p. 48.
[12] See Edwin B. Flippo, *The Principles of Personnel Management*, 2nd ed. (New York: McGraw-Hill Book Company, 1966), Chap. 7.

authority is similarly of prime importance. If sufficient authority has been delegated, accountability can then be exacted for performance results. Unity of command is essential to insure coordination of efforts. Single accountability for each person is desirable insofar as the size of the enterprise and the degree of specialization and technology permit.

With increasing size of organization, the tendency is in the direction of greater decentralization of authority and responsibility as well as more precise documentation of these relationships. In the following chapter, the various types of organization structure that can be developed among organization components will be discussed.

DISCUSSION PROBLEMS

1. Define and distinguish between substitutional and essential authority. What are likely to be the behavioral and classical views?
2. Discuss the concept of a plural presidency. What are the factors leading to the establishment of a presidential office?
3. When the requirements of a manager's position tend to exceed his capacities, what various organizational devices can be used to compensate?
4. Explain the derivation relationships among objectives, functions, responsibility, authority, and accountability.
5. Explain how and why the process of delegation does not relieve the manager of any of his responsibility.
6. What factors tend to move a firm toward decentralization of decision-making authority? What factors tend to move it toward centralization?
7. Indicate the nature and uses of organization documentation.
8. What are the behavioral objections to the concept of functional similarity? to co-equal authority and responsibility?
9. What is formal authority? What is the ultimate source of formal authority?
10. What are some difficulties often encountered in attempting to follow the guide of functional similarity in dividing up the workload?

SUPPLEMENTARY READING

Albanese, Robert, "Substitutional and Essential Authority," *Academy of Management Journal*, Vol. 9, No. 2 (June, 1966), 136–144.

Daniel, D. Ronald, "Reorganizing for Results," *Harvard Business Review*, Vol. 44, No. 6 (November–December, 1966), 96–104.

Dearden, John, "Computers: No Impact on Divisional Control," *Harvard Business Review*, Vol. 45, No. 1 (January–February, 1967), 99–104.

Hamilton, T. M., "Clarifying Responsibility Relationships," *California Management Review*, Vol. 10, No. 3 (Spring, 1968), 41–52.

Koontz, Harold and Cyril O'Donnell, *Principles of Management: An Analysis of Managerial Functions,* 4th ed., Chaps. 13, 14, and 17. New York: McGraw-Hill Book Company, 1968.

Melcher, Robert D., "Roles and Relationships," *Personnel,* Vol. 44, No. 3 (May–June, 1967), 33–41.

10

Organization Structure

Organizing has been described as the process of establishing relationships among functions, personnel, and physical factors. The primary formal relationships involved are responsibility, authority, and accountability. The immediate result of this process is the creation of some type of organization structure which consists of a formal set of relationships established to locate, position, and orient personnel as they execute work within the guidelines set up by organization goals.

In a sense, an organization structure can be compared to a harness for a team of horses. The harness defines the location of each horse, relates each horse to every other horse, and relates all horses to the common objective of moving the wagon forward. The goal is regulated teamwork in the maximization of efforts toward a common objective. Thus, when a person joins an organization, he has to submit to structure, regulations, and harnessing to a degree. He cannot be permitted to work on or at what he chooses, when he chooses, or how he chooses without some restriction as determined by organization goals. Though the structure is not rigid and the reins are held loosely, he must subordinate himself to some degree if organized activity is to be effected. We hope to obtain a measure of *both* coordination and cooperation, which necessitate a measure of subordination. Highly enthusiastic and cooperative personnel cannot work effectively if their work is uncoordinated and at cross purposes. In addition, such enthusiasm and a desire to cooperate would not last for long if there were no real accomplishment.

In theory, a structure should be designed where each person's efforts add to, but do not duplicate or offset, the efforts of others in his unit. The efforts of each unit should then merge effectively with those of other units to maximize accomplishment of departmental goals. The ultimate objective of the organizing function is to facilitate accomplishment of the basic objectives of the enterprise. Organization structure is an instrument of management, a means to an end.

All organization structures are composed of the same three relationships established among the same three components. If responsibility, authority, and accountability are prescribed in one way, we can develop *line organization structure*. If they are established among jobs, personnel, and physical factors in another way, we have *line and staff structure*. And if they are set up in a third possible manner, we can create a *functionalized structure*. These are the three basic types of organization structure, and each will be discussed below. In addition, there will be a discussion of two other types of structure, *project* and *committee*, which are sometimes used as supplementary appendages to the three basic types.

LINE ORGANIZATION STRUCTURE

Following the criteria established in Chapter 8, line organization structure can be defined as the structural relationships resulting from functional differentiation downward of primary or organic functions. It will be recalled that in a manufacturing concern the three functions of production, sales, and finance are usually regarded as being primary or line functions. Thus, a pure line organization would consist of people either performing one of these functions, or in the direct chain of command above. Fig. 10–1 shows a three-level line organization structure in simplified form.

FIGURE 10–1   LINE ORGANIZATION STRUCTURE

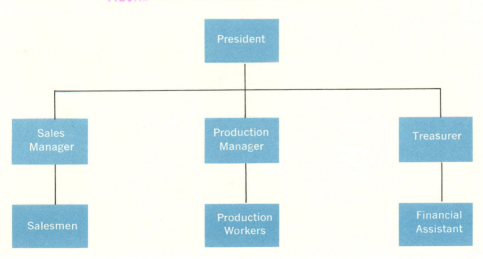

Bases of Departmentation

Thus far in this text, we have utilized the function as the prime basis for grouping to create jobs, sections, departments, and other organization elements. Other bases, however, can be adopted, such as (1) product, (2) geography, (3) customers, (4) time, and (5) numbers. When a firm is small, it typically begins as a line organization. Grouping is done on the basis of organic functions with the principle of functional similarity being paramount. Growth of the enterprise will usually lead to alternative grouping methods.

Departmentalizing on the basis of product or purpose requires that all functions bearing upon a particular product be grouped into a single coordinated unit. Thus, as indicated in Fig. 10–2, the second level of organization could consist of various product managers. Each of these product units has within it most of the required functions necessary for performance. Each has his own production and sales managers. Even though these divisions are a part of a single company, each may be established as a separate profit center; that is, they may be operated as separate companies for the most part. In this manner, stronger accountability for division results can be established inasmuch as each division is relatively free to deal or not deal with the other divisions in the company. For intra-company transactions, a comprehensive and accurate cost accounting system is an absolute prerequisite to maintenance of separate profit centers. The General Motors Corporation is an excellent example of a profit-center divisionalized enterprise. It will be noted, however, that the typical structure is a combination of bases, inasmuch as we have retained a centralization of the finance function on the second level along with the various groupings on the basis of product. This is, however, essentially a *product*-oriented structure, though *function* remains the basis for grouping within each product unit, and though it still provides the entire basis for finance.

This decentralized diversification is designed to produce such values as (1) development of a "whole" approach to each product including its development, production, and distribution; (2) more rapid decisions since the top level does not have to provide all coordination; (3) development of profit-oriented thinking closer to the point of operation, often resulting in demands for better justification of staff specialization; and (4) greater development and motivation of personnel, thereby contributing significantly to the executive talent pool of the enterprise. On the other hand, product divisionalization requires a larger supply of competent managers. It may also result in excessive duplication of specialized staffs and facilities in each of the divisions. It can also contribute to provincial thinking instead of company-wide concern, e.g., one division of a large corporation was so upset with the quality of raw materials received that

FIGURE 10–2   DEPARTMENTATION IN STRUCTURE

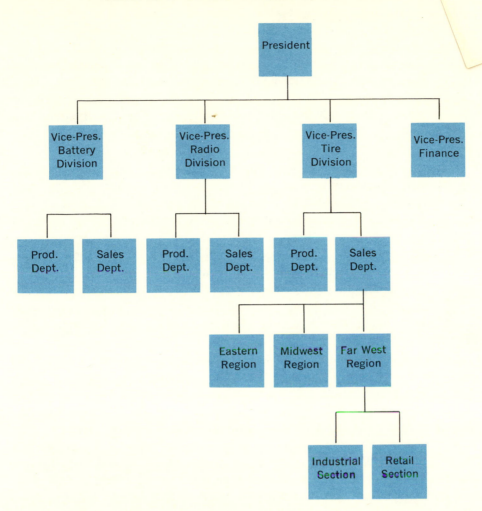

it was instituting legal action, not realizing that the supplier was a highly valued customer of two other corporate divisions. Some customers have been confused and dismayed when called upon by several different divisions of the same corporation, often using conflicting claims. Corporate divisions are also prone to give greater weight to short-term goals at the expense of investments whose payoff is farther in the future.

As indicated in the preceding chapter, there is no ideal mix of centralization, using the functional base, and decentralization, using the product rationale. When the total organizational task becomes too large and complex to be co-ordinated centrally, *some* portions will be broken loose with a consequent increase in risk and possible return. What portions and to what degree are questions involving a moving balance of values and disadvantages.

As organizations grow larger, there will be increasing decentralization in terms of geography as well as product. A unit can consist of all the activities within a certain geographic area or a certain plant which is separated from the rest of the company. The sales units of many firms utilize the geographical basis of departmentation. As shown in Fig. 10–2, the sales function within the Tire Division is further divided on the basis of geography with Eastern, Midwestern, and Far Western Managers. Thus, there is a combination of product, function, and geography for grouping activities in this organization.

A fourth basis, that of *customer*, can be exemplified by salesmen concentrating upon the consumer market for tires, while others work primarily with industrial users. This is shown on the fifth level of the chart in Fig. 10–2.

The other bases of grouping are less significant in their effect upon organization structure. However, it is apparent that one can divide into groups on the basis of sheer numbers. If, for example, there are 60 laborers digging ditches and performing various manual tasks, these men will probably be divided into smaller groups because of the span of control. The *time* basis recognizes the necessity of around-the-clock operation of some enterprises. A department may be set up on some other basis, e.g., function, but operate 24 hours a day. Therefore, we will need three shift foremen for the three separate groups.

Though a single comprehensive illustration has been used, it should be apparent that these various bases of grouping activities can be used at many and diverse places within any organization. A department store groups primarily upon the basis of product or commodity sold, but it also utilizes the customer base when it sets up a teenage shop or a bargain basement. The maintenance operation in a factory is established on the basis of function, but its own subdivision can be on the basis of geography, as certain groups of machinists and inspectors are assigned designated areas of the plant to patrol and maintain. In addition, a particular class of equipment may be so complex as to require specialized attention regardless of location. Thus, these specialists would be organized on the basis of product or purpose, while the rest are formed on the basis of geography.

Advantages of Line Structure

The primary advantage of the line organization structure is in its *simplicity* of relationships. Lines of accountability are clear and unmistakable. Responsibility and authority are more likely to be precise and understandable inasmuch as there exist no specialists who can cross organization lines. If one purpose of organization structure is to permit an effective relating of one person to another, there is an advantage when these relationships are simple enough to be readily understood by all.

A second advantage lies in the *speed* with which the organization can change direction and move. There are few people to consult when problems arise. We may not be able to get the latest and best scientific answer to a problem, but we do get an answer in a relatively short period. Sometimes speed and flexibility of movement more than make up for less precision and accuracy in deciding what is to be done.

Pure line organizations are small. Increasing size usually leads to the adoption of different forms. Thus, to the line organization can be attributed the advantages that accrue to small size. In the personnel area, for example, there is usually a greater feeling of closeness of management to the employee. The firm is also small enough for most people to be aware of what is going on. The larger the enterprise, the more impersonal and complex the relationship between labor and management.

A final comment about firms with line organization structures can be interpreted as either an advantage or disadvantage. The line organization permits and facilitates centralized control by one man. If that man is extremely able, he can effect a maximum of value throughout the firm. On the other hand, if he is less able, his limited ability will be felt throughout the structure.

Disadvantages of Line Structure

The basic disadvantage of line organization structure is, as implied above, its increasing lack of effectiveness as the enterprise grows in size. At some point, speed and flexibility do *not* offset lack of specialized knowledge and skill. Our all-around manager finds he can no longer fully cope with his job (see in Chapter 8 the discussion on the law of functional growth).

If the organization is still to remain purely line, one solution is for the central executive to seek help by creating additional levels of organization to spread the supervisory load. This, however, will result in a lengthening of the chain of command and a consequent loss of some of the values of speed, flexibility, and central control. In addition, the lack of the influence of staff specialists tends toward a provincial view of organization problems. The production man is concerned almost exclusively with his production problems, and the rest of the firm can look after itself. Sales personnel tend to have similar views, resulting in what some term "compartmentitis." All orientation is inward to the function and upward to the superior.

Thus, at some point in the growth curve of a firm, there will be a need for specialists in management. When provision is made for these specialists, one has altered the structure type from pure line to line and staff.

LINE AND STAFF STRUCTURE

Line and staff structure is a result of primary functional differentiation downward, *plus* secondary functional differentiation outward. A staff function is one that has been separated from a primary chain of command for purposes of specialization to produce economy and effectiveness of operation.

Types of Staff

Various methods of classifying types of staff have been proposed. One possibility is to differentiate on the basis of breadth of background—*general* staff and *specialized* staffs.

Someone in a general staff position usually possesses a background very similar to that of his line superior. His duty is to assist his superior in the function of coordination and control. In the military, the general staff is used as a coordinator of various specialized staffs in order to present a unified and consistent program to the line executive.[1]

In Fig. 10–3, two assistants to the president are indicated. If we assume that the first assistant's primary function is to aid the president in general coordination of the major functions, he can be designated a general staff man. If the second assistant's basic function is to be a legal advisor to the president, he would be a specialized staff man. Within the production division, the production control department performs a general staff function. It is the responsibility of this department to coordinate the various production sections with the specialized staffs of product engineering, industrial engineering, personnel, cost control, and materials.

There are usually more specialized staffs than general staffs. The typical conception of a staff man is one who knows more and more about less and less, until he knows everything about nothing. But as we have seen above, some staffs are of a general type requiring a broad background.

Within the specialized category, there are three subsidiary types: (1) advisory, (2) service, and, (3) control. It is possible, of course, though not usual, for a particular staff man or unit to perform all three of these functions.

An advisory staff man is a specialist who provides expert information and recommendations in his particular area. He makes studies, collects and interprets data, and suggests programs of action. Since his is a specialized viewpoint, the line superior must relate it to other general and specialized areas of

---

[1] Dale and Urwick feel that industrial managements could make more use of this concept. See Ernest Dale and Lyndall Urwick, *Staff in Organization* (New York: McGraw-Hill Book Company, 1960).

FIGURE 10–3 LINE AND STAFF STRUCTURE

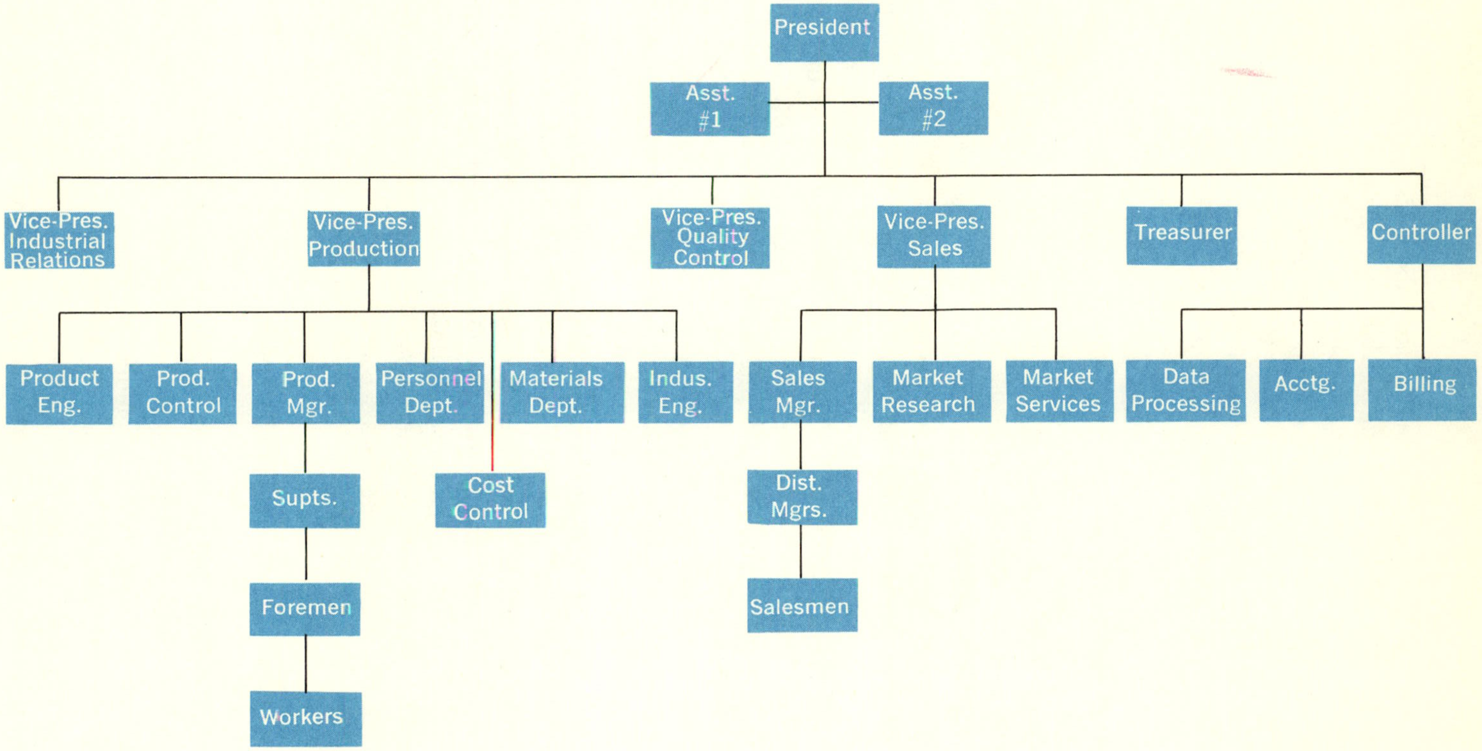

the organization. The specialist knows more about his speciality than his line superior, but the latter knows more about the general situation than the specialist. Examples of this type of staff would be the president's second assistant who specializes in legal matters (see Fig. 10–3), and an economist who has been employed to prepare business forecasts for the firm.

The second type of specialized staff performs some kind of facilitative service for the organization. Examples are personnel and materials departments. The staff personnel department procures employees, assists in their training, and administers wage and salary programs. When services are centralized and performed by a staff unit, it is important to define carefully what job is to be done and where the jurisdiction of the staff begins and ends. For example, if the materials purchasing function is centralized and performed by staff, should line supervisors be allowed to interview salesmen? Should line supervisors be permitted to contact and recruit potential employees when a central personnel department exists? What authority in hiring and purchasing should be given to staff and denied to supervisors? Moreover, in the large diversified organization, what purchases are to be made by central headquarters purchasing staffs, and what are to be delegated to divisional purchasers? Thus, there are higher staff-lower staff problems of division, as well as the more frequently noted line-staff difficulties. It is apparent that the service staff provides many opportunities for possible conflict between line and staff, more so than in the case of advisory staff. It is easier to reject advice than it is to reject service, particularly when that service is to be executed *only* by one central unit.

The third type of staff, control, provides the greatest chance for conflict between line and staff. Those on the control staff are functional specialists whose prime concern is with regulating some *phase* of organization activity. Quality control is an excellent example. Quality control personnel require a technical, specialized background and usually possess the authority to reject manufactured goods not made to approved specifications. Cost control is another good example of a specialized, control staff.

Principles of Line and Staff Relationships

It is apparent that the introduction of staff specialists into an organization complicates the clear and simple relationships of line structure. Experience has indicated that a series of formal guides or principles can help to ease any potential conflict between line and staff. Among these principles are the following: (1) staff advice, (2) limitation of staff economy, (3) compulsory staff advice, and (4) staff independence. The first two principles emphasize the organic and vital importance of the line functions; the second two insure that the values that are produced by staff units are properly utilized by the organization.

The *principle of staff advice* states that staff should not be given rights of command, but rather, rights of advice, suggestion, and recommendation. The personnel staff specialist recommends that a man be hired; he does not order it. The assistant to the president speaks in the name of his line chief and not in his own right. If the staff man seeks to issue orders, the integrity of the line is broken, resulting in a violation of single accountability, and possibly unity of command.

There are occasions, however, when the staff man is convinced of the merits of a recommendation he has made, and is not content to accept the rejection given by line personnel. Formally, his only alternative is to appeal to a common line superior. For example, let us assume that the industrial engineer in Fig. 10–3 has recommended to a production supervisor that the layout of his department be modified substantially. The supervisor considers this staff proposal and rejects it. The engineer will probably then attempt to persuade, argue with, and possibly pressure the supervisor to accept the new layout. If this fails, the engineer must decide whether his proposal is sufficiently important to merit appeal. Both men have a common line superior in the vice-president of production. An appeal can be presented and after hearing both sides, the vice-president can rule. If he decides in favor of the industrial engineer, the integrity of the line has been preserved, for the staff recommendation has been transformed into a line command. It is suggested, however, that formal appeals to a common superior be kept to a minimum. Such an act does not endear the engineer to the supervisor and future informal relationships are impaired. In addition, the vice-president doubtlessly would be impatient with persistent squabbling among his line and staff personnel. He would probably suggest that they both learn to work together without excessive use of the formal chain of command.

The second guide, the *principle of the limitation of staff economy,* also emphasizes the central role of line functions.[2] In order for the primary or line functions to be performed with *maximum* effectiveness, it is sometimes necessary for the supporting staff to operate with *less* than maximum economy. In other words, it is the function of staff to serve the line with expert advice and facilitative services. It is *not* the function of line to serve and adjust to staff. For example, the staff maintenance department could probably be operated more economically if it could regulate its work without adapting to the schedules of line personnel. Janitors would be hired to work only in the daytime and a row of offices would be cleaned up in sequence in the most economical manner. It matters little that executives and secretaries are inconvenienced;

[2] See Ralph C. Davis, *The Fundamentals of Top Management* (New York: Harper & Bros., 1951), p. 451.

maintenance must go through! This is obvious nonsense, but we do see the relationship of service. Maintenance often adjusts to the line by working at night and working *around* operations in order to minimize interference. This necessitates certain losses in economy. It also means that the size of maintenance or repair crews must approximate that necessary to care for peak loads, and not average loads. If we could smooth out maintenance requirements by storing machines to be repaired during slack periods, the size of crews could be reduced. But the line operator needs the machine *now,* and not a month later when the crew can get to it. Thus, the economy with which the maintenance department can be operated is *limited.*

The third principle suggested above serves to emphasize the values of staff. Even though the advice or service staffs have no command authority behind them, the line should listen. The *principle of compulsory staff advice* requires that line personnel listen and consider, but does *not* compel acceptance.[3] The theory is that if the advice and service is of superior caliber, issuing from the expertise of specialists, personnel will be influenced accordingly. Again, the line superior has a wider knowledge of events than does the staff specialist. The point is that the principle of compulsory staff advice rests on the theory of utilizing *all* talent that exists in an organization. Though line personnel may try to avoid specialized staff because of the latter's attempted revision of customary processes, or because of resentment at the loss of a function to staff, the principle requires that staff be heard. The specialist should not expect that his ideas will be bought wholesale without change. Whichever portion is useful will be accepted.

The final principle noted is concerned with freeing staff personnel from undue domination by line superiors. The *principle of staff independence* states that staff personnel should feel sufficiently secure to enable them to render truthful advice. There are some line superiors who demand a "yes-man" attitude on the part of their staffs. They want to hear *only* the advice that agrees with what they wish to do. In such an event, the line manager might just as well discharge his staff and save the money. The only true value being provided is the ego support that issues from a "belief" that several experts agree with him.

If, however, the line superior disagrees with a certain staff man's suggestions on *every* occasion, one or the other is destined to leave his position. The meaning of the relationship required by the principle is that the staff man feels that he *can* investigate and make truthful recommendations so that the organization can profit most from his expertise. He should not feel that he must study in depth his superior rather than his speciality.

These four principles constitute *broad* guides to action, and are not to be applied literally. In general, staff should attempt to avoid breaking the chain of

---

[3] See James D. Mooney, *The Principles of Organization* (New York: Harper & Bros., 1947), p. 119.

command, and should try to adjust to the line. And in general, the line should consult and work with staff, at the same time permitting a reasonable degree of freedom and voicing of conflicting opinions. Both line and staff must produce values within the organization. Though the incidence of such values is primary in the case of line, and secondary in the case of staff, recognition of the importance of these contributions is essential on the part of both groups if there is to be effective, organized action.

Advantages and Disadvantages of Line and Staff Structure

The primary advantage of the line and staff structure is the value issuing from expert specialization. The actions of the manager can become more scientific, through concentrated and skillful study of business problems. In addition the manager's effective span of control can be lengthened. Some types of staff operate as an extension of the manager's right arm, and assist in coordination and control.

The disadvantages of line and staff structure issue basically from the increased number and complexity of organization relationships. We have introduced various specialists who execute portions of functions extracted from existing chains of command. These staff personnel will know more about their specialties than will their line superiors. We must determine in some manner how they are to fit into the organization without destroying unity of command. The *right* of the line manager to command still remains, though his *ability* to do so may have been considerably diluted. Perhaps most of the disadvantages of line and staff structure issue from the particular people manning the structure. There is a tendency for the specialist to seek to enlarge his influence by usurping line authority in his speciality. This is compounded by a realization that the fundamental purpose of all staff is to produce greater economy and effectiveness of operation. This means that staff must attempt to introduce changes in the line, changes which result in more efficiency. These changes will not always be welcomed with open arms by line personnel. Thus, the introduction of specialized, non-command personnel into what was once a fairly simple organization structure serves to complicate relationships to a high degree.

FUNCTIONALIZED ORGANIZATION STRUCTURE

If the incumbent of a specialized function that has been differentiated outward from a primary chain of command is delegated *command* authority over others in regard to this speciality, a *functionalized* relationship has been created. Thus, in line organization there is limited specialization of management. In line and staff, we have introduced more specialization, but with only advisory authority; the integrity of the chain of command has been preserved. In the functionalized form, these specialists are given authority to issue orders in their own name. The chain of command is broken, thereby creating multiple accountability.

Nature of Functionalized Structure

There probably has never been a *completely* functionalized organization structure. Frederick Taylor almost created one with his eight functional foremen.[4] He broke the job of general foreman into eight narrower jobs. The worker therefore had eight supervisors, each with similar line authority. The principle of single accountability was violated on a wholesale basis. Perhaps it takes the genius of a Taylor to preserve unity of command with such a structure.

Even though few if any organizations are established on a completely functionalized basis, it is not unusual to functionalize the relationship between one or two specialists and the remainder of the organization. If a function is deemed to be of crucial importance, it may then be necessary for the specialist to serve in other than an advisory capacity. The violation of single accountability is undertaken deliberately. The possible losses issuing from confusion and conflicting orders from multiple sources may be more than offset by increased effectiveness in the specialty.

A good example of a function which is often functionalized is that of quality control. Not only has the function risen in structural level in many organizations, but its authority has often been increased sufficiently to merit the functionalized label. A staff quality control department would merely advise; if, however, that unit is empowered to issue orders in its own name, it can no longer be called staff. The chain of command has been split. As long as this splitting process is restricted, coordination and unity of action is not in excessive danger. If the function is extremely complex, highly important, or involves human life, organization members can realize the necessity of functionalized relationships and can work effectively under multiple bosses.

Many organizations who choose to utilize the functionalized relationships attempt to confine its impact to managerial rather than operative levels. Thus, the department supervisor may have to account to more than one boss, but his own subordinates are protected from this possible confusion. It is apparent that this type of authority relationship is difficult enough for members of management to understand without subjecting the operative level to it. No relationship is effective if it does not enhance cooperation and coordination. As indicated in Fig. 10–4, the functional specialist is not prevented from contacting directly the rank and file, but he is without the right to issue commands.

[4] Frederick W. Taylor, *Shop Management* (New York: Harper & Bros., 1911), pp. 99–109.

FIGURE 10–4   STAFF AND FUNCTIONALIZED RELATIONSHIPS

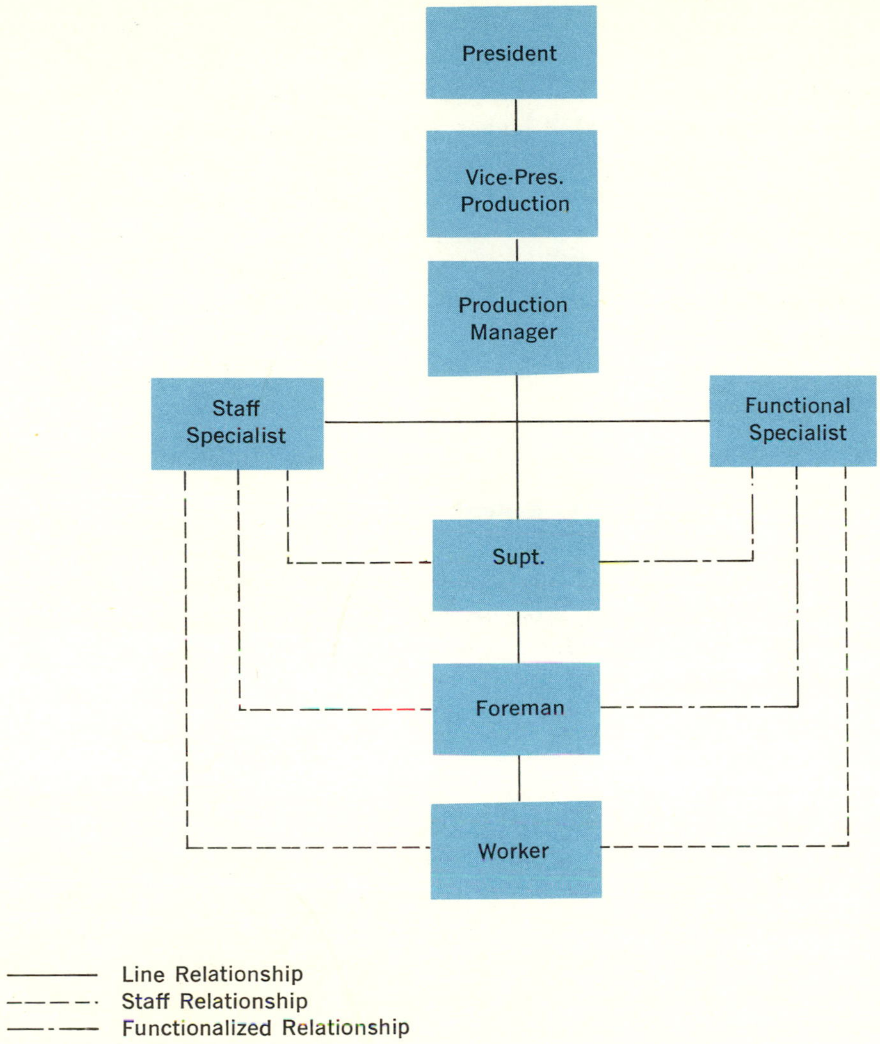

```
                        ┌──────────────┐
                        │  President   │
                        └──────────────┘
                        ┌──────────────┐
                        │  Vice-Pres.  │
                        │  Production  │
                        └──────────────┘
                        ┌──────────────┐
                        │  Production  │
                        │   Manager    │
                        └──────────────┘
┌──────────────┐                              ┌──────────────┐
│    Staff     │                              │  Functional  │
│  Specialist  │                              │  Specialist  │
└──────────────┘                              └──────────────┘
                        ┌──────────────┐
                        │    Supt.     │
                        └──────────────┘
                        ┌──────────────┐
                        │   Foreman    │
                        └──────────────┘
                        ┌──────────────┐
                        │    Worker    │
                        └──────────────┘
```

——————— Line Relationship
— — — · Staff Relationship
—— · —— Functionalized Relationship

His authority to require action in his specialized area is restricted to management levels. The staff specialist has only recommending authority to *all* personnel.

Advantages and Disadvantages of Functionalized Structure

The primary advantage of the functionalized structure is its maximum utilization of specialization. From the advisory authority of the staff specialist, we have moved to the command authority of the functional specialist.

Uniformity of action throughout the organization in the specialized function is greatly enhanced.

The disadvantages arise basically from the violation of the principle of single accountability, and a consequent endangering of unity of command. There is as well a greater potential for possible conflicts in command, and a tendency to keep authority centralized at higher levels in the organization. If used excessively, the line department supervisor may turn into a figurehead who merely communicates orders without participating in their determination. The structure can become tremendously complicated when there are corresponding functional specialists on multiple levels in the organization. The lower functional specialist may be subject to dual accountability—his line superior and his corresponding functional specialist on the next level up. Thus, this relationship should be used with caution and its need should be thoroughly ascertained prior to usage.

OTHER STRUCTURAL TYPES

Line, line and staff, and functionalized are the three basic structural types. All three can exist in a single organization. In addition to these types, there are other, supplementary structures. Among these are (1) the committee and (2) the project structure.

Committees

The committee is often presented as a separate type of organization structure. It can be defined as a group of persons, established on a standing or *ad hoc* basis, who discuss and develop solutions for problems requiring an integration of ideas and viewpoints. Such groups are usually set up as either line or staff, usually the latter, and thus do not constitute a separate and distinct structure.

Despite the problems of working as a group toward a decision, there are many legitimate uses to which a committee can be placed. Among these are:

1. Dealing with problems involving complex and diverse elements where no one person has the balanced perspective, and when the best solution is a compromise between legitimate but opposing viewpoints. For example, determining a correct policy on product diversification is highly adaptable to committee action where the legitimate, but often opposing, views of production, sales, engineering, and finance will be heard.

2. Dealing with problems of coordinating diverse functions. It is possible for

one supervisor, with an appropriate span of control, to attempt coordination. But often problems are so varied, wide, and complex that additional measures must be taken to insure coordination in terms of time and sequence of action. Where many elements and persons are involved, a committee can perform a useful function.

3. Securing acceptance of decisions. When one has had a part in the decision-making process as a committee member, he is more inclined to accept the resulting solution. A group decision on problems that involve highly subjective elements, such as determining who should be promoted to a higher position, often engenders greater acceptance than if it were made autocratically by a single individual.

4. Making more legitimate the exercise of authority and power. The board of directors is a line committee and one of its justifications is that it is an *elected* and representative body which can oversee the actions of the enterprise's management. This function is more acceptable to society when performed by a group of elected representatives rather than by a single individual. There are instances when these boards become "tired fictions," in effect appointed and controlled by the managements they are supposed to oversee. In such cases, the usefulness of the committee system is placed in considerable jeopardy.

Though the committee has a place in organization structure, it possesses a number of disadvantages. Among the more apparent is that it is a slow, expensive, and often painful process of reaching a decision. A single executive can reach decisions in a fraction of the time with much less direct expense. The committee also has the characteristic of divided responsibility; it is difficult to hold members accountable for the actions of the group. There is also a tendency to work toward the lowest common denominator, the compromise answer that everyone will accept, though the best answer is not always the most popular. There are also dangers of group domination by one or several members, and the possibility of continued indecisiveness leading to a break-down of group action. The latter disadvantage is sometimes used as a positive value by certain executives. If one wishes to do nothing about a problem, assigning the problem to a carefully chosen committee may accomplish this result (i.e., nothing) without giving the appearance of unwillingness to take action.

As indicated in the preceding chapter, there is a tendency to move to group, committee management at the presidential level in large organizations. The complexity and the significance of major decisions seem to require group deliberation despite the disadvantages of slowness and divided responsibility. In the United States, one man in the top management group is almost always designated as the final authority, e.g., president or chairman of the board. The basic concept of a single final authority is rarely given up completely. It is interesting to note, however, that various European managements have gone so far in the group management direction that the single final authority has been abandoned. In four of seventeen Dutch companies and five of thirty-three German firms, the top managing committee had no chairman.[5] In the remaining firms, all of whom used the plural executive concept, a chairman was designated as "first among equals." He acted as the moderator and the voice of the group. Such an approach demands teamwork in the application of multiple talents to major problems. It is also affected by the usual byproducts of slowness in decision making, log rolling, diffusion of responsibility, and frustration of strong individual entrepreneurial instincts. It is yet another attempt to introduce specialized talent into organizations requiring knowledgeable decisions and coordinated action. Though the approach to top management in the above cited firms is one of group democracy, there was little evidence that collegial decision making was carried very far down within the supporting hierarchies.

Project Structure

The various line, line and staff, and functionalized structures have been generally called "bureaucratic structures" by behaviorists. This goes back to the original use of the term by Max Weber at the turn of the century as he was emphasizing such characteristics as form, hierarchy, specialization of task, emphasis upon competence in manning, systems of rules, and impersonality of interpersonal relations.[6] Primary concern is with the establishment and distribution of authority to coordinate the enterprise, with a resulting emphasis upon vertical, rather than horizontal, relationships.

Behaviorists have been quick to point out the inhibiting effects of a hierarchy based on authority. Work processes may flow horizontally, diagonally, down, or up depending upon the problem and distribution of talents. Project structures have been introduced into more traditional structures in order to adapt to the requirements of work. The general result has been an enhancement of work effectiveness at some cost in clarity and understandability of organizational relationships.

Work projects are performed in all organizations. Procedures can be established which specify the sequential relationship of activities among various specialized parts of the enterprise. At times, the project gets lost, delayed, or

---

[5] F. Newton Parks, "Group Management, European Style," *Business Horizons,* Vol. 9, No. 3 (Fall, 1966), p. 85.

[6] H. H. Gerth and C. Wright Mills, trans., *From Max Weber: Essays in Sociology* (New York: Oxford University Press, 1946).

confused. No single agency is directly concerned with the entire project. Of course, top management is generally concerned with the long-term performance of various functional entities, and to a lesser extent with the specific performance of particular projects. If a management desires to emphasize strongly a specific project, a particular structure may be created. Such specific efforts are usually confined to undertakings that are (1) definable in terms of a specific goal, (2) somewhat unique and unfamiliar to the existing organization, (3) complex with respect to interdependence of activities necessary to accomplishment, (4) critical with respect to possible gain or loss, and (5) temporary with respect to duration of need.[7]

The project type of structure is a highly effective means by which all of the necessary talent and resources can be focused for a time on a specific project goal. When that goal is accomplished, the structure should be abolished. Some of the more commonly known uses of this concept were the task forces of World War II. The mission may be that of conquering a particular island in the Pacific. For this, a team is created composed of members of the Army, Navy, Marines, and Air Force. Each member is chosen for his particular capabilities in light of the goal to be accomplished and an organization structure is created. When the mission is accomplished, the task force is broken up and personnel are returned to regular organization components.

The most popular current use of this concept is in the aerospace industry where project teams are created for specific space or weapon systems or components thereof. For example, one type of skill that is of use in a space vehicle project is a "human-factors" specialist. This specialist reports to his regular human-factors supervisor who has charge of a department manned by psychologists, sociologists, anthropologists, and physiologists. Such a department would conduct studies on human adaptability to various environments which may be encountered with the products manufactured by the company. When a particular project team is formed, a specific human-factors specialist is assigned to it along with the other specialists, technical and managerial, needed to accomplish the goal. The human-factors specialist must meet the time and quality requirements of his project officer, while at the same time satisfying his regular supervisor on the general quality of work turned out. He secures his merit evaluations, compensation, and advancements from his regular supervisor who is influenced by reports from the various project officers for whom he has worked.

Project structure is an additional, supplementary, and horizontally oriented attachment to the existing, vertical traditional organization. The traditional, functional departments do the work, but the project officer is responsible for its application to his project. In simple terms, the project officer will specify *what*

---

[7] John M. Stewart, "Making Project Management Work," *Business Horizons*, Vol. 8, No. 3 (Fall, 1965), p. 54.

effort is needed and *when* it will be performed, while the concerned department managers may well decide *who* in their unit is to do the work and *how* it is to be accomplished. Home base for most personnel is the existing department, e.g., engineering, machine shop, purchasing, human factors, etc. Temporarily, they, or a portion of their time, are on loan to the project officer. The project officer slices through the organization in the specific interest of his one undertaking.

The greatest current use of this concept of organization is in industries with highly complex product systems. A survey of various forms in use shows four dominant types: (1) an *individual* project manager who has no activities or personnel reporting to him; (2) a *unit* project organization where the manager is provided with assistants who aid in scheduling, funds supervision, and coordination; (3) an *intermix* type when some of the basic operative functions are removed from existing departments and assigned full time to the project manager, while others remain more in the control of existing departments; and (4) an *aggregate* organization where all activities and personnel are assigned to the project manager.[8] The last form provides no unusual problem in terms of authority and coordination. It is still labeled the project approach because of its presumed temporary nature.

It is apparent that one of the crucial questions created by this form of structure is that of authority. A deliberate conflict has been established between the project officer and existing department heads.[9] The authority delegations are overlapping, presumably in the interest of assuring that all problems will be covered. Both project managers and department heads are virtually forced into using means *other* than formal authority. A survey of 46 companies revealed that negotiation, personality and persuasive ability, and respect for competence were relied upon heavily by reporting project managers.[10] Informal relationships become more important than formal prescriptions of authority. In the event of conflict and dispute, discussion and consensus are required rather than forcing of compliance through threat or punishment. This deliberate conflict was made evident in a detailed study of 26 project managers and 26 general managers in six defense/aerospace firms located in the western United States.[11] The percentage of agreement on the project manager's decision-making authority in crucial areas was about 80

[8] C. J. Middleton, "How to Set Up a Project Organization," *Harvard Business Review*, Vol. 45, No. 2 (March–April, 1967), p. 75.

[9] David I. Cleland, "The Deliberate Conflict," *Business Horizons*, Vol. 11, No. 1 (February, 1968), pp. 78–80.

[10] Richard M. Hodgetts, "Leadership Techniques in the Project Organization," *Academy of Management Journal*, Vol. 11, No. 2 (June, 1968), p. 215.

[11] Richard A. Goodman, "Ambiguous Authority Definition in Project Management," *Academy of Management Journal*, Vol. 10, No. 4 (December, 1968), pp. 395–407.

percent; that is, one-fifth of the managers in each company did not agree concerning his rights. Greatest disagreement concerned the project manager's rights in exceeding personnel ceilings during emergencies, canceling subcontracts and bringing the work in-house, and selecting subcontractors. His authority was more clear in such areas as initiating work in the supporting departments, assigning priorities for work in support areas, authorizing total overtime budget, authorizing subcontractors to exceed cost and schedules, and determining content of the original proposal for the project. He does not usually have final authority in make or buy decisions, canceling subcontracts, hiring additional people, or in determining the initial price of the proposal.

The project manager is fully responsible for the success of the project. The existing department manager is fully responsible for the technical excellence and quality of the tasks in his area of specialization. Operative personnel performing these tasks, often highly skilled technicians and professionals, are therefore accountable to multiple managers. The effectiveness of the concept in operation shows that man can work for two or more masters, and that a master can effectively influence those over whom he has no clear authority. The possibility of conflict and frustration is great, but the opportunity for prompt, expeditious, and effective accomplishment is even greater. The coordinative power of knowledge and expertise make up in part for the vagueness and complexity of formal organizational relationships. Both project officers and supporting managers must maintain an open mind and be willing to negotiate. Full and free communication, regardless of formal rank, is required among those working on the project. More attention is allocated to roles and competencies in relation to the project than to formal levels of authority. In essence, we move to the general atmosphere prescribed by behaviorists for the management of professionals. As a final note, it is interesting to see that as the size of the project increases, there is a reversion to the more traditional approaches of authority definition and impersonality.[12] It suggests the existence of some practical limitations upon the implementation of behavioral concepts.

MANNING THE STRUCTURE

On the basis of an analysis of objectives, functions have been determined and grouped, responsibility has been delegated, organizational rights have been prescribed, and provision for accountability has been made. The organization structure has been designed; to complete the organizing process, this structure must be manned.

The manning process is beyond the scope of this book, but its relation to the

[12] Hodgetts, "Leadership Techniques in the Project Organization," p. 218.

organizing process should be recognized and understood.[13] On the basis of the original layout of units of responsibility and authority, job descriptions and job specifications must be prepared. A job description is a statement of the functions and responsibilities required of the incumbent of a unit of work; it is a standard of function. A job specification is a statement of the human qualities necessary to execute these responsibilities; it is a standard of personnel. Thus, the classical approach is to design the job units according to principles, and deduce the type of people who can best fill the requirements.

With this specification of manning requirements, the next step is to recruit applicants for the job openings. If many apply, the chances for a successful matching of man and job will be improved. The many that apply must be screened in some fashion to determine whether they have the requisite qualifications. All screening devices, such as psychological tests, interviews, references, application blanks, and physical examinations, should issue from the job analysis. What does the opening require? What does this man possess in the way of qualifications? On this basis, screening is accomplished and the structure manned. There are a host of problems involved in this process such as (1) the possible inability to locate a man who matches the opening, thus necessitating a reorganization; (2) a personnel policy that requires use of present personnel rather than recruiting outsiders, thus necessitating alteration of ideal units of responsibility and authority; (3) the inability to measure precisely the characteristics of human beings; and (4) the inability to measure precisely the human requirements of the job. Nevertheless, the basic approach of job analysis, job description, job specification, recruitment, and screening is the fundamental one for manning the organization structure.

Summary

All organizations consist of basic factors and relationships. The factors of personnel, functions, and physical factors are combined by means of responsibility, authority, and accountability into a structural harness. The type of structure can be line, line and staff, or functionalized.

In the simple, direct line type, all personnel are performing basic, organic functions, or are located in a chain of command above these functions. The line and staff form introduces the complexities of specialists of an advisory service, or control nature. To indicate how these specialists should be tied into the structure, there are such basic guides as the following: (1) staff should be advisory; (2) staff should adjust its service to line requirements; (3) staff should be heard; and (4) staff should feel sufficiently secure to give truthful advice.

The functionalized form of structure takes fullest advantage of specialization

---

[13] For more complete coverage, see Edwin B. Flippo, *Principles of Personnel Management,* 2nd ed. (New York: McGraw-Hill Book Company, 1966), Chaps. 7–10.

while increasing organization complexity. When the staff specialist is given the authority to issue orders concerning his specialty, he is transformed into a functional specialist. This violates the principle of single accountability but does have the advantage of insuring uniformity and expertness in the particular function concerned.

Other supplementary types of structure are committees and project or task force structures. These are used on special problems where the above types of structures are deemed inadequate. After the structure has been designed, it must be manned with people. The classical approach is to locate people to fit the jobs developed from rational analysis. Once we have selected particular people to fill these openings, the stage has been set for informal organization. This subject will be covered at length in the following chapters.

DISCUSSION PROBLEMS

1. Indicate the various ways that specialized knowledge can be introduced into an organization.
2. How can an organization's need for coordination and control be reconciled with its need for highly specialized and skilled knowledge?
3. Can a committee make a good president? Discuss.
4. Identify and discuss the classical principles that guide in establishing line and staff relationships. Which ones defend the importance of line?
5. When organizing on the basis of product, what values are derived? What difficulties are encountered?
6. If a personnel manager asks that line foremen training classes be held at 8 A.M. daily because that is his slack period, what principle is he violating? How?
7. If the President of the United States uses his Council of Economic Advisers primarily for testifying before Congress in support of his economic programs, what principle is he likely to be violating? How?
8. Define and distinguish among line authority, staff authority, and functional authority. What is the justification for each?
9. What is organization structure? What are its uses? What are its undesirable side-effects?
10. What is the nature of the manning task created by formal organization structure?

SUPPLEMENTARY READING

Cleland, David I., "Understanding Project Authority," *Business Horizons,* Vol. 10, No. 1 (Spring, 1967), 63–70.

Gemmill, Gary R., "How Managers Use Staff Advice," *Personnel,* Vol. 45, No. 4 (September–October, 1968), 48–52.

Gilman, Glenn, "The Computer Revisited," *Business Horizons,* Vol. 9, No. 4 (Winter, 1966), 77–89.

Goodman, Richard A., "Ambiguous Authority Definition in Project Management," *Academy of Management Journal,* Vol. 10, No. 4 (December, 1967), 395–407.

Hughes, Everett C., "Preserving Individualism on the R&D Team," *Harvard Business Review,* Vol. 46, No. 1 (January–February, 1968), 72–82.

Middleton, C. J., "How to Set Up a Project Organization," *Harvard Business Review,* Vol. 45, No. 2 (March–April, 1967), 73–82.

Parks, F. Newton, "Group Management, European Style," *Business Horizons,* Vol. 9, No. 3 (Fall, 1966), 83–90.

Walker, Arthur H. and Jay W. Lorsch, "Organizational Choice: Product vs. Function," *Harvard Business Review,* Vol. 46, No. 6 (November–December, 1968), 129–138.

Section B

Informal Organization

In addition to the formal relationships established by the manager, the personnel within an organization will develop unofficial relationships that have great impact upon goal accomplishment (Chapter 11). Among the more significant informal relationships are those concerned with status, power, and politics (Chapter 12). And finally, the manager must be concerned with the human impact of the work systems that he has devised for use (Chapter 13).

11

Informal Organization

In the three preceding chapters, we have discussed the development of *formal* organization structure. We ended with the placing of people into the logically designed and related slots within that structure. Now the organization comes *alive* with the actions, sentiments, feelings, and attitudes of multiple and varied personalities. Formal organization consists of the official, authorized relationships prescribed by management. Informal organization consists of the myriad relationships, unofficial and unauthorized, created by the many individual personalities and groups within the formal organization. Without the formal, the informal would not exist. However, abolition of the informal organization would require (if you will) the abolition of people. It is the purpose of this chapter to examine the nature of informal organization, its values and costs, and some of the specific techniques of charting these relationships.

NATURE OF INFORMAL ORGANIZATION

It would be the height of naïveté for any manager to assume that he could prescribe and control every relationship among all persons within his employ. Relationships will spring up spontaneously, inevitably, and on a continuing basis. Some of these relationships are based on emotion: John Jones likes Joe Smith; he is indifferent to Jim Clark; and he detests Paul Black. Though in many instances there is no necessity for management to be concerned as to whether or not subordinates like each other, nevertheless their feelings will undoubtedly affect the quality of cooperation that exists among, for example, the four people above. Other informal relationships are sometimes termed "non-formal"; they constitute acts related to job performance which are not officially prescribed in the organization manual, standing operating procedure, or company policy.[1] Sometimes such acts serve to fill in structural gaps, since no official document can prescribe in minute detail every movement, thought, or decision that should be made in each instant of time. Still other informal acts can, of course, constitute violations of prescribed relationships; as when John Jones agrees to perform one of Joe Smith's official duties.

There is no choice as to whether or not there will be an informal organization. The traditional manager can, of course, attempt to design the formal structure as tightly as possible, thus seeking to minimize informal relationships. Or, on the other hand, the behaviorist may attempt to design the structure quite loosely in the interest of encouraging individual initiative and self-regulation. We must go back again to the basic question, raised in Chapter 6, concerning the nature of man. If one assumes that the typical man is shortsighted, lazy, selfish, and has poor judgment, one will attempt to structure the organization tightly and restrict the room in which to maneuver. If one assumes the opposite, one moves away from the precise, engineered model of structure, giving up some formal control so as to profit more from individual ingenuity, imagination, and responsibility. In either event, informal organization is a fact of organization life.

Although informal relationships are infinite and their nature is highly varied, attempts have been made to describe various types. Two basic relationships, status and power, will be discussed in the following chapter. In enlarging the formal concept of the job to include these additional variables, the sociologists have introduced the term "role." A role would consist not only of the formal description of the job, but also the normally expected behavior and attitudes of the job-holder. "Normally expected behavior and attitudes" can, of course, differ with the perspective of the observer. An executive will want his supervisors to act and think like managers, to be true to the role of supervisor. The supervisor's subordinates will have somewhat different role expectations for him, but they are often able to understand his behavior by viewing it as a part of his supervisory role. Most people must fill multiple roles. The worker in the shop is perhaps also a member of the union, a senior man in the group, and a shop representative on a production committee. Outside of the organization, his roles may be those of father, member of the church, officer in a lodge, and citizen.

In addition to interpersonal relationships within informal organization, there is a marked tendency to create another major component, the primary or social group. A social group exists when a relatively small number of people share

---

[1] Robert Dubin, *Human Relations in Administration* (Englewood Cliffs: Prentice-Hall, Inc., 1961), p. 84.

common values and develop a pattern of relationships solidifying the group and giving it a definite character of its own. Unless the employee is completely isolated, he probably will belong to one or more social groups within the enterprise. These groups are usually formed spontaneously and naturally, though their shaping can be influenced by formal management organization and physical layout. Norms of behavior are developed, and social pressures are applied to "nonconformists." Members of the group tend to be homogeneous, that is, the social distances between them are not great. Often informal leaders will develop, and their leadership is accepted out of respect and/or affection. Sociologists believe that the social unit, rather than the individual, is the basic component of effective organizations in action.

Thus informal groups tend to possess the following characteristics: (1) a tendency to remain small; (2) the satisfaction of group member wants; (3) the development of unofficial leadership; (4) a highly complex structure of relationship; and (5) a tendency toward stability.

Since interpersonal relationships are the essence of informal organization, the informal group must remain small enough so that its individual members can interact frequently.

Informal groups come into being primarily in response to the "extraorganizational" wants of its members. In the first place, interpersonal contacts provide some relief from boredom, monotony, and the pressures of formal organization. Second, opportunities for informal status are made available through the respect and prestige sought for within the group and accorded by it. In addition, a degree of personal security is provided—the group member knows that he is accepted as an equal by his peers. He can also take heart in the fact that the group can exert more influence and power against or for the formal organization than an individual can.

Inevitably, the informal group will develop unofficial leadership, often in multiple areas of activity. A spokesman for the group may present requests to official management; another member may be the informal leader in the area of dress and social habits. This type of leadership rests solidly upon acceptance by others rather than upon formal authority prescribed by management.

A final characteristic of informal organization is the group's basic tendency toward stability. It has been stated that informal groups tend to resist changes of all types by applying sanctions against group members to prevent deviation from group-held norms. There have been many instances where a nonconforming member was consigned to a state of social isolation for breaches of behavioral norms. Groups also tend to resist changes imposed from without by management or other agencies; consequently, many managers view informal groups as a negative force inhibiting dynamic and forward-looking management. But, on the other hand, this stability should be recognized as a state in which much productive work can be effected (management would call it "dynamic stability"). When changes are introduced so rapidly that they inhibit interpersonal relations and the formation of strong informal groups, the rates of absenteeism, turnover, and grievances tend to rise substantially while productivity decreases. It takes time to form strong interpersonal ties among people, but these ties can be broken overnight by official acts of management.

VALUES OF INFORMAL ORGANIZATION

It is fortunate that management does not have the option of destroying the informal organization, as it is the source of many positive values which can contribute to greater organizational effectiveness. Among these values are the following:

1. Enables the greater bulk of the organization's work to get done.
2. Patches up gaps and deficiencies in the formal structure.
3. Aids in lengthening the effective span of control.
4. Compensates for the unavoidable violation of some formal organizational principles.
5. Provides an additional channel of communication.
6. Provides necessary social values and satisfactions.
7. Stimulates better and more sensitive management.

These values will be discussed in the following sections.

Facilitates Accomplishment of Work

It is doubtful that any traditional management theorist ever imagined that he might insist on approving every move and word in advance. If people in any organization acted only when they were told to act, followed standard instructions to the letter at all times, and contacted others only when duly authorized, operations would quickly grind to a halt. However, the traditionalist does tend to rely more heavily on formal decisions and documents based upon a scientific study of business problems. He would leave less room for individual variations than a behaviorist would. Again, it is a matter of degree. When a traditionalist sees a largely unstructured situation, or one involving a violation of roles (such as the operative making management decisions or executing engineering work for which he has little formal background), he is immediately inclined to "clean up" the situation and bring order out of this "chaos." Unfortunately, this is often true, even where the productivity and creativity of this unstructured group is vastly superior to similar, but more highly regulated, groups. There are also occasions when the formal command is wrong or inadequate for the situation. If the atmosphere is heavily traditional, subordinates may exhibit "malicious obedience" through executing the command faithfully despite personal knowledge of inevitable failure. If more faith is placed in informal relationships, subordinates may voluntarily adapt the command to requirements of the actual situation. When loosely structured groups are able to achieve organization objectives more effectively in an informal manner, one must admit the superiority of the informal over the tightly structured. As indicated in Chapter 7, deviations from regulations should not be *automatically* classified as mistakes. What is needed is a *flexible* managerial approach based upon formal structuring, permitting and even encouraging deviations in the interest of material contributions toward organization goals.

Alleviates Deficiencies in the Formal Structure

As mentioned above, the formal organization often has within it a number of gaps which the informal can fill. For example, in traditional theory the job is designed along logical lines and a man is hired to fill it. Theoretically, the man is perfectly matched to the job. But, as a practical matter, this perfect fit rarely occurs. To compensate, the man usually reworks the boundaries of his job to attain some acceptable compromise. Thus, instead of the set of logically designed jobs depicted in Chapter 9, there may, in practice, be a number of oddly shaped jobs. Even with such personalization of the job, our main concern is whether the job requirements are being met. If the results are compounded of inefficient gaps and overlaps, management will have to enter the situation with more structuring.

As a tangible example of a gap in the formal structure, let us consider a person who is promoted to a position that exceeds his current capabilities. This is not an unusual occurrence in the armed services, for instance, where a young officer is appointed unit commander. The formal orders and regulations say that he *is* the commander, with certain responsibilities and authorities. If he admits his temporary inadequacies, he may obtain help from other officers and his enlisted personnel. For a while, he is not filling the position adequately. In effect, deficiencies in the formal structure have been alleviated by the officer's sharing decision making to a high degree with the first sergeant. It is hoped, however, that with further learning the informal may resemble the formal more closely. If not, then perhaps the first sergeant should be made commander legally as well as in fact.

There are additional examples of discrepancies between formal structures and those who work within them. A manager in one firm was excellent in direction and control, but realized his limitations in planning. In time, he discovered a subordinate who was adept in this area and moved to establish him as his planning assistant. Thus, realization of one's inability to fully meet job requirements, as laid down by the formal organization, leads in some instances to greater use of subordinate participation in management decision making.

Finally, quite often a job incumbent feels that another member of the organization is not living up to his assignment. Instead of reporting this to a superior, the job incumbent may pass over, or patch up, this difficulty by performing additional unofficial duties himself or by stimulating others to take on unofficial tasks. More than one employee in a business organization has been protected from official surveillance by these unofficial helpful acts of his colleagues. To reiterate, then, the informal organization deals with behavior as it *actually* occurs in an enterprise; the formal structure deals with behavior as it *should* occur.

Enables Lengthening of the Effective Span of Control

We indicated earlier that the caliber of subordinates is one of many factors that help to determine the effective length of a span of control.[2] We can now take into account the factor of informal relationships. The more the group learn to work together on their own, the greater the number of personnel who can be included in one executive's span. There is some disagreement on the current level of knowledge concerning effective small-group behavior, as exhibited by the contradictory statements of Suojanen and Urwick. As Suojanen states:[3]

The gist of the argument advanced here is that the span of control is no longer a valid principle of organization in view of the advances that have occurred in those social sciences that relate directly to administrative theory. The emergence of the primary group concept leads logically to group coordination.

To this, Urwick replies:[4]

[2] See Chapter 7.

[3] Waino W. Suojanen, "The Span of Control—Fact or Fable?" *Advanced Management,* Vol. 20, No. 11 (November, 1955), p. 13.

[4] Lyndall F. Urwick, "Span of Control—Some Facts About the Fable," *Advanced Management,* Vol. 21, No. 11 (November, 1956), p. 5.

Perhaps he will pardon an unconvinced "Span of Controller" from putting the simple question, "What advances in what social sciences since when?"

As individuals and small groups *do* learn to interact more effectively and are permitted to do so by their managers, the manager should be able to devote less time to coordination and integration, which could well contribute to a lengthening of his effective span. Advances in knowledge concerning the social or primary group add one more factor to consider in reaching a conclusion as to the effective span of control.

Compensates for Violations of Formal Organization Principles

The development of informal relationships also influences the effectiveness of certain traditional principles of formal organization. For example, it has been pointed out that the principle of parity of responsibility and authority is often violated.[5] As a result, the employee, in order to get his job done, tries to develop *informal* contacts with personnel over whom he has no formal authority. Favors are traded and friendships formed or simulated. One quickly learns that the formal prescription of authority often is not a sufficient base for operation. Yet this still does not negate the desirability of *attempting* an equation of responsibility and authority as the formal foundation upon which these informal relationships are to develop.

We mentioned before that as the size and complexity of business enterprises grow, single accountability becomes increasingly difficult to maintain. A man is often compelled to work for two or more bosses. And yet, just as development of informal relationships among *subordinates* enables a lengthening of the effective span of control, the development of informal working relationships among *superiors* may enable the retention of unity of command despite the violation of single accountability. If multiple bosses are well-coordinated on an informal basis, consistent orders can probably still be effected. Various industrial firms have developed a plural chief executive office. Needless to say, the members of this office must develop relationships over and above any formal ones prescribed by the organization manual. In these situations, the individual assumes a greater measure of importance, since informal relationships are person-centered and person-created. The number and nature of the relationships will vary with the situation. It is not a matter of formally defining a job, with assigned personnel assuming the characteristics of interchangeable parts. The importance of the person tends to increase while the importance of job-description precision tends to decrease.

[5] Douglas McGregor, *The Human Side of Enterprise* (New York: McGraw-Hill Book Company, 1960), p. 158.

Provides Additional Channel of Communication

The informal organization provides an additional channel of communication for the enterprise. To some traditional managers, the "grapevine" constitutes an obstacle to be destroyed, as they seek to channel and control most, if not all, communications through the official chain of command. However, the grapevine can add to organization effectiveness if the manager will study and use it. The grapevine is fast, highly variable, and usually accurate in the information it transmits (two studies have shown that when the information being conveyed concerns noncontroversial company data, it is accurate more than three-quarters of the time[6]). Keith Davis has concluded that most grapevines operate in a cluster-chain fashion; that is, one person operates as a source for many people, rather than for just one.[7] If management is to utilize the grapevine as a means of getting certain information to the employee group, it must find the source and make sure that truthful information is fed into it. If management is to utilize it as a means of determining what feelings the employees have, it must identify and tap the outlets. Certain people can be identified as one-way funnels; that is, they receive information and pass it on but do not feed back reactions. Others are two-way funnels, receiving and returning information.

The grapevine has certain disadvantages. It will spread rumors and false information as rapidly as it will facts. It also tends to outstrip formal channels on speed, enabling unauthorized personnel to receive information long before their supervisors do. To overcome this in one plant during collective bargaining periods, the management established a telephone number which the supervisors could dial daily to hear a tape of the latest information on the progress of bargaining. This enabled these supervisors to be at least equal to their subordinates in speed, thus maintaining or enhancing their status as managers "in the know." However, the employees made a game of trying to use this secret number, too. Management decided not to discourage this, since they preferred the employees to hear management views on the issues. And the information was made all the more attractive by the employees' feeling that they were obtaining it through unauthorized means. This is only one technique of feeding a grapevine; others are available to a management desiring to disseminate information through unofficial channels.

The use of the grapevine does not decrease the importance of the official channel of communication and command. The grapevine can spread much

---

[6] Eugene Walton, "How Efficient Is the Grapevine?" *Personnel*, Vol. 38, No. 2 (March–April, 1961), p. 48, and Keith Davis, *Human Relations at Work*, 3rd ed. (New York: McGraw-Hill Book Company, 1967), p. 224.

[7] *Ibid.*, p. 225.

information in a short period, but it cannot provide the authority that is necessary for much of the action that will take place.

Provides Means of Social Satisfaction

Over half of all voluntary resignations in many organizations occur within the first six months of employment. Some of these may be due to poor selection and placement techniques, resulting in a mismatch of man and job. Most, however, are the result of poor induction procedures, where the new employee is not aided in the process of joining one or more informal groups. Doing one's job well is undeniably one source of personal satisfaction. But if a company is so cold and impersonal that few informal, interpersonal contacts are permitted or encouraged, many new employees will seek employment elsewhere. Friendships, or at least speaking acquaintances, are highly essential to a satisfactory working environment for most people. The plant or office is a community of people. Only the informal relationships established by persons and groups can meet the needs of acceptance and gregariousness. Management can attempt either to aid or to hinder this process of establishing primary groups.

Like almost everything else in management theory, extremes are to be avoided. There can be too few informal contacts and groupings, resulting in a highly formal, cold, and impersonal organization. Or we can have too many, thus turning the workplace into a social circle with a detrimental effect upon work output. This is why management is still largely an art of apportioning.

Stimulates Better Management

Awareness of the nature and impact of informal organization often leads to better management decisions. Acceptance of the fact that formal relationships will not enable full accomplishment of organization tasks stimulates management to seek other means of motivation. If most of the work is done informally, the manager will seek to improve his knowledge of the nature of people in general and his subordinates in particular. If he realizes that organization performance can be affected by the granting or withholding of cooperation and enthusiasm, he will seek other means than the formal to develop desirable attitudes. He will not depend solely upon the authority of his position.

In addition, if he studies his groups, he will discover that just as there are individual personalities and differences, there are also group personalities and differences. Knowledge of these group characteristics will improve his management by enabling more accurate prediction of group behavior and reactions to his own orders and requests. Sayles discovered in one of his studies the following types of groups in one plant: (1) apathetic, (2) erratic, (3) strategic, and (4) conservative.[8] Apathetic groups were found to have relatively few grievances, but they exhibited signs of suppressed discontent and internal friction. There was no discernible informal leadership. The erratic groups exhibited inconsistent behavior, ranging from good relations with management to sudden and explosive rebellion. These groups tended to have highly autocratic informal leaders. Strategic groups showed well-planned and consistent grievance activity and a high degree of internal unity. They tended to apply continuous pressure on management for desired action. The conservative groups were the most stable and self-confident. Often management had more grievances against these groups than the groups had against management. They would pressure management when it was thought necessary for highly specific objectives.

The types of jobs and physical layout were two of the major factors affecting the formation of these various groups. The jobs of the apathetic groups were relatively low-skilled, low-paying, and located sequentially on a relatively long assembly line. The erratic groups held substantially similar jobs on short assembly lines subject to a high degree of worker control. The jobs of the strategic group were mostly separate individual operations involving substantial worker judgment; they were more important than the jobs of the preceding two groups and were well paid. The jobs of the conservative groups, which involved critical and scarce skills, were the top operative jobs in the plant.

It is difficult to separate the formal groups from the informal, for the types of jobs created by management, as well as the layout of the plant, have important repercussions on the formation and unity of informal groups. The manager must accept the group as an integral component of the total organization; he can no longer operate on an individual-to-individual basis. The groups must be studied to determine their makeup and characteristics in order to make the execution of the basic functions of management more realistic.

LOSSES FROM INFORMAL ORGANIZATION

The informal organization is not without its drawbacks when viewed in the light of the requirements of organized activity. Among the possible costs are the following:

1. Some informal relationships work counter to the basic goals of the organization.

[8] Leonard Sayles, *Behavior of Industrial Work Groups: Prediction and Control* (New York: John Wiley & Sons, Inc., 1958), pp. 7–39.

2. There is a lesser degree of predictability and control as compared to the theory of formal structure.
3. There is less interchangeability of individual personnel, thus reducing the number of practical alternatives for management.
4. There are costs involved in "lubricating" the informal organization.

These factors will be discussed in the following sections.

Works Counter to the Formal

It is apparent to most managers that individuals and groups can and sometimes do work contrary to the formal goals of an enterprise. If informal action could always be aligned with these formal goals, few would object to the encouragement and use of such action. However, there are such things as work restriction, pressuring other workers to exhibit disinterest in company requirements, disloyalty, insubordination, and unauthorized actions that work at cross-purposes with other functions in the organization.

Work restriction is not a creation of the modern labor union. It has always been a form of worker protest against some segment of the environment. When incentive systems are utilized, it becomes a particularly common type of employee reaction. Work restriction may result from the employee's fear of working himself out of a job, a desire to force concessions from management, a fear that management will demand greater productivity, or social pressures brought to bear on the employee. As will be discussed in a later chapter on first-level supervision, a foreman may tacitly permit, or even encourage, work restriction. It often makes his job easier by permitting a steady and predictable output, as well as by providing a basis for peace in the group.

In theory, each employee is as interested in and enthusiastic about his job as the manager is. In actual practice, this attitude is rare. Even if a particular employee is highly interested and would like to display enthusiasm and effort, the pressures of the group often dictate a different type of behavior. We are not implying that *all* informal practices are contrary to the requirements of logical organization. If such were the case, no organization could operate with any degree of effectiveness. However, we must recognize that the customs, habits, and beliefs of various groups within that organization will not always agree with the manager's set of customs and beliefs. It does little good to describe others as lazy, disinterested, and disloyal; one must make the attempt to understand why they exhibit such attitudes. And, as Dubin suggests, perhaps the manager must learn to accept such attitudes as a neutral element.[9] If the manager feels he must convert *all* employees to a point of view highly

---

[9] Dubin, *Human Relations in Administration,* p. 85.

favorable to the company, he will often do more harm than good. He must learn to ignore and tolerate attitudes that are contrary to his own. If one begins a crusade to convert all neutral attitudes into positive attitudes, the neutral groups may well grow smaller through wholesale defections to negative groups. Perhaps we should accept the idea that everyone can not and will not be as interested in and enthusiastic about his job as we are. And, as Argyris has indicated, some of the jobs that firms have created for their employees are such that it becomes very difficult to show any enthusiasm or interest.

Friendships and reciprocal cooperative relationships provide many of the elements of informal organization which facilitate work accomplishment. However, certain friendships can work counter to goal requirements and may have to be discouraged. There was, for example, the case of the department head who rode to work with one of his female subordinates. During these daily trips, she would question him closely about his problems and provide a substantial amount of advice. During the work day, she would often stop her own work to discuss a problem the department head was experiencing. She also attempted to issue orders to fellow employees. When higher management became aware of this friendship and its impact on operations and morale, it took action to alter this informal relationship. The department head was given a choice of giving up the friendship or giving up his job. Management usually holds that the manager should stand somewhat aloof from the employee group so as to avoid providing the basis for charges of favoritism and bias. A too close relationship also makes it difficult to do some of the undesirable things a supervisor is often called upon to do. This is particularly true for the supervisor promoted from the ranks, who will be required to break off friendships in the group. And yet this must be done, though gradually and tactfully, in order to avoid excessive resentment. Most subordinates understand the requirements of the supervisory role and accept the necessity for the break.

Another example of an informal relationship that worked counter to the requirements of formal management occurred in a laundry that employed a large number of female employees. The laundry manager had hired a new shirt-presser who seemed to be working out quite well. After three months on the job, she asked for a temporary leave to attend to some personal affairs. When she returned, she was reassigned to her old job. The next day, the manager was met by a delegation of seven women who issued an ultimatum: either the new shirt-presser must be fired or the department would resign en masse. The manager had no rational basis for discharging the woman, but he believed that the department *would* walk out. He knew it was an unfair decision and action, but he let the new shirt-presser go. Simultaneously, he resolved to break up this social group that was inhibiting his freedom to manage. Appreciating the influence of "human ecology," over the next several months he scattered individual members of this group, through transfers, to jobs all over the plant.

They were able to maintain contact during breaks and lunch periods, but gradually the strength of the ties diminished. Thus the manager was able to break up a social group which he believed was contributing more harm than good.

Reduces Degree of Predictability and Control

One of the basic purposes of organization is to insure predictability and control of individual behavior so that it will work effectively and cumulatively toward organization goals. We have introduced the human element and indicated that individuals and groups have many and varied reactions. Deviations from formal procedures and policies are not necessarily bad and will often contribute more than they cost. Acceptance of this view necessarily leads to a less controlled and less rigid situation.

The manager must learn to live with uncertainty *within* the firm as well as without. He usually accepts the necessity for uncertainty in relation to the market, the government, and the labor union. But he feels that he can control all that takes place within his own organization. We have introduced the idea that this is not so, that the intellectual formulation of a policy or plan does not insure its execution in the manner prescribed. The human element can and does add much to organization *effectiveness;* it also can and does add much to the degree of *uncertainty.* There are many managers who actually long for the predictability and precision of the machine that could replace all people. But it is apparent that the machine cannot provide the degree of flexibility, adaptability, and ingenuity that the human being can. The manager must reconcile himself to the fact that flexibility and ingenuity must lead to an increase in the degree of uncertainty, with a consequent decrease in predictability and control.

Lessens Interchangeability of Personnel

As indicated earlier in this chapter, the development of the informal group is a natural phenomenon. Man seeks to be accepted by his associates, and until he obtains a degree of acceptance he is often limited in his motivation and effectiveness. Once he becomes an integral part of a group, he is heavily influenced by that group's norms. In *The American Soldier,* a four-volume study of the United States Army during World War II, one of the major conclusions was that the natural unit of personal commitment was the informal group, *not* the total formal organization.[10] The soldiers reported that one of

---

[10] Samuel A. Stouffer, et al., *The American Soldier,* Vol. II (Princeton: Princeton University Press, 1949), p. 174.

the major reasons for moving forward in combat was to avoid letting the other fellow down. The solidarity developed in the natural or primary group greatly strengthened the motivation of individual members. The other major reason given was "to get the job done"—acceptance, in other words, of the formal organization goal.

The significance of this finding creates problems in interchangeability of personnel. If natural groups are broken up by moving individual members in and out of them, the degree of motivation and cooperation is reduced. If the number of such movements is high, it is also very unlikely that any strong natural groups will be developed, thus throwing the entire burden of accomplishment upon the formal organization and individual-to-individual relationships. This may well mean that management should think in terms of moving *groups* around, rather than individuals.

A second suggestion related to primary groups is that management should attempt to minimize the disruption of cooperative groups when changes in plant and procedures are initiated. The introduction of mass production assembly lines has been found to inhibit the formation of informal groups, since each man can relate effectively only with his two neighbors. Some have suggested that this physical arrangement has had much to do with the creation of apathetic attitudes, high turnover, and high rates of grievances.[11]

Management sometimes designs work teams in a manner that prevents the formation of natural groups. In an Indian textile mill, for example, one method of organization resulted in a high degree of specialization by the individual; each man was on his own. Production problems reached such proportions that a redesign of organization structure, to provide the basis for a greater degree of group interaction, was necessary.[12]

Physical barriers in the plant can also affect the formation of primary groups. In one company reported by Richards and Dobyns, a small number of clerical employees were physically isolated from the rest of the group.[13] All were performing substantially the same type of work, but nine of them were together in a separate place. A high degree of small-group loyalty resulted, with favorable effects on productivity. When a change in the physical layout was made so that these nine were more visible and less isolated, efficiency dropped markedly.

These illustrations point up the fact that if management wishes to capitalize upon the considerable values issuing from development of primary work groups, it must lose some flexibility in decision making. The group becomes a

[11] Frank J. Jasinski, "Adapting Organization to New Technology," *Harvard Business Review,* Vol. 37, No. 1 (January–February, 1959), pp. 79–86.

[12] A. K. Rice, *Productivity and Social Organization: The Ahmedabad Experiment* (London: Tavistock Publications, Ltd., 1959).

[13] Cara B. Richards, and Henry F. Dobyns, "Topography and Culture: The Case of the Changing Cage," *Human Organization,* Vol. 16 (Spring, 1957), pp. 16–20.

limiting factor just as important as the technical characteristics of a machine or work process. The formation of these groups can be inhibited, with possible reduced loyalty, higher turnover and absenteeism, and greater dissatisfaction. Or management can attempt to align its overall requirements with the conditions necessary for the development of natural groups and thus reap some of the benefits of informal organization.

Increases Costs of "Lubricating" the Informal Organization

This section emphasizes the point that special efforts will be required to facilitate the formation of positive informal relationships. Informal groups will usually indulge in gossiping, betting, and general horseplay. These are acts which, again, will tax the patience of the rigid, rational manager. Yet if an effective work group is to be established, some of these activities will have to be permitted and should even be encouraged. The manager must realize that, despite his concern for goal accomplishment, he must allow the group time and opportunity to maintain itself in good working order. Man can usually sustain action for a longer period of time under an informal atmosphere than he can when the situation is highly rigid, controlled, and formal.

MANAGEMENT AND THE INFORMAL ORGANIZATION

Both formal and informal organizations have values and costs. Formal organization is designed to enable effective execution of a high volume of planned tasks by multiple personnel. As such, it is adapted to yesterday's problems which are presumed to also be a large portion of tomorrow's tasks as well. But tomorrow's problems are not always foreseeable and controllable, thereby requiring a more flexible managerial attitude toward organization structure and organizational behavior.

Management must establish general guides in the forms of goals, policies, procedures, and structures. At the same time, it must develop means for combatting the pressures and habits through which people become prisoners of these guides. Essential to this is the recruitment and retention of inquiring and innovative personnel. Equally essential is the creation of an environment in which these personnel can thrive. This requires a tolerance for reasonable deviations from organization guides, a measure of freedom in which the limits of a job can be reworked, an absence of covert thought control, and provision for organizational conflict and dissent. Formal systems and procedures, though designed to promote operational effectiveness, can work counter to these supplementary values. John Gardner tells the story of a friend who, while located in the front lines in Germany during World War II, received a message telling him to proceed to London immediately. Upon going to Army head-quarters to obtain written orders for travel, he found that it had just been established and was in the throes of becoming organized. He also discovered that he had just thirty minutes to catch a plane while knowing that it usually required hours, and sometimes days, for a smoothly functioning headquarters to cut travel orders. After explaining his problem to the sergeant, the latter disappeared in the back room for a few minutes and then returned with the necessary orders. Mr. Gardner's friend exclaimed that he had never been in such an efficient headquarters, to which the sergeant replied, "Sir, it's just lucky for you we weren't organized!"[14] Obviously, all requests for travel orders could not be handled in this manner. Formal organization and systems must be established for repetitive activities. But it should be equally obvious that *some* requests *should* be handled in this manner.

In classical literature, conflict seems to be the antithesis of good organization. Cooperation, subordination, and coordination are the values to be derived from functional definition, commensurate authority and responsibility, single accountability, and an absence of gaps and overlaps in responsibility. This assumes that cooperation, subordination, and coordination are all being geared to a correct and true specification of goals and activities. If this assumption is not true, then dissent and conflict can lead to organizational renewal and revitalization.

If an organization member can object to a management directive, it *can* lead to a search for a new and better directive. It can also lead to managerial disapproval and reprimand of the objecting member. It behooves the manager to remember that subordinate criticisms can be right as well as wrong. If he never allows them to be heard, he will never find out which is the case. Though management directives are carved in tablets of formal authority, they do not necessarily always represent the truth in fluid and complex situations.

On the other hand, objections and contributions of particular organization members do not always represent the truth. The manager is an organization member who also has certain skills and information that are often not possessed by others. His position is unique in that he must *judge* the quality of the contributions of both himself and others. He has the responsibility for decision and is accountable for the resulting action. But even when he must reject criticisms and require subordination to official specifications, he would do well to defend his course of action through information and explanation, rather than authority. The ability to direct and control without sacrificing the values of individual freedom and dissent may be tantamount to having one's cake and eating it too. It is, nevertheless, the managerial stance necessary for an effective integration of formal and informal organizations.

[14] John W. Gardner, "Can Organization Dry Rot Be Prevented?" *Personnel Administration*, Vol. 29, No. 3 (May–June, 1966), p. 3.

CHARTING THE INFORMAL ORGANIZATION

Because of the complex and dynamic nature of people, the number of informal relationships established in any formal organization will be infinite. The manager, nevertheless, seeks some means whereby he can observe, record, and study these relationships, which affect the enterprise so greatly. Various methods of charting have been developed, each suited to a particular informal relationship. If to the formal relationships depicted upon the typical organization chart were added the many significant informal relationships, the formal chart would be obliterated. Perhaps, then, the total organization structure, both formal and informal, is so complex that it cannot be *completely* understood. For this reason, study of organization is usually segmented into such elements as responsibility, authority, status, feelings, power, and politics.

Examples of specific charting techniques are (1) the contactual chart, (2) the sociogram, and (3) the influence or power chart. There are doubtless others, and the manager can always improvise his own. Fig. 11–1 indicates the actual contacts between particular people in the organization. Note that all contacts do *not* go through formal channels. In some cases certain levels of

FIGURE 11–1   A CONTACT CHART

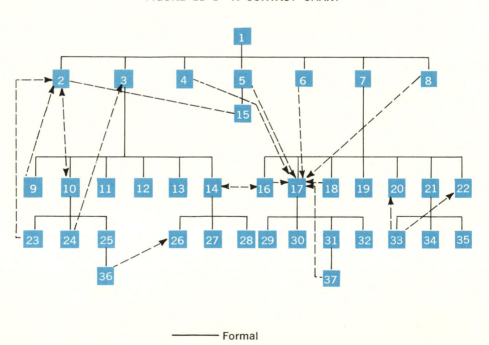

management are by-passed; others show cross-contact from one chain of command to another. One individual appears to be very popular—at least judging by the number of people seeking to contact him. What the chart does not show are the reasons for these contacts. Undoubtedly, some of them facilitate the accomplishment of work and would be highly acceptable to the traditional manager. Others are required by informal organization. And still others may work to the detriment of organization goals.

Fig. 11–2 depicts a slightly different type of informal relationship. This chart, a sociogram, shows the *feelings* of people toward each other. Employees are

FIGURE 11–2   SOCIOGRAM IMPOSED ON DEPARTMENTAL LAYOUT

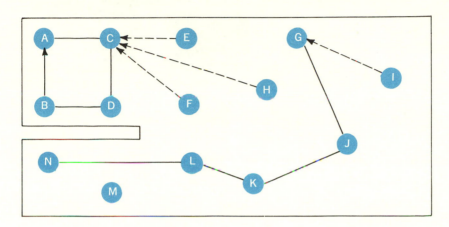

– – – – – One Way Relationship

————— Reciprocal Relationship

Chains—A, C, D, B; N, L, K, J. G: Star—C: Isolate—M

asked to indicate with whom they would like to work and associate, with whom they would *not* like to work, and to whom they are indifferent. In this manner, leaders and isolates can be uncovered and identified. Management has used sociometric measurement to form work teams; in one instance, the results were improvement in both productivity and worker satisfaction.[15]

A third chart is one that attempts to show levels of influence. It is a modified formal organization chart.[16] Fig. 11–3 shows the formal organization structure

[15] Raymond H. Van Zelst, "Sociometrically Selected Work Teams Increase Production," *Personnel Psychology*, Vol. 5, No. 3 (Autumn, 1952), pp. 175–185.
[16] For one use of this type of chart, see Melville Dalton, *Men Who Manage* (New York: John Wiley & Sons, Inc., 1959), pp. 21–22.

FIGURE 11–3   MILO FORMAL CHART SIMPLIFIED

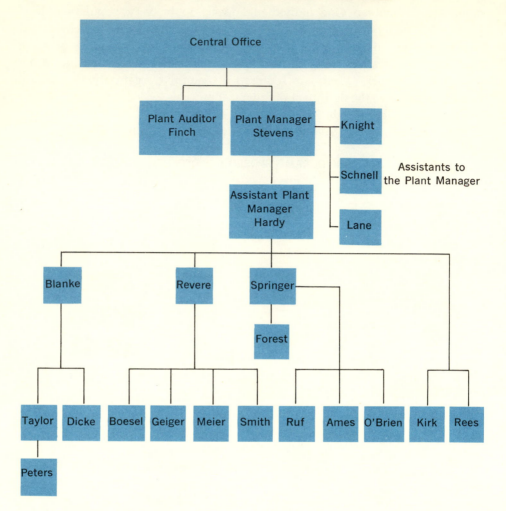

Source: Melville Dalton, *Men Who Manage,* p. 21. New York: John Wiley & Sons, Inc., 1959.

in simplified form for the Milo company; Fig. 11–4 indicates the influence or power level of these people. Note, for example, that, in the formal structure, Blanke, Revere, and Springer are equal. On the informal level, Springer is greatest in influence, with Blanke second and Revere last. The informal structure also shows that the assistant plant manager has equal influence with the plant manager.

In the following chapter, two of the more basic types of informal relationships, status and power, will be discussed. The last chart we discussed is, in effect, a power chart; but all three charts we have mentioned can give insight into the status relationships. These relationships are among the most important

FIGURE 11–4   MILO CHART OF UNOFFICIAL INFLUENCE

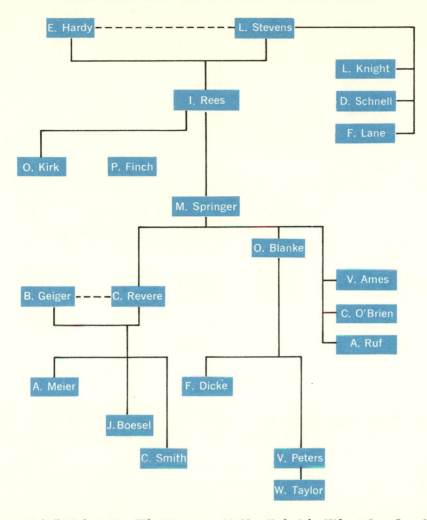

Source: Melville Dalton, *Men Who Manage*, p. 22. New York: John Wiley & Sons, Inc., 1959.

in operating organizations. Though the manager cannot possibly cope with every informal relationship, he can add materially to managerial effectiveness by concentrating upon a few.

SUMMARY

As broadly defined, informal organization consists of all relationships among people in an organization which are not officially established by management. Such relationships are formed by the particular individuals and groups manning particular structures.

The informal organization has much to contribute toward organization effectiveness in terms of (1) facilitating formal work; (2) fillings in gaps in the formal structure; (3) adding to the span of control; (4) compensating for violations of the principles of parity of responsibility and authority, unity of command, and single accountability; (5) providing a grapevine as an additional communication channel; (6) making the enterprise a more enjoyable place to work; and (7) stimulating management to do a better and more sensitive job.

The relationships created by members of an organization can also add to the costs of doing business—by informal work restriction, for instance. The primary group constitutes an additional limiting factor in decision making. These informal relationships are so many and so varied that management is called upon to absorb a large measure of uncertainty within its own organization. Yet if one is to obtain the most from the informal organization, some special attempts must be undertaken to keep the groups in good working order.

Any organization must have a rational, central objective to which all members should contribute in some manner. Even with the highest degree of good will and morale, some formal means of coordination must be present. Informal organization is in no way a substitute for formal organization. It is, rather, a highly important supplement. To see with depth of understanding in the organization, one needs both the formal and the informal views. In the following chapter, two of the more basic types of informal relationships will be discussed.

DISCUSSION PROBLEMS

1. In what ways does formal organization inhibit innovation and flexibility? In what ways does informal organization inhibit coordination and unity? Which set of values is more important?

2. In what ways does understanding informal organization contribute to more effective management?

3. Describe the primary or natural work group. How can management promote or inhibit formation of these groups? Why should they promote or inhibit them?

4. When the informal and the formal clash, how is the conflict to be reconciled?

5. What effect do informal organization concepts have upon the following: (a) span of control, (b) unity of command and single accountability, and (c) parity of authority and responsibility?

6. Is the grapevine of any value to a manager? How does it differ from the official channel of communication?

7. Distinguish among a sociogram, a contactual chart, and a power chart. Of what value are these to a manager?

8. How does knowing that a group is usually apathetic, erratic, strategic, or conservative contribute to a more effective management?

9. What is meant by "lubricating the organization"?

10. Cite examples of informal relationships patching up defects in the formal. Cite examples of informal organization working counter to the formal.

SUPPLEMENTARY READING

Bell, Gerald D., "Formality Versus Flexibility in Complex Organizations," in *Organizations and Human Behavior*, ed. Gerald D. Bell, pp. 97–106. Englewood Cliffs: Prentice-Hall, Inc., 1967.

Bennis, Warren G., "Organizational Revitalization," *California Management Review*, Vol. 9, No. 1 (Fall, 1966), 51–60.

Dalton, Melville, *Men Who Manage*, Chaps. 3, 8, and 9. New York: John Wiley & Sons, Inc., 1959.

Etzioni, Amitai, *Modern Organizations*, Chap. 4. Englewood Cliffs: Prentice-Hall, Inc., 1964.

Gardner, John W., "Can Organization Dry Rot Be Prevented?" *Personnel Administration*, Vol. 29, No. 3 (May–June, 1966), 3–13.

Jacoby, Jacob, "Examining the *Other* Organization," *Personnel Administration*, Vol. 31, No. 6 (November–December, 1968), 36–42.

Muti, Richard S., "The Informal Group—What It Is and How It Can Be Controlled," *Personnel Journal*, Vol. 47, No. 8 (August, 1968), 563–571.

Speroff, B. J., "Sociometry—A Tool of Leadership and Clique Identification," *Personnel Journal*, Vol. 45, No. 10 (November, 1966), 618–619.

12

Status, Power, and Politics

In the preceding chapter, we have seen how individuals and groups add supporting structures of their own to the formal organization. Many informal relationships appear to be casual and unsystematic, but, with time, patterns tend to develop. Three systematic informal (though not exclusively so) relationships will be discussed in this chapter: status, power, and politics. We should note that some of the more important sources of status and power are elements of formal organization developed by management. However, their classification as a part of informal organization is still justified on at least two bases. First, and most obvious, there are many informal sources of power and status. And second, these relationships, regardless of source, are relationships as seen and determined by the *people* in the enterprise. Restriction of one's view to strictly the formal would preclude many important aspects of status, power, and politics.

STATUS

Status can be defined simply as one's social rank or position in a group. It is an important relationship having much to do with the morale and efficiency of any organization, and is an inevitable component of human relationships in all walks of life, business and nonbusiness. In this section, we wish to examine the sources of status in business organizations, the symbols that denote status levels, and the functions of a status system. Certain applications to practical business problems will be presented in order to indicate the importance of the concept to the manager.

Sources of Status

As indicated above, the sources of status, or social rank, can be of both an informal and formal nature. Examples of these sources are as follows:

Formal Organizational Sources

1. Occupation or job
2. Organization level

Personal Sources

1. Education
2. Age
3. Seniority
4. Race
5. Religion
6. Parentage
7. Sex
8. Competence
9. Associates

It is apparent that certain jobs or occupations are accorded a higher prestige level than others. For example, white-collar jobs are usually more highly esteemed than blue collar. In one survey of public opinion, the position of highest prestige in the country was that of U.S. Supreme Court Justice and the lowest was that of shoe shiner.[1] Examples of various intervening jobs were college professor in eighth position, lawyer at eighteenth, electrician at forty-fifth, policeman at fifty-fifth, restaurant cook at seventy-first, singer in a night club at seventy-sixth, and garbage collector at eighty-eighth. Within particular companies, management has discovered, often in great surprise, the following status differentials: long distance telephone operators had higher social rank than operators handling local calls; cooks who worked on white meat had higher status than those who worked on dark; and cafeteria waitresses who handled fish dishes had less prestige that those who served beef. As can be seen, then, the status of one's occupation depends on the rank accorded it by *one's peers*, and not by management alone. The job assigned to a person as well as the level of organization on which it is placed are significant sources of status; in general, the higher the organization level, the higher the level of prestige. And yet, as we shall see below, one is naïve to assume that there is a perfect coincidence of formal job relationships and the status accorded a person holding that formal job.

The characteristics of the individual are important sources of social rank.

[1] Carroll L. Shartle, *Occupational Information*, 3rd ed. (Englewood Cliffs: Prentice-Hall, Inc., 1959), pp. 55–57.

There is a general respect in this society for the better educated, the older person, and the individual who has been in the organization for a longer period of time. These sources are widely found in our society as evidenced by such diverse examples as the impact of Sputnik in the 1950's, the favoring of the older son, and the honoring of one's parents. Whether one wishes to admit it or not, there are status hierarchies among and within races, religions, and nationalities. Again, these varying status levels are a result of general social attitudes of approval or disapproval. Though one may aspire to a society where all are completely equal, such a utopia remains highly unlikely until there are major changes in human personality. Fair or not, too, the man is generally accorded more prestige on a given job than a woman.

A particular individual can possess high status even though ensconced in a low status job. If one does a low status job extremely well, his skill is often generally recognized and respected. On the other hand, if the president of the firm bumbles and muddles through his responsibilities, his status level is substantially reduced. And finally, there is status that issues from one's associates. This is social rank that comes from friendship, kinship, or social organizations. Membership in a certain fraternity or club, and graduation from certain schools, are examples of status being assigned to a person on the basis of the status accorded the larger group. Membership in these groups is often predicted on possession of some of the other personal sources of status.

Symbols of Status

A status symbol is a visible, external denotation of one's social position. A stranger can enter an organization and if he is knowledgeable of status hierarchies, he can quickly obtain a social fix through a reading of the various symbols. However, one must recognize that systems of symbols often vary from firm to firm. For example, one would usually expect that the higher the status, the more elaborate the office furnishings. In Marquand's *Point of No Return*, however, the high status positions were given antique roll-top desks, while the lower jobs were equipped with new, shiny, modern furniture.[2] Symbols sometimes change with the times. The brass spittoon used to denote high status in the oil industry, but this has since been replaced, for better or worse, by a water carafe and tray. Among the more typical symbols are the following:

1. Job titles
2. Pay
3. Clothing
4. Size and location of desk or office
5. Location of parking space

2 John P. Marquand, *Point of No Return* (Boston: Little, Brown, 1949).

6. Type of company car assigned
7. Secretaries
8. Privacy
9. Furnishings, including rugs, pictures, tables, etc.
10. Privileges, including freedom to move about, not punching the time clock, and freedom to set own working hours and to regulate coffee break
11. Ceremonies of induction
12. Possessions such as home, private automobiles, stereos, etc.

Most of these symbols have to do with a business firm. But it should be apparent that status is a major factor in our entire society and is not confined to business organizations.[3] One feels that one is judged in general by the kind of car one drives, the home one keeps, and the clothes one wears.

Within the company, however, many of the symbols are within the control of the management, and constitute the basis for many bloody battles. Executives have gotten down on hands and knees to measure and compare sizes of offices. Windows are counted, steps from the president's offices are paced off, secretaries are sought, parking space is fought for, and company cars are wangled. A humorous, fictional example of status symbols by organization level is presented in Chart 12–1. Some reflection on this exhibit leads one to believe that there is more truth than fiction here.

Some managements have sought to abolish the whole problem of awarding status symbols by attempting to equalize all privileges, offices, and furnishings. Windowless buildings have been constructed, office sizes are completely standardized, and only one type of company car is available. However, as long as there are differences in status, some type of symbol will be worked out by the group. At the very least, we cannot all stand in one spot, and the distance one's office is located from the president's is often established as a symbol of social rank. The fact that the executive suite is frequently on the top floor is indication of these jobs being higher in status as well as otherwise. Other managements have attempted to bring order out of chaos by establishing a standard set of symbols for each major class of status. For example, Gulf Oil Corporation divides its management personnel into five levels for purposes of distributing company cars. Division managers can choose between Cadillacs and Imperials, while sales representatives must select from among the cheaper models of Chevrolet, Plymouth, and Ford.

Incongruency of Status Sources and Symbols

Status is a stratifying factor which necessarily establishes one of three relationships: superior, equal, inferior. When a person's status is fairly clear and

[3] See Vance O. Packard, *The Status Seekers* (New York: David McKay Co., 1962).

CHART 12–1 STATUS SYMBOLS

Visible Appurtenances	Top Dogs	V.I.P.'s	Brass	No. 2's	Eager Beavers	Hoi Polloi
Brief cases	None—they ask the questions	Use backs of envelopes	Someone goes along to carry theirs	Carry their own—empty	Daily—carry their own—filled with work	Too poor to own one
Desks, office	Custom made (to order)	Executive style (to order)	Type A, "Director"	Type B, "Manager"	Cast-offs from No. 2's	Yellow Oak—or cast-offs from Eager beavers
Tables, office	Coffee tables	End tables or decorative wall tables	Matching tables, type A	Matching tables, type B	Plain work table	None—lucky to have own desk
Carpeting	Nylon—1-inch pile	Nylon—1-inch pile	Wool-twist (with pad)	Wool-twist (without pad)	Used wool pieces—sewed	Asphalt tile
Plant stands	Several—kept filled with strange exotic plants		Two—repotted whenever they take a trip	One medium-sized—repotted annually during vacation	Small—repotted when plant dies	May have one in the department or bring their own from home
Vacuum water bottles	Silver	Silver	Chromium	Plain painted	Coke machine	Water fountains
Library	Private collection	Autographed or complimentary books and reports	Selected references	Impressive titles on covers	Books everywhere	Dictionary
Shoe-shine service	Every morning at 10:00	Every morning at 10:15	Every day at 9:00 or 11:00	Every other day	Once a week	Shine their own
Parking space	Private—in front of office	In plant garage	In company garage—if enough seniority	In company properties—somewhere	On the parking lot	Anywhere they can find a space—if they can afford a car

Source: Morris S. Viteles, "What Raises a Man's Morale," *Personnel,* published by the American Management Association, Inc. (January, 1954), p. 305.

220

known, he is high or low on most if not all of the status sources. These sources are therefore not incongruent. If he is high on some and low on others, it is difficult to ascertain whether he is a superior, a colleague, or an inferior. Some research studies have shown that where status hierarchies are clear and congruent, the amount of free interchange of information, suggestions, and help is materially reduced.[4] A clearly superior person attempts to retain the initiative and avoid closing the social distance between himself and others. An inferior tends to feel subservient and is restricted in his actions and comments. Only among equals is there usually a feeling of ease and relaxation which leads to mutual influence and helpfulness. In short, if the status hierarchy is as rigid and stratified as the formal organization hierarchy, the former works to hinder the organization. If the status of a person is not so clear, he can afford to ask for help from his supposed inferiors as well as offer suggestions to his supposed superiors.

There is also a second problem of incongruency between status sources and status symbols. As an example of this type, in some companies only members of top management are allowed to include their wives in their expense accounts for corporate trips. Some junior executives have followed the practice of bringing their wives along at personal expense without, of course, mentioning that fact to others. This caused considerable disgruntlement among those truly "deserving" of the symbol. There is also the company practice of providing country club memberships for certain executives. Others join the club at their own expense in order to share the possible benefits in social prestige from this symbol. Many of management's problems in status issue from the incongruency of sources with the accompanying symbols. These inconsistencies often issue from individual maneuvering for an undeserved symbol, with the assistance of an unclear system of symbols in the organization.

Status Functions

Though the development of status does contribute to some stratification and inflexibility in organizations, it also produces desirable values such as the following:[5]

1. Assists in meeting the needs of the individual ego.
2. Facilitates the process of communication.
3. Provides additional motivational devices for management.

[4] Louis B. Barnes, *Organizational Systems and Engineering Groups, A Comparative Study of Two Technical Groups in Industry* (Boston: Harvard Graduate School of Business Administration, 1960), Chap. 4.
[5] For a classic coverage of the function of status systems in formal organizations, see Chester I. Barnard, *Organization and Management* (Cambridge: Harvard University Press, 1948), Chap. 9.

Most people wish to be accorded some degree of respect by others. They want to have their abilities and accomplishments recognized, and status symbols constitute tangible evidence of this respect. In addition, we need to impute higher status to our formal superiors. The necessity of working for and taking orders from a superior who is not respected, let alone liked, does injury to the ego. A subordinate will often seek transfer to other positions, even with less pay and fewer privileges, in order to avoid this constant subordination to a person whom he cannot respect.

Status systems also facilitate the process of communication. We receive many messages daily from people not known personally. The status *title* of the person or position helps us to evaluate the worth of the message. For example, if the message is an analysis of a particular electronic mechanism, we will probably place less credence in it when signed by John Jones, plumber. If the report had been signed by John Jones, electrician, more faith in what it says will be forthcoming. But if signed by John Jones, electronic engineer, we believe what he says.

If we could not depend upon status titles to indicate the authenticity of the communication, life would be extremely difficult. When we go to a medical doctor for the first time, his advice is usually taken because he is an M.D., and not because we have evaluated his abilities. If the status of the person talking is known, the communication process is greatly facilitated.

Management has discovered that employees will strive for prestige and prestige symbols, as well as for more money. Therefore, nonfinancial incentives can be worked into a more comprehensive incentive system. A job title change is often as satisfying as more money. A change to a job of lesser pay but more prestige is often a change which a particular person will find satisfying, providing that the pay is still sufficient. It will be recalled that the need hierarchy indicates that other needs become apparent to the individual when lower needs have been reasonably well satisfied. Thus, status as a motivating tool has its greatest use in situations where monetary requirements have been met to a reasonable degree. If management is aware of status systems and the symbols which it can control, a more comprehensive and coordinated incentive system can be developed.

Status Applications

In a classic study of informal relationships in a restaurant, William F. Whyte demonstrated the interdependency of working procedures and status.[6] The guiding thesis underlying this study was that relations among people will work

[6] William Foote Whyte, "The Social Structure of the Restaurant," *American Journal of Sociology*, Vol. 54 (January, 1949), pp. 302–308.

more smoothly if higher status personnel usually *originate* action for lower status personnel. For example, in one restaurant, waitresses passed their customer orders on to countermen. This meant that the lower status female was initiating action for the higher status male. This provided the basis for much wrangling and bickering. When an intervening element was provided, such as a spindle for order slips or a high warming compartment so that waitresses and countermen had little contact, the amount of argument and controversy was materially reduced. In the kitchen, supplymen attempted to obtain food supplies from the chefs. This was in effect a low skilled male employee initiating action for the high skilled "kings" of the kitchen. Here again was the scene of many controversies as several supplymen enjoyed "needling" the chefs to "get a move on." Whyte reported that one supplyman had little trouble. He gave the chef the order and asked that *he* be called when it was ready, thus reversing the initiating process to conform with the ideal. When these various restaurant procedures were analyzed for their status implications, changes were introduced which substantially contributed to a more pleasant and effective working environment. As long as management needs people to man procedures, the human aspect is just as important as the technical.

In a case reported by Maier, employees of a public utility had established a status system within small working crews.[7] Each crew rode to job assignments in a truck under the direction of the senior man. The status source in this instance was seniority. The status symbol was seat location in the truck. The high status position held by the senior man was alongside of the driver in the cab. In the rear, the men were seated according to seniority, with the youngest at the very end. It was his task to open and close the tailgate for the other men. This system had been developed over the years and was unknown to management, until the order came down to the effect that the person seated in the cab must operate the tailgate. There had been too many ankle injuries resulting from climbing over and jumping down to the ground while the tailgate was up. This order meant that a *low* status task was to be performed by a *high* status person if that person remained in the high status seat location. Management had unknowingly disrupted the informal organization. Maier reported that the foremen who solved this dilemma most successfully were those who had no solution to present to the crews. These supervisors permitted the groups to talk the problem out among themselves and to determine a way in which the order could be met with the least damage to the status system. The informal organization is so diverse and complicated that only the members are fully aware of the social implications of changes. There was no standard, uniform solution to be applied to all crews. There was only the standard requirement that the gate

[7] Norman R. F. Maier, Allen R. Solem, and Ayesha A. Maier, *Supervisory and Executive Development* (New York: John Wiley & Sons, Inc., 1957), pp. 66–67.

would be operated by someone seated in the cab. In some cases, the senior man gave up his seat and the system of symbols changed. In others, he agreed to perform the duty if the group was successful in transforming it into a high status task (e.g., the senior man "looking after the troops").

These examples serve to illustrate the inevitability of status implications in organized activities of people. Needless roadblocks to cooperative action are thrown up when a manager refuses to consider the human implications of management decisions.

POWER

Like status, power is neither completely informal nor formal in nature. Power is the *capacity to apply influence or force to others.* As such, it includes, but goes beyond, the capacities provided by the formal organization, and, for this reason, is included in this section of the text.

Power is an emotionally laden term, particularly in cultures that emphasize individuality and equality. To label a manager as a "power-seeker" is to cast aspersions upon his motives and actions. Some of these negative connotations issue from older analyses that suggested that power is evil, that it corrupts people, that it is largely comprised of naked force, and that the amount is limited in supply. More modern analyses view power as an essential resource of society that can be subject to abuse.[8] Certainly, the modern business corporation constitutes an enormous concentration of economic power that has materially improved the standard of living of millions of people. When such concentrations lead to abuse, control rather than abolition would appear to be the more desirable course of action. Power can be a highly effective instrument for the good of mankind.

Power is essentially a relationship between people operating either as individuals or groups. The power of General Motors is exercised by human beings as is that also of the federal government. Thus, it is the capacity to affect the behavior of others. It can be viewed as both a latent potential and an actual activity. In many instances, the power-holder need not act to influence others; the latter anticipate his desires and act to avoid controversy or a risky showdown. Bertrand Russell has suggested that "the fundamental concept in social science is Power in the same sense in which Energy is the fundamental concept in physics."[9] However, it is far more difficult to measure power in social relationships than it is to measure energy in physics. Power does not merely consist of brute force, strength, coercion, and dominance. In many instances,

[8] Dow Votaw, "What Do We Believe About Power?" *California Management Review,* Vol. 8, No. 4 (Summer, 1966), p. 81.
[9] Bertrand Russell, *Power, A New Social Analysis* (London: W. W. Norton & Co., 1938), p. 12.

power is dependent upon acceptance of an influence by the recipient. As suggested above, it may be latent or used overtly. It can come from such diverse acts as the publication of a book, introduction of a new product, creation of a new idea, accomplishments of one's children, acceptance by a particular group, or appointment to a formal position. Precision of measurement may be restricted to such statements as the following: "as of the moment of observation, A has more power than C in connection with decision X under circumstances a', b', and c'."[10]

As implied by the above, power is not limited in total quantity. It is not always a win-lose proposition; if one has more power, it does not mean that someone else has less. When people band together to create an organized society, the amount of power is considerably increased. Obeying the commands of a policeman at an intersection does not mean that the motorist's total power has been reduced. Other motorists are prevented from interfering with his progress. The development of industrial technology by large business organizations has substantially increased the amount of power available. The single, lonely inventor is being replaced by the organized and affluent research and development departments in large enterprises. And when the single inventor does develop a new product, he is often powerless to make it widely available to the population without the aid of a large institution. The power of his new product coupled with the power of a large marketing organization may well add to the affluence of society in general.

Power is a resource that can be abused as well as used. Such abuses call for devices and techniques to restrain and control undesirable uses, and legitimatize its use in more constructive ways. In a sense, the balance of power among segments in our society permits greater freedom from governmental control for the manager. If society believes that the power of private business corporations is unfettered, it will tend to move toward a limitation or dilution of that power. This is one area where strong labor unions make a material contribution toward freedom for the manager. If there were no strong union movement to offset private management, it is doubtful if society would rest easy with the grant of power which private industry now has. Some private firms have larger budgets than some states in the union. This problem of general corporate power is compounded by the fact that many company boards of directors have become no more than cardboard fronts.[11] When the proxies for control are held by members of management, the board is not a legitimatizing power source elected by stockholders at large. There is no broad electorate against which the actions of the board and the management can be checked. In addition, there are some boards whose memberships are composed entirely of internal managers of the firm. Various writers in the field of management feel

[10] Votaw, *op. cit.*, p. 85.
[11] Peter Drucker, *The Practice of Management* (New York: Harper & Bros., 1954), p. 177.

that such power concentrations will not go long unchallenged by government.

One suggestion has been that the major stockholders, who often are the larger trust and pension fund administrators, organize to hire and pay professional directors who can provide an independent voice on these boards.[12] In this manner, the acts of management can be evaluated and passed upon by a board with real power. The alternative to this or some similar device, according to this writer, may be a government-appointed public director for these larger corporations, which may be increasingly regarded as quasi-public institutions because of the size of their expenditures and consequent impact upon the public at large.

Thus, in the general society, there is a problem of legitimatizing power which is held by the business manager. This can be done by either subjecting him to a broad power base, such as responsible stockholders or even the public at large, or by constructing a balance of power among big business, big unions, and big government. It is sobering for the businessman to reflect that some of his present freedom can probably be attributed to the rise of offsetting power sources which he often finds so objectionable.

Sources of Power

The sources of power are many and varied, and are not restricted to the legitimate ones provided by management. Among these sources are the following:[13]

1. Authority
2. Rewards and punishments
3. Expertise or skill
4. Function performed
5. Number of personnel performing
6. Friends and associates
7. Personality

The usual error of the traditionalist in management theory is to assume that power and authority are identical concepts. Undeniably, formal authority is a very important source of power, but *not* the only source. Power is the broader concept.

In the literature, there has arisen the term "informal authority." This concept

[12] Cf. Ernest Dale, *The Great Organizers* (New York: McGraw-Hill Book Company, 1960), Chap. 6.

[13] For other listings, see Harold Lasswell and Abraham Kaplan, *Power and Society* (New Haven: Yale University Press, 1950), p. 87; and John R. P. French, Jr. and Bertram Raven, "The Bases of Social Power," in *Studies in Social Power,* ed. Dorwin Cartwright (Ann Arbor: Institute for Social Research, 1959), p. 155.

serves to emphasize the influence which subordinates have with their superiors. An order is received from a superior and the subordinate can choose among several alternative actions: (1) he can *refuse* to obey, thus delegating no "informal authority" over himself; (2) he can *grudgingly* accept the order and execute it on a minimal basis; (3) he can accept and execute the order with a neutral or indifferent attitude; or (4) he can accept and execute the order with enthusiasm, intelligence, and ingenuity. The amount of "informal authority" granted the superior over himself is materially greater in the last alternative.

To be precise, however, for "informal authority" read *power*. Authority is a *formal* concept and issues from the formal organization. Authority is a *form* of power, but it is *institutionalized* power, obtained from one's superior and issued ultimately from society (see Chapter 9). The manager often has need for more influence than that issued to him formally by the organization; for he must realize that subordinates can give or withhold their cooperation, which, in effect, means giving or witholding power. But to term both formal and informal influence as (formal) authority only serves to confuse the issue.

In addition, then, to the formal source of power, there are many other means whereby an individual can influence or move others. The primary group has considerable influence when, for example, it can ostracize a person or give him the "silent treatment." Acceptance by this group is a reward avidly sought by most people.

Even though an individual has limited formal authority, his expertise in a particular area will also give him considerable influence or power. This is one of the major problems involved in line and staff relationships—the line has the power that issues from *authority* while the staff has the power that issues from *knowledge*. We have indicated in previous chapters the difficulty of preserving unity of command in this day of complexities issuing from technology and size. The formal *right* to manage a firm has remained, but the *capacity* to manage it has been diluted and spread among a number of experts. The man who *knows* has power regardless of the formal organization.

Power also issues from function. If a function needs to be performed, the performer has some influence. Failure to perform or variations in performance can affect others. Purchasing, for example, is a centralized staff function in many manufacturing organizations. The purchasing agent has substantial power by being able to determine who gets served first and how well. If we are functionally dependent upon another person, that person has a measure of influence through his ability and cooperation in executing those functions.

A particularly important function in all organizations is that of transmitting information. The person who transmits has considerable power inasmuch as he may filter, alter, or refuse to transmit data. In one particular company, the president discovered that he was often late in receiving significant information about his organization. He therefore appointed an assistant in charge of information. It was this assistant's task to assemble, analyze, and transmit significant information to his chief every morning. In a few years, the chief was moved up to chairman of the board and the information assistant was made president. His specialty, communication, was a function which had much to do with this move. With respect to this same function, it is important to note that *every* manager is dependent upon others for the information which is necessary for management. He cannot observe and collect all data personally. The higher his position in the organization, the more he must rely on others and their reports.

Dubin has pointed out that the number of people performing a particular function is an index of power.[14] If there is only one person available, that person possesses substantial power. If there are fifty people performing similar functions, the power of any one is not great; no one is indispensable when there are available substitutes.

At times a particular person has friends in high places. As such, he has a measure of power which issues from knowing the right people. This type of power is often termed "referent power." It is not as great as the power of the original source and is affected by others' estimates of the degree of closeness to that source. The son of the owner of the firm or the crony of the boss has a measure of influence which issues from this relationship.

Finally, the character and personality of an individual affect the degree of influence he has with others. If we like and respect another because of his age, competence, drive, education, and integrity, we are more willing to grant him influence over us. In theory, the scientifically selected and trained manager has the respect of all of his subordinates. In practice, such is often not the case. Another employee may be the informal leader in the department. He wields power which is not clearly seen and certainly not officially recorded. The astute formal manager often seeks the cooperation of such informal leaders in order to supplement his own institutionalized power.

Significance of Power to the Manager

As has been stated previously in this text, the traditional manager is often prone to view things as they should be, e.g., power equals authority. The behaviorists are inclined toward reporting things as they are, e.g., power equals authority plus many other unofficial factors. We are kidding ourselves if we think that the formal structure provides a complete picture of the influence structure of an organization. We must fill in the *names* on the chart and then attempt to ascertain the *real* power of these people. The resulting pattern is

[14] Robert Dubin, *The World of Work* (Englewood Cliffs: Prentice-Hall, Inc., 1958), p. 31.

unique to the particular organization. The standard sources help to explain from where that power issues, but the particular pattern will vary with different people and organizations.

Thus, the major value of knowing the power structure of a firm is to avoid mistakes resulting from naïveté. The organization chart shows that Jones is the top man, the president, of the organization. But it is important to find out as soon as possible that Smith, the vice-president, has equal power in most subjects. You must determine what matters to see Jones about and on what subjects Smith must be consulted. Reference should again be made to Figs. 11–3 and 11–4 for a contrast between the authority and power structures of one particular organization.

Another value issuing from a knowledge of power structures is that it tends to stimulate a more informed and sensitive manager. He recognizes that he cannot completely control any situation singlehandedly. He knows that rank and file employees have a measure of power in their ability to extend or withhold cooperation. The informal slowdown is a power act of major consequences. When individuals act in concert, their power is considerably greater than that issuing from the single person. The labor union movement is, of course, based upon this concept. Realization of the diffusion of power places greater emphasis upon the necessity for promoting cooperation in the pursuit of organization goals, and less upon the sanctions which can issue from the formal authority structures.

POLITICS

According to Webster, to be "politic" is to be "sagacious in promoting a policy; ingenious in statecraft; also, [concerned with] measures, plans, etc., shrewdly contrived, especially with regard to self-interest." In everyday parlance the title of "politician" is rarely one of high approbation. Yet politics and politicians are with us in all forms of organized activity, not only in those of government. Political action can and does provide positive values in the promotion of cooperation among individuals and groups with differing interests and objectives.

Pfiffner and Sherwood define politics as "the network of interaction by which power is acquired, transferred, and exercised upon others."[15] The term politics also suggests that these interactions occur in an area of *conflict*, and that the resulting power actions and interactions constitute one approach toward reconciliation.

[15] John M. Pfiffner and Frank P. Sherwood, *Administrative Organization* (Englewood Cliffs: Prentice-Hall, Inc., 1960), p. 311.

Role of Politics in Business Organizations

If all actions could be foreseen and prescribed for with accuracy, perhaps there would be little need for politics. This would also assume that all conflicts could be resolved in some rational manner acceptable to all. Inasmuch as neither of these two circumstances is likely, the individual will be asked to adjust and accommodate to varying conditions and pressures. Perhaps "adjustments and accommodations" are more understandable terms for this political process.

The complete elimination of conflict in business organizations is neither desirable nor possible. Even though we understand one another perfectly, conflict will not necessarily be eliminated between us. The boring utopia of complete harmony and agreement is not within the reach of man. Excessive agreement too often breeds rosy optimism and unjustified confidence. On the contrary, however, conflict can contribute in a positive fashion to organizational creativity and productivity. Conflict and disagreement force reexamination of basic ideas and philosophies, often resulting in modifications that benefit the organization as a whole. On the other hand, *excessive* conflict is the antithesis of organization, destroying more than it creates. The modern manager must accept conflict within the organization as a fact of life, but must seek methods of controlling and channeling it toward constructive ends.

One approach toward reconciling and living with conflict is that of accommodation or politics. Though going exclusively by the rule book could under certain circumstances be construed as one form of politicking, accommodation usually requires additional interactions to be forthcoming. It sometimes involves a bending of the rules, an exchange of favors, and offers of reward for the cooperation that management textbooks often indicate will be forthcoming automatically.

To make the implications of politics more concrete, let us assume the following example. An engineer heading up an industrial engineering department has developed a new procedure for processing work in a particular line executive's production department. According to the formal rules of the game, he would elect to follow the first suggestion in the following list. The others listed are not formally required and can be construed as various forms of "adjustment and accommodation":

1. The engineer submits the recommendation for approval by the line executive. He provides all of the supporting data and attempts to persuade him to his way of thinking. This failing, the engineer appeals to a common line superior who will decide the case and issue an order accordingly.

2. The engineer attempts to get to know the line executive on a personal basis. This involves casual conversation, inquiries about respective backgrounds, and the like.
3. The engineer attempts to *simulate* a friendship that he does not feel.
4. The engineer arranges to lunch with the line executive in the company dining room to promote his views on a casual basis.
5. The engineer invites the line executive to lunch away from the company premises at the former's own expense.
6. The engineer offers to exchange favors which are possible *within* the regular operating rules and policies, e.g., he agrees to do an immediate restudy of a particular job rate which has been resulting in serious difficulties between the line executive and the union.
7. The engineer agrees to favors involving a *slight bending* of the procedures and policies, e.g., agreeing to delay introduction of a new method and rate, even though fully developed and ready to go, at the request of the line executive.
8. The engineer agrees to a favor involving a more *serious bending* of the procedures and policies, e.g., "discovering" that the particular job rate mentioned in item six above is too tight, when it is not, and loosening it up for the benefit of the line executive.
9. The engineer agrees to cover for the line executive, e.g., the line executive wishes to use the industrial engineering department as an excuse for failing to meet schedules because of presumed work interferences.
10. The engineer, with the assistance of understanding accountants, agrees to a transfer of industrial engineering budget funds to the line executive's department.[16]

There are doubtlessly other possible actions that might be undertaken to persuade the line executive to cooperate. The available alternatives depend upon the extent of power possessed by the two parties. In instances where one has control over items or services which can be adapted to *personal* as well as organizational use, the power is even greater. There have been cases where personal furniture has been constructed on company time with company materials, as well as instances where personal cars have been repaired in company motor pools. The degree of politicking is limited not only by the formal organization restrictions, but by one's personal code of ethics and conscience as well.

That such actions as the above do exist in various business organizations is undeniable. Few businesses are run completely and rigidly by the book, and such practices cannot be condemned *per se*. Some accommodations are constructive, while others are perhaps destructive of both organized activity and individual morals.

---

[16] Such an instance was discussed by Melville Dalton in *Men Who Manage* (New York: John Wiley & Sons, Inc., 1959), p. 32.

Areas of Political Action

There are many potential areas of political action in business. Among the more commonly observed are:

1. Colleague versus colleague.
2. Superior versus subordinate.
3. Union versus management.
4. Line versus staff.

The numerous opportunities for political maneuvering among colleagues might involve promotions, budget allocations, or assignment of manpower and physical facilities. Concerning promotions, for example, a classicist would propose that position specifications should be written and the abilities of all candidates scientifically measured. A realist would contend that neither of these activities could be accomplished with exactness and accuracy. Consequently, much room is left for personal approaches to the problem. It has been observed that superiors making decisions about candidates for promotion tend to select personnel with characteristics and backgrounds like their own. Though it may be denied, in some companies memberships in the right political party, church, and country club are important variables.[17]

Where should the modern manager stand on politics and promotion? Though the processes are not exact and scientific, he must attempt to define carefully the job requirements, to insure equitable recruitment and as accurate a selection process as possible. With this, however, there is an inevitable degree of subjectivity which enters the decision-making process. As Dalton states:[18]

> [Higher] officers must consider the capacity of competing candidates to utilize and aid necessary cliques, control dangerous ones, etc. Too often the search for men who combine formal competence with this unspecified skill throws a top officer into despair. He is likely to put a premium on "loyalty" in terms of the candidate's seeing the job as he does. Wittingly or not, he begins to look for attitudes like his own as assuring a basis for understanding and cooperation.

[17] Vance Packard in his *The Pyramid Climbers* (New York: McGraw-Hill Book Company, 1962) suggests that some companies favor the WASP, that is, white, Anglo-Saxon, and Protestant. When any selection of major importance is made, the grapevine usually buzzes with various analyses of the bases for such an appointment.

[18] Dalton, *Men Who Manage*, p. 188.

Regarding the superior versus subordinate, the former has of course more institutionalized power, that is, formal authority, than the latter. Subordinates seek to reduce that power, or at least to soften its effects, through their ability to offer or withhold cooperation and obedience. At first, the struggle is usually informal. With increasing confidence, subordinates may attempt to formalize their power through representative groups or full-fledged labor unions. In colleges and universities, for example, these political struggles over power usually take place between the faculty and the school administrators. This is one explanation for the considerable use of faculty committees and senates. These are organizational devices which facilitate faculty participation and help in restricting unilateral action by college administrators. There are also, of course, many political struggles among faculty colleagues as they seek larger staff and budget allocations for their respective departments.

In the union-management political area, the union contract constitutes the formal law. Within these formal requirements, there is usually much room for maneuvering. In fact, one of the conclusions of the National Planning Association Committee on the Causes of Industrial Peace Under Collective Bargaining was that a more effective relationship resulted when *neither* party adopted a legalistic approach to the solution of problems.[19]

Obviously, the granting or withholding of concessions in the contract is the result of a power struggle known as "collective bargaining." Under the contract, grievances of particular individuals must be processed. The supervisor is under considerable pressure to keep the number of formal grievances down to a minimum. The union steward is under pressure to advance general union objectives and defend individual interests. Under these conditions, informal agreements between supervisor and steward are not unusual. The steward may agree not to press a particular grievance in return for a more valuable concession in another area. Or the word comes down from higher officials not to "rock the boat" while more important issues are under consideration. The steward has considerable power which issues from both the formal contract provisions and his personal influence over union members. The supervisor has the power which issues from formal authority, the ability to grant or withhold rewards, and the respect that his subordinates have for him as a person.

The political conflict between line and staff will be covered in the following chapter, which deals with the problems of specialization, since the development of specialists with restricted authority, but considerable powers issuing from expertise, also provides the basis for some interesting conflicts and accommodations.

[19] Clark Kerr and George Haverson, *Lockheed Aircraft Corporation and International Association of Machinists, Case Study Number 6* (Washington: National Planning Association, 1949), p. x: one of a series under the general title of *Causes of Industrial Peace Under Collective Bargaining.*

Values of Political Action

It is apparent that some degree of politics is a fact of organized life, regardless of the caliber of people involved or the degree of formalization of organization rules and regulations. No doubt some political maneuvering can make a *net contribution* toward organization effectiveness. Where there is head-on conflict and where some degree of cooperation is essential, concessions worked out between the parties often involve some bending or reinterpretation of the rules. On many occasions, the various conflicting interests are *all* highly legitimate and rest on solid ground. Some type of informal accommodation, compromise, or exchange is essential for a degree of reconciliation which permits the basic work of the organization to continue. One is usually safe, personally, if he sticks to the rule book and the letter of the law. Unfortunately, one also becomes known as a pathological bureaucrat who is more interested in being right, according to the rules, than he is in accomplishing the objective as revealed by the situation. On the other hand, organizations could devolve into complete chaos if everyone set himself up as a power politician above the law, the formal organization. It is clear that neither extreme is the answer.

An additional complicating factor is that of the individual conscience and code of ethics. If actions which would clearly operate to the net benefit of the organization happen to conflict directly with one's personal code of ethics, a serious question of choice has arisen. Fortunately, most of the actions required of the modern executive are compatible both with organization effectiveness and one's conscience, though not always with the formal procedures and policies.

Summary

In this chapter, three important types of relationships have been discussed: status, power, and politics. These relationships are classified as informal inasmuch as they are rarely spelled out in the official organization manual. Yet they are relationships which can aid or hinder the development of voluntary cooperation toward common objectives.

Status is social rank, and status systems will be developed by all groups where there are significant differences among personnel. Management orders and regulations should be designed so as to disrupt as little as possible these informal status relationships. The awarding of status symbols is an act which can have numerous and far-reaching repercussions upon employee morale.

Power is the capacity to apply effective force and influence. Authority is institutionalized power, and at the same time constitutes one of the major sources of power. Other important sources are expertise, functions, personality, and friends and associates. Just as Mooney considered authority to be the central principle of all formal organizations through providing the basis for insuring coordination, some behaviorists would consider power to be the central factor governing most human relationships.

As power moves into action, the result is politics and accommodation. When conflict is evident and inevitable, compromises and exchanges are often useful devices to insure some degree of cooperation toward common goals.

DISCUSSION PROBLEMS

1. In what way can status incongruency contribute to organizational effectiveness? In what way can it harm effectiveness?
2. Distinguish between status sources and symbols.
3. Discuss the positive and negative aspects of power. Should the general goal be the elimination of power over others?
4. What is meant by the statement that authority is institutionalized power?
5. If a staff specialist is having difficulty in convincing a line supervisor that he should take some specific action, what alternatives are open to him in the formal organization? in the informal organization? in his personal code of conduct?
6. Why does politics necessarily enter into the selection and promotion of executives?
7. Why does politics necessarily enter into the relationship between a shop supervisor and a union steward?
8. What is William F. Whyte's theory of status and procedural initiation?
9. Can conflict among people be eliminated in business organizations? Should it be? In case it cannot, what role should politics and accommodation play?
10. Cite the various sources of power, giving examples of each.

SUPPLEMENTARY READING

Dalton, Melville, *Men Who Manage,* Chaps. 2 and 3. New York: John Wiley & Sons, Inc., 1959.

Jay, Antony, *Management and Machiavelli*. New York: Holt, Rinehart, and Winston, 1967.

Litterer, Joseph A., "Conflict in Organization: A Re-Examination," *Academy of Management Journal,* Vol. 9, No. 3 (September, 1966), 178–186.

Mechanic, David, "Sources of Power of Lower Participants in Complex Organizations," *Administrative Science Quarterly,* Vol. 7, No. 3 (December, 1962), 349–364.

Mills, C. Wright, *The Power Elite*. New York: Oxford University Press, 1956.

Pfiffner, John M. and Frank P. Sherwood, *Administrative Organization,* Chaps. 15, 17, and 18. Englewood Cliffs: Prentice-Hall, Inc., 1960.

Strauss, George, "Tactics of Lateral Relationships: The Purchasing Agent," *Administrative Science Quarterly,* Vol. 7, No. 2 (September, 1962), 161–186.

Votaw, Dow, "What Do We Believe About Power?" *California Management Review,* Vol. 8, No. 4 (Summer, 1966), 71–88.

13

Specialization and Work Systems

The systems and patterns of work which resulted from management's application of the principles of division of labor, transfer of skill from man to machine, and interchangeable manufacturing, have had much to do with providing the United States with the most productive economy in the world. The effectiveness of scientific management procedures cannot be denied. But in recent decades, a nagging question has arisen. Can the tremendous results of such systems of work be maintained without a considerable cost in human values? Must man be, or is he indeed now, a victim of the procedures and mechanisms that science has created? Is it better to have a worker efficient from the scientific manager's viewpoint, however dissatisfied he is as a person? Or is it better to have the worker more satisfied at some *sacrifice* of technical efficiency? Or perhaps the effectiveness of the total system, technical and human, can be not only maintained, but enhanced by devoting greater attention to the human factor.

In this chapter, we propose to examine some of the human problems that issue from specialization and division of labor, such as the difficulties issuing from attempts to integrate *staff* specialists. We shall examine the human problems associated with work procedures and systems, such problems as the impact of automation.

Thus, the study of businesses can be approached in at least two different but contrasting ways, organizationally and operationally. As Chart 2–1 indicated, the basis for organization is the principle of functional similarity, which provides the rationale for establishing specialized jobs, departments, divisions, and other organization elements. Dividing up the total work load of an organization is essential if more than one person is required to execute it. Yet this very division creates certain obstacles and difficulties in putting it all back together again.

As seen from an operational viewpoint, certain sequences of functions must be developed to enable various project goals to be accomplished. Chart 2–1 indicated that while an employee is a member of the Milling Sub-Section, he is also the third step in a work procedure; he must relate to others on a horizontal basis. As long as people are involved in a work system, numerous human problems will develop which can hinder the technical workings of the system. This chapter proposes to deal with the impact upon human behavior of *organizing* on the basis of specialization as well as *operating* upon the basis of technically designed systems of work.

ROLE OF SPECIALIZATION AND WORK SYSTEMS

The values which issue from specialization were pointed out by Adam Smith in his *Wealth of Nations*. When one man concentrates upon a single task, he can produce more than if he spread his efforts over many and diverse tasks.

As indicated in Chapter 9, the basic guide for establishing organizational units is functional similarity. The desired value is productivity; the consequence is sometimes dysfunctional conflict issuing from varying views and scales of value. Specialization often results in strong, ingrained attachment to sub-goals of the enterprise which leads to an inversion of means and ends. Specialists are not immune to such ills as resistance to change that would decrease the importance of their speciality, and status anxiety as they compete with other specialists in the formal arena of the organizational hierarchy. Formal organization structure relies upon an imposed framework of authority to integrate various interdependent specialized functions. One behaviorist suggests that "modern organizations are modeled more on the parent-child relationship than on the adult relationship of specialist equals and colleagues."[1] It is suggested that problems engendered by specialization can be handled in ways other than by the use of formal authority.

Webber cites the instance of a manager of an engineering department who instituted a logging in-and-out register to control the frequent appeals of marketing personnel for engineering help on sales quotations.[2] The desired functional consequence was increased productivity of engineers through greater concentration on product design with less time devoted to solving

---

[1] Victor A. Thompson, *Modern Organization* (New York: Alfred A. Knopf, Inc., 1961), Chap. 4.
[2] Ross A. Webber, "The Roots of Organizational Stress," *Personnel*, Vol. 43, No. 5 (September–October, 1966), pp. 34–35.

routine sales quotation problems. The realized dysfunctional consequences were (1) resistance of sales personnel to the signing in and out process, (2) refusal of engineers to talk until sales personnel signed in, (3) an order from the marketing manager, at the request of the engineering head, to sign the register, (4) a marked reduction in the number of visits by sales personnel, (5) informal refusals of sales people to help engineers when the latter requested marketing information, and (6) reluctance on the part of sales personnel in quoting on customer product orders that required engineering assistance. Various sales managers indicated that if the problem had been discussed at the time of the introduction of the register, more cooperation would have been forthcoming. It is difficult to formally direct and order that cooperation be effected by multiple personnel in the innumerable transactions that must take place daily in any organization.

We have also advanced productivity through the application of the "transfer-of-skill" principle; that is, skill is transferred from man to a mechanism or machine. Machines can also be of a specialized type, still further enhancing quantity and quality of output. This latter principle has had a considerable effect upon the producing man, transforming him from the center of importance into an adjunct of the machine. The furthest application of the principle would be a *complete* transfer of skill to a machine which is self-operating and regulating—automation in other words. (The problems of this phenomenon will be discussed later in this chapter.)

These specialized machines and men will work for nought if they are not coordinated and unified. Thus, systems and procedures must be created to define the role of each productive unit and the precise sequences of operation. In many instances, this will mean a rigid and detailed regulating of all elements of the work system, both man and machine. This will insure coordination, though not necessarily cooperation. Each task will be done rapidly and uniformly at the right time and right place. The results in terms of production units are tremendous.

HUMAN PROBLEMS OF SPECIALIZATION

Specialization of functions, personnel, and physical factors is not without its drawbacks, drawbacks which are primarily in the human area.

Dependency Upon Others

Inasmuch as the total task has been split into so many subtasks, a whole host of interdependencies has been established. If one man fails to perform, he may seriously affect the total output. This places a considerable burden upon the manager to insure that such failures do not occur. It emphasizes the importance of maintaining reasonably peaceful and cooperative relationships among these dependent personnel. On the same basis, the individual firms in our economy are so specialized and interdependent that similar relationships between labor and management are essential to the welfare of the public. Imagine what would happen to the nation if the entire transportation industry were on strike—air, water, rail, truck, and bus. The economy would be strangled overnight. As we can see, then, division of the workload and consequent specialization has resulted in a spreading of the power through the establishment of dependent relationships. And as each specialist becomes *aware* of the power and influence that issue from his essential function, it becomes that much more difficult to *force* cooperation.

Narrow Perspectives and Orientations

Perhaps the foremost human relations difficulty to issue from specialization is the narrowness of viewpoint and limited perspective of the specialist. To become expert in a field, one must devote most if not all of one's time to study, learning, and practice. This necessitates a certain ignorance about other matters, thereby creating Veblen's "trained incapacity." Misunderstanding is fostered and specialists become impatient with each other as their specialties are not fully understood and appreciated.

Each man has a set of values developed from his experiences and education. Many of the conflicts and arguments among personnel in the same organization do not issue from basic dislike of or the inability to get along with each other. They more often come from a real misunderstanding of the other fellow's point of view, which is seen as narrow. One of the major and most difficult tasks of the manager is to provide a continuing education program for his specialists which will lead to a less provincial outlook. The functional analysis presented in Chapter 8 establishes the basis for this education in its attempt to distinguish between primary and secondary functions.

The narrow, though deep, orientation of the specialist also contributes to other problems. Often an expert literally cannot see the forest for all the individual trees. Knowing too much about his subject, he consciously or unconsciously avoids aspects of the problem outside his immediate range of knowledge. He tends to seek complexity at the expense of relatively common-sense solutions. The story is told of the sudden outbreak of dysentery in an army unit. Teams of experts were brought in to investigate. After detailed research by medical personnel and veterinarians, the mystery was solved by a line sergeant. He had observed that the trouble usually occurred on rainy days when the men lined up to enter the mess hall through an exit. This different route took advantage of shelter from the rain. As they passed the steamy soapy solution located by the exit to clean their messkits *after* eating, habit led many to dip their kits *before* eating. A specialized and knowledgeable expert has a tendency to seek the most deep and complex answers to problems in his specialty. He sometimes cannot see what an uninformed layman can.

The role of the *general manager,* then, becomes one of determining what portion of each expert's recommendations is the truth, and what part is error issuing from limited perspectives. The expert knows more than his superior about his specialty, but the manager must know more about the overall situation, which includes this specialty plus many others. The higher one rises in an organization, the more essential this particular managerial skill.

Communication Difficulties

Expertise in a particular field usually produces a system of terms and words which greatly facilitates communication among those in that field. Technical terms multiply like bacteria, yet they are essential for the development of interchange within the specialty. Unfortunately, these same terms tend to build a *wall* between the expert and the laymen, who are often experts themselves in *other* fields. Yet, if one is to integrate these experts into the general organization, there must be open lines of communication which overcome the difficulties of jargon. It is a rare ability (and one which should be treasured and developed) for an expert to be able to express complicated ideas in terms which nonexperts can understand. Too many are too impatient to make the attempt or to define the terms they are using.

Jurisdictional Disputes

Experts often war among themselves for territory to stake out, and specialization requires division of the field. Someone must mark off these divisions, and woe to those who attempt to invade a contiguous area. Sometimes smaller fields are carved from larger, thereby giving those specialists in the latter areas cause for resentment. For example, the industrial engineers have not all admitted the loss of the systems design field to other specialists. In colleges and universities, the industrial psychology department frequently offers courses similar to those found in business administration. Courses taught in industrial engineering are often similar to those in industrial management. When any one field is divided into specialties and sub-specialties, there will be hazy demarcations which will change as knowledge is advanced in the various fields. Specialization provides ample opportunities for jurisdictional disputes, and area experts are not necessarily skilled in consideration, tact, diplomacy, and generosity.

Psychological Fatigue

Much of the division of labor takes place in routine, operative jobs on production floors, offices, and assembly lines. Tasks have been designed which are so simple that muscular, rather than mental, memory is the prime requirement. The assembly line, which will be discussed in a later section, provides many examples of highly specialized, narrow, and shallow jobs. One factory in Texas derived considerable publicity when it "hired" and used chimpanzees on its mattress-stuffing lines for two days. The reactions of their "fellow employees" were somewhat mixed. In any case, such jobs often have a severe impact upon the worker, resulting in boredom, apathy, and general psychological fatigue. However, the production results of such systems of specialization have been so impressive that few, if any, managements will voluntarily give them up for the benefit of improved morale. The first approach to a problem of this type is usually that of more scientific placement. Some people like and can adjust to jobs which most others find monotonous. Other suggestions that have been tried involve greater diversification in job content. These approaches will be discussed along with the assembly line example later in this chapter.

Escape from Social Responsibility

Finally, a problem of major, general importance has resulted from the high degree of specialization prevalent in the economy and nation as a whole—the flight or escape from social responsibility. For example, the electronic engineer maintains that it would be foolish to hold him responsible for the psychological and sociological effects of automation. Designing the system is his specialty; its use is not. Or the scientists who developed the atom bomb disclaim responsibility for what is done with it, for this is not within their field. It is conceivable that a total result, which is highly objectionable socially, could be divided and compartmentalized into a number of segments, each to be executed by specialists who do *not* feel responsible for the whole. Ends are disassociated from means, whose cumulative effect brought these results about.

Within the firm, the technical specialist is often tempted to limit his responsibility to the technical aspects *only*. It is up to the line manager to place his technical innovations into effect. If troubles develop, the specialist attempts to

protect his idea, and attributes any difficulty to the ignorance and uncoopera-
tive nature of the people involved.

Line and Staff Conflicts

With the rapidly increasing complexity of business activities, it was inevitable, as we have noted, that many technical specialists would be added to
business organizations. Usually, these specialists are fitted into the organization
in a staff capacity. In traditional theory, these experts are without the authority
to force acceptance of their ideas. Formally, they have only the rights of
recommendation and appeal to common line superiors.

The addition of specialized staff personnel has produced a number of human
relations problems, many of which have already been discussed in connection
with specialization as a whole. More specifically, the definition of staff requires
that it be a function that has been *taken away* from an originally larger function. In addition, the objective of staff is to improve and change methods of
operation. This implies that staff knows *more* about business activities than do
those who are performing them. Improvement and change often mean doing
more work with the same or fewer personnel. Staff feels a pressure to justify its
own position by creating more economy and effectiveness through these
changes.

A third reason for conflicts between line and staff is the typical method of
manning staff positions in industry. In one study, it was discovered that staff
personnel as compared to line were (1) significantly younger; (2) better
educated in a formal sense; (3) more individualistic and restless; and (4)
different in mode of dress and personal habits.[3] Because of the technical
backgrounds required to fill these specialties, it was customary to recruit
primarily from colleges and universities, from both graduating students and
faculties. As a result, two different subcultures were established in the business
organization. This provided the basis for status conflict and lack of understanding, since changes were being suggested in line operations by people who were
younger, less experienced, better educated, and more individualistic.

Staff personnel also tend to move much more rapidly than line. Technical
specialists have usually been trained in the scientific method and proceed
about their work with dispatch. Because of this training and limited perspectives, they often view the answers they develop as the *only* answers possible.
They tend to discount the difficulties of acting upon their ideas, particularly
with reference to the human relations problems that ensue. Thus, the methods
of staff are rapid, methodical, and somewhat depersonalized, providing the

[3] Melville Dalton, "Conflicts Between Staff and Line Managerial Officers," *American Sociological Review,* Vol. 15 (June, 1950), pp. 342–351.

basis for futher conflict. In the opinion of line personnel, staff are too narrow and theoretical in their approach to practical operating problems.

One final source of difficulty is the organizational location of staff personnel. It will be recalled that staff functions can be evolved from the line at any level; but as the organization grows larger, there is a tendency to elevate staff to higher positions in the structure. In addition, the number of levels within a particular staff department is usually much fewer than in the line division to which it is attached. Thus, the typical staff man has a much shorter route to follow in contacting top management. Line personnel are frequently resentful of this closer relationship between top management and staff people and often impute a measure of power to the latter. Thus, a tendency develops to give staff recommendations more power than that which would issue from their formal authority. This is particularly true in matters which are so technical and complicated that line personnel have no alternative but to accept staff recommendations. Such relationships become transformed into functional relationships, rather than staff, with a consequent change from single to multiple accountability.

If there is to be coordinated and organized action, these potential areas of conflict must be controlled and directed along constructive channels. Among the various suggestions that have been made are the following:

1. Creation of special, formal coordinating agencies to integrate the various specialized units.
2. Broadening of backgrounds through line and staff rotation or special projects.
3. Political compromises.
4. More realistic organizational education, both within the firm and in colleges and universities.
5. Altering the behavior of staff to one of consultation and adaptation to client (line) requirements.

In organizing, functions that have been divided to achieve specialized productivity must be finally combined to achieve unity and coordination. In the formal hierarchical structure, the authority of superior managers is the basic means of combination. When demands for coordination exceed the capacity of the manager, new specialized coordinative units may be added. For example, Urwick and Dale have been in the forefront in advocating the creation of a general staff function in business similar to that in the military.[4] This general staff would assist in coordinating all the specialized staffs and help to provide a bridge between these staffs and the line. Thus far, this suggestion has not been widely adopted in industry on the top management

[4] Ernest Dale and Lyndall Urwick, *Staff in Organization* (New York: McGraw-Hill Book Company, 1960).

level, though a few firms, such as Koppers Company, have established some-thing similar to the military general staff. This same integrating help is re-quired in various parts of the organization. The responsibility of a production control department, for example, is one of coordinating such specialized units as product design, industrial engineering, purchasing, and quality control in their efforts to assist multiple line departments.

The behavior pattern of the integrating person is of crucial importance. Research has found that his style should fall between the extremes of the units with which he must deal; e.g., sales personnel are most concerned with sound personal relationships while production managers are more task-oriented and willing to sacrifice smooth interpersonal relations if required.[5] The integrator is more effective if he can cope with both patterns of behavior. He is also more effective if he has high prestige within the enterprise, is persuasive and verbally fluent, and is flexible in his ways of acting. Data also show that "there is a close relationship between the effectiveness of integration in an organiza-tion and the reliance of its members on confrontation as a way to resolve interdepartmental conflict."[6] Confrontation and discussion are preferred to either manipulated, smooth and friendly interpersonal relationships or the straight-forward use of authority.

Line and staff rotation has also been a favorite training program in the military. As the specialties become more complex, however, such rotation is very difficult to effect. Special attempts can still be made to provide staff personnel with significant experiences in working with line personnel and with opportunity for practical application of their ideas. In this manner, they would obtain a good grounding in human relations problems.

In the preceding chapter, various examples were given of political compro-mises between line and staff personnel. Most staff personnel discover rather quickly that other forces besides logic will be required to gain acceptance of their ideas. Some of the difficulties issuing from this initial naïveté could possibly be reduced by providing more realistic education and training in the colleges and universities from which most staff personnel are recruited.

The favored behavioral solution to line and staff conflict is the adoption of a consultative role by specialized staff.[7] This would require de-emphasis of police and surveillance activities as well as unwelcome entry into operating department activities. If the staff specialist is to succeed, he must demonstrate that his knowledge and service can work to the benefit of the using agency. There must be established a continuing relationship involving *joint* study of operating difficulties and an absence of threatening reports to higher line

[5] Paul R. Lawrence and Jay W. Lorsch, "New Management Job: The Integrator," *Harvard Business Review,* Vol. 45, No. 6 (November–December, 1967), p. 148.

[6] *Ibid.,* p. 149.

[7] Douglas McGregor, *The Professional Manager* (New York: McGraw-Hill Book Company, 1967), Chap. 7.

FIGURE 13–1   APPROACHES TO IMPROVING PRODUCTIVITY

Conventional Industrial Engineering	Behavioral Science Approach
• Cost reduction is the objective.	• The objective is to provide better tools for the manager, especially in cost and manpower control.
• The program is imposed from above.	• The program belongs to line management. The industrial engineer is a professional consultant to each level of line management, particularly to first-line supervision.
• The industrial engineer decides on the technique of measurement and what will be counted. The manager contributes only his knowledge of operations.	• The line manager is involved in day-to-day decisions on what to measure, how to count it, the measurement technique, and the reporting system.
• Performance reports are made by the industrial engineering department concurrently to all levels of management, and industrial engineers explain to top management reasons for variance in levels of performance.	• The performance report is issued by the line supervisor to his supervisor, who is responsible for any explanation, with assistance from the industrial engineer when desired.
• Standards (and resulting performance reports) will motivate increased productivity. (Carrot and stick approach.)	• Increased productivity stems from meaningful jobs, competent supervision, and effective teamwork. Standards may be helpful guidelines if the group has helped to create them.
• Build a job requiring efficiency, and let the worker adapt to it.	• In designing a job, take into account the technical requirements, organizational goals, and human motivation.
• The industrial engineer acts as an outside expert.	• The industrial engineer acts as a consultant.

Source: Reprinted by permission of the publisher from "A Team Approach to Improving Productivity," by S. L. Lieder and J. H. Zenger, *Personnel* (July–August, 1967), p. 72.

superiors. Similarly, the staff consultant should be free to withdraw from situations in which he feels he cannot be helpful. An example of a set of guidelines incorporating this viewpoint is shown in the right-hand column in Figure 13–1.[8] It is contrasted with the more traditional view on the left.

[8] Sharon L. Lieder and John H. Zenger, "Industrial Engineers and Behavioral Scientists: A Team Approach to Improving Productivity," *Personnel*, Vol. 44, No. 4 (July–August, 1967), p. 72. The firm involved is TRW Systems of Los Angeles. Similar efforts are being made by such firms as Eastman Kodak, Procter and Gamble, and Texas Instruments.

HUMAN PROBLEMS OF WORK SYSTEMS

In the field of organizing, personnel problems are often mishandled but rarely overlooked. The organizer recognizes that he has three important components—personnel, functions, and physical factors. In the field of operations, however, the systems designer is more prone to view his problems from a technical standpoint almost exclusively. The human element may be entirely overlooked as the mechanics of operational procedures are worked out to achieve system proficiency. This view is perhaps justified only in cases where there is complete automation and all people have been *eliminated*. Even here, the displacement is such that broad social problems are created by the "procedures expert," for whom people become *obstacles* to efficiency, rather than assets.

The systematic study of the human implications of procedural design has led to the discovery of various human problems which issue from work systems. The following are some of the more prominent:

1. The discipline imposed by the system and work place.
2. Impact of layout and space upon human needs.
3. Status problems in procedural initiation.
4. The integration of horizontal work flowing with vertical structuring of formal authority.
5. Worker insecurity.

System Discipline

We have indicated earlier that some of the higher needs of man issue from the ego, the desire to be somewhat independent, dominant, and recognized. There has been a trend in the direction of a more permissive and less autocratic management with the development of the human relations field. Yet, ironically, the concurrent tremendous advances in various technological fields have brought with them a discipline of the work place which can be as autocratic as that of any "bull of the woods" manager. It is obviously a more impersonal type of discipline, but it does demand that one stand there, not move about, and process each unit precisely and exactly according to the system instructions. The greater the specialization of labor, the greater the necessity for discipline and predictability of work behavior. Specialized tasks in themselves often lose their meaning to the performer. Many of the interviews conducted with assembly line workers report their hatred for the monster, the continuous conveyor.[9] The flow of work is a never-ending river;

[9] Cf. Charles R. Walker and Robert H. Guest, *The Man on the Assembly Line* (Cambridge: Harvard University Press, 1952).

any sense of pride in accomplishment is lost, for nothing is ever really completed. Thus, until utopian automation removes all workers completely from the work place, work systems, rather than the manager, will provide much of the discipline necessary to insure coordination.

Ecology

It was also pointed out earlier that one of the higher needs of man was that of association with others. However, technology again often serves to frustrate this need. On mechanized assembly lines, each worker can associate only with the worker ahead of him and the one behind; the creation of primary work groups is made more difficult. In the automated factory, fewer personnel will be required and they may be forced to work alone. One union in England submitted a new demand for "loneliness pay" because of the new work layout. Management should at least recognize that certain technical processes are frustrating the satisfaction of basic human needs. If these processes cannot be altered without sacrificing efficiency, perhaps other efforts can be made to enable contact and talk during elongated coffee breaks, to provide for relief workers, etc.

Work Initiation

It is difficult for high status personnel to be told to work, however impersonally, by people of lower status. Many procedures require this to happen, as for example the supplymen telling the cooks to hurry up with the order. Management should seek to alter or supplement work systems with as little disruption as possible of informal social relations. The human component of any system requires as much study as the physical factors.

Horizontal Work Flow vs. Vertical Control

The actual work of an organization is accomplished on a horizontal basis. A work project cuts across organization lines and moves from one level of organization to another, all in the interest of accomplishing a specific project goal. Thus, the vertical lines of accountability for a total project are difficult to integrate with the horizontal flow of the work itself. As work crosses organization jurisdictions, it is legally inspected for purposes of accountability. In this manner, the next unit of authority cannot claim that unacceptable work was received from the preceding unit. It is apparent that the formal authority structure necessary for the basic framework of the organization is not readily adaptable to the horizontal flow of work. For this reason, certain adaptations in structure have been innovated, an example of which is the project form discussed in Chapter 10. Some theorists have suggested almost complete elimination of formal structures in the interest of not hampering the work flow. It should be apparent that such an approach would throw up more obstacles than it would eliminate. A compromise solution must be worked out.

Worker Insecurity

And finally, there is the general problem of the impact of a specialized, highly mechanized work environment upon the personality of the worker. Job insecurities are increased where (1) the job is "engineered out," that is, the worker is told exactly what to do with little or no deviations permitted; (2) the system is apparently more important than any individual employee; (3) the worker has lost public identity for his job because it is so narrow and esoteric that the outside world would not understand what a "fin sticker" is, for example; and (4) the job requires muscular, rather than mental, attention, and ample time is allowed for imagined troubles. Overall, the worker senses a loss of control over himself and his future. He is a victim of the technical system. This is a very difficult problem with which to cope, and workers have provided some of their own solutions by forming labor unions to help regain some measure of control. Yet the strongest labor union possible can help little with respect to the individual problem of adjusting to a job which is boring, repetitive, and personally obnoxious to its incumbent.

THE ASSEMBLY LINE

As a tangible example of a work system which is both the hallmark of technical efficiency and the root of many human problems, the modern mechanically paced assembly line is non-pareil. The task of each person along the line is defined precisely, both in terms of methods and the time required for completion, through scientific management techniques of motion and time study. Usually, the skill required at each station is quite limited, for employees can learn to do most of the tasks in a matter of hours. The individual worker must keep up, for the product will continue along the line, with or without the part. Thus, the degree of interdependency is high inasmuch as trouble at any one station may necessitate the stopping of the entire line. Because of the high degree of subdivision and specialization of tasks, only surface mental attention is required. The employee may not even know what it is he is working upon;

his interest in the job and the organization is proportionately lessened and deadened.[10]

It is evident that the demands made upon the employee are low in terms of skill and participation and high in terms of tolerance to repetitious, controlled, and pressurized production. If the time standards are set tightly, even communication between the worker and his immediate neighbors is difficult.

A study by Guest and Walker showed that the absenteeism rate among workers on the assembly line was twice as high (3 percent) as the rate for those who worked *off* the line in such jobs as maintenance and stock (1.6 percent).[11] On the various production and assembly lines, there was some variability in conditions, e.g., some tasks were even more repetitive than others, some required more skill, some permitted more interaction with fellow workers, some were less paced mechanically, etc. When these production jobs were measured on the basis of such variables, personnel on the jobs which were most repetitious, mechanically paced, and with the least skill requirement and chance for personal interaction, had the higher absenteeism rates.

SOCIO-TECHNICAL SYSTEMS

In the past two decades, there has been an attempt by various researchers in the United States and Great Britain to establish a socio-technical approach to the design of work systems. It will be recalled that in the pioneering scientific management movement, the task to be performed was highly central to the theory of management developed by Taylor, Gilbreth, and others. A science of work was to be established by such specific techniques as motion analysis and time study. With the inducement of money, economic man would consent to undertake these scientifically determined tasks.

With the human relations research of the 1920's, the pendulum swung to the other extreme. Though the behaviorists involved in the Hawthorne experiments may not have intended that the task be subordinated to an unimportant role, it is nevertheless true that the consumers of this research concluded that human relations and the social environment were the most important factors to be considered by the effective manager. Managing literally became the art of managing *people* rather than managing *work*. Many concluded that employee morale was the fundamental determinant of productivity. An even greater impedance to the development of a meaningful theory was the inference that the scientific management approach worked completely *counter* to the development of constructive human relationships, that if we valued and moved

---

[10] See Walker and Guest, *The Man on the Assembly Line,* and Charles R. Walker and Robert H. Guest, *The Foreman on the Assembly Line* (Cambridge: Harvard University Press, 1956).

[11] Walker and Guest, *The Man on the Assembly Line,* p. 116.

toward organizational efficiency, we inevitably stunted human growth and development through imposed regimentation, however rational.

Thus, the excessively simple economic model of man proposed by the early scientific management movement was now joined by the excessively simple feeling or attitude model proposed by many behaviorists. These reviews set the stage for a third move of the pendulum to a more balanced and far more complex theory of managing. It was to be a theory that regards *both man and work* as inextricably intertwined and equally important.

The term "socio-technical" first appeared during the 1950's in the writings of various members of the Tavistock Institute of Human Relations in London.[12] As a unit of analysis, it encompasses both the social aspects emphasized by the behavioral scientists and the technological components which have always been valued by the scientific management school. The view is that both contribute significant and interacting elements of a total system, and neither can nor should be studied in isolation. The system is composed of men, machines, and goals, the boundaries of which are determined by commonality of goals, space, and time. In addition, the socio-technical system is an open one, subject to influences that exist outside of its immediate boundaries. Above all, the boundary is *not* to be drawn *between* man and the task.

The initial study of the Institute took place in the British coal mines and sharply demonstrated the effects that technology and the physical environment have on interpersonal relations. It was discovered in a controlled experiment that the effects of the technical task on worker output are mediated through an emerging social organization. This social organization of norms and values is heavily affected not only by the technology, but also by the physical environment, supervisory behavior, and the rewards system established by management.

To cite one illustrative example, the British researchers contrasted two technical systems of mining coal: (1) the conventional longwall which emphasized job and shift specialization, with coordination being provided by management, and (2) the composite longwall which emphasized organization by the mining cycle, the work to be coordinated within and by the cycle work group. The latter method was significantly better in such measured results as absence rates, state of cycle progress at end of shift, and general productivity.[13] The latter system provided the means for a sense of closure in finishing a unit of work; the group was responsible for a complete cycle of mining. It also provided for control by the group of many of its significant activities, such as individual task assignment and member selection. In effect, much of the managing process had been delegated to the group with subsequent opportunity for flexibility and self-control.

---

[12] E. L. Trist, G. W. Higgin, H. Murray, and A. B. Pollack, *Organizational Choice* (London: Oxford University Press, 1965).

[13] *Ibid.*, pp. 122–125.

In a related study by A. K. Rice in an Indian textile mill, it was discovered that organization on the basis of specialization resulted in less production than a different organization on the basis of a meaningful output unit.[14] The operation of weaving room equipment involved 12 specialized tasks for 240 looms. For example, a single weaver operated 30 looms, a battery filler cared for 50 looms, and a smash-hand tended 70 looms. The existing organization, based on this worker specialization, was operating at an efficiency index of 80. In the experiment, a part of the organization was altered to create an effective work group. All workers who were interdependent were made members of the same group and placed in charge of a specific bank of looms. As a result of this new organizational base (the bank of looms), more worker cooperation and coordination developed with a rise in efficiency from 80 to 95, and a drop in damage from approximately 30 to 20. In the remaining part of the mill where the old job specialization method of organization was still being used, efficiency stayed at about 80 and the damage rate continued at an average of 30. Just as the mining cycle constituted the meaningful work unit in the British coal mines, the bank of looms enabled worker understanding, cooperation, and commitment in the Indian textile mill.

JOB DESIGN

In the United States, this type of research is often termed "job design" rather than socio-technical systems. It is also more narrow and closely related to specific job tasks. Among the various approaches to job design that have been researched are the following:

1. The introduction of some variability in worker tasks through either job rotation or the employee working up the line.
2. Job enlargement.
3. Worker control over pace.
4. Information and orientation concerning the whole and its interrelated parts.

Variability in Worker Tasks

Since the jobs are routine and of limited skill requirement, it is possible to introduce some form of worker rotation. Note again, however, that the first approach should be that of improved placement. There are certain people who actually prefer to work on routine, repetitive, low-skill jobs, and who would object to any rotation. However, experience has indicated that the majority of

---

[14] A. K. Rice, *Productivity and Social Organization: The Ahmedabad Experiment* (London: Tavistock Publications, Ltd., 1959).

people are adversely affected psychologically by the tasks as designed and laid out on the modern assembly line.

In addition to work rotation, some men on the line have discovered that they can complete their tasks more rapidly than the standard times allowed, and thus can work up the line on units that have not reached their work stations. This permits both (1) some employee control over the job, and (2) a brief unscheduled work break.

Job Enlargement

We have in some instances perhaps passed the point of peak production in our progress toward specialization. As Fig. 13–2 indicates, productivity rises with increased specialization up to a point where it begins to decline. This decline may be from worker rebellion, boredom, and monotony. Thus, there are other variables in production efficiency besides specialization and the technical components. Perhaps a reversal of the specialization process to some degree may, through its impact upon human attitudes, raise the productivity curve.

FIGURE 13–2   SPECIALIZATION AND PRODUCTIVITY

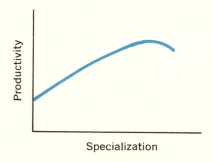

There has been some research and practical experimentation with this theory of job enlargement. One of the first companies involved was the International Business Machines Corporation. IBM attempted, for example, to integrate the set-up function in the drilling department with the tasks of operating machine tools. This meant the gradual elimination of the specialized set-up job. Over a ten-year period, the company altered the proportions from one set-up man per 22 operators, to one per 48, to no set-up men at all.[15] The drilling jobs became more interesting, and the pay was raised because of the increased skill requirements. Additional benefits included a better quality of product, less idle time, and improved employee morale.

[15] Charles R. Walker, "The Problem of the Repetitive Job," *Harvard Business Review,* Vol. 28, No. 3 (May, 1950), p. 57.

In another study conducted by Marks and reported by Davis, a controlled experiment was undertaken to compare the results of the modern assembly line with those of production under conditions of job enlargement.[16] The product involved was a hospital appliance assembled by nine operators located along a moving conveyor. In Fig. 13–3, the production rates under the assembly line set-up are reported in part *a* as an index of 100. The first variable introduced

FIGURE 13–3   AVERAGE DAILY PRODUCTIVITY INDEXES

N = number of days in each job-design period

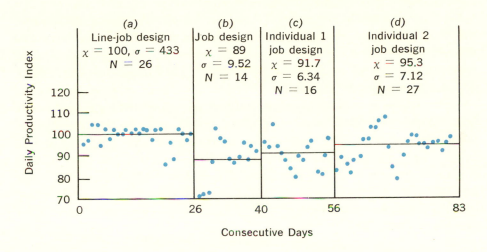

Source: Reprinted by permission of the publisher from "Job Design and Productivity: A New Approach," by Louis E. Davis, *Personnel*, March, 1957. © 1957 by the American Management Association, Inc.

was the elimination of the moving conveyor but with no job enlargement. Part *b* in Fig. 13–3 indicates that production dropped to approximately an index of 90. The second change introduced a high degree of job enlargement. Instead of one person doing one of nine tasks, each would assemble a complete appliance by performing *all* nine tasks. Part *c* indicates that the production rate rose to approximately 92, which is considerably below that of the traditional assembly line. Part *d* shows the results of this same system of job enlargement, but with the work taking place on the main floor rather than in a separate room as in the case of part *c*. With the further experience and the opportunities for interaction with more people, production rose to an index of 94, still below the original method. However, it should be noted in part *d* that the trend was upward and on certain days exceeded the amount under the conveyor production line. Job

[16] Louis E. Davis, "Job Design and Productivity: A New Approach," *Personnel*, Vol. 33, No. 5 (March, 1957), pp. 418–430.

enlargement was tried for 43 working days while the assembly line had been in operation for a number of years.

Another highly significant result of these changes in job design was an immediate increase in the quality of product under the system of job enlargement. Though quantity was slow in returning to former levels, there was an immediate drop in the number of rejects to *one-fourth* of the original amount. This could have come from both the increased interest in the job as well as the opportunity for management to impose more precise accountability. When one man makes the entire assembly, it becomes that much easier to discover causes for any rejects.

A final study to be cited is the enlargement of various assembly line jobs in a home laundry manufacturing firm.[17] Attempts were made during the space of five years to increase the number and variety of tasks. Employees were also given responsibility for pacing of work, determination of work methods, and passing upon the quality of completed products. For example, a pump assembly line of 6 operators required 1.77 minutes per unit. In moving from the assembly line to single operator work stations, the pump was assembled in one job of 35 elements requiring 1.49 minutes. In 13 other similar job changes, there was an average decrease in quality rejects from 2.9 to 1.4 percent, and an average decrease in output efficiency from 138 percent to 126 percent. In a study of employee reactions, the enlarged jobs were preferred over assembly line jobs primarily because of the benefits of self-pacing. It should be noted that the mixed results in terms of both quantity and quality are similar to the previously cited study.

Worker Control Over Pace

One possibility for meeting the requirements of the ego, without giving up the technology, is to *permit the group to regulate the pace* of the moving conveyor. William F. Whyte reports one interesting instance where this was tried.[18] The task involved painting toys which were moving along a conveyor line. Toys were carried on hooks, and the eight female employees located along the line would remove a toy, place it in a jig inside a painting cubicle, spray it, and then hang it back on the line. These eight women were paid on a group bonus plan but the anticipated development of group cooperation and high morale did not materialize. Turnover and absenteeism were high, as were the number of complaints submitted. One of the chief complaints was that the

[17] E. H. Conant and M. D. Kilbridge, "An Interdisciplinary Analysis of Job Enlargement: Technology, Costs, and Behavioral Implications," *Industrial and Labor Relations Review*, Vol. 18, No. 3 (April, 1965), p. 377.

[18] William Foote Whyte, *Money and Motivation* (New York: Harper & Bros., 1955), pp. 90–96.

pace of the line was too rapid. One meeting with these women ended with a suggestion that *they* be allowed to control the speed of the conveyor. This, naturally, was heresy to both managers and time study engineers. After much discussion and argument, it was agreed to give the system a try.

The eight women spent several coffee breaks in discussing what speeds to run the conveyor. A control mechanism was provided with the indexes of slow, medium, and fast. They decided that the first half-hour of the shift was to be at medium speed, the next 2½ hours at high, the half-hours before and after lunch at low, and the rest of the afternoon at high with the exception of the last 45 minutes at medium. Though the previously engineered standard would have been just above *medium* on the dial, the average that these women worked out was on the *high* side. Within a few weeks, these workers were producing 30 to 50 percent above the level originally expected. Their bonuses were of such size that it became embarrassing to management, since they were now earning more than many skilled workers in other parts of the plant. Much controversy ensued concerning this. Finally, the superintendent arbitrarily ruled that the painting operation be returned to its original state with the hooks moving at the time-studied standard speed. Production dropped immediately, and six of the eight girls quit within the next month.

This episode describes various elements which contributed toward more cooperation, elements which served to satisfy some of the basic needs of man (see Chapter 6). The right to control the pace is evidence of respect for human integrity. The opportunities given the workers to meet and discuss production problems among themselves and with management aided in forming a primary group. The varying of the pace from hour to hour is more nearly akin to human requirements. (The idea that a constant pace is more efficient is more characteristic of machines than of men.) However, delegating the right to control pace is antagonistic to the traditional scientific management approach. A manager decides and commands, and a subordinate accepts and follows. And finally, the considerable results that were accomplished threw the department out of balance with the rest of the organization.

Information and Orientation

Though the worker must perform a narrowly specified task that precludes closure, it has been suggested that a broader understanding of the whole will contribute to improved productivity and satisfaction. The effects of this type of role orientation were researched in a study conducted at General Electric.[19] Discussions were held among employees concerning how their work affected

[19] Melvin Sorcher and Herbert H. Meyer, "Motivation and Job Performance," *Personnel Administration*, Vol. 31, No. 4 (July–August, 1968), pp. 17–21.

that of subsequent work stations. They were also taken on a tour of other work stations to establish a more personal relationship with other employees. This orientation was conducted for eight groups of employees who had an unusually high amount of responsibility, discretion, variety, and physical movement in their jobs, as well as for six work groups in which the jobs were more typical of assembly work with little variety and movement. After orientation, significant improvements in quality were noted in both types of jobs, but the greatest improvement was in the more routine assembly type. In the eight weeks preceding the program, the average acceptance rate was 57.9 percent and 66 percent at two different control points. For the nine weeks following the program, acceptance percentages rose to 69.2 and 92.1, respectively. When the program was inaugurated in another department, it was found that reductions in defects were directly proportionate to the percentage of employees in a group who had happened to attend the orientation course. It was estimated that in all such programs, the return on the investment in role-training was about 50 to 1.

Both the socio-technical systems and job design approaches are consistent with the research and theories of Douglas McGregor, Abraham Maslow, Frederick Herzberg, and Rensis Likert. Louis Davis summarizes the implications of the British studies as follows:[20]

1. Develop composition of a group that enables self-regulation.
2. Provide for the full range of necessary skills.
3. Delegate authority for self-assignment of tasks and roles in the group.
4. Develop internal communication opportunities within the group.
5. Provide for a group monetary reward system.

The more specific job design studies suggest the following:

1. Broaden the job scope to include all tasks necessary to complete a significant unit which enables closure.
2. Introduce greater task variety.
3. Permit self-regulation of speed.
4. Permit self-determination of work methods and sequence.
5. Permit self-inspection of output.

It should be readily apparent that the above listed suggestions are compatible with Theory "Y," the hierarchy of needs leading to self-actualization, concentration upon motivators rather than hygiene factors, and supportive supervision. They all are designed to meet the need for completion of the whole task, the need for a measure of autonomy in the control of one's activities, and the need for satisfactory relationships with others.

[20] Louis E. Davis, "The Design of Jobs," *Industrial Relations,* Vol. 6, No. 1 (October, 1966), p. 44.

AUTOMATION

A second example of a work system which must be discussed in any text on human relations and management is that of automation. Mechanization is the process of transferring skill from men to machines so that the bulk of the work is accomplished by machines. Man is still needed to feed and control the machine, but often his task is of a low skill level, routine, and repetitive.

When so much skill is transferred to the machine that it no longer requires man to feed and control it, we have automation. Automation necessitates the introduction of some form of data processing: information at the work place is given to a control center where it is compared to standards; new information is then sent out automatically to regulate the working unit. It is a big leap to move from *machine* operation with *manual* control to *machine* operation with *machine* control. The ramifications are tremendous, and, for this reason, the period of the 1950's and 1960's has been referred to as the *second* industrial revolution.

The most striking result of automation is the tremendous increase in productivity per man-hour. An automobile company, for example, can produce an engine block from a rough casting in 14½ minutes as compared with 24 hours prior to automation.[21] Automation reduced the number of workers required to stuff frankfurters for a certain volume of production from fifty to seven or eight.[22] It is clear that if one wishes to continue to maintain and increase the economic standard of living, the introduction and promotion of automation is inevitable.

Again, however, the major problems involved in this work system are *human* rather than technical. The most dramatic problem is the technological unemployment that will occur from these sharp increases in productivity per man-hour. It has been estimated that all types of technological progress would permit the discharge of 1¼ million workers per year without any decline in output.[23] When we realize that the total labor force grows at a rate of more than a million a year, the problem of adjusting labor supply to employer demand is magnified.

Some experts believe that the unemployment problems resulting from automation are temporary, that the usual pattern of adjustment will follow; i.e., lower prices will lead to increased demand for goods, thus resulting in long range greater employment. If this proves to be true, it still does not take care of the short run during which time many workers will require help. Although

---

[21] Walter S. Buckingham, *Automation* (New York: Harper & Bros., 1961), p. 23.

[22] Town Hall, *Automation and the Worker,* Los Angeles, California (February, 1963), p. 5.

[23] Alvin H. Hansen, "Automation and the Welfare State," *New Republic* (April 10, 1961), p. 10.

there will be increasing opportunities for the better educated in the professional, technical, and skilled fields, and for new workers with appropriate backgrounds, it is the low skilled personnel who will experience the major difficulties. They will often have to be retrained or downgraded. Even retraining poses a problem, since many of these workers do not have the minimum necessary formal education. Automation thus engenders difficulties for society in general as well as business in particular.

Automation has had a considerable impact upon labor-management relations. The major demand of unions in recent years is that job rights for present personnel be protected. In some instances, this had led to featherbedding, the requirement of pay for work that is either not done or is unnecessary. In general, the union movement has not been opposed to automation, but has sought first, some control over its introduction in order to ease the impact upon workers, and second, some sharing of the cost burden for this introduction. In a few cases, managements have agreed to pay for the right to introduce technological improvements. For example, the Pacific Coast Longshore Agreement provided for a Mechanization Fund in 1960, where the employer in effect paid $29,000,000 for the right to introduce technical changes without fear of a strike. Armour and Company established an automation fund, in 1949, of a half-million dollars to be used for studying the problem and paying for the retraining and transfer of employees to other plants.

The burden of solving the problems of automation must be shared among industry, labor unions, and government. The impact of automation on the general unemployment level led to the Federal Manpower Development and Retraining Act of 1962. The approach here is to work through public employment agencies to determine what skills are in demand, to solicit applications from among displaced personnel, to organize and finance a training program, and to locate newly trained personnel in jobs. Though much remains to be done, training programs have already been undertaken for such diverse jobs as electricians, formal restaurant waiters, forestry aides, licensed practical nurses, and engineering aides.

Ultimately, the solution may well mean a shortening of the standard work week to something less than the standard 40 hours. A few industries have established a 36 hour week and some unions have demanded as few as 30. But here again, this problem of unemployment cannot be met in isolation from all other factors. Competition from industrial firms in other countries in the world will preclude the complete absorption of increased labor costs in consumer prices. Thus, the world political and economic situation influences attempts towards any permanent solution to the general problem of technological unemployment.

Within the individual firm, the possibility of solving some of the human problems appears to be much brighter. If the cooperation of the union has been obtained through both planned participation and the establishment of funds to aid the displaced, considerable progress has been made. Ordinarily, the impact can also be softened by restricting the hiring process and allowing the normal amount of resignations to reduce the labor force to the level needed. In-plant retraining and transfer programs can be worked out. Earlier retirement dates may be established along with a gradual reduction in hours to the degree that the market and competition will permit. Of course, these approaches do not solve the general problem in society. We still must create at least 2½ million new jobs each year to keep up with both technological progress and the growth of the labor force.

With respect to other human problems, automation requires management to view the components of the factory as a functionally interdependent unit rather than as a number of independent operations. This means that those working in an automated factory be *flexible* and *adaptable*. Greater interdependence means a greater need for cooperation and coordination. There may be a shift to more centralized decision making and less individual autonomy. The jobs may be more interesting and demanding, but they will also be more precisely tied into a larger system.

Management has also discovered that with a problem as large and as complicated as automation, the more participation in the problem-solving process, the better will be the acceptance of the answers. Some of the answers, though completely understood, will necessarily be bitter pills to swallow. Men will lose jobs which they have held for years or be downgraded to lower status and lower skilled jobs. They will see younger and better educated people enter the firm as higher paid employees in better jobs. Automation, with all its disruptive characteristics, is thus not only inevitable but also obliges management, along with labor and government, to aid those who are caught in this process of change.

Summary

The benefits of specialization and work systems are predominantly technical (improved production quality and quantity). The drawbacks and problems are predominantly human (the frustration of basic human needs, and unemployment). The goal must be an optimizing of human as well as technical values.

Specialization creates problems of dependency, narrowness of viewpoint, jargon, jurisdictional disputes, and psychological fatigue. The addition of staff provides a good example of the problem of integrating technical specialists into the broader organization.

Work systems create such human problems as increased discipline, frustration of gregarious needs, increased insecurity, and possibly the worker's complete elimination. The modern assembly line and automation, while leading to the highest economic standard of living in the world, are two outstanding examples of work systems that have caused a considerable number of human problems. A changing of exclusive emphasis from work to man has not been rewarding in terms of developing a meaningful management theory. The socio-technical approach, encompassing both man and technology as interrelated components, holds far greater promise for future research. It also is far more complex, thereby precluding quick and easy answers to very important problems.

DISCUSSION PROBLEMS

1. Discuss and interrelate the following propositions: (1) if the work is technically well designed, employee motivation is unimportant, and (2) if employees are well motivated, work design is unimportant.
2. Discuss the nature and significance of socio-technical systems. How does the British research differ from that conducted in the United States?
3. Discuss the effects of task variety and worker pacing upon attitudes and productivity.
4. What effect does information and orientation have upon attitudes and output?
5. Contrast the effects of job enlargement upon output quantity and quality.
6. Describe the role of staff acting as a consultant to line.
7. Describe the role of a formally designated integrator whose task is the reduction of interdepartmental conflict.
8. What are the various reasons for conflicts between line and staff personnel? What approaches can be taken to reduce these clashes?
9. What is the relationship between status and work procedures? layout and gregariousness? work flow and authority?
10. Distinguish between mechanization and automation. How do the human problems differ?

SUPPLEMENTARY READING

Baker, John K. and Robert H. Schaffer, "Making Staff Consulting More Effective," *Harvard Business Review*, Vol. 47, No. 1 (January–February, 1969), 62–71.

Davis, Louis E., "The Design of Jobs," *Industrial Relations*, Vol. 6, No. 1 (October, 1966), 21–45.

Lawrence, Paul R. and Jay W. Lorsch, "New Management Job: The Integrator," *Harvard Business Review*, Vol. 45, No. 6 (November–December, 1967), 142–151.

Lieder, Sharon L. and John H. Zenger, "Industrial Engineers and Behavioral Scientists: A Team Approach to Improving Productivity," *Personnel*, Vol. 44, No. 4 (July–August, 1967), 68–75.

Paine, Frank T. and Dennis R. Hykes, "Automation and Motivation: A Theory of Management," *Personnel Administration*, Vol. 29, No. 1 (January–February, 1966), 26–32.

Sorcher, Melvin and Herbert H. Meyer, "Motivation and Job Performance," *Personnel Administration,* Vol. 31, No. 4 (July–August, 1968), 9–21.

Webber, Ross A., "The Roots of Organizational Stress," *Personnel,* Vol. 43, No. 5 (September–October, 1966), 32–39.

Cases for Part III

OPTICS, INC.

This non-profit corporation was set up 10 years ago to develop an astronomical research facility for the United States. In this short time, it has developed the world's foremost center for astronomy.

In the past, construction of a telescope was the lifetime work of several people. Optics has now constructed 10 major instruments, with other telescopes in progress. This rapid growth has been due to continued financial support precipitated by the space race, but in greater part by the excellent staff organized to plan and direct the growth of the observatory. The professional staff is composed of a group of experienced astronomers and engineers well acquainted with astronomical instruments. This group is housed in a city office facility 80 miles from the observatory site. As the construction of the mountain facilities and telescopes are completed, the responsibility for the operation and maintenance is relinquished to a permanent staff living at the site.

The supervisory organization at the site is usually composed of a superintendent and two supervisors. One supervisor handles buildings and grounds, and the other is supervisor of the electricians and telescope maintenance people. The responsibilities of these jobs have continued to vary and change over the last several years as the mountain complex has grown and operating procedures have been developed.

During the construction phase, the supervisory staff was larger and consisted

263

of a Mountain Superintendent, construction inspectors, a mechanical supervisor, a head electrician, and a supervisor of the inspectors. As the greater part of the construction on the shops, homes, and telescopes was completed, the work load for these people lessened. The inspectors were let go, and at this same time the mechanical supervisor resigned for a better position elsewhere.

It was decided at this time by the management of Optics, in conference with the Mountain Superintendent, that Jim Handy, the head electrician, should combine his duties with those of the departing mechanical supervisor.

Since the combined staff of the electrical and mechanical groups numbered about 10 people and most were experienced employees having worked in the construction phase, no supervision problems were foreseen. At this time the only change in Handy's job was the combination of his former supervisory duties with those of supervising the maintenance mechanics. While *all* his time was now spent in supervision of the workers, his job title was not changed. In this manner, he was able to continue to be paid for his overtime hours and receive the higher hourly rate paid for construction work whenever the job justified this. Working in this way, Handy was able to bring his yearly wages to nearly that received by the Mountain Superintendent. Handy was believed to be a competent electrician, but was not well-liked by his subordinates or technicians from the downtown office. He was short-tempered and extremely critical of work not done his way.

Before the yearly wage and salary review, Handy asked that his job title be changed from head electrician and maintenance manager to a salaried position such as that accorded to the past mechanical supervisor. This was reviewed by management, and it was agreed to give him the salaried position along with a substantial raise above the basic rate he had been paid in the past. Since all his work had been of a supervisory nature for the past year, there were no indications at this time of any problems arising from the change.

Two weeks later when one of the engineering staff from downtown was sent to the mountain to check the cause of some shorting of electrical wires in a telescope, Mr. Handy refused to allow the downtown engineer to modify the wiring. After a heated argument about the competence, responsibility, and authority of the downtown group to work on existing equipment, Handy resigned his position.

When notified of this, the downtown Manager of Engineering Services talked to Jim as a friend and asked him to withhold his resignation until an investigation could be made of the problem. It then became apparent that Handy was discontent with his salary. He felt that he had received a pay cut when given the salaried position, since his income for the previous year was $3,000 higher with its construction and overtime wages than his new salary.

A management meeting was held two days later to discuss the possible effect Handy's resignation might have on the organization. At this meeting, varied opinions were expressed. These opinions ranged from the desire to fire him if he did not leave, to the desire to keep him at all costs. The people expressing these extremes of viewpoints were the directors of different telescope projects. In one case, the Astronomer-Director felt Mr. Handy had failed to perform his job properly and that several projects had not been completed on schedule. He also stated that Handy would not accept the fact that all astronomical equipment is experimental and as such must be built and rebuilt several times before it functions properly. These criticisms were later answered by Handy when he stated that the downtown group of astronomers and engineers never completed anything without later wanting to change it. He stated he "tried to avoid these projects until everyone made up their minds."

The viewpoint expressed by the other project directors was that Mr. Handy was doing a good job of maintaining his telescopes and that if he left, his knowledge of the mechanical and electrical aspects of the telescopes would be lost at a time when Optics was particularly short of capable and experienced electricians.

No action was taken in this meeting, but the majority of the management group felt that Handy should be kept if conveniently possible. The Administrating Director refused to raise Handy's salary since it was in line with other positions of equal responsibility, but a temporary increase was given based on the fact that Handy would have increased responsibilities while the Mountain Superintendent would be away for an extended period attending to building construction at another site. No action was taken regarding the conflict between the downtown engineering staff and Handy. For the time being, Handy withheld his resignation.

THE CLEAN ROOM

On January 8, 1965, the encoder department of Artex Corporation will move into a new building. One of the greatest improvements in the new over the old is an air-filtered clean room. The clean room is important because it is here that the fine precision parts of the encoder are cleaned and assembled. The parts are so small and intricate that even cloth lint will impair functioning. In the present building, the assembly is done in small booths set on benches; only the assembler's hands and the product parts are in the booth. This is undesirable because the location of the assemblers is in the same area where machining, drilling, and all other work is done. Although these individual booths improve the situation, many encoders still malfunction due to contamination, and have to be disassembled and cleaned again.

The new clean room is to be used only for encoder assembly. The people working in it must wear special lint-free smocks, furnished by the company, and special caps to prevent hair from getting into the parts. They must go through a lock before entering the clean room, because the air pressure inside is slightly higher than outside. This will allow the air to go out of the clean room every time the door is opened, so that no outside contamination can enter.

So far there seem to be few quality problems. A difficulty arises when the people who must work in the clean room are considered. They are not happy about the regulations to which they must conform. The regulations pertaining to the clean room are: no smoking, no purses allowed inside, no drinking of coffee, and no articles allowed inside except those connected with the work. Before entering the clean room, and while in the lock, their shoes must be vacuumed and a smock and cap put on. When leaving the clean room, the smock and cap must be taken off in the lock. The employees compare the new clean room to a prison. Some complain that whenever they want to smoke they must leave the clean room. Most of the women complain that they are reluctant to leave their purses in lockers outside the clean room.

To relieve the level of dissatisfaction, a union steward suggests that management should call a meeting of all the people concerned and ask for ideas as to how these inconveniences can be solved without decreasing production. This would allow employees to participate in the planning of procedures and cause them to feel that the company is interested in their problems. One possible solution suggested by the steward involves altered work schedules. Each man's schedule would include two separate types of work; one type would involve work within the clean room, and the second would involve work in the regular work area. In this way the assemblers could spend half their time outside the clean room and the other half inside. Those who are in the clean room would also get an extra ten-minute break to smoke or do whatever they wanted, whereas the people working outside would get only the regular breaks.

At the present time, because of the press of activities in moving into the new building, management is planning no action. Technological requirements make the clean room an absolute necessity. There has been no significant increase in the number of grievances or absences among assemblers.

JOB DESIGN

Fuel cells are a hand-fabricated product, subject to very rigid specifications, small tolerances, and repeated in-process inspections. In spite of every precaution possible during their construction, they are subject to defects and require many repairs after completion. Because of the skills and experience needed to assemble fuel cells and the time required, each builder works on only one operation. The first operation, called Operation A, is representative of all the other operations of manufacture.

Operation A is almost the same on every fuel cell, and there are dozens of differently shaped fuel cells, ranging in size from $2' \times 2' \times 2'$ to $10' \times 10' \times 10'$. A single layer of rubber-dipped, square-woven nylon fabric is made to fit exactly the contour of a multi-recessed, oddly configured form. Numerous sharp angles and projections, in addition to recesses, require many cuts in the fabric to insure a perfect fit to the form. The material is spliced together with a buna cement.

Constant changes in production schedules make it necessary for each operator to move from one type of cell to another frequently, and the length of time required for Operation A varies from 6 to 30 hours depending on the size and degree of configuration. Because of the length of time involved, and the fact that two shifts operate in the building department, sometimes 6 or 8 different employees will work on *one* Operation A before it is completed. It has been noted that there is a relationship between the number of operators working on each cell and the quality of the finished product: the *larger* the number, the *lower* the quality. The quality control department has suggested that each operator build her own cell from start to finish through Operation A to insure optimum quality.

It would be possible to assign an operator to one cell as it started through the assembly line, hold it for her at the completion of her shift, have her continue work on it the next day, and so on until the operation was completed by this one operator. It could be held for an extra day if she were absent or if she were assigned to another special job on any particular day. This solution would undoubtedly raise the quality of the product, but it would also *double* the inventory of in-process work. The question is—which alternative is to be followed? Shall the quality of the work be raised at the cost of doubling the inventory of cells-in-process? Should the present system be maintained? Or is there another alternative?

Management decided that the in-process inventory must not be raised and another course was selected. Operators on the two shifts were set up as teams. A first-shift builder is teamed with a second-shift builder. These teams are recognized by everyone. Each team works one cell through to completion, and no one else works on a team cell other than that team. The builders are coupled according to their individual skills, the best builders are teamed together, as are the lesser skilled. A spirit of competition is encouraged between teams. The teams which show the lowest quality receive the greatest amount of attention, inspection, and re-instruction by the supervisor in the area. Only in the event of absenteeism is a team broken into by other builders. Instead of waiting for assignment to a cell at the beginning of the shift, each builder starts working on the cell her teammate worked on during the preceding shift. When it is completed, usually during the shift rather than exactly at the end of a shift, the supervisor assigns the next cell on schedule, which is as close as possible to the finished cell in configuration. The load at the beginning of the shift is thus lightened for the supervisor as he does not have to assign everyone their day's work at one time. By keeping cells with practically the same configuration within the orbit of a team, a greater division of labor is accomplished as the teams become more skilled on cells of a general size and shape. As every cell is being worked on both shifts, there is no increase in the in-process inventory, while at the same time quality improves by limiting the building of any one cell to no more than two operators.

THE PRECURE PAINT JOB

In the manufacture of a fuel cell, just before it is cured, it is painted with a precure paint. This paint sets up within a matter of minutes, seals any slightly loose edges of outerply splices or lacing tabs, and imparts a glossy black finish to the cell. Ten or twelve years ago this operation had been performed by *female* employees, as part of the job of stripping and finishing the fuel cells. When cells are completed in this stripping and finishing operation, they must sit in storage for twelve hours before they can be precure painted. As the fuel cell business expanded during the Korean conflict, storage became a problem due to lack of space in the fuel cell building department. There was some available room in the building which housed the fuel cell curing heaters. After the cells were completed in the stripping and finishing operations they were moved to the cure room (about one-eighth of a mile from the fuel cell building department), where they sat for the required 12-hour drying time. So they would not have to be transported back and forth again, the precure paint operation was moved to the curing room area. Only two employees were needed to precure paint for 24 hours' production of fuel cells. There were no service men available in the curing room to turn the cells if female employees were used to paint them. For this reason, the piecework rates on precure paint were changed to conform to a man's base rate, and elemental times for self-service were added to the original times. Thus, precure painting became a *man's* job. This situation remained unchanged for over twelve years.

Last week, management decided that the opposite type of storage problem existed. There was excess room in the fuel cell building department, and no available storage room in the curing department. Accordingly, the self-service elements were *removed* from the precure paint rates, the rates were adjusted to conform to a female fuel cell builder's base rate, and the job was returned to the fuel cell building department as an integral part of the strip-finish operation as it was twelve years ago.

One of the two precure painters whose job was suddenly engineered out of existence was an executive board member of the local union, and the other was a chief steward. These men were given the opportunity of following their job—that is, they were given the opportunity of moving into the strip-finish area, which is regarded as a female job, and which carried a base rate 31½¢ lower than the male precure painter's base rate. Because servicing was also a good part of the precure paint rates when the job was performed by a man, these men were also given the alternative opportunity of transferring into the fuel cell building department as service men. One of the two was unable to do this due to a medical restriction on the amount of lifting he was allowed. Servicing in the fuel cell building department requires some very heavy lifting in order to change rolls of stock.

A meeting was called between the management of the fuel cell building department, the president of the local union, three divisional stewards, and the affected precure painter. At this meeting the union filed a total of five grievances, a sort of "shotgun offense" designed to secure the return of the precure paint job to the status of a man's job. At the same time the affected precure painter announced that he would transfer to the fuel cell building department as a strip-finish operator. There are twenty female employees and no men on the strip-finish operation.

THE R. H. FACTOR COMPANY

The R. H. Factor Co. is a large aerospace corporation located in the western United States. It has divisionalized its operation into five product areas, each at different locations. All the plants are within a 40 mile radius of corporate headquarters.

The company has approximately 50,000 employees with a divisional breakdown as follows: A. 15,000, B. 17,000, C. 10,000, D. 5600, E. 1800, and corporate headquarters 600.

The Air Force and the federal government presently account for over 90 percent of the sales. Contracts are for the most part cost-plus-fixed-fee with a definite trend toward the cost-plus-incentive-fee type.

Each division is currently doing its own purchasing. Recently an Air Force audit team uncovered several somewhat embarrassing purchases. In one case, purchases had been made at one division for 16,000 particular bolts at $14.00 per hundred, while at another division the identical item was purchased from a different supplier in quantities of 60,000 at $16.50 per hundred and 3000 at $27.00 per hundred.

At first the audit team had intended to make only a random check based on a limited sample of purchases; however, they were so disturbed at the results of the random audit that a more extensive evaluation was undertaken. It became readily apparent that, rather than the exception, the above-mentioned example was not an uncommon occurrence, especially for burden items.

Needless to say, there were a multitude of suppliers furnishing the same product to the various divisions at different prices. Consequently a formal complaint was registered and the management of the R. H. Factor Co. was expected to come up with a solution to the problem.

After careful consideration and extensive analysis, management decided that a complete reorganization of purchasing was needed. Centralized purchasing on an annual contract basis was selected as the foundation for a plan to resolve the problem.

1. The contracts would be for one year.
2. All the contracts would be on a fixed price basis and all orders would be placed at that price regardless of the quantity ordered.
3. All contracts would be awarded through competitive bidding.
4. Contracts for total company requirements would be placed with one source, unless service requirements and volume were such that one source could not handle it.
5. Contracts would be placed directly with manufacturers, rather than distributors, whenever possible.
6. Contracts would not be awarded unless at least $20,000 annually could be saved.
7. Items for contract would have to be used by two or more divisions.
8. Contracts would be awarded based on the recipient being the stocking supplier and providing all warehousing facilities.
9. All buying personnel would be required to procure against the annual contract, unless extenuating circumstances such as delivery or quality problems dictated otherwise.
10. Internal paperwork would be on a release basis against the open order, as opposed to writing a purchase order for every purchase.

Among the anticipated advantages to the R. H. Factor Co., were the following:

1. Better prices due to larger volume.
2. Reduction of paperwork and costs due to the release system.
3. Reduction of warehousing costs.
4. Reduction of the lead time needed for delivery.
5. Elimination of duplication of effort.
6. More time devoted by buyers to items not covered under contract.
7. Consistency of prices throughout the company rather than wide fluctuations.
8. Establishment of relationships with suppliers for a longer period of time, thus allowing the supplier to initiate imaginative cost-saving programs.

It was felt that the easiest way to get into the program was to begin with such items as stationery supplies, printed forms, maintenance items, data processing supplies, and reproduction papers. Upon digesting this, purchasing agents could then move on to more complex things such as engineering services and graphic arts and laboratory equipment.

In order to implement the program, one man at each division was assigned the task of "watchdog." His function was to answer all questions at the division level, resolve problems as they arose, serve as the communication link between the corporate office and the division. He was accountable to corporate headquarters but was physically situated in a division office. There were to be monthly meetings of the divisional administrations and the three-man staff at the corporate office. During these meetings, problems would be discussed and solved, experiences exchanged, suggestions made, and information passed along. The corporate officer in charge felt that the key to the success of the program would be the promotion of cooperation and acceptance rather than forced compliance.

DEPARTMENTAL SPECIALIZATION

In Towson's chain of department stores, the accent is truly upon customer service. All operating and management personnel are indoctrinated with this philosophy. Managers of departments are, of course, expected to provide a maximum of service at a minimum of cost.

In the Alford branch store, three of the service departments are located side by side: lay-away, car pick-up, and parts and repair. Though located together geographically, there is little or no interchange of personnel working in each department. The volume of business of each tends to fluctuate depending upon time of year, sales, holidays, etc. The busiest times for lay-away are during the "back-to-school" sale and just before Christmas. Parts and repair has most of its business just after Christmas and after every sale. Volume in this area is the most difficult to predict and it often fluctuates widely for no apparent reason. Car pick-up has many customers during all sales and promotion of large items.

John Carlson is a college student working in the lay-away department in the Alford branch. The following is his report of an episode that occurred one Christmas:

"Over the Christmas holidays we were faced with this situation. My immediate boss, having just taken over control of the department the previous month, naturally wanted to make a good showing and have as small an amount of hours worked as possible. I feel as though his objective of lowering the payroll from that of last year was out of line. Neither did he take into consideration that our total store sales were up for the complete year, including that of layaway. During November we were open on Wednesday and Saturday nights, which was not on the records of the previous year.

"The real problem began when we were to send out approximately 10,000 reminder notices telling the customers of their December 15 pick-up date for all Christmas lay-aways. For one thing, we were too short-handed to deal with the *usual* amount of customers and binning of the lay-away packages at this time of year. With the reminder cards to be written and with an increase in business, this, I felt, was too much. I made a suggestion, around the last week in November, that we soon put on some part-time help even if it was only a couple of girls to write out cards. At first my supervisor's reply was negative, saying 'by all of us working slightly harder and cooperating to the fullest extent, we could continue through the holidays with the same amount of man hours.'

"Within a week to ten days his decision was reversed by *his* supervisor, and the hiring of new help began. To start off, two girls were hired to write the reminder cards, and a short time later two fellows also were added to our division. As an end result we were literally swamped during the complete holiday season. The cards were late in being sent out, the binning was beyond our capacity, and the inexperienced help did us little good in working the counter and waiting on customers.

"Much of our confusion and delay of customer time could have been avoided had my superior not been so set on trying to make favorable impressions on the store manager that he completely disregarded our store motto and policy of 'customer service' and 'satisfaction guaranteed.' I feel this is very poor business when one man has been warned of the coming 'rush' and deliberately tries to set goals which could not possibly be reached.

"On many occasions, personnel in parts and repair tried to help out, but they only contributed to the confusion. It seems to me that the notion of 'planning ahead' and 'organizing' could be a little more evident in practice. I think I see how a smooth operation could be made out of this mess if the principles of management were only applied as they were written."

TECHNOLOGICAL CHANGE AND THE PUBLIC

Magino's is a specialty store catering predominantly to higher income female customers. The store has attempted to create and maintain an image of quiet, sophisticated quality with no stinting upon service. In a recent remodeling of the store, the old-fashioned elevators manned by operators were replaced with modern, efficient automatic ones that do not require the services of employees. The management had instituted this change for several reasons: (1) new elevators would eliminate the need for four elevator operators; (2) the wage of an elevator controller was eliminated; and (3) the new elevators fitted better into the newly remodeled store.

At 10 o'clock on the opening day after the remodeling, the store manager was summoned by a floor walker. One of the store's oldest and most valued customers had refused to enter the automatic elevator. She had insisted that she did not know how to operate an elevator, and felt that the entire operation was unsafe. She wondered why the service of the store had deteriorated so badly to permit unprofessional personnel to operate elevators. The store manager tried his best to calm the customer, and rode up the elevator to the desired fourth floor after assuring her that he was competent to operate the push button mechanism. She requested that he meet her when she had completed her shopping in order to operate the elevator on the return trip.

During the first week, there were a number of similar incidents involving old, established customers. There was a general feeling that the automatic elevator constituted a deterioration in the class of service normally expected from a store with the image of Magino's. Numerous letters of complaint were received, in addition to which several customers walked out of the store. Consequently, the problem was scheduled for discussion by the executive committee of the store.

Part Four

DIRECTING

Plans have been made, and an organization has been created to put them into effect. The next logical function of a manager is to stimulate the organization to undertake the work required. The traditional manager relies primarily on his own leadership ability to accomplish this, while the behaviorist places more faith in the self-motivation of subordinates.

Section A

Formal Direction

The manager has primary responsibility for initiating and guiding work toward the accomplishment of organization objectives. Since the traditional manager relies more on himself than on others, he issues orders and attempts to develop a climate in which these orders are readily accepted and executed (Chap. 14). Two important elements of that guiding climate are (1) a monetary compensation system that will stimulate the desired behavior (Chap. 15); and (2) a training program that will influence subordinates to react to situations in accordance with the desires of the leader (Chap. 16).

14

Leadership

We have shown that there are in theory two approaches to planning and organizing—the humanistic and the rationalistic. The third major function of management—directing—does not, however, even in theory, allow for two such possible approaches.

Direction can be defined broadly as the process of initiating action. Theoretically, we have already devised plans with due concern for the human element. We have established a sound formal structure of organization, with regard for such factors as status, power, accommodation, and politics. The firm is ready for some action to take place in accordance with those plans. Traditionally, then, the next and final function of the manager would be to *control* this action. In the past, the usual assumption was that if there were good plans and excellent organization, people would automatically and willingly start to work. But the human relations movement of the past four decades has distinguished a prior function, that of direction. The fact that the separation of a function having to do with stimulation and motivation is a product of the behavioral approach makes it difficult, therefore, to allow for both a traditional (rationalistic) and a behavioral (humanistic) approach.

Almost all writers and practitioners of traditional management theory devote considerable attention to the concept of leadership. Some of these writers, in fact, have tended to equate leadership with management as a whole. As we shall see, however, leadership is merely one aspect of a larger function—that of direction.

In this and the next two chapters, attention will be devoted to the more conventional concepts of leadership. The emphasis will be upon the leader's responsibility to stimulate action. At the same time, the behavioral modifications of this approach will be presented. This chapter will deal with commands, types and styles of leadership, and the differing skills required on the top and bottom levels of the organization. The traditionalists have long placed great confidence in money as a stimulating device; this will be discussed in the next chapter. And finally, we shall discuss training people to guide them in their work, with particular emphasis upon training in the area of human relations.

We shall then move on to discuss aspects of motivation, which did not receive great emphasis until recent decades. One major concept, heretical according to many traditional managers, is that of rank-and-file participation in management decisions. Communication skills and group dynamics, long taken for granted by too many managers, will be the subject of this section's concluding chapters.

Though there is no carefully delineated categorization in this third major management function (direction), we have attempted to differentiate between the elements emphasized by the traditionalists, in the first three chapters, and those stressed by the behaviorists in the following three. As a result, contrasts between the philosophies of the two groups should become apparent.

ORDERS

In the first book on general management theory, Henri Fayol established planning, organizing, commanding, coordinating, and controlling as the basic functions of management.[1] He recognized that commands or orders have to be given by the manager if anything is to happen. No matter how permissive and democratic a manager wants to be, he has to indicate what he wants done. The traditional manager includes not only *what*, but also *how*, while the behaviorists suggest that more freedom be permitted in the manner in which a job is done. McGregor recommends that, as often as possible, only the *objectives* be communicated, with subordinates being allowed to exercise self-direction and self-control.[2]

It is interesting to note that McGregor at one time expressed doubts about an idealistic world inhabited by Theory "Y's" who need little or no direction. Upon leaving the presidency of Antioch College, he wrote the following in 1954:[3]

[1] Henri Fayol, *General and Industrial Management* (New York: Pitman Pub. Corp., 1949, trans. from the French originally published in 1916).
[2] Douglas McGregor, *The Human Side of Enterprise* (New York: McGraw-Hill Book Company, 1960), Chap. 5.
[3] Douglas McGregor, *Leadership and Motivation* (Cambridge: The MIT Press, 1966), p. 67.

> Before coming to Antioch . . . I believed for example that a leader could operate successfully as a kind of advisor to his organization. Unconsciously, I suspect, I hoped to duck the unpleasant necessity of making difficult decisions, of taking responsibility for one course of action among many uncertain alternatives, of making mistakes and taking the consequences. I thought that maybe I could operate so that everyone would like me—that "good human relations" would eliminate all discord and disappointment. I could not have been more wrong. . . .

In his latter writings, however, he returned to the message of Theory "Y" in which he identifies more with subordinates than with their managers.

There is a significant place for the *order* in any theory of management. The order is the technical means through which a subordinate understands what is to be done. There should be, of course, not only understanding, but willing acceptance of the command. Thus we present the following characteristics of the "good" order.

The order should issue from the demands of the situation. Coming to grips with a situation requires, according to one author, "the ability and courage to face the facts in the situation, interpret the facts properly in the light of the situation's requirements, and follow the course of action they dictate."[4] If the order conforms to the requirements of the situation, it is not only a logical command, but is more acceptable to a subordinate. He sees himself as being ordered by the situation, not necessarily by an arbitrary and capricious manager.

The order should be clear, concise, consistent, and not unnecessarily detailed. Communication of orders by the superior, and understanding and acceptance by the subordinate, require that sufficient information be given to insure understanding. Too much information implies a lack of confidence in the subordinate and results in overdirection.

The tone of the order is important. The skilled manager does not make a "big thing" of the issuance of orders. He is confident of his power, position, and ability, and his instructions flow naturally. He does not flaunt his formal power in the face of his subordinates. Many executives have found that an atmosphere of suggestion, rather than outright command, stimulates better acceptance. If an order can be framed as an authoritative suggestion, it is much easier for the subordinate to accept it. In one study, however, the importance of this skill was minimized. Research revealed that on *half* of the occasions when the manager *thought* he was transmitting orders and instructions, his subordinates regarded them as information or advice.[5] This was a problem of

[4] Ralph C. Davis, *The Fundamentals of Top Management* (New York: Harper & Bros., 1951), p. 152.

[5] Robert Dubin, *Human Relations in Administration* (Englewood Cliffs: Prentice-Hall, Inc., 1961), p. 316.

communication and probably resulted from the subordinate's desire to protect his status.

If possible, the reason for the order should be given. Again, most people accept an order more readily if they understand the need for it. Orders sometimes become unrealistic as conditions change; if the subordinate knows the reasons and goals, he can adjust better or know when to ask for a reinterpretation. Of course, there are many occasions when information cannot be given, perhaps because of a need for secrecy, or the lack of such information, or a scarcity of time. If a manager is known for his willingness to share information, the subordinate will usually accept the necessity for its being temporarily withheld.

NATURE OF LEADERSHIP

As indicated above, the leader has always occupied a strong and central role in traditional management theory. There have been attempts to identify a leader type or a leader syndrome, a person who would be a leader anywhere, anytime, and under any conditions. There was a feeling that leaders were born rather than made. In recent decades, however, a considerable amount of money has been invested in research into leadership.[6] It was discovered that there can be no stereotypes, no easy relating of human characteristics to success. The general conclusion has been that leadership is a relationship among several complex elements, primarily those of (1) the leader, (2) the led, and (3) the situation. Each of these will be discussed briefly.

The Leader

Without doubt, the characteristics of the leader are important, but *not* as important as was once believed. Attempts to enumerate the traits of an effective leader have ranged over the usual elements—intelligence, self-confidence, sociability, will or perseverance, reality orientation, dominance, human relations attitude, and such. Lippitt reports that in 106 studies of leadership traits, only 5 percent appeared in four or more studies.[7]

Despite general agreement that there is no standard universal pattern of leadership traits, some authors still attempt to identify the four or five most

[6] Cf. Ohio State University leadership studies such as Ralph M. Stogdill, ed., *Leadership and Structures of Personal Interaction;* Bureau of Business Research, The Ohio State University, Research Monograph No. 84 (1957); and Ralph M. Stogdill, Carroll L. Shartle, and associates, *Patterns of Administrative Performance,* Bureau of Business Research, The Ohio State University, Research Monograph No. 81 (1956).

[7] Gordon Lippitt, "What Do We Know About Leadership?" in *Leadership in Action* (Washington: National Training Laboratories, National Education Association, 1961), p. 7.

crucial factors that greatly aid in success. Harrell concludes that the four major characteristics are strong will, extroversion, power need, and achievement need.[8] Keith Davis concludes that the major traits are intelligence, social maturity and breadth, inner motivation, and a human relations-oriented attitude.[9] Though such lists overlap considerably, these traits cannot explain the success, or lack of it, of all leaders in all situations. Without discounting the importance of the central figure—the leader—the correct answer requires a more comprehensive framework and analysis.

The Led

If there are no followers, there cannot be a leader. Leadership requires that the leader relate to people, and the successful relationship will vary in kind with the type of people. Certainly, the basic approach to manual laborers will have to be different from the one used to inspire research chemists. And a man who is a leader in one group may be rejected by another.

At the same time, it is important to note that any leader, while *of* the group, is also *apart* from the group. He is the only one in the group that must accept the responsibility for group goals. Each subordinate may be selfishly oriented and want to look after himself only. But the leader is a coordinator who must integrate, unite, and direct. Though he believes implicitly in the democratic approach, the power granted to him by the formal authority structure will impose a permanent barrier between him and the group. Though inextricably linked, then, the leader and the led are, at the same time, distinct elements and must be studied as such.

The Situation

Perhaps the most significant result of recent research into leadership is the development of the situation viewpoint, which maintains, in effect, that the situation (the problem and its environment) will structure the type of leadership that is called for. In this sense, a man may well be a leader in one situation and a follower in another. He may be a leader of the group at one time and find that his particular talents are not required at another.

Variances in situations have been the cause of much inexactness and ambiguity in leadership research. For example, the Ohio State leadership

[8] Thomas W. Harrell, *Managers' Performance and Personality* (Cincinnati: South-Western Publishing Co., 1961), p. 171.
[9] Keith Davis, *Human Relations at Work*, 3rd ed. (New York: McGraw-Hill Book Company, 1967), p. 99.

studies identified two important dimensions of leader behavior: (1) *initiating structure* which is the extent to which one defines and structures the roles and tasks through planning, scheduling, ordering, etc., and (2) *consideration* which is the degree to which the leader has developed personal relationships characterized by mutual trust, good rapport, and two-way communication with subordinates. A survey of numerous studies attempting to relate these dimensions to performance effectiveness shows few significant correlations.[10] Though they are two important elements of leadership behavior, it is apparent that they must be related to the situation.

Among the many situational variables that must be related to leadership behavior are (1) expectations of the led, (2) degree of task structuring imposed by technology, (3) pressures of schedules and time, (4) degree of interpersonal contact possible between leader and led, (5) degree of influence of the leader outside of the group, and (6) stages of organizational development. If a group expects and wants authoritarian leadership behavior, it is more likely to be satisfied with any type of leadership given. If they have less authoritarian expectations, a leader who strongly emphasizes initiating structure will be resented.[11] Research has also shown that when the work situation is highly structured by technology and the pressures of time, the supervisor who is high in consideration is more likely to meet with success as measured by absenteeism, turnover, and grievances. If task structuring precludes individual and group self-actualization, it will be useless to look for motivation from this source. Attention will have to be given to Herzberg's hygienic factors instead.[12] Another research study has shown that when subordinates have little contact with their supervisor, they prefer him to be authoritarian. But if they must work and interact continuously, they want him to be high in consideration.[13] However, consideration is insufficient if the leader lacks influence with his own superiors which would enable this concern to be profitable in terms of subordinate benefits.[14] And consideration is insufficient without initiating structure. In a study of 129 clerical employees, those who perceived a high level of consideration in their supervisor seemed to be more strongly motivated by initiating structure than those who perceived a low level of consideration.[15] In this study, consideration tended to correlate significantly with more of the higher

[10] Abraham K. Korman, " 'Consideration,' 'Initiating Structure,' and Organizational Criteria—A Review," *Personnel Psychology*, Vol. 19, No. 4 (Winter, 1966), pp. 361–379.

[11] U. G. Foa, "Relation of Workers' Expectations to Satisfaction with Supervisor," *Personnel Psychology*, Vol. 10 (1957), pp. 161–168.

[12] See Chapter 7.

[13] V. H. Vroom and F. C. Mann, "Leader Authoritarianism and Employee Attitudes," *Personnel Psychology*, Vol. 13 (1960), pp. 125–140.

[14] D. C. Pelz, "Influence: A Key to Effective Leadership in the First-Line Supervisor," *Personnel*, Vol. 29 (1952), pp. 209–217.

[15] Michael Beer, *Leadership, Employee Needs and Motivation* (Columbus, Ohio: Bureau of Business Research Monograph No. 129, 1966), pp. 43–44, 67.

order needs (esteem and self-actualization), while initiating structure correlated significantly with the security need. A combination of leadership behaviors tended to increase the overall level of satisfaction.

Lippitt and Schmidt have identified six stages of organizational development which require different kinds of leadership: (1) creation of a new organization, (2) survival of a continuing system, (3) attainment of stability, (4) gaining reputation and prestige, (5) achieving uniqueness and adaptability, and (6) contributing to society.[16] For example, the foundation of the General Motors Corporation required the talents of a "promoter" type of leader. From 1916 to 1920, William C. Durant, who was known for his sales promotion ability, was president. He used a "one-man," autocratic but dynamic approach. Dale reports that as General Motors grew and began to stabilize, some of Durants' shortcomings became all too apparent: (1) he failed to understand the use of accounting; (2) he had no interest in or conception of inventory control; (3) he failed to take expert advice; and (4) he failed to develop a stable organization.[17] The situation demanded a different type of leadership. The company needed structuring, and Alfred P. Sloan, Jr., filled the gap in the early 1920's. In an attempt to explain the phenomenal success of General Motors today, much credit is still being given to the organization work of Alfred Sloan.[18] And today, it is apparent that the leadership of General Motors must encompass a concern for statesmanship with respect to broad social objectives. Failure to recognize societal obligations would lead to a serious threat from the firm's environment in terms of both social approval and governmental control.

The leadership of various labor unions also has altered with situation changes. In the 1930's, unions were fighting for their existence, and a strong, dynamic, and often brutal type of leadership was called for. Today, many unions have carved out a secure position in the economy. It is true that some leaders do not understand or accept the fact that the need for their particular talents has passed. They continue to use the same old techniques despite the fact that they are no longer applicable to *this* situation. When this occurs, changing leaders will usually prove to be difficult and distasteful, but inevitable. There are, of course, some men who possess such a broad variety of leadership skills that they are able to adjust to varying places and times. Perhaps these are the born leaders; the great majority are more restricted in ability.

Within the industrial organization there are many different situations that call for different abilities. The leadership required of the first-level supervisor is

[16] Gordon L. Lippitt and Warren H. Schmidt, "Crises in a Developing Organization," *Harvard Business Review*, Vol. 45, No. 6 (November–December, 1967), p. 103.

[17] Ernest Dale, *The Great Organizers* (New York: McGraw-Hill Book Company, 1960), pp. 73–76.

[18] Robert Sheehan, "How General Motors Did It," *Fortune* (June, 1963), pp. 97–111.

not the same as that of top management. (This will be discussed and con-trasted in a later section.) Harrell concluded that the personalities of the successful managers in various functional fields were different as a result of the contrasting situations. Sales managers, for example, were interested in power, status, and persuasion; production managers, in things and numbers; finance and accounting managers, in bringing order out of chaos; and research and engineering managers, in abstract reasoning.[19] McGregor indicates that the situational approach to leadership should result in one major conclusion for today's management—*"provide a heterogeneous supply of human resources from which individuals can be selected to fill a variety of specific but unpredictable needs."*[20]

TYPES OF LEADERSHIP

The essence of leadership is stimulating and influencing others to become followers. In a sense, every man becomes a leader in some phase of his life when he motivates others. We have noted earlier that managers are *formally* designated leaders, while older and respected colleagues may often be in-formal leaders.

The type of approach used to influence others to follow provides the basis for one classification of leadership. If the approach is grounded primarily on fear, threat, and force, it is usually characterized as *negative*. If it is based primarily upon incentive, reward, and possible gain, it is described as *positive*.

Negative leadership, possibly because it is so tempting and easy to use, is widely found in all types of organizations. The layman expects leaders to use this type, since it fits one popular stereotype of manager. (Often one has been influenced in this way by one's own boss.) Negative leadership relies heavily upon control over those elements that can be taken away—a job, income, respect, and so forth. The manager who is a negative leader uses the formal authority of his position to reprimand, fine, hold up to ridicule, lay off, or discharge.

There is nothing inherently wrong with negative leadership. Fear can be used as a constructive force. All managers, good or bad, will have to use negative persuasion with some subordinates in some situations. The important item to note is that its appropriateness will vary with the leader, the led, and the situation. For example, as indicated in Fig. 14–1, the *degree of dependency* is a major factor. The more independent the follower, the less appropriate the use of fear. One does not threaten one's friends if one wishes them to remain

---

[19] Harrell, *Managers' Performance and Personality,* pp. 173–174.
[20] McGregor, *Leadership and Motivation,* p. 185.

FIGURE 14–1   AUTHORITY AND DEPENDENCE

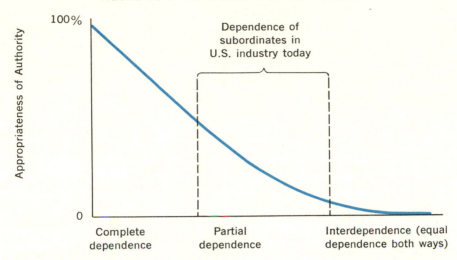

Source: Douglas McGregor, *The Human Side of Enterprise,* p. 25. New York: McGraw-Hill Book Company, 1960.

friends. At the other extreme, one can utilize fear with some impunity in the master-slave relationship, where the one is totally dependent upon the other.

In a broader sense, the use of fear is less appropriate with today's labor unions than it was when employees were weak and less well-organized. It is less appropriate in times of prosperity than in times of depression, and it is less appropriate in private industry than in the military, where the soldier must serve out his hitch. As Fig. 14–1 shows, McGregor concludes that the role of formal authority and fear as prime motivating devices is considerably restricted in this day and country. He suggests that the modern manager must adjust to the times and seek other means to gain a following.

Positive leadership is less widely used because of its complexity. It rests fundamentally upon an analysis of human needs (see Chapter 6). The positive leader, like the negative, wishes to influence a follower to execute some task that the organization *needs;* the leader studies the individual to determine what he *wants.* The leader must then select a want that can be provided by the organization and which will be granted *if* the task is performed in the manner desired by the organization. Dubin views this entire process as a problem of *exchange* between the individual and the organization.[21]

To take a simple case, the leader wants the subordinate to produce over 50 units per hour. He believes that the subordinate wants not only money to satisfy basic needs but also some measure of respect. Thus he agrees to pay him 5¢ per unit produced *and* to praise him publicly if excellent production rates are established. But, as stated, positive leadership is highly complex. Man

[21] Dubin, *Human Relations in Administration,* p. 47.

want money and recognition, but he also wants acceptance by his fellow-workers. He may discover that producing 50 units per hour is socially unacceptable, and the need to be accepted outweighs the need for more money and recognition. At this point, it is far too easy for the positive leader to change to a negative viewpoint—to rely upon fear and force. If he is to retain the positive approach, he must shift his focus from the individual to the group. Why is the production of 50 units per hour socially unacceptable to the group? What does the group want in exchange for what he, the leader, wants? The implications are endless. However complex, time-consuming, and frequently ineffective positive leadership may be, it has such a tremendous potential that continued study, experimentation, and application are worthwhile.

Many management practitioners and theorists believe that leadership in American industry must move further toward the positive approach. This is not just a reflection of the human relations movement and the growing recognition of the importance of the individual in business organizations; it is also a result of the decreased dependency of employees upon management. It rests on a firm belief that the avenue to greater human satisfaction, as well as greater productivity, lies in this positive approach. We can classify our profit system as a positively motivated system—the possibility of gaining the profit stimulates action. This would be in contrast to a negatively led system—the possibility of being ostracized if certain actions and results are not forthcoming.

MOTIVATION

The motivation to act cannot be observed; it can only be inferred by observing and analyzing actual behavior. Managers are position holders whose prime responsibility is the influencing of behavior along lines deemed appropriate to organizational goals. The actual effect of this influence comes from an assessment by the receiver (subordinate) of the following: (1) the anticipated *value* of the perceived outcome of the behavior, and (2) the strength of *expectancy* that the act will actually result in a realization of the outcome. In the example cited previously, producing 50 or more units per hour has various values for the worker under an incentive system. He will produce 50 or more units if he places higher value on the monetary return than he does on social approval. He must also determine whether he can exert enough effort to meet the standard, as well as decide if the money will actually be forthcoming. For example, if he is tied into a continuous assembly line over which he has no control, he would not expect to be able to vary his individual output. If he fears managerial rate slashing when standards are exceeded, he will not produce the specified amount. Vroom has suggested that the motivational force equals the value of the outcome multiplied by the strength of the expectancy that the outcome will be realized.[22]

If the manager is to motivate in a positive manner, he must have available a series of rewards or outcomes that employees value. He must also insure that desired behavior (work toward organizational goals) and the rewards are effectively related. The employee must perceive and understand this relationship if he is to be influenced. Among the various rewards that have been used in organizations are the following:

1. Judicious use of praise.
2. Public recognition of accomplishments.
3. Delegation of more responsibility.
4. Development of an atmosphere that suggests productivity and creativity.
5. A sincere interest in the people with whom one works.
6. Competition.
7. Information.
8. Money.
9. Security.
10. Participation.

It is not difficult to understand the theory behind each of these rewards. Their application in particular situations is an art that requires experience. As an approach to people, praise is based on the needs of the ego. If a task is accomplished in a superior fashion, the manager should note this and compliment the employee. But praise is an art that can be overused or misused crudely and without tact, or it can be skillfully given when deserved. All too often, good work is taken as the manager's due for the pay given, and poor work is immediately censured.

The need for recognition can also be satisfied by public recognition of accomplishment through announcements, awards, honors, and other means that tend to raise the subordinate in the eyes of his peers. In addition, praise received from the manager through a fellow employee is often more effective than that given directly by the leader himself. Delegation of responsibility also appeals to the ego by enhancing the need for dominance and independence. Of course, there is always the possibility that some men have little need for these things, particularly when they have always lived in an autocratic atmosphere. It would be difficult to influence them favorably through delegation of more responsibility, since they need security far more than they need independence. People react to positive motivation appeals in accordance with their individual needs. On the other hand, most people respond both more predictably and

[22] Victor H. Vroom, *Work and Motivation* (New York: John Wiley & Sons, Inc., 1964), Chap. 2.

more rapidly to the crack of the whip of an autocratic, negative leader. This helps to explain why there is a tendency to rely excessively upon the negative.

The next two items on our list—atmosphere and attitude—are necessarily harder to define. The development of a general atmosphere of productivity and creativity is the result of many different acts over a long period of time. An atmosphere can be characterized by an air of "relaxed mediocrity," or it can be one of "no nonsense" and "nose to the grindstone." It can be highly formal and cold, or warm and congenial, with everyone on a first-name basis. An energetic, hard-working, creative person can be slowed to a walk by working continuously with indolent, irresponsible, uninteresting people. Conversely, an able but lazy individual often can become more productive in a vibrant, inquiring, and working atmosphere.

Taking a sincere interest in people as individuals is also a general approach rather than a specific technique. People sense very quickly whether their supervisors are truly interested in them, or regard them merely as means, or often, obstacles, to the organization's ends. Small talk, inquiry into personal background, exchanging views, and experiences—all of these show interest in people. The charge that industry treats its employees as machines or numbers may be a bit overworked, but perhaps the basic human need for attention merits more response than it is now eliciting.

Some people like to compete and attempt to demonstrate their superiority, while others prefer the security of no competition. Industry has made ample use of formal competitions in sales, production, and safety contests. But the competitive appeal can also be used informally by subtle and judicious comparison of the varying quality of one person's efforts or the efforts of different people at the same task.

When the characteristics of a good "order" were discussed earlier in this chapter, we indicated that people usually like to know why they are told to do things. Sometimes, when a supervisor has not been given the reasons for an order he must pass on, he simply commands his subordinates to perform. If there are any questions, he may (1) tell them it is none of their business, (2) say that he doesn't know but it is a "typically asinine" order of top brass, or (3) tell them he does not know but is sure there are sound reasons that could not be communicated. Any manager's special leadership technique is based not only on his own attitudes and abilities but also on the situation as structured by *his* leaders.

Money can be used as a positive motivation tool, but this is not as simple as the traditional manager has always assumed. The problems involved in using money in this way will be covered in the following chapter.

Providing some degree of security is also an approach that can help to influence people positively. If a man is constantly and excessively worried about the security of his job and its income, he cannot do his best work on an extended basis. (Recall that the need for security is ranked second in the Maslow hierarchy.) On the other hand, too much security can be equally disastrous. A man who has absolutely no worries about retaining a job and advancing would usually require a strong character to continue to do good work.

Most behaviorists believe that participation in management decisions also is a positive approach to the problems of influencing employees. People are stimulated to take pride and interest in their work; more use is made of their talents. In fact, this tactic is so important and so widely advocated by the behaviorists that an entire chapter will be devoted to it in this book.

These examples of rewards do not constitute a precise pattern of positive motivation; they are rather a convenient point from which one can begin to analyze organizational behavior. Does the organization actually give rewards directly in proportion to the behavior desired? If the high quality worker receives the praise, recognition, concern, freedom, security, and money, and the poor producer does not, then they serve as stimuli to performance. Instead of being concerned with everybody's level of job satisfaction, it has been suggested that we should be mostly concerned with assuring that the *best* employees are most satisfied. "A man may know that he is regarded as one of the best employees, but this knowledge will do little to enhance his performance if his superior cannot provide him with sufficient rewards or opportunities to gain reward."[23] Intrinsic rewards, or the joys of accomplishing meaningful work, are also effective motivators. But their strength tends to diminish if not bolstered by extrinsic rewards under the control of the organization. And as indicated previously, the manager is also able to influence the obtainment of intrinsic rewards through his design of jobs within the formal structure.

There have been many studies that attempt to correlate job performance and job satisfaction. The correlations produced have been low, thus suggesting that job satisfaction does not necessarily lead to high performance. On the other hand, perhaps these low correlations are indicative of a poorly designed and administered rewards system. Instead of hypothesizing that high satisfaction will lead to high performance, perhaps the causal relationship is the reverse. Increased performance will lead to increased job satisfaction *provided* that the performance is appropriately rewarded.[24] If the correlation is low, then the manager should look to improve his motivational system.

[23] Lyman W. Porter and Edward E. Lawler, "What Attitudes Tell About Motivation," *Harvard Business Review*, Vol. 46, No. 1 (January–February, 1968), p. 124.
[24] *Ibid.*, p. 123.

STYLES OF LEADERSHIP

In addition to classifying leaders by the method of influence they attempt to use, we can also categorize them on the basis of the location of the *decision-making function*. Leaders can be characterized as (1) autocratic, (2) participative, or (3) laissez-faire.[25] Other terms are also used—"authoritarian" or "leader-centered" for autocratic, "democratic" for participative, and "free-rein" for laissez-faire.

Autocratic

With the autocratic leader, decision making is located solely with himself. Autocrats can be classified as three types: the hard-boiled, the benevolent, and the manipulator. The hard-boiled autocrat works rapidly and forcefully and makes heavy use of negative influences. He *gives* the orders and subordinates *take* them. The latter are often resentful and quarrelsome, and incipient revolt is ever present.

The benevolent autocrat, on the other hand, attempts to use many of the techniques of positive leadership. He makes ample use of praise, the pat on the back, and requests for personal loyalty to achieve acceptance of *his* decisions. Benevolent autocracy often occurs when a leader wishes to share decision making with his subordinates but does not know how to go about it. He thinks he is a participative leader, even though his actions label him an autocrat. Employees may be quite happy under this type of leadership, but they remain dependent upon the autocrat as leader. Indeed, he must take care to avoid subordinate lethargy because of this relationship.

A third variation would be the manipulative autocrat. Subordinates are made to *feel* that they are actually participating in decision making even though the manager is pulling the strings from a hidden position. As one manager said, "It took an hour of discussion before the group finally decided in the way that I wanted without me saying it." Of course, the danger of manipulation is the resentment of being "had" when it is eventually discovered.

---

[25] Though these types have long been recognized in practice, pioneering controlled research was undertaken in Iowa classrooms of 11-year-old children by Kurt Lewin, Ronald Lippitt and R. K. White. See Lewin, Lippitt, and White, "Patterns of Aggressive Behavior in Experimentally Created Social Climates," *Journal of Social Psychology* (Vol. 10, No. 2), and Ronald Lippitt, "An Experimental Study of Authoritarian and Democratic Group Atmospheres," *University of Iowa Studies in Child Welfare* (Vol. 16, No. 3).

Participative

The participative leader attempts to share some of the decision-making responsibility with his followers. He cannot do this for all decisions; but, when possible, he consults with the group on questions that interest them and to which they are able to make a contribution. His estimate of his subordinates' abilities is usually higher than the autocrat's is. He attempts to develop a general sense of responsibility for the accomplishment of group goals, using both praise and criticism, but he does this objectively and in relation to clear job assignments. Though decision making is shared, the ultimate responsibility for the decision still rests with the leader. This is the type of leadership that many believe has the greatest long-run promise for maximum gain. It is also the most difficult to practice and will be discussed at length in a later chapter.

Laissez-Faire

The laissez-faire leader attempts to pass the responsibility for decision making to the group. Though the formal principles of organization will never permit this to be done completely, this leader, in contrast to the first two types, does not wish either to make decisions alone or merely ask for advice. He wishes to *join* the group as a fellow participating member. He prefers to give little or no direction, while allowing his subordinates a great deal of freedom and leading with a very loose rein and little or no formal structuring. This type of leadership is extremely slow in process and often produces chaotic results. There is usually a great deal of buck-passing, many cynical comments, and little real interest in the job. Most people, regardless of level of ability, feel the need for some type of structuring. The demands of the ego are not usually such as to require an almost completely directionless situation.

As was true of positive and negative leadership, these three leadership styles cannot be condemned or upheld in toto for all problems and situations. There are, for instance, occasions when the autocratic approach is not only best; it is the only one possible. But except for the diehard autocrat, there are probably few leaders who are always autocratic, or always participative or laissez-faire. And yet industrial leadership has always been criticized for too much negative influence and too much autocracy. Today the indications are for more movement toward positive stimulation and participation without actually operating in a completely laissez-faire manner.

LEADERSHIP OF TOP MANAGEMENT

In discussing the situational theory of leadership, we indicated that circumstances at the top and bottom of large organizations are so different that they require different types of leaders. In the first chapter, we established the basic functions of all managers, president and supervisor alike, as planning, organizing, directing, and controlling. However, the first two functions are much more important at the top than at supervisory levels; the supervisor is often more concerned with direction and control.

Selznick has attempted to distinguish between institutional leadership and organization management.[26] To him, real leadership involves formulating the decisions that are of the greatest long-term importance for the organization as a whole. Examples are the determination of basic goals, recruitment of personnel who can advance these goals, defending the integrity of the institution, reconciliation of internal conflicts, and the degree of cooperation with other organizations.

In contrast to the institutional leaders, organization management is concerned more with the efficiency process of controlling the firm and directing it toward the known objectives. Thus leadership as such is found primarily, if not exclusively, at the top of the organization. In a sense, of course, using the broad definition of leadership given in this text, *all* managers are leaders of a sort. Selznick's definitions, however, do serve to describe and distinguish the drastically different types of problems and situations at the top and intermediate levels in an organization.

In adjusting to the different situations on different organization levels, Katz suggests that varying amounts of three basic skills—*technical, human,* and *conceptual*—are required.[27] Technical skill is the leader's ability and knowledge in the specific field he is managing. A production supervisor must know production, and a director of product development must know engineering. At the first level of management, technical skills are very important, for obviously the manager has to know something about what he is attempting to manage. But the higher one rises in the hierarchy, the less important the possession of technical skills becomes. In a sense, *managing*, rather than production, engineering, or sales, becomes the requisite technical skill. Most higher managers find it impossible to remain up-to-date in all the technical fields under their supervision and do a good job of managing as well.

Human skills involve the ability to motivate and integrate people into a work

[26] Philip Selznick, *Leadership in Administration* (Evanston: Row, Peterson, and Co., 1957), Chap. 2.
[27] Robert L. Katz, "Skills of an Effective Administrator," *Harvard Business Review,* Vol. 33, No. 1 (January–February, 1955), pp. 33–42.

situation. Since all managers must work with people, their need for these skills is self-explanatory—particularly on the lower levels of organization, where direction and control are primary. The higher manager must also be able to understand the requirements of and for constructive human relations, vis-à-vis a secretary or a vice-president; but he is *less* often called upon in this area.

The higher the management position in the organization, the greater the demand for conceptual skills—the ability to visualize, manipulate, and relate ideas—which are essential in making the critical decisions that Selznick regards as a key aspect of real leadership. They involve understanding abstract ideas, constructing models and relationships, and anticipating consequences of planned actions.

All leaders require these three skills (technical, human, and conceptual) but in amounts that vary with the level of the organization. Davis suggests that top and lower levels of management have equal requirements in the human skills areas.[28] The top managers have greater need of conceptual skills than of technical ones; the reverse is true for managers on the lower levels.

One final point should be made concerning the leadership situation at the very top of an organization. Each manager must divorce himself to some degree from his subordinates, but most have colleagues to share common problems, feelings, and experiences. The president, however, is alone. This isolation may contribute, in time, to a self-image of infallibility, particularly if he is an autocrat. His subordinates tell him what he wants to hear; he is seldom contradicted. Even if he enters the job with a fair degree of humility, this humility can eventually be replaced by an imperious self-confidence. This possibility reemphasizes the necessity for a strong board of directors who have the ability and power to work *against* as well as *with* the president.

SUPERVISORY MANAGEMENT

Moving from the top to the bottom level of management, we find the situation quite changed. The supervisor occupies a unique position. He is the *only* manager in the hierarchy who has *other management* personnel on one side and *non-management* personnel on the other. He is literally a man in the middle.

We have seen the nature of management demands for operating efficiency through scientific method planning, rational organization, etc.; the supervisor is under pressure *from his superior* to achieve these goals with his men. We have also seen the demands of individuals for security, recognition, independence, and acceptance; the supervisor is under pressure *from his subordinates* to protect them against management. He is pulled in two directions. The supervisor knows all too well the extent and nature of the power and authority of

[28] Keith Davis, *Human Relations at Work*, p. 103.

those over him in the hierarchy. Yet he also quickly becomes aware of the power of his subordinates to withhold cooperation and even to disrupt his area of operation. But in the last analysis he is more often *upward-oriented,* since the formal elements of power are more observable and immediate in their effect than the informal. This may result in alienation from his subordinates, who will look upon him as too company-minded.

Likert has reported some interesting research with respect to the effect of basic supervisory attitudes upon employee productivity.[29] He first classifies supervisors into two types—employee-centered and job-centered—and then defines these types further. Job-centered supervisors are concerned primarily with the performance of assigned tasks at the prescribed rates, using standard methods, conditions, and times. Employee-centered supervisors give their primary attention to the human aspects of the situation in an attempt to build an effective work group with high performance goals. No supervisor is exclusively job- or employee-centered, but a single approach is usually dominant. Fig. 14–2 shows one research experiment whose findings have been substantiated in repeat studies. In most of the studies conducted by the Institute for

FIGURE 14–2   SUPERVISION AND PRODUCTIVITY

NUMBER OF FIRST-LINE SUPERVISORS WHO ARE:

Source: Rensis Likert, *New Patterns of Management,* p. 7. New York: McGraw-Hill Book Company, 1961.

Social Research of the University of Michigan, the employee-centered supervisors produced better records in employee productivity, attitudes, and absences than those who were classified as job-centered.[30] It should be emphasized that employee-centered supervisors were not neglectful of the requirements of formal organization and did not engage in employee coddling. Rather, their awareness and concern for employees and the creation of a more permissive supervisory climate facilitated more effective accomplishment of high production goals.

[29] Rensis Likert, *New Patterns of Management* (New York: McGraw-Hill Book Company, 1961), Chap. 2.
[30] See D. Katz, N. Maccoby, G. Gurin, and L. G. Floor, *Productivity, Supervision, and Morale Among Railroad Workers* (Ann Arbor: Institute for Social Research, 1951), and D. Katz, N. Maccoby, and Nancy Morse, *Productivity, Supervision, and Morale in an Office Situation* (Ann Arbor: Institute for Social Research, 1950).

The supervisor has long been considered, at least in the literature, a key man in the management hierarchy. He is the management's immediate contact with the "troops," the person through whom orders are channeled. Over the years, the supervisor's job has become increasingly complex. He must work with a number of people who make different, often conflicting, demands upon him. We have seen how he is caught between higher management and his operative subordinates. With the continued trend toward complexity and specialization, various supervisory functions have been allocated to staff specialists. In large specialized companies, there are such staff aides for the production foreman as (1) product designers who indicate what he should produce; (2) quality control men who accept or reject what his men have made; (3) motion study and work simplification experts who set the methods of work; (4) time study men who tell him how much to demand of his people; (5) plant layout men who tell him where to locate his machines; (6) maintenance men who provide him with operable equipment; (7) purchasing people who supply him with appropriate materials; (8) personnel specialists who provide him with the people to man his department; and (9) production control dispatchers who tell him what jobs to do when.

In a previous chapter, we suggested that many operatives on modern assembly lines complain that their jobs have been "all engineered out." With the increasing proliferation of staff, there is a case for maintaining that the production foreman's job also has been "all engineered out." With all these experts about, it is little wonder that the supervisor is sometimes referred to as the forgotten man. His job appears to have become a marginal one. In the 1940's, many supervisors attempted to join employee labor unions or to organize foremen's unions. This short-lived attempt to separate themselves formally from management served to shock top management into a reevaluation of the supervisory position. Management reaffirmed that first-level supervisors were members of management and should consider themselves such. In many companies, supervisors were given better treatment, in terms of both status symbols and the controls exercised over them by higher management. But just to make sure, one provision of the Taft-Hartley Act of 1947 prohibited supervisors from joining employee labor unions. Supervisors still have the legal right to form a special supervisory union to deal with management, but these unions do not receive the protection of the Wagner and Taft-Hartley Acts.[31]

The supervisory task has been further complicated by the employee labor union movement. In addition to coping with his supervisor, his subordinates, and numerous staff specialists, the supervisor now must deal with the union steward. The power of labor unions has increased considerably within the past four decades, and the union representative is a force with which the supervisor

---

[31] See Chapter 25.

must reckon. The labor-management contract restricts all levels of management, particularly the supervisory. As indicated in a previous chapter, when two power sources collide, compromise and accommodation are often a necessary result.

Despite the erosion of the supervisory job through the growth of both unions and staff experts, there remains an important task for the supervisor to perform: he is still a key man who must build the bridge between employees and management. He must develop and maintain constructive human relationships on a day-to-day basis. Even with the occasional introduction of the human relations staff expert, the burden is on the immediate supervisor. Consequently, perhaps the modern supervisor should view the elimination of so many of his former tasks as the opportunity to specialize in his one major remaining task, human relations.

Because of the dilemma in which he finds himself, the supervisor requires understanding, help, and sympathy from his own superiors. Through less rigid formalization of requirements, he must be allowed to work out balances and compromises between opposing demands and people. An example may help clarify the problem. George Smith had asked his men to "take it easy" in order to "maintain the work flow." Although not overfriendly with his men, Smith was highly respected and liked. If he asked them to double their output during an emergency period, they would try their best and would often be able to do so. True, if a time study engineer had been turned loose in Smith's department, he probably would have been able, through tighter scheduling and standardization, to eliminate at least one milling machine operator out of the group of twelve. Higher management, however, though not fully informed on the details, was quite satisfied with Smith and his department. The general results, in terms of quality of product, meeting schedules, employee absenteeism, and grievance rates, were among the best. If management was aware of the "fat" in the department, they did not consider it worthy of an efficiency study.

This is a situation where the man in the middle worked out a solution that was acceptable to both his subordinates and his superiors. It is true that this solution did cost something in terms of money—the salary of one man. But what would happen if a staff expert were to enter the department, stop watch in hand, to pare out that extra man? Suppose we slice out all the fat in each man's job. Haven't we lost something equal to the saving? Again, this may be a case of "buying" cooperation. But it is strongly suggested that the most technically efficient and structured situation will cost something in terms of cooperation and motivation. Most supervisors are not fortunate enough to be able to work out a long-run balance of interests among the opposing forces as George Smith did. Some would claim he had sold out to the employees; others, that he was still too job-centered and company-minded. Perhaps he had only developed *the art of supervision* to effect a point of optimum return.

SUMMARY

Direction, the third major function of management, is the initiation of action in accordance with developed plans. Leadership is a major element of this initiation and is concerned with the relationships among the leader, the followers, and the situation. It is suggested that the situation is far more important in determining the leadership approach that will produce the desired values. The basic influences used to motivate can be classified as either negative or positive. Negative motivation is influencing others through fear. Positive motivation involves the relating of organization requirements with individual and group needs in order to work out an exchange that is profitable to both. The power of the motivational force is the product of perceived values of rewards and the expectancy that such rewards will actually be forthcoming. Typical rewards used in organizations are praise, information, concern, security, and participation.

A second classification of leadership rests on the locus of decision making. On this basis, such styles of leadership as have been identified include (1) hard-boiled autocracy, (2) benevolent autocracy, (3) manipulative, (4) participative, and (5) laissez-faire. Most theorists believe that the participative style has the greatest long-run potential.

Leadership at the top can be contrasted with leadership at the bottom of the organization. Top management requires conceptual skills in establishing the basic goals and image of the organization. Lower management requires more in the way of technical skills. Both require skill in human relations.

The supervisor is the man in the middle; he is between the demands of the organization as levied by his superiors and the wants of his subordinates as determined by basic human needs. His job has been complicated by the increasing number of staff specialists and the invasion of the labor union. The one major task that cannot be taken away is the responsibility for maintaining personal contact with rank-and-file employees. Often he requires skill in compromise and accommodation to work out a balance of forces on which he can build an effective unit.

DISCUSSION PROBLEMS

1. What is meant by the statement that the motivation force equals value of outcome multiplied by expectancy?
2. In diagnosing the situation to determine the appropriate leadership behavior, what factors should be considered?
3. What are the three types of autocrats and how do they differ?
4. Show the five styles of leadership on a continuum ranging from full leader control to full group control.
5. In what way could job performance be the cause of job satisfaction?
6. Indicate the varying needs for conceptual, human, and technical skills for the lower and higher levels of management.
7. Describe the unique position of the first-line supervisor.

8. Why is negative leadership more widely used than positive? Why is it becoming less appropriate in private industry?

9. Distinguish between "institutional leadership" and "organization management" as presented by Selznick.

10. Contrast the trait and situational approaches to leadership theory.

SUPPLEMENTARY READING

Bowles, Warren J., "The Management of Motivation: A Company-Wide Program," *Personnel,* Vol. 43, No. 4 (July–August, 1966), 16–26.

Fournet, Glenn P., M. K. Distefano, Jr., and Margaret W. Pryer, "Job Satisfaction: Issues and Problems," *Personnel Psychology,* Vol. 19, No. 2 (Summer, 1966), 165–183.

Hunt, J. G., "Breakthrough in Leadership Research," *Personnel Administration,* Vol. 30, No. 5 (September–October, 1967), 38–44.

Lawler, Edward E. and Lyman W. Porter, "The Effect of Performance on Job Satisfaction," *Industrial Relations,* Vol. 7, No. 1 (October, 1967), 20–28.

Lippitt, Gordon L. and Warren H. Schmidt, "Crises in a Developing Organization," *Harvard Business Review,* Vol. 45, No. 6 (November–December, 1967), 102–112.

Roberts, Karlene, Raymond E. Miles, and L. Vaughn Blankenship, "Organizational Leadership Satisfaction and Productivity: A Comparative Analysis," *Academy of Management Journal,* Vol. 11, No. 4 (December, 1968), 401–414.

Vroom, Victor H., *Work and Motivation,* Chap. 6. New York: John Wiley & Sons, Inc., 1964.

Zaleznik, Abraham, "Management of Disappointment," *Harvard Business Review,* Vol. 45, No. 6 (November–December, 1967), 59–70.

15

Compensation and Behavior

Managers in the American business system have long placed considerable faith in money as a motivation device. It is undeniable that money is effective in stimulating people to perform in ways the organization wants, but the relationship between compensation and performance is not a simple one.

In the hierarchy of human needs presented in Chapter 6, the physiological needs were deemed to be primary. Money can serve to satisfy these needs. However, as one need becomes reasonably satisfied, other *higher* needs begin to take its place, for the individual *cannot always* be influenced by the possibility of more money. He may feel at a particular time a greater need for acceptance by others, or for recognition for accomplishments, than for more money. Thus again do we get into the area of human relations.

In various morale surveys conducted in business firms, employees often report that their chief want is *not* money.[1] This does not mean that money is not important or basic. It does mean that in these particular companies, this need has been reasonably well met, and that other needs of a lower priority have now to be considered.

Nevertheless, every organization must attempt to obtain this "reasonable satisfaction" of the employee want for money. This must be taken care of before one can worry about acceptance, recognition, or self-actualization. In this chapter, we propose to outline the basic elements of a compensation

[1] Cf. William C. Menninger and Harry Levinson, *Human Understanding in Industry* (Chicago: Science Research Associates, 1956), p. 12.

program.[2] Our second purpose will be to examine the *human* problems which emanate from these programs. There are no answers to the question of money which are so scientific as to preclude the occurrence of human relations problems. However, we should make the attempt to structure compensation programs in a manner that will minimize these problems and enable monetary compensation to operate more effectively as a motivating influence.

MONEY AS A MOTIVATOR

As a result of behavioral research and writing, there has been a tendency to downgrade the importance of money as a motivator. The Herzberg theory of motivator and maintenance factors tends to place pay in the latter category. "It would seem that as an affector of job attitudes, salary has more potency as a job dissatisfier than as a job satisfier."[3] Thus, salary systems should be planned to prevent dissatisfaction rather than to encourage improved performance. The Maslow hierarchy of needs would also tend to downgrade the motivational qualities of money once a reasonable amount has been obtained. Both Herzberg and Maslow tend to emphasize the importance of higher needs of recognition and self-actualization which can issue from interesting and meaningful work.

On the other hand, pay can and does act to satisfy multiple needs. It obviously helps to meet the physiological and security needs, the importance of which tend to decline with increasing monetary income. But pay also begins to take on new meaning as an indicator of *recognition* and *justice*. Executives often want a six-figure salary, even at a comparative immediate economic loss because of the income tax. They know that such salaries appear in published financial statements. Research has indicated that when managers perceive that salary is actually geared to performance, it acts as an effective motivator.[4] However, the same study showed that at any given level of organization, pay often did *not* directly reflect variations in rated performances. When pay is not awarded according to performance, but is instead geared to age, seniority, or cost of living, then it certainly will not act as an effective motivator of performance.

If pay is directly related to performance, the recipient must perceive and

---

[2] Further details can be obtained from books on personnel management and wage administration. Cf. Edwin B. Flippo, *Principles of Personnel Management,* 2nd ed. (New York: McGraw-Hill Book Company, 1966), Chaps. 15–17, and David W. Belcher, *Wage and Salary Administration,* 2nd ed. (Englewood Cliffs: Prentice-Hall, Inc., 1962), Part I.

[3] Frederick Herzberg, Bernard Mausner, and Barbara Synderman, *The Motivation to Work* (New York: John Wiley & Sons, Inc., 1959), p. 82. *See also* Chapter 7 for an interpretation of this theory.

[4] Lyman W. Porter and Edward E. Lawler, *Management Attitudes and Performance* (Homewood: Richard D. Irwin, Inc., 1968), Chap. 4.

understand that such is the case if motivation is to follow. One of the most common policies in managerial compensation is that of secrecy. Executive paychecks usually receive very careful and guarded handling. Perhaps the firm is attempting to work both sides of the fence; higher quality performers are compensated well, but lower level performers are kept in the dark to avoid resentment. The latter are often given smaller increases accompanied with a word of encouragement. This approach is more pleasant and less stressful, but sometimes the results are dysfunctional. The higher paid performer does not really know that he is better compensated and may be resentful with consequent reduced motivation. The lower paid performer may feel that he is being rewarded for a continuation of his low level of performance.

In a study of 563 managers operating in organizations practicing salary secrecy, each was asked to estimate the average yearly earnings of (1) other managers at their own organizational level, (2) those one level above, and (3) those one level below.[5] When these estimates were compared with actual salaries, it was immediately clear that the secrecy policy had been successful in keeping the truth from the responding managers. However, the errors in estimating were not random. Managers *consistently underestimated* the pay of higher level managers and *overestimated* the pay of both peer managers and those at the next lower level. In reply to questions concerning their attitudes, they felt that there was too small a difference between their own pay and those of their peers and lower managers. Thus, even though pay is geared to organization level, secrecy may actually lead to dissatisfaction concerning perceived equity. It was also found that those managers who did possess an accurate picture of other managers' pay were more satisfied with their own pay than those who did not. Relative pay is an indicator of status and recognition. In another study of 1900 managers, highly paid foremen ($12,000 and over) were better satisfied with their pay than were lower paid company presidents (under $50,000).[6]

Compensation is also related to perceptions of justice and equity with respect to human inputs. People tend to evaluate their pay in terms of the relation between such inputs as skill, education, and effort, and the returns in money. In research conducted by Adams, it was found that employees will attempt to reduce any dissonance that may exist between pay received and pay expected.[7] With an experimental group of employees, he led them to believe that the pay awarded was significantly in excess of their qualifications. In one experiment, the overpaid group, compensated on an hourly basis, produced a

---

[5] Edward E. Lawler, "The Mythology of Management Compensation," *California Management Review*, Vol. 9, No. 1 (Fall, 1966), pp. 17–19.

[6] Edward E. Lawler and Lyman W. Porter, "Perceptions Regarding Management Compensation," *Industrial Relations*, Vol. 3, No. 2 (October, 1963), pp. 41–49.

[7] J. Stacy Adams, "Wage Inequities, Productivity, and Work Quality," *Industrial Relations*, Vol. 3, No. 2 (October, 1963), pp. 9–16.

quantity significantly in excess of an appropriately paid control group. In a second experiment under a system of individual piecework, the group with the excessively high piece rate tended to reduce dissonance by restricting output to place total pay in line with expectations. If an organizational member *feels* that his pay is low in relation to his human inputs, he may be tempted to slack off to an acceptable minimum, or even to improve the relation by "borrowing" various supplies from the organization. Certainly, Adams suggests a novel idea that planned overpayment of base pay may lead to increased motivation.

COMPENSATION SYSTEMS AND BEHAVIOR

There are various forms of individual and group behavior that managers deem appropriate and desirable in advancing the organization's goals. Whether viewed as a motivator or a hygienic maintenance factor, pay can be used in an attempt to effect this desired behavior. Although a particular pay plan may misfire and lead to dysfunctional behavior, attempts should be made to establish cause and effect relationships in advance, to be followed by constant surveillance of the behavior that ensues.

Though the number of specific pay systems is seemingly endless, they may be classified into three broad types.

1. Base pay or salary for the *job*.
2. Variable pay in recognition of the *individual* on the job.
3. *Supplementary* pay not directly related to the job or individual.

These are presented along with their sub-types and projected behavioral results in Fig. 15–1.

Every job calls for basic minimum compensation in terms of the human abilities and aptitudes necessary for its performance. Any person on a particular job, regardless of race, creed, color, sex, or age, should receive this basic minimum. It is primarily *job controlled,* and the best scientific methods that modern management has for determining the type of pay are job analysis and job evaluation. The outlines of these methods and the accompanying human problems will be discussed in the following section.

To provide for individual differences on the job, many organizations establish the opportunity for varying pay depending upon the person's characteristics and/or performance level. This will necessarily call for *measurement* of these characteristics and performances, a task which is indeed difficult. Measuring a job through job evaluation is much more simple than measuring a man in all of his complexities. Some firms attempt to evade this problem by permitting *no* varying compensation on a particular job. But they still must face the problem of determining who shall be advanced from one job to another. Most

FIGURE 15–1   COMPENSATION AND BEHAVIOR

Pay Plans	Projected Behavior

Base Pay (Job) . . . . Attraction to organization through meeting physiological and security needs
Satisfaction in terms of (1) relative pay of peers, superiors, and subordinates, and (2) inputs of skill, education, and effort.

Variable Pay (People)

┌ Seniority . . . . Stability of employment.
│ Long tenure.

├ Merit . . . . Higher quality of general performance.

└ Incentive

┌ Individual . . Higher Output.
│ Acceptable quality.

└ Group . . . . . Greater cooperation.
Higher quantity and quality of output.
Less waste.
Less resistance to change.
More suggestions.

Supplementary Pay

┌ Economic . . . . Maintenance of workforce.
│ (Pensions, Maintenance of morale.
│ insurance, etc.)

└ Time Off With Pay . . . . . Maintenance of workforce.
(Vacations, Maintenance of morale.
holidays, etc.)

organizations will recognize individual and group differences by providing variable pay for such items as seniority, general merit, and performance results. Such programs are variously designated as time pay, merit or performance rating, and incentive wages. These, too, will be outlined briefly to illustrate the problems that must be met to obtain some degree of human acceptance and satisfaction.

Finally, a third type of compensation has been developed to a high degree in the past three decades. Usually, this type is referred to as "fringe benefits." In a substantial number of business firms, this type of pay amounts to more than 25 percent of the total compensation and probably no longer deserves the designation of "fringe." A very brief coverage of these benefits will be presented to illustrate the philosophy of and reactions to this type of compensation.

BASE PAY FOR THE JOB

Before the base pay for a job can be established, the job itself must be fixed and described. This necessitates structuring by the manager as he organizes the firm. It introduces an element of rigidity and control to which many behaviorists object. But some degree of rationality and structuring must also be considered as a base from which to deviate in response to varying human needs.

Job Analysis

Job analysis is the process of studying and collecting information about the operations and responsibilities of a specific job. The job analyst does not seek to change or improve the job, for this is usually the province of either line management or other experts such as the motion study engineer.[8] Job analysis is usually deemed to be a personnel management task of determining what kinds and degrees of human abilities and aptitudes are required to perform the job at least at a minimal level of acceptance.

Through various research approaches such as interviews with the job incumbent, observation, logs, and questionnaires, the analyst collects information which will help to ascertain the type of person required by the organization. Among the subjects covered are: (1) an appropriate job title; (2) a short job summary; (3) sufficient information about duties performed to enable decision making about personnel requirements; (4) type of supervision given and/or received; (5) relation to other jobs, both organizationally and operationally; (6) equipment utilized; and (7) the surrounding working conditions. This information is presented in the form of a *job description* which is a standard of functions.[9] One example of this formal instrument was presented in Chart 9–2.

On the basis of a factual job description, decisions can be made by the manager concerning the level and type of abilities and aptitudes necessary to meet minimum job requirements. This process results in the creation of a *job*

---

[8] For problems in design of jobs, see Chap. 13.
[9] See Chap. 4.

specification, a standard of personnel. Specific standards are established in such areas as intelligence, experience, education, initiative, ingenuity, personality, physical strength, and dexterity. These specifications have many uses in addition to the one emphasized in this chapter. These include hiring, developing realistic training programs, evaluating the effectiveness of the organization structure, developing lines of transfer and promotion, and orienting new personnel on the job.

Job Evaluation

With the job description and specifications in hand, the manager is in a position to measure in some objective fashion the relative *value* of this job content. Job evaluation is the systematic process of measuring the worth of a job in relation to other jobs, both within and without a particular organization. The foundation of job evaluation is rationality. Its basic objective is *consistency* of base pay, both among jobs within the firm and with comparable jobs in other firms. Jobs are to be measured and pay established so that employees in more important jobs are paid more while those in less demanding jobs are paid proportionately less. Individual personalities, bargaining pressures, and sentimentality are to be minimized, if not eliminated, in this process, which is predicated on the belief that *more people will be better satisfied if pay rates are consistent* in terms of a systematic and rational measurement process. Ideally, pay is to rise as job demands increase (see Fig. 15–2).

FIGURE 15–2   THE PAY STRUCTURE

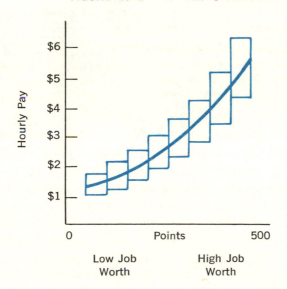

The rational manager has various alternative methods for going about this measurement process. The four commonly used approaches are (1) simple ranking of jobs, (2) job grading on the basis of pre-established job classes, (3) job-to-job comparison on a factor basis, and (4) the point system.[10] Before one can appreciate the clashes of interest between the individual personality and the rational compensation approaches of the scientific manager, some preliminary knowledge of these approaches must be possessed.

Measurement of Job Worth

In the more structured firms, jobs are analyzed and broken down into smaller job factors which can then be measured in a systematic fashion. These factors represent the requirements levied upon the job holder which he must contribute to, assume, or endure. They are usually of four types: (1) skill; (2) responsibility for material and other people; (3) physical, mental, and emotional effort; and (4) working conditions. A widely used list of requirements for operative jobs, the National Electric Manufacturers Association–National Metal Trades Association system, utilizes eleven sub-factors issuing from these four categories.[11]

CHART 15–1   SCALE OF VALUE FOR THE EDUCATION FACTOR
IN NEMA-NMTA JOB-EVALUATION SYSTEM

		Points		
14	28	42	56	70
Read, write, add, and subtract	Equivalent 2 years high school	Equivalent 4 years high school or 2 years plus 2–3 years trades training	Equivalent 4 years high school plus 4 years trades training	Equivalent 4 years university training

A committee of knowledgeable personnel prepares, for each factor, a group of scales consisting of a series of definitions and a value for each degree definition. An illustration of a scale for the education factor in the skill category is shown in Chart 15–1. The reliabilities of these scales are quite high; that is, any of several persons using these scales will obtain about the same answers.

[10] For additional detail, see Flippo, *Principles of Personnel Management*, Chap. 15.

[11] National Electrical Manufacturers Association, *Job-rating Manual and Hourly Job-rating Plan*, 1953; and National Metal Trades Association, *Wage and Salary Administration*, Industrial Relations Policies and Practices Bulletin No. 3, NMTA, Chicago, Ill.

All jobs to be included in the pay system are measured in terms of a common scale of values. These values are often expressed in terms of "points." Point totals for all jobs will produce a distribution along the abscissa in Fig. 15–2 from low to high. To translate these artificial points into dollars and cents, a wage survey for selected, representative, key jobs is usually made. Job evaluation is geared to the concept of the going pay rate in the market place for employee services. Those jobs requiring more of the previously listed factors command higher pay, since the supply of those with greater abilities is relatively limited. Wage and salary surveys are conducted among firms with which this particular organization must compete for personnel. Base pay is determined on a competitive basis for these key jobs, and then the pay of all other jobs is derived from these benchmarks. The technical method involves the plotting of going rates for the key jobs on a diagram, such as shown in Fig. 15–2, the construction of a pay curve connecting these job rates, and the interpolation of all other rates by reading up from the job locations on the abscissa to this pay curve.

At this point, if not before, the labor union usually enters the process of base pay determination. The *relative* pay rates should be established primarily on the basis of systematic job evaluation. The *absolute* levels of pay, that is, the pay curve itself, is usually a matter of negotiation with the union. The entire structure can be moved up, moved down, or left alone depending upon the outcome of these periodic union-management negotiations. This process is much easier when only *one* union represents all the jobs involved. One can imagine the difficulties that arise when various jobs in the *same* system are represented by from ten to fifteen separate unions, who vie with one another to obtain pay advantages.

Human Problems of Job Evaluation

Even though the above description has presented the bare bones of job evaluation, it is evident that we are dealing with a *systematic*, rather than scientific, process of pay determination. The process has high reliability, but its validity can only be determined by analyzing employee and market reactions to the rates finally established. If the rates are accepted as reasonable by the employees and if they serve to enable the firm to compete successfully in the labor market, the process can be presumed valid.

The first apparent problem in job evaluation, and one which usually issues from the latter's complexity and newness, is employee suspicion. Job evaluation, as we have mentioned, involves such concepts as job analysis, job descriptions, job specifications, job factors, scales with arithmetic or geometric progressions, wage surveys, etc. In addition, there is no legitimate basis for management's claiming that the results obtained are scientifically accurate beyond question. It can be successfully challenged by knowledgeable person-nel. Why should the factor of education be valued less highly than experience? Why not the reverse? The only good answer is that whatever system is de-veloped will apply equally to *all* jobs. Hopefully, the system will be objective and rational, unaffected by prejudice, caprice, and inconsistencies that "just happen."

The introduction of job evaluation is usually met with an *immediate increase in the number of grievances* concerning pay rates. This would appear to indicate its lack of validity. However, it should be realized that the evaluation process has introduced a sharpness and clarity in pay determination that did not exist before. The employee now has an objective basis upon which to rest a grievance. Prior to the systemization of pay structures, if the employee felt he was being discriminated against, he could only complain that the pay was not enough. Management could in turn reply that it *was* enough. With job evalua-tion, the employee can look at his job description and specifications and compare them with the degree definitions on the scales. If these items have been prepared in reasonably objective terms, the basis for claiming a discrep-ancy can be substantiated. Similarly, the basis for defending against the claim is also available. The best solution to this immediate rash of grievances is usually to *wait* and process each one carefully; the new structure may well allow for just such a procedure to be followed. After the first six months or so, the number of complaints tends to drop substantially.

The management drive toward rationality in the job analysis process pro-duces some additional problems. The job title, as far as the manager is con-cerned, is merely a useful label that helps to identify a category of work. For the purposes of hiring, training, job evaluation, etc., it should be *meaningful*. On the other hand, the job title is, to the job holder, a form of *status*. By improving technical identification for internal use, management often elimi-nates all meaning from the title for the job incumbent's friends and acquain-tances outside the firm. The manager would do well to realize that the title has other functions and values besides technical identification.

It has often been found that the values of rational management as reflected in the choice and weighting of job factors are in *conflict with the values of individuals and groups* performing these jobs. Management values skills, responsibility, effort, and adjustment to working conditions. The employee, in evaluating a job's worth, would accept these but would also add (1) super-visor of his job; (2) the quality of the department in which his job is located; (3) the sociability of fellow workers; (4) the steadiness of work; (5) how much overtime could normally be expected; and (6) whether the work output standards have been established tightly or loosely. Obviously, a job evaluation system cannot, for administrative purposes, include an unlimited number of job factors. Thus, it is apparent that worker values and management values will not always coincide.

At times the evaluation of jobs on a systematic basis will upset the traditional and accustomed lines of promotion. Davis reports an instance where the former relationship was promotion from addressograph operator to Clerk I, since the former was dirtier, noisier, and more monotonous.[12] On the job factor scales, these very conditions give the addressograph job more value and the relationship was reversed. This was very upsetting to the employees until management compromised by designating *both* jobs as entry jobs of substantially equal worth.

Finally, there is the problem of relating each person's present pay to the new, more systematic pay structure. An individual's pay may be too low in relation to the new structure, too high, or in line. There are few problems involved in adjusting pay upward to the new rate except insofar as the employee may feel he is owed back pay for all the years the job was out of line. The problem of the rate which is too high in relation to others (known as a "red circle" rate) is more difficult. The usual policy is to guarantee that no one's pay will be reduced as a result of job evaluation. This means that this "overpaid" employee must be (1) promoted to a job commensurate with his pay; (2) given additional responsibilities on his present job commensurate with his pay; (3) given no general pay increase when all others receive it; or (4) accepted indefinitely even though the pay is above the new structure. It is not worth the ill will of this one employee, particularly in view of his possible influence upon others, to risk a reduction in his particular pay rate. When and if the job becomes vacant, the rate can be placed in line.

Aids in Handling Job Evaluation Problems

Since the validity of the pay structure rests upon employee acceptance and satisfaction, the introduction of job evaluation is of crucial importance. In the first place, many firms encourage a maximum of *participation* in the process of establishing and administering the system. If there is a union, it may be consulted or at least informed. In the steel industry, for example, the entire system is a part of the labor-management contract and is administered in the various firms by a joint committee of union and company personnel. In this manner, the employees are encouraged to accept and trust a management device which is systematic rather than scientific. At the minimum, the union has the right to observe the system as it is designed and administered and process grievances for individual employees when it feels the system is working improperly.

The introduction of job evaluation will also require a considerable amount of publicity and education because of its newness and complexity. The elements of the system, as well as the basic philosophy, are usually presented in the

---

[12] Keith Davis, *Human Relations at Work,* 3rd ed. (New York: McGraw-Hill Book Company, 1967), p. 411.

form of pamphlets to demonstrate that management is hiding nothing. Group meetings to discuss its workings and impact are often held. Procter and Gamble, for example, allows its employees to select the companies that will be surveyed in the competitive wage and salary survey mentioned above.

Not only is there usually a guarantee that no one's pay will be reduced, but job evaluation is often introduced simultaneously with a general pay increase. The hope is that the employee will associate the system with the increase. And the system can be made more effective by compromises on the part of management when differences between employer and employee evaluation are uncovered. In one firm, for example, the system had assigned equal value to a number of jobs. The workers not only saw differences, but differences that varied from week to week. Management was sufficiently flexible to permit these differences to be recognized, and job assignments were altered from week to week on a seniority preference basis.[13]

In summary, job evaluation is a rational instrument for determining the base pay of jobs. Traditional managers believe that consistency will promote more satisfaction than would an unsystematic approach. Yet, a systematic approach will not do away with all dissatisfaction and will in fact work to create some of its own. Where human interests are concerned, *compromise and accommodation,* without giving up the essence of the system, will usually result in the greater value.

VARIABLE PAY FOR THE EMPLOYEE

When different men can perform at varying levels on the same job, provision should be made to recognize, stimulate, and compensate these differences. Programs of varying compensation have been developed on the basis of seniority, general merit or performance, and production output. The rate established through job evaluation is the base pay for the job regardless of the individual. Rate ranges may then be established around the wage curve to allow for variation. In the cases of seniority and merit, there are usually rate ceilings. (An example of this type of rate structure was given in Fig. 15–2.) In the case of incentive pay, there is *theoretically* no ceiling; the man is paid for what he does.

Seniority

Seniority is the length of recognized service in a particular organization. Different people have served a firm for different lengths of time, and the pay rate may be increased as the length of service increases, up to the rate ceiling.

[13] Leonard R. Sayles, "Worker Values in Job Evaluation," *Personnel,* Vol. 30, No. 4 (January, 1954), p. 272.

Using seniority as the basis for distinguishing among and compensating personnel has a number of advantages. First, it is an objective measurement. If specific rules of accumulation have been set up, there is little or no question concerning how much seniority each person has. One with five years, two months, three days, and two hours of service is clearly superior to another with five years, two months, three days, and one hour. Second, this approach transfers power from the manager to this objective system. Pay increases or promotions are no longer under the control of the "capricious and biased" supervisor. So long as the employee retains his job, the decisions are automatic. Third, the security of the individual is increased, for he knows what will happen and when.

A fourth value of the seniority system is that it makes for more peace and happiness among the greater majority of employees. If one were judging personnel by merit, a minority would be appraised as superior and would obtain more compensation. The majority is usually happier when length of service is the prime criterion. In addition, it is a part of our culture to respect age and seniority, and thus people are accustomed to accept decisions based upon time. And finally, the use of seniority as a method of decision making tends to promote long service and to reduce turnover; seniority is a valuable commodity which a man does not voluntarily surrender.

Though these values make a compelling case, traditional managements are usually opposed to a strict use of seniority in matters of pay. It does encourage long service, but not necessarily superior performance. The manager wants the job not only filled, but filled *well*. Seniority provides too much security and the younger, but often more able, personnel are discouraged upon entry. The alternative to measuring time of service is some system of measuring ability and performance. With this, however, the manager should clearly realize the nature of the situation when he chooses to follow merit over seniority. In the hope of stimulating better performance instead of longer service, he is trading a quiet, peaceful system for one which is difficult and often emotionally charged.

Merit or Performance Appraisal

Again, the purpose in this chapter is not to present a comprehensive coverage of systems of compensation. It is rather to provide a general approach in order to form the basis for analyzing their impact upon people. Though there are many systems for measuring a man's performance, the most widely used involves the establishment of *human factors* rather than job factors. In general, the former consist of two types: (1) such characteristics as intelligence, ingenuity, and personality; and (2) such contributions as quantity of work, quality, and responsibilities assumed. The modern trend is toward the latter inasmuch as they are not only more objective but stimulate less resentment on the part of the man being evaluated. When *characteristics* predominate in a system, the approach is more accurately termed "merit rating"; when contributions are emphasized, it is more appropriate to use the term "performance appraisal."

As in the case of job evaluation, scales [consisting of degree definitions and assigned values] are generally established for each selected human factor. The resulting totals of values, often points, are usually transformed into a restricted number of classifications in regard to performance, such as outstanding, superior, average, inferior, etc.

The problems engendered by merit or performance rating are many. First, it is not as reliable a measurement process as job evaluation. The reliability coefficients are rarely higher than .65 in human evaluation as contrasted with the .90's for job evaluation. Consequently, this known inaccuracy makes for employee distrust of the results. Second, the process of human evaluation must be undertaken by the immediate supervisor, and thus in an organization we have not one, but many evaluators. This can lead to inconsistencies within the same organization because of such rating errors as: (1) harshness on the part of a particular supervisor; (2) consistent leniency; (3) a tendency to evaluate everyone as average; (4) prejudice and bias issuing from race, sex, seniority, etc.; and (5) the sanction of one characteristic or contribution to color the overall evaluation excessively (the "halo error").

A third problem is the employee fear of management arbitrariness. Many would prefer to trust an objective system, such as seniority, rather than subjective evaluation. In addition, performance or merit appraisal is designed to benefit a minority of the group. In all likelihood, less than half will be rated as superior and deserving of advancement in pay or rank. As a result, we often encounter the pressures of the majority upon the minority not to make it "rough" on the rest by excessively superior performances.

A final problem is concerned with the process of communicating these ratings to the employee concerned. This is never easy since people would prefer not to be criticized, either constructively or destructively. Many supervisors dislike to participate in this process of talking over past performances with the subject employee. Yet, if one is to motivate personnel and execute the basic duties of a manager one must be able to inform the employee what management thinks of him and his performance. If the rating has been made in terms of human contributions, rather than characteristics, this will be considerably easier for both parties.

It will be noted that the above described approach to appraisal is traditional in that the superior sits in official judgment of the performance of the subordinate. Behaviorists contend that responsible Theory "Y" employees can be trusted to sit in judgment upon themselves. They would ask for not only a joint superior-subordinate establishment of performance goals at the beginning of an appraisal period, but also a joint conference discussing the quality of activity at the end. The discussion would be oriented more toward problem solving than approval, disapproval, or criticism, however constructive. Appraisal can be looked upon as a means of counseling and teaching for future improvement, as well as forming the basis of reward for performance in the past. With the increasing entry of technical, professional, and other white-collar employees into business organizations, there is a greater opportunity for adopting behavioral concepts of appraisal. Motivation is basically within the person. Management can only construct and operate an environment in which this motivation can hopefully be released.

The problem of measuring men and their performances are such that many firms have surrendered to the pressures of the majority and abandoned the process of merit or performance appraisal. Unions have made the drive for seniority control one of their major objectives. Yet, the organization *must* have acceptable performance, and must, therefore, utilize systematic performance appraisals. The potentialities in motivation of systematic appraisal are such as to encourage its use despite the numerous human relations problems involved. Human evaluation is fraught with problems, but it is a process which is essential to the development of *both* the man and the organization.

Incentive Systems for the Individual

There are also many systems of incentive pay that have been developed by scientific management. Such systems permit widely different pay on the same job for widely different levels of performance. We have discussed the problems of measuring the worth of the job and the man. Now we must add the problem of measuring the *normal output* to be expected from an *average man* expending *average effort* under *average conditions.*

One of the best methods that has been thus far developed in measuring output is time study.[14] If time study were completely scientific and accurate, many of the human problems would be reduced. However, various firms report that over half of all their grievances are concerned with incentive wages, and more particularly with the output standards as established by time study.

Though there are many systems of incentive pay, the most widely used is the piece rate, the employee being paid so much money for each unit of production. Theoretically, the sky is the limit in total compensation. For this system,

[14] For detailed presentations of the procedures and techniques of time study, as well as other approaches such as work sampling and synthetic time study through the use of therbligs, see such books as Benjamin W. Niebel, *Motion and Time Study,* 4th ed. (Homewood: Richard D. Irwin, Inc., 1967) and Ralph M. Barnes, *Motion and Time Study,* 6th ed. (New York: John Wiley & Sons, Inc., 1968).

we need two items of information: (1) the correct hourly pay rate from job evaluation; and (2) the correct hourly output from time study or some other research technique. For example, if the hourly rate is $3 and the output standard is 100, the piece rate is established as 3¢ per unit. Thus, if the man produces 200 per hour, he obtains $6, or twice the base.

Time Study Error

As suggested above, time study is not infallible. It involves a sampling of the work of a sample of the workforce. An "average" worker must be selected, and as he is being analyzed, his pace of work must be rated and converted to an "average." The problems of defining "average" are apparent. Allowances must also be provided for personal delays, for possible work interruptions, and for the fatigue that will accumulate during the day. Time study is a widely used technique in industry for establishing these work standards. More accurate answers can be obtained in this way than by guessing, relying upon experience, or allowing the worker to establish his own standard. Yet, it would be foolish to claim that time study results cannot be challenged.

When a time study engineer enters a production department, an informal war is often immediately declared. The employee views him as a management-sponsored mechanism that is merely taking money out of the employee's pocket. Consequently, the problems of accomplishing an accurate study are complicated by an understandable lack of full cooperation on the part of those studied.

Social Pressures and the Ratebuster

A second problem issues from the human need for acceptance. If a particular person responds to the incentive system as intended by management, he may well be a "ratebuster," or one who produces far in excess not only of the standard rate, but of the normal output of the majority of his associates. Other employees are fearful that management will raise the standard if anyone gets too far above the present one. Consequently, group social pressures, sometimes supplemented by physical ones, are brought to bear on the ratebuster. The power of such influences is illustrated in one case where a particular machine operator moved up to a pace greater than the normal production of 65 units per hour. She then was subjected to considerable abuse until she reduced her output to the normal amount. Sometime later, all the other operators in her group were transferred, leaving her alone. Within four days, she was producing 83 units per hour and sustained this rate from then on.[15]

[15] L. Coch and J. R. P. French, Jr., "Overcoming Resistance to Change," *Human Relations,* Vol. 1, No. 4 (1948), pp. 512–532.

A person who can maintain high performance levels in the face of pressures from the group must have a certain type of personality. To him, money must be more important than friends, communication with others, and acceptance. In one interesting study by Dalton, nine ratebusters were discovered in a group of 84 men in a Chicago plant.[16] Dalton found these men to possess, among other characteristics, the following: (1) they came from families of a higher socio-economic level; (2) they were more likely to be nominal Protestants than Catholics; (3) they were more likely to be Anglo-American; (4) they were normally Republicans who read a conservative newspaper; and (5) they were family men who were not "joiners" of organizations in the community. In theory, management should look upon the ratebuster with favor; he is responding to the system as designed. In practice, his presence is often so disruptive of the harmony and cooperation of the group that some managers are led to act against him. It is ironic to note that the ratebuster is the type of person for whom the incentive system was designed. If the standards are fairly established, there is little justification for not paying the production genius what he has earned. But there is, nevertheless, the tendency to sacrifice incentive pay plans as well as merit rating in the interests of peace and harmony.

Changes in Working Conditions

Employee reactions to incentive plans are also affected by their use in the past. These plans have always been a cornerstone of the scientific management movement, and Taylor has been credited with their introduction into American industry. Many followers of Taylor introduced them without the foundation of time-studied standards, and, as a result, were forced into widespread rate slashing of the worst sort. Employees often fear that the introduction of an incentive plan will require that they produce greater amounts for the same or even lower pay. Today, it is a common management policy to *guarantee that rates will not be changed except in the case of substantial changes in methods, machinery, or workplace.* Conditions are never static, and changes are constantly being introduced into the work situation. If we buy a new machine which enables the man to produce 200 units per hour with even less effort, the piece rate of 3¢ will have to be reduced, but not, of course, to the point where he will be making the same $3 per hour. It is customary to share the gains issuing from technology.

The problem of changes in working conditions is a major one. How large does a change have to be in order to be called "substantial"? Many changes are obviously of major proportions, but most are small and seemingly insignificant.

[16] Melville Dalton, "The Industrial 'Rate-Buster': A Characterization," *Applied Anthropology,* Vol. 7, No. 1 (Winter, 1948), pp. 5–18.

However, the accumulation of many small changes, often introduced informally, will lead to a serious deterioration of the accuracy of work standards. It
is not unusual for the employees to hide shortcuts in methods and tooling from
management, in order to win the informal war on incentive earning. Why
should they contribute to a reduction in their own rate? Some unions have
been able to obtain contract provisions which prohibit adjustment to changes
without their consent. For example, mechanization will permit a reduction
in a work crew from eight members to five. This means the elimination of
three jobs, and the union is tempted to press for "featherbedding," the
practice of requiring pay either for work not done or for work which is unnecessary. The employee and his union often feel that though the company
owns the equipment and the plant, *they* own the jobs. There is ample opportunity for constant, bitter, and often deadly conflict.

Consistency of Work Standards

Another problem of major proportion is that of consistency in work standards. We have spoken earlier of the attempts, through job evaluation, to derive
consistent base pay rates. Yet it is apparent that all of these attempts can be
negated through inconsistencies in the establishment of time-studied rates of
output. In the first place, not all jobs in a single organization ever are on
incentive pay. This could well mean that personnel on lower skilled jobs earn
more total pay because of the opportunities under the system. Those without
this opportunity feel resentful of these lower skilled personnel. Second, among
the jobs that are under incentive pay, there will be inconsistencies. A job just
recently studied is likely to have relatively tight standards, whereas one whose
standards were set some time ago is likely to have loosened somewhat.
Workers and supervisors alike know of these variations, and the allocation of
the jobs to particular people becomes a bone of contention. In the give and
take of compromise and accommodation, control over this allocation is one of
the major sources of power for the supervisor.

Work Restriction

In our discussion of standards, the concept of *work restriction* has appeared
throughout. This is the major weapon of the employees to be used against the
imposition of rationally determined standards. Work restriction is very widespread under incentive pay arrangements. A tabulation of individual earnings
in a group will usually show an abnormally high degree of concentration
around a certain figure.

In an interesting eleven month study by Roy, two clusters of earnings issuing from two types of work restriction were discovered.[17] Employees determined by trial and error which jobs were "gravy jobs" and which were "stinkers." A "gravy job" was one where they could easily produce above standard; thus, quota restrictions were imposed to hold earnings to a level which would not invite the time study engineers to restudy and lower the unit rate. Roy found that with experience the employees could meet this informal work restriction level in about six hours, thus necessitating a shrewdly camouflaged slowdown for the remaining two hours of the work day. On the night shift, there was less management control and the employee could sit, gossip, or read after the quota was met.

A "stinker" was a job where the rate was set so that it would require effort to make the guaranteed hourly rate. In addition to quota restriction, there was introduced here a second type of restriction termed "goldbricking." Employees made little or no effort to produce anywhere near standard, for the daily rate was guaranteed regardless of output. Thus, production was lost through "quota restriction" on the "gravy assignments," and it was also reduced by "goldbricking" on the "stinkers." He estimated that about half of the total jobs assigned were of each type, resulting in two earnings curves for each worker. Some managements even appear to encourage this restriction by saying that they will not pay for work in excess of a certain amount. This may issue either from a desire to have no ratebusters or from a realization that work standards have not been accurately established. However, even with the realization that work output is being informally controlled, many managements feel that the group accepted level is still higher than it would be under a non-incentive pay system. A 10 to 20 percent rise in productivity is not uncommon with the introduction of incentives. This rise is accompanied by increased administration costs resulting from both the process of establishing work standards and the ensuing problems of regulating and reporting individual outputs. But the costs most frequently deplored are those in the area of human relations—the bickering, warring, grieving, and general discontent. For this reason, some managements have turned to other approaches to motivate their personnel, one of which appears in the following section.

Incentives for the Group

Because of mechanization, automation, and discontent with individual incentives, there is a trend toward appealing to the group rather than each person separately. Two illustrations of this will be cited: production-sharing plans and profit-sharing plans.

[17] Donald Roy, "Quota Restriction and Goldbricking in a Machine Shop," *American Journal of Sociology,* Vol. 57, No. 5 (March, 1952), pp. 427–443.

Production Sharing. Perhaps the most famous production-sharing plan is the system developed by Joseph N. Scanlon in 1938.[18] The initial task was that of determining the overall *normal labor cost* per unit of output, based on past experience. If the entire production group, through greater cooperation and efficiency, could reduce the actual costs below this normal ratio, the amount saved would then be divided among the workers in the form of a bonus. In some instances, the savings would first be divided equally between the firm and the employee group, and the latter share allocated to individuals in proportion to base pay. Scanlon also developed a series of suggestion committees to stimulate and process ideas which would be forthcoming voluntarily. The total group would share in any improvements in efficiency, and thus no one would profit by hiding shortcuts to productivity. Under these arrangements, individual incentive plans are usually discontinued.

Perhaps the most interesting recent adaptation of the production savings approach was the plan inaugurated by Kaiser Steel in 1963. One of the objectives of the Kaiser management was to secure greater acceptance of mechanization and automation of manufacturing processes. A second goal was to stimulate both the submission of ideas and greater attention and will to work. A base period was selected, and it was agreed to share 32½ percent of any savings from improvements with the employees. This figure was the same as the past ratio of labor costs to total manufacturing costs. Individual incentive plans still existed, but the management objective was to gradually phase these out even to the extent of offering employees lump sum payments to change.

Profit Sharing. Profit-sharing plans go one step further by providing for a share, not in the savings in any one phase of the business, but rather in the *overall* results. Usually the company agrees to pay from 7 to 25 percent of total profits into a sharing fund for the employees.[19] This money is divided among all eligible personnel, usually on the basis of salary, seniority, or a combination of the two. Sharing is done on an annual basis, with most of the firms placing the share into a retirement trust for the employees. Some pay in cash at the end of each year.

There are various problems involved in the operation of these group plans which limit their motivational effect. In essence, we have added another problem in measurement. To the measurement of the job, the man, and the individual output, we now must add the measurement of the group or entire organization. There are similar problems concerning the *accuracy* of measurement. Does the amount of profit, for example, truly reflect employee efforts and thereby stimulate performance? If shares are divided on the basis of seniority or salary, an inefficient person will obtain just as much as a highly enthusiastic

[18] Fred G. Lesieur, ed., *The Scanlon Plan* (New York: John Wiley & Sons, Inc., 1958).
[19] Edwin B. Flippo, *Profit Sharing in American Business* (Columbus, Ohio: Ohio State University Bureau of Business Research, 1954), p. 38.

and effective one. The profits engendered by employee efforts could also be lost because of vagaries in market conditions or foolish buying by the purchasing agent. As a result, some choose *not* to classify profit or production-sharing plans as incentive arrangements.

This type of group compensation is an attempt to stimulate cooperation rather than competition. It is also an attempt to provide extra compensation over and above the market base rate for the entire group if the firm can afford it. Whether or not the organization can pay depends upon savings and profits made. With the continued advances in the direction of mechanization and automation, the popularity of individual incentives will decline as that of group type arrangements rises. These latter arrangements will, however, necessitate some sacrifice in the strength of stimulation for any one individual in the organization. Perhaps the force of group discipline, through the need for acceptance by one's peers, will provide an adequate substitute.

SUPPLEMENTARY COMPENSATION

The ingenuity of management and unions has resulted in a vast array of methods and systems for allocating monetary remuneration to employees. Base pay is fundamental and unavoidable. Variable pay involves various approaches towards the use of money as a motivating desire. But in the case of supplementary compensation not directly related to the job or performance, the development of ingenious ideas has reached a peak.

A series of studies by the U.S. Chamber of Commerce has shown the amount of supplementary compensation to have risen steadily to 20 or 25 percent of payroll.[20] Economic aids are provided such as pensions, life insurance, health and accident services, and support for employee credit unions. Time off with pay has been provided for vacations, holidays, illness, voting, lunch, rest, washup, clothes change, and involuntary layoffs under one year. Legally required payments are made for unemployment compensation, workmen's compensation, and old age and survivor's insurance. Recreational programs are made available in all sporting fields, social events such as dances and picnics, and special interest hobby groups. Employees are assisted with such facilitative and convenience services as hospitalization, housing, cafeterias, store, counseling, and education. One company even allocates an extra holiday to be taken on the employee's birthday. Another allocates four hours off with pay to attend a funeral, and eight hours if a pallbearer.

It is apparent that these forms of compensation range over a broad area of

[20] The 11th biennial survey conducted in 1967 among 1,150 business firms revealed that an average of 26.6 percent of total employee earnings was paid out in fringes. "Fringe Benefits Hit Record High," *Nation's Business,* Vol. 56, No. 9 (September, 1968), pp. 42–43.

activities and can easily consume a large share of the money available for employees. What is the relationship between this type of compensation and motivation? One possible answer is that the provision of these benefits will provide the employee with the atmosphere and security to encourage him to do his best work. An equally good assertion could be made that these payments encourage no better performance than the usual. There is an even less observable relationship here than in the cases of production-savings and profit-sharing plans. Perhaps we should not be so general and should attempt to analyze each plan to ascertain its effects. For example, a pension plan should enhance security and thus enable full attention to be devoted to the task. A recreation program should attract personnel and facilitate maintenance of good health and thereby promote good work. But even here, there is difficulty. In one company, the management found that the most enthusiastic of the participants in the recreation program were the poorest workers. And in another, the injuries sustained were such that they forced an abandonment of the sports program.

Many contend that the effectiveness of most of these types of programs cannot be proven. Such programs are installed at the demand or request of the labor union. This is in contrast with the 1920's when paternalistic managements introduced fringe benefits as a means of increasing the dependency of employees. If a particular company does not offer a widely popular plan, such as pensions or insurance, it is highly likely that they will suffer in the market place for employee services. It may well be that these plans do not motivate on the job so much as they prevent deterioration of the work force. They perform more of a maintenance function than a direction or motivation function. Their inclusion in this chapter is essential to complete the compensation triad: the job, the man, and the supplementary areas.

SUMMARY

It is difficult to summarize an entire field of study in one chapter, but our objectives have been limited. Money is *one* means of motivating a man to behave in the manner desired by the organization, and as such has received heavy emphasis by traditional managers. It can be a motivator only if (1) basic physiological and security needs are not reasonably satisfied, and (2) compensation is actually and perceptually geared to varying qualities of performance. In our increasingly affluent society, the second category or approach is the more meaningful one.

There are three general ways in which this money can be allocated: (1) base pay for the job; (2) variable pay for varying human characteristics or performances on this job; and (3) supplementary income not directly related to the particular job.

Scientific management has worked out, through job evaluation, a reasonably effective way of determining base pay for jobs. This effectiveness is determined by employee and manager acceptance and satisfaction with the pay established. Determining variable pay is a much more complex task, so complex that some organizations have given up and have elected to pay only the base rate. Yet if we are to take advantage of the money incentive, we must make the attempt to measure the man and reward behavior desired by the organization. There are three general bases for awarding variable pay: seniority, merit or general performance, and incentives based on output. Seniority rewards longevity of service and is easily administered. Merit pay rewards the man for behaving in a manner which the supervisor values. This type of compensation has many problems, not the least of which is the difficulty of precise measurement. Yet, evaluating the worth of subordinate performances is a task so closely akin to effective management that attempts of this type should be made even though not directly geared to pay.

Incentive pay for individuals has always been a cornerstone of the scientific management movement as founded by F. W. Taylor. Measurement of output is a process which is somewhat scientific, but has many arbitrary characteristics. Incentive pay is the locus of battles between the man and the organization. The employee's prime weapon in this conflict is the withholding of cooperation through restriction of output. Management defends itself by guaranteeing the employee that his rate will not be cut regardless of how much he produces. The steady introduction of innovations and changes contributes to the deterioration of the accuracy of such systems, however, thus complicating an already difficult situation. The trend seems to be in the direction of replacing individual incentives with group appeals.

Though profit sharing has long been a device used by a restricted portion of our economy, the attempts to appeal to broad group interests by means of money have received renewed emphasis in recent years. Finally, the broad field of fringe benefits has also enjoyed a steady and growing interest, particularly among labor unions and their members. Although the latter type of compensation stimulates little in the way of more effective performance, it may prevent any problem deterioration in performance levels.

DISCUSSION PROBLEMS

1. Discuss pay as both a motivator and a maintenance hygienic factor.
2. Even though pay is directly geared to varying levels of performance, how can pay secrecy invalidate the relationship?
3. What effect does perceived pay equity have upon employee performance?
4. What are the three types of variable pay plans? What types of organizational behavior are projected for each?
5. What are the three basic types of compensation? How are they interrelated?
6. Why are job evaluation approaches based on the concept of consistency and logic? What human problems can result?
7. Contrast seniority and merit systems in terms of human relations problems.
8. How does the behaviorist differ from the traditionalist in performance appraisal?

9. What are the human relations difficulties that issue from the installation and administration of individual pay incentive systems? How can these be reduced in
difficulty?

10. What is the nature and role of group incentive arrangements such as production-
savings and profit-sharing plans?

SUPPLEMENTARY READING

Flippo, Edwin B., *Principles of Personnel Management*, Chaps. 15–17. New York:
McGraw-Hill Book Company, 1966.

Gellerman, Saul W., *Management By Motivation*, Chaps. 9–11. New York: American
Management Association, 1968.

Jehring, J. J., "A Contrast Between Two Approaches to Total Systems Incentives,"
California Management Review, Vol. 10, No. 2 (Winter, 1967), 7–14.

Lawler, Edward E., "The Mythology of Management Compensation," *California
Management Review*, Vol. 9, No. 1 (Fall, 1966), 11–22.

Lawler, Edward E. and Lyman W. Porter, "Predicting Managers' Pay and Their
Satisfaction With Their Pay," *Personnel Psychology*, Vol. 19, No. 4 (Winter,
1966), 363–373.

Morton, Robert B., "Leveling with Others on the Job," *Personnel*, Vol. 43, No. 6
(November–December, 1966), 65–70.

Rodney, Thomas C., "Can Money Motivate Better Job Performance?" *Personnel
Administration*, Vol. 30, No. 2 (March–April, 1967), 23–29.

16

Training

As in the case of compensation, traditional managers have long placed great faith in training as a means of directing subordinates. Training is the process of increasing an individual's knowledge and skill in a particular area. Frank Gilbreth, pioneer in scientific management, not only made his life a search for the "one best way," but he believed that teaching this one best way was the means toward increased productivity. Unlike Taylor, he was convinced that if the employee used the methods developed, there was little need for time study and incentive wages to stimulate output.

Training has a number of values for *both* the organization and the individual. The organization hopes to gain through: (1) increased productivity; (2) reduced need for supervision; (3) enhancement of organizational stability and flexibility; and (4) heightened morale. The individual stands to gain through: (1) increased compensation resulting from better productivity; (2) greater freedom from supervision; (3) greater security of job opportunity; and (4) improved job satisfaction.

The increased productivity anticipated from training will be derived not only from improved quantity and quality of output but also from a reduction in waste of time, materials, and the utilization of equipment. If the man knows how to do the task correctly, as developed through scientific management studies, the likelihood is that quantity and quality will be improved. He will use less material, since scrap will be reduced, and will waste less time, since errors will be fewer. It has also been discovered that the number of accidents and injuries will be reduced if the employee not only knows how to use his equipment properly but also has constructive attitudes toward his job and the organization. This improvement in productivity should lead to more pay for the individual through such means as merit rating, promotion, or incentive wages. It should assist in improving his security either through assurance of retaining his present job or through promoting confidence in his ability to obtain other jobs in the competitive labor market.

This increase in the employee's skill will usually lead to greater freedom of operation, since there will be less need for close supervision. In effect, this constitutes exchanging the freedom to do a job in any fashion for the freedom to do the job in the prescribed manner without the manager watching every move.

If the work force has been well trained, the organization has benefited through further stability and flexibility.[1] Stability allows the organization to maintain effective operations, even though it may be losing key personnel, through a backlog of trained employees. Flexibility allows the organization to adjust to short-run variations in the amount of particular work to be done. Employees with multiple skills can then be easily shifted according to the immediate dictates of work volume. In addition, the employee's sense of security is increased, since a drop in his own work load will not necessarily require that he be laid off. Needless to say, organizational flexibility necessitates similar adaptability in equipment, layout, attitudes, and managerial skill as well.

THE TRAINING AND EDUCATION CONTINUUM

Training has been defined as a specific process of increasing one's skill and knowledge with reference to a specific job. It is apparent that both operatives and managers require a measure of training to meet standards of job performance. On the other hand, education is the process of increasing one's understanding and general knowledge of the total environment. It is less specific than training and is concerned more with developing general background and attitudes. We would like managers and operatives to have both a general understanding of the business environment and desirable attitudes toward their work and the organization. Thus, our goal is to develop personnel with the requisite *skill, knowledge,* and *attitudes* to perform effectively.

Training is more important than education for personnel with jobs on lower organization levels. There has been in recent years, however, a heightened interest in educating operative employees in such subjects as economic theory, political science, the profit system, and labor unionization. The manager of

[1] Ralph C. Davis, *The Fundamentals of Top Management* (New York: Harper & Bros., 1951), pp. 490–508.

today is more aware of the long-run importance of *attitudes* in addition to the more immediate values of *ability*.

On the higher levels of organization, education assumes greater importance. This is not only because of the increased importance of attitudes but also because of the increasingly broader nature of the tasks involved in these top positions. The president of a large corporation must be, among other things, a practical economist, a political scientist, and an internationalist. Thus, we often speak of *operative training* and *management development*. Training for specific skills is emphasized for the operative, and training *and* education are emphasized for the executive.

Though the burden for training must be assumed by the organization, the major responsibility for education falls upon formal schools and colleges. The difference between training and education is not a precise one; rather, it resembles a continuum ranging from general to specific, as suggested in Chart 16–1. When a person is taught how to assemble two parts and tighten a nut, this is obviously training of a highly specific nature; when he is enrolled in a university class in literature appreciation, this is obviously education of a rather broad nature.

It is apparent, however, that some business firms are engaged in education when they establish general courses for their personnel in such subjects as economics and government. Republic Steel, for example, has developed a comprehensive program for educating supervisors in the economics of the profit system. As this course is taught, Republic Steel is used as the primary example of a business enterprise, and it thus cannot be considered the same as a university course in economics. When firms seek to have college professors conduct such general courses, some professors insist that the courses be given at the college rather than on company property. They also prefer that the course be open to personnel of other companies. Both requests are in the interest of education rather than training. The firm, however, wants a compromise between the two, preferring a general course oriented toward its particular company and its problems. They are less interested in developing the "whole man" than they are in developing organizational effectiveness.

Within a college, there is usually a controversy between the proponents of general education and specialization in such areas as engineering, business administration, mathematics, etc. A few courses offered in some schools of business administration, insofar as they teach specific skills, tend to resemble training as much as they do education. A class in motion and time study, for example, will often instruct the student in the operation of a stopwatch. A wage and salary administration course may teach him how to execute a job description. It is apparent, of course, that even these specific techniques will not coincide with any particular firm's procedures for time study or job analysis, and thus their broad educational values are defended. But the conflict

CHART 16–1   THE TRAINING-EDUCATION CONTINUUM

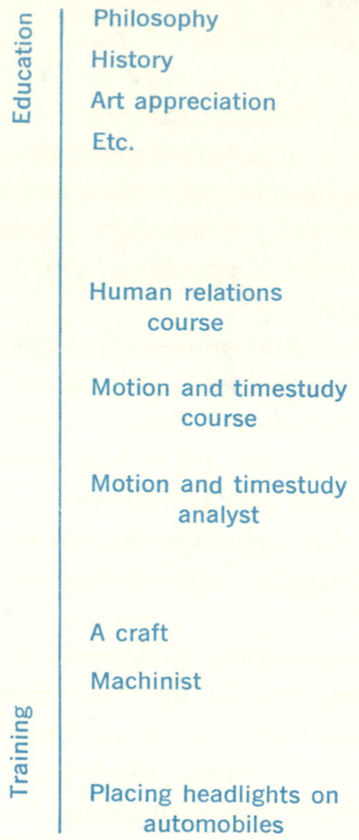

Education	Philosophy
	History
	Art appreciation
	Etc.
	Human relations course
	Motion and timestudy course
	Motion and timestudy analyst
	A craft
	Machinist
Training	Placing headlights on automobiles

Source: Edwin B. Flippo, *Principles of Personnel Management,* 2nd ed., p. 204. New York: McGraw-Hill Book Company, 1966.

between education and training is not easily resolved. Compromises have been worked out, usually on the basis that at least two of the four years of college should be devoted to truly *general* education. The remaining two are available for specialization nearer the center of the continuum. Even within these latter two years, there are differences in the degree of specialization. In business administration, for example, there is a *general* business field as well as various specialties such as marketing, finance, accounting, and personnel management. How much of these two years should be devoted to general business education and how much to the business specialty? Recent research reports in this field have suggested a year and a half in the general and not more than one semester in the specialty.[2] It is evident that this suggests a renewed emphasis upon the education, rather than training, role of institutions of higher learning.

[2] Robert A. Gordon and James E. Howell, *Higher Education for Business* (New York: Columbia University Press, 1959), and Frank Pierson, et al., *The Education of American Businessmen* (New York: McGraw-Hill Book Company, 1959).

A PHILOSOPHY OF TRAINING

With the responsibility for training recognized and accepted by most business organizations, efforts have been put forth to create systematic development programs. Many different programs have been devised for varying types of jobs and personnel, and these will be considered in the following section. Our purpose here is to emphasize a most important element of the training process, the *man* who is supposedly being developed.

Too many managers have taken the view that it is wholly within their power to develop another person. With this philosophy as a base, training and development "factories" were constructed. The raw material, the man, entered the organization, and after some preliminary induction, he was placed upon the development factory assembly line. Job analysis revealed that he needed certain knowledge and skills. The program was laid out in logical sequence, and the man was "beat upon" here, enlarged there, and "developed" in the image designed by his manager. These same managers, after viewing the resulting products, have lamented the passing of the man who was truly interested in advancing his own development. Many of the "products" had to be either rejected or restricted to tasks on a lower level than was originally intended. The development factories were re-examined, reorganized, and readjusted to correct the deficiencies that led to so many rejects.

We should note that the most important element in the development process is the individual and his background and attitudes rather than the specific program that may have been derived in the scientific manner. *The major type of development must be self-development.* If the man does not have the inner motivation to improve, his movement through the program will have little effect.

With this philosophy, a real question arises concerning the organization's responsibility for this development. Though the manager has no control over the trainee's private life, the environment of the firm is a major factor which can enhance or frustrate the will to improve. The reward system in the firm should be geared toward this improvement. More important is the creation of an open organization where a maximum interchange of information and feelings is made possible. We must assume that more of our personnel are of McGregor's Theory "Y" type, that they want to learn if they have the opportunity. And it is the organization's responsibility to provide the opportunity, to encourage them to take advantage of it, and to reward them when they do.

There are a considerable number of risks in adopting such a philosophy of development. In the open and less rigid organization, there will be less employee subservience, subordination, and loyalty, as well as more initiative and questioning of the status quo. There is also the possible loss of trained personnel, for they are in high demand everywhere. The manager may be tempted to withhold training opportunities for just this reason. To circumvent this possibility, the development of subordinates can be made a major responsibility of all managers through a system of recognizing and rewarding managers for their efforts in this regard. Managers should be asked periodically the nature of their efforts to stimulate subordinate development. Similarly, consideration should be given to the debilitating effect upon a unit's operating results of the transfer and promotion of competent personnel.

The development process should be a highly individualistic one. Often this is not completely possible when large numbers of men are involved, and it is less essential for personnel on the lower organization levels. But a variety of learning opportunities should be made available by the organization—either through an interested and helpful supervisor who views himself as a coach or through a tuition-paid night course in a local school.

Finally, the *individual* must also accept the fact that the door to development is operated from within. As indicated above, the manager has a set of intangible and difficult obligations to the trainee. But the maximum of opportunity can go for naught if the individual does not have the inner motivation and sense of responsibility to take advantage of these opportunities. He can ill afford to sit back and wait to be developed by the "factory," and he cannot view his development as a series of courses to take, books to read, and tests to pass. He must be concerned with *how* he can change. He is both discriminating and tolerant in his learning. He neither accepts without question everything his manager or instructor gives him, nor does he give up the entire process in disgust because some portion of it seems too theoretical or of little apparent worth on the job.

In universities, it has been discovered that more real learning takes place in classroom situations where the relationship of professor *over* student is less apparent, where the student can really question intensively the concepts being presented to him. This atmosphere may be more difficult to develop in the authority hierarchy of the business firm. If the trainee tends to question too much, the supervisor may in turn question his loyalty and willingness to follow orders. It is difficult for the manager to be both a supervisor, by virtue of his formal authority, and an instructor who views the trainee as the object of all developmental efforts. Yet the instructor must balance these two roles so as to acquire the maximum benefit from each.

TYPES OF TRAINING

As indicated above, business firms in the United States have developed a wide variety of specific methods for developing desired skills and attitudes. In general, it is possible to classify these methods into two basic categories: (1) those that mix training and operating values *on the job;* and (2) those that separate the two and concentrate upon development *off the job.* It should again be emphasized that the essential *organizational* purpose of *all* training is to *direct* and *control* employees. The manager must be reasonably certain that tasks performed will be in accordance with plans, policies, procedures, and programs.

Numerous training methods can be used with individuals in the midst of assigned tasks. Among these approaches are:

1. On-the-job experience, coaching, and understudy.
2. Job rotation.
3. Special assignments.

The primary value of on-the-job training is that the employee is highly motivated because of its obviously practical nature. Job rotation contributes to a broadening of his background in the different parts of the firm. Special assignments enable the bolstering of specific weaknesses.

Some training and development can better be done away from the work area. Special courses are often given in such subjects as management processes, mathematics, economics, and specific control techniques. Colleges and universities are quite active in providing live-in programs that get the executive away from the office for some introspection and free thinking. Various associations, such as the American Management Association and the Society for the Advancement of Management, offer many and varied opportunities for executive training and education. The typical company program usually involves a mixture of both on-the-job and off-the-job developmental approaches.

TRAINING IN HUMAN RELATIONS

As has been evident throughout this text, the modern manager has a great need for familiarity with the field of human relations. Regular classroom lecture and discussion courses have a role to play in advancing the level of *knowledge* about human relations. Their efficacy in improving skills and attitudes in this field is highly questionable, however. For this reason, other training methods, such as the following, have been developed:

1. The case-conference method.
2. The incident process method.
3. Role-playing.
4. Sensitivity training.
5. Structured insight.

Case-Conference Method

The case method of development utilizes case examples collected from various organizations for diagnostic purposes. The trainee must (1) identify the major and minor problems in the case; (2) filter out the significant facts from the insignificant; (3) analyze the issues and use logic to fill in the gaps in the factual presentation; and (4) arrive at some means for solving the identifiable problems.

The trainee will easily see that his fellow trainees usually differ with him about the case. He is thus taught tolerance of others' viewpoints as well as the difficulty of arriving at absolute answers to any human relations problem. He learns to express his views clearly because he is forced to defend them from the attacks of others. The instructor of a case course is a moderator rather than an instructor. If he is not to cut off all discussion, he must not reveal his own particular analysis of the issues until near the end of the session. He has a continuing function of summarizing and relating the various contributions that have been made.

In an interesting article on the case method of instruction, Alvin Brown deplores its use as a first course for trainees who have little or no background in the subject area.[3] Certainly, if any knowledge has been discovered through research and experience, trainees should first be exposed to it before attempting to tackle problems and cases. But certainly the appropriate use of concrete cases helps to make more realistic the artificial experiences of the classroom. Not only is the trainee provided with something in the nature of a bridge between theory and practice, he acquires practice in the problem-solving approach and in decision making.

Incident Process Method

One of the more unrealistic aspects of the case method of instruction is that of supplying the trainee with all the necessary facts of a particular case. In contrast, the central feature of the incident process method is to *force* the trainee *first* to determine what information he needs, and *second* to request the information before it is given to him. He is provided only with a precis of the case, such as: "John Smith, industrial engineer, discovered a missing tool in the locker of George Hall, skilled lathe operator." The trainee must then

[3] Alvin Brown, "The Case (or Bootstrap) Method," *Advanced Management,* Vol. 21, No. 7 (July, 1956), pp. 11–13.

determine what he wishes to know about this incident, such as the backgrounds of the two main participants and the atmosphere and policies of the organization. Pigors organizes the incident method as follows:[4]

1. Presentation of the incident to the trainees.
2. Fact-finding through questions asked by the trainees.
3. Definition of the problem by the group of trainees as a whole.
4. Individual, written decisions for the problem with supporting reasons.
5. Group discussion of the case and the decisions reached. If there are substantial differences in the individual decisions, these can be categorized in terms of basic approach. In this event, subgroups may be formed with leaders of each being asked to participate in a debate over the decisions.

Thus the case leader must be well prepared for the discussion. He must have answers for all questions, in the form of data previously prepared, or reasons for the unavailability of answers. Of course, no one in any practical situation ever has *all* of the facts. Managers and trainees alike will have to fill in some gaps with inferences and intuition based on past experiences.

The incident process method forces trainee fact-finding, but it reduces the amount of trainee preparation for a problem. Under the usual case method, the trainees are able to study the facts and issues for some time before discussion. This is obviously not possible under the incident process method.

Role-Playing

Both the case and incident process methods are artificial inasmuch as the trainee is not really involved. He is on the outside looking in, attempting to handle the concepts in a rational manner. Role-playing is an attempt to simulate for the trainee an actual situation from which he can, with the help of his fellow trainees and a skilled instructor, learn. The idea of role-playing was first used by J. L. Moreno in psychological therapy,[5] and it was later applied to training in human relations.[6]

Role-playing requires the trainee to carry out a thought or decision which he would merely verbalize in the two preceding methods. It emphasizes skill as well as knowledge. Reading a book on how to play golf can be of some

[4] Paul Pigors and Faith Pigors, *Case Method in Human Relations: The Incident Process* (New York: McGraw-Hill Book Company, 1961). (This method has been credited to the Pigors.)

[5] J. L. Moreno, ed., *Group Psychotherapy* (New York: Beacon House, Inc., 1945).

[6] For an excellent role-playing manual see Norman R. F. Maier, Allen R. Solem, and Ayesha A. Maier, *Supervisory and Executive Development* (New York: John Wiley & Sons, Inc., 1957).

assistance, but when one picks up the golf club he quickly realizes the short-comings of the purely intellectual approach. At this point he appreciates the significance of the gap between theory in the book and actual skill in swinging the golf club.

Role-playing usually involves constructing a situation in such a manner as to provide an opportunity for conflict. For example, a supervisor, on the advice of a motion and time study engineer, has decided to change the work methods of his subordinates. The supervisor's role may contain, among other items, such statements as, "You get along well with your men; this idea of the methods man makes pretty good sense for both the men and the company; the data provided by the expert are fairly clear." Roles are also provided for each of the men. One may exhibit great suspicion against the motion and time study expert. Another may be structured as a potential ally of the supervisor in the projected change. Still another may show a fear of working himself out of a job if methods are improved. All will probably reflect the usual human resistance to any change, good or bad. No dialogue is provided, and the trainees attempt to play themselves in the roles as structured. They are not actors. Each will have to respond to the impromptu statements and questions of the other role-players.

At times, multiple role-playing is of value. Several groups may role-play the same case simultaneously. In this way, contrasts in approaches and solutions can be made. For example, one supervisor may use a high pressure salesman-ship approach to convince his men, who in turn can be questioned concerning their reactions. Another may use a low pressure approach. And still a third may try an open, democratic, problem-solving approach using laissez-faire leadership tactics. The reactions of the participants can be examined to determine which approaches and what statements tended to be more constructive or destructive in terms of cooperation and acceptance. Another variation of basic role-playing is *skit completion* where dialogue is provided the participants up to a certain point, from which they are to carry on in the usual role-playing manner. Skit completion enables the instructor to focus the situation more precisely upon a particular problem.

The values of role-playing are many. As stated above, it constitutes an even better bridge between theory and practice. It is one thing to say, "I would apologize to the employee," and another to actually do it in an effective manner. It helps to increase the sensitivity of the trainee to the feelings of others by means of the feedback that occurs when the case is over and is being analyzed by the group. It may effect some attitude changes by forcing trainees into reversed roles (a domineering, autocratic supervisor might be assigned the role of an employee working for a domineering, autocratic supervisor). Role-playing makes possible the accumulation of some practical experience, even though simulated, without taking the risks of an actual situation. Various approaches can be tried to see which works best under what conditions. The advice of those with experience can be obtained with reference to particular statements, actions, and attitudes taken during the simulation. Role-playing may also provide some insight into one's self through discovering the impact made upon others during these sessions. Repeated exposure to various role-playing situations will help in achieving self-control.

There are, of course, problems and weaknesses in this type of training. Role-playing is still an artificial situation where the score really does not count. People are asked to *assume* roles and be regulated by the structure provided. Role-players will often say things that they would not dare say in an actual situation. Participants playing the roles of subordinates will ordinarily give the "supervisor" a much harder time than they actually would on the job. It is also difficult to introduce this type of training to experienced supervisors and executives. Many either discount its value as mere child's play or they "ham" the process up, playing for audience laughs. One possible way to move into role-playing from the more traditional and acceptable classroom type of training is to ask a particular trainee to get more specific in his answers to a case or question. When he says, "I would promote John Jones over Ray White," the instructor may ask him to phrase the remarks as he would actually say them. The instructor could then reply to those remarks and thereby create a form of role-playing. It is then a small step to move into more structured role-playing cases. The point, again, is that it is easy to verbalize rational concepts and very difficult to execute them.

Role-playing is a time consuming, expensive method of training. It may take two hours to make one basic point that could have been expressed in lecture in two minutes. However, not only is the point more likely to be retained when role-played, but actual practice has provided some increases in skill as well. But it is a method which is unsuited to the presentation of large amounts of information in a short period of time.

SENSITIVITY TRAINING

In 1946, Leland Bradford, Kenneth Benne, and Ronald Lippitt inadvertently developed the technique of sensitivity training as they were studying leaderless discussion groups. While trying to change behavior through reducing the restraining forces of buried fears, the feedback provided the group by outside observers was so revealing that an observer-moderator was placed in the group itself. Today such training is provided by National Training Laboratories, the American Management Association, and various universities and consultants throughout the country. Alternative titles frequently used are "T-group training" and "laboratory training."

As the title indicates, the general goal of sensitivity training is the development of awareness and sensitivity to behavioral patterns of oneself and others. Barriers that prevent this understanding are developed through a lifetime of interpersonal behavior and magnified by authority levels of formal organizations. More specifically, goals announced for this type of training have included (1) increased openness with others, (2) greater concern for needs of others, (3) increased tolerance for individual differences, (4) less ethnic prejudice, (5) awareness and understanding of group processes, (6) enhanced listening skills, (7) greater appreciation of the complexities of behaving competently, and (8) establishment of more realistic personal standards of behavior. With regard to the last item, it has been found that individuals rate themselves *lower* on trust and openness after sensitivity training than before. Instead of concluding that training was actually harmful, it is believed that trainees more fully appreciate the barriers to and complexity of *authentic* trust and openness after seeing and feeling it in a successful T-group.

Sensitivity training involves face-to-face learning about on-going behavior within a small group that meets for periods as long as a week or two. It is less artificial than role-playing inasmuch as the trainee plays *himself* rather than a structured role. A crucial factor in this approach is the complete absence of structure. There is no agenda and the moderator or trainer refuses to lead. Trainees come to the first meeting expecting to be guided and instructed by experts. The opening phase, however, is usually one of silence. The familiar structures and rationales have been removed. Silence is soon broken by someone asking for the purpose of the entire operation. The only replies are unofficial ones from other members of the group. There often follows an attempt to set up an informal pecking order as one participant suggests that each one introduce himself and provide a little background information. This subject is soon exhausted. One or more may again attempt to lead and influence the group. They are often met with resistance since they have no formal position of authority.

As indicated above, the primary subject for study in sensitivity training is the on-going behavior of the group and its several members and subgroups that may develop in time. The moderator-trainer is there to facilitate the feedback process so that each can learn how he is perceived by others. As will be stated later, he is also there to prevent serious psychological damage to particular persons who cannot bear up under the stresses created within the group. There always occurs a period of considerable frustration and conflict which generates a high level of insecurity and anxiety. This provides the opportunity for "gut-level" interchanges in such subjects as the need for intimacy and support, reactions to authority figures, and the need for control and dominance. The almost complete lack of structuring of the sessions usually forces someone to doubt the merits of the entire project and "blow his top." He and his behavior will probably become subject to group discussion and analysis. There is some likelihood that this person will acquire an ally or two, and the basis for a concrete analysis of cliques will have been provided. Each individual has a concept of himself when he enters sensitivity training and will doubtlessly attempt to defend that concept against all attacks. But these same defenses will probably be shaken from time to time by his fellow trainees. It is often a painful, but rewarding, experience to undergo.

In this type of training, the trainee should learn something about the personalities of others. His learning takes place on a *feeling level* rather than on an intellectual level as in the cases of other methods. He is experiencing these concepts rather than talking about them. With the help of the moderator and other trainees, he is led to appreciate the significance of these experiences. Tempers are frequently lost and one is forced to re-examine basic and long-standing attitudes and beliefs. The man who has long been accustomed to respect and acceptance is often shocked by the lack of enthusiasm with which his ideas are now received. He cannot order cooperation and acceptance in *this* group.

In successful T-groups, the period of frustration and conflict is followed by a time of cohesion and friendliness. Anxiety issuing from frustration can be alleviated only through close, supportive interaction with other people. In this period, there often develops a sense of purpose. This was stated by one participant in the following manner: "As corny as it may seem, and even with my predispositions to be careful, I developed a strong interest in and desire to help some members of the group."[7] It is hoped that trainees will learn to listen, to become more aware, to be more open and trusting, and to develop insight into their own personalities and their impact upon others. If a past behavioral style has not proved effective on the basis of feedback information, it is hoped that a different, more satisfactory one can be created. This can only be done with the supportive feedback of people who truly care and level in a constructive manner.

Sensitivity training has not received unanimous approval by industry leaders. It has been labeled "psychotherapy" rather than proper business training. Moderators have been criticized as being improperly grounded in psychology and psychiatric methods. It has been suggested that individual defense mechanisms that have been built up to preserve the personality over a period of years may be destroyed with little help being provided in replacing them with more satisfactory behavioral patterns. It is contended that one cannot exist without a few defenses such as rationalization, ambivalence, denial, suppression, and overcompensation. Frustration is an inevitable component of life and many of these mechanisms enable some degree of coping.

[7] William F. Glueck, "Reflections on a T-Group Experience," *Personnel Journal,* Vol. 47, No. 7 (July, 1968), p. 504.

In business organizations, managers frequently must make unpleasant decisions that work to the detriment of particular individuals and groups. Excessive empathy and sympathy will not necessarily lead to a reversal of the decision, and may exact an excessively high emotional cost for the decision maker. As one critic stated, "The normative prescriptions implied in laboratory training may be totally inappropriate for the business environment."[8] Many business organizations have internal environments characterized by competition and autocracy. The power inequality that goes with structure is not entirely compatible with openness, trust, and egalitarian ideology. In some instances, an effective manager must practice diplomacy through retaining a portion of the truth, or perhaps even telling different stories to two different persons or groups. Truth is not always most conducive to effective interpersonal and group relations. Sensitivity training would also tend to ignore organizational values that can issue from aggression, initiative, and the charismatic appeals of a particular leader.

There has been some research indicating the effectiveness of sensitivity training in changing attitudes and behavior of trainees. In a review of the very few studies available, Dunnette and Campbell conclude that, except in the case of ethnic prejudice, this type of training has not effected significant and lasting changes in attitude, outlook, and orientation.[9] In the Rubin study concerning prejudice, he measured self-acceptance and ethnic prejudice before and after training, and compared it with similar measures for an equivalent control group that experiences no formal training.[10] No changes were found in the control group, but there were substantial and significant changes toward *increased* self-acceptance and *decreased* ethnic prejudice after two weeks of T-group training for the other groups.

With respect to job behavior changes observed by peers, superiors, and subordinates, most research has shown that those undergoing sensitivity training were seen as making *more* changes than those not so trained. For example, Boyd and Elliss compared forty-two managers who experienced T-group training with twelve who had no training and ten who had been in a standard lecture-discussion human relations training program.[11] More observers reported job behavior changes for the T-group trainees (65 percent) than for the standard program trainees (51 percent) and the untrained (34 percent). Dunnette and Campbell cite three additional studies showing similar results.[12]

[8] John Drotning, "Sensitivity Training Doesn't Work Magic," *Management of Personnel Quarterly*, Vol. 7, No. 2 (Summer, 1968), p. 19.

[9] Marvin D. Dunnette and John P. Campbell, "Laboratory Education: Impact on People and Organizations," *Industrial Relations*, Vol. 8, No. 1 (October, 1968), p. 12.

[10] Irwin Rubin, "Increased Self-Acceptance: A Means of Reducing Prejudice," *Journal of Personality and Social Psychology*, Vol. 5 (1967), pp. 233–239.

[11] J. B. Boyd and J. D. Elliss, *Findings of Research into Senior Management Seminars* (Toronto: Hydro-Electric Power Commission of Ontario, 1962).

[12] Dunnette and Campbell, *op. cit.*, pp. 17–18.

Most of the observed behavioral changes were in the areas of greater openness, better understanding, and more consideration. There were no reported changes in analytical skills, ability to resolve conflict, or increasing overall effectiveness in the job. And as is always the case in researching complex behavior, unexpected findings are reported. Underwood found in one study that although T-group trainees were observed making more job changes than an untrained control group, more of the changes instigated by the latter were evaluated as enhancing overall job effectiveness (80 percent as compared with 67 percent).[13]

Many are agreed that sensitivity training does actually do something of significance to trainees. Serious psychological damage has been charged since there have been a few mental breakdowns among the thousands trained each year. House recommends that this heavy training weapon not be used without (1) careful study of the degree of interpersonal effectiveness *actually* needed in a particular job, (2) careful screening of participants to insure that they are mentally healthy to withstand the rigors of the technique, and (3) careful selection of trainer-moderators who are skilled in preventing psychological injury.[14] He feels that no one should be forced to undergo training against his will. But again in our hierarchical formal structures, expressions of a superior's opinion that consideration be given to attending can be construed as a mild suggestion by some and an outright command by another.

Structured Insight

It has been found that traditional methods of lecture, discussion, and case analysis are not as effective as sensitivity training in changing deep-seated attitudes about the nature of people. But the latter can be quite costly in terms of time, money, and psychological inputs. A third approach has been suggested that combines attitude changes with more structure in the training process. This approach usually begins with a systematic collection of the manager's attitudes and perceptions of peoples' characteristics and abilities in general, as well as preferred leadership styles in dealing with subordinates. This is done through a series of questionnaires using multiple choice, and sometimes forced-choice, techniques.

Information about the manager's expressed attitudes is fed back to him, and discussion is encouraged to compare attitudes and styles within the group. Comparisons are also made with various leadership models that the company

[13] W. J. Underwood, "Evaluation of Laboratory Method Training," *Training Directors Journal,* Vol. 19 (1965), pp. 34–40.

[14] Robert J. House, "T-Group Education and Leadership Effectiveness: A Review of the Empiric Literature and a Critical Evaluation," *Personnel Psychology,* Vol. 20, No. 1 (Spring, 1963), pp. 29–30.

or the training consultant may recommend. For example, in Blake and Mouton's Management Grid approach, an attempt is made to move the manager to a 9, 9 style that emphasizes equal concern for both people and output.[15] This is accomplished by group discussions of such subjects as the fundamental nature of man, conflicts between the individual and the organization, resolution of conflicts, self-actualization and job design, leadership styles, appraisal and development, and design of an organizational reward system.

In these discussions, many managers quickly realize that there are differences between what they say and what they believe and do. For example, many say that they favor subordinate participation, while at the same time report serious reservations concerning employee qualifications, ambition, and sense of responsibility. They also may realize that even though they tend to be directive with their own subordinates, they prefer their superiors to be more permissive. Discussions of this type may well lead to new insight and hopefully to a change in preferred leadership styles as measured by the original structured instruments.

PRINCIPLES OF TRAINING

The general objective of all training is to effect behavioral changes. Consequently, the principles of training find their base in the behavioral sciences.

One of the foremost principles of learning is that the trainee must be both motivated to be trained and sufficiently interested in the content of the program. We have emphasized earlier in this chapter that most development is self-development, and that each person must *want* to be changed. The content of the program must not only be sufficiently related to the goals and environment of trainees, but this relationship must be perceived and understood by these trainees. Often, classroom training is designated as "theory" and deemed to be completely unrelated to the practical environment. Thus, the initial contact in any type of training attempted must be concerned with demonstrating the necessity and pertinence of the behavioral changes desired. The relevance of these changes must also be re-enforced when the trainee returns to the job. Similarly, the goals of the training program must be reasonably consistent with the expectations of both the trainee's subordinates and his superior. If the changes to be effected are contrary to role expectations of either subordinates or superiors, the newly learned behavior will probably be of short duration.

Second, the trainee must be constantly informed concerning the progress of his development. He must feel that he is making progress; if he is not he should be told why. In fields where learning plateaus are common, he must be

---

[15] See Chapter 26 for a brief description of the Management Grid. For more details, see R. R. Blake and Jane Mouton, *The Management Grid* (Houston: Gulf Publishing Company, 1964).

encouraged during these periods when he feels no progress is being made. For operative jobs, learning curves which show normal progress are frequently used. The development of a manager, however, is considerably more complex and not as subject to categorization in terms of normal progress.

A third vital principle of training is that rewards must be related to progress in effecting behavioral changes. Without such reward, both the trainee and other organization members are likely to lose interest. One observes the rewards allocated to untrained personnel as compared with those awarded to the trained. Any significant discrepancy will seriously affect morale. Consequently, personnel possessing the power to allocate rewards must also be trained to value the objectives of such programs. When the content of a training program is inconsistent with the values of the manager, the latter will prevail, resulting in a waste of time and effort and in increased trainee frustration. For this reason, it has been suggested that training programs should begin at the top of an organization and work down to lower levels. When two or three levels of management are included in the same training sessions, status differences must be broken down. This combination has the value of committing both superior and subordinate to a new set of values *in the presence of each other*. This is much more compelling than if the same thing were done in separate groups.

Finally, within the various training sessions there are a number of frequently used learning principles. Development should proceed from the known to the unknown and from the simple to the complex. Not only does this facilitate learning, but it promotes trainee confidence in that he feels he can successfully effect behavioral changes. It has also been found that the higher the degree of trainee participation, through practice and discussion, the more effective and long lasting the behavioral changes. This subject of participation is significant in various areas of management as will be discussed in the following chapter.

It is apparent that training is not only a direction function which attempts to guide behavior, but it is also a process which in itself resembles the basic management process. The trainer, or manager, attempts to alter and control the behavior of the trainee, or subordinate, along certain desired lines. Thus, many of the general principles of management are also applicable to this single area of training.

EVALUATION OF TRAINING

Though it is easy to contend all education and training efforts are good, some attempt must be made to evaluate their effectiveness. At some point, the question must arise—has there been a behavioral change? And what criteria can be used as an index of this change?

In the case of operative training, where the emphasis is upon skill to do a particular job, reasonably accurate evaluation is possible. The indexes of quantity of work, quality of work, and scrap or reject rates will show whether there has been any improvement in skill as a result of training. Analysis of absenteeism and labor turnover rates may demonstrate morale values from this training. If the behavioral changes have been directed toward particular goals, such as safety improvements, more specific measures can be utilized. Accident frequency and severity rates are very useful criteria for judging the effectiveness of any safety effort. In addition, the opinions of the operatives' immediate supervisor should not be overlooked. Statistical data can go only so far, and the supervisor is usually a good judge of the skill level of his subordinates.

Training for executive jobs requires an intangible type of evaluation. It frequently resembles educational efforts which are more difficult to evaluate than specific training. A great deal of executive development in this country is taken on faith, though there is a trend in the direction of requiring proven value for dollars expended in this field.

One frequently used method of evaluating executive development programs is to secure the opinions of the trainees involved. In the greater bulk of evaluation attempts, these opinions have been highly favorable. Another approach is to secure some objective evidence of events that exhibit individual growth after training, e.g., number of promotions, pay increases, and increases in job responsibilities. Of course, the error here is that often very able people are selected to be trained, since most executive development programs are quite expensive. What would have happened to these particular people if they had *not* experienced this training? It could be that they would have been advanced anyway.

If training is to be evaluated in an objective fashion, data should be collected concerning the *behavior* of the trainee after training. This can then be related to the objectives of the training effort. Information can be collected from supervisors of trainees, colleagues, and subordinates. We still have the problem, of course, of determining whether these behavioral changes contributed to a more successful execution of organization tasks. The situational theory of leadership discussed in Chapter 13 would suggest that evaluation of this type of success would be very difficult indeed.

SUMMARY

Training is the process of increasing the skill and knowledge of a person to do a specific job. As such, it plays an important role in directing the efforts of subordinates toward the rationally determined objectives of the organization. Education is also a developmental process, but it is less specific in its directing capabilities, since it is concerned with increasing one's general background and understanding of the environment.

Due to the breadth and complexity of the management job, there are a large number of training and educational methods. On-the-job methods include experience, coaching, understudy, rotation, and special assignments. Training in the area of human relations is frequently done off the job, utilizing such methods as special courses, role-playing, cases, the incident process, structured insight, and sensitivity training. The last named is favored by most modern behaviorists since it has the greatest impact upon attitudes and behavior. Its goals of openness, trust, and sensitivity are also consistent with the behavioral approach to management.

In all training and educational attempts, the trainee is of central and crucial importance. We would hope that most trainees are Theory "Y" types and are both eager and able to learn. However, it should be realized that the culture, both general in society and specific within the firm, has a great deal to do with how he is to be classified.

Discussion Problems

1. How can training be classified as a part of the direction function?
2. Is training or education the more directive? Why?
3. What are the values of training to the individual? to the organization? Can training be disadvantageous to the organization?
4. Explain the statement that all significant development is self-development. What obligation does this impose upon the man? the organization?
5. Discuss the announced goals of sensitivity training. Relate them to the behavioral approach to management.
6. In what way does the processes of sensitivity training contribute to its announced goals?
7. Are the announced goals of sensitivity training compatible with modern business organizational life?
8. How does one go about the process of measuring the effectiveness of executive training techniques?
9. Contrast the case-conference approach to training with the incident process. Which is more near to the usual classroom situation?
10. How does the structured insight approach differ from sensitivity training? How is it similar?

Supplementary Reading

Drotning, John, "Sensitivity Training Doesn't Work Magic," *Management of Personnel Quarterly*, Vol. 7, No. 2 (Summer, 1968), 12–20.

Dunnette, Marvin D. and John P. Campbell, "Laboratory Education: Impact on People and Organizations," *Industrial Relations*, Vol. 8, No. 1 (October, 1968), 1–27.

Friedlander, Frank, "The Impact of Organizational Training Laboratories Upon the Effectiveness and Interaction of Ongoing Work Groups," *Personnel Psychology*, Vol. 20, No. 3 (Autumn, 1967), 289–307.

House, Robert J., "T-Group Education and Leadership Effectiveness: A Review of the Empiric Literature and a Critical Evaluation," *Personnel Psychology,* Vol. 20, No. 1 (Spring, 1967), 1–32.

Margulies, Newton and Anthony P. Raia, "Scientists, Engineers, and Technological Obsolescence," *California Management Review,* Vol. 10, No. 2 (Winter, 1967), 43–48.

Miles, Raymond E. and Lyman W. Porter, "Leadership Training—Back to the Classroom?" *Personnel,* Vol. 43, No. 4 (July–August, 1966), 27–35.

Stolz, Robert K., "Executive Development—New Perspective," *Harvard Business Review,* Vol. 44, No. 3 (May–June, 1966), 133–143.

Section B

Motivation

In recognition of both the power and abilities of subordinates, many managers have attempted to develop a degree of subordinate participation in managerial decisions and commands. The hope is thereby to increase motivation and to enhance the quality of decisions made (Chap. 17). The value of group, as opposed to individual, has also contributed to some modification in management philosophy (Chap. 18). And finally, in all attempts to direct or motivate, ideas must be communicated between manager and subordinate (Chap. 19).

17

Participation

One of the suggested techniques of positive motivation cited in Chapter 13 was that of greater employee participation in decisions that affect him. This is a theme which runs throughout the writings and research of the behaviorists. In Argyris's indictment of formal organizations and their negative effects upon human personalities, one of his suggestions for ameliorating these ills is more subordinate participation.[1] In Whyte's interaction method of analyzing organizational behavior, he consistently suggests that there should be more initiation of interactions from below in the hierarchy to approximate the number issuing from above.[2] And McGregor's plea for "management by integration and self-control" is a reflection of this same theme.[3] The behavioral theories of management have not as yet been fitted into any conceptual framework, as have the traditional theories.[4] Their contributions more often constitute bits and pieces of research which, as often as not, conflict with each other. The reason for this, claim the behaviorists, is that their suggestions and conclusions are based upon controlled research, while those of the traditionalists issue from armchair theorization. The latter can more easily be arranged into a beautifully

[1] Chris Argyris, *Personality and Organization* (New York: Harper & Bros., 1957), pp. 187–191.

[2] William Foote Whyte, *Men at Work* (Homewood: The Dorsey Press, Inc. and Richard D. Irwin, Inc., 1961), p. 561.

[3] Douglas McGregor, *The Human Side of Enterprise* (McGraw-Hill Book Company, 1960), Chap. 5.

[4] Cf. Ralph C. Davis, *The Fundamentals of Top Management* (New York: Harper & Bros., 1951), Chap. 1, and Harold Koontz and Cyril O'Donnell, *Principles of Management*, 4th ed., (New York: McGraw-Hill Book Company, 1968), Chaps. 2 and 3.

interrelated set of concepts. Nevertheless, behaviorists are almost unanimous in their opinion that managers and organizations should attempt to develop means which will facilitate the development of greater participation on the part of *all* members of an organization.

NATURE OF PARTICIPATION

There is some degree of participation by every member of any organization. We are not, however, talking about the kind of participation involved in the man on the assembly line performing his particular function in the context of the whole operation.

Harking back to Maslow's hierarchy of human needs, we recall that after reasonable satisfaction of his basic physiological and security needs, man becomes increasingly aware of the need to have some control over his life. A benevolent autocrat lets him know that he is a *human* factor in the organizational scheme but does not permit him to become an *adult* human whose ideas are solicited and utilized. Participation, in the sense in which it is discussed here, means that *the person is to give his thought and some portion of his emotions to the tasks of the organization.* It will require that managers share some of the decision-making process which traditional theory makes exclusively theirs.

One of the reasons given by Frederick Taylor for the introduction of scientific management was the inability of rank and file employees to make effective decisions about their work. Specialists began to devote themselves to motion study, time study, fatigue study, etc. It became management's duty to study and decide and the employee's duty to listen and comply. But this approach requires that the employee contribute his physical energy rather than his brains, his docile subservience rather than his initiative and enthusiasm. If we wish anything more, we must begin to share some of the decision-making responsibility with him. This may result not only in better decisions but also in a heightened sense of responsibility.

VALUES OF PARTICIPATION

The possible values of involving more people in the decision-making process lie in two areas: productivity and morale. With respect to the first area, improvements in productivity can issue from two sources: the stimulation of ideas and the stimulation of greater effort and cooperation.

Productivity

Acceptance of the philosophy of employee participation requires recognition that management does not have a corner on all of the ideas and talent in the organization. It is true that the major stock in trade of a scientific manager is ideas, but the people whose prime task is to execute can contribute more than mere acceptance and submission. Many employees complain about the unrealistic nature of an order or procedure yet are reluctant to submit suggestions for its alteration and improvement. In many instances this attitude issues from a feeling that management is not interested in what they think. In other cases, suggestions are withheld to avoid ostracism by the employee's peers. Though the scientific study may have been most thorough, decisions *do* have to be made in advance if separated from the work place. Time alone may make many decisions unrealistic. In addition, the executor often has access to information which is unavailable to the manager on a continuous basis. If management can develop more means of tapping the resourcefulness of *all* the people in an organization, and not just the portion designated as management and staff, the potentialities for improvements in productivity would be tremendous.

If employees are stimulated to participate in decisions affecting their work, they will often respond with increased effort in the execution of the organization's tasks. They have an added sense of responsibility resulting from the gratification of their need to be more independent. In one firm where the philosophy of participation was applied extensively, two interesting episodes illustrate productivity values issuing from this heightened sense of responsibility.[5] In a large electric utility, one of the continuous and irritating problems was the decision regarding the weather. Was it too bad, in terms of ice, sleet, snow, or rain, to order repair crews to climb the utility poles? The union contract stipulated that employees would not be asked to work in inclement weather. The problem was to determine whether the weather was sufficiently inclement to preclude work. There were many arguments at the work site, with consequent delays, much wasting of time, and a great deal of friction. On the advice of a consultant, the inclement weather issue was submitted to the entire employee group for discussion and analysis. On the basis of this group analysis, it was determined that the particular work crew at the site would be consulted by the foreman about the weather. After discussion and recommendation by the crew, it would be the foreman's responsibility to make the final decision. No hard-and-fast rule was established. After four years' experience, it was fully agreed that this approach had greatly reduced the number of arguments and the amount of time wasted. There were even

[5] Robert E. Schwab, "Participative Management—The Solution to the Human Relations Problem?" Speech before the Cincinnati chapter of the Society for the Advancement of Management (October 2, 1952), pp. 8–9.

instances when the foreman had to persuade the crew that the weather was too bad to climb the poles. The fear that the men would use the opportunity to "goof off" and refuse to climb even in good weather was ill-founded. All men have some sense of responsibility; this quality is not restricted to those who have been designated "managers."

In another instance in this same company, management was faced with the problem of stocking a reserve supply of coal in anticipation of a possible coal strike.[6] The 37 men involved were told the reasons for the extra effort. They were also informed that management did not know in fact what could really be expected from them during this emergency period. However, it was believed that a period of only three months was available to them for the establishment of a reserve supply. The group discussed the problem and directed various queries to management, one of which concerned the effect that this "crash" effort would have on their vacations. Management replied that they hoped that vacations could be eliminated during these three months, but any reasonable request would be respected. After further discussion, the group finally decided that they could stock 60 carloads of coal on each shift. This was even more than had been hoped for by management, which had considered a figure of 55 cars more likely. During these three months, the men worked seven days a week and exceeded the figure that they had set. The supervisors noted that the morale during this period was higher than it had been previously. A team spirit and improved attitudes were readily apparent.

In various controlled research experiments, similar improvements in productivity have been discovered with the introduction of greater employee participation. In one reported by Likert, data were collected from 31 geographically separated departments, varying in size from 15 to 50 employees, in a business firm that operated on a national basis.[7] The work performed in these departments was substantially the same. Group meetings held by the supervisors were used as an index of participation. The departments were classified into three types: (1) cluster "A" included the ten departments in which group meetings were considered by both the men and management to be worthwhile; (2) cluster "B" consisted of seven departments in which group meetings were never held; and (3) cluster "C" included 14 departments in which meetings were held but were considered by the men to be a waste of time, even though the supervisors contended the opposite. Fig. 17–1 shows the mean production rates of these three clusters, the rate for the departments emphasizing participation being the highest. It is interesting to note that a manager is better off with no participation, as in cluster "B," than with attempting to hold meetings where nothing seems to be accomplished. Such actions imply a

---

[6] *Ibid.*, pp. 9–10.

[7] Rensis Likert, *New Patterns of Management* (New York: McGraw-Hill Book Company, 1961), p. 119.

FIGURE 17–1   PRODUCTIVITY OF THE DIFFERENT
CLUSTERS OF DEPARTMENTS

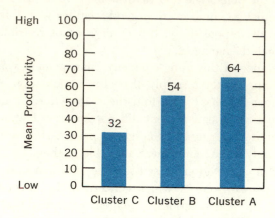

Department Clusters Based
on Group Meeting Method

Source: Rensis Likert, *New Patterns of Management,* p. 127. New York: McGraw-Hill Book Co., 1961.

manipulative approach where the men feel that management is really not interested in their ideas and is going through the participative motions in an attempt to stimulate their cooperation. When discovered, or even suspected, manipulation is ego-deflating and usually engenders resentment and hostility.

A well-known experiment in participation and productivity was conducted by Coch and French in a textile factory.[8] Four groups were established to determine the effects of varying degrees of employee participation on a change in work methods and accompanying piece rates. The first group, a control group, was approached by management in the usual manner: the new method and piece rate were prepared and installed by line management, methods engineers, and the training staff. With the second group, participation through representation in designing these changes was tried. A meeting was held and the need for change was presented dramatically by management. Management also presented, for group approval, a plan of approach for determining and implementing these changes. A few workers were selected by their fellow employees to work out details of the change, try the new methods, and train the other operators in the new procedures. In the third and fourth groups, *total participation* was attempted since they were smaller in size. A more personal and intimate atmosphere was established as all operators were to participate in the designing of new methods. The number of suggestions received was so great that the stenographer had difficulty in taking them down.

[8] Lester Coch and John R. P. French, Jr., "Overcoming Resistance to Change," *Human Relations,* Vol. 1, No. 4 (1948), pp. 512–532.

Though the previous output levels for *all four groups* were approximately 60 units per hour, 32 days after the changes were introduced, they were as follows:[9]

Control group	—48 units per hour.
Participation by representation	—68 units per hour.
Total representation, group 3	—74 units per hour.
Total representation, group 4	—72 units per hour.

Not only did the control group exhibit an absolute decline in output after the autocratically imposed change, but 17 percent of the employees quit during this period. There was also conflict with methods engineers, submission of grievances on the piece rates, and marked hostility against the supervisor. In contrast, the other groups exhibited a high degree of cooperation with both line management and the various staff specialists.

FIGURE 17–2   EFFECT OF CHANGE IN APPROACH UPON THE SAME GROUP

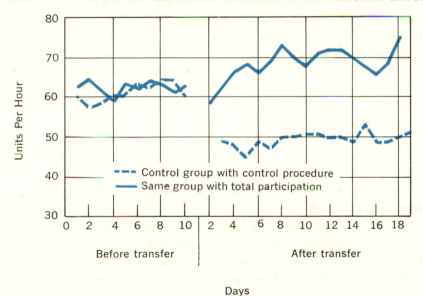

Source: Lester Coch and John R. P. French, Jr., "Overcoming Resistance to Change," *Human Relations,* Vol. 1, No. 4 (1948), p. 523.

A most interesting aspect of this study came from a further experiment with the personnel of the control group. These workers were finally transferred to a new job of comparable difficulty and the total participation approach was used to establish the methods. No reference was made to their past hostile behavior. As Fig. 17–2 indicates, this same group, using the participative approach,

[9] *Ibid.,* p. 522.

increased their productivity from 60 to 75 units. In addition, there were no resignations in the group during this nineteen-day experiment.

This firm, the Harwood Manufacturing Company, has continued to use the participative management approach to employees on all levels of the organization. Its basic leadership style as reported by upper managers, supervisors, and assistant supervisors, is one varying between consultative supervision and total participation.[10] In 1962, Harwood purchased the Weldon Company, a competitor in the pajama industry that had been experiencing a number of unprofitable years. Measurements of leadership styles used in the Weldon plant of 800 employees revealed a cross between exploitative and benevolent autocracy.[11] Harwood proceeded at once to try to change the philosophy of the Weldon managers, most of whom were retained. In two years time, the basic approach had been moved more closely to that of the purchasing company. This change was accompanied by a 30 percent increase in earnings of piece rate workers, a decrease in total manufacturing costs of 20 percent, a 50 percent decrease in labor turnover, and a change in profit as a percentage of investment from minus 17 percent to plus 15 percent. All these effects cannot be attributed to leadership style, but the chairman of the Harwood board is willing to credit a significant portion to the adoption of its participative management philosophy.[12]

Fleishman reports on another study in a dress manufacturing firm of 400 employees who are organized by the International Ladies Garment Workers Union.[13] This company's operations are characterized by frequent major style changes during each year which are usually accompanied by a drop in productivity until the new style has been mastered. Piece rates are negotiated with the labor union after completion of a learning period. Outside arbitrators determine such rates in case of management-labor disagreement.

In contrast to the more traditional approach to installing a style change, a participative experiment was conducted with a group of thirty sewing machine operators. This group was asked to perform the management tasks of establishing the sequence of operations, bundling methods, sorting, and pricing individual operations under the overall agreed upon dress piece rate. Based on past experience, management had anticipated that this particular style would require a production run of eight days. The participative group ran the entire lot of 750 dresses in only three days. There was almost no decrease in total piece rate earnings for the thirty women from the high level reached after extensive learning on the preceding style. When the more traditional method of

[10] Rensis Likert, *The Human Organization* (New York: McGraw-Hill Book Company, 1967), p. 34.
[11] *Ibid.*, p. 31.
[12] *Ibid.*, p. 38.
[13] Edwin A. Fleishman, "Attitude versus Skill Factors in Work Group Productivity," *Personnel Psychology*, Vol. 18, No. 3 (Autumn, 1965), pp. 253–266.

initiating change was used on the following lot of dresses, performance levels rose even higher. Continued use of the traditional approach did, however, lead to the conditions in effect prior to the experiment. The greater employee appreciation of management functions developed during the experiment had only a temporary effect after prior management approaches were reestablished.

Herzberg refers to the above forms of participation as "job enrichment." As noted earlier, job enlargment involves *horizontal* changes which introduce greater task variety. Job enrichment entails *vertical* changes leading to some degree of self-management. The employee is asked to participate in planning his work and measuring the results in terms of quantity and quality. Herzberg cites an example of a job enrichment project for stockholder correspondents.[14] Prior to a job change for the experimental group, indexes of performance level and attitudes toward the job were low. For one group, labeled the "achieving unit," correspondents were encouraged to answer letters in a more personalized way as compared to the former practice of following a standard form letter. They were also asked to assume responsibility for their own quality control through signing their own letters. These had previously been signed by supervisors. Employee subject matter experts were appointed to be consulted prior to one asking for help from supervisors. Specific high firm quotas for quantity of letters to be answered each day were eliminated in favor of general discussions concerning "a full day's work." And even these latter discussions were gradually eliminated. Six months after the beginning of this experiment, the performance index of the achieving unit stood at 90 as compared with 75 for a control group.

To cite other examples, the expansion of the work planning responsibilities of a group of ten female assemblers at Texas Instruments led to a reduction in assembly time for one product from 138 hours to 41 over a period of 9 months.[15] These employees had previously participated in a 24-hour training program in work simplification and cost reduction. Like Harwood Manufacturing, Texas Instruments is systematically attempting to manage in a consultative and participative manner. It also has a program of employee profit sharing through which monetary benefits of increased productivity can be shared. Non-Linear Systems of Del Mar, California attributes a 30 percent increase in productivity to a participative philosophy of management.[16] They also report that the job of specialized inspector has been eliminated and that customer complaints have been reduced over 70 percent.

A final example in a nonbusiness field shows some of the difficulties of

[14] Frederick Herzberg, "One More Time: How Do You Motivate Employees?" *Harvard Business Review*, Vol. 46, No. 1 (January–February, 1968), pp. 59–60.

[15] M. Scott Myers and Earl D. Weed, Jr., "Behavioral Change Agents: A Case Study," *Management of Personnel Quarterly*, Vol. 6, No. 3 (Fall, 1967), p. 16.

[16] "Can Employees Manage Themselves," *Dun's Review and Modern Industry* (November, 1965), pp. 59–60.

altering the environment to permit employee participation. In the typical mental hospital setting, the psychiatric aide is at the bottom of the hierarchy and makes relatively unimportant decisions. In an experiment at one Topeka hospital, the authority to make treatment decisions for schizophrenics was delegated directly from the hospital superintendent to the aide.[17] Psychiatrists, psychologists, nurses, social workers, and therapists were designated as *consultants* or resource people available to the aide for advice and assistance. Aides involved in the experiment were exposed to formal classes in psychopathology prior to the start of the project. The experiment was confined to one somewhat isolated ward in the hospital.

In the year following the introduction of the new approach, there was a marked improvement in the attitude and morale of the aides, and some noted improvement in the condition of the patients. By the close of the year, however, certain signs of deterioration began to be observed. Morale began to decline, efficiency began to drop, and there was a greater number of assaultive incidents among the patients. Expert observers concluded that the designated consultants (psychiatrists, nurses, etc.) as well as the administrators in the hospital were having a difficult time in sustaining the planned organizational relationship with the aide. It will be recalled that most of the hospital was being administered in the traditional manner. Many of the consultants did not fully accept the philosophy of decision making on the part of the unprofessionally trained aide. Hospital administrators concluded that such shifts in role expectations were feasible, but that they would require a far longer period of training and experience to implement than had been anticipated.

Morale

In these studies of productivity improvement, several references to morale were given along with production quantities. In these terms, participation helps to bring about the following:

1. Increased acceptability of management's ideas.
2. Increased cooperation with members of management and staff.
3. Reduced turnover.
4. Reduced absenteeism.
5. Reduced complaints and grievances.
6. Greater acceptance of changes.
7. Improved attitudes toward the job and the organization.

[17] William H. Key, Saul Siegel, and Nick Colarelli, "Power vs. Freedom: A Managerial Dilemma," *Personnel Administration,* Vol. 31, No. 3 (May–June, 1968), pp. 37–44.

Behaviorists have accused scientific managers of being too much concerned with the *quality* of decisions and not enough with their *acceptability* by those who are to execute them. If employees have had the opportunity of contributing something to the formation of a decision, they are more likely to accept and cooperate with the inevitable order that implements it. This is true even though the final decision is not identical with their own ideas, for at least they have been accorded the dignity and status of mature adults with something to contribute other than sheer physical energy. If ideas have been solicited, and none have been forthcoming, there is generally less reluctance to accept management's orders than if no interest in their opinions was shown.

We described above the manner in which the participative groups in the Coch and French study cooperated more fully with their supervisors and the various staff experts on changing methods and piece rates. In the electric utility company, a morale survey was conducted, the results of which are shown in Chart 17–1. Using the number of group meetings as the index of participation, note that there is a direct relationship between the degree of participation and the number of employees who say that their supervisor is good at handling people—83 percent for those supervisors who hold meetings often and 25 percent for those who practically never consult with their subordinates. An important variable, however, is the employee's view of the worthiness of such meetings. The supervisor who never held meetings was just as well off as the one who held them frequently when his subordinates felt that they were not worthwhile—25 percent in each case.

The Coch and French study also indicated a relationship between participation and turnover. The nonparticipation control group experienced a 17 percent separation rate in a short period of time after the autocratic introduction of the change. Man often seeks to reduce his frustration through escape—he

CHART 17–1 EFFECT OF MEETINGS ON ATTITUDE TOWARD SUPERVISOR

Frequency of Meetings	Meeting Seen as Valuable	Percent Saying Supervisor is Good at Handling People
Often	Yes	83
Frequently	Yes	70
Occasionally	Yes	61
Seldom	Yes	57
Frequently	No	25
Occasionally	No	20
Seldom	No	12
Practically Never	Yes and No	25

Source: Robert E. Schwab, "Participative Management: The Solution to the Human Relations Problem?" Speech before the Cincinnati chapter of the Society for the Advancement of Management, Oct. 2, 1952, p. 11.

quits. The utility company study showed a similar relationship between participation and absenteeism.[18] In departments where 70 percent of the employees felt free to discuss job problems with their superiors, the average was only *one* absence in a six-month period. Where only 30 percent felt free, the average was in excess of *four*. Intervening levels of freedom resulted in averages of two or three in the same six-month period.

In the stockholder correspondent study cited earlier, employees were asked if they felt that they were making a worthwhile contribution to their job.[19] A job reaction score for the experimental group rose from an index of 40 to 55 over a six-month period; there was no significant change for the control group. Another study of 315 managers in various companies revealed a significant relationship between their perceived *influence* in setting or changing departmental objectives, and the perceived *importance* of those objectives to total organizational efficiency.[20]

In general, the development of greater employee participation appears to have a direct and immediate effect upon employee morale. They take a greater interest in the job and the organization. They tend to accept, and sometimes initiate, changes not only because of their understanding of the necessity for change but also because their fear of insecurity has been reduced by knowing more about the change.

Participation in task planning and control is consistent with Herzberg's theory of motivational-maintenance factors. Studies of groups of employees at Texas Instruments indicate that the motivated workers are those most highly involved in job decisions concerning methods and results.[21] In one division of the company, department heads place the results of attitude surveys directly into the hands of six-man task forces authorized to meet as often as required on company time to analyze the results. The department head then shares survey results and task force interpretations and recommendations with his own superior. Any actions undertaken by management are communicated back to the original task forces. In effect, it turns the traditional flow of interpersonal initiations upside down. The image of the effective supervisory role in this company has been described as follows:[22]

A supervisor rarely motivates by exerting personal control on the subordinate. Rather he motivates by setting up a challenging job situation which

[18] Schwab, "Participative Management—The Solution to the Human Relations Problem?" pp. 12–13.

[19] Herzberg, *op. cit.,* p. 60.

[20] Gerald H. Graham, "Correlates of Perceived Importance of Organizational Objectives," *Academy of Management Journal,* Vol. 11, No. 3 (September, 1968), pp. 291–300.

[21] Scott Myers, "Who Are Your Motivated Workers?" *Harvard Business Review,* Vol. 42, No. 1 (January–February, 1965), pp. 73–88.

[22] Myers and Weed, *op. cit.,* p. 18.

leads to achievement, responsibility, growth and recognition. He does this by sharing information about organizational goals, arranging for equipment, supplies, and budgets, sustaining opportunities for self-development and acting as a mediator for unresolved conflict.

PREREQUISITES TO PARTICIPATION

These values of participation present a very rosy picture, but now it is necessary to fill in the shadows. There are certain prerequisites to and limitations on greater employee participation in decision making. Among the former are (1) sufficient time; (2) adequate ability and interest on the part of the participants; (3) rational requirements of structures and systems; (4) lack of the necessity for secrecy; and (5) reasonable security for the participants.

If immediate decisions are required, time cannot be spared for group participation. The manager decides what to do and issues the order accordingly. Even so, if the employee is made aware of the necessity for speed in a particular case, he will accept more readily the "autocratic" order.

Whether or not greater involvement in decision making can be developed is largely dependent upon the ability and interest of the participants, both subordinates and managers. This is not an easy concept to implement. Obviously, if the subordinate has neither knowledge of nor interest in a subject, there is little need to consult with him.

In the beginning, the switch from autocracy to participation will require some time for adjustment on the part of both parties, since participation requires the ability to govern oneself instead of leaning upon others. In addition, it requires time for the subordinate to learn to handle this new-found freedom and time for the supervisor to learn to trust his subordinate. If the electric utility had decided to pursue a program of greater participation, it would have had to live with *whatever* answer the employee group came up with. The management had hoped to get 55 carloads. If the group had decided upon only 48, management would be unable to say, "Well, 48 carloads are not enough. We were hoping for at least 55. That is what it will have to be." In such an event, management has revealed its use of "participation" as a manipulative device. It would want to know the employee's decision *only* if it agreed with a prior management decision. If management truly believes in a policy of participation, it will have to *pay* for the learning process by accepting the inevitable number of disappointments and extra costs; participation is, after all, an investment of a long-range nature.

Thus, prerequisites of participation for the subordinate are ability, knowledge, and interest in the subject at hand, a sense of responsibility, and the ability to communicate; and for the manager, a trust in the subordinate's ability and sense of responsibility and a willingness to stay with the approach for a reasonable period before giving up.

Additional limiting factors are the rational work system and structures. As the automobile comes down the line, one cannot permit freedom of employee decision concerning the execution of his assigned function. As indicated in Chapter 13, increased mechanization and automation in industry are introducing an impersonal discipline into modern organizations. Participation can be of help in determining if and how these systems are to be introduced. But once installed, the amount of freedom for both manager and operative has been reduced. There are no completely free, unlimited areas of action for participation. The distribution of disagreeable work assignments, for example, can be handled through consultation with the parties involved. These parties may even be allowed to prepare the assignment list. They cannot, however, decide that the tasks should *not* be done. The organization structure and policies provide the perimeters within which participation can be developed. In addition, there is also the limiting factor of secrecy. Though employees may have an interest in a subject, the demands of competition may require that information concerning it be suppressed.

As indicated in Fig. 17–3, the area of job freedom left to the incumbent may be quite restricted. His task is pregoverned by management directives, organization policies and procedures, the union contract, relations with the union steward, staff specialists, and the degree to which he can obtain the cooperation of subordinates.

And finally, it is illogical to attempt to secure suggestions and ideas about

FIGURE 17–3   LIMITS TO PARTICIPATIVE FREEDOM

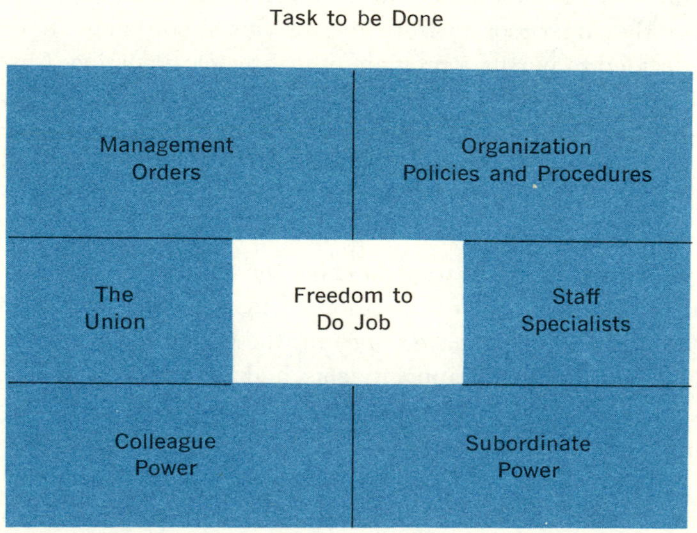

Task to be Done

Management Orders	Organization Policies and Procedures
The Union	Freedom to Do Job	Staff Specialists
Colleague Power	Subordinate Power

subjects and acts which tend to threaten the security of the individuals concerned. If a management is contemplating closing a plant two years hence, discussing the problem with employees *now* may do more harm than good. It is also useless to ask an employee for suggestions as to the manner in which he can best be fired, to take an extreme case.

RISKS OF PARTICIPATION

Traditional managers view the participation process as containing certain risks to the enterprise. One of these risks was cited above under the prerequisite of time; that is, until the employee develops a new sense of responsibility, there is the risk of bad decisions issuing from his participation. An immediate lack of responsibility is understandable if one has worked for an autocratic oppressor. If employees are apathetic or hostile, the attempt to engage them in the decision-making process is likely to prove disastrous. If, however, the attempt has been put forward sincerely, skillfully, and over a period of time, the chances are good that the desired results will occur.

There is also some risk of losing control over the direction of the enterprise when that control is shared with a large number of people. Yet, although the manager may in one sense have relinquished some of his formal power, in another sense he may gain the additional power that issues from the cooperation of his subordinates.

It should be noted, however, that at no time are all of the decisions made in a firm vested in management, with the operative's actions being only in response to such decisions. As Barnard pointed out long ago, a single command issued by management will result in literally thousands of decisions being made by those who are not supposed to decide.[23] Thus, if a utility manager orders that a pole be moved from one side of the street to another, perhaps 10,000 further decisions may be required by various personnel before the pole is finally set. Only the decisions that were difficult or involved controversy will be remembered. Training has supposedly been of assistance in helping these subordinates make the decisions that the manager would have made had he been on the site of the pole relocation.

Development of further subordinate participations also introduces risks issuing from slowness and inflexibility. The time necessary for consultation will cost something in terms of both money and the possible loss of immediate opportunities. Similarly, a history of employee consultation may restrict the organization's movements, since the group will feel aggrieved if autocracy is ever substituted for the participative process. For we are dealing not only with

[23] Chester I. Barnard, *The Functions of the Executive* (Cambridge: Harvard University Press, 1938), p. 198.

the determination and execution of necessary organization tasks but also with the establishment and maintenance of status and power systems.

Some behaviorists feel that most of the avowed risks of participation are in effect *rationalizations* to protect the manager's ego. Only he can make the best decisions, he feels, and it is unfortunate that other people are ever necessary to accomplish organization goals. If these people are required, the ego demands that they be submissive and subordinate to the superior directions of the formal leader. If this view has an element of truth, it may help explain why too few managers are willing to take the risk to test out participation as a way of managing. It would be foolish to insist that participation works in all situations and with all people, but it is equally shortsighted to refuse to experiment with the approach when the prerequisites have been realistically and reasonably met.

DEGREES OF PARTICIPATION

There are varying degrees of subordinate participation, which revolve basically around four elements: (1) *role* or part taken by the participants; (2) *organizational level* of the participants; (3) the *significance of the subjects and areas open* to participative decision making; and (4) the *frequency* with which

CHART 17–2   DEGREES OF PARTICIPATION

FACTOR	DEGREES		
	LOW	MODERATE	HIGH
Scope of usage	Narrow, minor matters	Selected subjects	Everything of real concern
Frequency of use	Rarely used	Occasional or periodic meetings	Consistently "way of life"
Persons involved	Select few / Top management	Select groups or committees	All supervisors / All employees
Part taken	Communication heard	Consulted (consultative management)	Group decision (democratic management)

Source: Robert E. Schwab, "Participative Management: The Solution to the Human Relations Problem?" Speech before the Cincinnati chapter of the Society for the Advancement of Management, Oct. 2, 1952.

participative attempts are made. An outline of three possible degrees for each of these elements is shown in Chart 17–2.

Role

The role of the participants in decision making is one of the most important elements determining the degree of participation. In general, three roles can be identified: (1) understanding the nature of and reasons for particular management decisions; (2) advising the manager prior to the time that the decision is made; and (3) exercising authority through voting upon the decision.

Complete autocracy would involve not only the decision's being made by the manager but also no communication of anything except the command to act. If the manager volunteers reasons for the decision, he is moving in the direction of greater participation. He realizes that his subordinates may be more inclined to cooperate more effectively if they are aware of the necessity for the decision.

In the last two decades, there has been a substantial amount of information given to the rank and file personnel in American business firms. Some of this is due to at least a minimal acceptance of a philosophy of participation. Perhaps more is due to a realization of the *power* of subordinates both as members of labor unions and as citizens with a vote at the polls. Most managers want their employees adequately informed concerning their side of fundamental questions *before* the employee exercises his choice in both governmental and union affairs.

The manager proceeds a step further if he approaches his subordinates for advice and information *prior* to his having reached a decision. This is often referred to as "consultative management." This can be done on an informal individual basis with degrees ranging from consulting *one* trusted employee to asking for the opinions of *all*. It can be done more formally through meetings with the entire group. Consultative management constitutes a merging of formal and informal organization; that is, the manager himself will make the decision only after having enlisted the aid and advice of those with knowledge and interest in the subject.

The logical culmination of employee participation would be decisions which are solely group-based. Yet even here, the very decision to allow such freedom to the group rests with the manager. Thus, in the final analysis he remains responsible for the decision and for the manner in which it is achieved.

Organization Level

When we speak of subordinates in the participation process, we should realize that most managers are also subordinate to higher managers. If only vice-presidents are permitted a voice in management decisions, the scope of such participation is not high. As additional organization levels are included in the decision-making process, the scope is, by definition, widened. Note that while the scope of participation can be broad, the effect of such participation on the organization is minimal. Similarly, participation can be relatively restricted to a small but important group, with the result of such participation being of critical concern to the organization.

We should recognize that there have been complete autocrats in charge of various organizations in which even vice-presidents were relegated to the role of mere clerks. One well-known president of a large retailing organization lost over ten of his vice-presidents through his refusal to share decision-making authority.

A study of 200 managers on different levels in 8 companies revealed that higher managers were more likely to use participative approaches than lower managers.[24] Upper managers demonstrated both greater freedom in decision making and a greater reliance upon subordinates for advice. If lower managers are merely to execute orders of higher executives, they will usually consult only with their superiors. If lower level managers are to use participative techniques, they must have some areas of final choice. When given final choice, they are more likely to consult with subordinates in the decision-making process.

Subjects

The topic under consideration by management determines the degree of participation. Obviously, such subjects as vacation schedules, disagreeable job assignments, and lunch periods do not constitute important areas of participation. If, however, the consultations are about such subjects as layoffs, production schedules, and recognition of labor unions, the level of participation is quite high.

Again, the usual participative situation involves a mixture of elements and degrees. On highly important subjects, management rarely goes to the rank and file for an authoritative decision. Of course, the National Labor Relations Act *requires* that a firm permit its employees to vote on whether or not a labor union should be recognized, but this is an exception not within management's authority to decide. On limited subjects, such as the lunch period schedule, authoritative decision making by, or at least in consultation with, the rank and file would not be unworkable.

[24] Vaughn Blankenship and Raymond E. Miles, "Organizational Structure and Managerial Decision Behavior," *Administrative Science Quarterly*, Vol. 13, No. 1 (June, 1968), pp. 106–120.

Frequency

Though, to some degree, the use or non-use of the participation process is controlled by the subject, few, if any, firms use the participative process constantly. Many in fact use it so rarely that their personnel never acquire any real skill in its application. In the latter event, personnel generally resent any effort to involve them in decision making. They feel that management is trying to put something over on them.

PARTICIPATION SYSTEMS

In addition to a participative attitude on the part of the immediate supervisor, various formal systems have been devised for the sharing of management decisions. Several of these are discussed below.

Multiple Management

This approach was first developed by Charles P. McCormick, president of McCormick and Company of Baltimore.[25] In taking over this organization from his uncle, McCormick was concerned about his own lack of knowledge in running the enterprise. As a partial remedy, he established, in 1932, a junior board of directors which, in effect, duplicated the existing board. This former group was given the authority to discuss all problems that the senior board could discuss, with the exception of wages and grievances. One of the basic objectives was to develop middle managers with broad, company-wide perspectives. (As such, this method could have been mentioned in the preceding chapter as a training technique.) However, a second objective was to permit sharing and participation in decision making, also on a company-wide basis. With respect to the degrees of participation, this system was established on a group advisory basis for *middle management personnel* who met periodically to discuss major matters of importance to the entire organization.

The junior board at McCormick consisted of 17 department managers or their assistants. Periodically, six of these members were dropped from the board by vote of the membership, and nominations and elections were conducted among the remaining 11 for their replacement. Membership in this group was considered an honor and a high status symbol and was prerequisite for entry to the senior board.

All recommendations had to receive a unanimous vote by the junior board.

[25] Charles P. McCormick, *Multiple Management* (New York: Harper & Bros., 1938).

suggestions forwarded were rarely turned down by the senior
~h the junior board was to perform an advisory function, it
~ ritually authoritative. Satisfactory experience with this
Cormick to establish more restricted boards for the
divisions.

an

1.   ın was briefly discussed earlier as a form of company-wide compensation (see Chapter 15). Money, however, was only one element. More
important, according to Scanlon, was a changed attitude on the part of
management and employees. No longer were managers to hold themselves
apart from employees as the only decision makers. Cooperation was to be the
order of the day. Staff engineers were to talk directly and in friendly fashion
with the machinists. A joint problem-solving approach was to be taken rather
than one of incentive wages, high pressure salesmanship, and outright commands. The point was made that the enemy of labor was *not* management and
vice versa, but it was rather the competitive firm that could make the same or
better product for a cheaper price.

One of the first successful installations of the Scanlon plan was at LaPointe
Machine Tool Company in Hudson, Massachusetts. At the time, Scanlon was a
United Steel Worker's official. This company was near bankruptcy, and the
work week had been cut back to four days. Something drastic was necessary to
save it, and the answer was to be an advanced form of employee participation.
The payoff in money was arranged as described previously—any savings from
improvements in general efficiency would be shared with everyone. But the
crucial factor was a change in attitude from internal cutthroat competition and
protection of status to one of mutual cooperation. The formal mechanism
consisted of a series of departmental committees, composed of the foreman
and a union representative and established for the purpose of soliciting and
processing suggestions for improvement. There was also a higher, plant-wide
screening committee for ideas falling outside the province of the department.
The accent was upon teamwork, both in terms of the spirit that prevailed and
in the formula for sharing any potential gains. This was not the traditional
form of suggestion committees and systems, which are more nearly akin to an
individual incentive system (*individuals* are stimulated to submit suggestions
for improvements in the hope of gaining monetary rewards). Such forms of
participation usually result only when the organization has its back against the
wall and is in serious difficulty. When conditions are more prosperous, management is usually not so willing to share its decision-making authority to this

degree, nor do the employees tend to develop such a high sense of joint responsibility for the welfare of the enterprise.

When lower managers are deficient in participative skills, it has been suggested that formal systems such as the Scanlon plan will insure a minimum of participation in the enterprise. Walton points out that on the average lower managers (1) tend to be more concerned about narrowing the status differences between them and subordinates, (2) can less afford to spend time in talking activities which are the prime currency of participative techniques, (3) are less likely to have the desired verbal skills, and (4) must deal with rank and file who are often less responsive to appeals of self-actualization.[26] Varying abilities and conditions would result in nonuniform leadership styles throughout the enterprise. On the other hand, a Scanlon arrangement requires that formal committees be established and consulted, thus assuring a minimum of participation for all employees despite varying skills and attitudes of supervisors. And as indicated earlier, such formal participation is directly tied to the reward of money, a symbol that is on the surface more fashionable to many than recognition, dominance, independence, or self-actualization. In summary, Walton feels that for middle and upper managers, the leadership style approaches have encouraging possibilities, while the formal Scanlon arrangements are inappropriate. For the first line supervisors, however, the leadership style approaches have pessimistic possibilities, while formal arrangements have greater potential as a beginning program. As both supervisors and subordinates approach the Theory "Y" model, participative techniques can be expanded beyond that formally required.

Special Committees

All formal systems of participation seem to involve the creation of a group or committee. It assures the participants that their contributions will be solicited on a continuing basis.

For particular subjects and problems, various firms have established a committee to participate in the decision-making process. Thus, safety committees are frequently set up to draw upon the backgrounds of all concerned in order to stimulate a degree of safety consciousness. During World War II, the dominant industrial problem was production. Consequently, many production committees, composed of workers and management personnel, were established to foster cooperation in the solution of production problems. The number of such committees has been greatly reduced in recent years, perhaps

[26] Richard E. Walton, "Contrasting Designs for Participation Systems," *Personnel Administration,* Vol. 30, No. 6 (November–December, 1967), p. 38.

because of our lack of knowledge and skill in participation. Furthermore, the unions have in general been opposed to any unilateral attempts by management to promote employee participation in management decisions. They are distrustful of the motives and suspect a diminution of loyalty to the union. If there is to be participation, they prefer that it be effected through the union's own organizational arrangements. The requirement of periodic collective bargaining, as well as the numerous grievance committee meetings, are evidences of participation through union representation.

To move to another field briefly, the use of groups and committees is a common administrative device in colleges and universities. The degree of faculty participation is usually much higher than would be the case in a private business firm. It is not unusual for a faculty committee to be empowered to search for a new president of the institution or a new department head. Usually the role is an advisory one but is greatly supplemented by powers issuing from persuasive abilities as well as by general faculty support. The task of merging the requirements for effective university management with the high degree of participation demanded by faculty members is so complex that academic administrators have become almost a different breed of managers. If the present trend in business toward greater participation continues, perhaps we will have to look to college presidents and deans for the experience and answers to the business problems of the future.

SUMMARY

As used in this chapter, participation is the process of involving more members of the organization in the decision-making function. It constitutes an attempt to secure an emotional and mental involvement in the work of the organization. The possible values issuing from this are an increase in productivity through greater effort and improved quality of ideas and the enhancement of morale, as reflected in the degree of cooperation, attitudes toward supervision and the job, absenteeism, grievances, turnover, and acceptance of change.

There are numerous limitations and risks to this process of participation. Time is required, both for the process itself and for learning how to consult and be consulted. Both the manager and the subordinate must possess the requisite skills and attitudes. Often the technical requirements of a situation preclude anything but autocracy. The major risk is the possible loss of control that may result from the sharing of decision making and reduced structuring.

One need not be for or against participation in toto. There are varying degrees revolving around the role of the participants, the organizational level, the subjects involved, and the frequency of such attempts at involvement. The roles may require listening to explanation of reasons for commands, advising the superior prior to determination of the command, or actually deciding as a group what the order should be. The organizational levels of participants can vary from top management to rank and file. Subjects can be of major importance or little consequence. Frequency of use can be rare or constant. Various examples of formal systems of participation are multiple management, the Scanlon plan, and special committees such as safety or production groups.

DISCUSSION PROBLEMS

1. Contrast the conditions affecting subordinate participation for both upper and lower level managers.
2. Define and distinguish between job enlargement and job enrichment.
3. What is the relationship between the Herzberg theory of motivation-maintenance factors and employee participation?
4. Discuss the importance of the time element in the participation process.
5. Distinguish between consultative and democratic management. What is the role of the hierarchy in each?
6. Indicate the degrees of participation for each element in the multiple management system of participation.
7. Contrast the first degree of participation with the last, on the basis of role, organization level, subject, and frequency.
8. Discuss the prerequisites and risks involved in employee participation.
9. What are the values of formal programs of participation over the consultative management style?
10. Analyze the Scanlon plan in terms of the degrees of participation involved.

SUPPLEMENTARY READING

Fleishman, Edwin A., "Attitude versus Skill Factors in Work Group Productivity," *Personnel Psychology*, Vol. 18, No. 3 (Autumn, 1965), 253–266.

Key, William H., Saul Siegel, and Nick Colarelli, "Power vs. Freedom: A Managerial Dilemma," *Personnel Administration*, Vol. 31, No. 3 (May–June, 1968), 37–44.

Likert, Rensis, *The Human Organization*, Chaps. 2 and 3. New York: McGraw-Hill Book Company, 1967.

Myers, M. Scott, "Every Employee a Manager," *California Management Review*, Vol. 10, No. 3 (Spring, 1968), 9–20.

Myers, M. Scott and Earl D. Weed, Jr., "Behavioral Change Agents: A Case Study," *Management of Personnel Quarterly*, Vol. 6, No. 3 (Fall, 1967), 12–19.

Newport, M. Gene, "Participative Management: Some Cautions," *Personnel Journal*, Vol. 45, No. 9 (October, 1966), 532–536.

Raia, Anthony P., "A Second Look at Management Goals and Controls," *California Management Review*, Vol. 8, No. 4 (Summer, 1966), 49–58.

Walton, Richard E. "Contrasting Designs for Participative Systems," *Personnel Administration*, Vol. 30, No. 6 (November–December, 1967), 35–41.

18

Group Dynamics

In the preceding chapter, we discussed one of the major recommendations of many of the behaviorists—increased employee participation. We also saw how many of the participative approaches involved groups rather than individuals. Here again we have a split between the traditionalists and the behaviorists. Traditional management theory has been strongly individualistic in its orientation, e.g., individual incentive wages, job specialization and functional definition, individual initiative and ingenuity, and authoritarian leadership. Groups are recognized, but only as official committees whose use should be kept to a minimum. On the other hand, behavioral scientists, particularly sociologists, have suggested that the natural organization unit, rather than the individual, is the primary group. Concepts of informal organization were added to the formal designs of management. As Likert states, "An organization will function best when its personnel function *not as individuals* but as members of highly effective work groups with high performance goals."[1] Likert does not visualize the organization structure in the usual individually-oriented, pyramidal fashion; rather, he views it as a series of interlocking groups. The manager is a "linking pin" between two or more such groups. He is simultaneously the leader of his own group and a participating member of his superior's group.

Because of the group's importance to both traditional and behavioral theories we shall attempt to discover how it operates, how its structures and procedures can influence results, and how it can be used, as well as misused, in advancing the organization's interests. We shall, in short, be dealing with the area of study known as "group dynamics."

[1] Rensis Likert, *New Patterns of Management* (New York: McGraw-Hill Book Company, 1961), p. 105. Emphasis added by author.

NATURE OF GROUP DYNAMICS

Though the interest in group dynamics has issued primarily from behaviorists, Mary Parker Follett attempted in the 1920's to incorporate groups as a significant component of a systematic approach to management.[2] Her contribution did not meet with great enthusiasm, for at that time the individual was considered the basic building block of organizations. In the late 1920's and early 1930's, Elton Mayo's studies at Western Electric further revealed the nature and significance of informal primary groups in business organizations.[3] These famous experiments, as well as the writings of Chester I. Barnard, stimulated an increased interest in the group.[4]

Study of the group and group processes was not identified as a separate field of research and inquiry until the late 1930's, with the work of Kurt Lewin and his associates. Lewin popularized the term "group dynamics" and aided in the establishment of the Research Center for Group Dynamics, the first organization devoted to the exclusive study of group phenomena.[5] Though there is the usual controversy over the credit for initiating a field of study, Lewin is considered by most to be the "father" of group dynamics.

A group can be defined as two or more people, interacting and interdependent, who have the ability to behave in a unified manner with a shared purpose or objective in mind. As the term "group dynamics" indicates, this process is not a static one, involving as it does a continuous change and adjustment of relationships within the group. Most of the research regarding these relationships has been devoted to groups of from two to a dozen members. Our emphasis here will be on the small, face-to-face groups which Likert considers to be basic to large organizations.

As Lewin has pointed out, the dynamic group is not merely the sum of the individual members; instead, it is a structure that issues from the interactions of these individuals. As such, it is both a result of individual personalities and behavior as well as a conditioner of that behavior. Most people tend to act differently as individuals than as members of a group; we should not assume, however, that a "group mind" exists or that the group as such can think. Thus the individual and the group should be studied as interrelated elements.

The goal of group dynamics is to study the elements and processes of groups

[2] Mary Parker Follett, *Creative Experience* (New York: Longmans, Green, and Co., 1924).
[3] See Chapter 1.
[4] Chester I. Barnard, *The Functions of the Executive* (Cambridge: Harvard University Press, 1947), Chaps. 4 and 5.
[5] Though founded at the Massachusetts Institute of Technology, the Research Center was moved to the University of Michigan after Lewin's death. Other similar groups are the Social Relations Laboratory at Harvard, Human Dynamics Laboratory at University of Chicago, Group Dynamics Center at Temple University, and the Research Center for Human Relations at New York University.

in order to formulate laws which influence and govern their operation. As such there are many factors which must be considered. Democratic leadership, for example, may be one possible variable, and the researcher would state, "If you use the democratic approach with a particular group working on a particular task, you will achieve a particular result." Similarly, attempts have been made to develop cause and effect relationships surrounding such variables as status congruency, cohesiveness, and size, among others. Many of these will be discussed below.

Cattell has suggested, as a means of signifying the dimensions of a group, the term "syntality, or the attributes of the group *as* a group, i.e., by its measured performance as an integrated whole."[6] Just as one must define the dimensions of an individual personality in order to understand a person and predict his behavior, so must one define the dimensions of group syntality in order to understand it and predict its behavior.

CHARACTERISTICS OF THE GROUP

In its basic sense of dynamic interaction of individuals in a face-to-face relationship, group dynamics has been going on since the beginning of man. Only in recent decades, however, has there been a systematic attempt to study these complex forces in order to understand how a group operates. Various disciplines have been involved, such fields as psychology, sociology, anthropology, social psychology, and psychiatry. As a result, certain basic elements of the group have been identified. Among these characteristics are group goals, structure, size, leadership, participants, cohesiveness, norms, and agreement. Each of these will be discussed below.

Group Goals

All group task-goals are necessarily derived from basic organization objectives (see Chapter 2), and provide the bases for continued interaction. Research has indicated that group members are more dedicated to goals which they have helped establish, than to those imposed upon them by others. However, the opportunity for participation in establishing goals is, in most instances, considerably restricted. Such opportunity is more prevalent in those organizations where time is available, or when management is unsure of organization objectives.

The nature of the task-goal will affect the group's membership, processes,

---

[6] R. B. Cattell, David Saunders, and Glen Stice, "The Dimensions of Syntality in Small Groups," *Human Relations,* Vol. 6, No. 4 (1953), pp. 331–356.

and norms. Delbecq identifies three general types of task-goals: (1) routine decision making, (2) creative decision making, and (3) negotiated decision making.[7] The first type is characteristic of most groups operating within the business firm. Specialized members are selected on the basis of contributions to the task-goal, e.g., developing an inventory policy or establishing a fringe benefit program. Group norms often emphasize professionalism of members, shared responsibility for the goal, and central coordination by a chairman. In creative decision-making groups, the selection of members is more heterogeneous to enable different viewpoints and frames of reference to focus on the problem. Norms usually support originality and unusual ideas, nonauthoritarian processes, openness in communication, deliberate separation of idea origination and evaluation, humor, and consensus. The goal in a negotiating group is reconciliation of differences between opposing factions, e.g., labor and management. Membership is usually equally divided and each individual sees himself as a representative of his faction. Processes should emphasize orderly communication, formalized procedures to handle disputes, and veto power by each faction. Norms often include acceptance of freedom to disagree, acceptance of necessity for partial agreements, and perception of conflict as being healthy rather than pathological. It is apparent that the formal task goal of a group provides the basic foundation for its makeup and operation.

Research has also suggested that if the group is to be utilized on a continuing basis, it must always have as a *secondary* goal that of maintaining itself. Excessive and continuous pursuit of the task-objective may do irreparable harm to the cohesiveness and effectiveness of group action. Consequently, the leader must provide time and means for stimulating some degree of group harmony. He may become impatient with idle chatter or the discussion of irrelevant issues but he must accept these activities as essential to this secondary goal. In addition, the effective group will recognize and deal with interpersonal, and potentially disruptive, conflict, instead of hiding or suppressing it. For the intellectual consideration of the task-objective will be facilitated by the release of emotional pressures within the group. In a study of 165 top executives in six companies, it was found that 84 percent felt it was a sign of immaturity to express feelings openly during decision-making meetings.[8] The classical approach to management tends to value cognitive rationality as being relevant and good, and emotional and interpersonal discussions as being irrelevant, immature, or not contributing to the task-goal. If human beings were able to completely segment and suppress their feelings toward other members of a group, perhaps these feelings would not constitute barriers to

[7] Andre L. Delbecq, "The Management of Decision-Making Within the Firm: Three Strategies for Three Types of Decision-Making," *Academy of Management Journal*, Vol. 10, No. 4 (December, 1967), pp. 332–338.

[8] Chris Argyris, "Interpersonal Barriers to Decision Making," *Harvard Business Review*, Vol. 44, No. 2 (March–April, 1966), p. 87.

effective discussion. Behaviorists would suggest that segmentation is not possible, and that feelings of irritation and ill will can contribute to withholding significant information, restricted commitment to the task-goal, and "one-upmanship" tactics while following a hidden agenda.

An interesting aspect of this group-maintenance goal is the so-called "goblet issue," where group members evaluate each other (as at a cocktail party, where the participants size each other up through their "goblets").[9] Although much time may be expended on so relatively unimportant an issue, the leader should be aware of its usefulness in permitting group members to learn about each other and the possible roles they are likely to play.

Structure

As with the overall organization, there are both formal and informal structures in small groups. In business organization groups, there is almost always a designated leader. Standard rules of procedure are frequently adopted to facilitate accomplishment of objectives. This obviously introduces an element of regimentation and restriction, just as does formal organization structure. Yet, one study showed that task-oriented groups produced greater personality and behavior changes than did free, unstructured group discussions.[10] Even more important there was greater participant satisfaction with a predetermined group goal and distinct progress toward that goal. In unstructured groups, on the other hand, participants were irritated and frustrated by the indefiniteness and excessive irrelevant social conversation.

Though the leader and formal procedures are visible, there is also an informal and less discernible structure in any group. The job held outside the group, the person's ascribed status, and interpersonal relationships, are all structural elements which will influence the outcome of group processes. Each member has other functions which he performs on a continuing basis, and which management, in structuring a group, must take into account. Thus, the impact of a senior man on the group will be materially different from that of a lower-echelon employee. When status, as determined by ability, and voting power are congruent, the group usually is more congenial and the members see themselves as gaining by the process.[11] When voting power is held by persons of little recognized ability, there is more tension and less satisfaction among group members.

There are also varying degrees of friendship among members of any group.

[9] William C. Schutz, "Interpersonal Underworld," *Harvard Business Review,* Vol. 36, No. 4 (July–August, 1958), pp. 123–135.

[10] John H. Mann, and Carola Honroth Mann, "The Importance of a Group Task in Producing Group-member Personality and Behavior Changes," *Human Relations,* Vol. 12, No. 1 (1959), pp. 75–80.

[11] Ralph V. Exline, and Robert C. Ziller, "Status Congruency and Interpersonal Conflict in Decision-making Groups," *Human Relations,* Vol. 12, No. 2 (1959), pp. 147–163.

Some research indicates that people tend to agree with those they like while rejecting the same idea as expressed by those they dislike. Thus power, status, friendships, and cliques all constitute elements of the invisible structure. One of the basic purposes of the "goblet issue" is to begin the assessment of some of these relationships.

Size

Most of the studies in group dynamics have been concerned with relatively small groups. The size of the group should be large enough to obtain sufficient ideas yet small enough not to hamper free communication and inhibit participation.

Research has indicated that the two-man group, the dyad, is dangerous, for without complete agreement such a group risks dissolution. The triad often results in two of its members pitted against the third, with an undue amount of power allocated to the second person on the majority side. Most studies of size have been concentrated upon groups of from two to twelve in number. It has been found that as size increases within this restricted range, the degree of consensus in group discussion decreases; factionalism and the formation of subgroups become definite possibilities. Increasing size works to the advantage of the autocratic leader since member tolerance for increased direction becomes greater.[12] In larger groups, members report greater feelings of insecurity and threat; only the more forceful members try to present their ideas. This combined with the tendency to form cliques or coalitions of subgroups often leads to political rather than analytical decisions.

In research reported by Bales, *five* members were considered optimum for discussion groups. When groups were of this size, members felt more comfortable and indicated that they had sufficient time for adequate discussion.[13] In addition, a strict deadlock is not possible, and the commonly observed 3–2 split does not isolate and alienate any single member.

Bales also stated that seven is the maximum; anything larger causes some personnel to discontinue talking to each other and to center their remarks on a few top men.

Bonner suggests that groups of from six to ten persons offer maximum conditions for interaction in problem solving.[14] This is less precise than Bales's conclusion and reflects the inexactness of research in this area. No precise optimum size has been discovered, but the ideal is reached when every member has the opportunity of contributing according to his maximum ability.

[12] J. K. Hemphill, "Relations Between the Size of the Group and the Behavior of 'Superior' Leaders," *Journal of Social Psychology*, Vol. 32 (August, 1950), pp. 11–22.

[13] Robert F. Bales, "In Conference," *Harvard Business Review*, Vol. 32, No. 2 (March–April, 1954), pp. 44–50. This was also confirmed in Donald E. Porter, "Information Distribution and Group Size," *Industrial Management Review*, Vol. 4, No. 2 (Spring, 1963), p. 16.

[14] Hubert Bonner, *Group Dynamics* (New York: The Ronald Press, 1959), p. 212.

Leadership

Though there has been some experimentation with leaderless groups, most researchers have concluded that every group requires some *central focus*. The first studies by Lewin and his associates varied the leadership element to ascertain its consequences on group processes. Such approaches as authoritarian, participative, and laissez-faire were introduced into controlled experiments, with the second approach resulting in a maximum of interaction and ideation.[15] Perhaps this is the source for the feeling that democratic management is *the* group dynamics technique though these experiments constitute only one of many research attempts to discover the laws of group processes. Some have in fact further concluded that the ideal leader is one who establishes a warm, intimate relationship with group members. Yet other studies have indicated that the psychologically-distant leaders were more effective in promoting group productivity than were those with closer ties to the group.[16]

Bales suggested that the center of focus should consist of *two* leaders since most groups have two objectives: the task and group maintenance.[17] Thus, the task leader would concentrate upon the formal goal, often with the result of achieving low popularity among group members, while the social leader would restore unanimity and congeniality. Though it is possible for both leadership functions to be performed by one person, Bales suggests it is more likely that they will be executed by two different people.

A still broader view of leadership suggests that in the effective group, all participants perform leadership functions at one time or another. Thus, if any participant encourages contribution, mediates disputes, or clarifies problems, he is, in this view, exhibiting leadership. Such a degree of participation is highly desirable for certain types of problems and situations, but it still does not reduce the need for a unifying and controlling leadership. It is also the task leader's duty to recognize the necessity for group maintenance, and thereby to stimulate some of the tension-relieving interactions and to develop a social leader as partner.

Participants and Participation

A group consists of both participants as well as leaders. We have indicated above that the size of the group is a major factor in determining the nature and

---

[15] See Chapter 14.

[16] Fred E. Fiedler, "The Leader's Psychological Distance and Group Effectiveness," in Dorwin Cartwright and Alvin Zander, *Group Dynamics,* 2nd ed. (Evanston: Row, Peterson, 1960), pp. 586–606.

[17] Bales, *op. cit.,* p. 47.

degree of member participation. The power and status structures are also important in that there tends to be greater participation when these relationships are substantially equal. Finally, participative leadership also tends to stimulate more member participation than does authoritarian.

The task objective constitutes an important determinant of member participation. If the objective is for the leader to inform the group of his decision, questions by the participants may suggest dissatisfaction, disagreement, and possible insubordination. If the objective is group problem solving, questioning would in this case be regarded as helpful. In the individual-versus-group controversy as applied to problem solving, the group has one possible advantage. With several minds being focused on a problem, there is a greater potential for disagreement than there is in individual thinking, the kind of disagreement which allows for the consideration of many alternative possibilities.

Benne and Sheats suggest a variety of operational functions for group members in discussion.[18] Again, these are divided along the lines of the two basic objectives, the group task and group maintenance. Among the group-task functions are those of researching, informing, clarifying, coordinating, orienting, testing, and summarizing. Among the group-maintenance functions are those of encouraging, mediating, and "gate-keeping," or providing everyone with a chance to speak. These are all desirable participant roles which will enhance group effectiveness. There is also behavior which can serve to block the attainment of both task and social objectives. The participants who exhibit such undesirable behavior have been variously labeled as pigeonholers, hairsplitters, fence sitters, orators, yes-men, sulkers, and needlers.

Figs. 18–1a and b provide two contrasting patterns of group participation. The first figure represents a discussion that is closely controlled by the leader. Everyone participates but each member communicates only with or through the leader. Fig. 18–1b portrays a freer discussion, where members talk to one another as well as to the leader. The leader may remain silent for considerable periods of time. (This pattern of participation is most helpful in problem-solving conferences.)

Cohesiveness

One group characteristic that has received much attention from researchers is that of cohesiveness, or the degree of attraction that the group has for each of its members. It is exemplified by such attitudes and actions as loyalty to the group, a feeling of responsibility for group endeavors, defending the group against outside attack, friendliness and congeniality, and a tendency to think in

---

[18] Kenneth D. Benne and Paul Sheats, "Functional Roles of Group Members," *Journal of Social Issues,* Vol. 4, No. 2 (Spring, 1948), p. 41.

terms of "we" instead of "I." If the group is to act in a unified manner, some degree of cohesion must be present.

The amount of cohesiveness is largely determined by the degree to which the group goals help satisfy individual needs. A constant management problem is that of relating the task objectives of various groups to the individual needs of group members. Informal groups are usually started because of an inability of official groups to meet all human needs. As indicated previously, abolition of these informal groups is neither possible nor desirable, particularly since the degree of cohesion in these unofficial groups is usually much higher than in the formal, official committees. Management would prefer to have such cohesion within its officially constituted groups, but the presence of task objectives makes this impossible. Action can be taken, however, to promote the attraction of official groups by (1) demonstrating the interdependency of task objectives and individual needs; (2) enhancing the status of the official groups; (3) stimulating greater member participation through participative leadership techniques; and (4) devoting greater attention to activities that promote group maintenance. Symptoms of low cohesiveness are the emergence of subgroups, cliques, factions, and lone wolves.

FIGURE 18–1   TWO PATTERNS OF PARTICIPATION

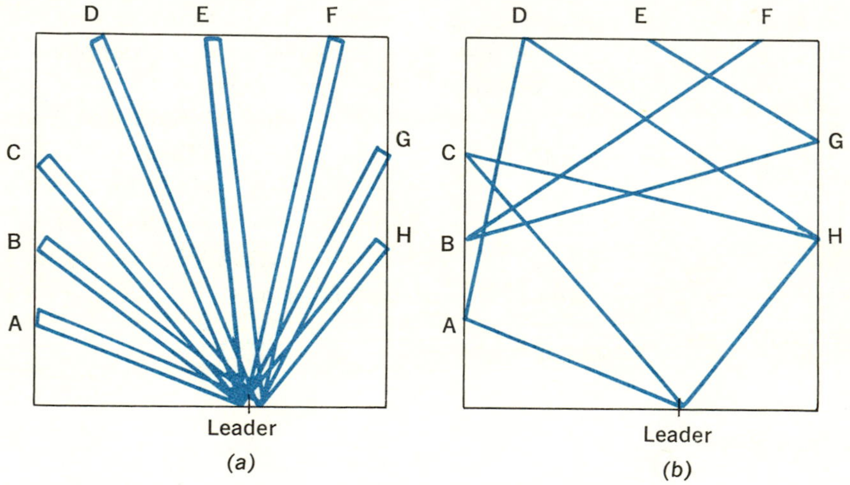

If cohesiveness is obtained for official, task-oriented groups, the organization stands to gain through increased cooperation and motivation. The greater the attraction the group has for its members, the greater its power to change, motivate, and control those members. It should be noted, however, that this same cohesiveness can work just as effectively *against* task objectives in groups that are oriented in an opposing direction.

Norms and Conformity

The tendency for behavior of group members to coincide with group norms can come from subtle pressures as well as from the need for some commonly-accepted truth. There are many problems and situations where the absolute truth is unknown or unavailable, and the individual can judge the validity of his opinion *only* by comparison with other opinions. If he is drastically out of line with the majority of his associates, his sense of security is in jeopardy. Asch has demonstrated that this phenomenon can occur even with decisions about factual matters.[19] A group of seven to nine college students were each given two cards. On one card was one black line; on the other, three lines of varying lengths. Each man was asked to choose the one line among the three that matched the length of the single line on the first card. In ordinary situations, people will make mistakes in this comparison less than one percent of the time. However, the test is structured in such a manner that all of the participants *but one* are instructed to agree with each other, right or wrong. The remaining one is the guinea pig whose resistance to group norms is being tested. Under the group pressures of majority opinion, the minority subjects swung to the majority's wrong opinion in over one-third of the cases. This is substantially greater than the normally expected one percent. If the minority member was provided with a partner, his resistance to the majority's erroneous opinion was materially increased.

Here again is the eternal dilemma of the individual—the conflict between the needs of the ego and the need for social acceptance. The group members must hold some common values, attitudes, and opinions, if they are to function in a unified manner. The individual needs social support and must accept some of these values, though at some cost to his individuality. The cry has long been against conformity, but the cause should be against *unnecessary and excessive conformity*. It is interesting to note that informal groups usually require *greater* conformity with respect to minor matters than do the official task-oriented groups designed by management.

Agreement

The pressures toward group norms tend to produce agreement. However, every group must have various formal mechanisms whereby specific agreements on task functions and objectives can be obtained. Voting is one way of

[19] Solomon E. Asch, "Studies in the Principles of Judgment and Attitudes: II. Determination of Judgments by Group and Ego-standards," *Journal of Social Psychology*, Vol. 12 (1940), pp. 433–465, and "The Doctrine of Suggestion, Prestige, and Imitation in Social Psychology," *Psychological Review*, Vol. 55 (1948), pp. 250–276.

determining the will of the group, but such a clearcut distinction between the "yeas" and the "nays" is often detrimental to future cooperation. Most small business groups prefer to work toward a *consensus* as determined by the group leader. Consensus means acceptance of the group's decision without the individual necessarily approving it personally. In reaching a consensus, each member must feel that the group understands his position and feelings on the question, and that the group should proceed in the generally agreed-upon manner even though he, personally, does not agree. It requires on his part an ability to think not only as an individual, but as a member of a cohesive group. Consensus necessarily requires active participation on the part of *every* member. The leader needs to know, in some way, where each person stands.

There are occasions in most groups when an impasse has been reached and a consensus cannot be determined. In different fields, various mechanisms have been established to resolve such fundamental disagreements—the mediator and arbitrator in labor relations, for example. The everyday operation of small groups within the business enterprise, however, does not usually allow for the entry of such third parties. Of course, the leader can always "solve" the impasse by dictating the answer. Yet, many managers desire to have the consensus support of the group. One suggested procedure for resolving such situations rests on the belief that many impasses come from misunderstanding and poor communication.[20] Thus the leader of the group may call upon a member of the *proposing* side to state his case fully without interruption or counter-statement. After this presentation, only three types of inquiries may be made by opponents: (1) questions of clarification of what was said, in order to promote understanding; (2) requests for information concerning the unique aspects of the proposal in comparison with past experiences; and (3) questions concerning the means required or available for testing the validity of the proposal. The result of this procedure is fuller understanding on the part of both the opponents and the proponents. In addition, the tensions resulting from the impasse are drained away in the inquiry period. The members are stimulated to look less at each other and more at the issues. This is no panacea for resolving basic disagreements, but it has helped one firm reduce the number of such impasses.

VALUES AND DANGERS OF THE GROUP

In the preceding discussion several advantages and disadvantages of group processes have been suggested or implied. It is appropriate at this point to contrast these values and dangers. Among the former are the following:

[20] Irving J. Lee, "Procedure for 'Coercing' Agreement," *Harvard Business Review,* Vol. 32, No. 1 (January–February, 1954), pp. 39–45.

1. Improved decisions, particularly in areas subject to a high degree of subjectivity.
2. Improved acceptance and motivation, both for members and non-members of the group.
3. Broadening of backgrounds and perspectives of group participants.
4. The facilitation of coordination of action.
5. The facilitation of the integrating of conflicting viewpoints.

Improved decisions are supposed to result from the joint and simultaneous impact of several minds on a common issue. In various experiments in problem-solving tasks, it has been found that groups obtain more accurate answers more quickly than do individuals working alone.[21] At the same time, it should be mentioned that without necessarily becoming a member of an organized group the individual can still have the advantages resulting from relationships with other people. Such informal ties, however, lack some of the effects of multiple minds working simultaneously on common issues in an organized, face-to-face manner.

On subjective issues, particularly those dealing with promotion or performance evaluation, the group can work to better advantage than can the individual. In such matters, one man usually cannot have all of the pertinent information, and a pooling of opinions and facts will lead to a better answer. In addition, since an absolute answer is impossible to achieve, group members and nonmembers alike are more inclined to accept the answer of a group over that of an individual.

We have indicated in the preceding chapter that subordinate participation in the discussion of problems often results in greater acceptance of resulting decisions. The utilization of groups for discussion purposes makes it evident to all that subordinate opinions are valued by the organization. Exposure to broad problems and the various viewpoints of multiple personnel constitutes a broadening experience for the members of a group, while it enhances individual judgment and facilitates cooperation. Group meetings are often essential to assist in coordinating various activities in terms of time and sequence of action. And finally, where conflicts of interests are concerned, mutual discussion in a face-to-face relationship is the best known means of reconciliation. We must keep in mind, however, that executive commands are quite ineffective in integrating interests. Commands can integrate action, but whether a man changes his mind or not is largely up to him.

Traditional management theorists and practitioners have long placed great faith in the individual, particularly the leader or manager. Various drawbacks of group processes have been presented, among them the following:

[21] Cf., Donald E. Porter, "Information Distribution and Group Size," pp. 12–16.

1. Division of responsibility which leads to reduced individual concern for problems and decisions.
2. A leveling effect which issues from the necessity to agree.
3. Pressures toward excessive conformity.
4. Pressures toward excessive conservatism.
5. Time and expense.
6. Manipulation of people.

One of the basic indictments advanced by traditionalists is the division of responsibility entailed in group decision-making and action. They maintain that *only* individuals can be responsible. The traditionalists also suggest that a group tends to bury issues that the manager prefers to postpone or avoid completely. Behaviorists reply that effective groups, if properly led, can and will develop a sense of responsibility. They concede that the manager is fully responsible for the decision, but this does not preclude use of groups for consultative purposes. As in the case of participative skills, however, it takes time and practice to acquire the leadership and membership skills for small group action. And until some degree of such skills is obtained, the indictment of unconcern and evasion of responsibility has merit.

Traditionalists also contend that the seeming necessity to agree will result in a decision based on the lowest common denominator. Most people prefer agreement to conflict and will hesitate to voice objections when they think the majority is headed in an opposite direction. Traditionalists have had visions of everyone going to a meeting wanting to do *only* what the group wants to do, in which event nothing is done. Students of group processes reply that the *effective* group has a healthy respect for the minority view, and that if disagreements are not encouraged, the group is *not* operating in a mature fashion. (An interesting question arises when the group establishes total individuality as a norm or standard. In this unlikely event, conformity would lead to a lack of uniformity. Certain types of psychological training groups have established such a norm for developmental purposes.) Behaviorists also point out that most people are usually members of multiple groups with frequently conflicting norms. In any event, we must have some agreement on basic values to provide the basis for cooperation and coordination, while doing away with conformity for its own sake.

Another accusation made against group decision making is that such decisions are usually more conservative than are individual decisions. The group will not take risks whereas one person will. Yet a series of interesting studies conducted by Marquis revealed the opposite conclusions.[22] Both college

[22] Donald C. Marquis, "Individual Responsibility and Group Decisions Involving Risks," *Industrial Management Review*, Vol. 3, No. 2 (Spring, 1962), pp. 8–24.

students and business managers were asked to make certain decisions involving varying degrees of risks. This was to be done on an individual basis. Afterwards, these persons met in groups to discuss and remake the same decisions. In the greater bulk of cases, the group decision resulted in exposure to a significantly higher degree of risk than did the individual decisions. It was hypothesized that the groups may have been acting irresponsibly since responsibility was divided. The experiment was altered to make the leader of each group fully accountable for the decision which would be made by him *after* discussion and consultation with the group. In these cases also, the decisions made with consultations were more risky than those made without. In short, the question as to whether groups or individuals are more conservative in approach is a problematic one.

It is apparent that group processes do consume time. An individual could make a decision in a few seconds, while the group, with the same amount of information, may take hours or days. The costs must be computed in terms of the time each executive spends away from his department in group sessions, and these costs must be more than offset by the values derived from group processes.

A final criticism of the group, amd more particularly of the study of group dynamics, is that skills developed in dealing with groups can easily lead to manipulation of people. A knowledgeable and unscrupulous leader or participant can maneuver other group members to achieve his own selfish ends. Of course, this depends on the leader and on the effectiveness of the group processes themselves. If *all* people can obtain more knowledge and skill by means of group action, the opportunities allowed the unscrupulous manipulator are materially reduced.

AN APPLICATION OF GROUP DYNAMICS— THE CONFERENCE

Though most organizations are replete with groups, particularly informal ones, perhaps the formally organized conference or committee is the type most commonly recognized by practicing managers. Both traditionalists and behaviorists realize a need for greater manager skill in conference leadership. In this section, we will discuss group dynamics in action as revealed in the problem-solving conference.

The problem-solving conference process can be divided into three basic parts: (1) formulation of the issues to be discussed; (2) exchange of information, opinions, and feelings by all participants; and (3) development of a solution.

Formulation of the Issues

In most organizations, the major responsibility for the formulation of the issue rests with the conference leader. Conferences are usually called for a definite purpose—the task-objective that issues from the work situation. The group should be informed concerning the specific goal and the areas in which it can operate. The group should also be informed as to whether its role is one of advice to the manager or one of actual decision making. Such information serves to reduce the ambiguity which frequently occurs at the beginning of most meetings.

The manager usually believes that he has correctly identified a problem. Discussion may reveal, however, that other problems are more fundamental, and that the suggested one is merely a symptom of the basic difficulty. Thus, conferences are generally more effective if the leader does not enter the process with fixed ideas. The attitude should be one of a *group* problem-solving approach. At times, he may confine himself to stating the goals for the group, while allowing the members to determine the problems and obstacles preventing their accomplishment. At the minimum, the leader should avoid statements that imply a preconceived answer, as well as those that serve to threaten the security of the group.

The Exchange

This phase of the conference is sometimes known as the "drawing-out" stage. The objective is to obtain the maximum number of facts, opinions, attitudes, and feelings of all members on the identified issues. All contributions should be welcomed at this stage *without evaluation*. It will be recalled from the discussion of brainstorming sessions that no negative criticism of suggestions was permitted. Imagination and judgment are both necessary to the creative process, but each tends to interfere with the other. Imagination works best if no judgment is permitted during the time when all ideas are being solicited.

The conference leader has an obligation to insure the maximum amount of member participation. He should be aware of his own status and power in relation to the rest of the group. If he is an organizational superior, he should be particularly careful in the early stages to provide no clues as to his own thinking. If all he wants is agreement with his own ideas, another meeting other than a conference is indicated.

One of the critical skills of the conference leader in the drawing-out phase is that of knowing how to ask questions. Various types of questions such as the following can be posed:

1. *Directed.* If certain people have not voiced any contributions, their participation may be encouraged by directing specific questions to them. If the leader is to determine whether or not there is a consensus, he must, after all, have some indication of the position of every member.

2. *Overhead.* The overhead question is one asked of the entire group with no specific person designated to answer. It is an invitation to general discussion. The leader may be aware of certain phases of the issue which have been neglected and may pose questions such as, "What do we know about . . . ?" and "Will this present any obstacle?" The overhead question shows a willingness of the leader to loosen his control over the discussion and thereby stimulate interchange among the members.

3. *Reverse.* A group member will frequently direct a question to the leader, particularly if the leader's status, power, and position are higher, and if the leader is known for his authoritarian techniques. If the leader does not wish to influence the decision at this point, the reverse question may be used. The ball is tossed back to the original questioner. Even though he says, "Well, I don't know about that; what do *you* think," it is usually apparent that he is not exhibiting a condition of ignorance. Some managers have the erroneous impression that not having an answer for anything and everything constitutes a weakness which places their capabilities in doubt. If he is to successfully draw out the contributions of the various group members, the leader will have to suppress his inclination to feed his own ego by acting as an oracle.

4. *Relay.* A variation of the reverse question is to toss the ball not back to the original questioner, but to a third party. Or the leader may elect to elevate the importance of the question by directing it to the group at large, thus transforming it into an overhead, relay question.

As the various contributions are received, it is important to keep the discussion focused on the issues rather than on the contributors. There is the usual temptation to applaud ideas expressed by friends and superiors, and to deprecate those advocated by enemies and inferiors. Ideas are thereby personalized and discussion of facts and issues suffers. It is also difficult for a contributor to discuss his own idea objectively, to disown it, and subject it to critical analysis by himself and the group. If the idea is criticized, he often feels that he, as well as the idea, is under attack. The leader and other group members can aid in the attempt to depersonalize contributions and restrict the discussion to the issues.

The apparent division of responsibility among all group members tempts some to let others carry the entire load of the discussion. Just as there are certain requirements for effective conference leadership, there are definite obligations for the effective conference participant. Among the skills and obligations of a good participant are:

1. To listen with understanding.
2. To exhibit a desire to know the views and feelings of others.
3. To operate as part of a group, rather than to dominate it.
4. To make an effective contribution by providing facts and views, suggesting possible solutions, and supporting or opposing suggestions of others.
5. To aid in the integrating of conflicting viewpoints by asking clarifying questions and noting areas of agreement.
6. To be tactful and civil by giving others an opportunity to speak, avoiding personal attacks on the motivations and integrity of speakers, and exhibiting some degree of self-control in personal conduct.

Solution

All discussions must end, hopefully with some degree of agreement. The leader should keep emphasizing the responsibility of the group as a whole in order to promote cohesiveness and overcome any tendency toward abdication of group responsibility.

Many leaders have found it a worthwhile technique to list the various suggestions on a blackboard. In this manner, the group can select from the list the ideas believed to be most valuable, *without* necessarily rejecting, one by one, all the remaining ideas. The person who contributed an idea not selected can still see that, if not selected, it was at least recognized and recorded. This small point aids in his accepting the group solution.

The weaknesses and strengths of all selected ideas should be examined in detail and an attempt should be made to have the group move to some conclusion. Formal voting should be avoided while the leader makes an effort to determine the consensus of the group.

The group will usually want to know what will happen to the agreed-upon solution. This is usually covered in the beginning, but the leader should again note its final disposition. For if the group is to operate effectively on a continuing basis, there must be some feedback concerning what happens to its recommendations.

Summary

The effective work group is an important element in the behaviorist's approach to management. Traditionalists have made use of such formal group conferences and committees. We have indicated in previous chapters concerning formal organization theory that the increasing size and complexity of modern business organization has led to the further use of management committees. One receives the impression that traditional managers have been *forced* into working with and through groups, while behaviorists *eagerly advocate* their use in ever wider areas. The proper attitude lies somewhere between these two extremes.

The possible values derived from the use of groups are improving decision making and acceptance and motivation of decisions, broadening backgrounds of group members, and the facilitation of coordination and integration of action and viewpoints. The group also has such dangers and disadvantages as the following: (1) a potential division of responsibility; (2) a leveling effect to secure agreement; (3) pressures toward conformity and manipulation; and (4) the expenditure of much time and money for every group meeting. It is an art to determine the mixture of individual and group efforts that will be most effective in accomplishing task-objectives on a continuing basis.

If groups are to constitute a significant portion of management theory, their elements and processes must be studied. The title of group dynamics has been applied to this field of study. Various significant group properties have been identified, such as the goal, the group's structure, size, type of leadership, participation, cohesiveness, norms, and agreement.

One of the most widely accepted formal groups is the problem-solving conference or committee, which involves an attempt to obtain maximum participation and contribution from each member. Its basic stages involve formulation of the issue, exchange, and solution. Multiple individuals operating in face-to-face situations can stimulate each other in the possible development of more effective answers to common problems.

DISCUSSION PROBLEMS

1. What effect does size of group have upon its processes?
2. What effect does the varying nature of the task goal have upon group membership, processes, and norms?
3. What role should open expression of emotional feelings have in group discussions within business firms?
4. Identify and discuss the two basic goals of any group. Which is primary?
5. What is "hidden agenda"? "the goblet issue"? "the leveling effect"?
6. Discuss the role of the group in management theory. How does the emphasis of the behaviorist differ from that of the traditionalist?
7. Identify and relate the concepts of cohesiveness and conformity within groups.
8. Why does Bales recommend at least two leaders instead of one for each group?
9. The question is a significant tool in the hands of the conference leader. What are the various types and how should they be used to stimulate the maximum participation?
10. Discuss values and disvalues of the group as an organizational device.

SUPPLEMENTARY READING

Argyris, Chris, "Interpersonal Barriers to Decision Making," *Harvard Business Review,* Vol. 44, No. 2 (March–April, 1966), 84–97.

Delbecq, Andre L., "The Management of Decision-Making Within the Firm: Three Strategies for Three Types of Decision-Making," *Academy of Management Journal,* Vol. 10, No. 4 (December, 1967), 329–339.

Delbecq, Andre L., "The World Within the 'Span of Control,'" *Business Horizons,* Vol. 9, No. 4 (August, 1968), 47–56.

Drought, Neal E., "The Operations Committee: An Experience in Group Dynamics," *Personnel Psychology,* Vol. 20, No. 2 (Summer, 1967), 153–163.

McGregor, Douglas, *The Professional Manager,* Chap. 10. New York: McGraw-Hill Book Company, 1967.

Oshry, Barry I., "Clearing the Air in Human Relations," *Business Horizons,* Vol. 9, No. 1 (Spring, 1966), 35–46.

Prince, George M., "How to be a Better Meeting Chairman," *Harvard Business Review,* Vol. 47, No. 1 (January–February, 1969), 98–108.

19

Communication

In all of the preceding discussion, it has been *assumed* that the manager and the subordinate were communicating with each other: the subordinate understood the manager's command and the manager understood the subordinate's contributions. This assumption that perfect communication is taking place is widespread in both theory and practice.

Though the subject of communication enters into every phase of management, this chapter will concentrate specifically upon its nature, significance, and problems. Communication is classified under the basic function of direction inasmuch as the issuance of orders and the eliciting of participative responses are totally dependent upon communication. Theoretically, the manager may develop his plans, procedures, and organization by himself, but when he wants to implement these, he must communicate his desires to others. Communication is a subject which has been emphasized greatly by the behaviorists, since both employee participation and group dynamics require communication skills of the highest order.

NATURE AND SIGNIFICANCE OF COMMUNICATION

The word communication comes from the Latin word *communis*, which means "common." Communication is therefore the act of imparting a common idea or understanding to another person. It covers any type of behavior that effects an exchange of meaning.

Communication has at least two purposes. First, it is the means whereby the *plan can be implemented* and action coordinated toward a common end. The traditionalist is likely to emphasize this particular purpose. But secondly, communication is the means whereby the members of an organization can be *motivated* to execute the plans willingly and enthusiastically. The manager may know the logical objectives and requirements of the formal organization; but, what is more difficult, he has to discover the needs and wants of the particular people on whom he is dependent for the accomplishment of these objectives. In addition, he must impart understanding of the reasons for the work and the values to be derived by the employee.

Observation of any organization on any given day can provide many instances of faulty communication; for perceptive skills, as well as good will and impeccable intentions, are required in communication. Perhaps the greatest error in communication is the one emphasized in the opening sentence of this chapter, the *assumption* that understanding exists. In one of Likert's studies (see Chart 19–1), 85 percent of the foremen covered reported that their men

CHART 19–1   EXTENT TO WHICH SUBORDINATES FEEL FREE TO DISCUSS IMPORTANT THINGS ABOUT THE JOB WITH SUPERIORS—AS SEEN BY SUPERIORS AND SUBORDINATES

	TOPSTAFF SAYS ABOUT FOREMEN	FOREMEN SAY ABOUT THEMSELVES	FOREMEN SAY ABOUT THE MEN	MEN SAY ABOUT THEMSELVES
Feel very free to discuss important things about the job with my superior	90%	67%	85%	51%
Feel fairly free	10	23	15	29
Not very free	..	10	..	14
Not at all free	..	..	..	6

Source: Rensis Likert, *New Patterns of Management,* p. 47. New York: McGraw-Hill Book Company, 1961.

felt very free to discuss important matters with them. Only 51 percent of the men agreed with this. Faulty perception is not confined to first level supervisors, for 90 percent of top staff officials indicated that the foremen they dealt with felt very free to discuss matters with them. However, only 67 percent of the foremen indicated that this was true.

A second example of faulty perception was obtained in another company, where first level foremen were asked to report on the feelings and attitudes of their men regarding good wages, security, promotion, appreciation of work done, and tactful disciplining.[1] The foremen ranked ten wants in the order they believed *the men* to desire them. To check the accuracy of the listing, the men were themselves asked to rank these same ten wants. A rank-difference correlation between the two lists was *minus* .35. Had the foreman made their estimates and then *reversed* them, they would have come closer to knowing how their men actually felt!

A follow up study some twenty years later revealed much improvement in supervisory empathy.[2] Projected worker rankings of these same ten wants by manufacturing supervisors correlated .88 with actual worker rankings. For a group of utility workers and supervisors, the correlation was .95. The improved correlations could be accounted for by increased supervisory training. It is interesting to note, however, that supervisors' projected ranking changed less during the twenty years than did actual worker rankings. Perhaps the workers have changed their views more than the supervisors.

However important accurate communication may be, it is no panacea for all problems of conflict and lack of motivation. Every field has its devotees, and there are some who see *every* problem as one of faulty communication. For example, if only Russia and the United States could fully understand each other, there would be no conflict. Or, if labor would only make the attempt to understand the necessities of operating a business in a competitive environment, and if the manager could understand perfectly the needs and wants of his personnel, peaceful cooperation would ensue. Obviously, perfect understanding, if such were possible, does not insure cooperation and the absence of conflict. There are usually conflicting values, portions of which will have to be sacrificed to attain minimum degrees of cooperation and coordination.

In the discussion of communication in this chapter, we shall confine ourselves to four phases: (1) subjects to communicate; (2) formal and informal structures for communication; (3) channels through which information can flow; and (4) the fundamental process involved in mutual understanding.

SUBJECTS

In the past, the manager has tended to communicate not much more than the orders necessary to effect his plans. Various factors have played a part in getting him to share more information, not only with his subordinates, but with

---

[1] *Foreman Facts*, Vol. 9, No. 21 (December 5, 1946), Labor Relations Institute. Also reproduced in *Management Review*, Vol. 43, No. 6 (June, 1954), p. 362, and William C. Menninger and Harry Levinson, *Human Understanding in Industry* (Chicago: Science Research Associates, 1956), p. 12.

[2] M. Schwartz, E. Janusaitis, and H. Stark, "A Comparison of the Perception of Job-Related Needs in Two Industry Groups," *Personnel Psychology*, Vol. 19, No. 2 (Summer, 1966), pp. 185–194.

the general public as well. One of these factors derives from the research of the behavioral scientists, who have demonstrated the motivational qualities of information. Human relations research also underscored the need for subordinates to be heard and understood by their supervisors, thus introducing a high degree of subjectivity into the organization's communication framework.

The depression of the 1930's also was a major factor in enlarging the scope of business communications, as the confidence of the American public in its private business system was severely shaken. Managements became more interested in informing both public and employees alike in order to demonstrate that the grant of power to run the economy was being well handled.

A third factor was the suddenly increased power of labor unions in the 1930's and 1940's. The union can often force a sharing of information through both economic and political pressures. The National Labor Relations Board, for example, has often ordered a company's management to open its records to the union in order that collective bargaining "in good faith" may be effected. Many managements have realized that union members are also their employees and have moved to effect an understanding with them to offset the increased power of labor union representatives.

Determining what specific subjects to inject into the communication channels of a company is a very difficult problem. The manager who believes that everything is suitable for transmission will not only clog the channels with insignificant trivia, but he may harm his operation by releasing information that should be retained. The National Association of Manufacturers has suggested that the following should be communicated: (1) information about the company—its operations, products, and prospects; (2) information about company policies and practices related to personnel and their jobs, such as vacations, seniority, pay systems, etc.; (3) information about specific situations that arise in the company, such as a change in management or alteration of a layout; and (4) information about the general economic system in which a company and its employees operate. Within these broad areas, many specific details must be attended to. For example, the management should inform its employees of the company's products, believing that their understanding will inspire interest, loyalty, and cooperation. But on the other hand, disclosure of future product plans may jeopardize the company's future in a highly competitive industry. In matters more closely related to the employee's interests, such as seniority and pay, the tendency is toward providing all information that could possibly be desired. In still another area, that of economic education, the management may typically wish to provide *more* information than the employee actually wants.

The two best guides for determining what information to provide derive from the objectives of coordination and motivation. What must personnel know in order to relate effectively to others and to the organization as a whole?

And secondly, what do employees *want* to know, before cooperation will be given willingly and with enthusiasm?

As the discussions presented in earlier chapters would suggest, the employee wants to know such things as (1) his standing in relation to the official, formal authority structure; (2) his standing in relation to the informal organization with respect to individual status, power, acceptance, etc.; (3) events which have bearing upon his future economic security; and (4) operational information which will enable him to develop pride in his job.

COMMUNICATION STRUCTURES

As indicated in Chapter 1, management is the monitoring agency for an organizational system of inputs, processings, and outputs. Information is of prime concern in this monitoring process. Initiation of processing requires the issuance of information that instructs and authorizes action to take place. During and after processing, information must be collected that can be compared with predetermined processing and output standards.

In the traditional framework, communications are largely structured; they go through authorized channels. As indicated in Fig. 19–1, the lines of authority

FIGURE 19–1   CHAIN-OF-COMMAND COMMUNICATION CHANNEL

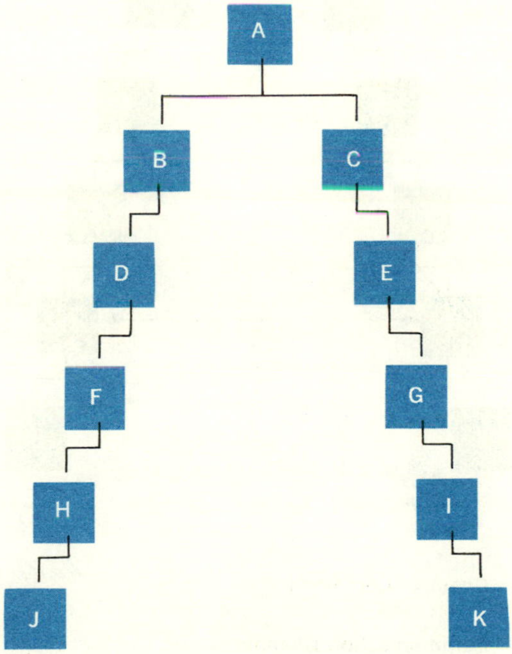

are also the lines of communication. This is necessary in order for the various managers to coordinate effectively the work in their various jurisdictions. Communications must be controlled so that work can be regulated and unity of command preserved.

Though the military organizations have a reputation for insisting that most communications flow through channels, probably no one has insisted upon complete adherence to these formal lines. Long ago, Fayol pointed out that following the line of authority could prove to be disastrously time-consuming when speedy decisions and actions are required. In Fig. 19–2, if *H* required an interchange of information with *I*, he would have to proceed through channels—*F* to *D* to *B* to *A* to *C* to *E* to *G* to *I*. In this manner, all supervisors would be informed and could approve, disapprove, or modify the interchange. In this manner also, the project may be dead by the time the interchange between *H* and *I* is effected. In addition, the various levels of supervision would have been swamped by an excessive amount of irrelevant information flowing through its communication stations. Fayol suggested that a "gang-

FIGURE 19–2   FAYOL'S "GANGPLANK"

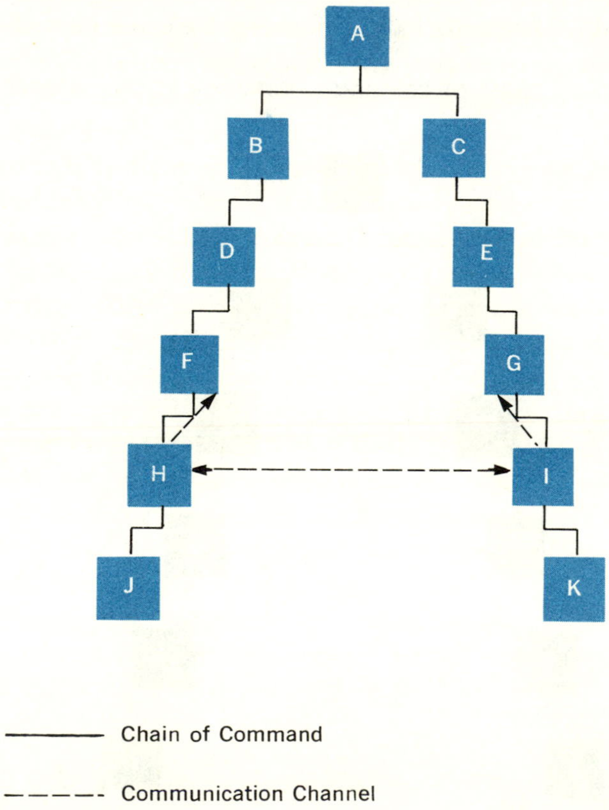

————— Chain of Command

— — — — Communication Channel

plank" be laid directly from *H* to *I* and the interchange effected immediately, as shown in Fig. 19–2. To provide for the protection of unity of command, the supervisors of *H* and *I* should be informed that the contact is being made. They should also be apprised of any significant agreements that have been reached.

It also happens on occasions that *A* wishes to instruct *H* to move immediately upon a project in his area. Going through channels may take too much time, and thus, a simultaneous release of authority to *H*, with informational copies to *B*, *D*, and *F*, will take care of both objectives—speed and coordination. Thus, provision must be made for diagonal as well as upward and downward flows of information. This formal system should be designed to handle the normally expected volume of orders, instructions, and reports. When channels become overloaded from unusual conditions, it has been observed that organizational responses are varied and include such reactions as the following: (1) omitting or filtering out certain information, (2) queuing or delaying responses during a peak period and then catching up later, (3) setting up some priority system of processing information inputs, (4) reducing processing standards to expedite flow, (5) establishing temporary additional channels, (6) escaping or retreating to formalistic procedures resulting in reducing the acceptance of information inputs, and (7) redesigning the entire communication system through enlargement, decentralization into smaller processing units, or changing the initiation of inputs, e.g., self-service in a library or market.[3]

The difficulties of confining communications to prescribed structures have led to the discovery by behaviorists that there are many *informal* communication structures in most organizations. Through the grapevine, a man can discover information that he may receive three days later through official channels (see Chapter 11). It has also been suggested by various behaviorists that there should be a *free flow* of communication without the restrictions of formal structures. In this way, all are knowledgeable and can coordinate and supervise themselves as well as develop a greater interest in the organization's work. This philosophy is consistent with the Theory "Y" type of personnel projected by McGregor, as well as with the advocation of a high degree of employee participation. It is also consistent with the behaviorists' philosophy of fewer restrictive controls and greater trust in subordinates.

There have been serious doubts raised concerning the practicability of a completely free flow of communications, no matter how enlightened the personnel involved. There is the danger, for example, of communicating so much information that it would be difficult to determine what is important and what is irrelevant.

---

[3] See D. Katz and R. L. Kahn, *The Social Psychology of Organizations* (New York: John Wiley & Sons, Inc., 1966), p. 231.

Yet, even in such highly unstructured situations, people *will* introduce structuring and restrictions on their own. Out of daily person-to-person interactions will develop a set of relationships which tend to facilitate effective action. The boss does not want to be told everything, and his subordinate will soon come to know what data and events he wishes to know. At times, the manager's set of expectations is outdated, e.g., in the small department he wishes to know almost everything that is going on, whereas in a larger department such an attitude would quickly have to be eliminated.

Research conducted by Bavelas, Guetzkow, Simon, and others has shown that structuring the flow of communication will lead to efficiency but not necessarily to high morale of all participants.[4] The experiment consisted of the establishment of various communication networks, three examples of which are shown in Fig. 19–3. The first network is most similar to the formal structure of a firm (four persons able to communicate with only a central fifth person). The second network in 19–3b is representative of the free-flow concept (everyone can communicate with each other). In the circular network of 19–3c, each person can communicate only with his two neighbors.

Each group's task differed from the others but was usually straightforward and simple. For example, five marbles of different colors were given to each person, only *one* of which was held in common by all. Each person had to discover this common color. It was found that the highly structured network, 19–3a, was not only the most accurate but also the fastest means of reaching a decision and communicating it to all persons. There was a tendency in the free-flow network for the group to choose a leader, but only after some experimentation. People will usually create a set of stable and restrictive relationships even when given the opportunity *not* to do so. It is interesting to note that the free-flow group would sometimes introduce innovations, more so than in the more structured networks. For example, the four persons reporting to an informally agreed upon central person would merely communicate the color they did *not* have rather than the five colors they did, thus saving a considerable amount of time.

In contrasting the highly structured and the free-flow networks, the former was faster and more accurate, at least in the beginning stages. However, the level of task *satisfaction* was significantly *higher* in the free-flow group. The participants may not have been particularly efficient, but they were enjoying the experiment. Again, this is illustrative of the clash between efficiency and morale. Participants involved in the circular network, 19–3c, were considerably

[4] Alex Bavelas, "Communication Patterns in Task-Oriented Groups," *Journal of Acoustical Society of America*, Vol. 22 (1950), pp. 725–730. And Harold Guetzkow and Herbert A. Simon, "The Impact of Certain Communication Nets Upon Organization and Performance in Task-Oriented Groups," in *Some Theories of Organization*, Albert H. Rubenstein and Chadwick J. Haberstroh, eds. (Homewood: The Dorsey Press, Inc., and Richard D. Irwin, Inc., 1960), pp. 259–277.

FIGURE 19–3 COMMUNICATION NETWORKS

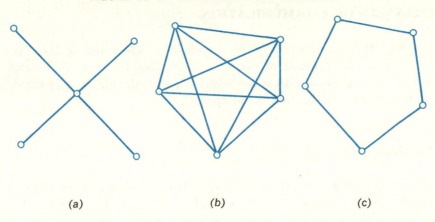

(a)   (b)   (c)

slower and made more mistakes.[5] They experienced the greatest difficulty in organizing their relationships, while the emergence of a leader was considerably delayed. When the problem to be solved is highly complex involving value judgments, it has been found that the free-flow structure enables reaching a decision more quickly.[6] Experimental groups were given complex problems such as a recommended action for an executive who has had an affair with his secretary, but desires to remain with his sensitive wife. Members of the groups were instructed that there were no correct or incorrect answers, and that a unanimous decision was desirable but not necessary. The average time for the group to reach a decision in the (a) network was 16.62 minutes as compared with 9.71 minutes for the (b) network; the difference in time was statistically significant. The percentage of disagreement with the group decision was 18.75 for the highly structured (a) network and 9.28 for the free-flow (b) structure.

In summary, some structuring of communication is essential to coordination and unity of command. Too much regimentation, however, not only is detrimental to morale but also represses innovative tendencies. As with most management problems, the probable correct solution requires an artful balancing of regimentation and freedom. Pfiffner and Sherwood suggest that the structured communication system should more closely resemble a series of chain-links rather than a single line.[7] In or about any one level, the information flow can be circular and relatively free, with the final decision resting with the manager.

[5] Rubenstein and Haberstroh, *Some Theories of Organization*, p. 269.
[6] Marvin E. Shaw, Gerard H. Rothschild, and John F. Strickland, "Decision Processes in Communication Nets," *Journal of Abnormal and Social Psychiatry*, Vol. 54 (1957), pp. 323–330.
[7] John M. Pfiffner and Frank P. Sherwood, *Administrative Organization* (Englewood Cliffs: Prentice-Hall, Inc., 1960), p. 306.

CHANNELS OF COMMUNICATION

An important component of communication structures is the channel through which the symbols of meaning are to flow between sender and receiver. If only superiors and subordinates are considered, these channels are logically of two types, downward and upward.

Downward Channels

The traditionalist is likely to emphasize the importance of the downward channels of communication. He is aware of the necessity for directing, i.e., for conveying management's orders and viewpoints to subordinates, believing that the logic of these orders will stimulate desired action. The manager must know well the subject he hopes to communicate and what type of reaction he desires. He must also have fully in mind the type of audience he is trying to reach, whether it is a staff engineer, a skilled mechanic, or a ditch digger. Timing is highly important, for a presentation which would be acceptable at one time might be highly repugnant at another. One company attempted to introduce a time-studied incentive plan simultaneously with the periodic collective bargaining sessions, with disastrous results. The channels and media of communication must also be selected. Among the various channels available to carry the information downward are the following:

1. *The chain of command.* Orders and information can be given face-to-face or in written fashion and transmitted from one level to another. This is the most frequently used channel and is appropriate on either an individual or a group basis.

2. *Posters and bulletin boards.* Many employees refuse to read such boards, and thus this channel is useful only as a supplementary device.

3. *Company periodicals.* A great deal of information about the company, its products, and policies can be disseminated in this manner. To attract readership, a certain percentage of space must be devoted to personal items about employees, and thus the periodical plays a part in developing the social life of the organization. Controversial issues, such as the union shop and featherbedding, could be discussed, but most companies are too much concerned with avoiding controversy.

4. *Letters and pay inserts.* This is a form of direct mail contact and is ordinarily used when the president of the organization wishes to present something of special interest. Letters are usually directed to the employee's home address. The use of pay inserts at least insures exposure to every employee.

5. *Employee handbooks and pamphlets.* Handbooks are frequently used

during the hiring and orientation process as an introduction to the organization. Too often, however, they are unread even when the firm demands a signed statement that the employee is acquainted with their contents. When special systems are being introduced, such as a pension plan or a job evaluation system, concise, highly illustrated pamphlets are often prepared to facilitate understanding and stimulate acceptance.

6. *Information racks*. In a relatively small number of organizations, racks containing free paperback literature of all types are provided. Mixed in with books on hobbies and sports are pamphlets on the profit system, the company, management techniques, and the like.

7. *Loudspeaker system*. The loudspeaker system is used not only for paging purposes, but also to make announcements while they are "hot." Such systems can also be misused, as in the case where the president of a company sent his greetings from his cool vacation place in the mountains to the hot, sweaty workers on the production floor.

8. *Grapevine*. Though the grapevine is an informal means of communication, it has been suggested earlier that management should "feed, water, and cultivate" its growth by providing factual information to combat rumors.

9. *Annual reports*. A perusal of typical annual reports would indicate that they are increasingly being written for the benefit of the employee and his union, as well as for the stockholder. It is a channel which appears to be designed for one group, the owners, to which others "tap in" hoping to obtain information not intended for them.

10. *The labor union*. The union can be very helpful in communicating certain philosophies to company employees. The union voice, added to the management voice, can be highly persuasive. On occasion, a union steward will do what he can to convince an employee of the groundlessness for his grievance. At the same time, however, there is a danger in too much over-cooperation between management and union, and the employee-union member will become increasingly distrustful of such a relationship.

There are doubtlessly many other channels that are used every day by management in attempting to communicate with subordinates. Middle and lower managers are usually contacted personally and through such written devices as memoranda, policy manuals, and authorized schedules. External means, such as radio, television, and the press, can be used to contact employees as well as the general public. With the multiplicity of channels and media and the changed philosophy toward a greater sharing of information, it is little wonder that some have concluded that we have effected "over-communication." Using the definition of communication given above, it would be more appropriate to refer to this as "over-publication." Communication requires that the information be received and understood, and the typical shotgun approach results in a lot of attempts being wasted. Management should judiciously choose the subjects to be communicated, determine the characteristics of the intended audience, and select a restricted number of the channels most likely to reach the minds of that audience. Management will never know if communication has been effected until it determines the audience's response through the use of upward channels.

The use of these downward channels is potentially damaging to effective communication. A fundamental source of difficulty is that of differing cultures. Management personnel with a bias toward efficiency might attempt to establish understanding with subordinates who are biased toward personal and economic security. Often *only* the manager understands what he is saying. His terminology reflects both his background and his scale of values, which can serve to confuse subordinates or engender resistance. Many management and staff personnel have never progressed through the lower ranks, having entered the organization from colleges and universities. They should be fully aware of the likelihood of being misunderstood while attempting to use these downward channels of communication.

Upward Channels

The behaviorists have emphasized the establishment of upward channels of communication from subordinate to supervisor. This is necessary not only to determine if subordinates have understood any information sent downward but also to meet the needs of the human ego. The entire chapter on participation represents a philosophy that requires more upward initiation of action. An upward flow of information is also necessary if management is to coordinate the various activities of the organization.

There are many channels from which to choose for the upward flow of information, feelings, and attitudes, some of which are listed below:

1. *The chain of command.* Theoretically, the flow of communication is two-way between superior and subordinate. The superior should have an open-door attitude as well as some of the skills of a counselor. If he has more courage, he may hold group meetings in which expression of gripes and attitudes is encouraged.

2. *The grievance procedure.* A systematic grievance procedure is one of the most fundamental devices for upward communication. The subordinate knows that there is some means whereby he may appeal beyond his own immediate supervisor. And if he has the backing of a labor union, he is even more encouraged to voice true feelings. The mechanics of such procedures will be discussed more fully in Chapter 25.

3. *The complaint system.* In addition to grievance procedures, some firms

encourage all types of upward communication by establishing means of preserving the identity of the complainant. "Gripe boxes" may be established into which an employee can place a written complaint or rumor which management will investigate. In one firm, a blackboard was divided into halves, one side being for employee complaints or rumors, the other for management's replies. An answer of some sort was guaranteed within a 24-hour period.

4. *Counseling*. Though all supervisors have a counseling obligation, the authority barrier makes true communication difficult. For this reason, special staff counselors may be provided to whom employees may go in privacy and confidence. This subject will be considered more fully in Chapter 22.

5. *Morale questionnaires*. This channel also preserves the identity of the employee when answering specific questions about the firm and its management. It will be recalled that morale questionnaires were discussed earlier in Chapter 6.

6. *An open-door policy*. An open-door attitude on the part of each supervisor toward his immediate subordinates is to be highly commended. With regard to higher management it is seldom used, since the employee is usually reluctant to bypass his immediate supervisor.

7. *Exit interview*. If the employee leaves the organization, there is one last chance in the exit interview to discover his feelings and views about the firm in general and his reasons for quitting in particular. Follow-up questionnaires are also used at times, for the employee will rarely give full and truthful information at the time of his departure. He must always remember that a work reference will be required and honest communication may jeopardize his future. After he has obtained another position, he may be more willing to give his true views on a questionnaire.

8. *Grapevine*. Though management may be reluctant to feed and cultivate the grapevine, it should *always* listen to it. The grapevine is a spontaneous and natural phenomenon which serves as a means of emotional release and provides management with significant clues concerning the attitudes and feelings of organization members. If the grapevine should ever become silent, *that* is the time to worry.

9. *Labor union*. A prime purpose of the labor union is to convey to management the feelings and demands of employees. Collective bargaining sessions constitute a legal channel of communication for any aspect of employer-employee relations.

10. *The Informer*. The communication barrier of formal hierarchy can be removed through the use of management informers among the rank and file. Their formal use has been in the field of labor relations and, hopefully, this use has diminished with the introduction of federal legislation. The use of this channel goes a questionable step beyond merely listening to the grapevine.

11. *The Ombudsman*. Though little used in this country, it has been suggested that corporate justice in nonunionized firms requires a special deputy of

the president to act as his eyes and ears. The ombudsman has been used mostly in Scandinavian governments to provide an avenue for citizen complaints and protests against unfair and depersonalized treatment by various bureaucratic officials. An ombudsman has only the rights of acceptance or rejection of individual complaints, investigation, and recommendation of action to the top organizational official. The ombudsman in the Danish government, for example, accepts and investigates only 15 percent of the complaints submitted, and recommends action in 5 percent of those investigated.[8] In many instances, lower managers in the hierarchy make voluntary adjustments precluding recommendations to the top official. The position of ombudsman has been recommended to business firms as a further indication of corporate interest and concern for the feelings of employees with respect to justice and fairness of treatment. Ombudsmen have also been established on various university campuses for the benefit of students.

There are many other specific avenues of communication that can be set up from subordinates to supervisors. There are also certain subtleties of which the manager should be aware. Thus, as subordinates contribute information to superiors, they know that it will be used for at least two purposes: (1) to aid management in controlling and directing the firm, and (2) to evaluate the worth of their performance. They are then tempted to filter, alter, and color information to have the fewest unfavorable effects upon themselves. In one study, it was discovered that the supervisors were considerably less aware of their subordinates' daily work problems when these subordinates were anxious to be promoted.[9] When employees did *not* care as much about their future within the firm, they were less prone to restrict or alter negative information concerning errors and problems. Thus we have the ironic situation where personnel who wish to progress in the organization respond favorably on such items as training, incentives, and suggestions, but unfavorably in reporting the factual information needed to coordinate and control the enterprise effectively. This problem is most prevalent in organizations where the pressures are great and the personnel highly ambitious.

Interaction theory emphasizes the importance of upward communication channels. When management dominates the communication process through downward channels, there tends to be greater subordinate dissatisfaction regardless of the quality of orders being communicated. Walker, for example, found that the better foremen on assembly lines were those who provided for reciprocal rather than unilateral interactions with their men.[10]

[8] Isidore Silver, "The Corporate Ombudsman," *Harvard Business Review,* Vol. 45, No. 3 (May–June, 1967), p. 78.
[9] William H. Read, "Upward Communication in Industrial Hierarchies," *Human Relations,* Vol. 15 (1961), pp. 1–8.
[10] Charles R. Walker, Robert H. Guest, and Arthur N. Turner, *The Foreman on the Assembly Line* (Cambridge: Harvard University Press, 1956).

THE FUNDAMENTAL PROCESS OF COMMUNICATION

Ideas must be translated into a set of symbols, which are then transmitted to the second person. He receives the symbols and attempts to decode them. If he obtains the idea as transmitted by the first person, communication has been effected. The first person can only learn of his success by receiving symbols returned by the second.

The basic elements of this process are portrayed in Chart 19–2. Communication must always take place between two or more people. Shouting for help on a desert island is not communication; similarly, if the professor lectures and no one listens or understands, there is no communication. The skills of communication, then, involve *sending* through speaking, writing, drawing, and acting— and *receiving* through listening, reading, and observing. The symbols may be either words or language, actions, pictures, or numbers.

CHART 19–2   THE COMMUNICATION PROCESS

SENDER⟶	TRANSMISSION OF SYMBOLS⟶	RECEIVER
1. Speaking	1. Words	1. Listening
2. Writing	2. Numbers	2. Reading
3. Acting	3. Actions	3. Observing
4. Drawing	4. Pictures	

Communication Symbols

Of the four symbols listed, perhaps words and actions are most important. As Korzybski pointed out, language is a map of the ideas conceived, *not* the ideas themselves.[11] When one looks at a map of Arizona, he is not looking at the state directly. But through the map, he can obtain a good impression of its contours and dimensions. If he truly wishes to see Arizona, he must travel over its mountains, valleys, and deserts. In viewing language as a map of ideas, we do not even have the advantage of a single, common map. The sender attempts to encode his ideas into a word map and sends this map to a second person. However, languages are very complex mechanisms, and the same word will not have the exact same meaning for everyone. And even if both parties are in agreement as to which formal meaning is involved, there are the differences in individual backgrounds which give varying connotations to words. The word "management," for example, may be defined by both parties as the planning, organizing, directing, and controlling of the activities of others. If the first party's parents have been managers and the second's parents have been labor

---

[11] Alfred Korzybski, *Science and Sanity*, 3rd ed. (Lakeville: The International Non-Aristotelian Library Publishing Co., 1948), p. 58.

union organizers, it is apparent that the word "management" will evoke drastically different meanings. It is difficult enough if words are representative of tangible objects such as chair, pencil, or hat.[12] But one can imagine the difficulties in using such terms as "liberal," "conservative," "philosophy," "group dynamics," and "communication."

An additional complicating factor is that of *context*. We are all aware of the dangers of quoting someone out of context. In a larger sense, one should decode symbols in relation to the time, place, and social framework in which they were sent. If the president of a company, for example, tries to fraternize with rank and file, one improper use of a term will destroy the rapport he is trying to establish. It is often safer to recognize and retain the necessary social distance. A manager who has been promoted from the ranks has a better chance of coping with the problem of context, since he is familiar with the environment of his subordinates.

The manager must also recognize that he communicates by what he does or does not do. If a man comes to work one day and finds his desk moved from a location in a private office to one in an open area, communication of a sort has taken place. If no verbal explanation accompanies the action, people will interpret it their own way; the missing symbol or signal will be supplied by the observer. And despite any verbal protestations to the contrary, such a move will likely be interpreted as a demotion for the man.

In one company, management had introduced a change in procedure for a small crew of men. The new method was timed and piece rates were established. None of the men produced more than half of the standard amount and were therefore on a time-wage basis rather than piece rates. They all filed grievances protesting the unfairness of the standard. Management tried everything it could think of to correct the problem, from all-day time studies to providing each man with a private instructor in the new method. A check on similar jobs in other companies revealed that the standard was in line. Thus, management concluded that a concerted work restriction was involved. The next move was one of communication through *action*. An engineer was sent to the production department, and he proceeded to measure various angles and spaces on the floor. He volunteered no information to the men. Finally, one man's curiosity got the best of him and he asked the engineer what he was doing. The engineer indicated that management wanted to see if there was sufficient room to locate certain machinery which could do the work of this crew of men. He continued about his business of measuring. The next day, all work crew members were producing amounts well *above* the established standard.

---

[12] A problem concerning a tangible good arose during World War II. Under the Lend-Lease Program, Great Britain ordered so many million bushels of corn, which were shipped to them by the United States. The problem of communication came to light when it was discovered that what the British call corn, we in the United States refer to as wheat.

Various pictures and illustrations can add to the effectiveness of communications. Business firms make use of such media as blueprints, posters, charts, and motion pictures. Graphs and charts offer clear, and at times the only, means of portraying multiple relationships. With such charts, contrasts can be seen and trends recognized more easily. Though words may be understandable, the receiver often prefers illustrations and thus opens his mind more readily to materials involving their use.

The final communication symbol, numbers, has been increasingly exalted in our modern society. It is deserving of separate emphasis.

Mathematics constitutes a language all its own, a language which has a higher degree of precision than words. This precision is largely *internal*, and dangers enter when external factors must be translated into numbers. As pointed out in Chapter 4, there are difficulties in translating business practices into linear equations to develop optimum solutions. Mathematics can add to the processes of judgment and communication, but it can never be a complete substitute for verbalizing, acting, and observing.

The number is often used to mislead as well as to communicate. In civil service examinations, for example, the person scoring 77½ is deemed superior to one scoring 77. There is a difference, but it undoubtedly is insignificant considering the state of the art of testing. The statistician can make use of either the mean, the median, or the mode, depending on which is best fitted to his purpose. Numbers can be combined with pictorial representation to mislead without actually lying. Huff's "Gee Whiz Chart" is a case in point.[13] If the slope of a line is too gentle to stimulate the observer's interest, the bottom portion of the chart can be cut off, the vertical spacing on the ordinate widened and the horizontal spaces shortened. With these misleading but not false changes, a gentle upward slope can be transformed into a mountain peak.

The number is a powerful symbol of communication, and today's business manager must be able to understand ideas that have been translated into this symbol. Presumably, greater knowledge of the number symbol will lead not only to better decision making and improved communication but also to a degree of sophistication which will make it more difficult to mislead with statistics.

Communication Skills

As indicated in Chart 19–2, one can communicate through the spoken word, the written word, actions, or illustrations. Naturally, the skills of speaking to individuals are somewhat different from those required in appearing before groups.

[13] Darrell Huff, *How to Lie with Statistics* (New York: W. W. Norton and Co., 1954), Chap. 5.

In speaking, one has the advantage of being able to obtain immediate feedback concerning the effectiveness of transmission. Facial expressions, questions, and replies can be evaluated to judge the degree of understanding established. In writing, this advantage is lacking. The writer must determine the characteristics of his audience and select words which he hopes will convey his meaning. Two somewhat mechanistic systems for judging the reading difficulty of written material are the Flesch system and the "fog index" suggested by Robert Gunning.[14] The Flesch system incorporates an analysis of sentence length, number of affixes, and number of human interest words used in the written presentation. Standards of readability are established for each of these factors, with seventeen words, for example, constituting the standard sentence length. The "fog index" is derived by determining the number of words in a hundred-word passage that have three or more syllables. This number is multiplied by 0.4. The answer roughly corresponds to the number of years of formal schooling required to read the passage with ease and understanding.

Using either of these systems, most best-selling novels test at seventh or eighth grade level. In an analysis conducted of United States Air Force documents, Air Force Regulations were placed at sixteenth grade level and Numbered Letters at eighteenth grade. As determined by the "fog index," *The Atlantic Monthly* magazine has a grade level of twelve; *Harpers,* eleven; *Time,* ten; *Reader's Digest,* nine; *Ladies Home Journal,* eight; and *True Confessions,* seven.[15]

The objective of both of these systems is to reduce the amount of pompous jargon and inflated prose. Of course, there is more to communication than can be revealed by these mechanistic counts of syllables and sentence lengths. The sender of symbols must have a clear and coherent grasp of the idea he hopes to transmit. The Flesch and Gunning indexes merely aid the writer in keeping his audience in mind.

Regarding the use of actions, often the manager is completely oblivious of their impact upon his subordinates. In any authority hierarchy, the formal leader is the center of attention for most subordinates. His actions will speak more loudly than his words.

In contrasting the skills of transmission and those of receiving, there has probably been too much attention given to the former. This would be consistent with the traditional philosophy which emphasizes the role of the leader. But communication cannot take place unless there is receipt and understanding by the other party. It has been observed that the average speaking speed is 120 words per minute. One is able to listen more than four times as rapidly.

[14] Robert Gunning, "How to Improve Your Writing," *Factory Management and Maintenance,* Vol. 110, No. 6 (June, 1952), p. 134.
[15] "Our Changing Language," *Machine Design* (July 20, 1967), p. 192.

The question therefore arises, what does the listener do with the free time that results from this difference in speeds?

At least three types of listening have been identified: marginal, evaluative, and projective. The speed of listening provides the opportunity for marginal listening, a dangerous type that can lead to misunderstanding of and even insult to the speaker. Evaluative listening requires the second party to allocate his full attention to the speaker. The excess time is devoted to evaluating and judging the nature of the remarks heard. Often, we are forming rebuttal remarks while the sender is still speaking, thus moving into a type of marginal listening. Instead of one idea being transmitted and held by two people, we often end up with two ideas, neither of which is really communicated to the other. If the listener allocates too much time to disapproving or approving of what he hears, it is doubtful if he has the time to understand fully. This is particularly true when the remarks are loaded with emotion or concern the security and status of the receiver.

The third type of listening holds the greatest potential for effective communication. The listener fully utilizes his time by attempting to *project* himself into the position of the speaker and understand what is being said from *his* viewpoint. He first listens *without* evaluation. After he feels that he understands what has been said, evaluation then can enter the process. Rogers suggested a rule to be followed to insure some degree of projective listening. "Each person can speak for himself only *after* he has related the ideas and feelings of the previous speaker accurately and to that speaker's satisfaction."[16] There is no necessity to agree with the statements, but there is every necessity to understand them from the speaker's standpoint. Only in this way is it possible to frame a reply that will actually respond to the speaker's remarks. Effective listening is *empathic* listening. It requires an ability to listen for feeling as well as for words. Sensitivity training, discussed in Chapter 16, can aid in the development of this skill.

There are other psychological barriers to this process of empathic listening. It requires courage for anyone, particularly a manager, to make a sincere attempt to project into the role of another person, e.g., a subordinate. He often fears that true understanding will alter his own feelings and convictions about a subject or about himself. The subordinate easily senses the presence of a closed mind, and this leads him to take even more extreme and objectionable positions in the discussion. Furthermore, many subordinates do not fully approve of all orders and wishes of their superiors. If an organization member does summon the courage to voice a criticism or an opposing view, a resulting rise in the emotions of the criticized superior often ensues. He is unable to lay aside his feelings to try to understand objectively the communication. It will be

---

[16] Carl R. Rogers and F. J. Roethlisberger, "Barriers and Gateways to Communication," *Harvard Business Review*, Vol. 30, No. 4 (July–August, 1952), p. 48.

recalled from the preceding chapter that one of the characteristics of a healthy group is the ability to bring intragroup conflicts to the surface in order that they may be discussed, understood, and perhaps resolved. In like manner, a characteristic of the mature personality is the ability to accept criticism without immediately throwing up emotional barriers which lead to further conflict. It has been found that mere acceptance of the criticism, without necessarily agreeing with what is said, leads to a reduction in the amount and severity of that original criticism. This in turn may stimulate the criticized superior to make concessions which may lead to both greater understanding and possible compromise adjustment.

Reading skills have received great attention in our society, particularly after the publicity given to the reading speed of a President of the United States. The amount of written material a manager must plow through seems to increase yearly, and some attempt should first be made to consolidate and reduce it. However, the ability to read rapidly and with understanding is an essential communication skill, particularly in larger organizations. It has been found that reading speeds can be doubled and tripled with little or no loss in comprehension.

As in the case of listening, there are too few attempts to increase skill in observation outside of training for law enforcement. Most people miss a great deal by not actually seeing what they are looking at. It was mentioned earlier that some managers are very adept at assessing the general atmosphere of an organization by merely strolling through its work places. Observation of furnishings, housekeeping, dress of personnel, and activities can convey much information. Using our powers of observation to supplement listening and reading will add immeasurably to our understanding of what is actually transpiring.

Summary

Communication is the process of effecting an interchange of understanding between two or more people. The development of an organization with subdivision of tasks gives rise to the need for communication. It provides the basis for the coordination of operations and the motivation of personnel.

Coordination demands some structuring of the organization's communication system. Yet, excessively regimented relationships lead not only to employee dissatisfaction but also to some inefficiency in decision making. A compromise between completely structured and completely free-flow communication is necessary.

The trend in American business is to share more information with both employees and the general public. Management has recognized that deeds alone are insufficient to sustain acceptance of the free enterprise system and the manager's role therein. Within the firm, two-way communication must be developed through the establishment of both upward and downward channels between superior and subordinate.

The essence of the process is the act of transmitting ideas and understanding from one person to another. This involves (1) encoding the idea into such symbols as words, actions, pictures, and numbers; (2) sending the signals through speech, writing, actions, or pictures; and (3) receiving and understanding through listening, reading, and observing. Though perfect communication can rarely if ever be effected, skill in the use of these symbols will help to reduce many of the barriers. A further need is the ability to empathize, to project oneself into the role of the listener and to heed feelings as well as logic. Communication is no panacea for all the ills of organizational conflict, but its improvement will help to separate and identify real conflicts from those created by misunderstanding.

DISCUSSION PROBLEMS

1. Relate the Maslow hierarchy of needs to the concept of channels of communication.
2. What is the role of communication in the monitoring of organizational processes? in the maintenance of organizational health?
3. Contrast and compare the appropriateness of communication networks on simple and complex problems requiring group decisions.
4. Discuss the nature and role of communication filters in upward and downward communication channels.
5. If perfect communication were feasible in an organization, would this serve to eliminate all conflict?
6. Discuss the concept that language is like a map.
7. What are the communication skills? Which are most generally emphasized in traditional training programs? Which are emphasized in sensitivity training?
8. Why is the best listening empathic in nature?
9. What is the nature and purpose of the Flesch and "fog index" systems?
10. Discuss the nature and role of a corporate ombudsman.

SUPPLEMENTARY READING

Anderson, John, "What's Blocking Upward Communications?" *Personnel Administration,* Vol. 31, No. 1 (January–February, 1968), 5–7, 19–20.

Brown, Warren B., "Systems, Boundaries, and Information Flow," *Academy of Management Journal,* Vol. 9, No. 4 (December, 1966), 318–327.

Bugental, Daphne E., Robert Tannenbaum, and H. Kenneth Bobele, "Self-Concealment and Self-Disclosure in Two Group Contexts," *California Management Review,* Vol. 11, No. 2 (Winter, 1968), 23–28.

Davis, Keith, "Success of Chain-Of-Command Oral Communication in a Manufacturing Group," *Academy of Management Journal,* Vol. 11, No. 4 (December, 1968), 379–387.

Silver, Isidore, "The Corporate Ombudsman," *Harvard Business Review,* Vol. 45, No. 3 (May–June, 1967), 77–87.

Sutton, Harold and Lyman W. Porter, "A Study of the Grapevine in a Governmental Organization," *Personnel Psychology,* Vol. 21, No. 2 (Summer, 1968), 223–230.

Vogel, Alfred, "Why Don't Employees Speak Up?" *Personnel Administration,* Vol. 30, No. 3 (May–June, 1967), 18–23.

Cases for Part IV

THE MENDEL REAL ESTATE COMPANY

Joe Ash obtained a job with the Mendel Real Estate Company in Los Angeles at the end of his junior year in college. The job was an opportunity to see California and was arranged by his father as a personal favor from the president, Mr. Mendel.

Upon arrival, Joe was taken first and directly to the president, Mr. Mendel, who greeted him cordially, told him a little about the organization, and finally took him to lunch. At this time, Joe learned that the whole organizational effort was directed at developing a 10,000 acre site in the Mohave desert, which Mr. Mendel and some associates had purchased from the Air Force directly after W. W. II. The general plan was to develop this site into a large metropolitan area. An architect had been hired and everything had been planned out to the smallest detail, including the future location of the business district, the width of the streets, park facilities, etc.

That afternoon after the brief orientation, Joe was introduced to several executives: Mr. Fred Johnston, the Sales Manager; Mr. Jim Johnston, the Sales Coordinator; and finally Mr. Miller for whom he was to work. Mr. Miller's function was rather strange in its uniqueness, for the advertising department had been recently created. Joe's first day was taken up with orientation, and the next few days were spent at "make work" tasks such as scanning all the various newspapers for any mention about the company's site. At this time, he was temporarily assigned to the desk of Mr. Miller's secretary who had quit just shortly before his arrival. He was also given the ambiguous title of "trainee" with a salary of $400 per month. The following events are in the words of Joe Ash.

"At first, Mr. Miller was extremely friendly and talkative, but after several days he began to warn me about doing a good job, keeping busy, and in general preached about almost everything. This had an effect on me, for in general I had a great desire to do well and be recognized for my work, partially due to the fact that the president of the company was a business friend of my father. It was this attitude that made some of the following incidents so frustrating for me.

"I noticed early that Mr. Miller liked to present a front of being extremely busy and hyperactive, running from office to office, and in general exaggerating certain movements. The advertising department was his own little domain and he was left to run it fairly much as he pleased. At this time, however, I had no real knowledge of his other less desirable behavioral patterns. It was only later on through several incidents, informal talks with employees, and general observations that showed me his true character, which tended to make him an extremely hard and unpleasant boss to work for.

"One of these first incidents was in the early 'make work' stage, when I was supposed to be scanning several newspapers. Often having nothing to do, I took to reading other material, and also catching up on my correspondence. One day Mr. Miller ran into the office, observed that I was writing letters, and became very flustered, saying that if Mr. Mendel ever noticed that I was not working, he would be reprimanded. Asking him what I should do, he replied 'I don't know, but just do something and look busy.' This put me in a very unsure position, for I didn't know how I should conduct myself, being given no directive line of action. It was at this time that I began feeling personally uncomfortable and unsure around Mr. Miller. I felt that I could not predict his next course of action. It was in this state of mind, one day, wishing to hustle in Mr. Miller's office, that my glasses dropped from my shirt pocket and broke on the floor, while Mr. Miller was on the phone. Seeing what had happened he laughed and told the party on the other line, 'Oh it's nothing, just one of the people here having a rough day.'

"Shortly after this incident a new secretary was hired for Mr. Miller, Miss Goldstein, a young, intelligent and quite independently minded college girl. For this reason, I was moved from Mr. Miller's office to a desk in the corner of the large central office. This move was a great relief to me for I was no longer in the immediate proximity of Mr. Miller, even though I was still directly subordinate and reporting to him. It was about this time that I noticed that Mr. Miller had alienated just about all the permanent rank-and-file who were very cold towards him, despite his occasional attempts at joking with them.

"At this time I had a second unpleasant experience with Mr. Miller. It was about the third week of my employ that Mr. Miller came to me and said: 'I have a very important, interesting, and responsible job for you that I wonder if you can handle.' This job entailed sorting all the pictures of the site in some logical fashion, marking them, and finally establishing a file cabinet for them. I told him that I was sure that I could do this successfully, but being somewhat unsure of myself, by then, I asked him exactly how he wanted me to go about this task. At this question he threw his hands up in disgust and chewed me out for not having any brains, initiative, or imagination. Then in a belittling fashion he spent several minutes explaining in great detail exactly what I should do, concluding with the statement that I was wasting too much of his time. This incident left a bad taste in my mouth and further colored my view towards Mr. Miller.

"A few days after the above incident, Miss Goldstein, who had been having frequent disagreements with Mr. Miller, abruptly quit, bringing the total of quits among Mr. Miller's secretaries in two months to three.

"It was a few days after Miss Goldstein's quitting that my final incident with Mr. Miller took place. At this time Mr. Miller decided to use me for delivering several advertising formats to the Los Angeles *Times*. Thus, I was to take a format to Mr. Stevens, the editor in charge. Mr. Stevens not being in the office, I left it with his assistant. Coming back to the office I told Mr. Miller, who became furious and chewed me out. He immediately called the newspaper office and found out that everything was o.k. This did not seem to satisfy him, and he continued to be angry that I had disobeyed his precise instructions. Thus, the next day, when I was again to deliver the ad format to the *Times*, Mr. Miller came out with a big brown manila envelope. Calling me from my desk to the middle of the office, he showed me the envelope and read his message, which was printed in large red letters, out loud, asking me if I could follow instructions, and if I adequately understood. No one laughed, but nevertheless I became extremely resentful of this treatment. Subsequently when Mr. Stevens was again not in the office, I told the assistant that I would wait and informed him of Mr. Miller's directive, at which he laughed. Then I proceeded to loiter away several hours, which gave me the feeling of getting back at the organization. After three hours of wasted time I called the office and explained to Mr. Miller that Mr. Stevens was out. He authorized me to leave the ad with the assistant and did not seem to be displeased with the fact that I had wasted several hours.

"Having turned all these unpleasant incidents over and over in my mind, I decided that I did not want to work for Mr. Miller any longer. Therefore, the next day I went directly to the office of the president and told him only that I wished to work part time. He immediately asked me if I truly wanted to work part time or if I wanted a more meaningful job. On this note, I admitted it was the latter, and told him about all that had happened with Mr. Miller. At this point he admitted that all this about Mr. Miller was true, and told me that I must never tell any of the other employees, but that Mr. Miller had long been under a psychiatrist's care and that this new position was an important chance for him to prove himself. Nevertheless I said that I still desired to be transferred. Thus I was transferred to the inventory control department upon which Mr. Miller, sensing what had happened, tried to be really friendly to me. However, I avoided all interaction with him as much as was possible."

THE 80th ANTIAIRCRAFT BATTALION

The 80th Antiaircraft Battalion was composed of a headquarters and four gun batteries. The battalion commander, Colonel Black, had a staff composed of personnel, intelligence, operations, and supply. In addition to the staff, there was an executive officer whose job it was to coordinate the activities of the staff. The mission of the battalion was to provide air defense of assigned targets. Colonel Black, as commander, was responsible to see that the battalion operated as a smoothly functioning team, always ready to perform its assigned mission.

The following account is by Major Johns, the operations officer. The operations officer is responsible for the planning and coordination of all combat and training activities of the battalion.

"The battalion had been ordered into the field to set up an air defense of an air base. No difficulty was encountered the day the battalion took up defensive positions. As far as I could determine, everything was proceeding smoothly as prescribed by battalion procedures. The battalion commander, Colonel Black, was away from the headquarters command post inspecting the operations of each individual gun battery in turn. This was the normal procedure for the battalion commander when setting up a defensive position.

"Shortly after the battalion had completed setting up its defense, Colonel Black came to the battalion command post looking rather perturbed. He entered the operations center and said to me, 'Johns, you let me down.' I asked him what he meant. He answered, 'You let me down. I was over watching Battery A set up their guns and I did not like the way their trucks were being dispersed. You know the proper procedures and so does Battery A. Why didn't they use them?' I then asked Colonel Black if he had spoken to the commander of Battery A about his dissatisfaction. Colonel Black answered, 'No you are my operations officer, and you let me down.' I told Colonel Black that I would take care of the situation. Colonel Black left and I called the commander of Battery A on the phone and told him that Colonel Black was displeased with the dispersal pattern of his trucks. I suggested to the commander that he straighten it out in accordance with prescribed battalion procedures. The commander of Battery A told me it would be accomplished without delay. The following day, Colonel Black informed me that Battery A had moved some of their trucks and he, Colonel Black, was pleased with the results.

"On many occasions Colonel Black would go to his staff officers when he was not satisfied with some battery operation rather than go to the commander concerned. It became common practice for the staff officer so contacted to suggest to the subordinate commander involved that the Colonel was displeased and suggest that the difficulty be corrected. The battalion functioned smoothly as a team in spite of Colonel Black's reluctance to criticize any of his subordinate commanders. It soon developed that any conflict between subordinate commanders and the staff was settled by the operations officer instead of the battalion commander. Colonel Black's relationship with his superiors was good and he had the reputation of having a battalion that was always ready and able to perform its mission."

A MANUFACTURED CRISIS

Dr. David Braun has been a member of the foreign language department of a Midwestern college for four years. This college has a student body of 5000 and is divided into four schools: arts and science, education, business administration, and fine arts. Professor Braun has been granted tenure at the Assistant Professor level. He has the general reputation of being a fine teacher, is quite popular with his students, and is accepted by his fellow faculty members. He has been the adviser of the student Spanish Society for two years.

One November day, the student president of the Spanish Society complained to Dr. Braun that he had been unable to get some organization material reproduced by the central duplicating agency of the college. This constituted a sudden change in policy and Miss Argon had not been able to supply him with a satisfactory reason for the change. She had indicated that she had received orders to discontinue doing student organization work. Dr. Braun said that he would look into the matter and, in the meantime, would take the material to be duplicated.

He telephoned Miss Argon and she referred him to her supervisor, Mr. Ralph Barnes. Dr. Braun went over to see the head of the duplicating center immediately after his next class. Mr. Barnes told Professor Braun that a study conducted by his office revealed an excessive amount of time being allocated to student organization work. Professor Braun said, "Is it not a duty of this college to support these student organizations in any way possible?" Barnes replied that he was not concerned with extra-curricular activities, that his job was to get the most for the college's dollar in the duplicating center. He felt that student organizations could well look after their own finances. Braun was dissatisfied with this argument, but left the administrator's office.

Professor Braun's next move was to take up the matter with his department head. The latter was sympathetic, but did not feel that any formal protest would be advisable. He discouraged any thought of contacting the Dean of Arts and Science on such a minor matter. Neither did he feel that an appeal to the college business manager would be of any value.

The next day, Professor Braun decided to take matters into his own hands. He took the written material in question to Miss Argon. He noted, as he entered the door, that three of the five girls were engaged in idle chatter. He asked Miss Argon if one of the girls did not have time to run off the Spanish Society's material. She replied rather abruptly that it was out of the question. At this point, Professor Braun demanded to know why the three girls were loafing. Miss Argon replied that *that* was *her* responsibility, not Professor Braun's. Professor Braun then proceeded to lecture her strongly to the effect that the only excuse for the existence of the duplicating center was to serve the educational objectives of the college. He also commented negatively upon the quality of the service in the past, the surly attitude of Miss Argon, and the inadequate cooperation received by the faculty. He said, "The material that I hold in my hand is *now* labeled 'institutional material' that *I* want for *my* use! I insist that it be taken and duplicated!"

Miss Argon was quite upset and near tears. She snatched the material out of Professor Braun's hands, turned on her heel, and went to the back of the room. Professor Braun announced in a loud voice, "I'll be back to pick it up Friday," and slammed the door as he left.

For two days, Professor Braun heard nothing from his "mad scene." He had hoped to change policy so that the student organization's work could be done. On the third day, two events took place: (1) he received the duplicated material in the interoffice mail; (2) there was an announcement in the student newspaper to the effect that a duplicating machine was to be set aside and allocated to student use. Stencils, typing, and labor for operating the machine had to be provided by the student organizations. Dr. Braun was surprised, but quite pleased with how the episode turned out.

INCENTIVE PAY

At Moore's Department Store there are basically three types of wages paid to salesmen, depending on the type and price of merchandise, and the knowledge and skill required to sell. The first type is an hourly wage and is used by the Candy, the Snack bar, the Tobacco, and Toy departments. The second classification of wages includes those departments that pay their salespeople a one percent commission in addition to the regular base pay. Such departments include Hardware, Sporting Goods, Housewares, and many of those dealing in soft lines. The third basic type is called the "big ticket departments" whose merchandise has an average price greater than the other departments. The commission class will vary from 5 to 10 percent. However, these commissions are not directly added to the salesman's base pay, but rather are paid on amounts sold over the salesman's quota. Departments of this type deal with Refrigerators, Ranges, Plumbing and Heating, Paint, Electrical Equipment, Vacuum Cleaners, Shoes, and Men's and Women's Apparel.

In the Electrical department, salesmen are on a 7 percent commission. Here, several problems have arisen among the salespeople as a result of the compensation system. The common argument is "whose customer is whose." Even though they all use business cards, problems still arise. Many times the customers will first say that they are "just looking." Unless the salesman sticks close by and tries to sell them the product, they will go on looking and another salesperson will ask if they can be of help. This will continue until such a time that the customer has made a choice and some salesman is free. The problem arises when one salesman spends some time with the customer answering questions and explaining the goods, and then has to leave him for some reason. Unless he asks him to wait a moment and then returns immediately, he is likely to get the most available salesman to help him, not realizing that the salesman is on a commission. If the first salesman is tied up with another customer and one of the other salespersons approaches his first customer—here is where the fight begins.

Another problem that arises is when a customer returns and asks for Mr. Jones, and Mr. Jones is off or out to lunch. It has been informally agreed that unless the customer's merchandise is wrapped up and tagged, the first salesperson will not get credit for the sale, even though he might have spent a great deal of time selling the customer. If, on the other hand, the order is already written up, then it will be rung up for him. But even with this agreement, there is still some cheating and arguments.

There is one additional problem—the handling of small purchases. When one works on an incentive basis, it is natural to want to avoid spending time on small purchase customers when you can possibly be talking to a customer who might make a large purchase. At present, there is no system as to how these small purchase customers should be handled, and it is quite unfair when one salesman cannot get away from the customers standing around the check stand. Many of the departments in the store have quick-service cashiers who do nothing but handle this type of customer; they are not paid commission, and instead receive a higher base rate. But in the Electrical department, management does not feel that there is a sufficient amount of work for a specialized small purchase cashier. In the meantime, there is considerable squabbling, but no real desire to change the incentive system. With a certain amount of scrambling, backbiting, and maneuvering, most salesmen can make a higher take-home pay than if they were on a fixed salary.

Part Five

CONTROL

The final function in the management process is that of assuring that directed action takes place in accordance with plans. The control of action necessitates managerial attention to both a **technical information process** concerned with the enforcement of standards, and a **cooperative process** concerned with the integration of individual and group interests.

Section A

Formal Control

The manager is responsible for insuring the accomplishment of group and organizational goals. To effect this, he must compare operating results with pre-established standards and take necessary corrective action (Chap. 20). One form of corrective action which the traditionalists have tended to emphasize is disciplinary action (Chap. 21).

20

Control

We have by now determined the organization objectives, along with the necessary policies, procedures, and programs for their accomplishment. To insure that the initiated action proceeds in the direction of these objectives, control is necessary. To many, this function is the essence of management. It should be apparent by now, however, that the satisfactory performance of planning, organizing, and directing can reduce the difficulty, as well as the significance, of the control function. All four functions are interrelated as links in a chain, and the poor accomplishment of any one can seriously affect the enterprise.

NATURE OF CONTROL

Control can be defined as the *regulating of activities in accordance with the requirements of plans.* The fundamental goal is to assure satisfactory accomplishment of the basic objectives of the organization. It therefore requires an awareness of actions that take place, the correlation of all these actions with respect to each other and in relation to the objective, and the removal of any obstacles to the attainment of goals.

It will be recalled from Chapter 1 that management is concerned with directing and monitoring a system of inputs, processes, and outputs. As indicated in Figure 1–1, the basis for monitoring is the collection and feedback of information concerning the nature of processes and outputs. Theoretically, every processing activity and output could be measured, reported, and compared to predetermined standards. In practice, only a portion is monitored; all activities are not equally important nor are they all subject to precision of measurement. As was emphasized in Chapter 2, the more precise and quantitative the measurement of an activity or output, the more likely that it will be subjected to close control. If measureable outputs are *not* the most important, there is the possibility of managerial monitoring leading to goal distortion.

The manager receiving the feedback of information acts in the manner of a servomechanism in correcting operations in accordance with programmed standards. Just as a room thermostat collects and compares temperature information with a preset standard and initiates more air inputs in case of perceived discrepancies, a manager also collects operating information and initiates corrective action in the case of perceived deficiencies. As behaviorists emphasize, the manager must not only be aware of outputs, he should also be concerned with proper maintenance of the processing organization which is largely comprised of human beings. This requires collection and feedback of information concerning such human assets as morale, loyalty, cooperation, and creativity.

A parallel can be drawn with the management of an automobile upon the highway. The automobile is a mechanical organization operating under the management of a driver. It is a means of achieving particular goals, e.g., transporting passengers to a particular destination. The driver-manager collects operating information with reference to this goal. Is he on the correct route? Is the car still on the road? Societal standards also affect the manager and his organization, e.g., speed limits and traffic lights. In the event of ascertaining that incorrect routes are being followed, or that the automobile is drifting off the roadway, or that the speed limit is being exceeded, the driver-manager must initiate corrective forces.

The automobile-organization must also be monitored and maintained to assure its continued effective functioning for this and other future goals. For this purpose, there are certain information collection devices such as the gasoline gauge, oil pressure indicators, and temperature dials or "idiot lights." If the driver-manager wishes to utilize his automobile-organization on a continuing basis, he must insure maintenance of minimum acceptable inputs of gasoline, oil, and water. It is unfortunate that we are usually more concerned and adept at machine organization maintenance than we are with human organization maintenance.

Coordination and control are often deemed to be the same function. However, it is more helpful to view coordination as a specialized aspect of the broader function of control. Coordination is concerned with the correlation of multiple activities, with time constituting a major factor. Planning and organizing have resulted in the division of the total task into a number of subdivisions, often minute in size. If each person performs the work required of him, but without regard to proper timing, it would be similar in effect to a football line whose members each charge ahead at slightly different times. A lot of energy is expended, but its cumulative effect is more nearly that of a single individual instead of the entire team. To coordinate efforts, two major factors are involved: (1) a definite sequence of activities, and (2) chronological time. Planning should indicate the order of events—i.e., which should come first and which should be performed simultaneously—while direction is concerned with releasing commands at the appropriate times in relation to this plan. Thus, planning, organizing, and directing provide the framework for coordination, which in turn insures that these sequences and times are met satisfactorily.

Control is concerned as well with making sure that plans are being met. The results of various activities within a set period of time are compared with what was planned. (These elements of control are not particularly glamorous and do not involve the direct action contacts which often accompany coordination.) And finally, when obstacles to the accomplishment of plans are discovered, control tries either to remove these obstacles or to alter plans in order to go around them. Thus, the four fundamental functions of management constitute a circular relationship. Control checks to see if planned goals have been attained; if not, it then follows a period of replanning, reorganizing, redirecting, and eventually, recontrolling. Though theoretically, one may discuss these functions separately, in practice it is difficult to determine clearly a marked dividing line. On one project, all four may be performed within an hour and not necessarily in the prescribed sequence. On another project, the planning phases may consume months or years with control problems arising only in the distant future.

Every manager has a control function which, along with direction, links two levels of organization. As indicated in Chart 20–1, each management level plans for, organizes, and directs the lower level. Lower levels of management of course require more specific planning, organizing, and directing. The immediate supervisor issues orders to his operative subordinates to execute the work generally planned by top management and more specifically planned by middle and lower management. *During* and immediately *after* this operative performance, information concerning results is sent up to the various levels of management. This enables the immediate supervisor to control within the limits of his specific plan. He must then report to higher management the information desired of his department. This information in turn enables higher levels of management to ascertain whether action is conforming to general plans and objectives and whether corrective measures need be taken.

In this chapter, the basic phases of the control process will be discussed. Since planning and controlling are so closely intertwined, this will first require

CHART 20–1   ORGANIZATION LEVELS AND LINKING MANAGEMENT FUNCTIONS

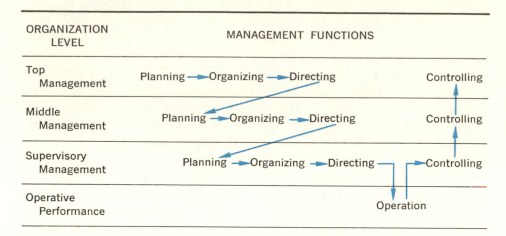

ORGANIZATION LEVEL	MANAGEMENT FUNCTIONS
Top Management	Planning → Organizing → Directing · · · · · · · · · · Controlling
Middle Management	Planning → Organizing → Directing · · · · · · · · · · Controlling
Supervisory Management	Planning → Organizing → Directing · · · · · · · · · · Controlling
Operative Performance	Operation

a reemphasis of the use of *standards*. With these standards as representative of the plan, the control process consists of the following three functions: (1) overseeing, (2) comparison, and (3) corrective action. Through the performance of these functions, information will be obtained as to operating results, comparisons will be made with standards, and corrective action will be taken if the two do not agree. The emphasis here is upon the formal and technical process. In Chapter 22, the human reactions will be examined in detail.

SETTING STRATEGIC CONTROL POINTS

It will be recalled from Chapter 5 that a complete program of standardization would involve specifications covering the basic components of the organization—personnel, functions, and physical plant. But more important are the standards which specify the type of performance *results* desired. In general, these standards of performance results are based on (1) quantity of output, (2) quality of work, (3) time or schedule of performance, and (4) monetary expenditures.

Here again in the matter of control, the traditionalists and the behaviorists part company. The latter emphasize the concept of *self-control* issuing from a large grant of freedom to subordinates. The traditionalists tend to move toward the other extreme of *imposed control*, of establishing standards for every act, and of retaining authority in the manager's hands. Neither extreme on such a control continuum is desirable or workable. Management must establish standards of expectations for the guidance of subordinates as well as for measurement and control purposes. Yet these standards or control points should *not* be established and enforced on every conceivable thought and action but should be individually selected in a *strategic* manner.

A strategic control point has a number of basic characteristics. First, it is a point established for *key* operations or events. Behaviorists are on sound ground in their indictment of many managers as establishing control points on too many operations. Some self-control is desirable for reasons of personnel development and motivation. Second, the strategic point should be located properly with respect to *timing* requirements. The application of this standard should enable action to be stopped or altered before serious damage is done and should prevent mistakes from being covered over by future work. For example, quality control points in production should be located at the receipt of materials, just after operations which are basic and have far-reaching effects on subsequent steps, and just prior to highly expensive operations. In short, strategic points should be selected which will enable the manager to retain the necessary minimum degree of control without subjecting every move to close regimentation.

The more effective strategic points are reasonably *comprehensive* in their coverage; that is, they indicate the level of performance for a broad spectrum of key events. At times this comprehensiveness conflicts with the need for proper timing. Net profit, for example, is a comprehensive strategic control point, indicating the progress of the entire enterprise. Yet, if one waits until the regular accounting period to obtain this figure, one loses control of the immediate future. A related factor is the *economy* of the application of control points. A comprehensive reading of all correspondence that enters or leaves the firm is rather expensive for the executive to effect. Not only is most of his time wasted on events that are unimportant, but the delays in processing correspondence are likely to interfere with effective functioning of the organization as a whole.

The selection of various strategic control points should also be *balanced*. If only credit losses are watched and controlled, for example, sales may suffer because of an overly stringent policy in accepting credit risks. If sales are emphasized out of all proportion, then credit losses will mount excessively. There is a tendency to effect excessive control over the tangible functions, such as production and sales, while maintaining too little control over the intangible, such as personnel development and other staff services. This often leads to a state of imbalance where production line executives are held to exact standards, and staff executives are seemingly given "blank checks." This is another source for possible conflicts among personnel in the organization.

Though the establishment of such points for a staff group is more difficult, standards of some type, qualitative if not quantitative, can be determined if the objectives are clearly specified. For example, the fundamental functions of a personnel department have been identified as procurement and development of personnel, compensation, integration, and maintenance.[1] For each of these functions, the following suggested control points could be used:

Procurement
1. Placement follow-ups to determine level of satisfaction of both new employee and supervisor.
2. Number of voluntary resignations and requests for transfer.
3. Number of involuntary layoffs.

Development
1. Productivity increases.
2. Scrap losses.
3. Adequacy of talent reservoir.

Compensation
1. Number of grievances related to wages.
2. Relation to community wage curve.
3. Incentive earnings, in terms of both amount of money and number of wage-earners.

Integration
1. Morale survey standards.
2. Levels of absenteeism, turnover, and tardiness.
3. Total number of grievances.

Maintenance
1. Accident frequency and severity rates.
2. Insurance premiums for workmen's compensation.
3. Degree of employee participation in service programs.

In addition to controlling each of these five functions, various companies have developed overall quantitative measures of the work of the personnel department. One example of this would be the Employee Relations Index of General Electric, a composite figure based on such factors as absences, separations, disciplinary suspensions, grievances, employee participation, etc.[2]

OVERSEEING

With standards available specifying desired results, the first logical phase of control after direction is overseeing the action that will follow or assuring that *appropriate* action is taking place.

Overseeing is accomplished largely through observation and through conferences between supervisor and subordinate. A large portion of the lower

---

[1] Edwin B. Flippo, *Principles of Personnel Management,* 2nd ed. (New York: McGraw-Hill Book Company, 1966), Chaps. 1 and 6.
[2] Willard Merrihue and Raymond Katzell, "ERI: Yardstick of Employee Relations," *Harvard Business Review,* Vol. 33, No. 6 (1955), p. 91.

level manager's time is devoted to this function. In fact, the positions of "group leader" or "labor pusher" are strictly concerned with overseeing the work ordered by the department head. Such additional specialization can aid in extending the department head's span of effective control.

The greatest opportunity for the discovery and correction of undesired deviations takes place while the work is being performed. If an entire lot of fifty units is completed by a worker, and inspection reveals that *all* fifty are too small, there is little that can be done about it. If, during the operation, someone had personally checked the work as to method and results, much material and labor would have been saved. The amount of overseeing necessary is dependent upon such factors as the skill and attitude of the worker, the skill of the manager, and the discipline of the work place. Well trained and experienced employees require less constant supervision. If the worker is controlled by mechanically paced assembly lines and automatic inspections, here again the amount of overseeing is considerably reduced. A further consideration as to the amount of control necessary is whether the employee is a Theory "X" or Theory "Y" type.

There are several differences between the overseeing and comparison phases of control. Though both involve relating what *is* going on to what *should be* going on, overseeing is effected *while the work is in progress.* Comparison comes later and relies upon reports of completed steps in a project or on the results of the entire project.

A second difference between the two functions is a result of this contrast in timing. Overseeing has to be accomplished by the immediate supervisor. Comparison, however, can be done not only by the supervisor but also by higher line managers or various staff officials. Since it relies upon reporting, it can be divorced physically from the point of operations.

Finally, overseeing requires face-to-face contacts and personal observation as the method of obtaining information. The manager must evaluate work in both qualitative and quantitative terms and must be adept in human relations skills. Comparison, however, is usually concerned with only a quantitative and statistical evaluation of actions that have reached some stage of completion. Though observation can be used to gain such information, it more frequently involves written reports, charts, graphs, telautographs, etc.

COMPARISON

Comparison is the function of determining the degree of agreement between performance results and performance standards and can take place on or away from the point of operation. It can be applied to the cumulative performance results of departments or of the entire organization, to completed specific projects or undertakings, or to some finite portion of such projects while in progress. The objective of comparison is to determine whether deviations from plans have taken place and, if necessary, to bring them to the attention of responsible officials.

Professor Ralph C. Davis has identified four fundamental phases of the comparison function:[3]

1. Receipt of raw data.
2. Accumulation, classification, and recording of this information.
3. Periodic evaluation of completed action to date.
4. Reporting the status of accomplishment to higher line authority.

Collection of Data

The first phase of comparison requires the establishment of a structured system of upward communication. The closer the control desired, the greater the need for speed, capacity, and accuracy in this communication system. If centralized control is desired, such a system is absolutely essential. Closed circuit television, for example, has enabled the continuous, and relatively inexpensive, collection of data on multiple operations or on events which were impossible to observe prior to its development. In general, information can be collected by means of direct observation, oral reports, or written reports. The large and rapid strides in improving communication devices has enabled the traditional manager to regain some of the control he had lost through the sheer size of the enterprise.

Classification of Information

The large volume of data which has been generated by computers and improved communication systems can literally snow a manager under. It can be handled and used *only* if classified in some meaningful manner. The purpose of classification is to enable the identification of significant deviations from plans.

The exception principle is a basic generalization of control which has long been emphasized by traditional managers. Most executives quickly recognize that they can neither do the work of their department nor oversee every action

[3] Ralph C. Davis, *The Fundamentals of Top Management* (New York: Harper & Bros., 1951), p. 721.

that takes place. More time must be devoted to the exceptions, the significant deviations from plans, policies, and standards of performance. The classification of information in ways that will reveal these deviations is prerequisite to the use of this exception principle.

The widespread use of various charts and graphs as a means of classifying information has aided in the rapid recognition of significant deviations. We shall later discuss examples of such devices, with one illustration for each of the four types of performance standards.

Comparison and Evaluation

A major problem concerning the evaluation of data collected and classified is that of the *timing* of comparisons. Continuous comparison is expensive, objectionable to subordinates, and usually unnecessary. Under conditions of close and centralized control, frequent collection of data and comparison of results to standards will be made. Where there is a greater delegation of responsibility to subordinates, such comparisons are less frequent. To some extent, the frequency is determined by the activity being controlled. The installation and administration of a psychological testing program, for example, will require a comparison period of several months, if not years; this much time is needed before sufficient data can be obtained to judge the worth of the tests. In quality control of production of parts with small tolerances, comparison with standards may occur every minute. Additional factors influencing frequency include the time required to complete identifiable units; the closeness of control desired; the availability of the information concerning performance results; the degree of standardization of methods and physical factors; and the degree of centralized control being attempted.

When comparisons are made and exceptions are discovered, there must be some determination of the *significance* of the deviations. Judgment and experience are necessary to determine which deviations require controlling action (see Chapter 7).

Reporting

In the event that a staff official, such as a production control specialist, discovers a significant deviation in plans, the fourth phase of comparison would naturally follow. He would report the difficulty to whichever line official has the necessary authority to institute corrective action. If the person discovering the deviation also has the power to make the correction, this fourth phase is merely implied.

Every manager requires a system of reports in order to maintain control. The exceptions should be highlighted for special attention. Note that both types of exceptions should be reported, the exceptionally good and the exceptionally bad. In addition, it is wise to require summary reports of *all* key events, whether exceptions or not. Though such events are not out of control, the manager should still be informed with regard for his amount of time and his desire. Evidence that attention is being given to everything provides a disciplinary and *controlling* influence upon subordinates. If the manager seems not to be interested in an operation which is proceeding according to plan, this frequently leads to a lack of interest and diligence on the part of the operator.

CORRECTIVE ACTION

Comparison may discover no significant deviations. In such a case, there is need only for the continuous influence of the manager's attention.

The function of corrective action is concerned with either correcting deviations from planned performance or altering the plan to allow for obstacles which cannot be removed. The goal is to restore effective, coordinated action.

Two general types of corrective action have been identified—immediate and basic. The type most frequently recognized is the immediate; something must be done *now* to correct the situation and get back on track. For example, a particular project is a week behind schedule and, if not corrected, will seriously affect other projects and necessitate extensive and far-reaching adjustments. The first problem is *not* to worry about *who* caused the difficulty, but rather to get the project back on schedule. Depending upon the authority of the official concerned, such corrections as the following may be ordered: (1) overtime hours may be authorized for project personnel; (2) additional men and equipment may be allocated; (3) a full-time expediter may be assigned to push the project personally; (4) an extra effort may be asked from all personnel, perhaps through the use of participation approaches (see Chapter 17); or, (5) failing all these, the schedule may have to be readjusted, thereby requiring changes all along the line.

After the degree of stress has lessened through any of the above measures, attention can then be devoted to the second type of corrective action. Just how and why did events stray from their planned course? What can be done to prevent a recurrence of this type of difficulty? Too often, the manager is caught up in the excitement of solving immediate problems, never taking the time to do some fundamental analysis of causes. Yet, the dull work of basic corrective action must be done for the sake of future economical and effective operations.

Upon investigation, the manager may discover various fundamental causes for the difficulty. The schedule may have not been met because of a certain department's actions which reflect a pattern of behavior that has been observed in the past. Or it may be discovered that not only was this particular project in trouble, but *most* of the projects in this company are behind schedule. In the first event, investigation may reveal that poor equipment in the one department or poor control on the part of the department supervisor is the major source of the trouble. Thus, basic corrective actions would involve new or improved equipment or new or improved management. Such action does not necessarily add anything to the project which revealed the difficulty; its primary effect is on all *future* projects that will flow through this department.

If most of the projects in a firm are usually behind schedule, an even more serious type of basic corrective action may be demanded, such as a drastic overhaul of general control procedures or a re-examination and reconstitution of sales policies and relationships between sales and production control. There might even be a reorganization of the entire company. In any event, the analysis of fundamental causes is basic to scientific management. It requires an investment in time and money which the necessities of daily routine will often prevent. For this reason, staff has been developed to undertake such work, and consultants are often hired to spot basic defects and recommend solutions.

Finally it should be emphasized that immediate corrective action should be undertaken *first*. Too often, a manager who has discovered trouble immediately demands to know *who* caused it and may take disciplinary action on the spot if he feels he has discovered the culprit. A sounder approach would be for the manager to confine himself to the *immediate* emergency. After he has some room and time in which to breathe, he can do a better job of administering whatever disciplinary action he feels necessary for the future of the organization. Often, in the lessened strain of the situation, he will decide that actions he had previously intended to take are detrimental to future effectiveness.

COMPARISON DEVICES

We noted that there are certain devices used in the classification phase of comparison. Inasmuch as the four types of performance results that should be controlled are quantity, quality, time, and costs, an example of a control device emphasizing each of these will be given. Many devices are designed to provide comparison for more than one of the standards. (These devices are intimately involved with *both* planning and control. As they are designed and set up, they represent a plan. As they are altered to reflect action results, they require control. Thus, they can be discussed in either the section on planning or the present one on control. Their use here is to demonstrate the process of comparison, evaluation, and corrective action.)

Quantity

As a device which will assist in controlling quantity of work, the Gantt Chart is widely known and used.[4] It is a highly adaptable classification instrument developed by Henry L. Gantt, pioneer of scientific management, and can be used to control such items as inventory quantities, project schedules, and machine or work center loading. In most instances, it is based on the concept of portraying work planned and work done in relation to each other and in relation to chronological time. As shown in a machine layout illustration in Fig. 20–1, a calendar scale for chronological time is provided across the top. For each machine listed on the left, a thin straight line shows the amount of work planned for it. The lower heavy line shows the amount of work completed. The heavy vertical line portrays the current date and will move steadily to the right with the passage of time. A brief look at such a chart will reveal machines that have done the planned amount of work and are on schedule, those that have done more than planned, and those that are behind schedule. The latter two categories are exceptions to the plan and may or may not be significant, depending upon managerial judgment. It is apparent that in specifying standards of quantity of work, it must be in relation to time, e.g., 50 units per hour.[5]

Quality

The most widely known control devices have been developed for the more quantifiable functions such as production and sales. Two of the most common *quality* comparison devices are the $\bar{X}$ and R Charts developed by Shewhart.[6] The quality of a product is the combination of attributes, such as form, dimensions, composition, and color, which distinguish it from other products.

[4] For a comprehensive coverage of the many things that can be done with a Gantt Chart, see Wallace Clark, *The Gantt Chart: A Working Tool of Management* (London: Sir Isaac Pitman and Sons, Ltd., 1946).

[5] Two somewhat mechanical adaptations of the Gantt Chart are the Produc-trol Board developed by the Wassell Corporation and Sched-U-Graph developed by Remington Rand Corporation.

[6] W. A. Shewhart, *Economic Control of Quality of Manufactured Products* (New York: D. Van Nostrand Co., 1931).

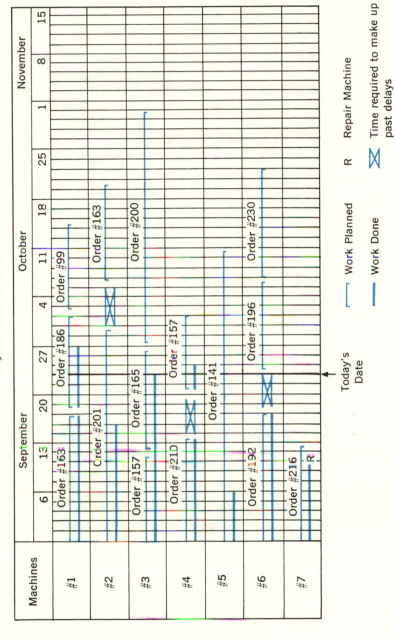

FIGURE 20–1 GANTT CHART

Layout Chart for Machine

FIGURE 20–2   X̄ CHART FOR QUALITY CONTROL

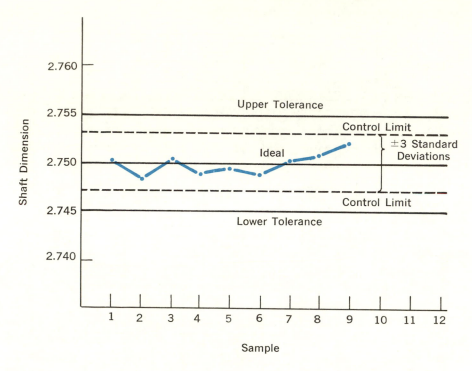

Sample

Fig. 20–2 is a portion of an X̄ Chart designed to facilitate comparing measurements of the average of a product's characteristics against the standards of quality specified. The product in question is a shaft and the principal quality attribute being subjected to control is its diameter. On the chart are horizontal lines showing the desired diameter (2.750 inches), the permissible deviations or tolerances ($\pm$.005 or 2.745 and 2.755), and the statistical quality control limits (2.750 inches $\pm$ three standard deviations or 2.746 and 2.754).[7] The derivation of these statistical control limits is beyond the scope of this book. Our purpose here is to provide an example of a control device which enables the comparison of quality produced with quality desired.

As indicated in Fig. 20–2, samples of shafts produced are taken periodically, perhaps every hour. The average of the sample is computed and plotted on the chart. It will be noted that the averages plotted are all within both the quality control limits and the tolerances permitted. However, they are moving steadily upward toward these limits. This may be caused by the wearing of a cutting tool, the loosening of a fixture, or any number of factors. If some correction of the work situation is not forthcoming, the shaft dimensions will be out of

[7] See Acheson J. Duncan, *Quality Control and Industrial Statistics,* rev. ed. (Homewood: Richard D. Irwin, Inc., 1959) for explanation of the derivation of these quality control limits.

control and will not meet standards. This type of comparison device can thus prevent deviations before they actually occur.

Time

The Gantt Chart discussed above is an excellent device for portraying and controlling time standards. A more recent adaptation of this approach is the Program Evaluation and Review Technique, commonly referred to as PERT.[8] It is most useful in planning and controlling large, complex projects, often involving separate companies, in which it is difficult to keep track of progress and coordinate the various efforts. Although first developed by the Navy Special Projects Office in 1958 for national defense projects, it has since been adapted to various business uses such as the construction of highways, the design and development of new products, and the production and staging of a Broadway play from manuscript to first night.

This approach to control tends to focus managerial attention upon such elements as (1) the interrelationships of multiple components of complex projects, (2) the shortest time to complete the overall project, (3) the ascertainment of possible slack times within particular components, and (4) the portions of the project most likely to impede or delay accomplishment of the overall result. It rests upon the exception principle when it highlights the critical components that can make or break the project. It is also concerned with more effective utilization of resources when it identifies facilities and resources that are not being fully applied.

A PERT network is a "flow diagram consisting of the activities and events which must be accomplished to reach the program objectives, showing their logical and planned sequences of accomplishment, interdependencies, and interrelationships."[9] The development of a network usually begins with the final project objective, e.g., in Fig. 20-3, it is event 70, the completion of pilot runs. An event is a point in time when something either begins or ends. It is usually represented by a circle and is given an identification number within the network. The numbering is in sequence in terms of time. An activity involves the expenditure of resources leading to the accomplishment of an event. Activities are indicated by straight lines connecting two events. Thus, a network is a number of events related to each other by activities.

Beginning with the ending event, the manager works backward to other events that must precede. For all events, one should ask the following questions: (1) What events and activities must take place *before* this one can

---

[8] See Harry F. Evarts, *Introduction to PERT* (Boston: Allyn and Bacon, 1964).

[9] *PERT Fundamentals,* Vol. III. (Washington: PERT Orientation and Training Center, 1963), p. 16.

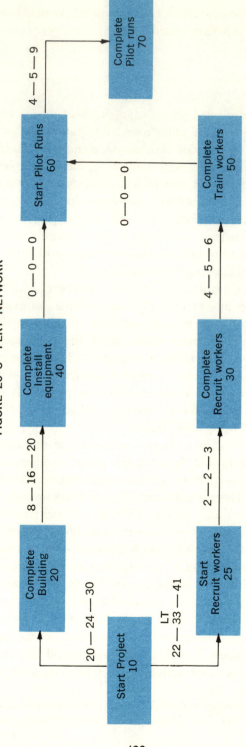

FIGURE 20–3   PERT NETWORK

Source: From Harry F. Evarts, *Introduction to PERT*, p. 34. © Copyright 1964 by Allyn and Bacon, Inc., Boston. Reprinted by permission of the publisher.

occur? (2) What events cannot be accomplished until *after* this event is completed? (3) What events can be done *concurrently* with this particular event? For example, in the construction of a house, the completion of a foundation must precede the construction of the frame; the frame must be completed before siding can be attached; and wiring and plumbing can be undertaken simultaneously. In Fig. 20–3, the recruiting of workers can take place while the building and equipment are being made ready.

The next step in PERT networking is the obtaining of time estimates for all activities. It is customary to develop three types of times from which a fourth, the expected time can be derived. These are (1) the optimistic time estimate, should everything go extremely well, (2) the most likely time, and (3) the pessimistic time, should everything go very badly. The expected time is derived through the following formula:

$$\text{Expected time} = \frac{Optimistic\ time + 4\ (Most\ likely\ time) + Pessimistic\ time}{6}$$

On the chart in Fig. 20–3, these times are represented by three figures on each of the activities. For example, it is most likely that completion of the building, event 20, will require 24 weeks. There is a slight chance that it will require only 20 weeks or as much as 30 weeks. The expected time is

$$\frac{20 + 24(4) + 30}{6}\ \text{or 24.3 weeks.}$$

With these sequences and times, a flow chart portraying the network of events can be established. The activity sequence that requires the longest total time span for the project is referred to as the critical path. In the network presented, the critical path is 10–20–40–60–70, and has a total optimistic time of 32 weeks, total pessimistic time of 59 weeks, a total most likely time of 45 weeks, and a total expected time of 45.1 weeks. It should be noted that the recruiting and training of workers does not take nearly as long as getting the production line ready. Workers need to be ready about 5 weeks before planned completion of the pilot runs. Rather than start recruitment at the same time as the project, a delay or lead time of about 33 weeks has been placed into the network as shown on the line connecting events 10 and 25. There is no slack or lead time in the critical path of any PERT network. If the time of the critical path can be reduced, the entire project can be completed more quickly.

Against this standard of expected times, progress information can be compared. The critical path is watched closely; facilities and manpower can be transferred to critical path activities when necessary, for the overall time of the project is controlled by the time for this critical path. The periodic comparison of progress to this overall time plan is essential to coordination of the many personnel and organization elements involved.

Cost

Though there are many control devices established for the control of costs or expenditures, perhaps the most widely known and used is the budget.[10] To illustrate again the very close relationship between planning and controlling, a budget constitutes a statement of *planned* expenditures of money, manpower, time, space, or equipment. Budgetary control is concerned with the subsequent comparison of actual or proposed expenditures with this plan. Most phases of the business can be reduced to expenditures of money. Among the typical budgets prepared in a business enterprise are those for sales, production, materials, labor, manufacturing expense, capital expenditures, and cash.

One of the greatest values of establishing a budget is that of forcing the manager to plan the future of his organization in fairly concrete and precise terms. Usually, expenditures are forecast on the basis of an anticipated volume of business, and all budgets ordinarily begin with the sales forecast. In order that these monetary standards may not become unusable, flexible budgets are often prepared for varying levels of business activity. The use of each budget as a comparison control device is relatively simple. Chart 20–2 shows a small portion of the total budget for an enterprise. Actual expenditures are compared column by column with planned expenditures, and significant deviations can be determined for future control reference. Budgets are also used as devices for controlling the present; *proposed* expenditures may, for example, not be within the budget. The manager proposing the exception will have to prove his case in order to secure approval of the deviation. On the other hand, expenditures within the budget have already received approval. It often happens that changing conditions no longer necessitate their expenditure, though approved, with a consequent danger of monies being spent unnecessarily or diverted into unauthorized channels.[11]

THE CONTROL SYSTEM

If control is to be effected on a continuous basis, some type of formal system must be established and maintained. Behaviorists have chafed considerably

[10] See such texts as Glenn A. Welsch, *Budgeting: Profit-Planning and Control* (Englewood Cliffs: Prentice-Hall, Inc., 1957), and J. B. Heckert and J. D. Willson, *Business Budgeting and Control,* 2nd ed. (New York: The Ronald Press, 1955).

[11] For examples, see Melville Dalton, *Men Who Manage* (New York: John Wiley & Sons, Inc., 1959).

CHART 20–2   BUDGETARY CONTROL

BUDGET
MACHINING DEPARTMENT
SYS. CO.

October 1 – 31

ITEM	BUDGET	ACTUAL	OVER	UNDER
Direct Labor	$ 6,000	$ 6,500	$500	
Indirect Labor	1,720	1,900	180	
Operating Supplies	250	500	250	
Maintenance	2,550	2,000		550
Misc. Expense	80	50		30
Total	$10,600	$10,950	Over $350	

about the degree of control actually introduced and administered in the formal hierarchies of business organizations. But it must be admitted that some central restraint is absolutely essential. The acceptance of this necessity is an additional mark of *maturity* that Argyris might add to his various dimensions.[12]

In discussing the subjects of standards and the phases of control, we have indicated some of the fundamental features of a control system. Basically, the philosophy on which the system should be founded must be one of learning from the past in order to control the future. A second essential element previously discussed is timeliness, the discovery and reporting of deviations *before* excessive costs are involved. In addition to these, a systematic approach should be: (1) adapted to the formal organization structure; (2) adjusted to informal organization relationships; (3) understandable to its administrators; (4) economical in operation; and (5) flexible in adapting to changing conditions.

It will be recalled that accountability is one of the three major formal relationships established by the organizing process. The reporting system for control must be adjusted, then, to formal lines of accountability. If significant deviations are discovered through comparison, there should be some means of associating them with the organization element responsible for the deviation. Naturally, the standards established for control should make sense in terms of this accountability. It does little good to place in the department head's budget expenditures over which he has absolutely no control.

Another related problem in organizing for control is the widespread use of staff officials to aid in controlling specific areas such as production scheduling and control, quality control, cost control, and the like. The subject of line and

[12] See Chapter 6.

staff conflicts was discussed in Chapter 13, and the control staffs are the source of many of the difficulties. Line personnel are told that staff personnel are advisory. They soon perceive that these staff people are seemingly in command over a particular specialized area. In theory, there is single accountability, but in practice, subordinate personnel often have to become skilled in working for two or more masters.

Adaptation of a control system to informal organization may well have to be done by the administrator of the control system. The ways and techniques of circumventing control techniques are legion. (An excellent description of some rather extreme activities of this type is given at length in Dalton's *Men Who Manage.*) The manager must accept the fact that he cannot control every event and act and will have to admit the *inadequacy* of the control system as a single approach. Resistance to controls will inevitably arise, and the system could be tinkered with forever to overcome each aberration as it is exposed. Some acceptance of behavioral theories will lead to more cooperation and coordination than would the use of the formal system alone. This subject will be discussed at length in Chapter 22.

It is apparent that any system must be understandable to its users if it is to be of value. Too often the staff specialist in control is carried away by his extensive knowledge, and designs control charts and graphs that are a joy to him but a horror to others. One might also point out that nonunderstandable controls are a needless expense.

Finally, conditions are never static. The system which proposes to aid in controlling events must be flexible to allow for varying factors. The budget is a case in point, wherein expenditure levels are established for varying percentages of capacity. If a control system is rendered useless by changes in conditions, it does not possess the characteristic of flexibility.

SUMMARY

Control is the restraint and regulation of activities in accordance with plans and objectives. It is totally dependent upon the prior existence of plans.

Standards are the specific and tangible representation of those plans. The standards of results—quantity, quality, time, and cost—are fundamental, and strategic control points concerning these must be established for key operations. These strategic points should be comprehensive, economical of operation, timely, and balanced in scope.

The manager closes the control loop through a feedback of critical information with respect to preestablished standards. This involves direct overseeing by immediate supervisors, periodic collection of data from all significant activities, and systematic comparison with standards. In the event of intolerable exceptions, the manager initiates corrective action in the form of new inputs or alteration of his expectations. Examples of various standard control devices include the Gantt Chart and PERT for quantity and time, Shewhart's $\overline{X}$ chart for quality control, and budgets for control of costs.

The standards, reports, and comparisons must be bound together into a system. Such a control system should enable timely discovery of deviations, should be directed to the future rather than the past, should be adapted to formal and informal organization relationships, and should be understandable and economical.

DISCUSSION PROBLEMS

1. What are the parallels between managing an organization and driving a car?
2. What are the parallels between maintaining a human organization and maintaining an automobile?
3. How do classicists and behaviorists differ in the *amount* of feedback that should be provided in managing an organization? the *frequency* of feedback? the *subjects* about which there should be feedback?
4. Discuss the relationship of the control function to the planning function; the direction function.
5. Describe a strategic control point.
6. For each of the standards of performance, describe a comparison device adapted to its control. What types of devices would you suggest be developed for controlling standards of personnel, functions, and physical factors?
7. Distinguish between overseeing and comparison in terms of time, goals, and organization.
8. Distinguish between immediate and basic corrective action. Cite examples of each type.
9. Design a PERT network for constructing a house requiring such events as completion of frame, wiring, plumbing, foundation, excavation, interior decorating, lath and plastering, siding, exterior painting, and landscaping.
10. For your next vacation trip home, describe the planning, organizing, directing, and controlling of events necessary to assure your arrival at a specific time.

SUPPLEMENTARY READING

Dickson, G. W., "Management Information-Decision Systems," *Business Horizons,* Vol. 9, No. 6 (December, 1968), 17–26.

Dusenbury, Warren, "CPM for New Product Introductions," *Harvard Business Review,* Vol. 45, No. 4 (July–August, 1967), 124–139.

Evarts, Harry F., *Introduction to PERT.* Boston: Allyn and Bacon, 1964.

Rhind, Ridley, "Management Information Systems," *Business Horizons,* Vol. 11, No. 3 (June, 1968), 37–46.

Schoderbek, Peter P. and Lester A. Digman, "Third Generation, PERT/LOB," *Harvard Business Review,* Vol. 45, No. 5 (September–October, 1967), 100–110.

Voris, William, *Production Control,* 3rd ed., Chaps. 1 and 10. Homewood: Richard D. Irwin, Inc., 1966.

21

Disciplinary Action

In a broad sense, disciplinary action could encompass any action designed to promote cooperation and obedience to rules, regulations, and commands. As such, it would include training activities as well as positive motivation techniques as discussed in Chapter 14. The discussion of disciplinary action in this chapter, however, will be confined to its negative aspects of correction and penalty.

PHILOSOPHIES OF DISCIPLINARY ACTION

A reconsideration of the basic philosophies of traditionalists and behaviorists will reveal differences in establishing the role of disciplinary penalties. In this book, we approach negative disciplinary action from the traditional viewpoint. Not only has such disciplinary action been greatly emphasized and used by traditional managers, but it is ordinarily most closely associated with the function of control. Long ago, Henri Fayol stated that "for control to be effective, it must be done within reasonable time and *be followed up by sanctions.*"[1] More recently, R. C. Davis indicated that because disciplinary action usually arises out of moves undertaken to implement the plan, it falls more within the area of controlling rather than of organizing.[2]

[1] Henri Fayol, *General and Industrial Management* (trans. by Constance Storrs from the French Edition of 1925) (New York: Pitman Publishing Company, 1949), p. 108. Emphasis added by the author.
[2] Ralph C. Davis, *The Fundamentals of Top Management* (New York: Harper & Bros., 1951), p. 737.

The fact that negative disciplinary action should occupy an important place in traditional theory is logical, for it rests upon the right or authority to apply sanctions and penalties. According to Mooney's philosophy of management, authority is the all-inclusive principle of organization from which all other principles can be derived.[3] If a subordinate acts in defiance of that authority, the immediate reaction is to preserve its integrity through the application of sanctions. Unity of command must be maintained and all those not conforming to the requirements for coordinated action must be made to change by the manager.

On the other hand, the behavioral writers of recent years have deplored what they feel to be the manager's excessive use of authority and misuse of the right to apply penalties. As one labor economist stated, "Industrial discipline has traditionally been both severe and irresponsible."[4] Psychologists have gone so far as to question the very basis of negative action.

In the human relations movement of the past three decades, there is little in the literature which supports even a necessary *minimum* of negative disciplinary action. Perhaps this is because of the belief that there has been an excess of negative action in the past, and if managers are to move from one extreme of a negative-positive continuum, they must do so completely.

Yet, negative disciplinary action does have an essential role in management theory, whether that theory is oriented toward the traditional or the behavioral. To deny its need in all organizations is to be naive and foolish. To rely upon it to the exclusion of all other conditioning activities is equally foolish and wasteful. Though Theory "Y" people are to be greatly desired, the fact is that all organizations have a number of Theory "X" people, not all of whom were the creations of the excessive use of authority by traditional managers. At the same time, it is undeniable that too many managers take the easy way out by condemning all deviations from plans as mistakes, shifting all blame for such deviations upon the shoulders of subordinates, and using their formal authority to apply penalties in retribution. There must be some middle ground upon which a more constructive use of essential negative disciplinary action can be based. Modern management is moving in the direction of a more enlightened philosophy because of the increasing inappropriateness of authority as the primary or sole basis for management. As has been pointed out earlier, such factors as the offsetting power center of the labor union and the increasing levels of education of the work force have compelled managers to seek other means of influencing behavior. But the need for negative disciplinary action can never be completely eliminated, and thus it is important to define its role in a balanced philosophy of management.

[3] James D. Mooney, *The Principles of Organization* (New York: Harper & Bros., 1947), p. 6.
[4] Orme W. Phelps, *Discipline and Discharge in the Unionized Firm* (Berkeley: University of California Press, 1959), p. 4.

NATURE OF DISCIPLINARY ACTION

Defined in its negative sense, disciplinary action is the application of penalties in order to condition future behavior, not only of the particular subordinate concerned but of the employee group as well. It should not be used as a form of retributive justice but should be construed as a form of education which serves to supplement self and group discipline. It was stated previously that all control activities should be oriented toward the future, that one cannot control the past. The goal of constructive disciplinary action should always be to determine what measures can be taken to influence favorable behavior in the future. If approached in this manner, the sanctions and penalties that may be applied are more likely to be accepted by the persons concerned.

Negative disciplinary action is one of the most difficult responsibilities of a manager, as it involves the use of direct and personal sanctions upon other people. Contrary to popular stereotypes, most managers do not enjoy this process and would prefer to avoid it. Their failure to take prompt negative action has in fact resulted in organizational losses. In a few cases, the flow of work has been altered to bypass an individual in the hope that he will take the hint and remove himself. On other occasions, a job has been abolished, thus necessitating a layoff. After the employee has left the organization, the duties may be reconstituted and a person hired under a slightly different job title. There are still other occasions when a resignation has been negotiated or the employee "promoted" to a less essential job. Some managers prefer to pay for the privilege of not discharging a man by giving him a salary without reference to what the employee may or may not contribute aside from staying out of the way.

In short, the manager must, as we have said, accept the need for some form of negative disciplinary action. Though the overwhelming majority of employees may be good industrious citizens, there will usually be a minority requiring more than positive stimuli. Fortunately, cases requiring penalties are few in terms of total employees and man-hours. And yet, these few cases are explosive in the extreme. Approximately half of all grievance cases appealed to an impartial arbitrator by the labor unions involve disciplinary action. What is even more sobering is that in approximately half of *these* cases, the individual's position is upheld and management is either reversed or its decision substantially modified.[5] With the union exercising a watch-dog function over the

---

[5] Cf., *Industrial Relations News* (August, 1960), and American Arbitration Association, *Procedural and Substantive Aspects of Labor-Management Arbitration: An AAA Research Report* (New York, 1957), p. 27.

disciplinary action taken by managers, it is important that it be undertaken in a judicious and fair manner.

REASONS FOR UNDESIRABLE BEHAVIOR

Why do people commit acts calling for disciplinary action? In many instances, the environments structured by management tend to evoke this type of behavior. For example, as Argyris has pointed out, management has sometimes structured jobs which are highly specialized, routine, and boring to many workers.[6] In addition, if it is a job which does not lead anywhere, the employee may express his resentment by striking back through acts which management cannot tolerate. A forward looking disciplinary attitude would consider, then, not only the illegality of the act but the possible reasons for that act. Perhaps either a modification of jobs can be introduced or an improved matching of man to job effected. In many instances, neither will be possible, in which case discipline will have to be applied—hopefully, again, with a degree of understanding. As Argyris points out, in time the offenders will probably change from an attitude of active rebellion to one of apathetic acceptance. This would be sufficient in terms of Dubin's notion that the majority of employees maintains only neutral attitudes toward the organization, its management, and their jobs.[7]

Much employee resentment can no doubt be attributed to the employee's frustration, to highly autocratic and domineering management. One reaction to frustration is that of escape, either by means of excessive absenteeism or tardiness. Gambling, drinking on the job, soldiering, and daydreaming may also constitute attempts to adjust to otherwise intolerable situations. Other offending acts are caused by fear—the fear of working oneself out of a job or the fear of the pressures of informal groups whose norms require rebellion against authority. Acts committed in obvious defiance of authorized orders and policies are not, as we can see, subject to simple analysis.

In the sections that follow, one approach to constructive disciplinary action will be presented. It will be divided into two parts: (1) guides to disciplinary action and (2) elements of a disciplinary action program. This approach, though positive and constructive, is entirely consistent with traditional management theory, as it emphasizes principles and preplanned programs. Though the behaviorists contend that no such principles have ever been validated, the study of managerial practices has resulted in generalizations derived from a distillation of these practices. These guides can definitely be applied to condition future behavior.

[6] See Chapter 6.
[7] See Chapter 6.

GUIDES TO DISCIPLINARY ACTION

Though the following generalizations have not been validated in controlled experiments, they are regarded by many experienced managers as practices and approaches which are more likely to help than to hurt. The objective in each is to penalize an act which is contrary to necessary organization norms and to take this action in such a manner as to educate and condition toward more desirable future behavior.

1. The manager should exhibit the attitude of assuming that all employees desire to conform to reasonable organization requirements.
2. The act, rather than the actor, should be condemned.
3. Promptness is important in taking negative disciplinary action.
4. Negative disciplinary acts should be administered in private.
5. Listening, understanding, and consulting have priority in cases seeming to call for disciplinary action.
6. Consistency and flexibility in the administration of disciplinary action is highly essential.
7. The application of a penalty should always carry with it a constructive element.
8. The manager should determine the degree of success or failure of the disciplinary action taken.

Manager Attitude

The basic attitude of the superior is a highly important factor in preventing or correcting negative behavior. First, the manager should borrow a page from McGregor and assume that all of his personnel, including past offenders, are basically industrious. If he regards the past offender with great suspicion, the latter will often continue to oblige him by providing the trouble he seems to expect. At the same time, the manager should make sure that whatever discipline he has imposed has been effectively communicated to and understood by the offending party.

Focus on the Act

As we have said, the act should be condemned as unacceptable rather than the offending employee. If he in fact is not acceptable, then he should be fired. If, however, we wish to utilize his service further, any disciplinary action should not jeopardize these same future services.

Promptness

Promptness in the application of disciplinary action should not preclude certainty about the validity of these actions. If one penalizes an employee unfairly or unnecessarily, the impact upon both him and his fellow employees is severe. Yet, on the other hand, if corrective punishment is too long delayed, the relationship between the penalty and the offensive act becomes hazy. The longer the delay, the more one forgets and the more it is felt that the punishment is not deserved. Though the distastefulness of negative disciplinary action leads many to postpone it as long as possible, this very postponement helps to destroy any positive educational effects for the future.

Privacy

One of the most frequently cited principles of disciplinary action is that concerning privacy. Inasmuch as such action definitely impinges upon the ego of the subordinate, it is usually better practice to administer it in private. In this way, the person concerned can save "face" among his colleagues even through the grapevine may carry the news of his chastisement. But like all principles of management, generalizations can be applied only to a degree. There are some people who are merely amused by a private reprimand. In such cases, a public reprimand may have a more desirable effect. For most people, however, behavior in the future is more likely to be improved if necessary disciplinary action is administered in private. There is less chance of future resentment and a greater possibility of future cooperation.

Careful Investigation

If the disciplinary interview is being conducted in private, the person involved must be asked for his side of the story. It is too easy in the heat of a situation for the manager to lose his temper. Let us assume, for example, that the subordinate has a history of tardiness for which he has been warned repeatedly. On one particular occasion when he is needed most, he is again late. Upon his reporting to work he is summarily dismissed and ordered to leave the premises. On this *one* occasion, however, he had an excellent reason for being late, and discipline on this occasion was patently unfair. Disciplinary action is such a volatile force that the manager must always be certain he is on solid ground. In addition, he should attempt to consult with other managers about difficult cases. Obtaining another's opinion is not necessarily a sign of weakness.

Consistency and Flexibility

The next two guides are both highly important, though somewhat conflicting. Consistency requires that offending persons be treated equally for similar offenses; it is based on a set of rules with corresponding penalties for first offense, second offense, etc. Equal treatment reduces the possibilities of favoritism, thereby stimulating greater group acceptance of penalties. Yet, people and conditions are *never* the same. For example, two individuals are both discovered away from their authorized work positions. One is rather retiring in nature, timid, and easily influenced by others. The other is brassy and self-confident. To mete out identical penalties would be *inconsistent* because of differences between the two cases. Or, one employee may have been with the company for six months, the other for 20 years. One may be a very low skilled, expendable employee and the other a key individual whose loss to the organization would be serious. Indeed, the offenses might have occurred at two different times, with one employee absent from his work place during a slack period and the other absent while things were highly rushed.

In considering a particular offense, the superior should be able to adjust to such elements as (1) the intent of the offender; (2) extenuating circumstances; (3) the past record of the offender; (4) whether this offense constitutes a test case and possible precedent for the future; and (5) whether a seemingly inconsistent treatment can be justified to the offender, the employee group, the union, and possibly an arbitrator. If the supervisor makes an attempt to administer completely identical penalties for seemingly identical offenses, he may be unduly severe with one and excessively lenient with the other. Consistency is highly important because it promotes predictability and acceptance. But because of the variability of people and situations, an element of flexibility must be present. This is not to say that in some organizations, where there has been considerable trouble between management and employees or management and union, a legalistic approach emphasizing consistency above flexibility may be necessary. If, on the other hand, relationships are better and if supervisors are skilled in human relations, more flexibility can be introduced. The ideal is, in short, "predictability but not inflexibility."

A Constructive Element

In the administration of disciplinary action, the penalty itself is negative in that it involves the loss of a privilege, reduced self-esteem, etc. But, if one is to remain true to the goal of conditioning future behavior, instead of merely punishing past acts, every penalty should carry with it a constructive element.

First, the manager should make sure that the offender understands that his act was contrary to formal organizational requirements and that such requirements are necessary to secure coordinated action. But more than this, the offending individual should be counseled concerning what behavior will be required of him and how he can best avoid similar disciplinary action in the future.

Follow-Up

Finally, there must be some attempt to ascertain the success of the managerial action taken (did the penalty have the requisite conditioning effect?). Yet the manager must be intelligent enough to follow up in a manner that does not invite the resentment which the first guide is designed to avoid. If he discovers that the offending individual has not changed and seems to be inviting more disciplinary action, he must re-examine what has transpired in an attempt to discover the causes of this attitude. Admittedly, in a competitive free enterprise situation, there are limits to this process of analysis in terms of both time and managerial skill. Yet these should not deter the manager from at least trying to come to terms with the offender and the reasons for the offense.

DISCIPLINARY STYLES

Just as there are general styles of leadership, a manager tends to develop a basic style in administering disciplinary action. Perhaps the easiest, but not necessarily the most effective, style is one of legalism. Rules are made to be enforced and the only problem is one of ascertaining the facts concerning the violation or lack of violation. Consistency of rule application is the keynote, e.g., a rule is a rule is a rule.

In an interesting experimental approach, Shull and Cummings have identified five disciplinary styles which can be located on a traditional-behavioral continuum.[8] The first on the traditional end is labeled "purely legalistic," and the approach is the one described above. The system is enforced and protected regardless of individual personalities and circumstances. Moving toward the behavioral end of the continuum, a second style of "legalistic-judicial" is identified. Concern for rule enforcement is dominant, but the manager will consider possible extenuating circumstances. A limited number of exceptions to automatic application of the penalty are made when there is factual evidence of events indicating that punishment would be unfair.

A third style is identified as "judicial-clinical." Using this approach, the

[8] Fremont A. Shull, Jr. and L. L. Cummings, "Enforcing the Rules: How Do Managers Differ?" *Personnel*, Vol. 43, No. 1 (March–April, 1966), pp. 38–39.

supervisor will consider subordinate *intent* as well as actual events. Punishment may be withheld if the manager feels that the subordinate violated the rule unintentionally. A fourth approach of "clinical-humanitarian" is definitely biased toward concern for effective conditioning of employee behavior in preference to concern for maintaining the system of rules. It assumes that most violations are accidental deviations that do not seriously affect the functioning of the system. However, there may be a few employees who seem to violate rules purposefully and selfishly even when the situation is under their control; they will have to be disciplined, though reluctantly. The final style of "purely humanitarian" is based on the concept that rules are for educational, guidance, and developmental purposes. It also assumes that all employees are mature, Theory "Y" types. There is no necessity for a legal authority to administer disciplinary action; rather the necessary discipline issues from either self-control or social discipline imposed by the group. It is also highly likely that employees had a significant role in the original establishment of organizational rules.

In identifying the style preferred by managers, Shull and Cummings presented four cases of rule violation. The rule involved is "an employee shall be fined five dollars for being tardy a third time, as well as for any subsequent dates, within any given six-month period."[9] Employee A is a highly respected, key man scheduled to retire within two years and has been aided by the company in purchasing a small farm 30 miles from the plant. He has been late three times due to heavy snows. Employee B is a better than average worker, and is late a third time because of the birth of a son. Employee C is an average worker who is also a union steward. He is late for a third time due to a flat tire, and produces evidence of this through a service station charge slip. Employee D is known as "the joker" of the crew and is late for a third time since his wife wanted to ride into town in order to shop.

The authors suggest that if all four employees are to be fined, the approach is legalistic. If all except Employee A are fined, the approach is legalistic-judicial. Employee A is excepted since the company contributed to the difficulty in helping to purchase the farm under its retirement program. If Employee B is also excepted, intent has been considered and the style is judicial-clinical. If only Employee D is fined, the approach is clinical-humanitarian since only the man who appears to have little regard for appropriate behavior is being penalized. If none of the four are fined, the style is purely humanitarian.

In research concerning this style continuum, it has been found that the larger the group of subordinates, the more likely the legalistic end of the continuum will be used. In addition, those managers on the legalistic end are more likely to score higher in such personality variables as aggression, domi-

[9] *Ibid.*, p. 36.

nance, and autonomy. Most businessmen reported that they were more likely to fine either all or none of the four, thus emphasizing consistency over flexibility.

Consistency of rule application is the easy way out for the supervisor. It may be the only way when a union is present or there are bad relations between subordinates and managers. Certainly, the more complex styles are the intermediate ones where the manager is attempting to maximize total value, that is, preserving the essence of the system while simultaneously meeting developmental needs of individuals. The supervisor should be neither completely oriented to the system nor exclusively concerned with needs and aspirations of people within the system. In making his decision, he must also attempt to assess the impact upon the remaining members of the group.

It has also been pointed out by politically-oriented behaviorists that disciplinary rules are bargaining chips given to immediate supervisors by the organization. Their lack of enforcement can be traded to subordinates in return for desired behavior. For example, even though there is a "no-floating around" rule during working hours, the supervisor may not "see" employees who sneak off for a smoke when production is up, employees are being cooperative, and things are going well. If the group or a particular individual becomes troublesome, the supervisor's eyesight improves and he invokes the prescribed rule. Employees are quick to assess the degree to which a supervisor is willing to develop an indulgency pattern in return for desired attitudes and behavior. Rules can be either used or not used, and both approaches have their values.

In a role-playing case concerning the enforcement of a safety rule, over 85 percent of 150 first-line supervisors indicated that they would not apply a penalty to a key man caught working without his safety glasses.[10] Devising a rule is an easy impersonal task; its enforcement is highly personal and difficult. In the area of safety in particular, the emphasis is usually upon education and development rather than enforcement. Perhaps the humanitarian style is more appropriate in safety because of the greater overlap of organizational and human interests.

ELEMENTS OF A DISCIPLINARY ACTION PROGRAM

Given the objective of disciplinary action, some formal provision for a program designed to attain this objective should be made. This program should contain the following elements:

1. Written rules and regulations.
2. Authorized penalties.

[10] R. H. Magee, "How to Build Motivation into Safety Rules," *Personnel Journal,* Vol. 46, No. 2 (February, 1967), p. 88.

3. Disciplinary action records.
4. Organizational relationships among:
   a. immediate supervisors
   b. higher management
   c. the personnel department
   d. the labor union
   e. the employee group
5. Right of appeal.

Disciplinary Code

If one is to influence behavior it is necessary for subordinates to be aware of the behavior desired by the organization. Various rules of conduct should be determined and specified in such areas as attendance, safety, housekeeping, etc. Many managers contend that the list of formal rules should be kept to a minimum in order not to suggest offensive acts, antagonize subordinates through emphasizing their employment in a rule-ridden organization, and in order to provide for the desired flexibility of disciplinary action discussed above.

Participation by employees and union representatives in the establishment of a code tends to increase cooperation and discipline. Employees and union representatives can be consulted as to the desirability and workability of specific rules suggested by management. In most such discussions, the employees themselves will have ideas which management has not suggested concerning additional codes.

One difficult task involves informing employees of the nature and meaning of codes of conduct. A popular approach is through use of the employee handbook, with supplementary explanations by personnel staffs and immediate supervisors. Furthermore, if there is an excessive number of rules, it is unlikely that all of them will be regularly enforced. Regarding enforcement of rules lying dormant on the books, employees deserve fair warning of their renewal. Rules should either be consistently enforced or removed from the code.

An interesting question is the degree of control that an organization can exercise over off-the-job behavior.[11] In specific cases appealed to an impartial industrial arbitrator, the general approach has been a functional rather than a physical separation of activities. If the off-the-job act adversely affects the enterprise, management can legally invoke organizational disciplinary action. For example, off-the-job communist activities are punishable only when the employer can provide tangible proof of damage. This has been difficult to prove in cases other than newspapers where their quasi-public nature enables

[11] John W. Leonard, "Discipline for Off-The-Job Activities," *Monthly Labor Review*, Vol. 91, No. 10 (October, 1968), pp. 5–11.

harm to be done to their reputations. In off-the-job fighting, the organization can discipline when supervisory personnel are involved; the company has the right to preserve its authority hierarchy. Fights among operative personnel are usually punishable only when they occur on plant property. In general, arbitrators are also reluctant to allow organizations to interfere with the private love life of employees. However, exceptions are permitted when "love triangles" contribute to real or anticipated organizational harm, e.g., an airline was permitted to enforce a rule to the effect that married crew members could not date hostesses.

Penalties

Management can avail itself of a variety of penalties which can condition behavior. Thus, it is not unusual for the list of rules to specify corresponding penalties. A list follows, in order of increasing severity, of penalties usually available:

1. Oral reprimand.
2. Written reprimand.
3. Fines.
4. Loss of privileges.
5. Layoff.
6. Demotion.
7. Discharge.

The oral reprimand can be of two types: (1) a tactful correction of a deviation by calling to the subordinate's attention the right way of operating or behaving and (2) reproof of the offender. With respect to reprimands, the manager can be quite flexible, varying from a mild form of correction to a severe "chewing out." As indicated earlier, a public reprimand is more severe than one administered in privacy, so much so that its use is not generally recommended.

If the offense is more serious, the reprimand may be written. Usually the employee is asked to sign the document or challenge it within a specified period of time. The supervisor's written reprimands are usually reviewed by higher management and the personnel department. After a designated period, such as six months, they should be allowed to expire if there have been no further offenses. If allowed to remain in the subordinate's personnel record for years, the severity of the penalty is likely to be far in excess of the seriousness of the offense.

Though many managements believe only in reprimands and discharges, feeling that the intervening penalties are more disruptive than corrective in nature, other penalties are available for consideration. The loss of privileges could include such items as (1) reduced overtime; (2) assignment to no-bonus jobs; (3) transfer to a less desirable shift; (4) loss of preference in machine assignments; (5) placement at the bottom of the seniority list; (6) loss of holiday pay; and (7) reduced vacation time. For such offenses as tardiness or leaving the work area without permission, fines bearing some relationship to the work time actually lost are sometimes levied.

The severest penalties are layoff, demotion, and discharge. Final approval of these penalties lies outside the authority granted to the immediate supervisor. Disciplinary layoff without pay can vary from a few hours to several days. Such layoffs are usually specified for repeated offenses. When the situation is highly volatile, some recommend the use of temporary suspensions in order to remove the offender from the scene. If, upon investigation, a severe penalty is found to be appropriate, the suspension can become a part of a layoff without pay. Otherwise, the suspended employee is reinstated with no loss of pay. His absence makes possible investigation and decision making in a relatively calm atmosphere.

Demotion as a disciplinary penalty is of highly questionable value. The effect on the employee is doubly severe in that he has not only lost face with his colleagues on a long term basis, but he is now "underplaced," i.e., assigned to a job for which he is overly qualified. Demotion for disciplinary reasons creates an organizational "sore" which can inflame and perhaps infect surrounding personnel as well. Most managers feel that if the offense is of such severity that a temporary layoff is inadequate, discharge is the only other alternative. Demotion should be used *only* in cases where the employee is unable to meet present job requirements or where reductions in the labor force require that those with seniority be kept.

Discharge constitutes industrial capital punishment; it involves loss of job and income, loss of seniority rights within the firm, and loss of any state unemployment compensation. As such, it should be used only for highly serious violations or chronic offenders who show no signs of improvement. Most organizations allow the immediate supervisor to discharge only members of his own department and not of the organization as a whole. Since the passage of the Wagner and Taft-Hartley Acts, all discharges have been reviewed by those familiar with labor law.[12] If any discharge can be reasonably interpreted as a means of interfering with union activity, it cannot be legally justified. The union contract usually specifies a managerial right to discharge for "just cause." However, "just cause" is subject to interpretation through the grievance procedure. If for no other reason, then, there should be a good working relationship between management and union.

[12] See Chapter 25 for a discussion of these acts and their effects.

Records

In a discharge case, records are highly important since the case will most likely be appealed to an arbitrator. Such records will often persuade the union not to fight a particular case, even though union representatives normally feel obliged to push such cases as far as possible. These records should provide at least two types of evidence: (1) an accurate statement of the offense or offenses, and the corresponding penalties, and (2) a statement of management's efforts to correct and condition the behavior of the offender through advice, warnings, and assistance. Evidence of a lack of such aid has led to the reversal or alteration of many managerial disciplinary actions.

Organization

In addition to the offending employee, there are at least five other important organization elements involved in the disciplinary situation: the immediate supervisor, higher management, the personnel department, the labor union, and the employee group. Many practitioners and theorists would insist that *all* disciplinary action must be administered by the immediate supervisor regardless of who might have observed the offense. This is consistent with the principles of unity of command and single accountability. The right to take disciplinary action, whether exercised or not, is considered to be a crucial component of leadership. And yet, in this there is a dilemma similar to the situation discussed in group dynamics, where dual leadership is required for task and social goals. Negative disciplinary action must be administered by the *same* person who is responsible for the technical guidance of the work. At the same time, the disciplined employee is often more resentful of the supervisor who *enforces* a rule than he is of the persons in higher management who may have *formulated* the rule. The supervisor is the person *directly* responsible for actions which conflict with the subordinate's self-esteem; relations between the supervisor and the subordinate must, of necessity, become strained after disciplinary action has been taken.

As indicated earlier, a formal code of conduct is an important part of any disciplinary action program. Few supervisors, however, will rigidly follow this code. Informal and often unvoiced exchanges are sometimes worked out. In return for greater indulgence from the supervisor, for example, subordinates will cooperate more fully and perhaps even assist in protecting the supervisor from the actions of higher management or staff departments. Many traditionalists look upon these exchanges with horror, and they can admittedly be carried to excess. But it is certain that if the supervisor proposes to become a martinet who never wavers in his blind enforcement of the law, he is asking for a considerable amount of trouble, or, at the least, a minimum amount of voluntary cooperation. It is, of course, difficult to state a point at which compromises with official rules should stop. In theory, one can easily state that such compromises should continue only insofar as the long-run interests of the organization are helped more than they are hurt. If the organization wishes to pursue a flexible disciplinary policy, there must be capable and experienced supervisors who can establish some pattern of indulgence. If, however, supervisors are of more limited ability in this area, they should adhere more closely to the rule book, with authority being retained by the higher organizational levels.

Higher management, of course, also plays a significant role in disciplinary action. Not only do they have much to do with the formulation and approval of the formal codes of conduct, but, more important, they must determine the degree to which they will *support* supervisors. Higher management may constantly reverse lower managers in response to pressures from others; this is the quickest way to destroy supervisory morale, and supervisors may as well be denied disciplinary rights. If management's policy is to emphasize flexibility, it must support the supervisor—unless he has made an extreme error in judgment, in which case an occasional review and approval of supervisory decisions is necessary.

The role of the personnel department should be one of advice and counsel to higher and lower management in the formulation and enforcement of disciplinary regulations. Taylor's original functionalized organization structure provided for a "shop disciplinarian," a position which may have avoided the dilemma posed by coupling the tasks of technical guidance and administration of discipline. However, the modern personnel department is usually not in the business of directly disciplining offending employees. Where a union is not present, a personnel department may defend the disciplined employees when it feels the supervisor has been unfair.

Labor unions definitely play a significant role in the maintenance of discipline in unionized firms. The union stands ready to support grievances for employees who they believe have been treated unfairly. This duty is highly important in winning and maintaining the confidence of union membership in the goals and policies of the union. In this area, the informal agreement also plays a part. A union may sacrifice the interests of a single employee for the long-run interests of the union. By failing to push a grievance, the union may receive a more significant concession from management. It is useless to deny that such informal agreements exist, though many management theorists deplore such activities. They can indeed be carried too far and transform the rational economic enterprise into a political arena. And yet, some bending of the rules may effect more progress toward organization goals than a pious insistence on a no-deviation policy.

Finally, the informal employee group is an organization element which cannot be ignored in the disciplinary process. Thus, management's decision in disciplinary cases is affected not only by the possible conditioning of the single offending employee's behavior, but also by the predicted impact of such a decision upon other employees. (Will the treatment of this case be accepted as fair by others not directly involved?) In addition, the group is powerful in the sense that it can aid or hinder the efforts of management to maintain discipline, for the individual may react more to the informal pressures of the group than he would to the formal edicts of management. When group norms are in conflict with management codes of conduct, the individual is torn between acceptance by the group and possible disciplinary action by management. The power of the informal group should be aligned when possible with organizational goals.

Right of Appeal

Finally, every disciplinary action program should make definite and formal provision for the right of employee appeal. The entry of the union into the disciplinary process has forced this upon many business organizations. Over 90 percent of firms with union contracts have formal grievance procedures leading to impartial arbitration by an outside third party. But even firms without unions should develop and publicize a procedure which will enable an employee to appeal beyond the immediate supervisor. This not only insures more equitable treatment through review by others but also stimulates greater employee acceptance of the entire disciplinary process.

To some, there is an inherent conflict between effective management and an employee's right of appeal. The fact that there is no appeal is supposed to insure prompt and complete cooperation and subordination to the correct and efficient commands of the manager. No alternative but compliance is always an attractive situation for a manager imbued with the ideas of efficiency and precision. And yet, the number of alternatives to compliance are becoming more plentiful as time goes by. Some have been initiated by government and labor unions; others, such as informal resistance, soldiering, apathy, and malicious obedience, have been developed by the employees themselves. Subordinates are likely to give more than is forcibly extracted from them if they feel that certain individual rights are recognized and observed by their leaders. A leader who is doing a fair and effective job will not be fearful of a review of his actions by others. The fact that the right of appeal has been developed so well in other areas within our society makes it doubly difficult to deny in the business field.

Summary

As is usually the case, there must be some compromise between extreme attitudes regarding disciplinary action. Negative disciplinary action has a definite and essential place in the management of any enterprise, but it is not the single, or even the most important, means of obtaining obedience to the wishes of management. Disciplinary action issues from and is representative of the formal authority of management. Such authority is invoked when actions detrimental to the organization are committed.

Discipline should be directed primarily toward conditioning future actions rather than toward mere punishment. There should be some attempt to understand why such acts were committed. In many instances, the management may have invited offenses through the environment which has been created. When disciplinary action is undertaken, the manager should (1) assume a normal attitude toward the subordinate after the offense has been corrected; (2) condemn the act rather than the actor; (3) take action promptly; (4) administer any necessary penalties in privacy; (5) insure that he understands the offender's side of the story; (6) apply any penalty with due regard for equity and consistency, while recognizing the importance of flexibility; (7) accompany any penalty with suggestions as to the avoidance of similar actions in the future; and (8) follow up to determine the success of the conditioning attempt.

All managers develop a disciplinary style that attempts to relate the needs of the organization to the needs of the individual. Certainly, the specific needs of the manager are also considered. These styles range from legalistic to humanitarian, and involve both judicial and clinical considerations. A pattern of indulgence with respect to rule enforcement is often adopted in exchange for cooperative and understanding behavior from the group.

If disciplinary action is to be handled well on a continuing basis, provision should be made for formal programming of many of its elements. Among the more important components of such a program are codes of conduct, authorized penalties, records of offenses and management actions to correct, and the right of appeal from supervisory decisions. Not only are the offending subordinate and the supervisor important organization elements in the disciplinary program; so too are the supervisor's superiors, the staff personnel department, the labor union, and the other employees not directly involved. Though most employees are basically industrious, a few will usually require stimuli other than those which have been labeled as positive. Management must correctly apportion positive and negative motivation to obtain the optimum result.

Discussion Problems

1. Why does an organization need a system of disciplinary rules?

2. How can a system of rules lead to their violation?

3. Identify varying managerial styles of disciplinary action. What are the considerations in adopting a particular style? Which are the easier ones?

4. Present the cases for both flexibility and consistency in administering disciplinary action.

5. What is a "pattern of indulgence" and what does a manager hope to gain from developing one?

6. Cite various guides of disciplinary action, indicating how each aids in conditioning future behavior in a constructive manner.

7. If a manager finds it difficult to get along with the union or the group, is the disciplinary program likely to emphasize consistency or flexibility? Why?

8. Discuss the nature and importance of the right of appeal in disciplinary action.

9. Discuss the roles of the supervisor, his manager, the personnel department, and the informal group in a disciplinary program.

10. Contrast the positions of a traditionalist and a behaviorist on the role of negative disciplinary action in managing an organization.

SUPPLEMENTARY READING

Davis, James W., Jr., "Rules, Hierarchy and Organization Climate," *Personnel Administration,* Vol. 31, No. 3 (May–June, 1968), 50–55.

Fisher, Robert W., "Arbitration of Discharges for Marginal Reasons," *Monthly Labor Review,* Vol. 91, No. 10 (October, 1968), 1–5.

Flippo, Edwin B., *Principles of Personnel Management,* 2nd ed., Chap. 20. New York: McGraw-Hill Book Company, 1966.

Leonard, John W., "Discipline for Off-the-Job Activities," *Monthly Labor Review,* Vol. 91, No. 10 (October, 1968), 5–11.

Magee, R. H., "How to Build Motivation into Safety Rules," *Personnel Journal,* Vol. 46, No. 2 (February, 1968), 88–91.

Shull, Fremont A., Jr. and L. L. Cummings, "Enforcing the Rules: How Do Managers Differ?" *Personnel,* Vol. 43, No. 1 (March–April, 1966), 33–39.

Steinmetz, Lawrence, "Is It Wrong to Fire a Manager?" *Management of Personnel Quarterly,* Vol. 7, No. 2 (Summer, 1968), 3–11.

Section B

Integration of Interests

Effective control must also include a concern for the attitudes and interests of organization members, particularly with respect to their reactions to the administration of standards (Chap. 22). There are often specific clashes of interests between individuals and the organization, and counseling constitutes one approach toward their integration (Chap. 23). There are also group interests which affect and sometimes conflict with management's desires for efficient action. Among the more important of these are various minority groups (Chap. 24) and organized labor unions (Chap. 25).

22

Subordinate Reactions to Control

In the preceding two chapters, we have discussed the essential nature of managerial controls imposed upon organization activities. The best of plans and intentions do not preclude the necessity for some observation of action and its necessary restraint and regulation. If these plans are carried out by machines and equipment exclusively, then this chapter would be unnecessary. Machines can receive commands, execute them according to program, report performance results, and respond to managerial or self-correction impulses. We are less concerned about subjective responses, particularly if the machine maintenance program has been effective.

If people are involved, however, management will have to be concerned with subordinate reactions to controls. People will often respond in illogical and unpredictable ways, at least from a managerial viewpoint. If the day should arrive when people can be programmed and controlled as effectively as machines, we not only will have greater control over enterprise activity, but will have created a situation marked by great dullness, boredom, and an excess of power for the manager.[1] Fortunately, that day is not here and one must be concerned with subordinate reactions to management control processes. Many of these reactions are such that management feels them to be unfounded in reality. Consequently, the following chapter will also consider counseling as a means of assisting individuals in adjusting to organization requirements. We shall see that though both traditionalists and behaviorists accept the need for counseling subordinates who do not respond to controls as intended, the philosophies concerning what constitutes effective counseling differ vastly.

[1] Several interesting novels have been written about this subject by such authors as Aldous Huxley and George Orwell.

TYPICAL REACTIONS TO CONTROL

It will be recalled from Chapter 6 that with an increased standard of living, the needs of the ego have assumed greater importance. These needs include (1) the opportunity to be recognized as a person of worth by one's associates; (2) the opportunity to maintain a sense of independence and control over one's life and destiny; and (3) the opportunity to achieve something of significance. It was also pointed out that the degree of intensity of these needs, as well as the particular modes of expression, are conditioned by the person's cultural background and previous experience. Thus, if the person's total experience has been within highly autocratic institutions, one might conclude from his behavior that his ego-needs were small or non-existent. He doubtlessly would not resist the inauguration of stringent management controls; on the other hand, neither would he necessarily exhibit any highly favorable attitudes or behavior. If, however, his background and experience have encompassed activities involving greater participation, his response to controls will tend to be comparatively free-wheeling.

Though one could maintain that most personnel in modern business firms are fully conditioned by autocratic institutions, it should be recognized that situations are changing rapidly. Management actions which were appropriate fifty years ago are highly inappropriate today. Personnel on all levels of the hierarchy are more highly educated. Offsetting power centers, such as the labor union, have become a significant and permanent part of the economy. It is also unlikely that progressive managements will be satisfied with the neutral attitudes of subordinates conditioned to highly controlled situations. Thus, today's manager must be concerned with possible employee responses to controls *other* than those planned for by management.

The clash between management's need to control for the sake of the enterprise and the subordinate's need to satisfy certain egoistic requirements establishes the basis for several possible subordinate reactions:

1. Purposeful deviations from authorized plans and orders.
2. Informal attempts to establish offsetting power centers.
3. Formal attempts to establish offsetting power centers.
4. Climbing the hierarchy to areas where controls are less oppressive.
5. Aggressive attack against the imposition of controls.
6. Apathy.
7. Escape through absenteeism and turnover.
8. Understanding compliance.

Purposeful Deviation

With regard to the first possible reaction, the nature and significance of the informal organization have been discussed previously in Chapter 11. But it should again be emphasized that the ego will lead some subordinates to purposefully deviate from the plans and orders of the manager. An objective of management control is thus to discover these deviations and determine what, if anything, should be done about them. Subordinates, on the other hand, often originate creative means and display remarkable initiative not only in employing unauthorized methods, but in preventing these deviations from being discovered by management. If the work done should not measure up to known management standards, for example, records and reports may be altered by subordinates. All managers must learn to understand that reported events are *not* identical with actual events.

Many purposeful deviations make a definite contribution toward organizational goals by (1) forcing an adjustment of managerial edicts to variabilities in the actual situation and (2) enhancing employee morale by allowing a degree of independence. It requires shrewd and experienced managers to determine whether discovered deviations are, in the long run, constructive or destructive.

It is also important to adopt a constructive managerial attitude toward unpurposeful deviations or mistakes. The right to fail or the right to be wrong is an essential part of learning under practical conditions. Naturally, a manager cannot tolerate constant and serious errors on the part of subordinates. But neither should he tolerate no error. "One of the greatest unmeasured losses in business and industry is the unrealized innovations inhibited by fear lest the attempt prove a failure."[2] Accepting successful behavior as the organization's due, and heavily penalizing mistakes will usually freeze the subordinate into routine, safe, and less profitable behavior patterns. Progress is often a response to challenge, and challenge entails risk of failure. If failures are not permitted, challenges will be ignored. Rather than prohibit failure, the manager should insist upon maximum learning from mistakes made by the subordinate.

Offsetting Power Centers: Informal

To offset pressures generated by controls, the individual may seek to join an informal group. If he discovers that others are under the same type and degree

[2] R. Alec Mackenzie, "The Right to be Wrong," *Personnel*, Vol. 45, No. 6 (November–December, 1968), p. 18.

of pressure, he is better able to adjust and accept this pressure. Thus, the manager who seeks to break up and abolish informal groups might also be eliminating one of the means whereby his subordinates can adjust satisfactorily to the formal commands he proposes to issue. The informal group can, of course, go further by instituting offsetting power measures and acts. The attempt on the part of management to enforce an objectionable work standard can be countered by an agreement among group members to resist these standards. At times, such resistance is accompanied by demonstrations, such as pounding on tote boxes, failing to attach parts to every third or fourth product on a moving assembly line, or a wildcat strike. Subordinates frequently reveal a high degree of creativity in devising means with which to convince management that a particular order is both undesirable and impossible of attainment. Tool bits are burned out at the speed desired by the subordinate, employees "drop" of exhaustion, the number of grievances rises out of all proportion to reality, and the frequency of visits to the dispensary tends to increase drastically. The worker must, of course, have the support of his group, for the manager is less able to deal with a group than with an individual. There is here, then, the foundation for a continued "war" between the formal control power of management and the informal resistance power of the subordinate groups.

Offsetting Power Centers: Formal

Once subordinates become aware of the extent and effectiveness of the power they possess, there is often a move to perpetuate it through formalization. This is why some managements are so intent upon *never* losing any of the informal skirmishes, though enough have been lost to provide the basis for an increased sharing of power between manager and subordinate. In some enterprises, employee representation plans have been established. In colleges and universities, these take the form of "faculty senates" which meet to advise the president on policies and actions. If there is full faculty support for these recommendations, the power of the representative group is materially increased. In business enterprises, it is more likely that these representative groups will be transformed into formally recognized labor unions. Chapter 25 will analyze further the nature and importance of this formal offsetting power center.

Climbing the Ladder

It is usually contended that management control is greatest and most oppressive at the lowest level in the hierarchy. Most of the analyses of the clash between the organization and the individual have centered on this lowest operative level, for it is here that work can be planned and regulated most closely. It is here that quantitative standards can be established and enforced, mechanical pacing can be introduced, and man can be watched as he works, sometimes with the assistance of closed circuit television. Thus, it has been suggested that one possible subordinate response is escape through climbing to higher levels in the hierarchy where there are fewer quantitative standards and no mechanical pacing.

It may well be that the subordinate will have to climb to the highest levels to acquire any significant measure of freedom. Schoonmaker contends that first-level and middle managers often have less freedom than rank and file employees.[3] Workers have unions to represent their interests against the interests of the organization. A managers' union is almost unheard of, particularly when foreman's unions were exempted from the protection of the National Labor Relations Board in the Taft-Hartley Act. When an individual attempts to negotiate with the corporation, the power is heavily on the side of the latter. Rank and file employees may speak against and criticize the organization with some degree of impunity; it is often expected of them. Similar expressions from a manager may be tantamount to dismissal; organizational loyalty, or at least lip-service thereto, is expected. The organization tends to interfere much more with the family and home life of managers than it does with workers. And many managers are frozen into their positions by extensive deferred compensation and pension plans. Finally, top management does all it can to convince lower managers that the interests of all managers and the organization are identical. Though this is not true, managers are more likely to accept this thesis than are rank and file employees, thus contributing to more docile acceptance of organizational edicts. Schoonmaker, like William H. Whyte, suggests that the manager must fight to preserve his individuality in the large organization. More specifically, he suggests that he fight primarily with respect to career planning and self-development. It is essentially a power analysis with the goal of increasing the power of the individual manager through making himself more valuable to multiple organizations. This would include (1) acceptance of some inescapable conflict with the organization, (2) acceptance that superiors are interested in the career of others only with respect to advancement of their own careers, (3) analysis of career goals, personal liabilities, and assets, (4) planning for opportunities both within and without the immediate organization, (5) willingness to participate in the "political game," and (6) constant monitoring of career progress.[4]

Leavitt and Whisler suggest that the jobs of middle level managers will be

[3] Alan N. Schoonmaker, "Individualism in Management," *California Management Review*, Vol. 11, No. 2 (Winter, 1968), p. 11.

[4] *Ibid.*, pp. 16–21.

subject to increasing measurement and control.[5] Just as Taylor attempted to perfect control of the operative employee, information technology and computers may lead to either the elimination or intensive programming and control of many jobs held by middle managers. There is little evidence thus far that indicates that the middle manager job is being eliminated, but the amount of control is increasing.

Robert Presthus also presents another interesting dilemma. In his book *The Organizational Society,* he identifies in most organizations three major types of individuals: (1) the upward mobile, (2) the indifferent, and (3) the ambivalent.[6] The upward mobile desires to climb higher in the organization, although he tends to accept the system of controls, satisfy his superiors, prefer the *status quo,* and view the organization as an instrument for personal satisfaction. Thus, to achieve greater freedom through promotion to higher levels, he must first appear to give up his freedom through adherence to the system of controls. Ambivalents, on the other hand, are more apt to move the organization toward change and innovation since they are more fully aware of ego-needs. To them, past practice is no guarantee of rationality and right. They tend to be more sensitive and more catholic in their views and will pursue personal goals with consequent reduced loyalty to the present organization. The implication is that traditional management will reward the conforming, upward-mobile type with advancement to levels of greater power and freedom and tend to regard the ambivalents with some suspicion. In short, one must conform now to be advanced later.

Aggressive Attack

A fifth possible reaction to the application of management control is aggressive rebellion. On the surface, this type would appear to be the easiest to handle because it can be so readily discovered. But as indicated in the preceding chapter on disciplinary action, such overt rebellion is not easy to correct, particularly when the controls themselves often serve to incite such behavior.

Another type of aggressive and non-constructive behavior by subordinates is an attempt to shift accountability or blame onto other shoulders. Too often, a meeting called to adjust these deviations deteriorates into individual attempts to shift responsibility to others; one subordinate might try to loosen controls in his area by tightening them in others. Some of this behavior is due to the essential nature of the formal control and accountability system, i.e., the need

---

[5] Harold J. Leavitt and Thomas L. Whisler, "Management in the 1980's," *Harvard Business Review,* Vol. 36, No. 6 (November–December, 1958), pp. 41–48.
[6] Robert Presthus, *The Organizational Society* (New York: Alfred A. Knopf, Inc., 1963), Chaps. 6, 7, and 8.

for answerability if a minimum degree of organizational control is to be attained. Yet, more of it is due to an excessively autocratic atmosphere. When the emphasis is placed more on ascribing blame than on solving operational problems, this type of aggressive and ulcer-creating activity is a typical result.

Finally, a third type of aggression is to mount an attack upon monetary compensation while resigning oneself to the impossibility of satisfying ego-needs. This will provide the means whereby the subordinate can satisfy his needs *outside* of the present organization. Some managers naturally deplore an excessive concern of subordinates for the dollar, for carried with it is a consequent unconcern for the welfare of the organization.

Apathy

There is, of course, the possible reaction of indifference or apathy toward both organization goals and potential conflicts between organization and individual needs. There is substantial agreement among psychologists and sociologists that this is the prevailing attitude of rank and file employees in industry.[7] Some are concerned about this attitude and feel that the organizational environment must be changed to stimulate greater interests, loyalty, and activity. Participation and job enlargement are favorite suggestions.[8] Others view apathy and indifference as inevitable components of those highly structured and controlled situations which must exist if coordinated activity is to be effected.[9] They concede that the work place for rank and file will never be a "central life interest" and that the worker will have to satisfy his ego *off* the job.

Absenteeism and Turnover

If the clash between organizational and individual needs is too severe, the individual can resolve his tension by partial or total escape through excessive absenteeism or resignation. These are reactions which management has long recognized as undesirable for the enterprise as well as the individual. Many research studies have been made concerning the true causes and the cures of absenteeism and turnover. Someone who quits a job because he can no longer tolerate his manager and the autocratic structure is not likely to admit it while

[7] Cf. Robert Presthus, *op. cit.*, Chapter 7, and Robert Dubin, *Human Relations in Administration* (Englewood Cliffs: Prentice-Hall, Inc., 1961), pp. 78–80.

[8] Cf. Chris Argyris, *Personality and Organization* (New York: Harper & Bros., 1957), pp. 187–200, and Rensis Likert, *New Patterns of Management* (New York: McGraw-Hill Book Company, 1961), Chaps. 2 and 7.

[9] Cf. Leavitt and Whisler, *op. cit.*, pp. 44–45, and Dubin, *op. cit.*, p. 79.

picking up his final paycheck. He is fully aware of the larger system of control, that his next job will be dependent upon recommendations from *this* firm. Thus, he tends to give a reason which is impersonal and does not suggest that he finds the enterprise or its management objectionable. It is a continuing research problem for management not only to identify the degree and location of turnover but to ascertain its fundamental causes.

Understanding Compliance

Finally, there is the distinct possibility of obtaining the type of reaction desired by the manager—understanding and intelligent compliance with directions and controls. It would certainly be unrealistic, as well as unfair, to contend that subordinate rebellion of one kind or another is the inevitable reaction to management controls. There are many subordinates who prefer to be directed by others. They have become used to autocratic institutions and would in fact be unhappy if the manager attempted to institute participation and permissive practices. There are also others who have an understanding of the control requirements of a formal organization and intelligently subordinate personal interests to the demands of this organization. These are the reactions which the traditional manager anticipates as he plans and controls the activities of subordinates. However, as has been repeatedly emphasized through this text, it is foolish to conclude that these anticipated responses will always occur. Thus, the manager must accept not only the fact that subordinate resistance will frequently occur but also that this rebellion can assume multiple forms.

There is, of course, a type of compliance which is undesirable from the standpoint of effective organized action. The pressures which frequently accompany controls naturally stimulate subordinates to provide the specific results demanded by the manager, even though the subordinates may be aware of the inappropriateness or imbalance of these demands. The goal of the employee becomes *not* one of doing what is best for the organization, but rather one of finding out what the manager wants and then giving it to him. If the manager should, for example, have a greater interest in quantity output than in meeting schedule, subordinates will tend to ignore or delay small orders and insert high volume runs to give the boss what he wants. If he prefers quantity production to preventive maintenance of equipment, they will run the machines until they disintegrate. If he prefers heavy output and gives only lip-service to safety procedures, the employees may give him what he wants but at the expense of heavy injuries.

There must be, then, a balanced set of standards and a comprehensive control system. The essential point made here is that control accompanied by heavy pressures will produce a subordinate reaction of prompt and specific compliance with managerial demands, rather than with the organization demands. Therefore, under these conditions, it is highly essential that the manager know what is best for the organization.

TYPE OF WORK

The nature of the work and surrounding situation not only affects the degree of control that can be established but also the attitude and reactions of the personnel involved. In highly repetitive, rigidly structured work, the tendency is to manage along formal and traditional lines, emphasizing precise scheduling, cost control, and detailed quality and output control. Though the attitudes of personnel may be hostile, their impact upon productivity is minimal because of the structure.

In the more highly varied jobs where the subordinate has a measure of freedom, behaviorists are certain that more permissiveness and less control will result in more productivity and creativity. Heavy pressures rarely result in favorable attitudes, and attitudes are more significant determinants of behavior in less structured situations. There should be an approach to control which is based more on cooperation than command and more on the individual's ability to regulate himself than on tightly structured controls imposed by others. The increases in productivity and creativity which issue from this approach cannot be as readily shown in varied jobs as can those resulting from structured, autocratic controls in repetitive jobs.

The different approaches to these two categories of work are also based upon a power analysis. When the task can be watched, measured, and paced, the employee has restricted power. When this is combined with conditions of job scarcity among the labor force, the power of the organization is greatly increased. This suggests an interesting question. Why should management be concerned with employee reactions so long as they do what they are told to do? In the regimented task environment, it is most likely that they will execute tasks as ordered. The manager does not expect and often does not want more; he does not expect and does not have to tolerate less. If the manager is concerned with reactions and attitudes under these conditions, the forces will have to come from either within himself or from outside the immediate organization. Some managers have codes of ethics which lead them to be concerned with subordinate satisfaction even when there is no monetary return to the organization. Perhaps a stronger force is existing or threatened pressures from without. Employees may well combine into formally organized labor unions who will force an organizational concern for their interests. Or employees and unions may attempt to obtain governmental intervention to force greater organizational adaptation to subordinate interests. Both of these latter forces have and will continue to be applied within our society. Thus the manager must be concerned with employee reactions even under conditions where he has almost total immediate control.

In considering the second type of job described above, it is apparent that the power of the job incumbent is greater. Since the task cannot be constantly watched, measured, paced, or even specified in advance, the organization is heavily dependent upon the incumbent for effective performance. As indicated in Fig. 22–1, there is a large area of overlapping interests between the organization and the individual. It is in this area that the behavioral pattern of management is most pertinent, e.g., subordinate participation in decision making, job enlargement and enrichment, self-control, etc. Much of the behaviorist's effort is directed toward demonstrating that the area of overlap is much larger than classical managers would believe, e.g., employee participation leads to higher quantity and quality of output. It should also be noted in Fig. 22–1 that there are interest areas where there is irreconcilable conflict. If individual interests lying outside the area of overlap are to be met by the organization, it will require the outside pressures of labor unions and government. We have seen this in such problems as subsidizing the hiring of disadvantaged groups and prohibiting discrimination in hiring on the bases of race, religion, nationality, and sex. It can, of course, be contended that these two examples lie within the area of overlap, that in the long run the organization will receive a significant return upon its investment. However, acceptance of this concept in the short run is not widespread, thereby leading to outside pressures to move the organization to desired social actions.

FIGURE 22–1   OVERLAPPING ORGANIZATIONAL
AND INDIVIDUAL INTERESTS

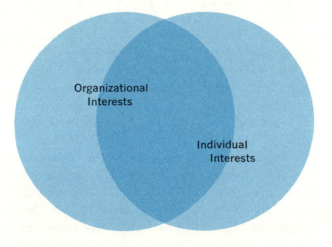

Organizational
Interests

Individual
Interests

In summary, the reasons for a greater manager concern for employee interests and reactions rests upon the bases previously given in Chapter 1: (1) improved productivity and profit in the areas of overlapping organizational and human interests, (2) outside pressures from labor unions and governments in areas outside the overlap, and (3) internal personal pressures of conscience and ethical codes leading to either a rationalization of overlap when such is not the case, or to an outright elevation of human values in relation to the technical and economic.

EXAMPLES OF CONTROL INSTRUMENTS AND REACTIONS

In Chapter 20, several examples of control instruments were presented to illustrate the problems of regulating quantity, quality, time, and cost. These factors must be subjected to some degree of control. As rational as the instruments of control are, they frequently bring about nonrational or emotional reactions. A few examples of these control instruments and the reactions they cause will be discussed briefly.

Budgets

Budgets, as discussed previously, force management to do an effective job of planning. They are also highly adaptable to control purposes, serving as a means of comparing actual results with predetermined standards of spending. There are, however, a number of side effects to budgetary control which are essentially human in nature.[10]

It must always be emphasized that any information that can be used to control the various *activities* of the firm can also be used to evaluate the worth of the *people* responsible for this action. Though the budget is set up on a balanced, coordinated basis for the welfare of the entire organization, each person tends to assume a more circumscribed attitude. They will explain away individual or departmental failures or attempt to shift the responsibility of failures either to other operating departments or to the persons responsible for the formation of the "unrealistic" budget. Thus, the budget establishes the framework for continued conflict within the organization. The very mention of the word "budget" tends to arouse antagonistic and emotional responses among those whose activities are being budgeted. As a result, staff personnel responsible for coordinating the preparation of the budget tend to become defensive while on the receiving end of much abuse. The problem is also

[10] Chris Argyris, "Human Problems with Budgets," *Harvard Business Review,* Vol. 31, No. 1 (January–February, 1953), pp. 97–110.

compounded by the fact that these same staff personnel are frequently in charge of the comparison phase of budgetary control. They must collect cost information and compare it with standards to discover exceptions. Their job becomes more complicated when staff budget personnel prefer to report these exceptions to their line superiors in order to *prove* that they are doing an effective job. A conference between budget personnel and lower officials may be more conducive to long-run cooperation, but it is not as effective as a formal report to higher management. Thus, staff-line conflicts serve to heighten the human problems involved in establishing budgets.

Argyris has reported other human difficulties growing out of the use of budgets in business.[11] Too often, budgets are rigid and excessively emphasize the past. While they usually report results, they do not give the reasons for the results. Whether or not the budget is realistic, it exists as a means of applying pressure to those who do not work within its pre-established framework. Thus, the budget is often viewed as something to be hated rather than as an instrument to assist in logical planning and control. Finally, there is a tendency to use the budget with the greatest pressure when times are bad. Costs must be cut in order to survive. It is during these same times that other pressures are felt by people, and the budget merely makes matters worse.

The fact that the budget tends to increase human problems is no basis for condemning its use. Some of these adverse effects can be reduced by more widespread subordinate participation in the preparation of budgets or by a change in emphasis in its enforcement. More attention can be given to the control and coordination of activities rather than to the determination of blame. In the final analysis, we cannot condemn completely the use of pressure as a constructive human relations approach; what should be condemned is an excessive use of pressure, to the degree that the budget loses many of its planning and control values.

Maintenance

As a second example of the varied and unexpected human reactions to a control system, we have Dalton's description of his experiences in an industrial plant.[12] Working as an employee of Milo (a fictional name), he observed an informal system of influence in the use of appropriated monies for the maintenance department. The responsibility for the allocation and control of maintenance tasks was located within the maintenance department, and considerable pressure for favored treatment was applied by operating executives. Aggressive and strong executives succeeded in obtaining more than their fair share of the

[11] *Ibid.*, pp. 97–98.
[12] Melville Dalton, *Men Who Manage* (New York: John Wiley & Sons, Inc., 1959), pp. 31–52.

appropriations, while less aggressive executives accumulated large backlogs of unfinished work orders. To correct this situation, a new department was created to control impartially the execution of maintenance work. Personnel in this department were even placed in a separate building to reduce pressures that might be brought to bear by operating executives. The net result was a *reversing* of positions of the high and low influence executives as the latter began to clear up their backlogs. The aggressive executives then began to attack the new control system as an example of red tape, as slowing down production, and as working from ill-conceived estimates. Finally, in response to a variety of informal pressures, the new system was abolished. It had been created to reduce costs, speed work, and check politics but was eventually undone by politics.

At this point, the scene of conflict switched to the relationship between the home office and the Milo plant as the former became interested in the maintenance problem. Within Milo it now became an issue of defending against the outside control of the home office, and internal bickering ceased. The home office concentrated on a single control point—the purchase of replacement parts. It first requested a listing of all parts costing $500 or more. Then, believing that a simple report would not lead to the necessary control, it created two new executive positions to administer the control program within the Milo plant. In an attempt to soften the shock of imposed control, the home office asked Milo officials to suggest possible choices for these two regulatory positions. Milo executives recommended two people who were generally regarded in the plant as mediocre personnel. Thus, those to be controlled hoped to soften pressures through influencing the selection of personnel responsible for the system's administration. These recommended appointments were approved by the home office.

The home office called for a first inventory of replacement parts, and the two newly appointed executives requested reports of plant officials. In view of the weakness of the new appointees, plant officials dragged their feet and refused to report the information. Finally, in desperation, the two executives reported the lack of cooperation to the home office. The result was an investigation and censure of plant officials. It was clear that regardless of their ability, they still had to be won over by the plant management. They were thus given a new office, flattered, and patronized. These attentions, accompanied by threats of reprisal, resulted in a promise of understanding cooperation on the part of the control executives.

Parts inventories were furnished to the home office. "Surprise" inspections ordered by the home office were, of course, made after the two executives were certain that the operating officials knew they were coming. A remarkably high degree of cooperation developed among the previously warring plant officials to protect against the pressures from above. The listings reported to the home office conformed closely to the "surprise" inventories. Thus, a working adjustment was effected. Reports flowed to the home office which, though not completely accurate, were good enough to permit planning and control within workable limits. The informal pressures and power exchanges enabled subordinate officials to operate within a personally constructed area of freedom.

Though not always as elaborate and involved as the example described above, attempts to loosen or shift control pressures are an inevitable fact of organized life. A manager would indeed be naive if he believed that his controls were working perfectly, with his subordinates responding logically, predictably, and in robot-like fashion. A degree of tolerance for resistance must be developed, without, of course, abdicating one's obligation to insure that enterprise objectives are met to some reasonable degree.

MANAGEMENT'S REACTIONS TO SUBORDINATE RESPONSES

The fact that there are many unanticipated subordinate reactions to controls provides the basis for analysis of *management* reactions to *their* reactions. A circular relationship often transpires. The manager plans and directs subordinates in the necessary work and establishes a system of controls. Such controls provide him with confidence that he is on top of the situation and that, even though he is not doing the work personally, it is being done as he has planned. Subordinates react in various ways, and subtle or blatant rebellion is not uncommon. If the control system is adequate, management will discover these undesired reactions. In line with the traditional philosophy, a crackdown is in order. New directions and tighter controls will usually be forthcoming. Heightened pressures by management tend, as we know, to stimulate further attempts on the part of subordinates to escape and to protect their own self-respect. If these escapes are discovered, still *more* stringent controls may be instituted. Katz describes this seemingly endless cycle as follows:[13]

1. The predetermined program is implemented. It is characterized by general, non-personal rules, division of labor, specialized competencies, and continuous checking to assure compliance.
2. Here the program immediately encounters unsought-for behavior as employees and subordinate managers seek to maintain their feelings of self-worth, their potential for self-determination, and their needs to have others acknowledge these capabilities.
3. Employees' reaction—Management's unilateral imposition of rules and detailed programming of behavior conflicts with employees' needs for self-determination and self-respect. Employees feel unappreciated, manipulated. They develop behavior patterns which enable them to resist rigid

[13] Robert L. Katz, "Toward a More Effective Enterprise," *Harvard Business Review,* Vol. 38, No. 5 (September–October, 1960), pp. 86–87.

task pressures and permit some degree of self-regulation through informal social relationships. Performance stabilizes at the minimum level tolerated by management. Employees tend to produce well below their capacities, have low involvement in their tasks, show little initiative, do only what they are directed to do.

4. Subordinate manager's reaction—Expected by top management to obtain the employees' compliance in the program without deviation, subordinate managers are likely to feel helpless, asked to do the impossible, and misunderstood. They try to escape their feelings of inadequacy by blaming "unreasonable and uncontrollable" employees or "unreasonable and unsympathetic" superiors. Depending on their temperament, individual managers will tend either to (a) insist on more precise performance of the program, instituting closer controls, closer supervision, more rigorous use of rewards and punishments, or (b) abdicate, contacting subordinates as little as possible, giving instructions, and then busying themselves elsewhere.

5. In either case, whether the subordinate manager cracks down or withdraws, his employees tend to react to his response by developing new behavior patterns. These patterns tend to stabilize at a new level of minimal performance and minimal satisfaction so that all the old problems remain while new anxieties are created.

6. At this point, top management becomes apprehensive and convinced that things are "out of control." Seeing widespread deviation from its predetermined program, top management is likely to respond to its anxieties by replacing the subordinate manager, applying more pressure for compliance, establishing more elaborate controls, or trying to train the subordinate manager in "how to get people to do what he wants them to."

7. Top management's action only serves to heighten the subordinate manager's anxieties and feelings of inadequacy. The proverbial "man in the middle," he finds his superiors expecting that he should be able to get his employees to perform strictly according to plan and his subordinates expecting that he should attend to their needs which underlie their deviation.

8. No matter what the subordinate manager does, the likely outcome is that employees will feel more unappreciated and misunderstood than before, the subordinate manager more helpless and insecure, and top management more anxious about its lack of control.

9. Top management responds by devising new predetermined programs, installing new controls, shuffling personnel, but not by questioning any of its original assumptions. Thus, the cycle of anticipated consequences starts all over again.

The pressure-escape-pressure cycle is established as inevitable and unending. However, it is more likely that a point of balance will be struck from time to time, providing thereby some satisfaction of both the organization's needs

FIGURE 22–2 A BALANCE OF PRESSURES

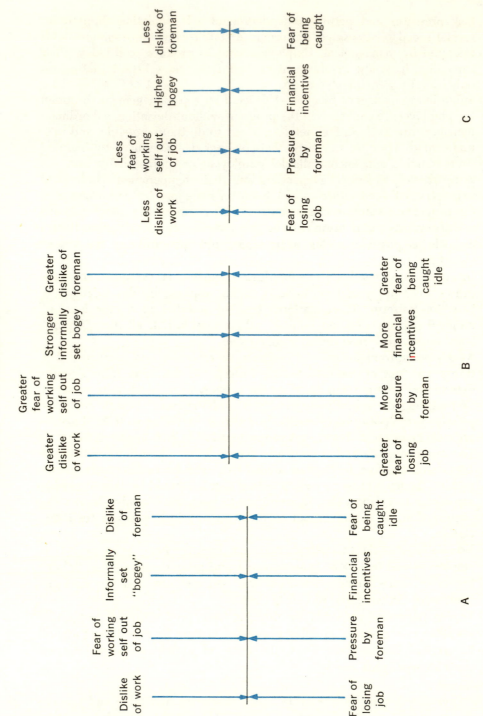

Source: George Strauss and Leonard Sayles, *Personnel*, p. 122. Englewood Cliffs: Prentice-Hall, Inc., 1960.

and the subordinate's needs. Management may well conclude that pressures cannot be increased endlessly, and employees will concede that some subordination and control are not only inevitable but necessary. As indicated in Fig. 22–2, these points of balance can vary from situation to situation. Each point of equilibrium is established as a balance between forces of management (pressures, insecurity, and financial incentives) and forces of subordinates (restriction of work, horseplay, and apathy). In all instances, the point is set at a level below capacity. If management wishes to raise productivity, one approach is as indicated in Fig. 22–2b—heightening pressures to force the output index up. These simultaneously stimulate an increase in the intensity of subordinate forces holding the index down. Thus, there is more production but also more pressure, more tension, and more rebellion. A second approach is suggested in Fig. 22–2c. Management tries to reduce the pressures which subordinates exert to hold productivity down by attempting to reduce their dislike of the job, the fear of working themselves out of a job, and their dislike for management and the necessary minimum controls. Typical recommendations made to accomplish this are more subordinate participation in decision making, job enlargement, and the creation of a more permissive atmosphere. In other words, behaviorists are demonstrating an agreement with traditionalists in *goals*—greater productivity and creativity. But they place less faith in the traditional approach of controls and pressures and seek to reduce subordinate resistance which tends to hold productivity down.

One possible view concerning the theory just described is that we must give up something desirable to gain some *other* desirable item, e.g., greater participation reduces resistance and increases cooperation, but it also reduces the degree of manager control. In a study reported by Likert, subordinates reported a lesser degree of *effective* control by supervisors who used excessive pressures. As indicated in Fig. 22–3, personnel feeling the *greatest* pressures reported that their supervisors had "some" influence over what actually went on in that department. Personnel feeling the *least* pressure indicated that their managers had a "great deal" of influence on what actually transpired. This study suggests that the typical fear of loss of control with the development of a more permissive climate has little foundation. Though increased participation will result in a reduction in the amount of *formal* control, the manager's actual *power* and *influence* will be increased through greater subordinate respect and cooperation.

SUMMARY

Control is an organic and fundamental function of management. When multiple personnel are supposed to be working toward a common objective, some coordination

FIGURE 22–3   EFFECT OF MANAGER PRESSURES ON MANAGER INFLUENCE

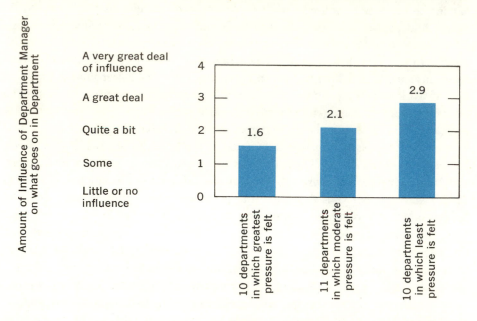

Degree of Unreasonable Pressure Felt for
Better Performance (as Seen by Men)

Source: Rensis Likert, *New Patterns of Management,* p. 57. New York: McGraw-Hill Book
Co., Inc., 1961.

and regulation are absolute necessities. And yet, the intrinsic nature of this
function, as compounded by specific techniques of execution, serves to impinge
upon the human ego and to reduce the opportunities for satisfying demands
made by the ego. Though many subordinates will react to controls as planned,
many others will attempt to escape through such activities as purposeful deviation
from plans, formal and informal development of offsetting power centers, attempts
to achieve greater independence, aggressive attack against the controls, apathy,
and escape through absenteeism and resignation. The manager must understand
the nature and reasons for each of these responses if he is either to take
necessary remedial action or merely to contain his own anxieties as he observes
behavior not in accordance with predetermined plans.

The concept of accommodation and balance of forces has merit in assisting
the manager to comprehend the nature of subordinate resistance. The type
of job, whether controlled or varied, will have much to do with the balance
of power, and consequently the degree of managerial concern with subordinate
reactions. Complete control by management must be accepted as an impossibility,
and resistance, resentment, and rebellion must be expected and anticipated. More
effort should be undertaken to reduce resistance and rebellion by similarly reducing
the need for it. This is contrary to the usual approach of meeting resistance
with force, which in turn stimulates more resistance and even greater force.
The manager must not rely on any one approach for accomplishing the ends

of organized activity. Pressure and force have a role to play in certain situations with particular people; but in still other situations with other personnel, pressure will stimulate more deviation than compliance, more rebellion than cooperation.

DISCUSSION PROBLEMS

1. What effect does the type of job have upon management's degree of concern with job incumbent attitudes?
2. When organizational and individual interests do not overlap, what forces are brought to bear upon the organization to force concern for individual interests?
3. Contrast the degrees of freedom from control of operative employees, middle managers, and top-level managers.
4. Describe the pressure-escape-pressure cycle.
5. If employees constantly do as they are told, should management be concerned with what they are thinking?
6. What is the nature of the suggested approaches and techniques that are supposed to break the pressure-escape-pressure cycle?
7. What is meant by the "right to fail"?
8. Distinguish the upward mobile from the indifferent and the ambivalent: What are the values of each to effective operation? What are the disadvantages?
9. What is the relation between personal defense mechanisms and subordinate reactions to controls?
10. Discuss the various kinds of purposeful deviations from plans and orders, indicating types that are constructive as well as those that are disadvantageous to the organization.

SUPPLEMENTARY READING

Argyris, Chris, *Integrating the Individual and the Organization*, Chap. 11. New York: John Wiley & Sons, Inc., 1964.

Becker, Selwyn and David Green, Jr., "Budgeting and Employee Behavior," *Journal of Business*, Vol. 35, No. 4 (October, 1962), 392–402.

Hicks, Herbert G. and Friedhelm Coronzy, "Notes on the Nature of Standards," *Academy of Management Journal*, Vol. 9, No. 4 (December, 1966), 281–293.

Jasinski, Frank J., "Use and Misuse of Efficiency Controls," in *Organizational Behavior and the Practice of Management*, eds. David R. Hampton, Charles E. Summer, and Ross A. Webber. Glenview, Ill.: Scott, Foresman and Company, 1968, pp. 245–255.

Mackenzie, R. Alec, "The Right to be Wrong," *Personnel*, Vol. 45, No. 6 (November–December, 1968), 15–19.

McGregor, Douglas, *The Professional Manager*, Chaps. 8 and 9. New York: McGraw-Hill Book Company, 1967.

Schoonmaker, Alan N., "Individualism in Management," *California Management Review*, Vol. 11, No. 2 (Winter, 1968), 9–22.

Strauss, George, "The Personality vs. Organization Theory," in *Individualism and Big Business*, ed. Leonard R. Sayles. New York: McGraw-Hill Book Company, 1963, pp. 67–80.

23

Change and Counseling

As the preceding chapters have emphasized, the function of management control is essential to the success of any enterprise. However, management cannot be concerned solely with observable actions. Activities are heavily influenced by the multitude and variety of attitudes that issue from human needs, wants, and experiences. A continuing theme of this text has been that of dealing with conflicts of interests—conflicts between the individual and the organization, one individual and another, and one group and another. Thus, management must be concerned not only with control but also with the integration of interests that are in real or apparent conflict.

In this chapter, two subjects, change and counseling, which both bear upon the task of integrating interests, will be discussed. The problems of change could well encompass this entire text: planning involves the determination of desired changes, organizing is concerned with their implementation, and direction and control insure that they be effected. It is important, however, to concentrate for a time upon change as it specifically affects individuals and groups in the organization.

CHANGE

Inherent in every organization is a certain fluidity which constitutes an evolutionary process of change. Man must always adjust to these seemingly insignificant changes through learning, development, adaption, and maturation.

The human problems of change, however, are most apparent in those areas where management itself has initiated the change. An example would be the development of staff from line. Conflict comes from the fact that the former, utilizing expert knowledge, is attempting to change the latter. The outside consultant is also hired to recommend and effect changes which will benefit the organization. The consultant, as an agent of change, has certain advantages over regular management and staff personnel. He is a stranger and can often obtain information which is denied to regular personnel, particularly in the areas of personal conflicts and feelings. He may even be more respected because of the very fact that he is a stranger.

Greiner has classified basic approaches to change in the manner emphasized throughout this text—a continuum ranging from traditional to behavioral.[1] On the traditional end are the unilateral actions of management. These would include: (1) by decree in an impersonal, formal, and task-oriented manner; (2) by replacement of key persons in the event that decree fails; and (3) by structural changes in jobs and formal relationships. On the extreme behavioral end, the impetus for change is almost totally with the changee. Examples of these patterns would be sensitivity training and individual fact-finding on problems about which the person has become aware in his environment. Toward the middle of the continuum are shared approaches between superior and subordinate, or change agent and changee. These would include group decision making for a problem defined unilaterally by superiors, and group problem solving where the superior permits participation in the definition of the problem. Other patterns could be added as previously discussed in Chapter 17, but the list as provided by Greiner would range from extreme traditional to extreme behavioral as follows: (1) decree, (2) replacement, (3) structure, (4) group decision making, (5) group problem solving, (6) fact-finding, and (7) sensitivity training. The last two involve substantial loss of control by the change agent.

In an analysis of eighteen studies of organization change, it was discovered that successful changes utilized patterns involving sharing approaches, that is, superiors sought participation of subordinates in decision making.[2] In the less successful attempts, the approaches were closer to either end of the continuum; five used unilateral approaches of decree, replacement, and structure, and two used sensitivity training or fact-finding and discussion.

Regardless of who may institute the change, the employee affected is compelled to react in some manner to the specific change that is proposed. As Roethlisberger's "X" Chart indicates in Fig. 23–1, his response is a function of both his background, including his needs and experiences, and the particular

---

[1] Larry E. Greiner, "Patterns of Organization Change," *Harvard Business Review*, Vol. 45, No. 3 (May–June, 1967), pp. 120–122.

[2] *Ibid.*, p. 125.

FIGURE 23–1 ROETHLISBERGER'S "X" CHART

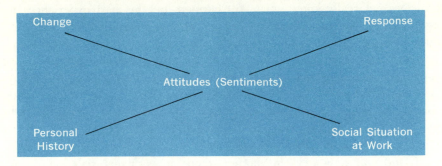

Source: R. J. Roethlisberger, *Management and Morale*, p. 21. Cambridge: Harvard University Press, 1946.

situation in which the change is introduced. One cannot predict from the technical content alone the employee's response. We may view the change "logically" and feel that any resistance is irrational. But we will never understand or be able to predict change responses unless something is known about the employee and his past experiences.

Resistance to Change

There are a number of possible sources for this often-encountered attitude of resistance to change. These sources include the following:

1. Insecurity.
2. Possible social loss.
3. Possible economic loss.
4. Stability of the situation.
5. Impact upon other portions of the organization.
6. Inconvenience.
7. The labor union.

Insecurity. Insecurity is usually suggested as the major source of general resistance. The present is known, understood, and has been absorbed. There is comfort in the *status quo;* man has worked out a relationship with it. Change introduces some degree of uncertainty. Organizations are so complex that a seemingly innocuous change, such as moving the location of the water cooler, can have far-reaching repercussions. To some, such a move is a symbol of management's unconcern for inconvenienced employees. To others, it means more traffic and interference around their work place. And to still others, it is another bit of evidence of the insufferable autocracy of management. Change, then, could involve a reduction in a current level of satisfaction. The changee often does not really know what will happen, but his past experiences have taught him to look for the worst. Change also suggests that either he or his methods are unsatisfactory, and thus he is condemned.

Social Losses. There are various kinds of social losses that can ensue from change. The mere fact that management wishes to impose a change is evidence of the employee's lack of independence. In addition, many of the modern technological changes tend to isolate even further the employee from his fellow workers.

Change will also involve altering informal relationships among personnel. A close friend may now work in another room, or work materials may now be received from a person of lower status. The complex of informal relationships described in Chapter 11 must inevitably be affected by the introduction of any change involving people. Established status symbols may be destroyed, or a lower status individual may be given a high status symbol. Social acceptance will be in jeopardy if a particular employee is favorable toward a change inaugurated by management while the majority of the group is not. The individual may have to choose between cooperation with management, and the friendship of his fellow workers. Thus what may seem desirable from a logical and technical view may meet with heavy resistance because the price in social relationships is too high.

Economic Losses. There are many changes introduced by management which inflict economic loss upon employees; in many cases, through technological advances, more work can now be done by the same or less personnel. Resistance to this kind of change is entirely understandable and most difficult to overcome. Even without the loss of job, change raises the possibility of reduced earnings, or of the same earnings accompanied by an accelerated pace or increased contribution.

Stability. If the organization's past history has been highly stable, it is doubly difficult to introduce a change. When personnel have not only adjusted to the *status quo,* but have begun to feel that it is a permanent situation, the inauguration of even the most minor change is considered to be revolutionary and highly disruptive. There are times, of course, when an organization which has pursued a policy of instituting changes fairly frequently has, in this manner, made changes a part of the *status quo.*

Unanticipated Repercussions. Few if any changes can be kept completely isolated; there are usually repercussions felt by other parts of the organization. These affected areas may bring about the downfall of the proposed improvement. For example, there is often a desire to change and improve supervisory practices; supervisors are therefore given a training course in human relations. Effecting changes in *supervisory* attitudes and methods is difficult enough; visualize, then, the difficulties which the supervisors in turn experience upon returning from the training course. Their subordinates had previously worked out a relationship with these superiors; now they do not know what to expect. The most admirable and correct action by the newly trained supervisor is likely to be met with a great deal of suspicion, particularly if it is inconsistent with the pattern of the past. Many attempts to change supervisory behavior have met with failure because other parts of the organization have been neglected in assaying the effect of the change.

Inconvenience. Despite possible social and economic losses, there is in any change a certain amount of inconvenience and extra effort required to make the adjustment. Old habits must be unlearned and new practices assimilated. Thus, inconvenience is a factor which will stimulate some resistance, but it is not the most fundamental source of opposition.

The Union. If there is present a labor union, its representatives are at times inclined to oppose on principle any change suggested by management regardless of the merits of the proposal. These representatives were not elected necessarily to cooperate with management and staff officials; their role is to protect the interests of the union member. The employee is usually more comfortable with a fighting union representative than he is with one inclined to cooperate with management on changes designed to promote the interests of the organization. Thus, it is expected that the union will produce some real or feigned resistance, even in cases where union leaders recognize that proposed changes are both good for union members and inevitable in their implementation.

Symptoms of Resistance

The sources of resistance to change are many and complex. The symptoms are more easily observed. There may be a considerable amount of griping and quarreling about the change, and a thousand and one reasons may be volunteered as to why the change will never work. At times, aggresive cliques are formed to combat the innovation and resistance may be undertaken subtly through skillful sabotage and purposeful poor work. Concerted slowdowns and wildcat strikes are power moves designed to influence management in its proposals and actions.

If management views the symptoms as fundamental problems, they will be at a loss in attempting to resolve the situation. For example, the many reasons given as to why the change will never work can be discussed and most, if not all, of them destroyed through rational analysis. Yet, it soon becomes apparent that the real source of resistance has to do less with rational analysis than with intuitive feelings. If management never attempts to ascertain the source of these feelings, it will forever be treating the symptom rather than the cause.

Suppression of symptoms without removing the cause merely channels the rebellion into other and often unexpected areas.

Approaches Toward Reducing Resistance

One Monday morning, employees of a midwestern railroad arrived at their office at the usual time. They tried the door and were surprised to find it locked. Soon they discovered a notice attached to the corridor wall which read essentially that effective immediately this office of the company had been eliminated. The rooms were empty and all equipment had been moved to a more central office some 600 miles away. No one was laid off, but if an employee wished to retain his job, he would have to be on the train the next afternoon headed for the consolidated central office. Should an employee wish to resign, his personal effects in his desk would be mailed back to him. Over the preceding weekend, moving vans had cleared the local office of all equipment and had transported it to the new office.

This, of course, is one way to introduce a change. The change may be technically justified, assuming the railroad is in serious financial difficulties. The manner of introducing the change is, however, subject to criticism. The Chamber of Commerce of the city attempted to expel the railroad from membership. In another state where the same events took place, members of the state legislature attempted to pass a bill prohibiting the removal of the railroad office from the state. The company's general approach was to make the change an accomplished fact, utilizing the power of the "new" *status quo.* Rapidity of execution was, they felt, the only answer to resistance which could never be overcome anyway.

Various suggestions have been made to soften the impact of a change. The problem is one of satisfying multiple needs of the organization and its members. Among the suggestions proposed are the following:

1. *Make changes in response to the law of the situation.* The first suggestion is that changes should issue from the facts of the situation rather than the whim or caprice of some executive. This also implies that needless, trivial changes should be avoided. If employees can perceive that alterations are necessary, however undesirable in terms of insecurity, they are more likely to make an effort to adjust.

2. *Disturb only minimally existing customs and informal relationships.* The culture developed by a group has real value from the viewpoint of organizational effectiveness, and management should work in consonance with these beliefs when possible. For example, a warehouseman has been accustomed to controlling the inventory of copper rod by means of two stripes drawn on the

wall.[3] There are more scientific ways of doing this, and one was worked out on paper using formula relationships among costs, volume, etc. The recommendation for change met with much resistance despite the knowledgeable and logical arguments set forth by the staff expert. Had the proposal been couched in terms the employee could understand, i.e., the two stripes on the wall, it probably would have been accepted. Perhaps the stripes were located at the wrong heights and the scientific approach could have placed them more accurately. As it was, the warehouseman refused to change a system with which he was comfortable and secure, regardless of any proven economic waste.

There are numerous other examples of technical changes which were modified to reduce resistance issuing from custom and culture. When safety shoes were first introduced, few employees would wear them willingly because of their appearance. When they were redesigned to resemble dress shoes, much of this resistance faded. Civilian consultants working with military personnel are more easily accepted if they are accorded a fictional rank, such as major or colonel. Instead of disparaging these customs and beliefs as "ignorance" or "stubbornness," the manager should reduce his own difficulties first by accepting the many values of group culture as providing a measure of security for individual members, and, second, by modifying his change to disturb this culture the least. If he once was a part of the employee's culture, e.g., a foreman promoted from the ranks, he is more likely to understand and appreciate the values of this approach. At times, selected personnel can be approached to aid in convincing a group of the advisability of a change. A staff expert, for example, may permit a line executive to announce a change, rather than present it as the proposal of an outsider. This may be difficult for the staff man to accept, but it will often reduce resistance to the idea. In addition management should be aware of the value of doing the least damage to existing status symbols. In the event one must be destroyed or reallocated, full explanations, preferably issuing from the law of the situation, will reduce any potential adverse impact. If the parking location of foremen must be moved to a less convenient spot, for example, perhaps reserved spaces can be introduced to preserve some semblance of a status symbol.

It is often advisable for a change to be introduced on a trial basis in order to encourage acceptance. Familiarity, through experience, with the nature of the change, as well as the assurance that one is not stuck with it, may reduce some of the insecurity. The manager must also appreciate the importance of allowing enough time for the change to be digested; he cannot expect complete understanding immediately.

3. *Provide information in advance about the change.* Such information can include the reasons requiring the change, its nature, planned timing, and likely

[3] J. M. Juran, "Improving the Relationship Between Staff and Line," *Personnel*, Vol. 32, No. 6 (May, 1956), pp. 515–524.

impact upon plant and personnel. Not all changes can be fully exposed and explained in advance of implementation. Secrecy may be necessary because of competitive reasons or when the change involves a particularly severe loss for those affected. For example, it was determined by one management that the closure of a plant would be necessary in approximately two years. The announcement of this fact, along with full explanation of reasons, brought about an immediate and severe drop in morale and production, as well as an increase in the number of resignations. Information should be provided, but its timing is difficult when the change will be heartily disliked by all.

4. *Encourage employee participation in establishing the change and/or its introduction.* At times, information is not enough to dispel anxiety. Facts presented by the manager may not be accepted as facts by the employees. In one company, a staff personnel expert suggested that additional older females be hired, and proceeded to substantiate this recommendation with all facts bearing upon absenteeism, productivity, turnover, etc.[4] There was much resistance provided by line superintendents, all contending that the evidence would prove that older female employees were undesirable. The staff man cut off his presentation of facts and suggested that a study might be made by the superintendents concerning how much the firm was *losing* by utilizing the older females they now had. Thus, the line superintendents were to discover their own facts. The net result was that each superintendent discovered for himself that the older female was an excellent employee in terms of absentee-ism, turnover, and productivity. All resistance to the proposed change in hiring practices faded.

The work of Kurt Lewin and other group dynamics researchers has suggested that participation in the determination and implementation of change will reduce resistance.[5] There is a feeling of lessened pressure upon employees and greater understanding of the nature and probable impact of the change. There is also likely to be an increased sense of pride since the change was worked out through consultative practices.[6]

5. *Attempt to satisfy multiple needs simultaneously.* Change is ordinarily introduced to advance the organization's interests, while often leading to economic loss for the employee. Many firms may, however, guarantee against such loss, e.g., no one will be laid off as a result of automation and other technological innovations. Or, in case of a change in methods or standards of performance, a worker's present earnings may be guaranteed. It is possible, of course, to go further by assuring employees that gains from changes will be shared (see Chapter 15). The employee is encouraged to accept, and even

[4] A. J. Marrow, and John R. P. French, "Overcoming a Stereotype," *Journal of Social Issues,* Vol. 1, No. 3 (1945), pp. 33–37.
[5] See Chapter 18.
[6] See Chapter 17.

suggest, changes on the promise of a share in the gains through productivity bonuses.

6. *Provide for means of releasing tensions resulting from the introduction of change.* There will always be some types of losses against which there can be no guarantee. Management should, therefore, be aware of the necessity for the release of emotional tensions surrounding these losses. Management should not attempt to meet hostility with hostility, nor emotions with logic. After the resentment has been aired, it is then possible that the employee may finally accept the change.

7. *Negotiation.* Finally, resistance to change can be reduced through the process of negotiation—an exchange of values. Negotiation is the primary means used by labor unions to effect modification of proposed management changes, and consequently increase the chances of their acceptance by union members. In return for accepting many changes in work rules, the West Coast employers provided a $29,000,000 benefit fund to aid longshoremen through early retirement and a type of annual wage guarantee.[7]

On a more restricted front, there are numerous daily exchanges between labor representatives and management designed to make more palatable the introduction of changes. To some, negotiation is the only answer to reducing resistance to change. Indeed, negotiations can help greatly to reduce *overt* resistance. But if the causes of such resistance still remain unchanged, the problem frequently will assume a new form. Apathy, griping, sloppy work, and quarreling can still occur, even though a deal has been worked out between labor and management. In effect, the union member may feel that he has *two* agents of change to deal with now, instead of just management alone.

Lewin breaks down the problem of change into three major parts: (1) unfreezing the present level; (2) moving to the new level; and (3) refreezing group life at the new level.[8] Before undertaking a change, management should first devote more attention to the unfreezing process, the reduction of possible resistance to changes of the *status quo*. Unfreezing is perhaps the most important part of the change process. It was pointed out earlier in this text that many attempts at executive training (hopefully a process of change) are undertaken away from the job at some remote spot in order to promote the unfreezing process. In coercive organizations, unfreezing can be promoted by undermining and isolation of social support of peers. This was a common and effective practice of Chinese communists during the Korean conflict. Behaviorists prefer that unfreezing be accomplished primarily though self-insight and awareness, believing that only if the person truly wants to alter his behavior will the

---

[7] Gerald G. Somers, Edward L. Cushman, and Nat Weinberg, eds., *Adjusting to Technological Change* (New York: Harper & Row, 1963), p. 82.

[8] Kurt Lewin, "Frontiers in Group Dynamics," *Human Relations*, Vol. 1 (1947), p. 34.

change be effective and long lasting. Such a process is most likely when the environment is characterized by trust and support. The moving phase provides the changee with the direction of change desired. Here, external pressures of reward and punishment can be utilized, as well as internal pressures of identification with ideal persons or organizations. The final stage of refreezing attempts to create a new stability, a new *status quo*. Change will persist only when provided with internal and external reinforcement. If the executive trainee actually changes while at a sensitivity training conference, the change will persist only if reinforced by the environment to which he returns. It must also be remembered that the new frozen stability will itself someday be subjected to a new sequence of unfreezing, moving to the new level, and refreezing as conditions evolve.

COUNSELING

Counseling is a major tool to be used in the discovery and integration of conflicts between the individual and his environment. We are primarily concerned with the organization environment, although emotional conflicts in the home can often be carried to the workplace, to the detriment of productivity.

Traditional and Behavioral Approaches to Counseling

The view that the traditional manager is completely autocratic and tough-minded in his approach to directing and controlling subordinates is an erroneous one. Traditional managers have long been aware of emotional conflicts on the job, and have attempted in their own way to reduce their impact. Western Electric is credited with the best known counseling program, which grew out of the famous experiments of the latter 1920's and early 1930's.[9] It is interesting to note that this program has been largely discontinued. It grew from its inception in 1936 to a maximum total of 55 counselors serving 21,000 employees in 1948.[10] With a new management taking over, the number of counselors was gradually reduced to zero in 1956. Dickson and Roethlisberger concluded that the program was highly successful in solving personal problems in a clinical situation, but the policy of counselor nonintervention in managerial processes precluded communication and discussion of many highly significant problems.[11] The new management felt that supervisors should assume a

[9] Helen Baker, *Employee Counseling: A Survey of a New Development in Personnel Relations* (Princeton: Industrial Relations Section, Princeton University, 1944), p. 11.
[10] William J. Dickson and F. J. Roethlisberger, *Counseling in an Organization* (Boston: Harvard University Division of Research, 1966), pp. 4–7.
[11] *Ibid.,* p. 477.

greater responsibility for human and labor relations, and thus the counseling function was returned to the line as a result of abolishing the staff. It should be noted that the function was not abolished, rather its organizational assignment was altered. (See Chapter 8.)

The traditional approach to counseling is consistent with the previously described traditional philosophies of planning, organizing, directing, and controlling. The manager wishes to know as quickly as possible the nature of the difficulty. With his superior knowledge of position and background, he immediately "understands" the problem, formulates the "correct" answer, and proceeds to persuade the employee to perceive this answer in the same way as he does. This approach is usually labeled "directive counseling."

The behaviorist, with his fundamental trust in the abilities of all men, relies more heavily upon the employee to solve his own problem. Rather than act as an initiator and problem solver, he views his role as one of sympathetic and active listening. This approach is termed "nondirective counseling." Both types of counseling will be discussed in the following sections.

Directive Counseling

After a preliminary statement of the nature of the difficulty by either the directive counselor or the employee, the former controls the discussion. He may seemingly permit the latter to volunteer solutions by directing a series of leading questions. For example, the employee's difficulty may be one of chronic tardiness. The directive counselor, after condemning the behavior, may ask why he has this difficulty. This will often result in a noncommittal response. The counselor then fires a series of rapid leading questions—Did you oversleep? Were you ill? Did you have car trouble? Is it the children? Are you overworking? etc. Not only does the process usually *not* lead to a discovery of the source of the trouble, it suggests to the employee a series of possible excuses that his manager-counselor might find acceptable.

The major tools of correction used by the directive counselor upon discovering the nature of the difficulty are advice, warning, exhortation, praise, and reassurance. All these actions emphasize the superior position of the counselor and the dependent one of the employee. The manager presumes he can fully understand the fundamental nature of the difficulty, and can determine and implement changes in attitudes or actions which will resolve the conflict. For the most part, however, he provides advice which is in response to his *own* needs, rather than to the needs of the employee.

At times, the directive counselor will make use of praise and reassurance in order to encourage the employee to overcome his problems, or to realize that no problem exists.

Directive counseling is consistent with the image of an all-knowing and all-powerful superior. The discussion can be as brief as the counselor wishes; whether or not the advice, praise, censure, exhortation, or reassurance is accepted depends upon the employee.

Nondirective Counseling

The philosophical framework of nondirective counseling is consistent with the behavioral approach to management theory. It rests upon a fundamental respect for the individual, a belief in his ability to solve his own problem with the aid of a sympathetic listener, and emphasizes the role of the counselor as one of understanding rather than passing judgment. The goal is to facilitate development of *self-insight*.

In the nondirective counseling discussion, the roles of counselor and employee are more nearly equal; there is no attempt to create a superior-subordinate relationship. Carl Rogers has broken the nondirective counseling session into three parts: (1) the release of tension; (2) the development of insight; and (3) the formation of new plans and choices.[12]

The nondirective counselor assumes that the employee is in the best position to know and understand his own problem. He must be essentially an interested and active listener, preferably one with the power to offer whatever help might be necessary. This requires a somewhat permissive, friendly atmosphere, with actions and statements which exhibit continuing interest but *not* judgment. Silence is also an invitation for the employee to speak further. At times, the counselor may make a summary statement, being ever careful that it is truly reflective and not altered in any essential manner. Probing questions are more directive but are often helpful in obtaining a fuller statement—such questions as "Could you tell me more about . . . ?" or "I'm a stranger to this situation, and could you fill me in on . . . ?" The counselor should learn to listen for feelings as well as for words.[13] Hopefully, as the employee verbalizes his problem, the situation will clarify itself and both he and his counselor will have a truer awareness of what lies behind the difficulty. The employee need no longer be defensive and can devote his energies to discovering insights about himself or the particular problem.

A difficult task for the counselor, particularly if he is a manager, is the handling of *negative* feelings. The employee may attack the organization, other employees, or the counselor himself. The natural tendency is to refute these accusations and demonstrate logically, or with the use of authority, that the

---

[12] Carl R. Rogers, *Counseling and Psychotherapy* (Boston: Houghton Mifflin Co., 1942.) See Chaps. 6, 7 and 8.

[13] Norman R. F. Maier, *Principles of Human Relations* (New York: John Wiley & Sons, Inc., 1954), p. 421.

employee is in error. If this should occur, the counselor has become directive. If he wishes to profit from the values of nondirective counseling, he must keep himself under restraint and accept these negative expressions as representative of the employee's feelings. He, of course, should not appear to agree or disagree with them, but should try to understand why they are being expressed. Though it is difficult for many managers to accept, having to listen to negative expressions is *not* evidence of reduced managerial authority. If he but continues to listen, it is almost certain that these hostile expressions will diminish and the discussion will turn to more fruitful areas.

As a result of the new insight gained by the employee, he can develop new plans, actions, or attitudes. At this point, the counselor may be of assistance by insuring that the employee has considered as many alternatives as possible. He may ask, "What would happen if you did what you suggest?" or "Have you considered such and such?" The expression of these probes must not, of course, reveal a bias toward any of the alternatives. There are occasions, however, when the counselor becomes convinced that resolution of the problem will require action by the *organization* rather than reorientation by the individual. In this event, it is helpful if the counselor has the authority to inaugurate such organizational changes. There is still a third possibility, that of arriving at no acceptable solution. In this event, the use of nondirective counseling might be condemned as worthless. But at least it can be said that listening does little actual harm and has the possibilities of doing considerable good.

Organization for Counseling

We have now reached the point, after having decided on the better type of counseling, of choosing the appropriate counselor. The two most apparent choices are either the immediate supervisor or a staff personnel counselor. In addition, there is a certain amount of counseling done by friends and acquaintances, as well as by outside professional personnel such as psychiatrists, psychologists, and representatives of religious organizations.

We have noted that nondirective counseling has many advantages over directive counseling. To achieve the necessary permissive, confidential, and non-judgmental atmosphere, many have concluded that specialized staff personnel constitute the best organizational arrangement. A staff psychologist can set up a zone of neutrality, while the immediate supervisor must work with the framework of his formal authority. On the other hand, the staff personnel counselor has little or no authority to institute organizational changes, a fact which is also apparent to the employee. The staff counselor must preserve the identity of the employee and can only make general reports to line management. In effect, then, communications are going up one channel—employee to personnel counselor—and possible action down another—supervisor to employee. For these reasons, the immediate supervisor is viewed by some as the most effective counselor. This was the conclusion of the new management of the Western Electric Company when it abolished its huge program of staff counseling.

When supervisors accept a counseling obligation, the temptation is to assume a directive role for it is difficult to be directive on the plant floor and nondirective in the office. The supervisor protests that nondirective counseling is fine in theory, but impractical in operation inasmuch as he is lacking in both skill and time. And, as indicated above, with the authority allocated to him, he could never hope to create a truly free and permissive atmosphere.

Keith Davis has proposed as one answer to this dilemma a third type of counseling which he has termed "cooperative counseling," lying somewhere between directive and nondirective counseling (see Chart 23–1).[14] Cooperative counseling begins with exclusive emphasis upon the nondirective approach. The employee is encouraged to voice his difficulties, and the supervisor accepts as his first role that of listening actively, interestedly, and intelligently. In all his actions, the supervisor must demonstrate an interest in and receptivity to subordinate problems, an attitude which in no way conflicts with his superior organizational position. Thus may be derived some of the values of emotional release and clarified thinking. When the supervisor is certain that he understands the problem, or when he is rushed for time, it is difficult for him to continue to allow the subordinate to talk. But it is essential for the supervisor to accept the concept that the subordinate must be allowed to speak without interference and with encouragement.

After the supervisor is certain that he has heard as much as the counselee will provide, he may assume a more directive role in cooperative counseling. He may reassure the employee that the problem is not really insoluble, or he may provide more information about the broader situation. If he concludes that some action is necessary, he will do this as the employee's supervisor rather than his counselor. The supervisor must demonstrate a willingness to listen and a desire to come to some conclusion that helps the employee and is

CHART 23–1   THE COUNSELING CONTINUUM

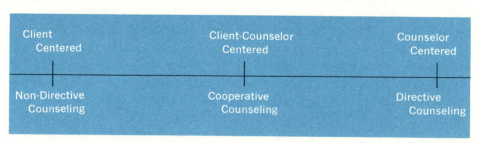

[14] Keith Davis, *Human Relations at Work,* 3rd ed. (New York: McGraw-Hill Book Company, 1967), pp. 361–362.

consistent with the needs of the organization. If the problem is a sensitive one, whose causes are outside the organization, e.g., trouble with family, the supervisor's role should be one of sympathetic listening *only*. Providing advice in this area is to be avoided. If the problem seems to require a major reorientation of values, the supervisor should recognize his lack of ability as a nondirective counselor and refer the employee to skilled help either within or without the organization.

Thus, the type of counseling that is appropriate to the immediate supervisor should be neither completely directive nor completely nondirective in nature. *It is employee-centered in the beginning and supervisor-organization-centered in the end*. It may not be as effective as the purely nondirective approach, but it will do less harm than the purely directive approach. At least the supervisor will have more information than he had before, and will acquire a greater understanding of the needs of his men. The danger, of course, is that supervisors will become more employee-centered than organization-centered.

A Note of Caution

Lest the preceding discussion imply that skilled counseling constitutes a panacea for all conflicts of interest, a word of caution is in order. Dealing with the values and emotions of human beings is one of the most complex tasks imaginable. It is highly doubtful that the typical manager will *ever* acquire the necessary skill to become a professional counselor. Such a profession requires long years of specialized training, education, and experience. Though a counseling obligation does exist for the manager, he must not attempt to convert the manager-subordinate relationship into one more closely resembling the doctor-patient role. If he attempts to become a lay-doctor, the subordinate may well make demands upon him that he will find difficult to meet, which in turn will increase the amount of resentment. The lay-doctor also risks loss of organizational perspective and may be unduly and excessively influenced in the direction of meeting the needs of the individual. On the other hand, the subordinate may be led into revealing things about himself that he will regret at a later time. Upon further consideration, he may become ashamed of having unburdened his innermost feelings to an organizational superior. A common reaction is avoidance of further contact with the supervisor, thus contributing to a deterioration of the situation.

SUMMARY

Change is an inevitable component of life both within and without the business institution. The very essence of management is to change conditions by directing resources toward a predetermined goal. Scientific management has largely been concerned with the quality of such changes, with the objective of deriving the most beneficial plans and actions. However, when human beings are involved with such changes, an additional problem arises—resistance to any alteration of the *status quo*. This resistance is derived from a general feeling of insecurity which issues basically from lack of knowledge about the particular change and fear of possible economic, psychological, and social loss. Resistance can be reduced by providing more complete information about proposed changes, stimulating participation in change determination, maintaining respect for the customs and culture of those affected by the change, attempting to reduce economic and social losses, and providing for release of the tensions that build up in the process of changing.

Counseling is one of the more effective approaches toward the reduction of conflicts of interests issuing from change. Both traditionalists and behaviorists are in favor of change, but they differ in the manner of its determination and introduction. Both agree that counseling is desirable to facilitate employee adjustment to changed situations, but they differ in the type of counseling most appropriate. Directive counseling, generally favored by the traditionalist, rests on the philosophy that the manager can best understand both the situation and the individual problems arising therefrom. An answer can be quickly derived which will suit both individual and organizational requirements. The efficacy of this approach is apparent in taking authoritative action; its values in altering the attitudes, beliefs, and values of the employee are questionable.

Nondirective counseling, generally advocated by the behaviorists, rests on the belief that the individual can best understand his own emotional problems and work out an effective solution to them. This is done with the aid of a nondirective counselor whose major contribution is that of active listening. Active listening requires a sympathetic, interested, and non-judgmental attitude. It is time-consuming, however, and necessitates a high degree of skill on the part of the counselor.

The major counseling effort must be undertaken by the immediate supervisor, who is lacking in both time and skill to use the nondirective approach. The staff counselor has the time and skill, but not the formal position to evoke change in the technical and organizational environment. Thus, a compromise type of counseling, using both the directive and nondirective approaches, is suggested for use by the immediate supervisors. The supervisor, who is predisposed to directive counseling, must move further toward the nondirective end of the counseling continuum, without, however, being transformed into a purely nondirective counselor. With the nondirective method as a base, the resulting directive action or advice will be more meaningful and more appropriate.

DISCUSSION PROBLEMS

1. Contrast traditional and behavioral patterns of introducing change.
2. Compare the continuum of change introduction by Griener with the continuums of participation discussed in Chapter 17.
3. In what ways can an organization unfreeze a person and prepare him to receive change? What ways are inappropriate for an open organization in a democratic society?
4. Was the great counseling program of Western Electric a success or failure? Why?

5. Contrast the traditional and behavioral approaches to counseling.

6. What is the role of advice in both directive and nondirective counseling?

7. What are the respective roles of counselor and counselee in both directive and nondirective counseling?

8. In what specific ways can a manager act to reduce both economic and social losses that may issue from a change?

9. Contrast the values of the supervisor as a counselor versus those of the staff professional counselor of the personnel department.

10. What is the significance of the statement that the change agent should adapt to the culture of the change? Cite illustrations of such adaptations.

SUPPLEMENTARY READING

Dale, Leon A., "The Supervisor as Counselor," *Personnel Administration,* Vol. 30, No. 6 (November–December, 1967), 6–12.

Dickson, William J. and F. J. Roethlisberger, *Counseling in an Organization,* Chap. 14. Boston: Harvard University Division of Research, 1966.

Greiner, Larry E., "Patterns of Organization Change," *Harvard Business Review,* Vol. 45, No. 3 (May–June, 1967), 119–130.

Hay, John E. and Miles D. Kumnick, "Counseling Industrial Managers with Q Sorts," *Personnel Journal,* Vol. 45, No. 9 (October, 1966), 558–561.

Lawrence, Paul R., "How to Deal with Resistance to Change," *Harvard Business Review,* Vol. 47, No. 1 (January–February, 1969), 4–12, 166–176.

Lundberg, Craig C., "Notes on Behavioral Change," *Personnel Administration,* Vol. 31, No. 3 (May–June, 1968), 45–48.

Lundberg, Craig C. and Robert E. Sproule, "Readiness for Management Development: An Exploratory Note," *California Management Review,* Vol. 10, No. 4 (Summer, 1968), 73–80.

24

Minority Groups

One of the foremost problems of our day is the integration of minority groups into the entire fabric of our society. We have been dealing thus far with various human problems of integrating individuals and groups with the formal organization. The essential nature of minority groups, however, lies *outside* the business environment, e.g., particular nationality, color, age, etc. The very fact that such groups are composed of a minority creates the additional problem of integrating *one* group with *another*. Some managements have indicated that though they wish to introduce and assimilate a minority group, the majority of employees will not permit it. This attitude will be examined at length later in the chapter. Though management has always felt a responsibility to integrate, in some manner or other, the *individual* and the *business organization,* either through positive or negative means, the obligation of integrating a *minority group* with a *majority group* is often less apparent.

SIGNIFICANCE OF DISCRIMINATION

Discrimination for and against particular persons and groups is practiced daily in every facet of our society. Decisions have to be made concerning hiring, firing, layoff, assignments, promotions, etc. Certain bases of discrimination are helpful toward increasing productivity, while others are both morally and economically harmful. We would hope that in making typical personnel decisions, few would object to discrimination based on ability and performance. But even here, the inroads of seniority in decision making have been marked, a subject which has been discussed previously in this text. Other bases are not directly connected with the job and organization, and their use is subject to more question. Thus, the Federal Government, several states, and many more cities have passed legislation prohibiting discrimination in employment for such reasons as race, religion, nationality, color, sex, and age.

On the other hand, there have been various laws which seek to promote discrimination on the basis of some off-the-job factor, which force the employer to consider variables other than ability and productivity. Most states have laws regulating the hiring and placement of women and children, the purpose being to protect the long-run interests of society. Consequently, a company may wish to avoid employing women and thereby dispense with additional separate physical facilities, restriction on hours, inspection by state officials, etc. Veterans are given preferential hiring rights in public service jobs in compensation for *past* service rendered to the country. Thus, a veteran may secure a position in preference to another who is more qualified.

Discrimination not based on job-related characteristics and contributions, then, is *wasteful* and *ineffective*. Talents are either misused or lost to society. There is also a substantial loss, social as well as economic, to the individuals and groups that have been shunted into less desirable positions. It is ironic that a long period of discrimination against a particular group will produce individuals lacking in ability and qualifications, which, in turn, will provide an "objective and acceptable" reason for further and continued discrimination. A vicious cycle is created which is very difficult to break. Pressures may have to be exerted by a substantial portion of our society to provide for the effective employment of minority groups.

The individual firm is a part of the nation's economy, and the economy is a part of the nation's total society. The first objective of the economy is to create and distribute economic goods and services at the lowest possible costs and prices. Yet, society will dictate that these economic processes be effected in a manner *consistent* with broader and more fundamental goals. Thus, if a society—national, state, or local—determines that discrimination for non-job reasons will not be permitted, the industrial firm has an obligation to adjust its activities to these objectives. It will be pointed out later in this chapter that most of these required economic adjustments can be justified on purely economic grounds; that is, nondiscrimination will *enhance* the productivity of the enterprise. But even if a change in employment practices should result in increased costs to the firm, society can dictate that social goals supersede the economic, and that the objectives of the economic system be *subordinate* to the general objectives of the total society.

TYPES OF MINORITY GROUPS

Though there are numerous non-job characteristics on which one can base his decision making and thereby practice discrimination, the following are some of the most prevalent.

1. Race
2. Religion
3. Nationality
4. Age
5. Women
6. Physical disability

Each of these will be discussed, with the greatest emphasis being allocated to the first. Discrimination in employment on the basis of race and color is currently one of the most pressing issues, and deserves extensive consideration.

RACE

Because of the energy with which their leaders are currently attacking the problem of employment discrimination, the Negro would constitute the best single illustration of a minority racial group.

Policy

In recent years, there has been a substantial quickening of the pace with which the Negro has pushed to reduce discrimination. Public schooling, housing, and public accommodations have received most of the attention thus far, but it is a certainty that private employment will acquire increasing significance. It does little good to open the schools, housing, hotels, and restaurants if the Negro is financially unable to use them. In the past few years, there has been a growing tendency toward the use of the economic boycott or "selective buying" on the part of the Negro consumer to force employers either to employ a greater proportion of Negroes or to promote more to higher positions. It has been the practice to establish certain quotas, in hiring or promotion, with which the employer must comply if the boycott is not to be imposed. When the product sold is a consumer good, such as gasoline or bread, these boycotts have met with a great deal of success in forcing managements to alter hiring practices.

In general, employers resist the idea of forced integration on a quota basis. They point out that the quotas levied often exceed the number of normal openings available. They also protest on the basis of inadequate qualifications of Negro applicants, maintaining that they are frequently more limited than those of white applicants. They argue for a *non-discriminating hiring policy* to be administered as they would any other personnel policy, with the emphasis upon ability and performance. The Negro, however, remains impatient with the present pace of integration and resorts to economic pressures to promote acceleration.

A review of various economic data will reveal the reason for this impatience. The Negro rate of unemployment is usually about double that of the white employee, for he is usually placed in jobs at the lower end of the pay scale, jobs most subject to layoff.

In the years between 1955 and 1965, employment of nonwhite workers increased at a substantially faster rate than for white workers. The ratio of nonwhite workers to total employment rose from 10.2 to 10.7 percent.[1] However, nonwhite workers continue to be disproportionately concentrated in the lower skilled blue-collar and service jobs. For example, 6.8 percent of nonwhites are in professional and technical jobs as compared with 13 percent of the whites; 31.7 percent of nonwhites are in service occupations as compared with 10.7 percent of the whites. Approximately 60 percent of the white labor force have high school diplomas, as compared to 40 percent of the nonwhite. There has, however, been significant progress in equalizing educational backgrounds. In 1952, the median years of school completed for whites and nonwhites in the labor force stood at 11.4 and 7.6, respectively; by 1967, these had increased to 12.3 and 10.8.[2] To compensate for these conditions, various Negro organizations, such as the Urban League, have pushed for a kind of "Marshall Plan" for the Negro; i.e., Negro employment should be *subsidized* by the employer. He should hire Negroes who may be less well qualified than competitive whites, and finance their training to develop the desired skills. Again, most employers and unions visualize a very difficult process in effecting an elimination of discrimination, without complicating it through inaugurating discrimination in reverse.

Despite these differences in philosophy, it is certain that the integration of the Negro into American industry will be accelerated. Firms can adopt varying viewpoints and policies such as the following: (1) continued discrimination even where controlling legislation exists; (2) a minimum degree of acceptance sufficient to meet legal requirements; (3) complete elimination of all discrimination, but with no specific action being undertaken—the firm's doors are merely opened; (4) a no-discrimination policy plus a plan of active and

---

[1] Joe L. Russell, "Changing Patterns in Employment of Nonwhite Workers," *Monthly Labor Review*, Vol. 89, No. 5 (May, 1966), pp. 503–4.

[2] Harvey R. Hamel, "Educational Attainments of Workers," *Monthly Labor Review*, Vol. 91, No. 2 (February, 1968), p. 28.

aggressive recruitment of qualified Negro personnel; and (5) the adoption of the Negro "Marshall Plan" to make up for past deficiencies—both preferential hiring and layoff to maintain and increase the Negro percentage.

The first policy is entirely possible because of the inexactness of hiring, placing, and promotion procedures. A person can be rejected because of race or color, and presumably be informed that rejection was due to inadequate experience, education, or some other objective factor. It is difficult to prove discrimination in any one specific case if the employer has been adept in covering his tracks. The second possible policy would be followed by the firm that is against any regulatory legislation, and studies the law to ascertain the minimum level of activity necessary to avoid legal action. The third policy is the one most likely to be adopted. The firm alters past practices by their *elimination;* supervisors, interviewers, and other managers are re-oriented to become color-blind. But no further action is taken. Often, the firm is surprised when few, if any, Negroes apply for jobs under the changed policy. They have found that they must aggressively advertise and promote their openness, and approach the recruitment of Negroes as a separate and special effort. Job openings will have to be run in Negro newspapers as well as in the metropolitan dailies. The image of the firm must be altered in the Negro community. The fifth policy is the one promoted by various Negro groups, but is, as we said, usually rejected by both employers and unions.

In a survey of 184 firms varying in size from 50 to over 500 employees, Luthans found that two-thirds reported having a specific non-discrimination policy.[3] Over 80 percent of these had placed the policy in writing. This would tend to locate them at the third level of policy cited above. Approximately 60 percent of the total number of firms indicated that they were at the fourth level, that is, their policy was supplemented with specific programs in recruitment, hiring, training, and promotion. However, it was reported that most of these firms were quite vague and inconclusive in describing the content of these programs, thus suggesting that they are still at the third level. Only about one-fourth appeared to have well planned and documented approaches toward reducing discrimination in employment. There were only a very few who indicated that they gave preference to minority groups despite differences in qualifications. It would appear that any type of "Marshall Plan" will require the active sponsorship of government and large sized businesses.

As an example of a special large-scale attempt by government and business to promote employment of the hard-core unemployed, the Job Opportunities in Business Sector (JOBS) program established in 1968 is the most outstanding. The task of government under this program is to identify and locate the hardcore unemployed, 80 percent of whom are Negro. The Federal Government

[3] Fred Luthans, "A New Look at Antidiscrimination Politics and Programs," *Personnel Journal,* Vol. 47, No. 12 (December, 1968), pp. 877–881.

has appropriated $350 million to subsidize unusual costs of training such as the teaching of basic reading and writing skills, personal counseling, and transportation services. The task of business is to provide the jobs and training. The implementing agency is the National Alliance of Businessmen which is composed of approximately 1,000 businessmen on loan from their regular jobs for periods of six months or longer. Henry Ford II, the head of NAB, has reported successful placement of 61,000 hard-core jobless in the first ten months of operation. Goals set by the President of the United States are 100,000 by mid-1969, and 500,000 by mid-1971.

Perhaps the most difficult aspect of the above specified task is the long-term retention of the newly hired person in the company. Over 85,000 were hired to obtain the 61,000 retentions cited above. After much experimentation, it has been found that highly personalized coaching and support are the keys to long job tenure. Turnover of those with personal coaches has averaged 18 percent as compared to 72 percent without them.[4] More specifically, an effective program would require such elements as (1) a specific job that the trainee knows that he is going to get, (2) training at a level slightly above that required to do the job in order to provide trainee confidence and supervisory acceptance, (3) job instruction primarily through demonstration, (4) frequent recognition of progress during training, and (5) special personal help in handling problems both within and without the company.[5] International Harvester, for example, launched a "New Start" program as a part of the NAB effort.[6] The company will receive over a half-million dollars from the Labor Department to provide pre-job training over and above normal training to be financed by the company. Special attempts to provide personal help are provided in the following ways: (1) a company representative telephones the recruit the night before he is to report for training and then picks him up the next morning, (2) attempts are made to recruit groups of friends rather than single workers, (3) company representatives mediate with police in the event that trainees have such difficulties, (4) breakfasts are served during the first week of training in order to develop the same habit of eating, (5) counseling is given in such areas as personal hygiene, buying on credit, banking, and diet, and (6) in the fourth and final week of pre-job training, the trainee is given a volunteer "buddy" from the department to which he will be assigned. The buddy is responsible for getting him to and from work, and orienting him to the plant during the eight-week on-the-job training period. Plant managers and first-level super-

---

[4] Frank Riessman, "New Careers: A Workable Approach to Hard-Core Unemployed," *Personnel*, Vol. 45, No. 5 (September-October, 1968), p. 4.

[5] James D. Hodgson and Marshall H. Brenner, "Successful Experience: Training Hard-Core Unemployed," *Harvard Business Review*, Vol. 46, No. 5 (September-October, 1968), pp. 152–153.

[6] "How to Turn Dropouts into Steady Workers," *Business Week* (August 31, 1968), pp. 64–68.

visors receive briefings on the reasons for and nature of the pre-job training. Of the 145 men hired thus far under the "New Start" program, only 17 have quit or been fired. Under a previous, less personal program, the record was 44 separations out of 50 hires.

Legislation—States

As has been indicated, there are several states that have passed fair employment practices laws. These include Alaska, Arizona, California, Colorado, Connecticut, Illinois, Indiana, Kansas, Nevada, Michigan, Minnesota, New Jersey, New Mexico, New York, Ohio, Oregon, Pennsylvania, Rhode Island, Washington, and Wisconsin. The oldest law of this type is that passed in New York in 1945.

The emphasis in each of these states has been upon education and persuasion to influence employers to alter discriminatory practices. The administering body is usually a commission whose objective is to protect the right of all persons to obtain and hold employment without discrimination on account of race, religion, color, creed, national origin, or ancestry. In many states, the law is directed not only toward employers but toward employment agencies, unions, and other employees as well. If a particular person feels that he has been rejected by an employer for reason of these non-job characteristics, he has the right of filing a complaint with this commission. The latter will conduct an investigation and if evidence is discovered substantiating the complaint, it attempts to conciliate with the respective firm. In most instances, this will insure the desired alteration of policies and procedures. In one survey of the experience of seven states and two cities, all but six of 5900 complaints were settled by informal conciliation.[7] Though there are fines and jail sentences authorized under most of these laws, the most powerful instrument of persuasion is possible damage to the firm's reputation and corporate image in the community.

If the employer feels strongly that he is not in violation of the law, the next step is for the commission to conduct a hearing and receive testimony. The commission may then issue a cease and desist order and/or an order to redress the wrong; e.g., fill the first available job vacancy with the complainant. In the previously cited study, five of the six complaints that went to formal hearings resulted in cease and desist orders.[8] These orders are enforceable through the state courts and the injunction process. Violations of such injunctions can

[7] Monroe Berger, *Effects of Fair Employment Legislation in States and Municipalities* (Washington: Government Printing Office, Staff Report, U.S. Senate, 82nd Congress, 2nd Session, 1952), pp. 14–15.
[8] *Ibid.*, p. 15.

result in fines or jail sentences. Research into the first ten years of experience under the New York laws reveals no jail sentences and very few fines.[9] Only in extremely rare cases has there been any resort to actual prosecution since the accent is upon education and conciliation.

With respect to the impact of such regulatory commissions, states having such laws have moved faster and further in the direction of opening employment doors to all persons regardless of race, religion, or nationality. In a study of the policies and practices of some forty-four companies with respect to the hiring of Negroes, state laws were given substantial credit for these firms embarking upon a formal program to reduce discrimination. Approximately half reported that their programs were instituted in order to comply with the law.[10] However, more reported that the basic cause was a fundamental economic need for labor. Other reasons were the desire to attract Negro customers and enhance public relations, specific pressures from outside Negro organizations, and the moral principles of the company's management.

Legislation—Federal

In 1964, major Federal civil rights legislation was passed by Congress. Though provisions concerning discrimination in public accommodations took effect immediately, those guaranteeing equal employment in business were delayed. In 1968, the last phase of the act became effective. It is unlawful for companies with twenty-five or more employees that are engaged in interstate commerce, to discriminate in any aspect of employment on the basis of race, color, religion, sex, or national origin. The Civil Rights Act proposes to eliminate discrimination in hiring, firing, apprenticeship programs, promotion, and job classification systems. Administration of the act is in the hands of a five-member Equal Employment Opportunity Commission.

Two other pieces of Federal legislation are also important in this field. The Walsh-Healey Act, which applies to firms having government contracts in excess of $10,000, provides the vehicle through which contractors can be regulated in their hiring practices. The major force is the threat of cancellation of current contracts and future blacklisting for further government business. The large size of the Federal budget tends to increase the effect of this law.

The Wagner and Taft-Hartley Acts, discussed more fully in the following chapter, have established a series of unfair labor and management practices that can be prohibited through the National Labor Relations Board and injunc-

[9] "California Fair Employment Practices," Merchants and Manufacturers Association Survey Analysis No. 45 (July, 1959), p. 3.

[10] Paul H. Norgren, et al., *Employing the Negro in American Industry* (New York: Industrial Relations Monograph No. 17, Industrial Relations Counselors, Inc., 1959), p. 36.

tions of the Federal Courts. In 1964, the Board revoked the certification of a labor union on the ground that it refused to process a grievance for a Negro employee of the Hughes Tool Co. of Houston, Texas. This precedent-establishing decision may open up a broad new battleground in the fight against employment bias.

Introduction of a Minority Group

Assuming that a firm wishes to embark upon the task of introducing a minority group for the first time, it is wise to be aware of possible *human relations difficulties*. Advance planning and preparation can serve to smooth the transition. In almost every case, management is fearful of "disintegration" through rejection by the present majority group. In the previously cited study of 44 firms, almost all managements reported that even though some trouble generally developed, it was nowhere near the magnitude that they had anticipated.[11] In general, managements are *overly fearful* of possible trouble. This emphasizes the obligation of management to *lead* in this area and not just react to possible power acts of the present employee group.

The first essential of such an introductory program is the adoption of a definite policy by top management. This serves the same purpose for the firm as the state law does for the community. If trouble does arise, supervisors are given more confidence by the existence of an explicit directive from top management. If persuasion fails, they can use the policy to force at least a minimum degree of acceptance.

The communication of the policy is of central importance. All managers must *understand* that the policy exists. As has been suggested previously, attitude changes are effected more readily through processes of discussion and conference, rather than through orders and commands. The philosophy and techniques of group dynamics can serve to develop supervisory understanding and acceptance of minority group members. Willing acceptance is always preferable to forced obedience. However, subordinate managers must be assured that top management means what they have said and promulgated. Employment agencies and the union must also be informed and convinced. As usual, actions in hiring and upgrading will mean far more than a planned publicity campaign alone.

A key issue is the *pace* with which minority members will be introduced into the firm, in terms of number, time, and degree of concentration. Two firms in Ohio happened to embark at about the same time upon a project of introducing Negro employees. Both plants had within them a substantial number of

[11] *Ibid.,* p. 94.

white Southern migrants, and both managements anticipated trouble. One firm decided to move quickly. On one Monday morning, the present employees were presented with an accomplished fact—some eight Negroes reported to work on jobs normally allocated to white employees. At first, there was a considerable amount of confusion and tension. For a time, a wildcat strike was feared. Management, however, had informed supervisors in advance and had worked with union leaders. As far as the employees were concerned, the pace was fast, the numbers great, and entry was localized in one department. No work stoppage ensued, although tension did remain high for two weeks.

The other firm pursued a different course. One Negro was hired and it was assured in advance that he was *more* than adequately qualified. He was placed into a nonsensitive job where he was not required by the work flow to interact extensively with fellow white employees. It was, however, a job which had been normally allocated to white employees. The way was prepared in advance by informing and educating employees as well as supervisors. After a period of little or no tension, this lone Negro was accorded a degree of acceptance by his immediate fellow workers. Management then brought in a second Negro and placed him in a different department. Various managements have discovered that the vanguard of these entrants should not be placed on sensitive jobs which require their checking and reviewing the work of other employees, e.g., an inspector of quality or a time card clerk. Many firms consider it best to place Negroes in various departments, thus preventing the establishment of white and non-white cliques. The single initial Negro entrant occupies a lonely and vulnerable position, for pioneering in any area is always difficult.

One could state that both of these approaches to integration worked successfully since there were no definite work stoppages. Yet, despite the pressures for greater speed by outside Negro groups, the employer usually favors a more gradual pace in terms of time and number. Most managers place greatest emphasis upon demonstrated successful performance by the minority employee, to be followed by gradually increasing interpersonal contacts with the majority group. At the same time, they wish to achieve a state of normalcy as quickly as possible inasmuch as the economic objectives, reducing costs and increasing profits, are still major organization objectives.

As noted earlier, a fair employment policy for a firm will require alteration of recruiting and hiring procedures, and the state employment agency must be informed. It is often desirable to work with Negro organizations such as the Urban League, predominantly Negro high schools, churches, and colleges. Successful programs have utilized such unusual approaches as the following: (1) Pacific Telephone and Telegraph Company uses walking employment offices—Spanish and Negro recruiters go to peoples' homes, barbershops, poolrooms, and bars, (2) Michigan Bell sends recruiting trailers to the ghetto areas, (3) Westinghouse Electric provides one-day plant orientation sessions for students from predominantly Negro high schools, and (4) General Electric took legal steps to open up housing for a newly hired Negro engineer.[12]

In the placement process, application blanks will have to be altered to eliminate questions bearing upon race, religion, and nationality, and interviewers will have to be retrained to assure equal treatment of all applicants. The problem of securing *qualified* Negroes has previously been mentioned. Often, their schooling and work experience are more limited than that of whites, and the employer will have to decide how far he will go in subsidizing this group. If the Negro applicant must be rejected on the basis of inadequate qualifications, frankness is important. Acceptance of such rejections is facilitated if it is realized that other Negroes have already been hired successfully by the firm. The Negro is sensitive because of past discrimination and any rejection must be handled skillfully. At the least, careful rejection records must be kept, particularly in states having fair employment practices legislation.

Concerning introduction and orientation of the new Negro employee, the supervisor is of utmost importance. Certainly, the new employee must be carefully oriented. Though technically qualified, he may need help in adjusting not only to the industrial environment, but to the probable "cold" initial acceptance by the majority. He should be placed in a department where the supervisor is both sympathetic to the 'company policy and respected by his present subordinates. The supervisor should speak frankly of possible prejudice and the necessity for patience and good performance. He should indicate that he and the company will not tolerate fellow employee actions when they definitely interfere with work processes or when they make it too uncomfortable for the new employee to carry on. If overt resistance is encountered, firm action in consonance with the policy is an absolute necessity. In regard to the employee himself, the manager should expect acceptable levels of job performance, criticize constructively when necessary, and handle disciplinary problems in the same manner as he would those of majority members.

Job Performance

With respect to the performance of the Negro employee, the evidence indicates that when he is properly placed, he works as well as anyone. Regarding the study of 44 firms cited earlier, Chart 24–1 shows that the Negro employee was similar to or better than white co-workers in overall performance, work quality and pace, job attitudes, accident record, illnesses, and turnover. His record was poorer in both wage assignments and absenteeism. But here again, a fair and firm company disciplinary policy can correct the

[12] Theodore V. Purcell, "Break Down Your Employment Barriers," *Harvard Business Review,* Vol. 46, No. 4 (July–August, 1968), pp. 71–72.

latter two difficulties. Two more recent studies show similar results. A survey of 74 firms that had employed Negroes from the Watts area in Los Angeles was conducted in 1966.[13] Twenty percent of the personnel directors and 40 percent of first-level supervisors indicated that the Negro was a "good worker"; 71 percent and 56 percent, respectively, said that he was "average." Only two percent reported that he was "poor." Over four-fifths of both personnel directors and supervisors reported that the Negro employee produced the same or better quantity and quality of output as other employees. As in the previously cited study, there were more difficulties in the area of absenteeism. In addition, there were more negative reports on promotability and willingness to assume responsibility, though in each case over half of those reporting indicated that the Negro employee was the same or better.

CHART 24–1   PERFORMANCE OF NEGRO EMPLOYEES RELATIVE TO WHITE CO-WORKERS

Performance Factor	No. of Reporting Establishments on Each Factor	Number Appraising Performance of Negro Employees Relative to White Co-Workers As		
		The Same or Better	Worse	Conflict in Views
Overall Performance	31	25	3	3
Quantity (pace) of Work	24	21	2	1
Quality of Work	25	24	1	. .
Job Attitudes	24	15	6	3
Absenteeism	30	17	10	3
Accidents and Illnesses	16	15	1	. .
Turnover	26	19	5	2
Wage Assignments	22	8	14	. .

Source: Paul H. Norgren, Albert N. Webster, Roger D. Borgeson, and Maud B. Patten. *Employing the Negro in American Industry.* New York: Industrial Relations Monograph, No. 17, Industrial Relations Counselors, Inc., 1959, p. 116.

The National Industrial Conference Board invited 96 well known firms throughout the nation to participate in a research project concerning their experiences with Negro employment.[14] Of the 47 who chose to reply, 46 of the chief executives and 42 of the personnel directors indicated that the Negro employee was either a "good" or "average" employee. Reports that the Negro employee was the same as others were given by 43 of the 47 companies on the

[13] William H. Reynolds, "Experience of Los Angeles Employers with Minority Group Employees," *Report to Management No. 16* (Los Angeles: University of Southern California Research Institute for Business and Economics), pp. 26–27.

[14] Stephen Habbe, "Company Experience with Negro Employment," *Studies in Personnel Policy No. 201* (New York: National Industrial Conference Board, 1966), pp. 130, 134, 146.

issue of reporting to work on time, 34 on attendance, 43 on quantity of work, 41 on quality, 40 on getting along with others, 16 on promotability, and 24 on willingness to assume responsibility. Thirty-four of the companies indicated that they were willing to go beyond the requirements of the state and federal civil rights acts in eliminating discrimination and prejudice. Two-thirds of the company presidents indicated that the company should pay for any extra training required.

The critical factor is that of qualifications at entrance. Though the Negro constitutes ten percent of the nation's population and work force, his general qualifications in terms of education and experience are more limited than those of whites. These limitations are due to aspects of our society which have hampered the Negro in so many areas. Inadequate schooling, for example, was the first problem attacked in the current drive toward equal opportunity. Negro families have had to adapt to low incomes and restricted job opportunities, and, as a result, often do not encourage their children to prepare for occupations outside of the Negro community. If higher education is sought, it is frequently in the professions, such as law or medicine, for which the Negro community has a need. Negroes tend to shy away from preparation for technical industrial jobs requiring an engineering or scientific background. This portion of the cycle—limited education leading to limited qualifications leading to continued discrimination on the basis of qualifications—must be broken if any degree of success is to be attained in opening up employment.

RELIGION AND NATIONALITY

In the first ten years of experience under the New York fair employment practices law, some discrimination was discovered by the commission in 45 percent of the 2772 complaints submitted.[15] Only 16 percent of these involved religion and 13 percent national origin, as compared with 71 percent for race.

Again, it is a part of our national philosophy to permit and encourage freedom of religious belief. And almost all of us have heritages going back to some other nation. Yet, there have been business organizations identified as being a "Catholic firm" or a "Jewish organization." Though there is less discrimination in initial hiring, there is more in upgrading to higher jobs, particularly those in the management ranks. The election of a Catholic president of the United States aided greatly in reducing the tendency toward making religion an issue in decision making. However, it may be more difficult to eliminate altogether discrimination because of religion and national origin. For differences in religion and nationality can be buried, and discrimination is more difficult to detect.

[15] "California Fair Employment Practices," *op. cit.,* p. 3.

OLDER EMPLOYEES

Though not currently as pressing as the issue of race, the problem of age will slowly and steadily become paramount in industrial employment. Over 40 percent of the labor force is older than 45, and half are over 40. Generally, workers over 45 tend to experience more than normal difficulties in obtaining a new job. The age of the entire population is steadily advancing, and the percentage over 45 will become increasingly larger. The political power of such a group is becoming more apparent. On June 12, 1968, the Age Discrimination in Employment Act became effective. It bans age discrimination in employment for employers of 25 persons or more in industries affecting interstate commerce. The law is also applicable to employment agencies and labor organizations. There are the usual exceptions in the cases where age is a *bona fide* occupational qualification, e.g., safety requirements calling for a younger man. Existing employee benefit plans such as pensions and insurance are also not affected if their design was not intended to evade the purpose of the act. However, no such plan can excuse the failure to hire an individual because of his age. They may be hired without necessarily including them in the pension or insurance plan, or they may be included with a reduced coverage. Several states also have laws prohibiting discrimination on the basis of age. Again, these laws are as difficult to enforce as those in regard to race, religion, and nationality. Though questions of age are removed from the application blank, shrewd guesses can be made by studying the applicant's background in work experience and schooling.

Though everyone ages at the same pace chronologically, there are significant differences in actual physiological and mental aging. There is a serious waste of human resources when decisions are made solely on the basis of chronological age. It may be even a greater waste inasmuch as we are throwing away the years of experience obtained by these older workers.

Performance of Older Workers

Various reasons have been given for preferring younger employees to older. Among these are the following: (1) the younger can do more and better work; (2) the younger are more adaptable and flexible; (3) the younger are in better health and are less prone to absenteeism, accidents, and turnover; (4) group life insurance rates would rise if older people were hired; and (5) pension costs would mount with the introduction of older workers.

Much research has been done to test the validity of these reasons. With respect to quantity and quality of output, almost all research projects are in agreement that the older worker is the equal of the younger.[16] The older worker offers in addition a maturity derived from experience. Since industry is becoming increasingly mechanized, there is less need for the employee to offer brute physical strength, and there is a greater demand for such knowledge and experience.

Adaptability and flexibility are more closely related to personality than to chronological age. There are rigid and inflexible younger persons, just as there are older employees who are set in their ways. It would be more appropriate to approach each person as an individual rather than as a stereotype. The data with respect to absenteeism rates show *no* significant difference between older and younger employees. Older workers are *less* prone toward accidents than are the younger.[17] Caution and experience usually overcompensate for any loss in agility and dexterity. Older workers are also usually superior in terms of labor turnover inasmuch as they are ironically fully aware of the discrimination that exists, and thus are more appreciative of the job they now hold.

The possible costs with respect to group life insurance and pensions are not as formidable as believed. The hiring of older employees will not suddenly convert the firm to an old-age home, and group life insurance premiums go up a negligible amount with the introduction of older employees. The pension constitutes a more difficult problem if the employer and labor union insist on an equal pension for *all* retiring employees. If varying pension benefits are permitted, based on varying lengths of service, the costs would not increase. A variable annuity could be provided based on average earnings and length of service. The inflexibility of present pension arrangements should not be allowed to prevent utilization of a valued human resource.

Retirement

Though it does not appear to be so to the young, compulsory retirement at some fixed age is a form of discrimination. The day after becoming 65, one is presumed no longer capable of meeting job requirements. At the time of retirement, most employees report a desire to continue to work beyond the compulsory retirement age. This effort to remove the older worker from the work force is also aided by the Old Age and Survivors Insurance provision of the Social

---

[16] See Ronald E. Kutcher and James F. Walker, "Comparative Job Performance of Office Workers by Age," *Monthly Labor Review*, Vol. 83, No. 1 (January, 1960), p. 40; Leonard Z. Breen and Joe L. Spaeth, "Age and Productivity Among Workers in Four Chicago Companies," *Journal of Gerontology*, Vol. 15, No. 1 (January, 1960), pp. 68–70; and U.S. Department of Labor, Bureau of Labor Statistics, *Job Performance and Age: A Study in Measurement*, Bulletin No. 1203, September, 1956.

[17] Henry D. Sayer, "Is Workmen's Compensation a Barrier to Employment of the Elderly?" *Never Too Old* (New York State Joint Legislative Committee on Problems of the Aging, 1949), p. 122.

Security Act, which provides for losses in benefits if more than a designated amount is earned in covered employment. There is no such limit on income from stocks, bonds, rents, and royalties.

There are at least three possible policies which can be adopted with respect to retirement ages: (1) mandatory retirement at some fixed age, usually 65; (2) flexible retirement, with the man working as long as he is able and willing; and (3) some type of compromise such as automatic retirement unless the worker receives special dispensation. The advantage of the first policy is in its ease of administration; there is no question as to what will occur at age 65. The disadvantages lie in the loss of experienced talent to the company and in the loss of morale and income to the retiree. The major administrative difficulty in flexible retirement is in obtaining a reliable and valid measure of actual physical and mental aging, one that is acceptable to the company, the employee, and the union. The problem here is similar to the seniority-versus-merit issue. One is easy to administer but results in certain performance losses, while the other is very difficult to operate, yet can lead to greater performance effectiveness. With the chronological age of the population steadily advancing, management should be more willing to take another look at the issue of fixed versus flexible retirement.

FEMALE EMPLOYEES

Since World War II, the number of employed female workers has been so great that reference to them as a minority group is probably no longer valid. Approximately one-third of the nation's work force is comprised of women. The largest single group is employed in clerical positions, and thus constitutes a majority group in many offices. Still there are approximately 20 states with laws that prevent employers from paying, for the same amount of work, less money to women than to men. On the other hand, there are many states with legislation protecting the female employee through the imposition of restrictions upon employers; e.g., 21 states regulate night work for women, 26 prohibit working in hazardous occupations, 27 provide for meal periods, 12 regulate rest periods, and 46 have laws governing the provision of such physical facilities as the number of seats and restrooms.[18] These laws, though designed for the long-run protection of society, often work to the detriment of employing female workers because of the additional burdens imposed upon the employer.

There are many difficulties derived from the employment of women, particularly when women are given jobs normally allocated to men. Some managers

[18] U.S. Department of Labor, *1960 Handbook on Women Workers.* Bulletin 275, Women's Bureau, Washington, D.C. (1960), pp. 121–132.

feel that the female will be more emotional and sensitive, and, as a result, less objective. There is always the possibility that she will replace some man, thus depriving him of an income necessary to support a family. Her absenteeism and turnover rates are higher than for her male counterpart. Most of these conclusions are, however, based on stereotypes; the only fear which is based on facts is that of absenteeism and turnover; various studies have shown these rates to be higher on the average than those for men.[19] But even here, the better approach is to consider each employee, male or female, individually.

HANDICAPPED WORKERS

The employment of the physically handicapped rests soundly upon economic, as well as humanitarian, grounds. All research on this topic has demonstrated that physically handicapped employees, when properly placed, are equal to or better than unimpaired employees in terms of productivity.[20] In addition, they demonstrate even *better* records in terms of absenteeism, turnover, and accidents. Because of past discriminatory practices, the handicapped employee values his job highly and his dedication to the task is inspiring to his fellow employees. One firm, for example, hired a polio victim as a radio mechanic. In over eight years on the job, he was never late or absent even though he had to arrive at the company parking lot approximately forty-five minutes early to allow enough time to walk to his post on crutches. Another company hired a typist who had the use of only one hand. She was obviously slower than her fellow typists, and made up for it by giving a full eight hours of work to her employer. Not only was she able to meet productivity requirements, but she had a salutary effect upon fellow workers who had been in the practice of extending 15-minute breaks to 30 minutes, and half hour lunches to whole hours.

Research has indicated that the fears regarding possible higher accident rates for the handicapped are groundless. Again, if correctly placed he is a valued employee. The "if," however, is the crucial factor. Employing the physically handicapped will require some restudy of jobs and perhaps some reallocation of tasks to fit particular impairments. Thus, the employer may have to assume an additional hiring cost. But on the other hand, there have been many occasions when such a restudy of jobs more than justified its costs. For example, in one department with rather noisy processes, the turnover rate

[19] U.S. Department of Labor, Women's Bureau, *Monthly Labor Review* (August, 1955), p. 889; and Dale Yoder, H. G. Heneman, Jr., John G. Turnbull, and C. Harold Stone, *Handbook of Personnel Management and Labor Relations* (New York: McGraw-Hill Book Company, 1958), pp. 14–35.

[20] Cf., Verne K. Harvey, "Government Procedure in Hiring the Handicapped," *Valor* (August, 1956); and Yoder, Heneman, Turnbull, and Stone, *op. cit.*, pp. 7–23.

was very high even though management had done all it could to reduce the source of noise. It was discovered that employees with some impairment in hearing were more stable in employment and attendance, and became less emotionally upset on the job. There are various jobs that the physically handicapped can do *better* than the normal employee, but even when he is merely an equal, his superiority in the other phases of employment makes him a highly desirable resource.

SUMMARY

To the problem of integrating the *individual* with the *formal organization* must be added the one of *integrating* a *minority group with a majority*. There is no basis, either economic or moral, for discriminating against any group because of one or more non-job characteristics. The most pressing current problem in this regard is that of introducing and integrating members of minority races into industrial firms. This has become a major issue because of the marked increase in activity in recent years on the part of minority races to gain equal employment opportunities.

In all cases, whether in regard to race, religion, color, nationality, sex, age, or physical impairment, research as indicated that *performance results are a factor of individual ability and not of a group stereotype*. The older worker is an able worker, just as is the female, the handicapped, or the member of a minority race or religion. Thus, the manager has no sound economic basis for discrimination.

The remaining barrier is one of rejection of the minority member by the majority group. Since there is no economic justification for discrimination and since the principles and beliefs of general society are contrary to such discrimination, it falls upon private management to *lead* in this regard. It has been found that managements tend to be overly fearful of disastrous consequences when the introduction of a minority group is contemplated for the first time. Careful thought, planning, and action can lead to a successful merging of various groups. As long as the business society is to remain a part of general society, *other obligations must be recognized beyond the goals of creating and distributing an economic product for a profit.*

DISCUSSION PROBLEMS

1. Discuss the five levels of policy on discrimination in hiring with respect to legality, equity, and effectiveness.
2. Describe the roles and relationships between business and government in the Job Opportunities in Business Sector program.
3. What is the significance of personal support in the hiring of the hard-core unemployed?
4. How does the Negro employee compare with others in terms of overall effectiveness, quantity and quality of work, attendance, promotability, and willingness to accept responsibility?

5. What types of problems are encountered in an active program of nondiscrimination in a company which has previously had little experience in this regard?

6. Distinguish between the problems of integrating the individual with the organization, and integrating a minority group with a majority.

7. Contrast the problems and values of mandatory retirement versus flexible retirement of older employees.

8. Refute the argument that the older worker is a less desirable worker; that physically handicapped workers are less desirable; that female employees are less desirable.

9. If the elimination of all non-job bases of discrimination results in increased costs of doing business in our society, who should absorb these costs? Will private business accept them? Will government have to subsidize business? Or do we determine (rationalize?) that we will profit in the long run?

10. Contrast the values of slow and rapid paces in introducing members of a minority group into a business organization.

SUPPLEMENTARY READING

Dailey, Charles A., "Prejudice and Decision Making," *Personnel Administration*, Vol. 29, No. 5 (September–October, 1966), 6–13.

Guion, Robert M., "Employment Tests and Discriminatory Hiring," *Industrial Relations*, Vol. 5, No. 2 (February, 1966), 20–36.

Habbe, Stephen, "Company Experience with Negro Employment," *Studies in Personnel Policy No. 201*. New York: National Industrial Conference Board, 1966.

Hodgson, James D. and Marshall H. Brenner, "Successful Experience: Training Hard-Core Unemployed," *Harvard Business Review*, Vol. 46, No. 5 (September–October, 1968), 148–156.

Luthans, Fred, "A New Look at Antidiscrimination Policies and Programs," *Personnel Journal*, Vol. 47, No. 12 (December, 1968), 877–881.

Purcell, Theodore V., "Break Down Your Employment Barriers," *Harvard Business Review*, Vol. 46, No. 4 (July–August, 1968), 65–76.

Reynolds, William H., "Experience of Los Angeles Employers with Minority Group Employees," *Report to Management No. 16*. Los Angeles: University of Southern California Research Institute for Business and Economics, 1967.

Russo, Sabatino A., "The Mature Woman: An Asset to Industry," *Personnel Journal*, Vol. 47, No. 12 (December, 1968), 853–856.

25

The Labor Union

A second type of *group integration problem* concerns the labor organization. We have discussed previously the tendency of people to form cliques and groups, in order to meet both social and security needs. These groups possess a power to affect and modify the edicts of management and the effectiveness of formal organization. Labor unions constitute a formalization of these groupings. Once the formal union is created and recognized by the organization's management, the latter must begin to *integrate the interests and objectives of the union with the interests and objectives of the organization.*

NATURE OF A LABOR UNION

A labor union is an organization of employees formed to promote, protect, and improve, through collective action, the social, economic, and political interests of its members. On the surface, the union represents a set of interests which appear to be directly contrary to the interests of management and the organization. The union proposes to restrict management's decision-making power on those matters which affect the economic and social interests of its members. We have seen in numerous cases where the interests of the organization do not always parallel the interests of employed personnel. The union can intensify and dramatize these conflicts.

In the early days of unionization in this country, a major objective was the *social* one of brotherhood and fraternity. Often, the organization would broaden this objective to include "uplift unionism," a desire to redo society through proposed reforms in land, currency, and debtor laws. These social objectives are still of real concern today, but more specific interests have assumed primary importance.

The major interest of the present-day labor union is an *economic* one, or "business unionism." Through collective organization and action, the union attempts to improve income of employees individually and collectively, reduce the number of working hours, and generally improve all aspects of working conditions. It insures that employee opinions and feelings will be voiced from a *position of strength* which a single individual could not hold alone. The union also provides *security* against unilateral and arbitrary management action. Thus, the ego needs of subordinates are partially fulfilled when they can feel sufficiently independent to challenge the decisions and actions of their superiors. Though a management, on its own, may voluntarily provide all that is desired in terms of wages, hours, and working conditions, it can *never* gratify the employee's need to stand on his own feet and speak from a position of power.

In the past three decades, a third major objective of the union has been added, that of improving through *political* action the status of employed personnel. The Congress of Industrial Organizations entered national and local politics with great energy, and supported such pro-labor laws as the National Labor Relations Act, the Social Security Act, and the Fair Labor Standards Act. The American Federation of Labor changed its "no politics" policy with the passage of the Taft-Hartley Act, a bill which both the AFL and the CIO vehemently opposed. These two labor groupings merged in 1956 to form the AFL–CIO. Organized labor today is highly interested and active in politics on all levels to promote the interests of employed personnel through legislative and administrative action. The general goals are still the same, but the techniques and pressures are directed not only toward the business organization, but toward the electorate and the elected as well.

In general, there are two basic types of labor unions, the craft and the industrial. These are often referred to as horizontal and vertical, respectively. The craft union organizes all employees engaged in a single occupation; it therefore cuts across many companies and industries (carpenters or machinists). A business firm may be forced to deal with as many as 15 different labor unions, any one of which can strike and close the plant through the establishment of picket lines.

The industrial union is vertical in the sense that it includes all workers of a particular company and/or industry regardless of occupation. It thus constitutes a mixture of skills and lacks the homogeneity of craft organization. Examples of industrial unions are the United Automobile Workers, United Mine Workers, and United Steel Workers.

It is apparent that these two types of union structures are designed to *conflict* with each other in jurisdiction. If a craft organization is formed and recognized in a plant represented by an industrial union, a portion of the group is sliced out and separated from the larger industrial organization. When the AFL and the CIO merged in 1956, the reconciliation of such jurisdictional disputes proved to be a difficult and continuing problem. Chart 25–1 portrays the basic organization structure of the current AFL–CIO. This is a federation of some 140 independent, international unions with the power being located primarily at this international level. Each international is composed of from ten to 2000 local unions established to deal and negotiate with local plant managements. There are times when a local union will disagree with its international, a situation which adds to management's difficulty in attempting an agreement and integration of interests.

In addition to the main line of communication—AFL–CIO headquarters to international union to local union—the chart shows various intermediate levels of organization that work for inter-union cooperation or regional, state, and local levels. Those internationals that have special interests in common, such as in the various metal trades, form departments to facilitate coordinated policy and action. These departments represent one formal attempt on the part of the AFL–CIO to integrate its multiple and diverse international unions into an effective unified whole.

DEVELOPMENT AND STATUS OF LABOR UNIONS

The status of organized labor in the United States in terms of membership stood at 19,100,000 in 1966, the highest numerical total in its history.[1] The previous high was in 1956 when a total of 18,500,000 members was reached. In the intervening ten years the membership of unions had actually dropped, reaching such levels as 17.6 million in 1962 and 17.9 million in 1964. Most of the members, some 14 million, are in unions affiliated with the AFL–CIO; the remaining are in separate unions such as the Teamsters, United Mine Workers, railway brotherhoods, numerous smaller independents, and the United Automobile Workers. The last named is the most recent to break away from the large federation. One-third of all union members in the United States are in the states of New York, California, and Pennsylvania. Approximately 22.7 percent of the total labor force is organized into unions. This represents a decline from a high of 25.2 percent reached in 1956.

The development of organized labor in the United States dates back to the very beginning of this country.[2] During most of the nineteenth century, unions

[1] Report of the Bureau of Labor Statistics of the Department of Labor cited in *Business Week* (December 14, 1968), p. 158.
[2] See Foster R. Dulles, *Labor in America* (New York: T. Y. Crowell Co., 1949), and Harry A. Millis and Royal E. Montgomery, *The Economics of Labor,* Vol. III, *Organized Labor* (New York: McGraw-Hill Book Company, 1945) for two interesting and excellent coverages of labor history.

CHART 25–1 STRUCTURE OF THE AFL–CIO

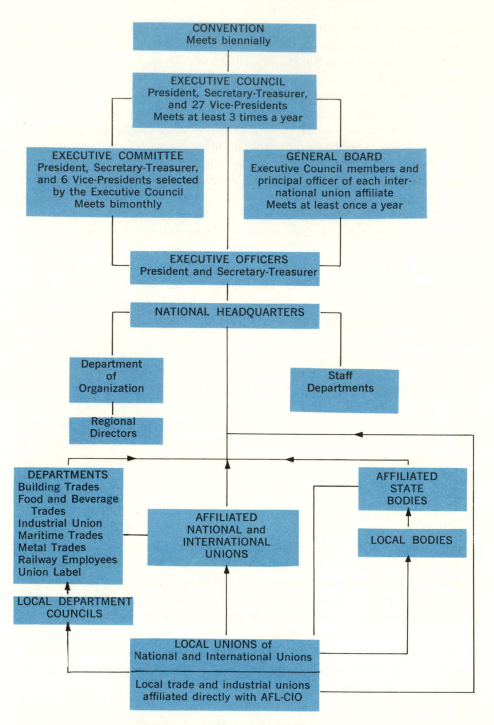

Source: U.S. Department of Labor, *Directory of National and International Labor Unions in the United States, 1963.* Bulletin No. 1395 (May, 1964), p. 43.

grew at a slow pace. The reasons were many: (1) periodic depressions and panics led union members to break ranks to obtain any kind of employment; (2) immigration from the East supplied workers willing to take less than the union demanded; (3) the frontier to the West drained off men when the employer made things difficult; (4) the general public attitude favored the rights of private property and was impatient with attempts of unions to restrict these rights; (5) management worked hard at combatting union activity; and (6) government maintained an unfavorable attitude toward labor organization. All these factors served to slow the growth of unions, and as each was modified or eliminated, labor organizations tended to grow.

By 1916, there were approximately three million labor union members.[3] In the next five years, total membership almost *doubled* as a result of wartime prosperity and favorable government attitudes toward unionization. Many managers concluded that the "hot war" against unions was not working well. Some switched to paternalism, a philosophy of labor-management relations emphasizing a fatherly and protective attitude which could be construed as a form of "cold war" against unions. In a sense, such programs were designed to prove to the employee that he had no need for an outside protector. During the 1920's and early 1930's, there was a decline in union membership, until, in 1932, the total dropped to fewer than three million. *Twelve years later, there were approximately fifteen million union members.* The most influential factors contributing to this five-fold increase were favorable public attitudes, passage of the National Labor Relations Act in 1935 (the Magna Charta of labor), and wartime prosperity. The right to organize without interference from management was guaranteed by the government. Strikes for recognition were replaced by secret ballot elections, most of which were won by unions. Collective bargaining was pronounced our national policy and employee-employer relationships were to be established on a bilateral basis. *Management's right to decide in a major area of business was reduced and rigorously regulated.*

Between 1945 and 1966, the total membership in organized labor increased, though the proportion of the labor force in unions has declined. The number of recognition elections won by unions declined from over 90 percent to approximately 55 percent. The failure of unions to keep pace with the growth of the labor force can be attributed to a number of factors. First, the industries where unionization has been strong are manufacturing, transportation, construction, and mining. In 1950 these industries provided about one-half of all payroll employment, but in recent years this has declined to approximately 43 percent. These are the industries that have been hardest hit by mechanization and automation. Manufacturing, for example, had seven percent more workers in 1962 than in 1950, but output was over 50 percent higher.[4] With this decline in

[3] Millis and Montgomery, *The Economics of Labor,* Vol. III, *Organized Labor,* p. 132.
[4] *Business Week* (December 1, 1962), p. 19.

the percentage of blue-collar employees, labor has had to turn increasingly to the organization of white-collar workers. Office and professional personnel are much more difficult to organize, however, because of their traditional identification with management. In addition, the image of labor unions that has resulted from the long, bitter, and often bloody fights for recognition is not necessarily attractive to white-collar employees. A second reason for the decline is that the large employing units are for the most part fully organized. Any additional growth will have to come at increasingly higher-per-person organizing costs. And finally, organized labor has been under heavy fire from congressional committees, and the resulting adverse publicity has hurt their standing with the general public. The Taft-Hartley Act of 1947 and the Labor-Management Disclosure Act of 1959 both had a part to play in restricting the power and freedom of American labor unions.

Concentration upon the number of members alone does not reveal the full story of the power and status of organized labor. Though less than a fourth of the labor force is organized, these existing unions do sit upon the life lines of the nation's economy. One strong labor union leader has indicated an interest in forming a federation of unions in trucking, railroads, airlines, and ships. If this were done, an organization totaling approximately five million members could have the potential power of freezing the nation over night. Organized labor is also very strong in such basic industries as steel, automobiles, and electrical equipment.

INFORMAL AND FORMAL RELATIONSHIPS BETWEEN UNION AND MANAGEMENT

Under the balloting procedures established by the National Labor Relations Act, a union-management relationship can be established by law. The employer is *forced* to recognize and negotiate an agreement with union representatives. There are, of course, a number of informal relationships that can be established. Management, for example, can adopt an attitude of *militant* opposition. The union wishes to restrict the decision-making rights of management, though it represents only *one* of many groups with a legitimate interest in organizational decisions. Management may react by doing all it can to eliminate the union. It legally has the right to speak out against the organization, while avoiding threats and promises; voluntarily provide a comprehensive personnel benefits program so long as it is not initiated during the election campaign; and do everything possible to influence employees away from the union. At least 12 months after a certifying union election, an employer may petition for a new election if he feels there is a possibility that the union no longer represents a majority. There are also certain activities which are illegal, such as searching out and discharging active union members, making threats against the employee group if the union is supported, and promising rewards if the union is de-certified. The union has the option of filing charges of unfair labor practices against management before the National Labor Relations Board, the administering agency for the NLRA.

The union will do all it can to assure its survival. For a time, union security and survival will take precedence over advancing the economic and social interests of its members. Harbison and Coleman have discovered that militant opposition often gradually changes into one of three other relationships: armed truce, working harmony, or union-management cooperation.[5] *Armed truce* is the next logical relationship after militant opposition; the battle is over for the moment. A contract has been signed and management attempts to preserve its traditional prerogatives and authority in running the company. Union officials are dealt with only to the extent the law requires. With the passage of time and continued support of the union by employees, there is the likelihood that the relationship will ripen into one of *working harmony*. It is difficult for management to accept at first the invasion of their organization by an outside group. After working with the union representatives for a time, however, there often grows a measure of respect for their skill, knowledge, and dedication to the philosophies of labor organization. Once the union is granted a degree of security so that it need not fear undermining, there is a definite possibility of developing a cooperative, working relationship. Many feel that a formal union shop is prerequisite to this working harmony relationship. There is the hope that the employees will develop and maintain a *dual* loyalty to both the company and the union.

In a few instances, working harmony may develop into *union-management cooperation*. In working harmony, management and union negotiate, give and receive, and make exchanges and accommodations on the basis of varying amounts of power. In union-management cooperation, instead of applying pressure upon each other, both groups apply pressure upon a common set of problems. Both accept a common responsibility for increasing productivity, reducing waste, safety, security, etc. When bargaining takes place, it is more likely to be based on facts rather than outrageous demands.

This degree of cooperation is usually not obtained until the organization is in serious danger of going out of business, and everyone works to assure the survival of management, the union, and the business organization. When, however, the organization is reasonably prosperous and there is disagreement concerning the allocation of income and rewards, there is likely to be simply a workable harmony. In general, management gets the type of relationship that it wants. A fighting militant management will beget a fighting militant union. If

[5] Frederick H. Harbison and John R. Coleman, *Goals and Strategy in Collective Bargaining* (New York: Harper & Bros., 1951).

working harmony is desired, the obligation is usually upon management to make the *first* move by allowing a sufficient amount of union security.

The informal attitudes of management and organized labor toward each other are usually codified by means of the labor contract. There are a number of possible types of union security clauses, among which are the following:

1. Open shop.
2. Simple recognition shop.
3. Agency shop.
4. Maintenance-of-membership shop.
5. Union shop.
6. Closed shop.

The *open shop* exists where no union is formally recognized. Such shops can either be truly open or restricted legally or illegally. If open, management, without interference or encouragement, permits employees to determine whether or not they wish to form or join a union. If the shop is restricted, management is militantly prohibiting the entry of a union, and as indicated above, there are legal means to actively oppose a union. There are also certain activities prohibited by law, such as the use of threats or promises and the use of "yellow dog contracts," wherein the new employee agrees beforehand not to join a union. The open shop is fair game for the union organizer.

The *simple recognition* shop is one in which a union has been formally recognized by management as the official and exclusive bargaining agent of all employees in its jurisdiction. Since the passage of the NLRA, recognition is gained through elections administered by the National Labor Relations Board. This board establishes election procedures, regulates campaign activities, certifies those who are eligible to vote, and conducts the secret ballot. If more than 50 percent of the voting employees favor the union, the employer must formally recognize and deal with this union as though it represented *all* 100 percent of the employees. Prior to the NLRA, a strike was usually necessary to exact recognition from an employer. The simple recognition shop has a minimum of 12 months security—an employer cannot petition for another election in less time. The union wants more security than this, and protests the existence of "free riders," or employees represented who have elected *not* to join the union.

The *agency shop* is one answer to the free rider argument. *All* employees pay dues whether or not they are union members. In effect, all pay an agency fee to the union for representation services rendered. However, there is no compulsion for anyone to actively join the union. Thus, non-union members are not subject to required attendance at union meetings, union assessments, and union disciplinary action. This shop constitutes a stronger degree of security than simple recognition, but not enough security to satisfy most labor unions.

Another type of compromise relationship is the *maintenance-of-membership shop.* This is a compromise between the union's desire for compulsory membership and management's wish to preserve freedom of choice. In this arrangement, there is no requirement that employees join the union; but when and if they do, they are frozen into membership for the life of the labor contract. Usually when the contract expires, there is a short escape period when employees may withdraw. Thus, the membership of the union is maintained for the life of the contract. This type of shop has, then, an element of freedom and an element of compulsion.

The *union shop* is a form of compulsory unionism. The employer may hire whom he will, but within a stipulated period of time, usually 30 days, employees must join the union or forfeit their jobs. In the construction industry, this period can be shortened to seven days.[6] Assuming there were no new employees in the past 30 days, all employees are members of the union and must remain so.

The *closed shop* is the strongest degree of union security and is outlawed by the Taft-Hartley Act. Under this arrangement, an employee must be a union member *at the time of hiring;* the union becomes the *only* source of labor for the employer. Though this shop is illegal, it exists in fact in a few industries, particularly construction, maritime, and printing. The clause is not in the labor contract, but hiring practices and work rules make it in effect a closed arrangement.

Inasmuch as less than one quarter of the labor force is organized, it is evident that the open shop is the most common formal management-union arrangement. Legally, the employer is free to make unilateral decisions concerning employees and employment. We have seen, however, that the manager does *not* possess all the power in an organization, and he is *never* completely free to make decisions without considering the power of subordinates. In those companies that do recognize and deal with labor unions, most of the formal arrangements are of the union shop type. The Bureau of Labor Statistics reported in recent years that of 1631 contracts surveyed, 71 percent provided for the union shop, 8 percent for maintenance-of-membership, 20 percent for simple recognition, and one percent for agency shop.[7] There have been later estimates by other observers that the proportion of agency shops has risen to nearly 5 percent. Many of these constitute a transformation of simple recognition shops into an agency arrangement as a means of offsetting the free rider argument.

It is apparent that the majority of American employers who deal with unions have accepted, through collective bargaining, the principle of *compulsory union membership.* Such agreements cover approximately three quarters of the total union membership. The NLRA requires the employer to grant the simple

---

[6] Title VII, Public Law 86–257.

[7] *Personnel,* Vol. 37, No. 2 (March–April, 1960), p. 60.

recognition shop if an election is won by the union, but there is no law requiring him to grant any degree of union security beyond this. Thus, one could conclude that the typical informal management-union relationship is one of working harmony and the typical formal relationship is the union shop. The most common processes through which these relationships are made effective are collective bargaining and the grievance procedure.

COLLECTIVE BARGAINING

It is the public policy of the United States that the determination of various relationships between employer and employee shall be made through the medium of collective bargaining. There are, however, few if any black-and-white answers to most questions that arise in this area. For example, there is no scientific formula that will tell exactly what a worker's wage should be. Job evaluation, time study, wage surveys, and other scientific management techniques provide a great deal of data to be considered, but there is no objective, correct answer. In this and many other matters, we cannot be certain that the manager will arrive at the correct answer by himself. For that matter, it is not certain that collective bargaining will produce the correct answer. But at least the voicing of all interests will probably lead to a more acceptable decision, which in effect makes it a more correct answer. It is also helpful if each of the interested voices has sufficient *power* to make sure that the voice is heard and respected, but not to the point where one can dominate the other.

Collective bargaining is a process in which representatives of labor and business meet to negotiate an agreement or contract. The term "collective" indicates that representatives are attempting to negotiate for groups of persons. The NLRA levies upon management the responsibility of bargaining "in good faith." The Taft-Hartley Act has a similar requirement for the labor union to bargain "in good faith." What is and is not good faith has become a matter of case-by-case determination by the National Labor Relations Board.

The process of collective bargaining can be segmented into certain fundamental stages:

1. The pre-negotiation phase.
2. Selection of negotiators.
3. Strategy.
4. Tactics.
5. The contract.

The *pre-negotiation* phase for a new agreement actually begins with the signing of the last contract, labor relations being a full-time job for management. It is obviously a full-time and specialized task for union representatives as well. Data on subjects as wages, hours, pensions, vacations, insurance, etc., must be carefully maintained by management. The day should be past when the labor union representative walks into a bargaining session armed to the teeth with a vast array of data, and the management representative walks in armed with only a lawyer. Lawyers are of value in bargaining sessions, but more particularly for their ability in assessing opposing personalities and evaluating statements of the opposition, than for anything else. However, collective bargaining is not essentially a legal process even though the net tangible result is a contract. What is being negotiated is a set of formal relationships, and their inevitable accompanying informal ones, with which the two parties must live on a day-to-day basis. Negotiators must have substantial factual knowledge of working conditions, past employer-employee relationships, personal characteristics of opposing negotiators, and economic conditions in the community, state, and nation. For example, it is likely that representatives of an industrial union will have a social philosophy emphasizing the interests of the rank and file in both economic and political terms. It is also likely that they will have substantially *less* power to commit the union than would the representatives of a craft union. The craft union is usually most interested in wages, hours, and working conditions. Not only must the labor organization be analyzed, but the background and personalities of particular union representatives must be studied as well.

The *selection of negotiators* for the actual bargaining process is the next important phase. On the company side, he may be any one of several people, such as the industrial relations director, the vice president of production or some other line function, an executive vice president, or the company attorney. The *team* or *committee* approach is frequently used to broaden the base and facilitate *education* and *communication* among management personnel. Because of the very nature of the bargaining process, which involves demands and rebuttals, delays for the re-evaluation of positions or the analysis of surprise proposals are desirable. The company representative can always indicate a lack of authority to commit the enterprise, and the consequent necessity of checking with a superior. Many consider it sound practice to keep the company president out of the negotiation process for if he is present, he may be forced into an instant answer on an issue that should have a more careful evaluation. Similarly, the union representative can always delay to check a counter-offer with the rank and file.

On the union side, the committee approach is also frequently used. It often includes business agents, shop stewards, president of the local, representatives of the international office, and, at times, rank and file members. The business agent and the international representatives are full-time, paid specialists of the union.

The basic strategy of the bargaining process is established by mapping out the fundamental plan and policies to be followed with respect to long-term labor-management relations, as well as the particular bargaining session that is pending. *Tactics* are the particular actions used at the bargaining table and these should conform in general to the outline of the strategy. The basic elements of any strategic plan would involve (1) the maximum concessions that can be granted to filed or anticipated labor demands; (2) the maintenance of management's basic right to manage the organization and the avoidance of mutual agreement clauses; (3) the degree to which the company employees and the general public will be kept informed by management on the progress of negotiations; and (4) the adoption of the basic attitude of not being overly fearful of the strike threat. The strike is the most potent economic weapon in the hands of the union, and management must be ever aware of its potential usage. There is a basic process, much of it psychological in nature, through which a union and its membership must go before there is a walkout. In general, management should not be so fearful of a possible work stoppage that the mere threat of one will send them scurrying to give greater concessions than are legitimately fair or necessary.

The tactics of bargaining would include such questions as (1) whether to have extended sessions; (2) whether to agree clause by clause or to give tentative agreement subject to a period of the entire package; (3) whether to offer far less than what will probably be agreed upon; and (4) whether, and to what degree, to engage in haggling, horse trading, pounding the table, shouting, and other dramatic performances to impress bargaining opponents. Though logic and scientific management would suggest an absence of tactics designed to mislead, past experience would indicate that such activities will continue to be used because of the very nature of the process. If both parties would ascertain *all* of the facts, and if both would be completely objective and willing to accept the direction that those facts indicate, perhaps the writing of the labor agreement could be reduced to an automatic and scientific procedure. Such a situation is not likely to occur, at least in the foreseeable future.

The labor-management *contract* stipulates in formal terms the nature of the relationships among union, management, and employee-union members. Most contracts include clauses covering the following areas: recognition and union security, rates of pay, hours of work, overtime, holidays, vacations, seniority, grievances, management prerogatives or responsibilities, safety and health, promotion, transfer, and layoff and discharge. As can be seen, the number and importance of such relationships are great.

PRESSURES TO AGREE

The labor union also adopts certain strategies and tactics to force an agreement on terms most acceptable to it and its members. They demand more in the expectation of getting less, make tentative agreements subject to ratification by total membership, and haggle and make exchanges and deals with management. Bargaining is essentially a political process as indicated in Chapter 12. In addition to these maneuvers, there are stronger pressure techniques, such as strikes, picketing, and boycotts. Strikes represent the ultimate economic weapon—the complete withdrawal of the labor resource and the attempted denial to the employer of substitute labor. In addition to the kind of strike which contributes to a high degree of union security, there are *economic* strikes designed to force higher wages and improved working conditions, *jurisdictional* strikes intended to force allocation of jobs to one union over another, *wildcat* strikes that are unauthorized by the union and represent spontaneous local objections to management acts, and *sympathetic* strikes by unions not directly involved in the primary dispute. The last three types are either illegal under the Taft-Hartley Act or fall outside the labor-management agreement.

Picketing is a device that is used to keep the business organization closed during the process of a strike. If the employer makes no attempt to operate during a work stoppage, picketing is usually peaceful. A back-to-work movement by the employer often stimulates the addition of an excessive number of pickets, and violence sometimes results. Picketing is designed to represent the union's right of free speech to advertise that a labor disagreement exists; it is not supposed to halt the entrance and exist of personnel. A secondary boycott is an effort through which pressure is applied by third parties to force the primary disputing employer to grant concessions to the union. Such third parties can be customers of the company or other business organizations who deal with the employer. The Taft-Hartley Act sought to make such secondary pressures illegal and to keep the dispute confined to the two primary parties involved.

When disagreements between labor and management become serious and begin to affect the welfare of a significant portion of the community, authorized third parties may enter the dispute, e.g., mediators and arbitrators. *Mediation* is a process whereby the third party attempts to stimulate the two primary parties to reach some type of agreement. The decision is to be made by the two parties and *not* by the mediator. He is strictly neutral and can only listen, suggest, communicate, persuade, and keep the parties talking to each other. *Arbitration* is a process in which the third party acts as a judge and renders a decision which ends the dispute. He holds hearings, collects facts, and decides what the two primary parties will do. Obviously, arbitration involves a far greater degree of authority delegated to outside third parties than is true of mediation.

The formulation of a new contract is so important that labor and management are both very reluctant to turn to arbitration. Thus, mediation is the process most widely used to assist in resolving disagreement over new contracts. Many of the mediators are provided by governmental agencies, such as the Federal Mediation and Conciliation Service and the various state mediation services. When labor contracts need interpretation as various specific disputes arise, an arbitrator is often used to provide the answer. This constitutes a lesser grant of power inasmuch as it is restricted to narrow disputes arising under an existing contract.

When the dispute over a new contract continues despite all efforts toward settlement, a strike will often begin. Excessively long strikes in basic industries, such as steel or coal, and even short strikes in industries such as transportation, can cause great harm to the nation's economy. In such a situation, the President of the United States is empowered under the Taft-Hartley Act to declare a national emergency and ask for a Federal Court injunction to terminate the stoppage for eighty days. If no agreement is reached with the aid of fact-finding boards and pressures of public opinion, the union is free to resume the strike after the eighty days. However, it is inconceivable that if a national emergency still exists, the nation's interests will be sacrificed in the interest of free collective bargaining. If the two parties are unable to reach an agreement voluntarily, the odds are that the government will substitute compulsory arbitration for the free collective bargaining process in these basic industries. A recent example of this took place in the railroad industry when an arbitration panel was established under a special federal law to decide upon the introduction of certain work rules. But even in this unusual case, the objectionable nature of the procedure was made evident by the fact that such arbitration decisions would be in effect for only two years, after which time the two parties would be free once more to bargain over these issues. If this freedom is to be preserved, a greater concern for the public interests must be made evident by responsible action on the part of both parties, labor and management.

ADMINISTRATION OF THE AGREEMENT

Though the union is designed to be a democratic organization through popular election of various officials, it is nevertheless a formal hierarchy not unlike the business organization. There are superiors, subordinates, multiple levels of authority, and varying degrees of functional specialization. It has also been discovered that the administrative attitudes of union officials toward rank-and-file union members are similar to those of business managers toward rank-and-file subordinates. Various research studies have shown that business managers tend to favor some form of subordinate participation in decision making, but at the same time are rather skeptical that the process will actually enhance organizational effectiveness.[8] A recent research study by Miles and Ritchie shows very similar attitudes held by a sample of 83 union officials.[9] These union leaders felt strongly that rank-and-file members should be encouraged to participate in decision making. They were also certain that this would have a highly favorable effect upon morale. However, neither craft nor industrial leaders felt that the *quality* of decisions would improve as a result of this participation. These same attitudes were held by higher union officials as they viewed the capabilities of shop stewards and committeemen. "The official tends to advocate allowing those below him some participation in decision making in order to maintain their loyalty, increase their morale, and enhance the likelihood that they will go along with his decisions. However, doubting their basic capabilities for sound judgment and their perspective and insight into organizational problems, he does not actually expect their participation to result in improved decisions."[10] The occupant of any administrative position in any type of formal organization tends to feel the weight of his responsibility for decision making. Though intellectually he is able to see the logic and potential values of subordinate participation, in practice he is reluctant to share his rights.

Thus far we have been concerned with the problem of integrating a group, the labor union, with the business organization in order to achieve the necessary degree of cooperation toward common and essential goals. The formal ending of this process would appear to take place with the signing of the labor contract, with or without the aid of outside third parties and power moves such as lockouts, strikes, picketing, and boycotts. As many have stated, however, the signing of the contract is a single milestone in the *continuing process* of union-management negotiation. Under the contract, there will arise numerous problems of interpretation and application, with disagreements over the handling of individual cases. Consequently, an important part of each contract is to make definite provision for the processing of specific disagreements, or *grievances*. The resulting grievance procedure is a basic mechanism which enables the resolution of problems and the integration of individual and union interests with the interests of the organization.

A grievance is a complaint, valid or not, which the employee feels has not been handled fairly and in accordance with the contract. It is usually *expressed* formally and in writing.

---

[8] See Raymond E. Miles, Lyman W. Porter, and James A. Craft, "Leadership Attitudes Among Public Health Officials," *American Journal of Public Health*, Vol. 53 (December, 1966), pp. 1990–2005 and Raymond E. Miles, "Conflicting Elements in Managerial Ideologies," *Industrial Relations*, Vol. 4 (October, 1964), pp. 77–91.

[9] Raymond E. Miles and J. B. Ritchie, "Leadership Attitudes Among Union Officials," *Industrial Relations*, Vol. 8, No. 1 (October, 1968), pp. 108–117.

[10] *Ibid.*, p. 115.

It is to management's advantage that clashes of interest be discovered and reduced if not eliminated. One of the major values of the labor union is the provision of *courage* and *support* which enable the employees to voice and formalize specific discontents. A formal grievance procedure is usually established, a simplified version of which is depicted in Chart 25–2. Details vary from firm to firm, depending upon size of firm and union and management's philosophy of line and staff organization. Such a procedure guarantees a type of *judicial justice* to supplement the administrative justice which every manager presumably exercises. It provides the basis for an employee appeal beyond the jurisdiction of the immediate supervisor, and thereby assists in reducing any friction which may have adverse effects upon productivity and cooperation. The grievance procedure usually constitutes a series of *conferences* among interested parties. When conflicts of interest exist, discussion and personal interchange of views hold the greatest potential for resolution and integration.

The initial step or conference in the typical procedure takes place among the aggrieved employee, the union steward, and the first level supervisor. Logic would suggest that the supervisor approach the grievance in the manner of a problem to be solved, following the usual steps of (1) defining the nature of the dissatisfaction; (2) obtaining the facts through interview, a study, and observation; (3) analyzing the facts and reaching a decision; (4) applying the decision; and (5) following up the case to determine if the disagreement has

CHART 25–2   A GRIEVANCE PROCEDURE

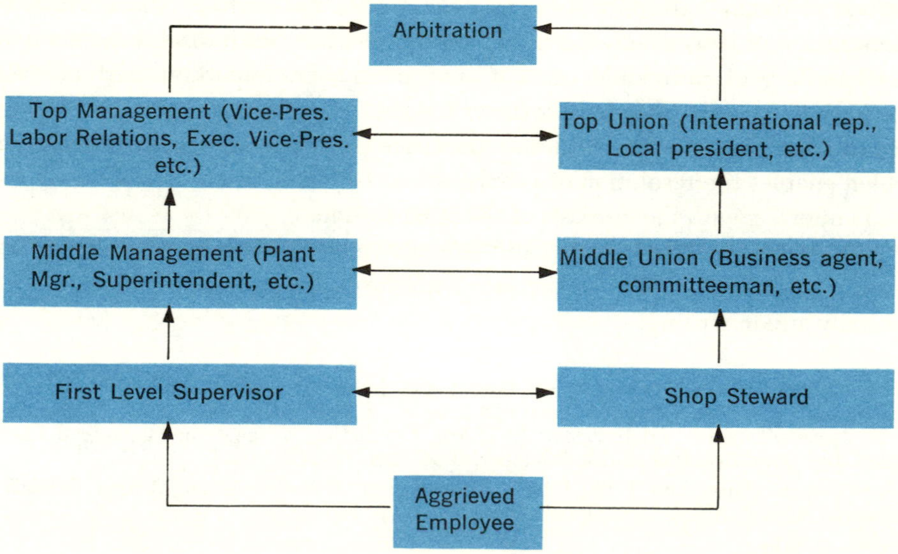

been successfully resolved.[11] Logic can contribute a great deal even to problems that are essentially human in nature. But as has been continuously emphasized, logic has its shortcomings when dealing with emotions and clashes of wills and interests. The greatest opportunity for a satisfactory integration lies in this initial step where *informal compromises* can be worked out. *Political exchanges* are not uncommon between the steward and the supervisor, sometimes to the detriment of a particular employee but to the advantage of long-run interests of the majority. The steward is an elected union official whose continuance in office is affected by his degree of disassociation from management. He sometimes pushes questionable grievances in the interest of satisfying his political constituents. The steward has a legal obligation to represent all employees in his jurisdiction, whether they are union members or not.

The intermediate step, or steps, involves conference among higher management and union officials. Whereas the steward is a regular company employee who has the additional task of representing union interests, higher union officials, such as the international representative and the union business agents, are often full-time specialized employees of the union. On the management side, the organization's interests may be represented by such personnel as a line superintendent, plant manager, or personnel manager. The use of the personnel manager in a decision-making capacity would violate certain principles of line and staff relationships discussed earlier in this text. However, several business firms do this in order to meet union specialization with management specialization.

The final step within the company is a conference between the highest union officials and the highest management representative. The specific grievance now constitutes a definite issue and it is very difficult to secure a voluntary integration of interests at this point. In the absence of settlement between the two parties, the alternatives are dropping the issue and living with the dissatisfaction, strike, or arbitration. In over 90 percent of the more than 100,000 labor contracts in this country, strikes are prohibited with respect to grievances, and arbitration by an impartial third party is substituted in their place.

The arbitrator is selected by both parties jointly and his compensation is usually financed equally. Some industries have permanent full-time arbitrators, while most employ them on a case-by-case basis. Once the arbitrator's decision is issued, it is binding on both parties if the contract is not to be violated. The fact that over 90 percent of all contracts provide for this *industrial judicial system,* as a substitute for economic force, gives cause for optimism and encouragement in the field of labor-management relations. This judicial complex has been created in the short space of less than 30 years.

[11] For elaboration on these steps as applied to grievances, see Edwin B. Flippo, *Principles of Personnel Management* (New York: McGraw-Hill Book Company, 1966), Chap. 20.

SUMMARY

The labor union stands as evidence that the business manager by himself has failed to integrate perfectly individual interests with organizational interests. The labor organization is formed to advance and protect the political, social, and economic interests of employees. Not only does it assist in assuring greater gratification of economic needs, it also provides the degree of independence and freedom from unilateral, arbitrary management that the individual requires. For many years, business managements were successful in containing the union movement through both positive and negative means. But with the protection provided by the government in the 1930's, the size and strength of the movement quintupled almost overnight.

The manager must now deal with his employees as individuals, as members of informal groups, and as members of a formal group recognized and protected by law. Collective bargaining in good faith is required on questions affecting the status of employees, and this area of required negotiation tends to grow with every decision of the National Labor Relations Board. Some authors have suggested a basic pattern of labor-management relations development, from authoritarian to paternalistic to constitutional to participative management. Constitutional management would require a sharing of rule-making power with the union, the current situation as required by law. Participative management would involve a further degree of sharing which might transform the business organization into a joint venture. We have not reached a state of joint management as yet, and there is considerable doubt as to the desirability of such a degree of sharing.

It is necessary, however, to formulate and apply a philosophy of labor relations that is both realistic and consistent with the framework of modern society. This philosophy will include such elements as management acceptance of the union as the official representative of the employees' collective interests, the union's acceptance of management as the primary planners and controllers of the enterprise, acceptance by both parties of the principle of free collective bargaining and free enterprise consistent with the public interest, emphasis upon a problem-solving rather than a legalistic approach to issues, and a full awareness of the obligations of both management and union representatives to employees, customers, stockholders, and the general public. This philosophy should provide a constructive approach to both the process of collective bargaining and the day-to-day administration of resulting contractual agreements. It would also provide for a legitimate role for third parties, mediators and arbitrators, in assisting in the resolution of problems and the integration of interests.

DISCUSSION PROBLEMS

1. Describe the current status of the labor union movement with respect to membership, organization, and goals.

2. Contrast the roles and attitudes of business managers and union leaders. How do they differ? How are they similar?

3. Assuming the most scientific and enlightened management possible, of what value is a labor union to an employee?

4. What evidence is there that the most common informal relationship between a labor union and a business management is one of working harmony?

5. Define and distinguish between mediation and arbitration. What are their roles with respect to bargaining over new contracts, and the settlement of grievances under an existing contract?

6. What are the reasons for the declining percentage of the labor force found in labor unions? What changes in union objectives and policies will be necessary to counteract this trend?

7. What are the alternatives to free collective bargaining in the matter of determining labor-management problem solutions? What are the probabilities of these alternatives coming to pass?

8. What is the status of compulsory union membership in the United States? What does the law require with respect to union recognition?

9. Define the varying types of informal relationships that may exist between a union and a management.

10. Define the varying types of formal relationships that may exist between a union and a management with respect to union security.

SUPPLEMENTARY READING

Eisinger, Richard A. and Marvin J. Levine, "The Role of Psychology in Labor Relations," *Personnel Journal,* Vol. 47, No. 9 (September, 1968), 643–649.

Miles, Raymond E. and J. B. Ritchie, "Leadership Attitudes Among Union Officials," *Industrial Relations,* Vol. 8, No. 1 (October, 1968), 108–117.

Prasow, Paul and Edward Peters, "The Development of Judicial Arbitration in Labor-Management Disputes," *California Management Review,* Vol. 9, No. 3 (Spring, 1967), 7–16.

Ross, Philip, "The NLRB and the Duty to Bargain," *Monthly Labor Review,* Vol. 89, No. 11 (November, 1966), 1241–1245.

Rossman, Herbert D., "You Can't Fire Us—We Just Quit," *Personnel Journal,* Vol. 47, No. 4 (April, 1968), 242–248.

Sorcher, Melvin and Roy deBrauwere, "Cementing Union-Management Relationships at the Bottom," *Personnel Journal,* Vol. 46, No. 10 (November, 1967), 649–652.

Cases for Part V

A SPECIAL PROJECT

The Harwell and Johnson dairies were in the process of merging and the Mountain Bank had been chosen to handle the work. Part of its duties consisted of calling in the old stock of the two companies and issuing new certificates to the stockholders.

To accomplish this, the bank temporarily moved six of its full-time employees along with a supervisor, Mrs. Cox, into a large, unoccupied room away from the main office building. The bank also started hiring temporary employees to help in issuing the new stock certificates and put them under the supervision of Mrs. Cox.

All the temporary help was acquired through an employment agency, Employers' Overload, which specialized in obtaining such help for businesses. Since it was summertime, most of the temporary employees were college students or were other relatively young people who had some office skills. The full-time employees were all in their mid-twenties with the exception of Mrs. Cox, who was in her fifties.

Technically the temporary workers were working for Employers' Overload as they received their checks from the agency, but operationally these workers received all their instructions from Mrs. Cox or the full-time employees of the bank. After the number of temporary employees reached about 20, Employers' Overload decided that it would send someone over to supervise them. The agency sent a Mr. Williams, who was in his fifties, to do this job.

Mr. Williams called a meeting and explained to the temporary workers that it was his duty to see that the bank was getting a fair share of work from them and that he would check on their sign-in times, coffee breaks, and lunch hours. Other than that, Mr. Williams did the same type of work as the other temporary workers. He was not an executive or full-time employee of Employers' Overload, and the agency had hired him for this particular purpose.

Before Mr. Williams came, there was a fairly lax attitude about getting to work exactly on time and extending coffee breaks and lunch hours. Mrs. Cox did not seem to mind if the workers took a few extra minutes off or showed up a few minutes late for work. Besides, the workers were becoming more familiar with their jobs each day and output was increasing steadily.

When Mr. Williams arrived, however, he started insisting upon everyone being exactly on time for everything. He instructed the temporary workers to write down to the exact minute their sign-in and sign-out times although it was the bank's policy that the time be recorded to the closest 5-minute interval. Mr. Williams and Mrs. Cox rarely consulted each other, and she was slightly amused more often than not when Mr. Williams cornered an employee and tried to tell him what to do about signing-in.

The workers resented Mr. Williams and no one seemed to accept his authority or seemed to respect him, as he himself was late to work on several occasions. One morning, one of the temporary workers, who was not at the first meeting called by Mr. Williams, showed up late for work, and Mr. Williams immediately asked for an explanation. The two started to exchange words and began talking very loudly. Finally, the worker in an angry voice questioned Mr. Williams' authority and asked for his credentials. Mr. Williams in an equally angry tone pointed to a military medal pinned on his coat and shouted, "This is all the credentials I need!" and threatened the worker with physical violence. At these remarks, the worker walked away. Mr. Williams then tried to telephone someone at the office of Employers' Overload, but he could not get in touch with anyone. He then pretended to forget the incident and tried to go about his job in the usual manner.

THE HEAVY EQUIPMENT COMPANY

The Heavy Equipment Company was founded shortly after the Civil War as a manufacturer of a revolutionary rock drill used in the mining industry. Because of the knowledge of hydraulics and pneumatics required for their primary product, over the years they gradually acquired the knowhow and manufacturing ability in many related industrial fields. Today they manufacture and sell pumps, compressors, condensers, turbines, and a line of construction equipment to industrial users on a worldwide basis. Because of the international aspects in the mining industry the Heavy Equipment Co. was early in establishing its reputation overseas and now has 35 wholly owned autonomous companies and over 70 distributors in foreign countries. With sales of over $450 million and approximately 35 percent earned by the international division, they are very eager to hire and train people who can sell in these international markets.

In 1964 the Heavy Equipment Co. hired Arturo Gomez through their college recruiter. Art's background was such that it appeared he would be a great asset to the company in their Latin American market. He was born and raised in Puerto Rico and had attended high school and college in the U.S.A. As a result he was completely bi-lingual with no accent in either language. After completing his engineering degree he had started for his M.B.A. but decided that the time, effort, and value of this second degree was less important than going to work and making some money.

After a three month formal training program consisting of classroom lectures on the various products, he was assigned to the international division in New York City. This assignment was to last six months to one year during which time he would work in four or five product departments learning engineering applications and pricing methods.

In the international division he was first assigned to work with Cliff Brown, who at the time had been with the company about a year and a half. Cliff spent the better part of the first day explaining to Art the various procedures for making quotations, introducing him to the various secretaries and clerks, and explaining the filing systems. The second day Cliff went through two basic pump quotations, showing Art the engineering calculations and the detailed price make-up. At this point he came across an ideal request for a quotation for a pump to a customer in Panama. To quote Cliff:

"I thought I would turn him loose on this one because everything was right. He was slated for Latin America, he had shown a good basic knowledge of hydraulics, and had not had any questions on the previous two price make-ups. In addition this request had all the pertinent information required to make a complete quotation, which happened very seldom in the international markets. Therefore, I gave him the price book and work sheets to let him handle this without help. I told him to prepare everything for the typist but to let me check it before we had it typed. I would check with him periodically but he said he was doing all right. At this point I got busy and had to leave the office for some time, and when I returned he had already had the quote typed. I told him I wanted to check it before he put it in the mail but he assured me that everything was correct. Nevertheless, I decided to check it and found that just about every calculation and price were wrong."

Cliff didn't mention the sloppy work to his boss thinking that Art would improve as he learned the importance of *detail* in an engineered quotation.

However, he did alert his fellow workers whom Art would soon be training under, that he had a sound engineering background but to be sure to check the work given him before sending it out of their respective departments.

Art stayed in New York for almost a year and did get his training as was promised. It soon became common knowledge that his work was far below standard but he was nevertheless scheduled to get a sales territory in South America. This meant he would get a substantial raise in pay and the people in the New York product departments would suffer because of his sloppy work when they tried to answer his inquiries from the field. During all this time (over one year), his immediate superiors responsible for his training and subsequent promotion were completely unaware of Art's basic weakness.

THE GRIEVANCE

The union steward on the second shift in the production department of a large manufacturing concern is also a quality inspector. She inspects in various departments, one of which is under the jurisdiction of a husky, red-headed, female supervisor, an attractive woman who uses the supervising tactics of the old "bull-of-the-woods" type of boss. The union steward-quality inspector is known for having a temper to match that of the red-headed production supervisor. Each of these women work for different departments and different foremen, the supervisor being in the jurisdiction of superintendent Tom Jones. The following is his report.

"One afternoon, just after I had arrived at work and was taking a verbal turnover from the day-shift foreman as we walked through the building area, the divisional steward for the union, a rough and tumble, difficult individual whose philosophy of life consists solely of bitterness against all corporations, approached us and handed me a written grievance. It stated very simply, and cryptically, 'We protest the action of a company supervisor in threatening a bargaining unit employee.' The union's divisional steward very brusquely stated, 'I'll be in tonight to meet with you on this grievance. I'd like to get it into the Personnel Department the first thing in the morning.' I was stone cold on the whole thing. I didn't have the slightest idea what the grievance was all about.

"I decided that my best defense would be a good offense, and that I must 'get there fustest with the mostest.' First, I queried every supervisor to find which one was accused of threatening an employee. The red-head gave me part of the answer I was looking for. She had done the threatening. She had told the union steward-quality inspector that unless she quit trying to supervise and stuck to her own job, she would see to it that the inspector had nothing to inspect all night but black paint (a distasteful job to inspectors because of the time and effort involved). Beyond admitting that she was the supervisor under fire, the red-head would say nothing except that she had a good reason for making the threat. Now I had to get the rest of the story.

"I next went to the painter who was being followed in her work by the aggrieved inspector and asked her if she had heard any argument between her supervisor and the inspector. She had. She eagerly volunteered the information that the inspector had been trying to tell the painter just what cells she should and should not paint, in order to make her own job as easy as possible. When she was confronted by the supervisor and told not to schedule the painter, but to stick to her inspection job, the inspector became very abusive in her language. The painter remembered one thing in particular which the inspector had told the supervisor—'You think you carry a lot of weight around here, but the only weight you pack is in that big, fat shape you live in!' I asked the painter if she would be willing to repeat what she had heard for a written record, and the painter said she would be glad to. She was very loyal to the supervisor. I took her to the office, made a written interview report of her statements, and had her sign it. I was ready for the divisional steward.

"The quality inspector-union steward came into the office with the divisional steward about an hour later to carry out the necessary formality of the first step in the grievance procedure. It was obvious from his opening statement that the inspector had told him only part of the story. He began with wild, belligerent statements about having supervisors fired, toned it down gradually to having the supervisor brought before the Personnel Director, and then ended by demanding an apology from the supervisor to the inspector. I let him do all the talking. When he was quite finished, and had thoroughly committed himself to the cause of the inspector, I handed him a copy of the interview report I had written on the painter. He read it, looked daggers at me, then turned to the inspector and asked her if she had made the remark about the supervisor's weight-carrying ability. The inspector said she had, and added, 'I told her to go to hell, too. You forgot to put that in the report.' The divisional steward was shaken. His case had vanished into thin air. It was now my turn to talk. I told the division steward that it was normal procedure to discuss grievances verbally with the foreman before filing the formal grievance. The whole thing could have been avoided, including his trip into the plant at night to discuss the problem. I also told him that a copy of the interview written about the painter would be put in the personnel folder of the inspector along with a copy of the grievance meeting minutes, in the event the inspector decided to do any more swearing at a supervisor. The divisional steward told me that he would like to talk to the inspector alone for a few minutes. He did so. Upon their return to the office, he asked permission to withdraw the grievance. This was done. I think that I taught the steward a lesson."

THE COMPANY QUEEN

The time is June 1964; the event is the choosing of a queen for the company picnic which is to be held in July. The method of choosing the queen is through votes of company personnel. The company has suggested that the queen was not to be chosen primarily on the basis of physical appearance but in terms of cooperation, pleasantness, and generally favorable attitudes. The contest created quite a furor among the women of the plant; petty arguments arose, jealousy reared its ugly head, and some caustic and critical remarks were heard.

The case in question concerns Sadie Smith who was a good worker, pleasant, and cooperative, and had been with the company for three years. She had set her heart on being selected queen, but instead of emphasizing her assets, she started vindictive rumors about her opponents and generally upset the girls on the line. As would be expected, she was *not* chosen queen and thus started a long trail of unpleasant events.

After the picnic was over, her uncooperativeness, rumor mongering, and unpleasantness continued. Her work fell in quality and quantity, while the quality of work of those who worked in her area of influence was disintegrating rapidly.

In the opinion of her supervisor, the company had three alternative solutions to the problem. First, they could fire her. Second, they could put her in an area with personnel who would be indifferent to her attitudes. Third, they could isolate her, that is, have her work with men.

He believed that firing her would be wrong because she had proven herself to be a good worker and very cooperative. Also he felt the company was partially to blame for having a ridiculous queen contest to begin with; management should have foreseen the consequences.

The company finally adopted the second alternative, that of transferring her to another area. This is the case as of now. The situation is better, though still not peaceful. The girls in this area do not take sides, but do listen to Sadie's story. They are at this time becoming weary of her complaining and beginning to resent her. The move was partially successful because her own work and attitude did improve to a degree.

Her former supervisor still contends that the third alternative should have been put into effect. This alternative would involve transferring her to a section where only men technicians work, and when they could utilize the services of a wire girl on a full-time basis. Under normal procedures, this section does not have a permanent wire girl, but asks the production department for such a girl to do routine wiring. This has resulted in a full-time job being filled by whichever girls could be freed from production. His alternative for placing

Sadie into this job permanently would have several possible advantages. It would allow the technician's area to have a wire girl at their disposal at any time, and also would not disrupt the production line each time a wire girl was needed. It would place Sadie in an area where there are no other women to whom she could complain and gossip. Being the only woman in the group would also give her ego a boost because the men technicians would "kid" with her, and therefore make her feel important. Her supervisor felt that this would distract her mind from the bitterness of the contest and enable her to produce up to her capabilities. Her association with the other women during coffee break and lunch period would be more amiable because everyone, including possibly Sadie, would now like to forget the unpleasant situation. This alternative would allow Sadie to revert to being a pleasant and cooperative worker without losing face. Management, however, is unwilling to take the supervisor's advice. They feel that Sadie has been given another chance with her present transfer, and have instituted a series of warnings which will result in her dismissal if there are no favorable behavioral changes forthcoming.

THE GINA CARSON CASE

Gina Carson was an excellent employee in every respect. She had worked in the production department for over ten years, was highly skilled, and did high quality work. Her only time off was during last year when she was on sick leave for several months. Upon her return, however, she lost no time in getting back into her old pattern of good work.

Beginning several months ago, Gina began to express dissatisfaction with various minor elements of her job. Because of her worth as a worker, every attempt was made to placate her and to iron out her difficulties, most of which proved to be largely imaginary.

Several weeks ago a rush order was scheduled on an item which had been obsolete for over three years. Gina was one of the few workers with a clear recollection of the production details of this item, and so she was temporarily transferred to the rush job. She was told that she had been selected because of her skill, and would be paid 95 percent of her classification average earnings (C.A.E.) in accordance with the terms of the current union contract. This rate of pay constituted a substantial increase over her usual earnings.

Gina seemed highly upset over the move, protested that she didn't remember the job well enough, claimed that her earnings would be adversely affected, and demanded that she be paid at the rate for experimental work, 100 percent of C.A.E. Her supervisor talked to her several times, but no amount of reasoning and logic would ease her complaints. She "collared" anyone and everyone passing by, delivering long-winded tirades to anyone willing to listen.

As a result, she produced about one-fourth of her normal day's work. At the end of her shift she turned in a claim for full C.A.E. on her timecard. At the supervisor's request the timekeeping department lowered this claim to the correct 95 percent of C.A.E. and sent her a notice of the change.

The union filed a grievance the next morning, claiming that Gina was performing experimental work, even though the item was identical with that produced several years ago. This grievance was not pushed energetically with management even though Gina had been a long-time union member.

Gina became even more distraught on the second morning following the grievance. Her union steward's sympathy toward her complaints seemed to reinforce all of her gripes. Further discussion among Gina, her supervisor, and the superintendent, elicited no response beyond a few well-chosen epithets regarding the probable ancestry of certain members of management.

Two hours later, without any warning, Gina walked into the department supervisor's office, threw her tools down on his desk, and said, "I can't stand this stinking place another minute! I quit!" She then walked out.

One union steward ran for the telephone to call for reinforcements, and another fell into step with Gina as she stomped out. He talked her into going to the Personnel Department where she was met by the just-summoned union president and several division stewards.

In the Personnel office Gina made some very hysterical observations about the company and the character traits of all management members. Her husband was called to come and get her, and when he arrived she gave him the worst tongue-lashing of all. Eventually she went home, avowing loudly that she would never return.

The following facts came to light upon further investigation. At the time of her sick leave last year, Gina had undergone a complete hysterectomy. Upon her recovery and return to work her doctor strongly advised a series of hormone shots to counter the effects of the operation. Gina refused, stating that she didn't want or need any shots.

By agreement between the union and the company, Gina is officially on sick leave. She has shown no evidence of wishing to return to work.

Part Six

CONCLUSION

Though one may separate traditional and behavioral approaches in theory and discussion, they are inextricably intertwined in practice. It has been the goal of this book to develop a more effective balance between both of these **essential** approaches to management.

26

Management: An Integrated Behavioral-Traditional Approach

Henri Fayol has been credited with authoring the first book on general management theory.[1] He set the pattern for the classical or traditional approach, identifying five major functions of management: planning, organizing, commanding, coordinating, and controlling. Taylor, Gantt, and Gilbreth were specifically concerned with improving the effectiveness of managing the production function. The emphasis of all these men was upon logical, rational analysis of business problems and upon controlling the future through effective planning.

In the past four decades, a number of other schools of management thought have sprung up, so many that the resultant controversy has been termed by one writer as "the management theory jungle."[2] One of the first of these new approaches was that of the behaviorists, who felt that they had discovered a fundamental flaw in the traditional approach—lack of appreciation of the importance and complexity of the human element in organizations. This approach has in turn been subdivided into psychological and sociological aspects, depending upon the emphasis given. More recently, the development of computer technology has spawned a mathematical school, with emphasis upon operations research, gaming, queuing theory, etc., as a way of making management more objective. Closely allied with this approach are members of the decision school who feel that decision making is both the core of management and the most significant avenue to research about management. There

[1] Henri Fayol, *General and Industrial Management* (New York: Pitman Pub. Co., 1949, trans. from the French originally published in 1916).
[2] Harold Koontz, "The Management Theory Jungle," *The Journal of the Academy of Management,* Vol. 4, No. 3 (December, 1961), pp. 174–188.

has been a substantial amount of warfare among these schools in the journals as each attempts not only to build up its approach, but also to destroy opposing theories. Naturally, the first and most widely accepted school, the traditional, has received the most abuse from the invading psychologists, sociologists, economists, and mathematicians.

There is a belief that each of these schools is dealing with *separate* aspects of the management task, and that there should thus be a kind of "intellectual free enterprise" in order to stimulate the greatest amount of research and advancement. On the other hand, the *practicing* manager feels a real need for a *general* theory of management inasmuch as he is usually not able to separate these aspects in actual practice. All schools have developed fundamental theorems, but the interrelationships among these discoveries are unclear. One author suggests that we should admit the existence of conflict among the schools, and should not attempt to put together things that appear to be incompatible.[3] This would result in the development of a number of meaningful theories, rather than just one.

It is apparent that the manager must undertake a single integrated task. He cannot say that "today I will be rationally oriented toward the organization's needs, tomorrow I will be people-oriented, and on the following day I shall solve problems with the computer and my slide rule." He must *practice* a general philosophy of management whether a unified theory exists or not.

One of the foremost characteristics of a theory of general management should be its potential usefulness to the practicing manager. The interdisciplinary warfare mentioned above is fun for the researcher and academician, but confusing and demoralizing to the manager who is seriously interested in improving his approach to organizational problems. Since the traditional or classical approach has always been a pragmatic one, it would appear that this school would provide the *overall* framework into which the human, mathematical, and decision-making elements can be fitted. Though the behaviorists have often questioned the entire basis of the traditional approach, the traditionalists do not usually reject outright the contributions which the various special disciplines have made. However, these contributions are viewed as *modifications* of and *supplements* to classical theory rather than as a complete reversal and substitution.

INTEGRATIVE APPROACHES

It is suggested that the greatest philosophical conflict among these schools lies between the behavioral and traditional approaches. Members of the latter

---

[3] John M. Pfiffner and Frank P. Sherwood, *Administrative Organization* (Englewood Cliffs: Prentice-Hall, Inc., 1960), p. 464.

school are basically inclined toward the utilization of rational techniques, quantitative or otherwise, in the determination of organizational plans and frameworks. Perhaps they are not as sophisticated in mathematical technique as members of the quantitative school, but they "buy" the basic logic of the approach. On the other hand, the clash between behaviorists and traditionalists is readily apparent. The latter tend to regard organization subordinates as limited in viewpoint and ability, thus requiring decisions and controls by the manager. Behaviorists tend to prefer McGregor's Theory "Y" viewpoint, emphasizing that the basic nature of man is one of goodness, creativeness, responsibility, and energy. The technical effectiveness of the traditional approach is readily apparent, particularly in business organizations. Behaviorists contend that such effectiveness is achieved with unnecessary sacrifice of the human assets of loyalty, pride, and good mental health. Both schools have a measure of the truth.

In recent years, there have been various attempts to develop conceptual frameworks for integrating the values pursued by the behavioral and traditional approaches. Much has been made of an inevitable clash between the needs of the organization and the needs of organization members. Both constitute important and legitimate sets of needs, but the particular manner of integration and reconciliation has been up for debate.

Among the varying proposed methods of integrating these two schools are the following:

1. The Fusion Process, advocated by Bakke.
2. The Modified Theory of Management, advanced by Likert.
3. An Overlay Approach, developed by Pfiffner and Sherwood.
4. Management by Task, presented by Leavitt.
5. The Managerial Grid, designed by Blake and Mouton.
6. The "Mix" Model of Argyris.
7. The Stogdill Model.

Each of these will be discussed briefly along with a summary of the basic approach advocated in this text.

The Fusion Process

Reference has been made earlier to the fusion process as a phenomenon that begins when the individual enters the organization.[4] This approach accepts as logical and rational the demands of formal organization for patterned and predictable human behavior. It also accepts and considers the requirements of

[4] See Chapter 7.

the individual, his physiological, social, and egoistic needs. Both sets of requirements must and will be satisfied to a reasonable degree, with a resulting high degree of fusion. If they are completely incompatible there is likely to be a parting of the ways through resignation or dismissal of the individual. As indicated in Chapter 7, Bakke and Argyris have developed scales to measure the degree of fusion present.

Fig. 26–1 portrays the essentials of the fusion process as a combination of two simultaneous sub-processes—a *socializing* one effected by the organization as it adapts the person to its ends, and a *personalizing* one effected by the individual as he adapts the organization to his ends. Through assignment of formal functions and rank, the organization hopes to regulate and control behavior along planned and predictable patterns. Through actual conduct and standing in the social organization, the individual hopes to achieve a reasonable satisfaction of physiological, social, and egoistic needs.

The model in Fig. 26–1 attempts to explain a process which inevitably occurs

FIGURE 26–1   THE FUSION PROCESS

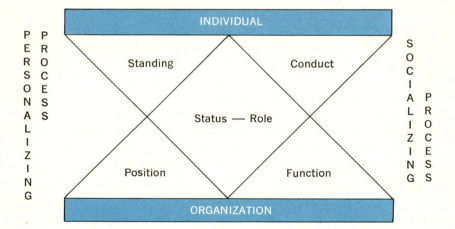

Source: E. Wight Bakke, *The Fusion Process*, p. 20. New Haven: Labor and Management Center, Yale University, 1953.

in every organization. The use of the model and accompanying scales of measurement enables management to effect a more perfect fusion. Additional emphasis is given to individual needs, in addition to that normally assigned to organization requirements.

In the final analysis, however, fusion is concerned more with results than with particular approaches to management functions. A further implication might be that total fusion is far superior to any conflict; as we have discussed, this may not necessarily be true. There are many occasions when the manager fully realizes that his departmental fusion score will be low for perfectly satisfactory reasons; he can always raise the score by reducing or altering requirements to adhere more reasonably to individual wants. Or organization demands can be held constant, while the search is continued for personnel who in turn adhere to these demands. The fusion process is a valuable addition to the theory of management and deserves a place as an integrative approach. However, it is more descriptive than normative, and thus somewhat limited as a general approach for the practicing manager.

Modified Theory of Management

A considerable amount of research into management processes and results has been directed by Rensis Likert in the Institute for Social Research at the University of Michigan.[5] He, too, has emphasized the short-sightedness of traditional managers in their job-oriented approach to goal accomplishment. His research reveals that the traditional approach, though admittedly effective, tends to evoke resentment, hostility, and eventual revolt on the part of subordinates. He suggests that the impressive results of traditional management are obtained only through a *liquidation of human assets*. All traditional managers are fully aware of the possibility of dissipating physical assets in the interests of short-run profits. Likert emphasizes that they should be equally aware of the probability of dissipating human assets, such as loyalty and voluntary cooperation, in the interests of short-run productivity.

Morse and Reimer report on a year-long study of varied management practices and results that was undertaken in four parallel clerical divisions with a total of 500 employees.[6] Each division was responsible for substantially the same type of work and had employees of comparable ability. In two of the divisions, an attempt was made to modify traditional management practices in favor of a participative and supportive approach. Managers were given training in group methods and participation techniques, and attempted to push decision making down to lower levels in the division. These were the "participative divisions." In contrast, the other two divisions were "hierarchically-controlled," and the manager attempted to increase the closeness of supervision and centralization in decision making. Furthermore, motion and time studies were widely used to establish new standards on these clerical jobs.

[5] Rensis Likert, *New Patterns of Management* (New York: McGraw-Hill Book Company, 1961).

[6] Nancy Morse and E. Reimer, "The Experimental Change of a Major Organizational Variable," *Journal of Abnormal Psychology*, Vol. 52 (1956), pp. 120–129.

At the end of one year's experience, the hierarchically-controlled divisions' productivity had increased by 25 percent. This was accomplished through a directive that the number of personnel would be cut one-fourth with no reduction permitted in the total output—time-study had revealed that this was possible. In the two participative divisions, productivity had increased by an average of 20 percent, one division increasing 25 percent and the other 15 percent. Thus, a case could be made for the autocratic, hierarchical approach in the short run. However, further measurements initiated by researchers revealed that the 25 percent increase obtained by the hierarchically-controlled divisions involved a considerable cost in human assets. Study of these divisions revealed (1) a marked increase in labor turnover; (2) decreased loyalty to the firm and division; (3) a decreased feeling of responsibility to see that the work gets done; (4) decreased employee satisfaction with supervisors; and (5) negative attitudes toward the highly productive employees in the division. Similar study of the participative divisions revealed the opposite conditions.

Likert suggests that if the experiment had been continued for a second or third year, the participative divisions would have shown a higher increase in productivity. Production in the hierarchically-controlled divisions would have declined as the adverse employee attitudes were felt more deeply. Thus, Likert suggests a theory which is, in a sense, one of "long-term management." A manager's effectiveness must, of course, be measured in terms of such immediate variables as output quantity, quality, time, and costs. But this is not enough. Likert's approach would include measurement of other variables whose importance becomes apparent primarily in the long run. Among these are the following:[7]

1. Extent of loyalty to and identification with the institution and its objectives.
2. Extent to which members of the organization at all hierarchical levels feel that the organization's goals are consistent with their own needs and goals, and that the achievement of the company's goals will help them achieve their own.
3. Extent to which the goals of units and of individuals are of a character to enable the organization to achieve its objectives.
4. Level of motivation among members of the organization with regard to such variables as:
   a. Performance, including both quality and quantity of work done;
   b. Concern for elimination of waste and reduction of costs;
   c. Concern for improving product;
   d. Concern for improving processes.

[7] Rensis Likert, "Measuring Organizational Performance," *Harvard Business Review* (March–April, 1958), pp. 49–50.

5. Degree of confidence and trust among members of the organization in each other and in the different hierarchical levels.
6. Amount and quality of teamwork in each unit of the organization and between units.
7. Extent to which people feel delegation is being effectively achieved.
8. Extent to which members feel that their ideas, information, knowledge of processes, and experience are being used in the decision-making processes of the organization.
9. Level of competence and skill of different groups in the organization to interact effectively in solving problems and other tasks.
10. Efficiency and adequacy of the communication process upward, downward, and sidewise.
11. Level of the leadership skills and abilities of supervisors and managers, including their basic philosophy of management and orientation toward the processes of leadership.
12. Aptitude scores of the members of the organization. If aptitude scores are obtained as people join the organization, then trends in these scores will show whether the current management is improving the basic quality of the personnel through its hiring practices or is letting quality deteriorate through unfavorable turnover.

Thus, the manager will be asked to show effectiveness in two areas, the organizational and the human. Both areas are compatible in the long run even though conflict may appear to be evident in the short run. The approach for integrating these two sets of values has been labeled "System IV" by Likert. System I is an autocratic approach, System II is benevolently autocratic, System III involves consultative supervision, while System IV advocates democratic decision making through group participation and supportive relationships between superior and subordinates. It is apparent that the four systems follow the basic styles of leadership discussed in Chapter 14.

Organization Overlays

Another attempt at integrating various approaches to management theory is the use of organization overlays. This concept is best illustrated by Pfiffner and Sherwood.[8]

The formal organization as described in Chapters 8 through 10 is seen as the fundamental and basic structure of relationships among personnel, jobs, and physical factors, constituting an *official* attempt by management to establish

---

[8] Pfiffner and Sherwood, *Administrative Organization,* Chapter 2.

patterned and predictable behavior. Like most critics of the traditional approach, Pfiffner and Sherwood feel that to stop the analysis of organization at this point is to deal with only a fraction of reality. They suggest additional important patterns of relationships. Some of these are not officially established by management, but are nevertheless vital, inevitable, and essential:[9]

1. The sociometric network, which is composed of individual and group feelings of attraction or rejection.
2. The system of functional contacts between intellectual leaders who, without direct responsibility for the work done, exert influence on others.
3. The grid of decision-making centers, composed of a series of horizontal and vertical interactions resulting in a decision's being made at some particular point.
4. The pattern of power or influence among all individuals and groups.
5. All types and channels of communication which reveal who talks to whom about what.

Each of these patterns, grids, networks, or systems can be theoretically portrayed in the same fashion as the basic formal organization structure. The sociometric network, for example, can be laid over the basic formal structure. This is followed by each of the other overlays in turn, with a resulting picture of extreme complexity. Pfiffner and Sherwood suggest that if *all* the overlays are comprehensive and accurate, the net result would be a picture so complex that it is *opaque*.[10] This would at the least demonstrate the difficulties inherent in the integrative process, as well as suggest the impossibility of its complete understanding. Fig. 26–2 is a rudimentary and hypothetical portrayal of a formal structure with various network overlays.

The use of overlays emphasizes the inevitability of significant relationships other than the formal, and demonstrates the high degree of difficulty involved in comprehensive analysis. On the other hand, such an approach is of little help in actually integrating classical and neoclassical approaches to management theory and practice. It has been suggested that because of the complexity of interrelationships, each of the grids and networks must be studied separately and individually. After a reasonable understanding of each in theory, the student would then be aware that all operate and interact simultaneously in actual practice. (The *science* of management is now replaced by the art of management.) The overlay technique is also limited in that only the organizational portions of management processes are emphasized, even though the technical content of plans, programs, policies, and controls are highly essential to a comprehensive management theory.

[9] *Ibid.*, p. 19.
[10] *Ibid.*, p. 19.

FIGURE 26-2 FORMAL AND INFORMAL NETWORK OVERLAYS

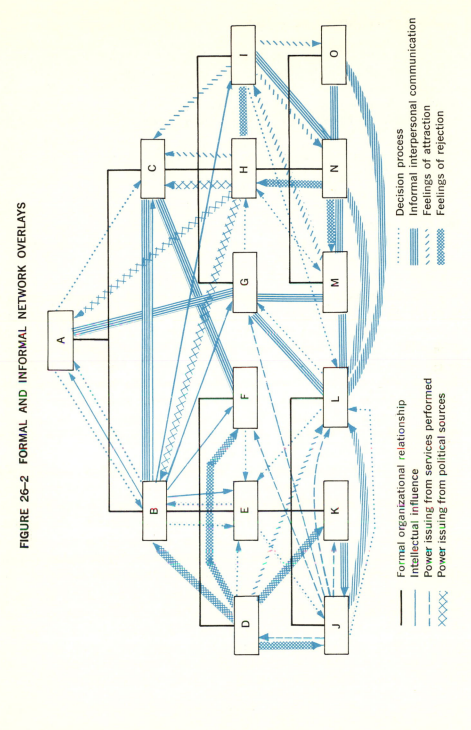

Formal organizational relationship

Intellectual influence

Power issuing from services performed

Power issuing from political sources

Decision process

Informal interpersonal communication

Feelings of attraction

Feelings of rejection

Management According to Task

Harold J. Leavitt has attempted to bridge the gap between the traditionalists and behaviorists in still another manner.[11] He notes the implication on the part of both schools that the management approach should be uniform. The traditionalists argue in favor of logical planning, clear job assignments, and reasonably comprehensive and close controls. The behaviorists differ materially on these subjects, generally favoring a greater degree of freedom and participation on the part of all organization members. *Both,* Leavitt contends, *are in error* in emphasizing that one should *always* be directive or *always* be participative.

In many situations, the closely controlled, directive approach may well be the most economical and efficient, in the long run as well as in the short. Certainly, traditional management has in the past been highly successful. In other situations, particularly when tasks are complex and the caliber of personnel high, the participative or behavioral approach is most economical and effective. Many behaviorists hailed the introduction of participative philosophies in the burgeoning research and development departments of modern manufacturing firms as the "beachhead" from which a general invasion would grow. Yet, while many managements continue to be very participative in their philosophies of managing research departments, they are at the same time very directive and restrictive in managing their production divisions. Both approaches are valid when the conditions appropriate to their use are present.

Thus, management by task should not be uniform, but should vary according to complexity, time available, caliber of personnel, goals, degree of repetitiveness of operations, size of organization, type of technology, and the political, social, and economic environment.[12] The manager should be trained in all schools and be taught to recognize significant variables. He should accept the task of selecting the most effective approach or approaches. We again place a considerable burden upon the practicing manager to determine the process which best integrates all values. This assumes, of course, that the "correct" scale of values can be determined in every situation. When technical and economic values clash clearly with moral and human considerations, what is an effective integration to one man will be objectionable to another. If the manager has been trained heavily in the traditional approach, he may be concerned more with economic and technical gains than with interpersonal relationships. If he has been grounded in the behavioral sciences, he will necessarily be

---

[11] Harold J. Leavitt, "Management According to Task: Organizational Differentiation," *Management International,* No. 1 (1962), pp. 13–22.
[12] See Howard M. Carlisle, "Measuring the Situational Nature of Management," *California Management Review,* Vol. 11, No. 2 (Winter, 1968), pp. 45–52.

concerned with technical and economic values, but will place more emphasis on these interpersonal relationships.

The Managerial Grid

Blake and Mouton use the device of a two dimensional grid to portray the relationship between organizational demands (concern for production) and human demands (concern for people.)[13] The grid is a 9×9 checkerboard, with concern for people shown on the vertical scale and concern for production on the horizontal. A score of 1 indicates low concern and a score of 9 shows high concern. On this basis, five styles of managerial behavior can be identified as follows:

1,1 The manager who has little concern for either people or production.
9,1 The manager who stresses operating efficiency through controls in situations where human elements cannot interfere.
1,9 The manager who is thoughtful, comfortable, and friendly, and who has little concern for output.
5,5 The manager who attempts to balance and trade off concern for work in exchange for a satisfactory level of morale.
9,9 The manager who seeks high output through the medium of committed people, a commitment achieved through mutual trust, respect, and a realization of interdependence.

The first four styles do not represent integrations of organization and human demands. Only the last depicts a successful integration in the eyes of Blake and Mouton. In this scheme, organizational and human values would appear to be accorded *equal* status (9,9), neither being subordinate to the other. The grid provides an excellent conceptual device for undertaking the orientation and training of managers with respect to the various styles available. This is true although a particular firm's philosophy would not accept the 9,9 style in its operations.

The "Mix" Model

Argyris has been among the leaders in highlighting the lack of congruence between the needs of traditionally managed organizations and the needs of healthy, mature human beings. As indicated in Chapter 6, he asserts that such

---

[13] Robert R. Blake and Jane S. Mouton; Louis B. Barnes and Larry Greiner, "Breakthrough in Organization Development," *Harvard Business Review*, Vol. 42, No. 6 (November–December, 1964), p. 133.

organizations serve to elicit human behavior characterized by passivity, dependence, minimal control, short-term perspective, and psychological failure. On the other hand, he indicates that the mentally healthy person is one who is aware of and accepts self, is able to influence his environment, has an appreciation for long-range goals, and has a high quality of concern for other people. He also hypothesizes that there is a greater possibility of integrating the individual and the organization if individuals aspire toward positive mental health, and if the organization is structured in a manner that enables this aspiration to be effected.

In the "mix" model, six dimensions of essential organization properties are proposed: (1) from a condition where one part of the organization controls the whole, to where the whole is created and controlled through interrelationships of the parts; (2) from an awareness of a plurality of parts to an awareness of a pattern of parts; (3) from attempts to achieve objectives related to parts to achieving objectives related to the whole; (4) from a condition where members are unable to influence internally-oriented core activities, to where they can be influenced as desired; (5) from a condition where members are unable to influence externally-oriented core activities, to where they can be influenced as desired; and (6) from a condition where core activities are influenced by the present, to where they are influenced by the past, present, and future.[14]

It is suggested that the organization is more in accord with the needs of healthy individuals if it is designed along the lines of the latter half of each of the six continuums. This would mean a reduction in the power of the manager, less competition among organization members, a greater concern for the total organization, more trust and openness among all personnel, more self-control, and more participation in matters affecting the interests of both the organization as a whole and its constituent members. On the other hand, Argyris contends that traditionally managed organizations are more in line with the needs of immature people who possess poor mental health. His model for a more effective organization is based on a definition of good mental health. To the degree that such "good mental health" is not actually held by organization members, to that same degree the recommended organization would be inappropriate, at least in the short run.

The Stogdill Model

Stogdill presents an organizational model in which human values tend to be equated in importance with organizational values.[15] He finds it *impossible* to explain organization behavior in terms of the single output of productivity. The

[14] Chris Argyris, *Integrating the Individual and the Organization* (New York: John Wiley & Sons, Inc., 1964), p. 150.

[15] Ralph M. Stogdill, *Individual Behavior and Group Achievement* (Oxford, Eng.: Oxford University Press, 1959), p. 13.

elements of the suggested model are divided into three categories: member inputs, mediating variables, and group outputs. Inputs are composed of member performances, interactions, and expectations. These inputs are arranged in both formal and informal role structures composed of functions, status, responsibility, and authority, thereby creating the mediating variables. Three separate group outputs are identified as (1) productivity, (2) morale, and (3) integration. Morale is defined in terms of the degree of freedom accorded members while pursuing organizational tasks, while integration is a measure of the cohesiveness and unity of the group. Thus, the organization is viewed as an instrument designed to achieve multiple end goals, *both* technical and human.

Stogdill also emphasizes the importance of the relationship between mediating structures and end outputs, suggesting that both low and high degrees of structure will be detrimental to productivity, morale, and integration. Low degrees or loosely structured organizations are generally preferred by behaviorists in the interests of self-control and independence. Tight structuring is usually preferred by traditionalists in the interests of coordination and direction toward central goals. Thus, the intermediate degrees of structure are proposed by Stogdill as most conducive to effectiveness for *both* the organization and its members.

THE CONTINUUM AS AN INTEGRATING CONCEPT

It is the thesis of this text that there can be an effective operational merger of the traditional and behavioral approaches to management. Traditional or classical theorists have provided a basic framework of presentation and analysis whose value is too great to be discarded. Instead of advocating its complete elimination because of certain shortcomings, it would be more realistic to *modify* the approach by incorporating the research findings of the behaviorists.

One of the foremost shortcomings of the behaviorist approach has been its lack of any organized framework. If traditionalists have been too "macro" in their sweeping approach, behaviorists have been too "micro" in concentrating upon multiple, separate, and unrelated details. Although the validity of many of the individual research findings of the behaviorists cannot be denied, they can only be of practical use insofar as they are integrated with the operationally-oriented traditional approach. Thus, there is need for a "neo-classical" or "neo-traditional" approach to management.

From the above brief description of various integrative attempts, it seems apparent that behavioral and traditional theories of management *both* have considerable value for the manager. Perhaps the manager should have a number of styles in his managerial repertoire and be able to diagnose when each is appropriate. For the greater bulk of situations, however, the effective approach is neither completely behavioral nor completely traditional. It is in these situations that human and organizational values should be balanced or, more preferably, integrated.

The concept of the continuum is a useful one for illustrating various degrees of integration. For example as shown in Fig. 26–3, a continuum for the element of decision making can be established. The purely behavioral extreme on the left is depicted by collegial decisions with all personnel involved. This position rests upon the attitude that man is basically able, energetic, and responsible—the Theory "Y" of McGregor. On the other extreme, the traditional position is represented by decision making by the manager. This rests not only on the assumption that the decision will then be made by the most able and best informed, but also on the necessity for central coordination of all action. Neither extreme of such a continuum leads to optimum effectiveness in most situations. It is suggested in the illustration that the relationship is curvilinear, with optimum effectiveness lying within the intermediate range.

In some of the integrative schemes, particularly the managerial grid, modified theory, and fusion process, measures are established for the two sets of values, human and technical. The implication is that *both* are desired *end outputs* of organized action. This is in contrast to the view that human values are to be achieved as a *means* to the end of technical efficiency.

Unless one is naively optimistic, it must be admitted that situations arise, at

FIGURE 26–3   A DECISION-MAKING CONTINUUM

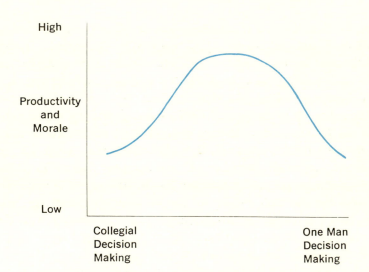

Source: Edwin B. Flippo, "Integrative Schemes in Management Theory," *Academy of Management Journal*, Vol. 11, No. 1 (March, 1968), p. 96.

least in the short run, where a maximization of technical values will lead to a reduction of possible human values, and vice versa. This is depicted in Fig. 26–4, on a control continuum. With complete individual freedom and self-

FIGURE 26–4   A CONTROL CONTINUUM

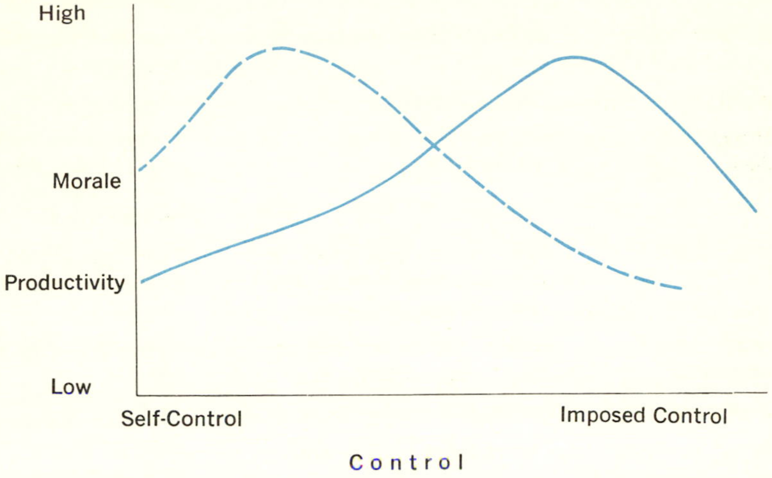

Source: Edwin B. Flippo, "Integrative Schemes in Management Theory," *Academy of Management Journal*, Vol. 11, No. 1 (March, 1968), p. 98.

control, ego needs of independence and dominance are more fully met, resulting in greater employee satisfaction. Technical efficiency, however, may suffer through poor coordination and absence of regulation by a central body. On the other extreme of the continuum, imposed control serves to frustrate egoistic needs but may well lead to an extraction of a prescribed level of output. Thus, the curves of production and morale may not coincide as is the case in Fig. 26–3. When there is a direct clash between sets of values, compromise and accommodation at less than the maximum level for each is necessary. It is conceptually possible to prepare continuums for many factors in managerial situations, as suggested in Chart 26–1. As an educational device, the continuum has great value. For operational use, there must be developed units of measurement of each factor as well as the correct shape of the effectiveness curves for both human and organizational values.

MANAGEMENT: AN INTEGRATED APPROACH

The approach advocated in this text has been based upon a subdivision of each of the four traditional functions of management. In planning, the advan-

CHART 26–1   MANAGEMENT: AN INTEGRATED APPROACH

Item	Item Continuums	
	Probable Area of Optimum Effectiveness	
	Classical	Behavioral
Nature of Man	Limited, indolent, in conflict	Responsible, energetic, able, cooperative
Hiring Personnel	Job is of central importance	Man is of central importance
Central Work Unit	The individual	The group
Organizational Complexity	Simple, clear, official relationships	Highly complex pattern of authority, power, status, and sociometric relationships
Degree of Structuring	Tight, precise organizational and operational procedures, systems, and structures	Few loose guides geared to objectives
Politics and Accommodation	Elimination through formal structures and controls	Essentials of organized life
Type of Influence Used	Authority	Power
Leadership	The leader is the manager	Multiple leaders, official and unofficial
Leadership Style	Autocratic	Democratic
Motivation	The manager motivates	The environment enables self-motivation
Decision Making	Centered in the manager	Collegial
Communication	Through the official, controlled network	Free, open, and unrestrained
Control	Precise, prompt, comprehensive, pressurized	Self-control
Conflict	Encouragement of "organization men"	Encouragement of conflict as inevitable and essential factor of progress

tages of the essentially rational approach are evident. An organization requires logic in prescribing objectives, developing programs, designing procedures, and establishing policies to guide personnel in their work. There *must* be a central focusing of all activities, thereby assuring the inevitability of *some* degree of restriction and control. But, because the human being is an organizational resource, one which traditionalists have underestimated in value, planning should be modified not only to incorporate a more thorough and realistic study and adjustment of individuals and groups to logically planned activities, but also to stimulate a greater sharing in the very process of planning itself.

Certainly, it does not require a wholesale abolition of traditional theory to recognize that thinking and planning talent exists to some degree in *all* personnel, and not solely in those formally designated as "managers." Yet, someone or some group must assume the responsibility for centralizing and approving the final plan toward which *all* will work. If this focus is lacking, it will be found that much bickering and working at cross purposes will result, even in a group of highly talented and intellectual personnel. Thus, there must be an *initiation* of a planning process, and a *final* determination of what plan should be approved for implementation. These functions are primarily, but not exclusively, the responsibilities of the manager. The actual process of developing the plan for possible approval can involve a greater role for any and all personnel, depending upon their interests and abilities, the problem, and the time available.

No one denies the necessity for *organizing* the efforts of multiple personnel toward a common goal. Again, the initial foundation must be a formal one based on a division of labor and a logical grouping of activities. The literature in formal organization is voluminous, involving treatment of functionalization, the process of establishing such formal relationships as responsibility and authority, and the alternative types of formal structures available. On the other hand, the contributions of the behaviorists in this function have also been great. Their first major point is that organizational relationships are established by *all* personnel, and not just by management alone. Informal relationships are thus added to, rather than substituted for, the formal. Of course, if there were no officially prescribed structure, there would be no framework on which the status, communication, sociometric, and power networks could be hung. In fact, if there was no officially designated objective, there would be no need for any type of organizing process, formal or informal.

The task of integrating formal and informal organizations is perhaps more difficult than that of merging the varying viewpoints in planning, directing, and controlling. Yet again, the manager must organize, and he will proceed with that portion that he recognizes must be done—the formal. There are no formulae developed to indicate to what degree this formal process must be altered by his knowledge of the power, status, and sociometric networks. But it *will be* modified in practice if not in theory.

The behavioral school can be given a portion of the credit for the separation and development of the *direction function* as one deserving equal attention along with planning, organizing, and controlling. Many traditionalists see two or three major functions, e.g., planning, organizing, and controlling. It was assumed that if plans were logical, and if tasks were clearly allocated, subordinates would automatically start to work both willingly and effectively. Those traditionalists who differentiated a separate direction function were likely to entitle it "command," implying a restrictive approach. They also tended to allocate an excessive amount of emphasis on monetary motivation as the basic approach to direction, while the behaviorists identified the physiological needs as primary. But the theory and practice of direction cannot stop here. Special study and efforts must be put forth to motivate personnel in today's modern business organization. These personnel are generally better educated, have received a reasonable amount of monetary reward, are relatively mobile, and have a measure of security generated through both informal and formal organization. Thus, the recognition and gratification of social and egoistic needs must be forthcoming.

Though McGregor, Likert, and other behaviorists have argued for more faith in men on the part of the manager, it would be sheer folly to modify the management process out of existence; he must be allowed to *control*. Even if one could assume that all personnel were able, enthusiastic, and cooperative, there will be unforeseen events that will force a collection, classification, and comparison of results to the plan, with a view toward possible corrective action. Thus, a system of communication is necessary to enable the manager to be apprised of operating results. Behaviorists also suggest that the control environment is not the sole creation of the manager, that he is influenced by attitudes of groups and individuals as well as by objective events. For example, the degree of closeness of control has important effects upon employees; pressure-oriented controls will stimulate resentment. The traditionalist is asked to modify his complete faith in control systems in favor of a greater degree of trust in the capabilities and good will of all personnel.

Behaviorists have also suggested that a major and continuing task of management is to maintain a reasonable integration of interests. This necessitates a willingness on the part of management to become aware of individual and group interests through grievance systems, counseling, relationships with organized labor unions, etc. Particular difficulties in this regard have been forced upon the modern manager in the form of organized minority groups and organized labor unions. In sum, the essence of an integrated approach to management is the balancing of values attained through restrictive and permissive means.

A FINAL WORD

Dalton, in one of his studies, analyzed the impact of a wage incentive system upon 84 production personnel.[16] Nine of these people were "ratebusters" who had chosen to produce to the maximum possible despite the social pressures of the group. Twenty-six restricted production, thereby clearly hoping for group acceptance rather than management's motivation. Of the remaining fifty

---

[16] Melville Dalton, "The Industrial 'Ratebuster': A Characterization," *Applied Anthropology,* Vol. 7, No. 1 (Winter, 1948), p. 17.

middle performers, *nine* had active ulcers. *None* of the ratebusters or restricters had this difficulty. Members of the central group were torn between the wish to satisfy traditional management in producing high output and the desire to conform to the wishes of the employee group.

Thus, if one is clearly and irrevocably a traditionalist, he is likely to be comfortable, though incorrect or incomplete. The same can be said of a staunch behaviorist. The real world suggests that both sets of values must be satisfied to a reasonable degree, and that their reconciliation is not an easy one. Thus, the "integrated" manager and researcher are often beset with doubts as to the correctness of a course of action. When any two areas are merged and integrated, mistakes are bound to occur. Like the fictional scientist who attempted to cross an abalone with a crocodile in the attempt to obtain an "abadile," something may go wrong, thereby creating the undesirable counterpart. It is our sincere hope that such has not been the case in this book.

DISCUSSION PROBLEMS

1. Is it possible to managerially eliminate all conflict from a business organization? Why or why not?
2. Which integrative models tend to suggest that both technical and human values can be maximized simultaneously?
3. Identify the significant differentiating element of each of the seven integrative models.
4. Why must one be concerned with integrating traditional and behavioral approaches?
5. Behaviorists have been credited with stimulating traditionalists to separate and identify one of the four major management functions. How did this come about?
6. Discuss the continuum as an integrating concept. What are its values and shortcomings?
7. How is the Argyris "Mix" Model related to his thesis of a clash between organizations and mature personalities?
8. If one accepts Leavitt's thesis of accepting all schools and managing by the situation, what important task remains for the manager?
9. In what way does the Stogdill model differ from those of Bakke, Blake and Mouton, and Argyris with respect to the concept that all values can be maximized?
10. Some have suggested that the theoretical description of communism given by Karl Marx would tend to place him as an extreme behaviorist. Discuss.

SUPPLEMENTARY READING

Bennis, Warren, "Organizations of the Future," *Personnel Administration,* Vol. 30, No. 5 (September–October, 1967), 6–19.

Blake, Robert R., Jane S. Mouton, Richard L. Sloma, and Barbara Peek Loftin, "A Second Breakthrough in Organization Development," *California Management Review*, Vol. 11, No. 2 (Winter, 1968), 73–78.

Carlisle, Howard M., "Measuring the Situational Nature of Management," *California Management Review*, Vol. 11, No. 2 (Winter, 1968), 45–52.

Flippo, Edwin B., "Integrative Schemes in Management Theory," *Academy of Management Journal*, Vol. 11, No. 1 (March, 1968), 91–98.

Graves, Clare W., "Deterioration of Work Standards," *Harvard Business Review*, Vol. 44, No. 5 (September–October, 1966), 117–128.

Myers, Charles A., "Behavioral Sciences for Personnel Managers," *Harvard Business Review*, Vol. 44, No. 4 (July–August, 1966), 154–162.

Roberts, Karlene, Raymond E. Miles, and Vaughn Blankenship, "Organizational Leadership Satisfaction and Productivity: A Comparative Analysis," *Academy of Management Journal*, Vol. 11, No. 4 (December, 1968), 401–414.

Strauss, George, "Human Relations—1968 Style," *Industrial Relations*, Vol. 7, No. 3 (May, 1968), 262–276.

Name Index

Adams, J. Stacy, 301
Albanese, Robert, 156, 168
Alexis, Marcus, 66
Anderson, John, 405
Ardrey, Robert, 93
Argyris, Chris, 92, 96, 110, 111, 114,
    115, 344, 369, 383, 441, 463, 467,
    475, 554
Asch, Solomon E., 375

Baker, Helen, 486
Baker, John K., 260
Bakke, E. W., 115, 545, 546
Bales, Robert, F., 371, 372
Barnard, Chester I., 221, 357, 367
Barnes, Louis B., 91, 221, 553
Barnes, Ralph M., 77, 313
Bavelas, Alex, 392
Bayes, Thomas, 63
Becker, Selwyn, 475
Beer, Michael, 91, 282
Behling, Orlando, 117
Belcher, David W., 300
Bell, Gerald D., 215
Benne, Kenneth D., 333, 373
Bennis, Warren G., 215, 561
Berelson, Bernard, 47
Berger, Monroe, 500
Blake, R. R., 338, 553, 562
Blankenship, L. Vaughn, 298, 360, 562
Bobele, H. Kenneth, 405
Bonner, Hubert, 371
Borgeson, Roger D., 505
Bowles, Warren J., 298
Boyd, J. B., 336
Bradford, Leland, 333
Brady, Rodney H., 41, 52
Brauwere, Roy de, 531
Brayfield, Arthur H., 87
Breen, Leonard Z., 508

Brenner, Marshall H., 499, 512
Brown, Alvin, 330
Brown, Warren B., 405
Buck, Vernon E., 28
Buckingham, Walter S., 257
Bugental, Daphne E., 112, 405

Campbell, John P., 336, 341
Carlisle, Howard M., 552, 562
Cartwright, Dorwin, 13, 226, 372
Cattell, R. B., 368
Centers, R., 112
Chartier, Roger, 118
Churchman, C. West, 18, 52, 65
Cleland, David I., 18, 188, 191
Coch, L., 314, 348, 349, 353
Colarelli, Nick, 352, 365
Coleman, John, R., 519
Conant, E. H., 254
Coronzy, Friedhelm, 475
Craft, James A., 527
Crockett, Walter H., 87
Cummings, L. L., 445, 455
Cushman, Edward L., 485
Cyert, Richard M., 41

Dailey, Charles A., 512
Dale, Ernest, 137, 176, 226, 243, 283
Dale, Leon A., 493
Daniel, D. Ronald, 168
Dalton, Melville, 211, 215, 231, 232,
    235, 242, 315, 434, 436, 468, 560
Dauw, Dean, 52
Davis, James W., Jr., 455
Davis, Keith, 137, 201, 281, 293, 309,
    405, 490
Davis, Louis E., 253, 256, 260
Davis, Ralph C., 23, 40, 42, 71, 75, 137,
    139, 148, 179, 279, 324, 344, 424, 438

Subject Index